A History of

Mediaeval Jewish Philosophy

A HISTORY OF

MEDIAEVAL JEWISH PHILOSOPHY

by ISAAC HUSIK

A TEMPLE BOOK

ATHENEUM, NEW YORK, 1973

Published by Atheneum
Reprinted by arrangement with
The Jewish Publication Society of America
Copyright © 1916 by The Macmillan Company
Copyright © 1940 by
The Jewish Publication Society of America
All rights reserved
Library of Congress catalog card number 58-8533
ISBN 0-689-70102-0
Manufactured in the United States of America by
The Murray Printing Company,
Forge Village, Massachusetts
Published in Canada by McClelland and Stewart Ltd.
First Atheneum September 1969
Second Printing April 1973

TABLE OF CONTENTS

PREFACE

No excuse is needed for presenting to the English reader a History of Mediæval Jewish Philosophy. The English language, poor enough in books on Jewish history and literature, can boast of scarcely anything at all in the domain of Jewish philosophy. The Jewish Encyclopedia has no article on Jewish philosophy, and neither has the eleventh edition of the Encyclopedia Britannica. Hastings' Encyclopedia of Religion and Ethics will have a brief article on the subject from the conscientious and able pen of Dr. Henry Malter, but of books there is none. But while this is due to several causes, chief among them perhaps being that English speaking people in general and Americans in particular are more interested in positive facts than in tentative speculations, in concrete researches than in abstract theorizing—there are ample signs that here too a change is coming, and in many spheres we are called upon to examine our foundations with a view to making our superstructure deep and secure as well as broad and comprehensive. And this is nothing else than philosophy. Philosophical studies are happily on the increase in this country and more than one branch of literary endeavor is beginning to feel its influence. And with the increase of books and researches in the history of the Jews is coming an awakening to the fact that the philosophical and rationalistic movement among the Jews in the middle ages is well worth study, influential as it was in forming Judaism as a religion and as a theological and ethical system.

But it is not merely the English language that is still wanting in a general history of Mediæval Jewish Philosophy, the German, French and Italian languages are no better off in this regard. For while it is true that outside of the Hebrew and Arabic sources, German books and monographs are the *sine qua non* of the student who wishes to investigate the philosophical movement in mediæval Jewry, and the present writer owes very much to the researches of such men as Joel, Guttmann, Kaufmann and others, it nevertheless remains true that there is as yet no complete history of the subject for the student or the general reader. The German writers have done thorough and distinguished work in expounding individual thinkers and problems, they have gathered a complete and detailed bibliography of Jewish philosophical writings in print and in manuscript, they have edited and translated and annotated the most important philosophical texts. France has also had an important share in these fundamental undertakings, but for some reason neither the one nor the other has so far undertaken to present to the general student and non-technical reader the results of their researches.

What was omitted by the German, French and English speaking writers was accomplished by a scholar who wrote in Hebrew. Dr. S. Bernfeld has written in Hebrew under the title "Daat Elohim" (The Knowledge of God) a readable sketch of Jewish religious philosophy from Biblical times down to "Ahad Haam." A German scholar (now in America), Dr. David Neumark of Cincinnati, has undertaken on a very large scale a History of Jewish Philosophy in the Middle Ages, of which only a beginning has been made in the two volumes so far issued.

The present writer at the suggestion of the Publication Committee of the Jewish Publication Society of America has undertaken to write a history of mediæval Jewish rationalistic philosophy in one volume —a history that will appeal alike to the scholar and the intelligent non-technical reader. Treating only of the rationalistic school, I did not include anything that has to do with mysticism or Kabbala. In my attempt to please the scholar and the layman, I fear I shall have succeeded in satisfying neither. The professional student will miss learned notes and quotations of original passages in the language of their authors. The general reader will often be wearied by the scholastic tone of the problems as well as of the manner of the discussion and argument. And yet I cannot but feel that it will do both classes good—the one to get less, the other more than he wants. The latter will find oases in the desert where he can refresh himself and take a rest, and the former will find in the notes and bibliography references to sources and technical articles where more can be had after his own heart.

There is not much room for originality in a historical and expository work of this kind, particularly as I believe in writing history objectively. I have not attempted to read into the mediæval thinkers modern ideas that were foreign to them. I endeavored to interpret their ideas from their own point of view as determined by their history and environment and the literary sources, religious and philosophical, under the influence of which they came. I based my book on a study of the original sources where they were available—and this applies to all the authors treated with the exception of the two Karaites, Joseph al Basir and Jeshua ben Judah, where I had to content myself with secondary sources and a few fragments of the original texts. For the rest I tried to tell my story as simply as I knew how, and I hope the reader will accept the book in the spirit in which it is offered—as an objective and not too critical exposition of Jewish rationalistic thought in the middle ages.

My task would not be done were I not to express my obligations to the Publication Committee of the Jewish Publication Society of America to whose encouragement I owe the impulse but for which the book would not have been written, and whose material assistance enabled the publishers to bring out a book typographically so attractive.

ISAAC HUSIK.

PHILADELPHIA,
    July, 1916.

This new edition is a reprint of that of 1916, corrected, and with Bibliography brought up to date.

March, 1930.

Professor Husik planned to make a number of minor changes in this volume; but he died (on March 22, 1939) without having realized this intention. The Jewish Publication Society of America thereupon decided to reprint the volume without change, except for bringing the bibliography up to date. To this task Professor Harry A. Wolfson of Harvard University lent his invaluable aid, and the Publication Committee herewith expresses to him its profound thanks.

December 1, 1941.

INTRODUCTION

The philosophical movement in mediæval Jewry was the result of the desire and the necessity, felt by the leaders of Jewish thought, of reconciling two apparently independent sources of truth. In the middle ages, among Jews as well as among Christians and Mohammedans, the two sources of knowledge or truth which were clearly present to the minds of thinking people, each claiming recognition, were religious opinions as embodied in revealed documents on the one hand, and philosophical and scientific judgments and arguments, the results of independent rational reflection, on the other. Revelation and reason, religion and philosophy, faith and knowledge, authority and independent reflection are the various expressions for the dualism in mediæval thought, which the philosophers and theologians of the time endeavored to reduce to a monism or a unity.

Let us examine more intimately the character and content of the two elements in the intellectual horizon of mediæval Jewry. On the side of revelation, religion, authority, we have the Bible, the Mishna, the Talmud. The Bible was the written law, and represented literally the word of God as revealed to lawgiver and prophet; the Talmud (including the Mishna) was the oral law, embodying the unwritten commentary on the words of the Law, equally authentic with the latter, contemporaneous with it in revelation, though not committed to writing until many ages subsequently and until then handed down by word of mouth; hence depending upon tradition and faith in tradition for its validity and acceptance. Authority therefore for the Rabbanites was two-fold, the authority of the direct word of God which was written down as soon as communicated, and about which there could therefore be no manner of doubt; and the authority of the indirect word of God as transmitted orally for many generations before it was written down, requiring belief in tradition. By the Karaites tradition was rejected, and there remained only belief in the words of the Bible.

On the side of reason was urged first the claim of the testimony of the senses, and second the validity of logical inference as determined by demonstration and syllogistic proof. This does not mean that the Jewish thinkers of the middle ages developed unaided from without a system of thought and a *Weltanschauung*, based solely upon their own observation and ratiocination, and then found that the view of the world thus acquired stood in opposition to the religion of the Bible and the Talmud, the two thus requiring adjustment and reconciliation. *No!* The so-called demands of the reason were not of their own making, and on the other hand the relation between philosophy and religion was not altogether one of opposition. To discuss the latter point first, the teachings of the Bible and the Talmud were not altogether clear on a great many questions. Passages could be cited from the religious documents of Judaism in reference to a given problem both *pro* and *con*. Thus in the matter of freedom of the will one could argue on the one hand that man must be free to determine his conduct since if he were not there would have been no use in giving him commandments and prohibitions. And one could quote besides in favor of freedom the direct statement in Deuteronomy 30, 19, "I call heaven and earth to witness against you this day, that I have set before thee life and death, the blessing and the curse: therefore choose life, that thou mayest live, thou and thy seed." But on the other hand it was just as possible to find Biblical statements indicating clearly that God preordains how a person shall behave in a given case. Thus Pharaoh's heart was hardened that he should not let the children of Israel go out of Egypt, as we read in Exodus 7, 3: "And I will harden Pharaoh's heart, and multiply my signs and my wonders in the land of Egypt. But Pharaoh will not hearken unto you, and I will lay my hand upon Egypt, and bring forth my hosts, my people, the children of Israel, out of the land of Egypt by great judgments." Similarly in the case of Sihon king of Heshbon we read in Deuteromony 2, 30: "But Sihon king of Heshbon would not let us pass by him: for the Lord thy God hardened his spirit, and made his heart obstinate, that he might deliver him into thy hand, as at this day." And this is true not merely of heathen kings, Ahab king of Israel was similarly enticed by a divine instigation according to I Kings 22, 20: "And the Lord said, Who shall entice Ahab, that he may go up and fall at Ramoth-Gilead?"

The fact of the matter is the Bible is not a systematic book, and principles and problems are not clearly and strictly formulated even in the domain of ethics which is its strong point. It was not therefore a question here of opposition between the Bible and philosophy, or authority and reason. What was required was rather a rational analysis of the problem on its own merits and then an endeavor to show that the conflicting passages in the Scriptures are capable of interpretation so as to harmonize with each other and with the results of rational speculation. To be sure, it was felt that the doctrine of freedom is fundamental to the spirit of Judaism, and the philosophic analyses led to the same result though in differing form, sometimes dangerously approaching a thorough determinism, as in Hasdai Crescas.[1]

If such doubt was possible in an ethical problem where one would suppose the Bible would be outspoken, the uncertainty was still greater in purely metaphysical questions which as such were really foreign to its purpose as a book of religion and ethics. While it was clear that the Bible teaches the existence of God as the creator of the universe, and of man as endowed with a soul, it is manifestly difficult to extract from it a rigid and detailed theory as to the nature of God, the manner in which the world was created, the nature of the soul and its relation to man and to God. As long as the Jews were self-centered and did not come in close contact with an alien civilization of a philosophic mould, the need for a carefully thought out and consistent theory on all the questions suggested was not felt. And thus we have in the Talmudic literature quite a good deal of speculation concerning God and man. But it can scarcely lay claim to being rationalistic or philosophic, much less to being consistent. Nay, we have in the Bible itself at least two books which attempt an anti-dogmatic treatment of ethical problems. In Job is raised the question whether a man's fortunes on earth bear any relation to his conduct moral and spiritual. Ecclesiastes cannot make up his mind whether life is worth living, and how to make the best of it once one finds himself alive, whether by seeking wisdom or by pursuing pleasure. But here too Job is a long poem, and the argument does not progress very rapidly or very far. Ecclesiastes is rambling rather than analytic, and on the whole mostly negative. The Talmudists were visibly puzzled in their attitude to both books, wondered whether Job really existed or was only a fancy, and seriously thought of excluding Ecclesiastes from the canon. But these attempts at questioning the meaning of life had no further results. They did not lead, as in the case of the Greek Sophists, to a Socrates, a Plato or an Aristotle. Philo in Alexandria and Maimonides in Fostat were the products not of the Bible and the Talmud alone, but of a combination of Hebraism and Hellenism, pure in the case of Philo, mixed with the spirit of Islam in Maimonides.

And this leads us to consider the second point mentioned above, the nature and content of what was attributed in the middle ages to the credit of reason. It was in reality once more a set of documents. The Bible and Talmud were the documents of revelation, Aristotle was the document of reason. Each was supreme in its sphere, and all efforts must be bent to make them agree, for as revelation cannot be doubted, so neither can the assured results of reason. But not all which pretends to be the conclusion of reason is necessarily so in truth, as on the other hand the documents of faith are subject to interpretation and may mean something other than appears on the surface.

That the Bible has an esoteric meaning besides the literal has its source in the Talmud itself. Reference is found there to a mystic doctrine of creation known as "Maase Bereshit" and a doctrine of the divine chariot called "Maase Merkaba." [2] The exact nature of these teachings is not known since the Talmud itself prohibits the imparting of this mystic lore to any but the initiated, *i. e.*, to those showing themselves worthy; and never to more than one or two at a time.[3] But it is clear from the names of these doctrines that they centered about the creation story in Genesis and the account of the divine chariot in Ezekiel, chapters one and ten. Besides the Halaka and Agada are full of interpretations of Biblical texts which are very far from the literal and have little to do with the context. Moreover, the beliefs current among the Jews in Alexandria in the first century B. C. found their way into mediæval Jewry, that the philosophic literature of the Greeks was originally borrowed or stolen from the Hebrews, who lost it in times of storm and stress.[4] This being the case, it was believed that the Bible itself cannot be without some allusions to philosophic doctrines. That the Bible does not clearly teach philosophy is due to the fact that it was intended for the salvation of all men, the simple as well as the wise, women and children as well as male adults. For these it is sufficient that they know certain religious truths within their grasp and conduct themselves according to the laws of goodness and righteousness. A strictly philosophic book would have been beyond their ken and they would have been left without a guide in life. But the more intellectual and the more ambitious are not merely permitted, nay they are obligated to search the Scriptures for the deeper truths found therein, truths akin to the philosophic doctrines found in Greek literature; and the latter will help them in understanding the Bible aright. It thus became a duty to study philosophy and the sciences preparatory thereto, logic, mathematics and physics; and thus equipped to approach the Scriptures and interpret them in a philosophical manner. The study of mediæval Jewish rationalism has therefore two sides to it, the analysis of metaphysical, ethical and psychological problems, and the application of these studies to an interpretation of Scripture.

Now let us take a closer glance at the rationalistic or philosophic literature to which the Jews in the middle ages fell heirs. In 529 A. D. the Greek schools of philosophy in Athens were closed by order of Emperor Justinian. This did not, however, lead to the extinction of Greek thought as an influence in the world. For though the West was gradually declining intellectually on account of the fall of Rome and the barbarian invasions which followed in its train, there were signs of progress in the East which, feeble at first, was destined in the course of several centuries to illumine the whole of Europe with its enlightening rays.

Long before 529, the date of the closing of the Greek schools, Greek influence was introduced in the East in Asia and Africa.[5] The whole movement goes back to the days of Alexander the Great and the victories he gained in the Orient. From that time on Greeks settled in Asia and Africa and brought along with them Greek manners, the Greek language, and the Greek arts and sciences. Alexandria, the capital of the Ptolemies in Egypt after the death of Alexander, and Antioch, the capital of Syria under the empire of the Seleucidæ, were well-known centres of Greek learning.

When Syria changed masters in 64 B. C. and became a Roman province, its form of civilization did not change, and the introduction of Christianity had the effect of spreading the influence of the Greeks and their language into Mesopotamia beyond the Euphrates. The Christians in Syria had to study Greek in order to understand the Scriptures of the Old and the New Testaments, the decrees and canons of the ecclesiastical councils, and the writings of the Church Fathers. Besides religion and the Church, the liberal arts and sciences, for which the Greeks were so famous, attracted the interests of the Syrian Christians, and schools were established in the ecclesiastical centres where philosophy, mathematics and medicine were studied. These branches of knowledge were represented in Greek literature, and hence the works treating of these subjects had to be translated into Syriac for the benefit of those who did not know Greek. Aristotle was the authority in philosophy, Hippocrates and Galen in medicine.

The oldest of these schools was in Edessa in Mesopotamia, founded in the year 363 by St. Ephrem of Nisibis. It was closed in 489 and the teachers migrated to Persia where two other schools became famous, one at Nisibis and the other at Gandisapora. A third school of philosophy among the Jacobite or Monophysite Christians was that connected with the convent of Kinnesrin on the left bank of the Euphrates, which became famous as a seat of Greek learning in the beginning of the seventh century.

Christianity was succeeded in the Orient by Mohammedanism, and this change led to even greater cultivation of Greek studies on the part of the Syrians. The Mohammedan Caliphs employed the Syrians as physicians. This was especially true of the Abbasid dynasty, who came into power in 750. When they succeeded to the Caliphate they raised Nestorian Syrians to offices of importance, and the latter under the patronage of their masters continued their studies of Greek science and philosophy and translated those writings into Syriac and Arabic. Among the authors translated were, Hippocrates and Galen in medicine, Euclid, Archimedes and Ptolemy in mathematics and astronomy, and Aristotle, Theophrastus and Alexander of Aphrodisias in philosophy. In many cases the Greek writings were not turned directly into Arabic but as the translators were Syrians, the versions were made first into Syriac, and then from the Syriac into Arabic. The Syrian Christians were thus the mediators between the Greeks and the Arabs. The latter, however, in the course of time

far surpassed their Syrian teachers, developed important schools of
philosophy, became the teachers of the Jews, and with the help of the
latter introduced Greek philosophy as well as their own development
thereof into Christian Europe in the beginning of the thirteenth
century.

We see now that the impulse to philosophizing came from the
Greeks,—and not merely the impulse but the material, the matter
as well as the method and the terminology. In the Aristotelian writings we find developed an entire system of thought. There is not a
branch of knowledge dealing with fundamental principles which is not
there represented. First of all Aristotle stands alone as the discoverer
of the organon of thought, the tool which we all employ in our reasoning and reflection; he is the first formulator of the science and art of
logic. He treats besides of the principles of nature and natural phenomena in the Physics and the treatise on the Heavens. He discusses
the nature of the soul, the senses and the intellect in his "Psychology."
In the "History of Animals" and other minor works we have a treatment of biology. In the Nikomachean and Eudemian Ethics he analyzes the meaning of virtue, gives a list and classification of the virtues
and discusses the *summum bonum* or the aim of human life. Finally in
the Metaphysics we have an analysis of the fundamental notions of
being, of the nature of reality and of God.

The Jews did not get all this in its purity for various reasons. In
the first place it was only gradually that the Jews became acquainted
with the wealth of Aristotelian material. We are sure that Abraham
Ibn Daud, the forerunner of Maimonides, had a thorough familiarity
with the ideas of Aristotle; and those who came after him, for example
Maimonides, Gersonides, Hasdai Crescas, show clearly that they were
deep students of the ideas represented in the writings of the Stagirite.
But there is not the same evidence in the earlier writings of Isaac
Israeli, Saadia, Joseph Ibn Zaddik, Gabirol, Bahya Ibn Pakuda,
Judah Halevi. They had picked up Aristotelian ideas and principles,
but they had also absorbed ideas and concepts from other schools,
Greek as well as Arabian, and unconsciously combined the two.

Another explanation for the rarity of the complete and unadulter-
ated Aristotle among the Jewish thinkers of the middle ages is that
people in those days were very uncritical in the matter of historical

facts and relations. Historical and literary criticism was altogether unknown, and a number of works were ascribed to Aristotle which did not belong to him, and which were foreign in spirit to his mode of thinking. They emanated from a different school of thought with different presuppositions. I am referring to the treatise called the "Theology of Aristotle,"[6] and that known as the "Liber de Causis."[7] Both were attributed to Aristotle in the middle ages by Jews and Arabs alike, but it has been shown recently [8] that the former represents extracts from the works of Plotinus, the head of the Neo-Platonic school of philosophy, while the latter is derived from a treatise of Proclus, a Neo-Platonist of later date.

Finally a third reason for the phenomenon in question is that the Jews were the pupils of the Arabs and followed their lead in adapting Greek thought to their own intellectual and spiritual needs. It so happens therefore that even in the case of Abraham Ibn Daud, Maimonides and Gersonides, who were without doubt well versed in Aristotelian thought and entertained not merely admiration but reverence for the philosopher of Stagira, we notice that instead of reading the works of Aristotle himself, they preferred, or were obliged as the case may be, to go to the writings of Alfarabi, Avicenna and Averroes for their information on the views of the philosopher. In the case of Gersonides this is easily explained. It seems he could read neither Latin nor Arabic[9] and there was no Hebrew translation of the text of Aristotle. Averroes had taken in the fourteenth century the place of the Greek philosopher and instead of reading Aristotle all students read the works of the Commentator, as Averroes was called. Of course the very absence of a Hebrew translation of Aristotle's text proves that even among those who read Arabic the demand for the text of Aristotle was not great, and preference was shown for the works of the interpreters, compendists and commentators, like Alfarabi and Avicenna. And this helps us to understand why it is that Ibn Daud and Maimonides who not only read Arabic but wrote their philosophical works in Arabic showed the same preference for the secondhand Aristotle. One reason may have been the lack of historical and literary criticism spoken of above, and the other the difficulty of the Arabic translations of Aristotle. Aristotle is hard to translate into any language by reason of his peculiar technical terminology;

and the difficulty was considerably enhanced by the fact that the Syriac in many cases stood between the original Greek and the Arabic, and in the second place by the great dissimilarity between the Semitic language and its Indo-European original. This may have made the copies of Aristotle's text rare, and gradually led to their disuse. The great authority which names like Alfarabi, Avicenna and Averroes acquired still further served to stamp them as the approved expositors of the Aristotelian doctrine.

Among the Arabs the earliest division based upon a theoretical question was that of the parties known as the "Kadariya" and the "Jabariya." [10] The problem which was the cause of the difference was that of free will and determinism. Orthodox Islam favored the idea that man is completely dependent upon the divine will, and that not only his destiny but also his conduct is determined, and his own will does not count. This was the popular feeling, though as far as the Koran is concerned the question cannot be decided one way or the other, as it is not consistent in its stand, and arguments can be drawn in plenty in favor of either opinion. The idea of determinism, however, seemed repugnant to many minds, who could not reconcile this with their idea of reward and punishment and the justice of God. How is it possible that a righteous God would force a man to act in a certain manner and then punish him for it? Hence the sect of the "Kadariya," who were in favor of freedom of the will. The Jabariya were the determinists.

This division goes back to a very early period before the introduction of the Aristotelian philosophy among the Arabs, and hence owes its inception not to reason as opposed to religious dogma, but to a pious endeavor to understand clearly the religious view upon so important a question.

From the Kadariya, and in opposition to the Aristotelian movement which had in the meantime gained ground, developed the school of theologians known as the "Mutakallimun." They were the first among the Arabs who deliberately laid down the reason as a source of knowledge in addition to the authority of the Koran and the "Sunna" or tradition. They were not freethinkers, and their object was not to oppose orthodoxy as such. On the contrary, their purpose was to purify the faith by freeing it from such elements as obscured in their minds the purity of the monotheistic tenet and the justice of God. They started where the Kadariya left off and went further. As a school of opposition their efforts were directed to prove the creation of the world, individual providence, the reality of miracles, as against the "philosophers," *i. e.*, the Aristotelians, who held to the eternity of motion, denied God's knowledge of particulars, and insisted on the unchanging character of natural law.

For this purpose they placed at the basis of their speculations not the Aristotelian concepts of matter and form, the former uncreated and continuous, but adopted the atomistic theory of Democritus, denied the necessity of cause and effect and the validity of natural law, and made God directly responsible for everything that happened every moment in life. God, they said, creates continually, and he is not hampered by any such thing as natural law, which is merely our name for that which we are accustomed to see. Whenever it rains we are accustomed to see the ground wet, and we conclude that there is a necessary connection of cause and effect between the rain and the wetness of the ground. Nothing of the kind, say the Mutakallimun, or the Mu'tazila, the oldest sect of the school. It rains because God willed that it should rain, and the ground is wet because God wills it shall be wet. If God willed that the ground should be dry following a rain, it would be dry; and the one is no more and no less natural than the other. Miracles cease to be miracles on this conception of natural processes. Similarly the dogma of creation is easily vindicated on this theory as against the Aristotelian doctrine of eternity of the world, which follows from his doctrine of matter and form, as we shall have occasion to see later.

The Mu'tazila were, however, chiefly known not for their principles of physics but for their doctrines of the unity of God and his justice. It was this which gave them their name of the "Men of Unity and Justice," *i. e.*, the men who vindicate against the unenlightened views of popular orthodoxy the unity of God and his justice.

The discussion of the unity centered about the proper interpretation of the anthropomorphic passages in the Koran and the doctrine of the divine attributes. When the Koran speaks of God's eyes, ears, hands, feet; of his seeing, hearing, sitting, standing, walking, being angry, smiling, and so on, must those phrases be understood literally? If so God is similar to man, corporeal like him, and swayed by passions. This seemed to the Mu'tazila an unworthy conception of God. To vindicate his spirituality the anthropomorphic passages in the Koran must be understood metaphorically.

The other more difficult question was in what sense can attributes be ascribed to God at all? It is not here a question of anthropomorphism. If I say that God is omniscient, omnipotent and a living God, I attribute to God life, power, knowledge. Are these attributes the same with God's essence or are they different? If different (and they must be eternal since God was never without them), then we have more than one eternal being, and God is dependent upon others. If they are not different from God's essence, then his essence is not a strict unity, since it is composed of life, power, knowledge; for life is not power, and power is not knowledge. The only way to defend the unity of God in its absolute purity is to say that God has no attributes, *i. e.*, God is omniscient but not through knowledge as his attribute; God is omnipotent but not through power as his attribute, and so on. God is absolutely one, and there is no distinction between knowledge, power, and life in him. They are all one, and are his essence.

This seemed in opposition to the words of the Koran, which frequently speaks of God's knowledge, power, and so on, and was accordingly condemned as heretical by the orthodox.

In the tenth century a new sect arose named the "Ashariya" after Al-Ashari, its founder. This was a party of moderation, and tended to conciliate orthodoxy by not going too far in the direction of rationalistic thinking. They solved the problem by saying, "God knows through a knowledge which is not different from his essence."

The other problem to which the Mu'tazila devoted their attention was that of the justice of God. This was in line with the efforts of the Kadariya before them. It concerned itself with the doctrine of free will. They defended man's absolute freedom of action, and insisted on justice as the only motive of God's dealings with men. God must be just and cannot act otherwise than in accordance with justice.

In reference to the question of the nature of good and evil, the orthodox position was that good is that which God commands, evil that which God forbids. In other words, nothing is in itself good or evil, the ethical character of an act is purely relative to God's attitude to it. If God were to command cannibalism, it would be a good act. The Mu'tazila were opposed to this. They believed in the absolute character of good and evil. What makes an act good or bad is reason, and it is because an act is good that God commands it, and not the reverse.

The foregoing account gives us an idea of the nature of the Mu'tazilite discussions of the two problems of God's unity and God's justice. Their works were all arranged in the same way. They were divided into two parts, one dealing with the question of the unity, and the other with that of justice. The proofs of the unity were preceded by the proofs of God's existence, and the latter were based upon a demonstration that the world is not eternal, but bears traces of having come to be in time. These are the earmarks by which a Mu'tazilite book could be recognized, and the respect for them on the part of the philosophers, *i. e.*, the Aristotelians, was not great. The latter did not consider them worthy combatants in a philosophical fight, claiming that they came with preconceived notions and arranged their conceptions of nature to suit the religious beliefs which they desired to defend. Maimonides expresses a similar judgment concerning their worthlessness as philosophical thinkers.[11]

This school of the Mutakallimun, or of the more important part of it known as the Mu'tazila, is of great interest for the history of Jewish rationalism. In the first place their influence on the early Jewish philosophers was great and unmistakable. It is no discovery of a late day but is well known to Maimonides who is himself, as has just been said and as will appear with greater detail later, a strong opponent of these to him unphilosophical thinkers. In the seventy-first chapter of his "Guide of the Perplexed," he says, "You will find that in the few works composed by the Geonim and the Karaites on the unity of God and on such matter as is connected with this doctrine, they followed the lead of the Mohammedan Mutakallimun. . . . It also happened, that at the time when the Mohammedans adopted this method of the Kalam, there arose among them a certain sect, called Mu'tazila. In certain things our scholars followed the theory and the method of these Mu'tazila."

Thanks to the researches of modern Jewish and non-Jewish scholars we know now that the Rabbanite thinker Saadia and the Karaite writers, like Joseph Al Basir and Jeshuah ben Judah, are indebted far more to the Mohammedan Mu'tazilites than would appear from Maimonides's statement just quoted. The Rabbanites being staunch adherents of the Talmud, to the influence of which they owed a national and religious self-consciousness much stronger than that of the Karaites, who rejected the authority of tradition, did not allow themselves to be carried away so far by the ideas of the Mohammedan rationalists as to become their slavish followers. The Karaites are less scrupulous; and as they were the first among the Jews to imitate the Mu'tazila in the endeavor to rationalize Jewish doctrine, they adopted their views in all details, and it is sometimes impossible to tell from the contents of a Karaite Mu'tazilite work whether it was written by a Jew or a Mohammedan. The arrangement of the work in the two divisions of "Unity" and "Justice," the discussion of substance and accident, of the creation of the world, of the existence, unity and incorporeality of God, of his attributes, of his justice, and of human free will, are so similar in the two that it is external evidence alone to which we owe the knowledge of certain Karaite works as Jewish. There are no mediæval Jewish works treating of religious and theological problems in which there is so much aloofness, such absence of theological prepossession and religious feeling as in some Karaite writings of Mu'tazilite stamp. Cold and unredeemed logic gives the tone to the entire composition.

Another reason for the importance of the Mu'tazilite school for the history of Jewish thought is of recent discovery. Schreiner has suggested [12] that the origin of the Mu'tazilite movement was due to the influence of learned Jews with whom the Mohammedans came in contact, particularly in the city of Basra, an important centre of the school. The reader will recall that the two main doctrines of the Mu'tazila were the unity of God and his justice. The latter really signified the freedom of the will. That these are good Jewish views would of course prove nothing for the origin of similar opinions among the Mohammedans. For it is not here a question simply of the dogmatic belief in Monotheism as opposed to polytheism. Mohammedanism is as a religion Monotheistic and we know that Mohammed was indebted very much to Jews and Judaism. We are here concerned with the origin of a rationalistic movement which endeavors to defend a spiritual conception of God against a crude anthropomorphism, to vindicate a conception of his absolute unity against the threatened multiplication of his essence by the assumption of eternal attributes, and which puts stress upon God's justice rather than upon his omnipotence so as to save human freedom. Another doctrine of the Mu'tazila was that the Koran was not eternal as the orthodox believed, but that it was created. Now we can find parallels for most of these doctrines. Anthropomorphism was avoided in the Aramaic translations of the Pentateuch, also in certain changes in the Hebrew text which are recorded in Rabbinical literature, and known as "Tikkune Soferim," or corrections of the Scribes.[13] Concern for maintaining the unity of God in its absolute purity is seen in the care with which the men of the Agada forbid any prayer which may have a semblance, however remote, of dualism.[14] The freedom of the will is clearly stated in the Rabbinic expression, "All is in the hands of God except the fear of Heaven." [15] And an apparently deterministic passage in Job 23, 13, "But he is one and who can turn him, and what his soul desireth, even that he doeth," is explained by Rabbi Akiba in the following manner, "It is not possible to answer the words of him who with his word created the world, for he rules all things with truth and with righteousness." [16] And we find a parallel also for the creation of the Koran in the Midrashic statement that the Torah is one of the six or seven things created before the world.[17]

These parallels alone would not be of much weight, but they are strengthened by other considerations. The Mu'tazilite movement seems to have developed among the ascetic sects, with the leaders of whom its founders were in close relation.[18] The ascetic literature bears unmistakable traces of having been influenced by the Halaka and the Agada.[19] Moreover, there is a Mohammedan tradition or two to the effect that the doctrine of the creation of the Koran and also of the rejection of anthropomorphism goes back to a Jew, Lebid-ibn Al-A'sam.[20]

More recently still * C. H. Becker proved from a study of certain Patristic writings that the polemical literature of the Christians played an important rôle in the formation of Mohammedan dogma,

* Cf. Zeitschrift für Assyriologie, 1912, 175 ff.

and he shows conclusively that the form in which the problem of freedom was discussed among the Mohammedans was taken from Christianity. The question of the creation or eternity of the Koran or word of Allah, is similarly related to the Christian idea of the eternal Logos, who is on the one hand the Word and the Wisdom, and is on the other identified with Jesus Christ. And the same thing holds of the doctrine of attributes. It played a greater rôle in Christian dogma than it ever did in Judaism prior to the philosophic era in the middle ages. To be sure, the Patristic writers were much indebted to Philo, in whose writings the germ of the mediæval doctrine of attributes is plainly evident. But the Mohammedan schools did not read Philo. It would seem, therefore, that Schreiner's view must be considerably modified, if not entirely rejected, in view of the later evidence adduced by Becker.

The more extreme doctrines, however, of the more orthodox Ashariya, such as the denial of natural law and the necessity of cause and effect, likewise the denial of man's ability to determine his actions, none of the Jews accepted. Here we have again the testimony of Maimonides, who, however, is not inclined to credit this circumstance to the intelligence and judgment of his predecessors, but to chance. His words are, "Although another sect, the Ashariya, with their own peculiar views, was subsequently established among the Mohammedans, you will not find any of these views in the writings of our authors; not because these authors preferred the opinions of the first named sect to those of the latter, but because they chanced first to become acquainted with the theory of the Mu'tazila, which they adopted and treated as demonstrated truth."[21]

The influence of the Kalam is present in greater or less degree in the philosophers up to Abraham Ibn Daud and Maimonides. The latter gave this system its death blow in his thoroughgoing criticism,[22] and thenceforth Aristotelianism was in possession of the field until that too was attacked by Hasdai Crescas.

Another sect of the Mohammedans which had considerable influence on some of the Jewish philosophical and ethical writers are the ascetics and the Sufis who are related to them. The latter developed their mode of life and their doctrines under the influence of the Christian monks, and are likewise indebted to Indian and Persian ideas.[23]

In their mode of life they belong to the class of ascetics and preach abstinence, indifference to human praise and blame, love of God and absolute trust in him even to the extent of refraining from all effort in one's own behalf, and in extreme cases going so far as to court danger. In theoretical teaching they adopted the emanatistic doctrine of the Neo-Platonic School. This has been called dynamic Pantheism. It is Pantheism because in its last analysis it identifies God with the universe. At the same time it does not bring God directly in contact with the world, but only indirectly through the powers or $\delta\upsilon\nu\acute{\alpha}\mu\epsilon\iota\varsigma$, hence *dynamic* Pantheism. These powers emanate successively from the highest one, forming a chain of intermediate powers mediating between God and the world of matter, the links of the chain growing dimmer and less pure as they are further removed from their origin, while the latter loses nothing in the process. This latter condition saves the Neo-Platonic conception from being a pure system of emanation like some Indian doctrines. In the latter the first cause actually gives away something of itself and loses thereby from its fulness. The process in both systems is explained by use of analogies, those of the radiation of light from a luminous body, and of the overflowing of a fountain being the most common.

The chief exponent of the ethics of the Sufis in mediæval Jewish literature is Bahya Ibn Pakuda. In his ethical work "The Duties of the Hearts," he lays the same stress on intention and inwardness in religious life and practice as against outward performance with the limbs on the one hand and dry scholasticism on the other, as do the Sufis. In matters of detail too he is very much indebted to this Arab sect from whose writings he quotes abundantly with as well as without acknowledgment of his sources except in a general way as the wise men. To be sure, he does not follow them slavishly and rejects the extremes of asceticism and unworldly cynicism which a great many of the Sufis preached and practiced. He is also not in sympathy with their mysticism. He adopts their teachings only where he can support them with analogous views as expressed in the Rabbinical writings. which indeed played an important rôle in Mohammedan ascetic literature, being the source of many of the sayings found in the latter.[24]

The systems of thought which had the greatest influence upon Jewish as well as Mohammedan theology, were the great systems of

Plato (especially as developed in Neo-Platonism) and Aristotle. These two philosophies not merely affected the thinking of Jew and Mohammedan but really transformed it from religious and ethical discussions into metaphysical systems. In the Bible and similarly in the Koran we have a purely personal view of God and the world. God is a person, he creates the world—out of nothing to be sure—but nevertheless he is thought of doing it in the manner in which a person does such things with a will and a purpose in time and place. He puts a soul into man and communicates to him laws and prohibitions. Man must obey these laws because they are the will of God and are good, and he will be rewarded and punished according to his attitude in obedience and disobedience. The character of the entire point of view is personal, human, teleological, ethical. There is no attempt made at an impersonal and objective analysis of the common aspects of all existing things, the elements underlying all nature. Nor is there any conscious effort at a critical classification of the various kinds of things existing in nature beyond the ordinary and evident classification found in Genesis—heaven and earth; in heaven, sun, moon and stars; on earth, grass, fruit trees, insects, water animals, birds, quadrupeds, man. Then light and darkness, the seasons of the year, dry land and water.

In Greek philosophy for the first time we find speculations concerning the common element or elements out of which the world is made—the material cause as Aristotle later called it. The Sophists and Socrates gave the first impulse to a logical analysis of what is involved in description or definition. The concept as denoting the essence of a thing is the important contribution Socrates made to knowledge. Plato objectified the concept, or rather he posited an object as the basis of the concept, and raised it out of this world of shadows to an intelligible world of realities on which the world of particulars depends. But it was Aristotle who made a thoroughgoing analysis of thing as well as thought, and he was the master of knowledge through the middle ages alike for Jew, Christian and Mohammedan.

First of all he classified all objects of our experience and found that they can be grouped in ten classes or categories as he called them. Think of any thing you please and you will find that it is either an object in the strict sense, *i. e.*, some thing that exists independently of anything else, and is the recipient of qualities, as for example a man, a mountain, a chair. Or it is a quantity, like four, or cubit; or a quality, like good, black, straight; or a relation like long, double, master, slave; and so on throughout the ten categories. This classification applies to words and thoughts as well as to things. As an analysis of the first two it led him to more important investigations of speech and thinking and arguing, and resulted in his system of logic, which is the most momentous discovery of a single mind recorded in history. As applied to things it was followed by a more fundamental analysis of all real objects in our world into the two elements of matter and form. He argued as follows: nothing in the material world is permanent as an individual thing. It changes its state from moment to moment and finally ceases to be the thing it was. An acorn passes a number of stages before it is ripe, and when it is placed in the ground it again changes its form continually and then comes out as an oak. In artificial products man in a measure imitates nature. He takes a block of marble and makes a statue out of it. He forms a log into a bed. So an ignorant man becomes civilized and learned. All these examples illustrate change. What then is change? Is there any similarity in all the cases cited? Can we express the process of change in a formula which will apply to all instances of change? If so, we shall have gained an insight into a process of nature which is all-embracing and universal in our experience. Yes, we can, says Aristotle. Change is a play of two elements in the changing thing. When a thing affected with one quality changes into a thing with the opposite quality, there must be the thing itself without either of the opposite qualities, which is changing. Thus when a white fence becomes black, the fence itself or that which undergoes the change is something neither white nor black. It is the uncolored matter which first had the form of white and now lost that and took on the form of black. This is typical of all change. There is in all change ultimately an unchanging substratum always the same, which takes on one quality after another, or as Aristotle would say, one *form* after another. This substratum is *matter*, which in its purity is not affected with any quality or form, of which it is the seat and residence. The forms on the other hand come and go. Form does not change any more than matter. The changing thing is the composite of matter and form, and change means separation of the actual components of which one, the form, disappears and makes room for its opposite. In a given case, say, when a statue is made out of a block of marble, the matter is the marble which lost its original form and assumed the form of a statue. In this case the marble, if you take away both the previous form and the present, will still have some form if it is still marble, for marble must have certain qualities if it is to be marble. In that case then the matter underlying the change in question is not pure matter, it is already endowed with some primitive form and is composite. But marble is ultimately reducible to the four elements, fire, air, water, earth, which are simpler; and theoretically, though not in practice, we can think away all form, and we have left only that which takes forms but is itself not any form. This is matter.

Here the reader will ask, what kind of thing is it that has no form whatsoever, is it not nothing at all? How can anything exist without being a particular kind of thing, and the moment it is that it is no longer pure matter. Aristotle's answer is that it is true that pure matter is never found as an objective existence. Point to any real object and it is composed of matter and form. And yet it is not true that matter is a pure figment of the imagination; it has an existence of its own, a potential existence. And this leads us to another important conception in the Aristotelian philosophy.

Potentiality and actuality are correlative terms corresponding to matter and form. Matter is the potential, form is the actual. Whatever potentialities an object has it owes to its matter. Its actual essence is due to its form. A thing free from matter would be all that it is at once. It would not be liable to change of any kind, whether progress or retrogression. All the objects of our experience in the sublunar world are not of this kind. They realize themselves gradually, and are never at any given moment all that they are capable of becoming. This is due to their matter. On the other hand, pure matter is *actually* nothing. It is just capacity for being anything, and the moment it is anything it is affected with form.

It is clear from this account that matter and form are the bases of sublunar life and existence. No change, no motion without matter and form. For motion is presupposed in all kinds of change. If then all processes of life and death and change of all kinds presuppose matter and form, the latter cannot themselves be liable to genesis and decay and change, for that would mean that matter is composed of matter and form, which is absurd. We thus see how Aristotle is led to believe in the eternity of matter and motion, in other words, the eternity of the world processes as we know them.

Motion is the realization of the potential *qua* potential. This is an Aristotelian definition and applies not merely to motion in the strict sense, *i. e.*, movement in place, or motion of translation, but embraces all kinds of change. Take as an example the warming of the air in a cold room. The process of heating the room is a kind of motion; the air passes from a state of being cold to a state of being warm. In its original state as cold it is potentially warm, *i. e.*, it is actually not warm, but has the capacity of becoming warm. At the end of the process it is actually warm. Hence the process itself is the actualization of the potential. That which is potential cannot make itself actual, for to make itself actual it must be actual, which is contrary to the hypothesis of its being potential. Potentiality and actuality are contradictory states and cannot exist side by side in the same thing at the same time in the same relation. There must therefore be an external agent, itself actual, to actualize a potential. Thus, in the above illustration, a cold room cannot make itself warm. There must be some agency itself actually warm to cause the air in the room to pass from cold to warm. This is true also of motion in place, that a thing cannot move itself and must be moved by something else. But that something else if itself in motion must again be moved by something else. This process would lead us to infinity. In order that a given thing shall be in motion, it would be necessary for an infinite number of things to be in motion. This is impossible, because there cannot be an infinite number of things all here and now. It is a contradiction in terms. Hence if anything is to move at all, there must be at the end of the finite chain a link which while causing the next link to move, is itself unmoved. Hence the motion existing in the world must be due ultimately to the existence of an unmoved mover. If this being causes motion without being itself in motion it does not act upon the bodies it moves as one body acts upon another, for a.body can move another body only by being itself in motion. The manner in which the unmoved mover moves the world is rather to be conceived on the analogy of a loved object moving the loving object without itself being moved. The person in love strives to approach and unite with the object of his love without the latter necessarily being moved in turn. This is the way in which Aristotle conceives of the cause of the world's motion. There is no room here for the creation of the world. Matter is eternal, motion is eternal, and there is an eternal mind for the love of which all motions have been going on eternally.

The unmoved mover, or God, is thus not body, for no body can move another body without being itself in motion at the same time. Besides, all body is finite, *i. e.*, it has a finite magnitude. A body of infinite magnitude is an impossibility, as the very essence of body is that it must be bounded by surfaces. A finite body cannot have an infinite power, as Aristotle proves, though we need not at present go into the details of his proof. But a being which causes eternal motion in the world must have an infinite power to do this. Hence another proof that God is not corporeal.

If God is not subject to motion, he is not subject to change of any kind, for change involves motion. As matter is at the basis of all change God is without matter, hence he is pure form, *i. e.*, pure actuality without the least potentiality. This means that he is what he is wholly all the time; he has no capacities of being what he is at any time not. But if he is not corporeal, the nature of his actuality or activity must be Thought, pure thinking. And the content of his thought cannot vary from topic to topic, for this would be change, which is foreign to him. He must be eternally thinking the same thought; and the highest thought it must be. But the highest thought is himself; hence God is pure thought thinking himself, thought thinking thought.

The universe is in the shape of a sphere with the earth stationary in the centre and the heavens revolving around it exactly as appears to us. The element earth is the heaviest, hence its place is below or, which is the same thing, in the centre. This is its natural place; and its natural motion when away from the centre is in a straight line toward the centre. Water is the next heaviest element and its natural place is just above earth; hence the water in the world occupies a position spherical in shape round about the earth, *i. e.*, it forms a hollow sphere concentric with the earth. Next comes the hollow sphere of air concentric with the other two. Its natural motion when away from its place in the direction of the earth is in a straight line toward the circumference of the world, not however going beyond the sphere of the lightest element of all, namely, fire. This has its natural place outside of the other elements, also in the form of a hollow sphere concentric with the other three. Its natural motion is in a straight line away from the centre of the world and in the direction of the circumference. Our earth, water, air and fire are not really the elements in their purity. Each one has in it also mixtures of the other three elements, the one which gives it the name predominating.

All minerals, plants and animals are formed from these four elements by various combinations, all together forming the sublunar world or the world of generation and decay. No individual thing in this world is permanent. All are subject to change and to ultimate destruction, though the destruction of one thing is the genesis of another. There is no annihilation.

The causes of the various combinations of the elements and the generation and destruction of mineral, plant and animal resulting therefrom, are the motions of the heavenly bodies. These are made of a purer substance than that of the four elements, the ether. This is proven by the fact that the heavenly bodies are not subject to change or destruction. They are all permanent and the only change visible in them is change of place. But even their motions are different from those of the four elements. The latter are in a straight line toward the centre or away from it, whereas the heavenly bodies move in a circle eternally around the centre. This is another proof that they are not composed of the same material as sublunar bodies.

The heavens consist of transparent spheres, and the stars as well as the planets are set in them and remain fixed. The motions of the heavenly bodies are due to the revolutions of the spheres in which they are set. These spheres are hollow and concentric. The outermost sphere forming the outer limit of the universe (the world is finite according to Aristotle) is studded with the fixed stars and moves from east to west, making a complete revolution in twenty-four hours. This motion is transmitted to the other spheres which carry the planets. Since, however, we notice in the sun, moon and the other planetary bodies motions in the contrary direction in addition to that from east to west, there must be other spheres having the motions apparent to us in the positions of the planets borne by them. Thus a given body like the sun or moon is set in more than one sphere, each of which has its own proper motion, and the star's apparent motion is the resultant of the several motions of its spheres. Without entering into further details concerning these motions, it will be sufficient for us to know that Aristotle counted in all fifty-five spheres. First came the sphere of the fixed stars, then in order the spheres of Saturn, Jupiter, Mars, Mercury, Venus, Sun, Moon.

God himself sets the outer sphere in motion, or rather is the eternal cause of its motion, as the object of its desire; and in the same way each of the other motions has also its proper mover, likewise a pure form or spirit, which moves its sphere in the same incorporeal and unmoved manner as God.

Thus we have in the supra-lunar world pure forms without matter in God and the spirits of the spheres, whereas in the sublunar world matter and form are inseparable. Neither is found separately without the other.

In man's soul, however, or rather in his intellect we find a form which combines in itself the peculiarities of sublunar as well as celestial forms. When in contact with the human body it partakes of the nature of other sublunar forms exhibiting its activity through matter and being inseparable from it. But it is not destroyed with the death of the body. It continues as a separate form after death.

The soul, Aristotle defines as the first entelechy of the body. The term entelechy which sounds outlandish to us may be replaced by the word realization or actualization and is very close in meaning to the Aristotelian use of the word form. The soul then, according to Aristotle, is the realization or actualization or form of the body. The body takes the place of matter in the human composite. It has the composition and the structure which give it the capacity for performing the functions of a human being, as in any other composite, say an axe, the steel is the matter which has the potentiality or capacity of being made into a cutting instrument. Its cutting function is the form of the axe—we might almost say the soul of the axe, if it were not for the circumstance that it cannot do its own cutting; it must be wielded by someone else.

So far then the human soul forms an inseparable unit with the body which it informs. As we do not think of the cutting function of an axe existing apart from the axe, so neither can we conceive of sensation, emotion or memory as existing without a body. In so far as the soul is this it is a material form like the rest, and ceases with the dissolution of the body. But the soul is more than this. It is also a thinking faculty. As such it is not in its essence dependent upon the body or any corporeal organ. It comes from without, having existed before the body, and it will continue to exist after the body is no more. That it is different from the sensitive soul is proven by the fact that the latter is inherent in the physical organ through which it acts, being the form of the body, as we have seen. And hence when an unusually violent stimulus, say a very bright light or a very loud sound, impinges upon the sense organ, the faculty of sight or hearing is injured to such an extent that it cannot thereafter perceive an ordinary sight or sound. But in the rational faculty this is not the case. The more intense the thought occupying the thinking soul, the more capable it becomes of thinking lesser thoughts. To be sure, the reason seems to weaken in old age, but this is due to the weakening of the body with which the soul is connected during life; the soul itself is just as active as ever.

We must, however, distinguish between two aspects of the rational soul, to one of which alone the above statements apply. Thought differs from sensation in that the latter perceives the particular form of the individual thing, whereas the former apprehends the essential nature of the object, that which constitutes it a member of a certain class. The sense of sight perceives a given individual man; thought or reason understands what it is to be a member of the human species. Reason therefore deals with pure form. In man we observe the reason gradually developing from a potential to an actual state. The objects of the sense with the help of the faculties of sensation, memory and imagination act upon the potential intellect of the child, which without them would forever remain a mere capacity without ever being realized. This aspect of the reason then in man, namely, the passive aspect which receives ideas, grows and dies with the body.

But there is another aspect of the reason, the active reason which has nothing to do with the body, though it is in some manner resident in it during the life of the latter. This it is which enables the passive intellect to become realized. For the external objects as such are insufficient to endow the rational capacity of the individual with actual ideas, any more than a surface can endow the sense of sight with the sensation of color when there is no light. It is the active intellect which develops the human capacity for thinking and makes it active thought. This alone, the active intellect, is the immortal part of man.

This very imperfect sketch of Aristotle's mode of approach to the ever-living problems of God, the universe and man shows us the wide diversity of his method from that with which the Jews of Biblical and Rabbinic tradition were identified. Greek philosophy must have seemed a revelation to them, and we do not wonder that they became such enthusiastic followers of the Stagirite, feeling as they must have done that his method as well as his results were calculated to enrich their intellectual and spiritual life. Hence the current belief of an original Jewish philosophy borrowed or stolen by the Greeks, and still betraying its traces in the Bible and Talmud was more than welcome to the enlightened spirits of the time. And they worked this unhistorical belief to its breaking point in their Biblical exegesis.

Aristotle, however, was not their only master, though they did not know it. Plotinus in Aristotelian disguise contributed not a little to their conception of God and his relation to the universe. The so-called "Theology of Aristotle" [25] is a Plotinian work, and its Pantheistic point of view is in reality foreign to Aristotle's dualism. But the middle ages were not aware of the origin of this treatise, and so they attributed it to the Stagirite philosopher and proceeded to harmonize it with the rest of his system as they knew it.

Aristotle's system may be called theistic and dualistic; Plotinus's is pantheistic and monistic. In Aristotle matter is not created by or derived from God, who is external to the universe. Plotinus derives everything from God, who through his powers or activities pervades all. The different gradations of being are static in Aristotle, dynamic in Plotinus. Plotinus assumes an absolute cause, which he calls the One and the Good. This is the highest and is at the top of the scale of existence. It is superior to Being as well as to Thought, for the latter imply a duality whereas unity is prior to and above all plurality. Hence we can know nothing as to the nature of the Highest. We can know only *that* He is, not *what* he is. From this highest Being proceeds by a physical necessity, as light from a luminous body or water from an overflowing spring, a second *hypostasis* or substance the *nous* or Reason. This is a duality, constituting Being and Knowledge. Thus Thought and Being hold a second place in the universe. In a similar way from Reason proceeds the third hypostasis or the *World-Soul*. This stands midway between the intelligible world, of which it is the last, and the phenomenal world, of which it is the first. The Soul has a dual aspect, the one spiritual and pertaining to the intelligible world, the other, called *Nature*, residing in the lower world. This is the material world of change and decay. Matter is responsible for all change and evil, and yet matter, too, is a product of the powers above it, and is ultimately a derivative of the Absolute Cause, though indirectly. Matter is two-fold, intelligible and sensible. The matter of the lower world is the non-existent and the cause of evil. Matter in a more general sense is the indeterminate, the indefinite and the potential. Matter of this nature is found also in the intelligible world. The Reason as the second hypostasis, being an activity, passes from potentiality to actuality, its indeterminateness being made determinate by the One or the Good. This potentiality and indeterminateness is matter, but it is not to be confused with the other matter of the phenomenal world.

Man partakes of the intelligible, as well as of the sensible world. His body is material, and in so far forth partakes of the evil of matter. But his soul is derived from the universal soul, and if it conducts itself properly in this world, whither it came from without, and holds itself aloof from bodily contamination, it will return to the intelligible world where is its home.

We see here a number of ideas foreign to Aristotle, which are found first in Philo the Jew and appear later in mediæval philosophy. Thus God as a Being absolutely unknowable, of whom negations alone are true just because he is the acme of perfection and bears no analogy to the imperfect things of our world; matter in our world as the origin of evil, and the existence of matter in the intelligible world—all these ideas will meet us again in Ibn Gabirol, in Ibn Daud, in Maimonides, some in one, some in the other.

Alike in respect to Aristotle as in reference to Plotinus, the Jewish philosophers found their models in Islamic writers. The "Theology of Aristotle" which, as we have seen, is really Plotinian rather than Aristotelian, was translated into Arabic in the ninth century and exerted its influence on the *Brethren of Purity*, a Mohammedan secret order of the tenth century. These men composed an encyclopædia of fifty-one treatises in which is combined Aristotelian logic and physics with Neo-Platonic metaphysics and theology. In turn such Jewish writers as Ibn Gabirol, Bahya, Ibn Zaddik, Judah Halevi, Moses and Abraham Ibn Ezra, were much indebted to the Brethren of Purity. This represents the Neo-Platonic influence in Jewish philosophy. The Arab Aristotelians, Al Kindi, Al Farabi, Avicenna and Averroes, while in the main disciples of the Stagirite, were none the less unable to steer clear of Neo-Platonic coloring of their master's doctrine, and they were the teachers of the Jewish Aristotelians, Abraham Ibn Daud, Moses ben Maimon, Levi ben Gerson.

One other phase must be mentioned to complete the parallelism of Islamic and Jewish philosophy, and that is the anti-philosophic attitude adopted by Judah Halevi and Hasdai Crescas. It was not a dogmatic and unreasoned opposition based simply upon the un-Jewish source of the doctrines in question and their incompatibility with Jewish belief and tradition, such as exhibited itself in the controversies that raged around the "Guide" of Maimonides. Here we have rather a fighting of the philosophers with their own weapons. Especially do we find this to be the case in Crescas who opposes Aristotle on philosophic grounds. In Judah Halevi similarly, though with less rigor and little technical discussion, we have nevertheless a man trained in philosophic literature, who found the philosophic attitude unsympathetic and unsatisfying because cold and impersonal, failing to do justice to the warm yearning after God of the religious soul. He could not abide the philosophic exclusion from their natural theology of all that was racial and national and historic in religion, which was to him its very heart and innermost essence.

In this attitude, too, we find an Arab prototype in the person of Al Gazali, who similarly attacked the philosophers on their own ground and found his consolation in the asceticism and mysticism of the Sufis.

We have now spoken in a general way of the principal motives of mediæval Jewish philosophy, of the chief sources, philosophical and dogmatic, and have classified the Jewish thinkers accordingly as Mutakallimun, Neo-Platonists and Aristotelians. We also sketched briefly the schools of philosophy which influenced the Jewish writers and determined their point of view as Kalamistic, Neo-Platonic or Aristotelian. There still remains as the concluding part of the introductory chapter, and before we take up the detailed exposition of the individual philosophers, to give a brief and compendious characterization of the content of mediæval Jewish philosophy. We shall start with the theory of knowledge.

We have already referred to the attitude generally adopted by the mediæval Jewish thinkers on the relation between religion and philosophy. With the exception of Judah Halevi and Hasdai Crescas the commonly accepted view was that philosophy and religion were at bottom identical in content, though their methods were different; philosophy taught by means of rational demonstration, religion by dogmatic assertion based upon divine revelation. So far as the actual philosophical views of an Aristotle were concerned, they might be erroneous in some of their details, as was indeed the case in respect to the origin of the world and the question of Providence. But apart from his errors he was an important guide, and philosophy generally is an indispensable adjunct to religious belief because it makes the latter intelligent. It explains the why's and the wherefore's of religious traditions and dogmas. Into detailed discussions concerning the origin of our knowledge they did not as a rule go. These strictly scientific questions did not concern, except in a very general way, the main object of their philosophizing, which was to gain true knowledge of God and his attributes and his relation to man. Accordingly we find for the most part a simple classification of the sources of knowledge or truth as consisting of the senses and the reason. The latter contains some truths which may be called innate or immediate, such as require no experience for their recognition, like the logical laws of thought, and truths which are the result of inference from a fact of sensation or an immediate truth of the mind. To these human sources was added tradition or the testimony of the revealed word of God in the written and oral law.

When Aristotle began to be studied in his larger treatises and the details of the psychology and the metaphysics became known especially through Averroes, we find among the Jews also an interest in the finer points of the problem of knowledge. The motives of Plato's idealism and Aristotle's conceptualism (if this inexact description may be allowed for want of a more precise term) are discussed with fulness and detail by Levi ben Gerson. He realizes the difficulty involved in the problem. Knowledge must be of the real and the permanent. But the particular is not permanent, and the universal, which is permanent, is not real. Hence either there is no knowledge or there is a reality corresponding to the universal concept. This latter was the view adopted by Plato. Gersonides finds the reality in the thoughts of the Active Intellect, agreeing in this with the views of Philo and Augustine, substituting only the Active Intellect for their Logos. Maimonides does not discuss the question, but it is clear from a casual statement that like Aristotle he does not believe in the independent reality of the universal (Guide III, 18).

In theoretical physics the Arabian Mutakallimun, we have seen (p. xxii), laid great stress on the theory of atom and accident as opposed to the concepts of matter and form by which Aristotle was led to believe in the eternity of the world. Accordingly every Mutakallim laid down his physical theory and based on it his proof of creation. This method was followed also by the early Jewish thinkers. The Karaites before Maimonides adopted the atomic theory without question. And Aaron ben Elijah, who had Maimonides's "Guide" before him, was nevertheless sufficiently loyal to his Karaite predecessors to discuss their views side by side with those of the Aristotelians and to defend them against the strictures of Maimonides. Saadia, the first Rabbanite philosopher, discusses no less than twelve erroneous views concerning the origin and nature of the world, but he does not lay down any principles of theoretical physics explicitly. He does not seem to favor the atomic theory, but he devotes no special treatment to the subject, and in his arguments for creation as opposed to eternity he makes use of the Kalamistic concepts of substance and accident and composition and division. The same is true of

Bahya Ibn Pakuda. Joseph Ibn Zaddik is the first who finds it necessary to give an independent treatment of the sciences before proceeding to construct his religious philosophy, and in so doing he expounds
the concepts of matter and form, substance and accident, genesis and
destruction, the four elements and their natures and so on—all these
Aristotelian concepts. Ibn Daud follows in the path of Ibn Zaddik
and discusses the relevant concepts of potentiality and actuality and
the nature of motion and infinity, upon which his proof is based of
the existence of God. Maimonides clears the ground first by a thorough criticism and refutation of the Kalamistic physics, but he does
not think it necessary to expound the Aristotelian views which he
adopts. He refers the reader to the original sources in the Physics
and Metaphysics of Aristotle, and contents himself with giving a list
of principles which he regards as established. Aristotle is now the
master of all those who know. And he reigns supreme for over a
century until the appearance of the "Or Adonai" of Hasdai Crescas,
who ventured to deny some of the propositions upon which Maimonides based his proof of the existence of God—such, for example, as
the impossibility of an infinite magnitude, the non-existence of an
infinite fulness or vacuum outside of the limits of our world, the
finiteness of our world and its unity, and so on.

These discussions of the fundamental principles of physics were
applied ultimately to prove the existence of God. But there was a
difference in the manner of the application. During the earlier period
before the "Emunah Ramah" of Abraham Ibn Daud was written,
the method employed was that of the Arabian Mutakallimun. That
is, the principles of physics were used to prove the creation of the
world in time, and from creation inference was made to the existence
of a Creator, since nothing can create itself. The creation itself in
time as opposed to eternity was proved from the fact of the composite
character of the world. Composition, it was said, implies the prior
existence of the constituent elements, and the elements cannot be
eternal, for an infinite past time is unthinkable. This method is
common to Saadia, Bahya, Joseph Ibn Zaddik, and others.

With the appearance of Ibn Daud's masterpiece, which exhibits
a more direct familiarity with the fundamental ideas of Aristotle,
the method changed. The existence of God is proved directly from

physics without the mediation of the doctrine of creation. Motion proves a mover, and to avoid an infinite regress we must posit an unmoved mover, that is, a first mover who is not himself moved at the same time. An unmoved mover cannot be corporeal, hence he is the spiritual being whom we call God. Ibn Daud does not make use of creation to prove the existence of God, but neither does he posit eternal motion as Aristotle does. And the result is that he has no valid proof that this unmoved mover is a pure spirit not in any way related to body. This defect was made good by Maimonides. Let us frankly adopt tentatively, he says, the Aristotelian idea of the eternity of the world, *i. e.*, the eternity of matter and motion. We can then prove the existence of an unmoved mover who is pure spirit, for none but a pure spirit can have an infinite force such as is manifested in the eternal motion of the world. Creation cannot be demonstrated with scientific rigor, hence it is not safe to build so important a structure as the existence of God upon an insecure foundation. Show that eternity of the world leads to God, and you are safe no matter what the ultimate truth turns out to be concerning the origin of the world. For if the world originated in time there is no doubt that God made it.

Thus Maimonides accepted provisionally the eternity of matter and motion, but provisionally only. No sooner did he prove his point, than he takes up the question of the world's origin and argues that while strict demonstration there is as yet none either for or against creation, the better reasons are on the side of creation.

Gersonides, on the other hand, was a truer Aristotelian than Maimonides and he decided in favor of the eternity of matter, though not of this our world.

The Jewish Mutakallimun, as we have seen, proved the existence of God from the fact that a created world implies a creator. The next step was to show that there is only one God, and that this one God is simple and not composite, and that he is incorporeal. The unity in the sense of uniqueness was shown by pointing out that dualism or pluralism is incompatible with omnipotence and perfection—attributes the possession of which by God was not considered to require proof. Maimonides, indeed, pointed out, in his opposition to the Mutakallimun, that if there is a plurality of worlds, a plurality of

Gods would not necessarily be in conflict with the omnipotence and perfection of each God in his own sphere (Guide I, 75), and he inferred the unity of God from his spirituality.

The simplicity of God was proved by arguing that if he is composite, his parts are prior to him, and he is neither the first, nor is he eternal, and hence not God; and the incorporeality followed from his simplicity, for all body is composite. Maimonides proved with one stroke God's existence, unity and incorporeality. For his argument from motion leads him to conceive of the first mover as a "separate" form or intellect. This clearly denotes incorporeality, for body is composed of matter and form. But it also denotes unity, for the immaterial is not subject to numerical distinction unless the one be the cause and the other the effect. But in that case the cause alone is God.

Next in importance to the proof of God's existence, unity and incorporeality, is the doctrine of attributes. We have seen (p. xxiii) how much emphasis the Arabian Mutakallimun placed upon the problem of attributes. It was important to Jew, Christian and Mohammedan alike for a number of reasons. The crude anthropomorphism of many expressions in the Bible as well as the Koran offended the more sophisticated thinkers ever since Alexandrian days. Hence it was necessary to deal with this question, and the unanimous view was that the Biblical expressions in question are to be understood as figures of speech. The more difficult problem was how any predicates at all can be applied to God without endangering his unity. If God is the possessor of many qualities, even though they be purely spiritual, such as justice, wisdom, power, he is composite and not simple. The Christian theologians found indeed in this problem of attributes a philosophical support for the doctrine of the Trinity. Since God cannot be devoid of power, reason and life, he is trinitarian, though he is one. The difficulty was of course that the moment you admit distinctions within the Godhead, there is no reason for stopping at three. And the Jewish critics were not slow to recognize this weakness in the system of their opponents. At the same time they found it necessary to take up a positive attitude toward the question of attributes so as to harmonize the latter with God's absolute unity. And the essence of the solution of the problem was to explain away the attributes. Saadia says that the ascription of life, power and knowledge to God does not involve plurality in his essence. The distinction of three attributes is due to our limited mind and inadequate powers of expression. In reality the essence of which we predicate these attributes is one and simple. This solution did not seem thoroughgoing enough to Saadia's successors, and every one of the Jewish philosophers tried his hand at the problem. All agreed that the attributes cannot apply to God in the same signification as they have when we use them in our own experience. The meaning of the term attribute was investigated and the attributes were divided into classes, until finally in the system of Maimonides this question too received its classical solution. God is conceived as absolutely transcendent and unknowable. No positive predicate can apply to him so as to indicate his essence. We can say only what he is not, we cannot say what he is. There is not the faintest resemblance between him and his creatures. And yet he is the cause of the world and of all its happenings. Positive attributes signify only that God is the cause of the experiences denoted by the attributes in question. When we say God is just we mean that he is not unjust, and that he is the cause of all justice in the world. Hence Maimonides says there are no essential attributes, meaning attributes expressive of God's essence, and the only predicates having application are negative and such as designate effects of God's causal activity in the world. Gersonides was opposed to Maimonides's radical agnosticism in respect of the nature of God, and defended a more human view. If God is pure thought, he is of the nature of our thought, though of course infinitely greater and perfect, but to deny any relation whatsoever between God's thought and ours, as Maimonides does, is absurd.

From God we pass to man. And the important part of man is his soul. It is proved that man has a soul, that the soul is not material or corporeal, that it is a substantial entity and not a mere quality or accident of the body. Both Plato and Aristotle are laid under contribution in the various classifications of the soul that are found in Saadia, in Joseph Ibn Zaddik, in Judah Halevi, in Abraham Ibn Daud, in Maimonides. The commonest is the three-fold division into vegetative, animal and rational. We also find the Platonic division into appetitive, spirited and rational. Further psychological details and descriptions of the senses, external and internal, the latter embracing the common sense, memory, imagination and judgment, are ultimately based upon Aristotle and are found in Judah Halevi, Abraham Ibn Daud and Maimonides, who derived them from Avicenna and Alfarabi. In the Neo-Platonic writers, such as Isaac Israeli, Solomon Ibn Gabirol, Joseph Ibn Zaddik, Moses Ibn Ezra, Pseudo-Bahya, Abraham Bar Hiyya, and so on, we also find reference to the World Soul and its emanation from Intelligence. In the conception of the human soul the Jewish philosophers vary from the Platonic view, related to the Biblical, that the soul is a distinct entity coming into the body from a spiritual world, and acting in the body by using the latter as its instrument, to the Aristotelian view that at least so far as the lower faculties of sense, memory and imagination are concerned, the soul is the form of the body, and disappears with the death of the latter. The human unit, according to this opinion, is body-and-mind, and the human activities are psycho-physical and not purely psychical as they are according to Plato. Some writers occupying intermediate positions combine unwittingly the Platonic and Aristotelian views, or rather they use Aristotelian expressions and interpret them Platonically (Saadia, Joseph Ibn Zaddik, Hillel ben Samuel).

As the influence of the Arab Aristotelians, Alfarabi, Avicenna and especially Averroes, began to make itself felt, the discussions about the Active Intellect and its relation to the higher Intelligences on the one hand and to the human intellect on the other found their way also among the Jews and had their effect on the conception of prophecy. Aristotle's distinction of an active and a passive intellect in man, and his ideas about the spheral spirits as pure Intelligences endowing the heavenly spheres with their motions, were combined by the Arabian Aristotelians with the Neo-Platonic theory of emanation. The result was that they adopted as Aristotelian the view that from God emanated in succession ten Intelligences and their spheres. Thus the first emanation was the first Intelligence. From this emanated the sphere of the fixed stars moved by it and the second Intelligence. From this emanated in turn the sphere of Saturn and the third Intelligence, and so on through the seven planets to the moon. From the Intelligence of the lunar sphere emanated the Active Intellect and the sublunar spheres of the four elements. These Intelligences were identified with the angels of Scripture. With some modifications this theory was adopted by the Jewish Aristotelians, Abraham Ibn Daud, Maimonides, Levi ben Gerson.

The Active Intellect was thus placed among the universal Intelligences whose function it is to control the motions of the sublunar world, and in particular to develop the human faculty of reason which is in the infant a mere capacity—a material intellect. Sensation and experience alone are not sufficient to develop the theoretical reason in man, for they present concrete, individual material objects, whereas the reason is concerned with universal truth. The conversion of sense experience into immaterial concepts is accomplished through the aid of the Active Intellect. And at the end of the process a new intellect is produced in man, the Acquired Intellect. This alone is the immortal part of man and theoretical study creates it. Averroes believed that this Acquired Intellect exists separately in every individual so long only as the individual is alive. As soon as the individual man dies, his acquired intellect loses its individuality (there being no material body to individuate it) and there is only one acquired intellect for the entire human species, which in turn is absorbed into the Active Intellect. There is thus no individual immortality. Maimonides, it would seem, though he does not discuss the question in his "Guide," shared the same view. Gersonides devotes an entire book of his "Milhamot Adonai" to this problem, but he defends individuation of the acquired intellect as such and thus saves personal immortality.

The practical part of philosophy, ethics, the Mutakallimun among the Arabians discussed in connection with the justice of God. In opposition to the Jabariya and the Ashariya who advocated a fatalistic determinism denying man's ability to determine his own actions, some going so far as to say that right and wrong, good and evil, are entirely relative to God's will, the Mu'tazila insisted that man is free, that good and evil are absolute and that God is just because justice is inherently right, injustice inherently wrong. Hence reward and punishment would be unjust if man had not the freedom to will and to act. The Karaites Joseph Al Basir and Jeshua ben Judah discuss the problem of the nature of good and evil and vindicate their absolute character. God desires the good because it is good, and it is not true that a thing is good because God has commanded it. Freedom of man is a corollary of the goodness of God. The Rabbanites take it for granted that good is good inherently, and God desires and commands it because it is identical with his wisdom and his will. Freedom of man does follow as a corollary from the justice of God and it is also taught in the Bible and the Talmud. The very fact of the existence of a divine law and commandments shows that man has freedom. And those passages in Scripture which seem to suggest that God sometimes interferes with man's freedom are explained away by interpretations *ad hoc*. Our own consciousness of power to determine our acts also is a strong argument in favor of freedom. Nevertheless the subject is felt to have its difficulties and the arguments against free will taken from the causal sequences of natural events and the influence of heredity, environment and motive on the individual will are not ignored. Judah Halevi as well as Abraham Ibn Daud discuss these arguments in detail. But freedom comes out triumphant. It is even sought to reconcile the antinomy of freedom vs. God's foreknowledge. God knows beforehand from all eternity how a given man will act at a given moment, but his knowledge is merely a mirror of man's actual decision and not the determining cause thereof. This is Judah Halevi's view. Abraham Ibn Daud with better insight realizes that the contingent, which has no cause, and the free act, which is undetermined, are as such unpredictable. He therefore sacrifices God's knowledge of the contingent and the free so as to save man's freedom. It is no defect, he argues, not to be able to predict what is in the nature of the case unpredictable. Maimonides cannot admit any ignorance in God, and takes refuge in the transcendent character of God's knowledge. What is unpredictable for us is not necessarily so for God. As he is the cause of everything, he must know everything. Gersonides who, as we have seen, is unwilling to admit Maimonides's agnosticism and transcendentalism, solves the problem in the same way as Ibn Daud. God knows events in so far as they are determined, he does not know them in so far as they are contingent. There is still another possibility and that is that God knows in advance every man's acts because no act is absolutely free. And there is an advocate of this opinion also. Hasdai Crescas frankly adopts the determinist position on the basis of God's knowledge, which cannot be denied, as well as of reason and experience, which recognizes the determining character of temperament and motive. But reward and punishment are natural and necessary consequences, and are no more unjust than is the burning of the finger when put into the fire.

In respect to the details of ethical doctrine and the classification of the virtues, we find at first the Platonic virtues and their relation to the parts of the soul, in Saadia, Pseudo-Bahya, Joseph Ibn Zaddik and even Abraham Ibn Daud. In combination with this Platonic basis expression is given also to the Aristotelian doctrine of the mean. Maimonides, as in other things, so here also, adopts the Aristotelian views almost in their entirety, both in the definition of virtue, in the division of practical and intellectual virtues, and the list of the virtues and vices in connection with the doctrine of the mean. As is to be expected, the ultimate sanction of ethics is theistic and Biblical, and the ceremonial laws also are brought into relation with ethical motives. In this rationalization of the ceremonial prescriptions of Scripture Maimonides, as in other things, surpasses all his predecessors in his boldness, scientific method and completeness. He goes so far as to suggest that the institution of sacrifice has no inherent value, but was in the nature of a concession to the crude notions of the people who, in agreement with their environment, imagined that God's favor is obtained by the slaughter of animals.

Among the peculiar phenomena of religion, and in particular of Judaism, the one that occupies a fundamental position is the revelation of God's will to man and his announcement of the future through prophetic visions. Dreams and divination had already been investigated by Aristotle and explained psychologically. The Arabs made use of this suggestion and endeavored to bring the phenomenon of prophecy under the same head. The Jewish philosophers, with the exception of Judah Halevi and Hasdai Crescas, followed suit. The suggestion that prophecy is a psychological phenomenon related to true dreams is found as early as Isaac Israeli. Judah Halevi mentions it with protest. Abraham Ibn Daud adopts it, and Maimonides gives it its final form in Jewish rationalistic philosophy. Levi ben Gerson discusses the finer details of the process, origin and nature of prophetic visions. In short the generally accepted view is that the Active Intellect is the chief agent in communicating true visions of future events to those worthy of the gift. And to become worthy a combination of innate and acquired powers is necessary together with the grace of God. The faculties chiefly concerned are reason and imagination. Moral excellence is also an indispensable prerequisite in aiding the development of the theoretical powers.

Proceeding to the more dogmatic elements of Judaism, Maimonides was the first to reduce the 613 commandments of Rabbinic Judaism to thirteen articles of faith. Hasdai Crescas criticised Maimonides's principle of selection as well as the list of dogmas, which he reduced to six. And Joseph Albo went still further and laid down three fundamental dogmas from which the rest are derived. They are the existence of God, revelation of the Torah and future reward and punishment.

The law of Moses is unanimously accepted as divinely revealed. And in opposition to the claims of Christianity and Mohammedanism an endeavor is made to prove by reason as well as the explicit statement of Scripture that a divine law once given is not subject to repeal. The laws are divided into two classes, *rational* and *traditional;* the former comprising those that the reason approves on purely rational and ethical grounds, while the latter consist of such ceremonial laws as without specific commandment would not be dictated by man's own reason. And in many of these commandments no reason is assigned. Nevertheless an endeavor is made to rationalize these also. Bahya introduced another distinction, viz., the "duties of the heart," as he calls them, in contradistinction to the "duties of the limbs." He lays stress on intention and motive as distinguished from the mere external observance of a duty or commandment.

Finally, some consideration is given in the works of the majority of the writers to eschatological matters, such as the destiny of the soul after death, the nature of future reward and punishment, the resurrection of the body and the Messianic period, and its relation to the other world. This brief sketch will suffice as an introduction to the detailed treatment of the individual philosophers in the following chapters.

MEDIÆVAL JEWISH PHILOSOPHY

CHAPTER I

ISAAC ISRAELI

We know next to nothing about the condition of the Jews in Mohammedan Egypt in the ninth and tenth centuries. But the fact that the two first Jewish writers who busied themselves with philosophical problems came from Egypt would indicate that the general level of intellectual culture among the Jews at that time was not so low as the absence of literary monuments would lead us to believe. Every one knows of Saadia, the first Hebrew grammarian, the first Hebrew lexicographer, the first Bible translator and exegete, the first Jewish philosopher of mediæval Jewry. He was born in Egypt and from there was called to the Gaonate of Sura in Babylonia. But not so well known is his earlier contemporary, Isaac ben Solomon Israeli, who also was born in Egypt and from there went later to Kairuan, where he was court physician to several of the Fatimide Califs. The dates of his birth and death are not known with certainty, but he is said to have lived to the age of one hundred years, and to have survived the third Fatimide Calif Al-Mansur, who died in 953. Accordingly we may assume the years of his birth and death as 855 and 955 respectively.

His fame rests on his work in theory and practice as a physician; and as such he is mentioned by the Arab annalists and historians of medicine.[26] To the Christian scholastics of mediæval Europe he is known as the Jewish physician and philosopher next in importance to Maimonides.[27] This is due to the accident of his works having been translated into Latin by Constantinus Afer,[28] and thus made accessible to men like Albertus Magnus, Vincent of Beauvais, Thomas Aquinas and others. For his intrinsic merits as a philosopher, and particularly as a Jewish philosopher, do not by any means entitle him to be coupled with Maimonides. The latter, indeed, in a letter which he wrote to

Samuel Ibn Tibbon, the translator of the " Guide of the Perplexed," expresses himself in terms little flattering concerning Israeli's worth as a philosopher.[29] He is a mere physician, Maimonides says, and his treatises on the *Elements*, and on *Definitions* consist of windy imaginings and empty talk. We need not be quite as severe in our judgment, but the fact remains that Israeli is little more than a compiler and, what is more to the purpose, he takes no attitude in his philosophical writings to Judaism as a theological doctrine or to the Bible as its source. The main problem, therefore, of Jewish philosophy is not touched upon in Israeli's works, and no wonder Maimonides had no use for them. For the purely scientific questions treated by Israeli could in Maimonides's day be studied to much better advantage in the works of the great Arabian Aristotelians, Al Farabi and Avicenna, compared to whom Israeli was mediocre. We are not to judge him, however, from Maimonides's point of view. In his own day and generation he was surpassed by none as a physician; and Saadia alone far outstrips him as a Jewish writer, and perhaps also David Al Mukammas, of whom we shall speak later. Whatever may be said of the intrinsic value of the content of his philosophical work, none can take away from him the merit of having been the first Jew, so far as we know, to devote himself to philosophical and scientific discussions, though not with the avowed aim of serving Judaism. The rest was bound to come later as a result of the impulse first given by him.

The two works of Israeli which come in consideration for our purpose are those mentioned by Maimonides in his letter to Samuel Ibn Tibbon spoken of above, namely, the "Book of the Elements," [30] and the "Book of Definitions." [31] Like all scientific and philosophic works by Jews between the ninth and thirteenth centuries with few exceptions, these were written in Arabic. Unfortunately, with the exception of a fragment recently discovered of the "Book of Definitions," the originals are lost, and we owe our knowledge of their contents to Hebrew and Latin translations, which are extant and have been published.[32] We see from these that Israeli was a compiler from various sources, and that he had a special predilection for Galen and Hippocrates, with whose writings he shows great familiarity. He makes use besides of Aristotelian notions, and is influenced by the Neo-Platonic treatise, known as the "Liber de Causis," and derived from a work of Proclus. It is for this reason difficult to characterize his standpoint, but we shall not go far wrong if we call him a Neo-Platonist, for reasons which will appear in the sequel.

It would be useless for us here to reproduce the contents of Israeli's two treatises, which would be more appropriate for a history of mediæval science. A brief *résumé* will show the correctness of this view. In his "Book of the Elements" Israeli is primarily concerned with a definite physical problem, the definition of an element, and the number and character of the elements out of which the sublunar world is made. He begins with an Aristotelian definition of element, analyzes it into its parts and comes to the conclusion that the elements are the four well-known ones, fire, air, water, earth. Incidentally he seizes opportunities now and then, sometimes by force, to discuss points in logic, physics, physiology and psychology. Thus the composition of the human body, the various modes in which a thing may come into being, that the yellow and black galls and the phlegm are resident in the blood, the purpose of phlebotomy, the substantial character of prime form, that the soul is not an accident, the two kinds of blood in the body, the various kinds of "accident," the nature of a "property" and the manner in which it is caused—all these topics are discussed in the course of proof that the four elements are fire, air, water, earth, and not seed or the qualities of heat, cold, dryness and moisture. He then quotes the definitions of Galen and Hippocrates and insists that though the wording is different the meaning is the same as that of Aristotle, and hence they all agree about the identity of the elements. Here again he takes occasion to combat the atomic theory of the *Mu'tazila* and Democritus, and proves that a line is not composed of points. In the last part of the treatise he refutes contrary opinions concerning the number and identity of the elements, such as that there is only one element which is movable or immovable, finite or infinite, namely, the power of God, or species, or fire, or air, or water, or earth; or that the number is two, matter and God; or three, matter, form and motion; or six, viz., the four which he himself adopts, and composition and separation; or the number ten, which is the end and completion of number. In the course of this discussion he takes occasion to define pain and pleasure, the nature of species, the difference between element and principle. And thus the book draws to a close. Not very promising material this, it would seem, for the ideas of which we are in search.

The other book, that dealing with definitions of things, is more promising. For while there too we do not find any connected account of God, of the world and of man, Israeli's general attitude can be gathered from the manner in which he explains some important concepts. The book, as its title indicates, consists of a series of definitions or descriptions of certain terms and ideas made use of by philosophers in their construction of their scheme of the world—such ideas and terms as Intelligence, science, philosophy, soul, sphere, spirit, nature, and so on. From these we may glean some information of the school to which Israeli belongs. And in the " Book of the Elements," too, some of the episodic discussions are of value for our purpose.

Philosophy, Israeli tells us, is self-knowledge and keeping far from evil. When a man knows himself truly—his spiritual as well as his corporeal aspects—he knows everything. For in man are combined the corporeal and the spiritual. Spiritual is the soul and the reason, corporeal is the body with its three dimensions. In his qualities and attributes—" accidents " in the terminology of Israeli—we similarly find the spiritual as well as the corporeal. Humility, wisdom and other similar qualities borne by the soul are spiritual; complexion, stature, and so on are corporeal. Seeing that man thus forms an epitome, as it were, of the universe (for spiritual and corporeal substance and accident exhausts the classes of existence in the world), a knowledge of self means a knowledge of everything, and a man who knows all this is worthy of being called a philosopher.

But philosophy is more than knowledge; it involves also action. The formula which reveals the nature and aim of philosophy is to become like unto God as far as is possible for man. This means to imitate the activities of God in knowing the realities of things and doing what the truth requires. To know the realities of things one must study science so as to know the various causes and purposes existing in the world. The most important of these is the purpose of the union in man of body and soul. This is in order that man may know reality and truth, and distinguish between good and evil, so as to do what is true and just and upright, to sanctify and praise the Creator and to keep from impure deeds of the animal nature. A man who does this will receive reward from the Creator, which consists in cleaving to the upper soul, in receiving light from the light of knowledge, and the beauty of splendor and wisdom. When a man reaches this degree, he becomes spiritual by cleaving to the created light which comes directly from God, and praising the Creator. This is his paradise and his reward and perfection. Hence Plato said that philosophy is the strengthening and the help of death. He meant by this that philosophy helps to deaden all animal desires and pleasures. For by being thus delivered from them, a man will reach excellence and the higher splendor, and will enter the house of truth. But if he indulges his animal pleasures and desires and they become strengthened, he will become subject to agencies which will lead him astray from the duties he owes to God, from fear of him and from prayer at the prescribed time.

We look in vain in Israeli's two treatises for a discussion of the existence and nature of God. Concerning creation he tells us that when God wanted to show his wisdom and bring everything from potentiality to actuality, he created the world out of nothing, not after a model (this in opposition to Plato and Philo), nor for the purpose of deriving any benefit from it or to obviate harm, but solely on account of his goodness.

But how did the creation proceed? A fragment from the treatise of Israeli entitled "The Book of Spirit and Soul"[33] will give us in summary fashion an idea of the manner in which Israeli conceived of the order and connection of things in the world.

In the name of the ancients he gives the following account. God created a splendor. This having come to a standstill and real permanence, a spark of light proceeded from it, from which arose the power of the rational soul. This is less bright than the splendor of the Intelligence and is affected with shadow and darkness by reason of its greater distance from its origin, and the intervening Intelligence. The rational soul again becoming permanent and fixed, there issued from it likewise a spark, giving rise to the animal soul. This latter is endowed with a cogitative and imaginative faculty, but is not permanent in its existence, because of the two intervening natures between it and the pure light of God. From the animal soul there likewise issued a splendor, which produced the vegetative soul. This soul, being so far removed from the original light, and separated from it by the Intelligence and the other two souls, has its splendor dimmed and made coarse, and is endowed only with the motions of growth and nourishment, but is not capable of change of place. From the vegetative soul proceeds again a splendor, from which is made the sphere (the heaven). This becomes thickened and materialized so that it is accessible to the sight. Motion being the nature of the sphere, one part of it pushes the other, and from this motion results fire. From fire proceeds air; from air, water; from water, earth. And from these elements arise minerals, plants and animals.

Here we recognize the Neo-Platonic scheme of emanation as we saw it in Plotinus, a gradual and successive emanation of the lower from the higher in the manner of a ray of light radiating from a luminous body, the successive radiations diminishing in brightness and spirituality until when we reach the Sphere the process of obscuration has gone so far as to make the product material and visible to the physical sense. The Intelligence and the three Souls proceeding from it in order are clearly not individual but cosmic, just as in Plotinus. The relation between these cosmic hypostases, to use a Neo-Platonic term, and the rational and psychic faculties in man Israeli nowhere explains, but we must no doubt conceive of the latter as somehow contained in the former and temporarily individualized, returning again to their source after the dissolution of the body.

Let us follow Israeli further in his account of the nature of these substances. The Intelligence is that which proceeds immediately from the divine light without any immediate agency. It represents the permanent ideas and principles—species in Israeli's terminology —which are not subject to change or dissolution. The Intelligence contains them all in herself eternally and immediately, and requires no searching or reflection to reach them. When the Intelligence wishes to know anything she returns into herself and finds it there without requiring thought or reflection. We can illustrate this, he continues, in the case of a skilful artisan who, when he wishes to make anything, retires into himself and finds it there. There is a difference, however, in the two cases, because Intelligence always knows its ideas without thought or reflection, for it exists always and its ideas are not subject to change or addition or diminution; whereas in the smith a difficulty may arise, and then his soul is divided and he requires searching and thinking and discrimination before he can realize what he desires.

What has been said so far applies very well to the cosmic Intelligence, the νοῦς of the Neo-Platonists. It represents thought as embracing the highest and most fundamental principles of existence, upon which all mediate and discursive and inferential thinking depends. Its content corresponds to the Ideas of Plato. But the further account of the Intelligence must at least in a part of it refer to the individual human faculty of that name, though Israeli gives us no indication where the one stops and where the other begins.

He appeals to the authority of Aristotle for his division of Intelligence into three kinds. First, the Intelligence which is always actual. This is what has just been described. Second, the Intelligence which is in the soul potentially before it becomes actual, like the knowledge of the child which is at first potential, and when the child grows up and learns and acquires knowledge, becomes actual. Third, that which is described as the second Intelligence. It represents that state of the soul in which it receives things from the senses. The senses impress the forms of objects upon the imagination (φαντασία) which is in the front part of the head. The imagination, or phantasy, takes them to the rational soul. When the latter knows them, she becomes identical with them spiritually and not corporeally.

We have seen above the Aristotelian distinction between the active intellect and the passive. The account just given is evidently based upon it, though it modifies Aristotle's analysis, or rather it enlarges upon it. The first and second divisions in Israeli's account correspond to Aristotle's active and passive intellects respectively. The third class in Israeli represents the process of realization of the potential or passive intellect through the sense stimuli on the one hand and the influence of the active intellect on the other. Aristotle seems to have left this intermediate state between the potential and the eternally actual unnamed. We shall see, however, in our further study of this very difficult and complicated subject how the classification of the various intellects becomes more and more involved from Aristotle through Alexander and Themistius down to Averroes and Levi ben Gerson. It is sufficient for us to see here how Israeli combines Aristotelian psychology, as later Aristotelian logic and physics, with Neo-Platonic metaphysics and the theistic doctrine of creation. But more of this hereafter.

From the Intelligence, as we have seen, proceeds the rational soul. In his discussion of the general nature of the three-fold soul (rational, animal and vegetative) Israeli makes the unhistoric but thoroughly mediæval attempt to reconcile Aristotle's definition of the soul, which we discussed above (p. xxxv), with that of Plato. The two conceptions are in reality diametrically opposed. Plato's is an anthropological dualism, Aristotle's, a monism. For Plato the soul is in its origin not of this world and not in essential unity with the body, which it controls as a sailor his boat. Aristotle conceives of the relation between soul and body as one of form and matter; and there is no union more perfect than that of these two constituent elements of all natural substances. Decomposition is impossible. A given form may disappear, but another form immediately takes its place. The combination of matter and form is the essential condition of sublunar existence, hence there can be no question of the soul entering or leaving the body, or of its activity apart from the body.

But Israeli does not seem to have grasped Aristotle's meaning, and ascribes to him the notion that the soul is a separate substance perfecting the natural body, which has life potentially, meaning by this that bodies have life potentially before the soul apprehends them; and when the soul does apprehend them, it makes them perfect and living actually. To be sure, he adds in the immediate sequel that he does not mean temporal before and after, for things are always just as they were created; and that his mode of expression is due to the impossibility of conveying spiritual ideas in corporeal terms in any other way. This merely signifies that the human body and its soul come into being simultaneously. But he still regards them as distinct substances forming only a passing combination. And with this pretended Aristotelian notion he seeks to harmonize that of Plato, which he understands to mean not that the soul enters the body, being clothed with it as with a garment, and then leaves it, but that the soul apprehends bodies by clothing them with its light and splendor, and thus makes them living and moving, as the sun clothes the world with its light and illuminates it so that sight can perceive it. The difference is that the light of the sun is corporeal, and sight perceives it in the air by which it is borne; whereas the light of the soul is spiritual, and intelligence alone can perceive it, not the physical sense.

Among the conceptual terms in the Aristotelian logic few play a more important part than those of substance and accident. Substance is that which does not reside in anything else but is its own subject. It is an independent existence and is the subject of accidents. The latter have no existence independent of the substance in which they inhere. Thus of the ten categories, in which Aristotle embraces all existing things, the first includes all substances, as for example, man, city, stone. The other nine come under the genus accident. Quantity, quality, relation, time, place, position, possession, action, passion—all these represent attributes which must have a substantial being to reside in. There is no length or breadth, or color, or before or after, or here or there, and so on except in a real object or thing. This then is the meaning of accident as a logical or ontological term, and in this signification it has nothing to do with the idea of chance. Clearly substance represents the higher category, and accident is inferior, because dependent and variable. Thus it becomes important to know in reference to any object of investigation what is its status in this respect, whether it is substance or accident.

The nature of the soul has been a puzzle to thinkers and philosophers from time immemorial. Some thought it was a material substance, some regarded it as spiritual. It was identified with the essence of number by the Pythagoreans. And there have not been wanting those who, arguing from its dependence upon body, said it was an accident and not a substance. Strange to say the Mutakallimun, defenders of religion and faith, held to this very opinion. But it is really no stranger than the maintenance of the soul's materiality equally defended by other religionists, like Tertullian for example, and the opposition to Maimonides's spiritualism on the part of Abraham ben David of Posquières. The Mutakallimun were led to their idea by the atomic theory, which they found it politic to adopt as more amenable to theological treatment than Aristotle's Matter and Form. It followed then according to some of them that the fundamental unit was the material atom which is without quality, and any power or activity in any atom or group of atoms is a direct creation of God, which must be re-created every moment in order to exist. This is the nature of accident, and it makes more manifest the ever present activity of God in the world. Thus the "substantial" or "accidental" character of the soul is one that is touched on by most Jewish writers on the subject. And Israeli also refers to the matter incidentally in the "Book of the Elements." [34] Like the other Jewish philosophers he defends its substantiality.

The fact of its separability from the body, he says, is no proof of its being an accident. For it is not the separability of an accident from its substance that makes it an accident, but its destruction when separated. Thus when a white substance turns green, the white color is not merely separated from its substance but ceases to exist. The soul is not destroyed when it leaves the body.

Another argument to prove the soul a substance is this. If the soul were an accident it should be possible for it to pass from the animal body to something else, as blackness is found in the Ethiopian's skin, in ebony wood and in pitch. But the soul exists only in living beings.

We find, besides, that the activity of the soul extends far beyond the body, and acts upon distant things without being destroyed. Hence it follows that the soul itself, the agent of the activity, keeps on existing without the body, and is a substance.

Having made clear the conception of soul generally and its relation to the body, he next proceeds to treat of the three kinds of soul. The highest of these is the rational soul, which is in the horizon of the Intelligence and arises from its shadow. It is in virtue of this soul that man is a rational being, discriminating, receptive of wisdom, distinguishing between good and evil, between things desirable and undesirable, approaching the meritorious and departing from wrong. For this he receives reward and punishment, because he knows what he is doing and that retribution follows upon his conduct.

Next to the rational soul is the animal soul, which arises from the shadow of the former. Being far removed from the light of Intelligence, the animal soul is dark and obscure. She has no knowledge or discrimination, but only a dim notion of truth, and judges by appearance only and not according to reality. Of its properties are sense perception, motion and change in place. For this reason the animals are fierce and violent, endeavoring to rule, but without clear knowledge and discrimination, like the lion who wants to rule over the other beasts, without having a clear consciousness of what he is doing. A proof that the animals have only dim notions of things is that a thirsty ass coming to the river will fly from his own shadow in the water, though he needs the latter for preserving his life, whereas he will not hesitate to approach a lion, who will devour him. Therefore the animals receive no reward or punishment (this in opposition to the Mutakallimun) because they do not know what to do so as to be rewarded, or what to avoid, in order not to be punished.

The vegetative soul proceeds from the shadow of the animal soul. She is still further removed from the light of Intelligence, and still more weighed down with shadow. She has no sense perception or motion. She is next to earth and is characterized by the powers of reproduction, growth, nutrition, and the production of buds and flowers, odors and tastes.

Next to the soul comes the Sphere (the heaven), which arises in the horizon and shadow of the vegetative soul. The Sphere is superior to corporeal substances, being itself not body, but the matter of body. Unlike the material elements, which suffer change and diminution through the things which arise out of them as well as through the return of the bodies of plants and animals back to them as their elements, the spiritual substances (and also the sphere) do not suffer any increase or diminution through the production of things out of them. For plants and animals are produced from the elements through a celestial power which God placed in nature effecting generation and decay in order that this world of genesis and dissolution should exist. But the splendor of the higher substances, viz., the three souls, suffers no change on account of the things coming from them because that which is produced by them issues from the *shadow* of their splendor and not from the essence of the splendor itself. And it is clear that the splendor of a thing in its essence is brighter than the splendor of its shadow, viz., that which comes from it. Hence the splendor of the vegetative soul is undoubtedly brighter than that of the sphere, which comes from its shadow. The latter becomes rigid and assumes a covering, thickness and corporeality so that it can be perceived by sight. But no other of the senses can perceive it because, although corporeal, it is near to the higher substances in form and nobility, and is moved by a perfect and complete motion, motion in a circle, which is more perfect than other motions and not subject to influence and change. Hence there is no increase or diminution in it, no beginning or end, and this on account of the simplicity, spirituality and permanence of that which moves it. The Intelligence pours of her splendor upon it, and of the light of her knowledge, and the sphere becomes intelligent and rational, and knows, without investigation or reflection, the lordship of its Creator, and that he should be praised and glorified without intermission. For this reason the Creator assigned to the Sphere a high degree from which it cannot be removed, and gave it charge of the production of time and the four seasons of the year, and the month and the day and the hour, and made it ruler of the production of perishable things in this world of generation and dissolution, so that the upper souls may find bodies to apprehend, to clothe with their light, and to make visible in them their activities according to the determination of God.

The Sphere by its motion produces the four elements, fire, air, water, earth; and the combinations of these in various proportions give rise to the minerals, plants and animals of this world, the highest of whom is man.

That the elements are those mentioned above and nothing else is proved by the definition of element and its distinction from "principle." A principle is something which, while being the cause of change, and even possibly at the basis of change, is not itself subject to change. Thus God is undoubtedly the cause of everything that happens in the world. He may therefore be called a principle of the world, but he does not enter with his essence the changing things. Hence it is absurd to speak of God as an element of the sublunar world. Matter, i. e., primary formless matter, does enter all changing things and is at the basis of all change; but it does not itself change. Hence matter also is a principle but not an element. An element is something which is itself a composite of matter and form, and changes its form to become something else in which, however, it is contained potentially, not actually. The product ultimately goes back to the element or elements from which it was made. When we follow this resolution of a given composite into its elements back as far as we can until we reach a first which is no longer produced out of anything in the same way as things were produced from it, we have the element. Such is the nature of fire, air, water, earth. All things are made from them in the manner above indicated. But there is nothing prior to them which changes its form to become fire, continues to reside potentially in fire and returns to its original state by the resolution of fire. The same applies to the other three.

The matter is now clear. The elements stand at the head of physical change and take part in it. Prior to the elements are indeed matter and form, but as logical principles, not as physical and independent entities. Hence it would seem, according to Israeli, that matter and form are side-tracked in the gradual evolution of the lower from the higher. For the elements, he tells us, come from the motion of the Sphere, the Sphere from the shadow of the Soul, the Soul from the shadow of the Intelligence, the Intelligence is created by God. To be sure he tells us that the Sphere is not body, but the matter of body. Yet the Sphere cannot take the place of prime matter surely, for it is undoubtedly endowed with form, nay is rational and intelligent, as we have seen.

When Israeli says that prior to the four elements there is nothing but the Omnipotence of God, he means that the sublunar process of change and becoming stops with the elements as its upper limit. What is above the elements belongs to the intelligible world; and the manner of their production one from the other is a spiritual one, emanation. The Sphere stands on the border line between the corporeal and the intelligible, itself a product of emanation, though producing the elements by its motion—a process apparently neither like emanation nor like sublunar becoming and change.

Creation in Israeli seems to be the same as emanation, for on the one hand he tells us that souls are created, that nothing precedes the four elements except the Omnipotence of God, and on the other that the elements come from the motion of the Sphere, and the souls issue from the shadow of the Intelligence. For matter and form there seems to be no room at all except as logical principles. This is evidently due to the fact that Israeli is unwittingly combining Aristotelian physics with Neo-Platonic emanationism. For Aristotle matter and form stand at the head of sublunar change and are ultimate. There is no derivation of matter or form from anything. The celestial world has a matter of its own, and is not the cause of the being of this one except as influencing its changes. God is the mover of the Spheres, but not their Creator, hence he stands outside of the world. This is Theism. In Israeli there is a continuity of God, the intelligible world and the corporeal, all being ultimately the same thing, though the processes in the two worlds are different. And yet he obviates Pantheism by declaring that God is a principle not an element.

We said before that Israeli takes no avowed attitude to Jewish dogma or the Bible. He never quotes any Jewish works, and there is nothing in his writings to indicate that he is a Jew and is making an effort to harmonize Judaism with philosophy and science. In words he refers to creation *ex nihilo*, which is not necessarily Jewish, it might be just as well Mohammedan or Christian. But in reality, as we have seen, his ideas of the cosmic process are far enough removed from the orthodox doctrine of creation as it appears in Bible and Talmud.

Incidentally we learn also something of Israeli's ideas of God's relation to mankind, of his commandments, and of prophecy. God created the world, he tells us, because of his goodness. He wanted to benefit his creatures. This could not be without their knowing the will of God and performing it. The will of God could not be revealed directly to everybody because the divine wisdom can speak only to those in whom the rational soul is mistress and is enlightened by the Intelligence. But people are not all of this kind; for some have the animal soul predominating in them, being on that account ignorant, confused, forward, bold, murderous, vengeful, unchaste like animals; others are mastered by the vegetative soul, i. e., the appetitive, and are thus stupid and dull, and given over to their appetites like plants. In others again their souls are variously combined, giving to their life and conduct a composite character. On this account it was necessary for God to select a person in whom the rational soul is separated, and illumined by the Intelligence—a man who is spiritual in his nature and eager to imitate the angels as far as it is possible for a man to do this. This man he made a messenger to mankind. He gave him his book which contains two kinds of teaching. One kind is spiritual in its nature, and needs no further commentary or interpretation. This is meant for the intellectual and discriminating. The other kind is corporeal, and requires spiritual interpretation. This is intended for the various grades of those who cannot understand directly the spiritual meaning, but who can grasp the corporeal teaching, by which they are gradually trained and prepared for the reception of higher truths. These people therefore need instructors and guides because a book alone is not sufficient for the purposes of those who cannot understand.

Dreams and prophecy are closely related, hence an explanation of the former will also throw light on the latter. A dream is caused by the influence of the Intelligence on the soul in sleep. The Intelligence receives its knowledge directly from God, and serves as a mediator between him and the soul, like a prophet who mediates between God and his creatures. In communicating to the soul the spiritual forms which it received from God, the Intelligence translates them into forms intermediate between corporeality and spirituality in order that they may be quickly impressed upon the common sense, which is the first to receive them. The common sense stands midway between the corporeal sense of sight and the imagination, which is in the anterior chamber of the brain, and is known as phantasy (Aristotelian φαντασία).

That the forms thus impressed on the common sense in sleep are intermediate between corporeal and spiritual is proved by the fact that they are different from the corporeal forms of things seen in the waking state. The latter are obscure and covered up, whereas those seen in sleep are finer, more spiritual and brighter. Proof of this is that a person sees himself in sleep endowed with wings and flying between heaven and earth. He sees the heavens opening and someone speaking to him out of the heaven, and so on. There would be no sense in all this if these phenomena had no spiritual meaning, for they are contrary to nature. But we know that they have real significance if interpreted by a really thoughtful person. The prophets also in wishing to separate themselves from mankind and impress the latter with their qualities, showed them spiritual forms of similar kind, which were preternatural. Hence all who believe in prophecy admit that dreams are a part of prophecy.

Now these intermediate forms which are impressed upon the common sense in sleep are turned over by it to the phantasy and by the latter to the memory. When the person awakes, he recovers the forms from the memory just as they were deposited there by the phantasy. He then consults his thinking power; and if this is spiritual and pure, the Intelligence endows him with its light and splendor and reveals to him the spiritual forms signified by the visions seen in sleep. He is then able to interpret the dream correctly. But if his powers of thought are not so good and are obscured by coverings, he cannot properly remove the husk from the kernel in the forms seen in sleep, is not able to penetrate to the true spirituality beneath, and his interpretation is erroneous.

This explanation does not really explain, but it is noteworthy as the first Jewish attempt to reduce prophecy to a psychological phenomenon, which was carried further by subsequent writers until it received its definitive form for the middle ages in Maimonides and Levi ben Gerson.

To sum up, Israeli is an eclectic. There is no system of Jewish philosophy to be found in his writings. He had no such ambitions. He combines Aristotelian logic, physics and psychology with Neo-Platonic metaphysics, and puts on the surface a veneer of theistic creationism. His merit is chiefly that of a pioneer in directing the attention of Jews to the science and philosophy of the Greeks, albeit in Arab dress. There is no trace yet of the Kalam in his writings except in his allusions to the atomic theory and the denial of reward and punishment of animals.

CHAPTER II

DAVID BEN MERWAN AL MUKAMMAS

Nothing was known of Al Mukammas until recently when fragments of his philosophical work were found in Judah ben Barzilai's commentary on the Sefer Yezirah.[35] The latter tells us that David Al Mukammas is said to have associated with Saadia, who learned a good deal from him, but the matter is not certain. If this account be true we have a second Jewish philosopher who preceded Saadia. His chief work is known by the title of "Twenty Chapters," fifteen of which were discovered in the original Arabic in 1898 by Abraham Harkavy of St. Petersburg.[36] Unfortunately they have not yet been published, and hence our account will have to be incomplete, based as it is on the Hebrew fragments in the Yezirah commentary above mentioned.

These fragments are sufficient to show us that unlike Israeli, who shows little knowledge of the Mu'tazilite discussions, Al Mukammas is a real Mu'tazilite and moves in the path laid out by these Mohammedan rationalists. Whether this difference is due to their places of residence (Israeli having lived in Egypt and Kairuan, while Al Mukammas was in Babylon), or to their personal predilections for Neo-Platonism and the Kalam respectively, is not certain. Saadia knows the Kalam; but though coming originally from Egypt, he spent his most fruitful years in Babylonia, in the city of Sura, where he was gaon. The centres of Arabian rationalism were, as we know, the cities of Bagdad and Basra, nearer to Babylon and Mesopotamia than to Egypt or Kairuan.

The first quotation in Judah ben Barzilai has reference to science and philosophy, their definition and classification. Science is the knowledge of the reality of existing things. It is divided into two parts, theoretical and practical. Theoretical science aims at knowledge for its own sake; practical seeks an end beyond knowledge, viz., the production of something. We call it then art. Thus geometry is a science in so far as one desires to know the nature and relations to each other of solid, surface, line, point, square, triangle, circle. But if his purpose is to know how to build a square or circular house, or to construct a mill, or dig a well, or measure land, he becomes an artisan. Theoretical science is three-fold. First and foremost stands theology, which investigates the unity of God and his laws and commandments. This is the highest and most important of all the sciences. Next comes logic and ethics, which help men in forming opinions and guide them in the path of understanding. The last is physics, the knowledge of created things.

In the ninth and tenth chapters of his book Al Mukammas discusses the divine attributes. This was a very important problem in the Mu'tazilite schools, as we saw in the Introduction, and was treated in Mu'tazilite works in the first division, which went by the title of "Bab al Tauhid," the chapter on the unity.

God is one—so Al Mukammas sums up the results of his previous discussions—not in the sense in which a genus is said to be one, nor in that in which a species is one, nor as the number one is one, nor as an individual creature is one, but as a simple unity in which there is no distinction or composition. He is one and there is no second like him. He is first without beginning, and last without end. He is the cause and ground of everything caused and effected.

The question of God's essence is difficult. Some say it is not permitted to ask what God is. For to answer the question what a thing is is to limit it, and the limited is the created. Others again say that it is permitted to make this inquiry, because we can use in our answer the expressions to which God himself testifies in his revealed book. And this would not be limiting or defining his glory because his being is different from any other, and there is nothing that bears any resemblance to him. Accordingly we should answer the question what God is, by saying, he is the first and the last, and the visible and the hidden, without beginning or end. He is living, but not through life acquired from without. His life is not sustained and prolonged by food. He is wise, but not through acquired wisdom. He hears without ears, sees without eyes, is understanding in all his works, and a true judge in all his judgments. Such would be our answer in accordance with God's own testimony of himself.

We must on no account suppose that the expressions living, wise, seeing, hearing, and so on, when applied to God mean the same thing as when we ascribe them to ourselves. When we say God is living we do not mean that there was a time when he was not living, or that there will be a time when he will not be living. This is true of us but not of God. His life has no beginning or end. The same thing applies to his wisdom. It is not acquired like ours, it has no beginning or end, and is not subject to error, forgetfulness, addition or diminution. It is not strange that his attributes should be so unlike ours, for it is fitting that the Creator should be different from the thing created, and the Maker from the thing made.

We must, however, analyze the matter of divine attributes more closely. When we say God is living, we may mean he is living with life as his attribute, i. e., that there is an attribute life which makes him living, or we may deny that there is any such attribute in him as life, but that he is living through himself and not through life as an attribute. To make this subtle distinction clear we will investigate further what is involved in the first statement that God is living with life. It may mean that there was a time when God was not living and then he acquired life and became living. This is clearly a wrong and unworthy conception. We must therefore adopt the other alternative, that the life which makes him living is eternal like him, and hence he was always living from eternity and will continue to be living to eternity. But the matter is not yet settled. The question still remains, Is this life through which he lives identical with his being, or is it distinct from his being, or is it a part of it? If we say it is distinct from his being, we are guilty of introducing other eternal beings beside God, which destroys his unity. The Christians are guilty of this very thing when they say that God's eternal life is the Holy Ghost, and his eternal Wisdom is the Son. If we say that his life is a part of his being, we do injury to the other aspect of his unity, namely, his simplicity. For to have parts in one's being implies composition. We are forced therefore to conclude that God's life is identical with his being. But this is really tantamount to saying that there is no attribute life which makes him living, or that he is living not through life. The difference is only in expression.

We may make this conception clearer by illustrations from other spheres, inadequate though they be. The soul is the cause of life

to the body, i. e., the body lives through the soul, and when the latter
leaves it, the body loses its life and dies. But the soul itself does
not live through anything else, say through another soul. For if this
were the case this other soul would need again another soul to make it
live and this again another, and so on *ad infinitum,* which is absurd.
The soul lives through itself. The same thing applies to angels. They
live through their own being; and that is why souls and angels are
called in the Sacred Scriptures spirits. A spirit is something that is
fine and light and incomposite. Hence their life cannot be due to
anything distinct from their being, for this would make them composite.

This statement, however, that souls and angels are living through
their own being must not be understood as meaning that they have no
creator who gave them being and life. The meaning merely is that
the being which God gave them is different from the being he gave
to bodies. Bodies need a soul to become living, the soul is itself living.
So in material things, also, the sun shines with its own light and not
with light acquired. The odor of myrrh is fragrant through itself, not
through anything else. The eye sees with its own power, whereas man
sees with the eye. The tongue does not speak with another tongue,
man speaks with a tongue, and so on. So we say of God, though
in a manner a thousand-fold more sublime, that he is living, but not
with a life which is distinct from his being; and so of the other attributes, hearing, seeing, and so on, that we find in the Scriptural praises
of him.

It is necessary to add that as on the one hand we have seen that
God's attributes are identical with his being, so it follows on the other
that the various attributes, such as wise, seeing, hearing, knowing,
and so on, are not different from each other in meaning, though distinct in expression. Otherwise it would make God composite. The
reason we employ a number of distinct expressions is in order to remove
from God the several opposites of the terms used. Thus when we say
God is living we mean to indicate that he is not dead. The attribute
wise excludes folly and ignorance; hearing and seeing remove deafness
and blindness. The philosopher Aristotle says that it is truer and more
appropriate to apply negative attributes to God than positive. Others
have said that we must not speak of the Creator in positive terms

for there is danger of endowing him with form and resemblance to other things. Speaking of him negatively we imply the positive without risking offence.

In the sequel Al Mukammas refutes the views of the dualists, of the Christians and those who maintain that God has form. We cannot afford to linger over these arguments, interesting though they be, and must hurry on to say a word about the sixteenth chapter, which deals with reward and punishment. This no doubt forms part of the second Mu'tazilite division, namely, the "Bab al 'Adl," or section concerning God's justice.

He defines reward as the soul's tranquillity and infinite joy in the world to come in compensation for the sojourn in this world which she endured and the self-control she practiced in abstaining from the pleasures of the world. Punishment, on the other hand, is the soul's disquietude and sorrow to the end of days as retribution for indulging in the world's evil pleasures. Both are imposed by God with justice and fairness. It is fitting that the promises of reward and threats of punishment consequent upon obedience and disobedience should be specified in connection with the commandments and prohibitions in the Scriptures, because this is the only way to train the soul to practice self-control. A child who does not fear his teacher's punishment, or has no confidence in his good will will not be amenable to instruction. The same is true of the majority of those who serve kings. It is fear alone which induces them to obey the will of their masters. So God in commanding us to do what is worthy and prohibiting what is unworthy saw fit in his wisdom to specify the accompanying rewards and punishments that he who observes may find pleasure and joy in his obedience, and the unobservant may be affected with sorrow and fear.

As the world to come has no end, so it is proper that the reward of the righteous as well as the punishment of the wicked should be without end. Arguments have been advanced to show that unlike reward which is properly infinite as is becoming to God's goodness, punishment should have a limit, for God is merciful. On the other hand, it is claimed on the basis of the finiteness of human action that both reward and punishment should be finite. But in reality it can be shown in many ways that reward and punishment should be infinite.

Without naming all the arguments—as many as ten have been advanced—in favor of this view, we may urge some of the more important.

It was God's own goodness that prompted him to benefit mankind by giving them laws for their guidance, and not any prior merits on their part which gave them a claim on God's protection. God himself is not in any way benefited by man's obedience or injured by his disobedience. Man knows that it is for his own good that he is thus admonished; and if he were asked what reward he would like to have for his good deeds he would select no less than infinite happiness. Justice demands that punishment be commensurate with reward. The greater the reward and the punishment the more effective are the laws likely to be. Besides in violating God's law a person virtually denies the eternity of him who gave it, and is guilty of contempt; for he hides himself from men, fearing their displeasure, whereas the omnipresence of God has no deterring effect upon him. For such offence infinite punishment is the only fit retribution.

The question whether the soul alone is rewarded or the body alone or both has been answered variously. In favor of the soul alone as the subject of reward and punishment it has been urged that reward raises man to the grade of angels, who are pure spirits. How then can the body take part? And punishment must be of the same nature as reward. On the other hand, it is claimed that the Bible says nothing of man being raised to the status of angels, and we know in this world of physical reward and punishment only. The Garden of Eden of which the Bible speaks is not peopled with angels, and that is where the righteous go after death.

The true solution is that as man is composed of body and soul, and both share in his conduct, reward and punishment must attach to both. As we do not understand the nature of spiritual retribution so the composite is equally inconceivable to us. But everyone who believes in the resurrection of the dead has no difficulty in holding that the body has a share in future reward and punishment.

CHAPTER III

SAADIA BEN JOSEPH AL-FAYYUMI (892–942)

Saadia was the first important Jewish philosopher. Philo of Alexandria does not come within our purview as he was not mediæval. Besides his work is not systematic, being in the nature of a commentary on Holy Writ. Though Philo was a good and loyal Jew, he stood, so to speak, apart from the real centre of Jewish intellectual and spiritual development. He was on the one hand too closely dependent on Greek thought and on the other had only a limited knowledge of Jewish thought and tradition. The Bible he knew only in the Greek translation, not in the original Hebrew; and of the Halaka, which was still in the making in Palestine, he knew still less.

It was different with Saadia. In the tenth century the Mishna and the Talmud had been long completed and formed theoretically as well as practically the content of the Jew's life and thought. Sura in Babylonia, where Saadia was the head of the academy, was the chief centre of Jewish learning, and Saadia was the heir in the main line of Jewish development as it passed through the hands of lawgiver and prophet, scribe and Pharisee, Tanna and Amora, Saburai and Gaon. As the head of the Sura academy he was the intellectual representative of the Jewry and Judaism of his day. His time was a period of agitation and strife, not only in Judaism but also in Islam, in whose lands the Jews lived and to whose temporal rulers they owed allegiance in the East as well as in Spain.

In Islam we saw in the introduction how the various schools of the Kadariya, the Mu'tazila and the Ashariya arose in obedience to the demand of clarifying the chief problems of faith, science and life. In Judaism there was in addition to this more general demand the more local and internal conflict of Karaite and Rabbanite which centred about the problem of tradition. Saadia found himself in the midst of all this and proved equal to the occasion.

We are not here concerned with the vicissitudes of Saadia's personal life or of his literary career as opponent of the Karaite sect. Nor can we afford more than merely to state that Jewish science in the larger sense begins with Saadia. Hebrew grammar and lexicography did not exist before him. The Bible had been translated into several languages before Saadia's day, but he was the first to translate it into Arabic, and the first to write a commentary on it. But the greatest work of Saadia, that which did the most important service to the theory of Judaism, and by which he will be best remembered, is his endeavor to work out a system of doctrine which should be in harmony with the traditions of Judaism on the one hand and with the most authoritative scientific and philosophic opinion of the time on the other. Israeli, we have seen, was interested in science before Saadia. As a physician he was probably more at home in purely physical discussions than Saadia. But there is no evidence that he had the larger interest of the Gaon of Sura, namely, to construct a system of Judaism upon the basis of scientific doctrine. Possibly the example of Islam was lacking in Israeli's environment, as he does not seem to be acquainted with the theories and discussions of the Mutakallimun, and draws his information from Aristotelian and Neo-Platonic sources. Saadia was in the very midst of Arab speculation as is evident from the composition of his *chef d'œuvre*, " Emunot ve-Deot," Beliefs and Opinions.[37]

The work is arranged on the Mu'tazilite model. The two main divisions in works of this character are *Unity* and *Justice*. The first begins with some preliminary considerations on the nature and sources of knowledge. It proceeds then to prove the existence of God by showing that the world cannot have existed from eternity and must have been created in time. Creation implies a creator. This is followed by arguments showing that God is one and incorporeal. The rest is devoted to a discussion of the divine attributes with the purpose of showing that God's unity and simplicity are not affected by them. The section on unity closes with a refutation of opposing views, such as those of the dualists or Trinitarians or infidels. The section on Justice centres about the doctrine of free will. Hence psychology and ethics are treated in this part of the work. To this may be added problems of a more dogmatic nature, eschatological and otherwise. We shall see in the sequel that Saadia's masterpiece is modeled on the same plan.

But not merely the plan and arrangement of his work give evidence of the influence upon Saadia of Islamic schools, many of his arguments, those for example on the existence of God and the creation of the world, are taken directly from them. Maimonides, who was a strong opponent of the Mutakallimun, gives an outline of their fundamental principles and their arguments for the existence, unity and incorporeality of God.[38] Some of these are identical with those of Saadia. Saadia, however, is not interested in pure metaphysics as such. His purpose is decidedly apologetic in the defence of Judaism and Jewish dogma. Hence we look in vain in his book for definite views on the constitution of existing substances, on the nature of motion, on the meaning of cause, and so on. We get a glimpse of his attitude to some of these questions in an incidental way.

The Mutakallimun were opposed to the Aristotelian theory of matter and form, and substituted for it the atomic theory. God created atoms without magnitude or quality, and he likewise created qualities to inhere in groups of atoms. These qualities they called accidents, and one of their important discussions was whether an accident can last more than a moment of time. The opinions were various and the accidents were classified according to their powers of duration. That is, there were some accidents which once created continued to exist of their own accord some length of time, and there were others which had to be re-created anew every moment in order to continue to exist. Saadia does not speak of matter and form as constituting the essence of existing things; he does speak of substance and accident,[39] which might lead us to believe that he held to the atomic theory, since he speaks of the accidents as coming and going one after the other, which suggests the constant creation spoken of by the Mutakallimun. On the other hand, when he answers an objection against motion, which is as old as Zeno, namely, how can we traverse an infinitely divisible distance, since it is necessary to pass an infinite number of parts, he tells us that it is not necessary to have recourse to the atomic theory or other theories adopted by some Mu'tazilites to meet this objection. We may believe in the continuity and infinite divisibility of matter, but as long as this divisibility is only potentially infinite, actually always finite, our ability to traverse the space offers no difficulty.[40] Finally, in refuting the second theory of creation, which combines Platonism with atomism, he argues against an atomic theory primarily because of its implications of eternity of the atoms, but partly also on other grounds, which would also affect the Kalamistic conceptions of the atoms.[41] These points are not treated by Saadia expressly but are only mentioned incidentally in the elucidation of other problems dealing with the creation of the world and the exist· ence of God.

Like Israeli Saadia shows considerable familiarity with Aristotelian notions as found in the Logic, the Physics and the Psychology. It is doubtful, however, whether he really knew Aristotle's more important treatises at first hand and in detail. The "Categories," a small treatise forming the first book of Aristotle's logic, he no doubt knew, but the other Aristotelian concepts he probably derived from secondary sources. For while he passes in review all the ten categories showing that none of them is applicable to God,[42] we scarcely find any mention of such important and fundamental Aristotelian conceptions as matter and form, potentiality and actuality, the four causes, formal, material, efficient and final—concepts which as soon as Aristotle began to be studied by Al Farabi and Avicenna became familiar to all who wrote anything at all bearing on philosophy, theology, or Biblical exegesis. Nay, the very concepts which he does employ seem to indicate in the way he uses them that he was not familiar with the context in which they are found in the Aristotelian treatises, or with the relation they bear to other views of Aristotle. Thus no one who knew Aristotle at first hand could make the mistake of regarding his definition of the soul as making the latter an accident.[43] When Saadia speaks of *six* kinds of motion[44] instead of *three*, he shows clearly that his knowledge of the Aristotelian theory of motion was limited to the little of it that is contained in the "Categories."

We are thus justified in saying, that Saadia's sources are Jewish literature and tradition, the works of the Mutakallimun, particularly the Mu'tazilites, and Aristotle, whose book on the "Categories" he knew at first hand.

Saadia tells us he was induced to write his book because he found that the beliefs and opinions of men were in an unsatisfactory state. While there are some persons who are fortunate enough to possess the truth and to know that they have it and rejoice thereat, this is not true of all. For there are others who when they have the truth know it not, and hence let it slip; others are still less fortunate and adopt false and erroneous opinions, which they regard as true; while still others vacillate continually, going from one opinion and belief to another. This gave him pain and he thought it his duty to make use of his limited knowledge to help them. A conscientious study of his book will tend to remove doubt and will substitute belief through knowledge for belief through tradition. Another result of such study, not less important, will be improvement of character and disposition, which will affect for the better a man's life in every respect, in relation to God as well as to his fellow-men.[45]

One may ask why it is that one encounters so many doubts and difficulties before arriving at true knowledge. The answer is, a human being is a creature, i. e., a being dependent upon another for its existence, and it is in the nature of a creature as such that it must labor for the truth with the sweat of its brow. For whatever a man does or has to do with is subject to time; each work must be accomplished gradually, step by step, part by part, in successive portions of time. And as the task before him is at the beginning complex, he has to analyze and simplify it. This takes time; while certainty and knowledge cannot come until the task is accomplished. Before that point is reached he is naturally in doubt.[46]

The sources of truth are three. First is that to which the senses testify. If our normal sense perceives under normal conditions which are free from illusion, we are certain of that perception.

The judgment is another source of truth. There are certain truths of which we are certain. This applies especially to such judgments of value, as that truth is good and falsehood is bad. In addition to these two sources of immediate knowledge, there is a third source based upon these two. This is logical inference. We are led to believe what we have not directly perceived or a matter concerning which we have no immediate knowledge of the second kind, because we infer it from something else which we have perceived or of which we have immediate certainty. Thus we believe man has a soul though we have never seen it because we infer its presence from its activity, which we do see.

These three sources are universal. They are not peculiar to a given race or religious denomination, though there are some persons who deny the validity of some or all of them. We Jews believe in them and in still another source of truth, namely, authentic tradition.[47]

Some think that a Jew is forbidden to speculate or philosophize about the truths of religion. This is not so. Genuine and sincere reflection and speculation is not prohibited. What is forbidden is to leave the sacred writings aside and rely on any opinions that occur to one concerning the beginnings of time and space. For one may find the truth or one may miss it. In any case until a person finds it, he is without a religious guide; and if he does find what seems to him the truth and bases his belief and conduct upon it, he is never sure that he may not later be assailed by doubts, which will lead him to drop his adopted belief. But if we hold fast to the commandments of the Bible, our own ratiocination on the truths of religion will be of great benefit to us.[48]

Our investigation of the facts of our religion will give us a reasoned and scientific knowledge of those things which the Prophets taught us dogmatically, and will enable us to answer the arguments and criticisms of our opponents directed against our faith. Hence it is not merely our privilege but our duty to confirm the truths of religion by reason.[49]

Here a question presents itself. If the reason can discover by itself the truths communicated to us by divine revelation, why was it necessary to have recourse to the latter? Why was it not left to the reason alone to guide us in our belief and in our conduct? The answer is, as was suggested before, that human reason proceeds gradually and does not reach its aim until the end of the process. In the meantime one is left without a guide. Besides not everybody's reason is adequate to discover truth. Some are altogether incapable of this difficult task, and many more are exposed to harassing doubts and perplexities which hinder their progress. Hence the necessity of revelation, because in the witness of the senses all are equally at home, men and women, young and old.[50]

The most important fact of religion is the existence of God. We know it from the Bible, and we must now prove it by reason. The proof is necessarily indirect because no one of us has seen God, nor have we an immediate certainty of his existence. We must prove it then by the method of inference. We must start with something we do know with certainty and proceed from it through as many steps of logical inference as may be necessary until we reach the object of our search.[51]

The world and the things in it are directly accessible to our senses and our judgment. How long has the world been in existence and how did it come to be? The answers to these questions also we do not know through our senses, and we must prove them by a chain of reasoning. There are several possibilities. The world just as it is may have existed from eternity. If so nobody made it; it just existed, and we have no proof of God. The world in its present form might have proceeded from a primitive matter. This hypothesis only removes the problem further back. For, leaving aside the question how did this prime matter develop into the complex world of our experience, we direct our attention to the prime matter itself, and ask, Has it existed from eternity or did it come to be? If it existed from eternity, then nobody made it, and we have no proof of a God, for by God we mean an intelligent being acting with purpose and design, and the cause of the existence of everything in creation. The third alternative is that whether the world was developed out of a primitive matter or not, it at any rate, or the primitive matter, as the case may be, was made in time, that is, it was created out of nothing. If so there must have been someone who created it, as nothing can create itself. Here we have proof of the existence of God. It follows therefore that we must first show that the world is not eternal, that it came to be in time, and this is what Saadia does.

Here are some of his proofs. The world is finite in magnitude. For the world consists of the earth, which is in the centre, and the heavens surrounding it on all sides. This shows that the earth is finite, for an infinite body cannot be surrounded. But the heavens are finite too, for they make a complete revolution in twenty-four hours. If they were infinite it would take an infinite time to complete a revolution. A finite body cannot have an infinite power. This Saadia regards as self-evident, though Aristotle, from whom this statement is derived, gives the proof. Hence the force or power within the world which keeps it going is finite and must one day be exhausted. But this shows also that it could not have gone on from eternity. Hence the world came to be in time.[52]

Another proof is based on the composite character of all things in heaven and earth. Minerals, plants and animals are made up of parts and elements. The heavens consist of spheres, one within the other. The spheres are studded with stars. But composition implies a time when the composition took place. In other words, the parts must have been there first and somebody put them together. Hence the world as we see it now is not eternal.[53]

A special form of composition, which is universal, is that of substance and accident. Plants and animals are born (or sprout), grow and decay. These manifestations are the accidents of the plant or animal's substance. The heavenly bodies have various motions, lights and colors as their accidents. But these accidents are not eternal, since they come and go. Hence the substances bearing the accidents, without which they cannot exist, are also temporal like them. Hence our world is not eternal.[54]

Finally, past time itself cannot be eternal. For this would mean that an infinite time has actually elapsed down to our day. But this is a contradiction in terms. What is already accomplished cannot be infinite. Infinity is possible only as a potentiality, for example, we may speak of a given length as infinitely divisible. This merely means that one may mentally continue dividing it forever, but we can never say that one has actually made an infinite number of divisions. Therefore not merely the world, but even time must have begun to be.[55]

It will be seen that the first three arguments prove only that the world in the form which it has now is not eternal. The possibility is not yet excluded of an eternal matter out of which the world proceeded or was made. The fourth argument proves a great deal. It shows that nothing which is subject to time can be eternal, hence not even prime matter. God can be eternal because he is not subject to time. Time, as we shall see later, cannot exist without motion and moving things, hence before the world there was no time, and the fourth argument does not apply to premundane existence.

To complete the first three arguments Saadia therefore proceeds to show that the world, which we now know came to be in time, must have been made by someone (since nothing can make itself), and that too out of nothing, and not out of a pre-existing eternal matter.

If an eternal matter existed before the world, the explanation of the origin of the world is open to two possibilities. One is that there is nothing outside of this matter and the world which came from it. This is absurd, for it would mean that an unintelligent dead thing is the cause of intelligence and life in the universe. We must therefore have recourse to the other alternative that someone, an intelligent being, made the world out of the primitive, eternal matter. This is also impossible. For if the matter is eternal like the maker of the world, it is independent of him, and would not be obedient to his will to adapt itself to his purpose. He could therefore not make the world out of it.

The only alternative left now is that the author of the universe is an intelligent being, and that nothing outside of him is eternal. He alone is responsible for the existence of the world, which was at one time nothing. Whether he first created a matter and then from it the universe, or whether he made the world outright, is of secondary importance.[56]

There is still a possibility that instead of making the world out of nothing, God made it out of himself, *i. e.*, that it emanated from him as light from the sun. This, as we know, is the opinion of the Neo-Platonists; and Israeli comes very close to it as we saw before (p. 6). Saadia is strongly opposed to any such doctrine.

It is unlikely, he says, that an eternal substance having neither form, condition, measure, place or time, should change into a body or bodies having those accidents; or that a wise being, not subject to change or influence, or comprehensibility should choose to make himself into a body subject to all of these. What could have induced a just being who does no wrong to decree that some of his parts should be subject to such evils as matter and material beings are afflicted with? It is conceivable only in one of two ways. Either they deserved it for having done wrong, or they did not deserve it, and it was an act of violence that was committed against them. Both suppositions are absurd. The fact of the matter is that the authors of this opinion to avoid the theory of creation *ex nihilo* went from the frying pan into the fire. To be sure, creation out of nothing is difficult to conceive, but this is the reason why we ascribe this power to God alone. To demand that we show how this can be done is to demand that we ourselves become creators.[57]

The question what existed in place of the earth before it was created evinces ignorance of the idea of place. By place is meant simply the contact of two bodies in which the one is the place of the other. When there is no earth and no bodies there is no such thing as place.

The same thing applies to time. Time means the persistence of existing things in heaven and earth under changing conditions. Where there is no world, there is no time. This answers the objection raised by some, namely, how is it possible that before all these bodies were made time existed void of objects? Or the other difficulty which is closely related, viz., Why did not God create the world before he did? The answer to both is, there was no before and there was no time, when the world was not.

The following question is a legitimate one, Why did God create all things? And our answer is, there was no cause which made him create them, and yet they were not made in vain. God wished to exhibit his wisdom; and his goodness prompted him to benefit his creatures by enabling them to worship him.[58]

We have now proved the existence of God as the cause of the existence of all things. We must now try to arrive at some notion of what God is as far as this is in our power. God cannot be corporeal or body, for in our proof of his existence we began with the world which is body and arrived at the notion of God as the cause of all corporeal existence. If God himself is corporeal our search is not at an end, for we should still want to know the cause of him. Being the cause of all body, he is not body and hence is for our knowledge ultimate, we cannot go beyond him. But if God is not corporeal, he is not subject to motion or rest or anger or favor, for to deny the corporeality of God and still look for these accidents in him is to change the expression and retain the idea. Bodily accidents involve body.[59]

The incorporeality of God proves also his unity. For what is not body cannot have the corporeal attributes of quantity or number, hence God cannot be more than one.[60] And there are many powerful arguments besides against a dualistic theory.

A unitary effect cannot be the result of two independent causes. For if one is responsible for the whole, there is nothing left for the other, and the assumption of his existence is gratuitous. If the effect consists of two parts of which each does one, we have really two effects

But the universe is one and its parts cannot be separated.[61] Again, if one of them wishes to create a thing and cannot without the help of the other, neither is all-powerful, which is inconsistent with the character of deity. If he can compel the other to help him, they are both under necessity. And if they are free and independent, then if one should desire to keep a body alive and the other to kill it, the body would have to be at the same time alive and dead, which is absurd. Again, if each one can conceal aught from the other, neither is all-knowing. If they cannot, they are not all-powerful.[62]

Having proved God's existence, unity and incorporeality, he proceeds to discuss his most essential attributes, which are, Life, Omnipotence, and Omniscience. These easily follow from what was said before. We cannot conceive a creator *ex nihilo* unless he is all-powerful; power implies life; and the thing made cannot be perfect unless its maker knows what it is going to be before he makes it.

These three concepts our reason discovers with one act of its thinking effort, for they are all involved in the concept, Maker. There is no gradual inference from one to the other. The reason we are forced to use three expressions is because of the limitations of language. Hence it must not be thought that they involve plurality in God. They are simply the implications of the one expression, Maker, and as that does not suggest plurality in God's essence, but signifies only that there is a thing made by the maker, so the three derivative terms, Living, Omnipotent, Omniscient, imply no more.

The Christians erred in this matter in making God a trinity. They say one cannot create unless he is living and wise, hence they regard his life and his wisdom as two other things outside of his essence. But this is a mistake. For in saying there are several attributes in him distinct one from the other, they say in effect that he is corporeal—an error which we have already refuted. Besides they do not understand what constitutes proof: In man we say that his life and his knowledge are not his essence because we see that he sometimes has them and sometimes not. In God this is not the case. Again, why only three? They say essence, life, wisdom; why do they not add power, or hearing and seeing? If they think that power is implied in life, and hearing and seeing in wisdom, so is life implied in wisdom.

They quote Scripture in their support, for example, the verse in

II Samuel (23, 2), "The *Spirit* of the Lord spoke through me, and his *Word* was upon my tongue." "Word" denotes, they say, his attribute of wisdom, and "Spirit" his life, as distinct persons. But they are mistaken. The expressions in question denote the words which God puts into the mouth of his prophets. There are other similar instances which they cite, and in their ignorance of Hebrew take metaphorical expressions literally. If they are consistent, they should add many more persons in the Godhead, in accordance with the many phrases of the Bible concerning the hand of God, the eye of God, the glory of God, the anger of God, the mercy of God, and so on.[63]

The above discussion, as also that of Al-Mukammas (p. 19), shows clearly the origin of the doctrine of attributes as well as its motive. Both Al-Mukammas and Saadia and the later Jewish philosophers owed their interest in this problem primarily to the Mohammedan schools in which we know it played an important rôle (see Introduction, pp. xxiii, xxvi). But there is no doubt that the problem originated in the Christian schools in the Orient, who made use of it to rationalize the dogma of the Trinity.

There is extant a confession of faith attributed to Jacob Baradæus (sixth century), the founder of the Syrian Church of the Monophysites or Jacobites, in which the phrase occurs that the Father is the Intellect, the Son is the Word and the Holy Ghost is Life. In the works of Elias of Nisibis of the Nestorian Church, who lived shortly after Saadia (975–1049), we also find a passage in which the three expressions essence, life and wisdom are applied to the three persons of the Trinity. The passage is worth quoting. It reads as follows: "As the essence of God cannot receive accidents, his life and his wisdom cannot be accidents. But whatever is not accident is either substance or person. Hence as the essence of the Creator and his life and his wisdom are not three substances or three accidents, it is proved that they are three persons."[64]

Monotheism was a fundamental dogma of the Mohammedan faith. Hence it was necessary for their rationalizing theologians to meet the Trinitarians with their own weapons and show that the multiplicity of the divine attributes which they could not deny, since the Koran was authority for it, does in no way affect God's unity. The problem was quite as important for Judaism as it was for Islam, and for the same reason. Hence Saadia's insistence that inadequacy of language is alone responsible for our expressing God's essential attributes in the three words, Living, Omnipotent, Omniscient; that in reality they are no more than interpretations of the expression Maker.

We have now shown that God is one in the two important senses of the word. He is one in the sense that there is no second God beside him; and he is one in his own essence, *i. e.*, he is simple and not composed of parts. His Life and his Power and his Wisdom are not distinct one from the other and from his essence. They are all one. We have also proved God's incorporeality. Nevertheless Saadia is not satisfied until he has shown in detail that God cannot be compared to man in any sense, and that the anthropomorphic expressions in the Bible must not be taken literally. In reference to Biblical interpretation Saadia makes the general remark that whenever a verse of Scripture apparently contradicts the truths of reason, there is no doubt that it is figurative, and a person who successfully interprets it so as to reconcile it with the data of sense or reason will be rewarded for it. For not the Bible alone is the source of Judaism, Reason is another source preceding the Bible, and Tradition is a third source coming after the Bible.[65]

In order to show that God is not to be compared to any other thing in creation Saadia finds it convenient to use Aristotle's classification of all existing things under the ten categories.[66] Everything that exists is either a substance, or it is an accident, *i. e.*, an attribute or quality of a substance. Substance is therefore the first and most important of the categories and is exemplified by such terms as man, horse, city. Everything that is not substance is accident, but there are nine classes of accident, and with substance they make up the ten categories. The order of the categories as Aristotle gives them in his treatise of the same name is, substance, quantity, quality, relation, place, time, position, possession, action, passion. If these categories include all existing things and we can prove that God is not any of them, our object is accomplished. The one general argument is one with which we are already familiar. It is that God is the cause of all substance and accident, hence he is himself neither the one nor the other. Scripture supports our view, as in Deuteronony 4, 15: "Take ye therefore good heed of yourselves; for ye saw no manner of form on the day that the Lord spake unto you in Horeb out of the midst of the fire: lest ye corrupt yourselves, and make you a graven image in the form of any figure, the likeness of male or female, the likeness of any beast that is on the earth, the likeness of any winged fowl that flieth in the heaven; the likeness of anything that creepeth on the ground, the likeness of any fish that is in the water under the earth: and lest thou lift up thine eyes unto heaven, and when thou seest the sun and the moon and the stars, even all the host of heaven, thou be drawn away," etc. And tradition is equally emphatic in this regard. Our sages, who were the disciples of the prophets, render the anthropomorphic passages in the Bible so as to avoid an objectionable understanding. This is particularly true of the Aramaic translation of the Targum.

Such terms as head, eye, ear, mouth, lip, face, hand, heart, bowels, foot, which are used in relation to God in the Bible, are figurative. For it is the custom of language to apply such terms metaphorically to certain ideas like elevation, providence, acceptance, declaration, command, favor, anger, power, wisdom, mercy, dominion. Language would be a very inadequate instrument if it confined itself to the literal meaning of the words it uses; and in the case of God we should be limited to the statement that he is.

What was said of the nouns above mentioned applies also to other parts of speech, such as verbs attributing human activity to God. Such phrases as " incline thine ear," " open thine eyes," "he saw," " he heard," "he spoke" are figurative. So the expression, "the Lord smelled," which sounds especially objectionable, denotes acceptance.

The theophanies in the Bible, where God is represented under a certain form, as in Ezekiel, Isaiah and Kings, do not argue against our view, for there are meant specially created forms for the benefit and honor of the prophet. This is what is meant by the " Glory of the Lord," and "Shekinah." Sometimes it is simply a created light without an individual form. When Moses asked to see God, he meant the created light. God cannot be seen with the eye nor can he be grasped in thought or imagination. Hence Moses could not have meant to see God, but the created light. His face was covered so that he should not be dazzled by the exceeding splendor of the beginning of the light, which is too much for a mortal to endure; but later when the brightest part passed by, the covering was taken off and Moses saw the last part of the light. This is the meaning of the expression in Exodus 33, 23, "And I will take away mine hand, and thou shalt see my back: but my face shall not be seen."

Having treated of God as the creator of the world and having learned something about his attributes, we must now proceed to the study of man, or which is the same thing, to an investigation of God's relations to the rational part of his creation in the sublunar world. That man is endowed with a soul cannot be doubted, for the activities of man's soul are directly visible. The problem which is difficult is concerning the nature of the soul.[67] Here opinions differ, and some regard the soul as an accident of the body, some think it is a corporeal substance like air or fire, while others believe there is more than one soul in man. It will be our task to vindicate our own view against these erroneous ideas. The soul is too important in its functions to be an accident. It is neither air nor fire because it has not the properties of these bodies. And if the soul consisted of two or more distinct parts, the perceptions of sense would not reach the reason, and there would be no co-operation between these two powers. The true view is therefore that the soul of man is a substance created by God at the time when the human body is completed. The soul has no eternal existence before the body as Plato thought, for nothing is eternal outside of God, as we saw before. Nor does it enter the body from the outside, but is created with and in the body. Its substance is as pure as that of the celestial spheres, receiving its light like them, but is much finer than the substance of the spheres, for the latter are not rational, whereas the soul is. The soul is not dependent for its knowledge upon the body, which without the soul has neither life nor knowledge, but it uses the body as an instrument for its functions. When connected with the body the soul has three faculties, reason, spirit and desire. But we must not think with Plato that these powers form so many divisions or parts of the soul, residing in different parts of the body. All the three faculties belong to the one soul whose seat is in the heart; for from the heart issue the arteries, which give the body sense and motion.

The soul was put in the body because from its nature it cannot act by itself; it must have the body as its instrument in order thereby to attain to perfect happiness, for the soul's functions either purify or defile it. When the soul leaves the body she can no longer repent; all this must be done while she is in the body. Being placed in the body is therefore a good for the soul. If she were left alone, there would be no use in her existence or in that of the body, and hence the entire creation would be in vain, which was made for the sake of man. To ask why was not the soul made so as to be independent of the body is foolish and tantamount to saying why was not the soul made something else than soul. The soul is not in any way harmed by being with the body, for the injury of sin is due to her own free will and not to the body. Moreover, the body is not unclean, nor are the fluids of the body unclean while in the body; some of them are declared in the Bible to cause uncleanness when they leave the body, but this is one of those ordinances which, as we shall see later, are not demanded by the reason for their own sake, but are specially commanded for a different purpose. As for the sufferings which the soul undergoes by reason of her connection with the body, some are due to her own negligence, such as cold, heat, and so on, others are inflicted by God for the soul's own good so that she may be later rewarded.

We see here, and we shall learn more definitely later, that Saadia is opposed to the view of the ascetics—a view Neo-Platonic in its origin—that matter and body as such are evil, and that the constant effort of man must be to free the soul from the taint of the body in which it is imprisoned, and by which it is dragged down from its pristine nobility and purity. Saadia's opposition to the belief in the pre-existence of the soul at once does away with the Neo-Platonic view that the soul was placed in the body as a punishment for wrongdoing. The soul was created at the same time with the body, and the two form a natural unit. Hence complete life involves both body and soul.

We have seen that God's creation of the world is due to his goodness. His first act of kindness was that he gave being to the things of the world. He showed himself especially beneficent to man in enabling him to attain perfect happiness by means of the commandments and prohibitions which were imposed upon him. The reward consequent upon obedience was the real purpose of the commandments.[68]

The laws which God gave us through the prophets consist of two groups. The first embraces such acts as our reason recognizes to be right or wrong, good or bad, through a feeling of approval or disapproval which God planted in our minds. Thus reason demands that a benefactor should receive in return for his goodness either a kind reward if he needs it, or thanks if he needs no reward. As this is a general demand of the reason, God could not have neglected it in his own case, and hence the commandments that we should serve him, that we should not offend or revile him and the other laws bearing on the same subject.

It is likewise a demand of the reason that one should prevent the creatures from sinning against one another in any way. Murder is prohibited because it would lead to the destruction of the race and the consequent frustration of God's purpose in creating the world. Promiscuous association of the sexes is prohibited in order that man may be different from the lower animals, and shall know his father and other relatives that he may show them honor and kindness. Universal stealing would lead to indolence, and in the end would destroy itself when there is nothing more to steal. In a similar way we can explain all laws relating to social dealings among mankind.

The second group of laws has reference to acts which are inherently neither right nor wrong, but are made so by the act of God's commandment or prohibition. This class may be called *Traditional* in contrast to the first, which we shall name *Rational*.

The traditional laws are imposed upon us primarily so that we may be rewarded for obeying them. At the same time we shall find on careful examination of these laws that they also have a rational signification, and are not purely arbitrary. Thus the purpose of sanctifying certain days of the year, like Sabbaths and holy days, is that by resting from labor we may devote ourselves to prayer, to the acquisition of wisdom, and to converse with our fellows in the interest of religion. Laws of ceremonial purity have for their purpose to teach man humility, and to make prayer and the visitation of holy places more precious in his eyes after having been debarred from his privileges during the period of his uncleanness.

It is clear that we should not know how to perform the traditional commandments without divine revelation since our own reason would not have suggested them. But even in the case of the rational laws the general principles alone are known to us from our own reason but not the details. We know in general that theft, unchastity, and so on, are wrong, but the details of these matters would lead to disagreement among mankind, and hence it was necessary that the rational laws also be directly communicated to us by divine messengers.

The divine messengers are the prophets.[69] They knew that their revelations came from God through a sign which appeared at the beginning of the communication and lasted to the end. The sign was a pillar of cloud or of fire, or an extraordinary bright light, as we learn in the case of Moses.

The genuineness of a prophet's message is tested first of all by the nature of the content, and then by his ability to perform miracles. The Israelites would not have believed Moses, notwithstanding his miracles, if he had commanded them to commit murder or adultery. It is because his teaching was found acceptable to the reason that the miracles accompanying it were regarded as a confirmation of Moses's divine mission.

The Jewish Law[70] contains three elements, all of which are necessary for effective teaching. First, the commandments and prohibitions, or the laws proper; second, the reward and punishment consequent upon obedience and disobedience; and third, examples of historical characters in which the laws and their consequences are illustrated.

But the written law would not accomplish its purpose without belief in tradition. This is fundamental, for without it no individual or society can exist. No one can live by what he perceives with his own senses alone. He must depend upon the information he receives from others. And while this information is liable to error either by reason of the informant being mistaken or his possible purpose to deceive, these two possibilities are eliminated in case the tradition is vouched for not by an individual, but by a whole nation, as in the case of the Jewish revelation.

As Saadia's emphasis on tradition, apart from its intrinsic importance for Judaism, has its additional motive in refuting Karaism, so the following discussion against the possibility of the Law being abrogated is directed no doubt against the claims of the two sister religions, Christianity and Mohammedanism.[71]

Abrogation of the law, Saadia says, is impossible. For in the first place tradition has unanimously held to this view, and in the second place the Law itself assures us of its permanent validity, "Moses commanded us a law, an inheritance for the assembly of Jacob" (Deut. 33, 4). The law constitutes the national existence of our people; hence as we are assured by the Prophets that the Jewish nation is eternal, the Law must be likewise. We must not even accept the evidence of miracles in favor of a new law abrogating the old. For as we saw before, it was not primarily Moses's miracles that served to authenticate his teaching, but the character of the teaching itself. Now that the law of Moses stood the test of internal acceptability and external confirmation by the performance of miracles, its declaration of permanent validity cannot be upset by any new evidence even if it be miraculous.

Man [72] alone of all created things was given commandments and prohibitions, because he is superior to all other creatures by reason of the rational faculty which he possesses, and the world was created for him. Man's body is small, but his mind is great and comprehensive. His life is short, but it was given him to assist him to the eternal life after death. The diseases and other dangers to which he is subject are intended to keep him humble and God-fearing. The appetites and passions have their uses in the maintenance of the individual and the race.

If it is true that God gave man commandments and that he rewards and punishes him according to his conduct, it follows that unless we attribute injustice to God he must have given man the power to do and to refrain in the matters which form the subject of the commandments. This is actually the case and can be proven in many ways. Everyone is conscious of freedom in his actions, and is not aware of any force preventing him in his voluntary acts. The Bible testifies to this when it says (Deut. 30, 19), "I have set before you life and death . . . therefore choose thou life," or (Malachi 1, 9), "From your hand has this thing come." Tradition is equally explicit in the statement of the Rabbis (Berakot 33b), "Everything is in the hands of God except the fear of God." To be sure God is omniscient and knows how a given individual will act in a given case, but this does not take away from the freedom of the individual to determine his own conduct. For God's knowledge is not the *cause* of a man's act, or in general of a thing's being. If that were so, all things would be eternal since God knows all things from eternity. God simply knows that man will choose of his own free will to do certain things. Man as a matter of fact never acts contrary to God's knowledge, but this is not because God's knowledge determines his act, but only because God knows the final outcome of a man's free deliberation.

Since it is now clear from every point of view that God does not interfere with a man's freedom of action, any passages in the Bible which seem to indicate the contrary are not properly understood, and must needs be interpreted in accordance with the evidence we have adduced from various sources including the Bible itself. Thus when God says (Exod. 7, 3) "I will harden the heart of Pharaoh," it does not mean, as many think, that God forced Pharaoh to refuse to let Israel go. The meaning rather is that he gave Pharaoh strength to withstand the plagues without succumbing to them, as many of the Egyptians did. The same method should be followed with all the other expressions in the Bible which appear to teach determinism.

A man's conduct has an influence upon the soul, making it pure or impure as the case may be.[73] Though man cannot see this effect, since the soul is an intellectual substance, God knows it. He also keeps a record of our deeds, and deals out reward and punishment in the world to come. This time will not come until he has created the number of souls which his wisdom dictates. At the same time there are also rewards and punishments in this world as an earnest of what is to come in the hereafter.

A man is called righteous or wicked according as his good or bad deeds predominate. And the recompense in the next world is given for this predominating element in his character. A righteous man is punished for his few bad deeds in this world, and rewarded for his many good deeds in the world to come. Similarly the wicked man is paid for his good deeds in this world, while the punishment for his wickedness is reserved. This answers the old problem of the prosperity of the wicked and the misery of the righteous in this world.

There are also sufferings of the righteous which are not in the nature of punishment for past conduct, but in view of the future so as to increase their reward in the world to come for the trials they endured without murmuring. The sufferings of little children come under this head.

On the other hand, a sinner is sometimes well treated and his life prolonged for one of the following reasons: To give him time to repent, as in the case of Manasseh; that he may beget a righteous son, like Ahaz, the father of Hezekiah; to use him as God's tool to punish others more wicked than he—witness the rôle of Assyria as Isaiah describes it in chapter ten of his prophecies; for the sake of the righteous who is closely related to him, as Lot was saved for the sake of Abraham; or in order to make the punishment more severe later, as in the case of Pharaoh.

That there is another world after this one in which man is rewarded and punished can be proved from reason, from Scripture and from tradition.[74] It is not likely from what we know of God's wisdom and goodness that the measure of happiness intended for the soul is what it gets in this world. For every good here is mixed with evil, the latter even predominating. No one is really content and at peace in this world even if he has reached the top of the ladder of prosperity and honor. There must be a reason for this, which is that the soul has an intuitional longing for the other world which is destined for it. There are many things from which the soul is bidden to abstain, such as theft, adultery, and so on, which it desires, and abstention from which causes it pain. Surely there must be reward awaiting the soul for this suffering. Often the soul suffers hatred, persecution and even death for pursuing justice as she is bidden to do. Surely she will be rewarded. Even when a person is punished with death for a crime committed in this world, the same death is inflicted for one crime as for ten crimes. Hence there must be another world where all inequalities are adjusted.

It is also evident that the men of the Bible believed in a hereafter. Else why should Isaac have consented to be sacrificed, or why should God have expected it? The same applies to Hananiah, Mishael, and Azariah, who preferred to be thrown into the fiery furnace rather than fall down in worship before the golden image of Nebuchadnezzar; and to Daniel who was thrown into the den of lions for disobeying the order of the king and praying to God. They would not have done this if they did not believe in another world, where they would be rewarded for their sufferings in this one.

Tradition and the Rabbinical literature are filled with reference to a future world. We need mention only one or two. In the Ethics of the Fathers (ch. 4) we read that this world is like the vestibule to the other world. Another statement in the Talmudic treatise Berakot (p.17a) reads that "in the world to come there is no eating and drinking, nor giving in marriage, nor buying and selling, but the righteous sit with their crowns on their heads and enjoy the splendor of the Shekinah."

With regard to the condition of the soul after death and the nature of reward and punishment in the next world, there is a variety of opinions. Those who hold that the soul is corporeal or that it is an accident of the body believe it is destroyed with the death of the body. We have already refuted their opinion. Others, like the Platonists, the Dualists and the Pantheists, who believe in the pre-existence of the soul either as a separate entity or as a part of God, hold that after the death of the body the soul returns to its original condition. Our belief as stated above (p. 37) is opposed to this. But there are some calling themselves Jews who believe in metempsychosis, that the soul migrates from one person to another and even from man to beast, and that in this way it is punished for its sins and purged. They see a confirmation of their view in the fact that some persons exhibit qualities which are characteristic of lower animals. But this is absurd. The soul and the body form a natural unit, the one being adapted to the other. A human body cannot unite with the soul of an animal, nor an animal body with a human soul. They try to account by their theory for the suffering of little children, who could not have sinned in their own person. But we have already explained that the suffering of children is not in the nature of punishment, but with a view to subsequent reward, and they must admit that the first placing of the soul in the body and giving it commandments is not in the nature of compensation for any past merit, but with a view to later reward. Why not then explain the suffering of children in the same way? [75]

As the body and the soul form a natural unit during life and a man's conduct is the combined effort of the two constituent parts of his being, it stands to reason that future reward and punishment should be imposed upon body and soul in combination. Hence the doctrine of the resurrection of the body, which is alluded to in the Bible and made into a religious dogma by the Rabbis, has support also in the reason.[76] Many objections have been advanced against it, but they can be easily answered. The strongest objection might seem to be that which attempts to show that resurrection is a logical contradiction. The argument is that the elements making up a given body during life find their way after the death of the person into the body of another, to which they are assimilated and of which they form a part. Hence it is impossible to resurrect two bodies out of the material common to both. But this argument is untrue to fact. Every human body has its own matter, which never enters into the composition of any other body. When the person dies and the body decomposes, each element returns to its place in nature, where it is kept until the resurrection.

But there is another event which will happen to Israel before the time of the resurrection. In accordance with the promises of the Prophets we believe that Israel will be delivered from exile by the Messiah.[77] Reason also supports this belief, for God is righteous, and since he has placed us in exile partly as a punishment for wrongdoing, partly for the purpose of trying us, there must be a limit to both.

Messiah the son of David will come, will deliver Jerusalem from the enemy and settle there with his people. When all the believing Israelites have been gathered from all the nations to the land of Palestine, then will come the resurrection. The Temple will be rebuilt, the light of the Shekinah will rest upon it, and the spirit of prophecy will be vouchsafed to all Israel, young and old, master and servant. This blessed period will last until the end of time, *i. e.*, until this world will give place to the next, which is the place of reward and punishment.

We describe the future habitation and status of the soul as Garden of Eden (Paradise) and Gehenna.[78] The former expression is intended to suggest happiness, there being nothing pleasanter in the world than a garden. The term Gehenna is associated in the Bible with Tofteh, which was a place of impurity not far from the Temple. In reality, however, God will create a substance which will combine light and heat in such a way that the righteous will enjoy the light only, while the wicked will be tortured by the heat. All this Saadia infers from Biblical passages.

There will be no eating and drinking in the next world, and hence no need of a heaven and an earth like ours, but there will be place and time, since creatures cannot do without it. There will be no succession of day and night, for these are of use only for our present life and occupations, but will be unnecessary there. There will, however, be a special period for worship.

Reward and punishment in the next world will both be eternal. It stands to reason that God should *promise* eternal reward and punishment so as to inspire mankind with the highest possible degree of hope and fear, that they may have no excuse for not heeding the commandments so forcibly impressed upon them. Having made the promise, his justice prompts him to fulfil it, and those who suffer have themselves to blame.

We have now completed in outline Saadia's system of Judaism. There are many details which we necessarily had to leave out, especially in the more dogmatic part of his work, that dealing with specific Jewish doctrines, which he constructs on the basis of Rabbinical literature and Biblical allusions interpreted so as to harmonize with the statements of the Rabbis. Many questions specifically theological and eschatological assumed importance in his mind by reason of his surroundings. I mean the Mohammedan schools and sects, and the Karaite discussions which were closely modelled after them. The most important part of his system philosophically is that which deals with creation and the attributes of God. His discussions of the soul and of free will are less thorough, and the details of his doctrines of resurrection, future reward and punishment, the redemption of Israel and the Messiah are almost purely dogmatic. For a scientific ethic there is no room at all in the body of his work. A man's conduct is prescribed for him in the divine commandments, though in a general way the reason sees the right and the wrong of the so-called rational group of laws. Still as an after thought Saadia added a chapter to the "Emunot ve-Deot" in which he attempts to give a psychological basis for human conduct. Noting the various tendencies of individuals and sects in his environment to extremes in human behavior, some to asceticism, some to self-indulgence, be it the lust of love or of power, he lays emphasis on the inadequacy of any one pursuit for the demands of man's complex nature, and recommends a harmonious blending of all things for which men strive.[79]

God alone, he says, is a real unity, everything else is by the very reason of its being a creature essentially not one and simple, but composite and complex. So man has a love and desire for many things, and also aversion for many things. And as in other objects in nature it takes a combination of several elements to constitute a given thing, so in man it is by a proper systematization of his likes and dislikes that he can reach perfection of character and morals. It cannot be that God intended man to pursue one object all his life to the exclusion of all others, for in that case he would have implanted only one desire in man instead of many. You cannot build a house of stones alone neither can you develop a perfect character by one pursuit and one interest.

Pursuit of one thing is likely to result in harm, for example, over-indulgence in eating brings on disease. Wisdom is therefore needed in regulating one's conduct. The principle here is control of one's likes and dislikes. Of the three faculties of the soul, reason, spirit and desire, reason must be the master of the other two. If any matter occurs to a person's imagination, he must try it with his reason to see whether it is likely to benefit or injure him, and pursue or avoid it accordingly. If, on the other hand, he allows the lower parts of his soul to rule his reason, he is not a moral man.

The reader will recognize Plato in the last statement. The division of the soul into the three faculties of reason, spirit and desire is Platonic, as we have already seen, and the attempt to base an ethic on the proper relation between the powers of the soul also goes back to Plato. But Saadia tries to show that the Bible too favors this conception.

When Ecclesiastes tells us (1, 14), "I have seen all the works that are done under the sun; and, behold, all is vanity and a striving after wind," he does not mean that there is nothing worth striving after, for he would then be condemning the objects of God's creation. His meaning is that it is vain to pursue any one thing to the exclusion of every other. He then proceeds to name three prominent objects of pursuit, wisdom, pleasure and worldly gain—all is vain when taken by itself. A proper combination of all is to be recommended as is delicately hinted in the same book (2, 3), "I searched in mine heart how to cheer my flesh with wine, mine heart yet guiding me with wisdom, and how to lay hold on folly."

CHAPTER IV

1. *Joseph Al-Basir (11th century)* [80]

Joseph ben Abraham, euphemistically surnamed on account of his blindness, al-Basir (the seer), was a Karaite and lived in Babylonia or Persia in the beginning of the eleventh century. His philosophical work is closely modelled on the writings of the Arabian Mutakallimun, the Mu'tazilites. Unlike Saadia, who tacitly accepts some of their methods and views, al-Basir is an avowed follower of the Kalam and treats only of those questions which are common to Jew and Mohammedan, avoiding, for example, so important an issue as whether it is possible that the law of God may be abrogated—a question which meant so much to Saadia. The division of his investigation into the two parts, Unity and Justice, is a serious matter with him; and he finds it necessary to tell us in several instances why he chose to treat a given topic under the one or the other heading. In spirit and temperament he is a thoroughgoing rationalist. Brief and succinct to the point of obscurity, he betrays neither partiality nor emotion, but fearlessly pushes the argument to its last conclusion and reduces it to its lowest terms.

Saadia (above p. 28) puts revelation as a fourth source of truth parallel to sense, judgment and logical inference. To be sure he, in one instance (p. 35), speaks of the reason as preceding the Bible even as tradition follows it, but this is only a passing observation, and is properly corrected by the view expressed elsewhere (p. 28) that while a Jew is not forbidden to speculate, he must not set the Bible aside and adopt opinions as they occur to him. Al-Basir does not leave the matter in this unsettled condition. He definitely gives priority— logical priority, to reason. Knowledge, he says, must precede revelation. The prophet as the messenger of God cannot be believed on his word, for the opponent may have the same claim. Not only must the prophet authenticate his mission by the performance of a miracle which cannot be explained by natural means, but we must know besides that he who sent him has our good at heart and would not deceive us. A knowledge of the existence, power and wisdom of the creator must therefore precede our belief in the prophet's mission. To take these truths from the words of the prophet and then give him credence because God sent him would be reasoning in a circle. The minimum of knowledge therefore which is indispensable before we can make any appeal to the words of the prophet is rational proof of the existence, power and wisdom of God. Having this minimum the person who is not practiced in speculative investigation may rely for the rest of the creed, for example, the unity of God and his other attributes, upon the words of the Bible. For if we know independently that God is Omnipotent and Omniscient, and the prophet can substantiate his claim to be a divine messenger by the performance of genuine miracles, his reliability is established and we are safe in accepting all that he has to say without proof; but the fundamental thing to do is to establish the prophet's reliability, and for this an independent source of evidence is necessary. This is the reason.

Our problem therefore is to prove the power and wisdom of God, which will imply his existence. We cannot do this directly, for we cannot see God. Hence the only method is to prove the existence of a powerful and wise creator through his creation. We must prove his power in doing things which we cannot do, such as the ability to create our bodies. But for this it is necessary to show that our bodies— and the same will apply to the other bodies of the world, and hence to the world as a whole—were created, *i. e.*, that there was a time when they were not. This leads us to an analysis of the constituents of body. All bodies consist of atoms and their "accidents," or conditions and qualities. The primary accidents, which are presupposed by all the rest, are the following four, combination, separation, motion and rest. Without these no body can exist, for body is the result of a combination and separation of atoms at rest or in motion. But combination and separation are the acts of a combiner and separater, as we can infer from the analogy of our own acts. Our acts have ourselves as their creators, hence the acts visible in the combinations and separations of atoms to form bodies must also have their creator.

The attributes of the creator we infer from the nature of his work. So we call God "Powerful," meaning that he had the power to create the world. As creation denotes power, so the success and harmony of the product argues wisdom; and this power and wisdom thus established are not disproved by an occasional production or event which is not perfect, a monstrosity for example, or disease and suffering. We say in reference to these that God must have a deeper object in view, to inspire mankind with the fear of God, and in order to increase their reward in the next world.

The attribute of Life follows from the other two, for life denotes the possession or capacity of power and knowledge.

Thus al-Basir has the same three essential attributes as Saadia. His proof of the existence of God is also identical with one of the proofs of Saadia. But he shows himself a more loyal follower of the Kalam by frankly adopting the atomic theory, whereas Saadia opposes it (p. 25).

Other predicates of God are perception, will, unity, incorporeality and eternity.

Perception is one of the most important expressions of life, but it must not be confused with knowledge or wisdom. The latter embraces the non-existent as well as the existent, the former the existent only. It is in virtue of the former attribute that we speak of God as "hearing" and "seeing."

"Willing" is another attribute of God, and those are wrong who identify God's will with his knowledge, and define God's willing to mean that his works take place in accordance with his knowledge. God's will must be a special attribute since we see in creation traces of free will. To be the will of God it must not reside in anything different from God, and yet it cannot inhere in God as the subject, for only body is capable of being the subject of accidents. The only solution, therefore, is that God exercises his voluntary activity through a will which he creates, a will not residing in any subject.

This discussion of the nature of God's will seems a case of hair splitting with a vengeance, and al-Basir is not the author of it. As in his other doctrines so in this also he is a faithful follower of the Mu'tazila, and we shall see more of this method in his discussion of the unity of God despite the plurality of his attributes.

But we shall first take up the attributes of incorporeality and eternity, which can be dismissed in a few words.

God is eternal because the only other alternative is that he is created. But if so there is a creator, and if the latter is again created, he must likewise have a creator, and so we are led to infinity, which cannot be, the infinite regress being in all cases an impossibility according to an axiom of the Kalam. We must, therefore, have an eternal creator somewhere, and he is God.

From God's eternity follows his incorporeality, for we have shown before that all body is created, since it presupposes combination and separation, and the latter a combiner and separater.

When we speak of the unity of God we mean first that there is no second God, and then that his own essence has no composition or plurality in it. Two Gods is an absurdity, for the one might desire what the other does not, and he whose will predominates is the real God. It is no objection to say that in their wisdom they would never disagree, because the *possibility* is there, and this makes the above argument valid. Again, if there were two Gods they would have to be completely alike in their essential attributes, and as space cannot hold them apart, since they are not bodies, what is there to constitute them two?

The other problem, of God's simplicity, is more difficult. Does not the multiplicity of attributes make God's essence multiple and composite? The form which this question took was this. Shall we say that God is omnipotent through Power, omniscient through Knowledge, and so on? If so, this Power, Knowledge, etc., are created or eternal. If the Power, say, is created, then God must have had power in order to create it, hence was powerful not through Power. If the Power is eternal, we have more than one God, and " Power " as an eternal would also be Wise and Living, etc.; Wisdom would also be powerful, living, etc., and so on with the other attributes, a doctrine closely bordering on Christianity and reminding one of Augustine. The principle of monotheism could not allow such a conception as this. If Power is neither created nor eternal, it follows that God is omnipotent not through Power as an external cause or a distinct entity, but through his own essence. The attributes Power, Wisdom, Life, are not anything distinguishable from each other and from God's essence. They are modes or conditions of God's essence. and are known along with it.

The same considerations which prompted us to conceive God as one and simple, make impossible the belief in the eternity of God's word. This was a point much discussed in the Mohammedan schools, and was evidently directed against Christianity, where the Word or Logos was identified with the second person in the Trinity. Eternity, Al-Basir says, is incompatible with the idea and purpose of speech. God speaks with a word which he creates. This adds no new predicate to God, but is implied in his Power. The attribute omnipotent implies that when he wills he can make himself understood by us as we do through speech.

We notice that Al-Basir is more elaborate in his discussion of the attributes than Saadia, and like Al-Mukammas he makes use of the formulæ of the Kalam, " omnipotent not with Power, omniscient not with Wisdom." Saadia does not follow the Kalam so closely, but is just as emphatic in his endeavor to show that the three essential attributes are only verbally three; conceptually and really they are one.

The doctrine of the attributes brings to a close the section on unity, and the second division of the investigation is entitled Justice and Fairness. The main problems here are the nature of good and evil and the relation of God to them, the question of free will and other subordinate topics, theological and eschatological.

With regard to the first question two extreme positions are possible, which were actually held by Mohammedan schools of Al-Basir's day. One is that nothing is good or bad in itself, our reason not recognizing it as such; that the divine command or prohibition makes the thing good or bad. Hence, the representatives of this opinion say, God, who stands above his commands and prohibitions, is not bound by them. Good and bad hold for the subject, not for the author. The acts of God do not come within the classification, and hence it is possible that God may do what we regard as injustice. Some, in their endeavor to be consistent and to carry the argument to its last conclusion, did not even shrink from the *reductio ad absurdum* that it is possible God may lie; for, said they, if I promise a boy sweet-meats and fail to keep my promise, it is no worse than if I beat him.

for this school there is no problem of evil, because ethical distinctions do not apply to God's doings. Whatever God does is good. The other school came under the influence of Greek thought and identified the idea of God with the idea of the Good. They maintained that from the nature of God's essence it was not only his duty to do the good, but that it was impossible for him to do anything else. Doing good is a necessity of his nature, and our good and evil are also his good and evil. Ethical values are absolute and not relative.

Neither of these radical views can be maintained. The first is refuted by its own consequences which only very few of its advocates were bold enough to adopt. The possibility of God telling a falsehood, which is implied in the purely human validity of good and evil, is subversive of all religion. God would then cease to be trustworthy, and there would be no reason for giving him obedience. Besides, if revelation alone determines right and wrong, it would follow that if God chose to reverse his orders, our moral judgments would be turned the other way around, good would be evil, and evil good. Finally, if good and bad are determined by the will of God only, those who do not believe in revelation would be without an idea of right and wrong, but this is manifestly not true.

But the other opinion, that God is compelled by the necessity of his nature to do the good, is also erroneous. In the first place it detracts from God's omnipotence to say he cannot do wrong. Besides, if he is compelled by an inner necessity to do the good, he must always have done this, and the world would have existed from eternity. It is just as wrong to say that it is the duty of God to do what is good and useful for man. For this is due to a confusion of the good or generous with the obligatory. Any deed to which no blame attaches may be called good. If no praise attaches to it either, it is indifferent. If it is deserving of praise and its omission does not call forth blame, it is a generous act. A duty is an act the omission of which deserves blame.

Now the truth in the question under discussion is midway between the two extremes. God is able to do good as well as evil, and is under no necessity. The notions of right and wrong are absolute and not merely relative. God never does wrong because evil has no attractive power *per se*. Wrong is committed always as a means to an end, namely, to gain an advantage or avoid an injury. God is not dependent upon anything; he needs no advantages and fears no injuries. Hence there is nothing to prompt him to do wrong. The good on the other hand attracts us by its inherent goodness, not for an ulterior end. If the good were done only for the sake of deriving some benefit external to the good itself, God, who is self-sufficient, would not do anything either good or evil. God does the good always and not the bad, because in his wisdom he sees the difference between them. It was a deed of generosity in God to have created the world and given life to his creatures, but it was not a duty.

This conception of the nature of good and evil leaves on our hands the problem of evil. Why does a good God permit disease and suffering to exist in the world? In particular, how explain the suffering and death of innocent children and harmless animals?

The answer of Al-Basir is that infliction of pain may under certain circumstances be a good instead of an evil. In human relations a person is permitted to inflict pain on another in self-defence, or to prevent the pain from becoming worse, as, for example, when a finger is amputated to save the hand. The infliction of pain is not only permitted, it becomes a duty in case of retribution, as in a court of justice; and finally it is permitted to inflict temporary pain if it will result in a greater advantage in the future. The last two cases apply also to God's treatment of his creatures. Disease and suffering are either punishment for offences committed, or are imposed with a view to later reward. In the case of children the last explanation alone is applicable. They will be rewarded in the next world. At the same time the parents are admonished to repentance and good conduct.

The most difficult question of the section on justice is that of free will and foreknowledge. Is man master of his actions? If so, how can we reconcile this with God's omniscience, who knows beforehand how the person will act at a given moment? Is man free to decide at the last moment in a manner contrary to God's knowledge? If so, we defend freedom at the expense of God's omniscience. If man is bound to act as God foreknew he would act, divine knowledge is saved, man's freedom lost. Al-Basir has no doubt man is free. Our own consciousness testifies to this. When we cut off our finger bitten by a snake, we know that we ourselves did it for a purpose, and distinguish it from a case of our finger being cut off by order of an official, before whom we have been accused or maligned. One and the same act can have only one author and not two, and we know that we are the authors of our acts. There is a much closer connection between an agent and his act than between a knower and his knowledge, which may be the common property of many, and no one doubts that a man's knowledge is his own.

The dilemma above mentioned with its two horns, of which one denies God's knowledge, the other man's freedom, is puzzling enough, to be sure. But we are not bound to answer it since it is purely hypothetical. We do not know of a real instance in which a man's decision tended to be contrary to God's foreknowledge of its outcome. Just as we should refuse to answer the question whether an actual case of injustice on the part of God would prove his ignorance or dependence, because we know through irrefutable proofs that God is wise and without need; so here we say man has freedom though God knows he will act thus and so, and refuse to say whether in case the unbeliever turned believer it would prove God's ignorance or change in his knowledge.

God's creation was a pure act of grace. But once having done this and communicated to us a knowledge of himself and his will, it is now his duty to guide us in the right path, by sending us his prophets. The commandments and prohibitions must never be contrary to the knowledge of reason. We must see in the commandments means of guidance, in the prohibitions a protection against destructive influences. If they had not this rational basis, we do not see why God should have imposed them upon us.

Having given us reason to know his being, and having announced his truth through the prophets, it is his duty to reward those who knew him and were obedient, eternally in the next world, and to punish eternally the unbeliever. If one has merits and sins, they are balanced against each other. If the sinner repents of his evil deeds, it is the duty of God to accept his repentance and remit his punishment.

2. Jeshua ben Judah [81]

Jeshua ben Judah or, as he is known by his Arabic name, Abu al-Faraj Furkan ibn Asad, was likewise a Karaite, a pupil of Joseph

Al-Basir, and flourished in Palestine in the second half of the eleventh century. His point of view is essentially the same as that of his teacher, Al-Basir. He is also a follower of the Mu'tazilite Kalam and as strong a rationalist as his master. He agrees with Al-Basir that we cannot get certain knowledge of the creation of the world and the existence of God from the Bible. This information must come originally from rational speculation. It should then be applied to the miracles of the prophets so as to prove the authenticity of their mission and the truth of their announcements.

He adopts the atomic theory, though he is opposed to the view that atoms are created ever anew by God from moment to moment, and that there is no natural and necessary sequence or continuity in the phenomena of the world or qualities of bodies, all being due to habit and custom induced in us by God's uninterrupted creations. As in his philosophical discussions he is a follower of the Kalam, so in his legalistic works he is indebted to the Mohammedan schools of religious law.

Like Al-Basir, Jeshua ben Judah regards as the corner stone of his religious philosophy the proof that the world was created, *i. e.*, that it is not eternal. His arguments are in essence the same, though differently formulated. In their simplest form they are somewhat as follows. The world and its bodies consist of atoms and their accidents. Taking a given atom for the sake of argument we know that it is immaterial to it, so far as its own essence is concerned, whether it occupy one place or another. As a fact, however, it does occupy a definite place at a given moment. This must be due to a cause. And as the atom in question in the course of time changes its place, this shows that the cause which kept it in the former place has disappeared and given way to a new cause, and so on. In other words, the successive causes which determine the positions and motions of the atoms are not permanent, hence not eternal but created. The necessary inference is that the atoms or the bodies, which cannot exist without these created causes (else they could not occupy one place rather than another), must also be created.

Another form of the argument for creation is this. The eternal has no cause. It exists by virtue of its own essence, and is not dependent on anything else. If now the atoms were eternal, they would have to persist in the same condition all the time; for any change would imply a cause upon which the atom is dependent, and this is fatal to its eternity. But the atoms do constantly change their condition and place. Hence they are created.

If the things of the world are created, someone must have created them. This is clear. But there may be room for the supposition that this creative agency is a "*cause*," *i. e.*, an impersonal entity, which by necessity produces other things from itself. Hence we must hasten to say that this conception of the Creator is impossible because incompatible with our results so far. A necessarily producing cause cannot be without creating, hence an eternal cause implies an eternal effect—which contradicts our idea of a created world proved above. We say, therefore, that the Creator is not a "cause" but an "agent," *i. e.*, one acting with will and choice.

God is incorporeal because body consists of atoms, and atoms, we have shown, are created. Besides, if he were corporeal, he could not create bodies any more than we can. He would furthermore be limited to a definite place, and the same arguments cited above to prove that atoms are dependent on a cause would apply to him. Finally we as corporeal beings cannot exert an influence on objects except by coming in contact with them. God causes the seed to grow without being in contact with it. Hence he is not body, and the scriptural passages apparently teaching the contrary must be explained otherwise.

Jeshua ben Judah likewise agrees with Al-Basir in regarding the nature of good and evil as absolute, not relative. Like his master he opposes those who make God's command and prohibition the sole creators of good and evil respectively, as on the other hand he refuses to agree with the view that God is bound by necessity to do the good. Our reason distinguishes between good and evil as our senses between white and black.

Among other arguments in favor of the absolute character of right and wrong, which we have already found in Al-Basir, appears the following. If good and evil mean simply that which God commands and prohibits respectively, and the distinction holds only for us but not for God, it follows that God may do what we think is evil. If this be so, we have no ground for believing in the good faith of the prophet—God might have sent him to deceive us—and the alleged basis of right and wrong is removed.

We conclude therefore that good and evil are absolute and are bind-ing upon God as well. God can do evil as well as good, but being omnipotent he can accomplish his purpose just as easily by doing good as by doing evil, and hence surely prefers to do good. Besides, all evil doing is the result of some need, but God has no needs, being self-sufficient, hence he does not do evil.

It follows from the above that God had a purpose in creating the world. For an act without a purpose is vain and hence bad. This purpose cannot have been egoistic, since God is without need, being above pleasure and pain. The purpose must therefore have been the well-being of his creatures.

CHAPTER V

SOLOMON IBN GABIROL

With Gabirol the scene of Jewish intellectual activity changes from the east to the west. Prior to the middle of the tenth century the centre of Jewish learning was in Babylonia. The succession of Geonim in the Talmudical schools of Sura and Pumbadita, and particularly the great fame of Saadia, made all the other Jewish communities of the world look to Babylonia as the spiritual centre. They considered it a privilege to contribute to the support of the great eastern academies and appealed to their spiritual heads in cases of doubt in religious matters. Some of this glory was reflected also upon the neighboring countries under Mohammedan domination, Palestine, Egypt, and Kairuan or northern Africa to the west of Egypt. Thus all the men, Rabbanites as well as Karaites, whom we treated so far lived and flourished in the east in one of the four countries mentioned. Christian Europe was intellectually on a low level, and as far as scientific studies were concerned, the Jews under Christian rule were no better than their temporal rulers.

But a new era dawned for Jewish literature with the accession to power of the Umayyad caliph Abd al Rahman III, as head of Mohammedan Spain or Andalusia. He was a liberal man and a patron of learning. Hasdai ibn Shaprut, a cultured and high-minded Jew, was his trusted adviser, and like his royal patron he protected and encouraged Jewish learning, Talmudical as well as scientific. When Moses ben Enoch, a learned emissary from the Babylonian Academy, was ransomed by the Jewish community of Cordova and made the head of a Talmudical school in that city, the beginning of the end of Babylonian Jewish supremacy was at hand. Moses ben Enoch the Talmudist, Menahem ben Saruk, the grammarian and lexicographer, and Dunash ben Labrat, the poet—all three under the distinguished patronage of Hasdai ibn Shaprut—inaugurated the long line of Spanish Jewish worthies, which continued almost five centuries, constituting the golden era of Jewish literature and making of Spain the intellectual centre of all Jewry.

Solomon ibn Gabirol was not merely the first Jewish philosopher in Spain, he was the first Spanish philosopher, that is, he was the first philosophical writer in Andalusia. Ibn Badja, the first Mohammedan philosopher in Spain, was born at least a half century after Gabirol. The birth of Gabirol is generally placed in 1021 and his death in 1058, though some have put it as late as 1070.

The fate of Gabirol in the history of Jewish literature was a peculiar one. Highly celebrated as a synagogal poet in the Sephardic as well as Ashkenazic community, his fame as a great philosopher was early overshadowed by his successors, and his chief work, the "Fountain of Life," was in the course of time quite forgotten. The Arabic original was lost and there was no Hebrew translation. The Tibbonides, Judah, Samuel and Moses, who translated everything worth while in Jewish philology, science and philosophy from Arabic into Hebrew, either did not know of Gabirol's masterpiece or did not think it important enough to translate. To judge from the extant fragments of the correspondence between Samuel ibn Tibbon and Maimonides, it would seem that both were true; that is that Samuel ibn Tibbon had no access to Gabirol's "Fons Vitæ," and that if he had had such access, Maimonides would have dissuaded him from translating it. Maimonides actually tells his translator [82] that the only books worth studying are those of Aristotle and his true commentators, Alexander of Aphrodisias, Themistius, Averroes. Alfarabi and Avicenna are also important, but other writings, such as those of Empedocles, Pythagoras, Hermes, Porphyry, represent a pre-Aristotelian philosophy which is obsolete, and are a waste of time. The books of Isaac Israeli on the "Elements" and on "Definitions," are no better, seeing that Israeli was only a physician and no philosopher. He is not familiar with the "Microcosmus" of Joseph ibn Zaddik, but infers from a knowledge of the man that his work is based upon the writings of the "Brothers of Purity"; and hence, we may add, not strictly Aristotelian, and not particularly important. Not a word is here said about Gabirol, apparently because Samuel ibn Tibbon had not inquired about him. But from Maimonides's judgment concerning the works of "Empedocles," we may legitimately infer that he would have been no more favorable to Gabirol; for, as we shall see, Gabirol's system is also based upon a point of view similar to that of the so-called "Empedocles." What the Tibbonides left undone was, however, partially accomplished about a half century later by the commentator and critic Shem Tob Falaquera (1225–1290). Apparently in agreement with Abraham ibn Daud that Gabirol's profuseness in his philosophic masterpiece made it possible to reduce it to a tenth part of its size, Falaquera did not find it necessary to translate the whole of the "Mekor Hayim" into Hebrew, giving us instead a translation of selected parts, which in his estimation contained the gist of Gabirol's teaching. The absence of a complete Hebrew translation of Gabirol's philosophical work meant of course that no one who did not know Arabic could have access to Gabirol's "Mekor Hayim," and this practically excluded the majority of learned Jews after the first half of the thirteenth century. But the selections of Falaquera did not seem to find many readers either, as may be inferred from the fact that so far only one single manuscript of this translation is known.

En revanche, as the French would say, the Christian Scholastics of the thirteenth century made Gabirol their own and studied him diligently. His fundamental thesis of a universal matter underlying all existence outside of God was made a bone of contention between the two dominant schools; the Dominicans, led by Thomas Aquinas, opposing this un-Aristotelian principle, the Franciscans with Duns Scotus at their head, adopting it as their own. "Ego autem redeo ad sententiam Avicembronis," is a formula in Duns Scotus's discussion of the principle of matter.[83]

The translation of Gabirol's philosophy into an accessible language, which was not considered desirable by Jews, was actually accomplished by Christians. About a century before Falaquera a complete translation into Latin was made in Toledo of Gabirol's "Fountain of Life," under the title "Fons Vitæ." This translation was made at the instance of Raymond, Archbishop of Toledo in the middle of the twelfth century, by Dominicus Gundissalinus, archdeacon of Segovia, with the assistance of a converted Jewish physician, Ibn Daud (Avendehut, Avendeath), whose name after conversion became Johannes Hispanus or Hispalensis. Unlike the Hebrew epitome of Falaquera this translation was not neglected, as is clear from the rôle Gabirol's philosophy plays in the disputations of the schools, and from the fact that there are still extant four manuscripts of the complete translation, one of an epitome thereof, and there is evidence that a fifth manuscript existed in 1375 in the Papal library.[84] As Ibn Sina was corrupted by the Latin writers into Avicenna, and Ibn Roshd into Averroes, so Ibn Gabirol became in turn, Avencebrol, Avicembron, Avicebron; and the Scholastics who fought about his philosophy had no idea he was a Jew and celebrated as a writer of religious hymns used in the synagogue. He was regarded now as a Mohammedan, now as a Christian.

This peculiar circumstance will help us to get an inkling of the reason for the neglect of Gabirol's philosophy in the Jewish community. It is clear that a work which, like the "Fons Vitæ," made it possible for its author to be regarded as a Mohammedan or even a Christian, cannot have had the Jewish imprint very deeply stamped upon its face. Nay more, while the knowledge of its having been translated from the Arabic may have been sufficient in itself to stamp the author as a Mohammedan, there must have been additional indications for his Scholastic admirers to make them regard him as a Christian. An examination of the work lends some semblance of truth to these considerations.

Gabirol nowhere betrays his Jewishness in the "Fons Vitæ." He never quotes a Biblical verse or a Talmudic dictum. He does not make any overt attempt to reconcile his philosophical views with religious faith. The treatise is purely speculative as if religious dogma nowhere existed to block one's way or direct one's search. Abraham Ibn Daud, the author of the philosophical treatise "Emunah Ramah" (The Exalted Faith), and the predecessor of Maimonides, criticises Gabirol very severely, and that not merely because he disagrees with him in the conception of matter and finds Gabirol's reasoning devoid of cogency and logical force—many bad arguments, he says, seem in the mind of Gabirol to be equivalent to one good one—but principally because Gabirol failed to take a Jewish attitude in his philosophizing, and actually, as Ibn Daud tells us, maintains views dangerous to Judaism (below, p. 198).

This will easily account for the fact that Gabirol, celebrated as he was as a poet, was lost sight of generally as a philosopher. The matter is made clearer still if we add that his style in the " Mekor Hayim" is against him. It is devoid of all merit whether of literary beauty or of logical conciseness and brevity. It is diffuse to a degree and frequently very wearisome and tedious. One has to wade through pages upon pages of bare syllogisms, one more flimsy than another.

Finally, the point of view of Gabirol was that of a philosophy that was rapidly becoming obsolete, and Maimonides, the ground having been made ready by Ibn Daud, gave this philosophy its death-blow by substituting for it the philosophy of Aristotle.

We now understand why it is that, with few exceptions here and there, Gabirol's philosophical work was in the course of time forgotten among the Jews, though his name Avicebron as well as some of his chief doctrines were well known to the Scholastic writers. To be sure, even students of Scholastic literature had no direct access to Gabirol's treatise as it was never printed and no one knew whether there were still any manuscripts of it extant or not. The only sources of information concerning Avicebron's philosophy were Aquinas's refutations, and Duns Scotus's defence, and other second-hand references in the writings of the Scholastics. Who Avicebron was no one knew. It was not until 1819 that Amable Jourdain,[85] in tracing the history of the Latin translations of Aristotle, came to the conclusion that more must be known about the philosophy of Avicebron's "Fons Vitæ" if we intended to understand the Scholastics. In 1845 Solomon Munk discovered in the national library at Paris the epitome of Falaquera mentioned above, and comparing it with the views of Avicebron as found in the discussions of the Scholastics, made the important discovery that the mysterious Avicebron was neither a Mohammedan nor a Christian but a Jew, and none other than the famous poet Solomon ibn Gabirol. Then began a search for copies of a Latin translation, which was rewarded amply. Both Munk and Seyerlen discovered manuscript copies of the " Fons Vitæ," and now both the Hebrew epitome of Falaquera and the Latin translation of Gundissalinus are accessible in print.[86] So much for the interesting history of Gabirol. Now a word as to his views.

Shem Tob ibn Falaquera, in the brief introduction which he appends to his epitome of the "Mekor Hayim" says, "It seems to me that Solomon ibn Gabirol follows in his book the views of the ancient philosophers as we find them in a book composed by Empedocles concerning the 'Five Substances.' [87] This book is based upon the principle that all spiritual substances have a spiritual matter; that the form comes from above and the matter receives it from below, *i. e.*, that the matter is a substratum and bears the form upon it." He then adds that Aristotle attributes a similar view to his predecessors, but that this view is inconsistent with Aristotle's own thinking. For in his opinion what is material is composite and possessed of potentiality. Hence only those things have matter which are subject to generation and decay, and in general change from one state to another.

Without going into detail as to the nature of this work of Empedocles named by Falaquera as the source of Gabirol's views—expositions of these so-called Empedoclean views and fragments from Empedocles's book have been found in Arabian and Hebrew writers [88]—it is sufficient for us to know that it has nothing to do with the real Empedocles, the ancient Greek philosopher; that it was another of the many spurious writings which circulated in the middle ages under famous names of antiquity; and that like the "Theology of Aristotle," and the "Liber de Causis," mentioned in the Introduction (p. xx), it was Neo-Platonic in character.

Thus Gabirol was a Neo-Platonist. This does not mean that he did not adopt many important Aristotelian conceptions. Neo-Platonism itself could not have arisen without Aristotle. The ideas of matter and form, and potentiality and actuality, and the categories, and so on, had become the fixed elements of philosophical thinking, and no new system could do without them. In this sense Plotinus himself, the founder of Neo-Platonism, is an Aristotelian. When we speak of Gabirol as a Neo-Platonist, we mean that the essence of his system is Neo-Platonic. He is not a dualist, but a monist. God and matter are not opposed as two ultimate principles, as they are in Aristotle. Matter in Gabirol is ultimately identified with God. In this he goes even beyond Plotinus. For whereas in Plotinus matter occupies the lowest scale in the gradation of being as it flows from the One or the Good (*cf.* Introduction, p. xxxviii), and becomes equivalent to the non-existent, and is the cause of evil, in Gabirol matter is the underlying substance for all being from the highest to the lowest, with the one exception of the Creator himself. [89] It emanates from the essence of the

Creator, forming the basis of all subsequent emanations.[90] Hence the spiritual substances of the celestial world, or, to use a more technical and more precise term—since spirit is not located in heaven or anywhere spatially—the intelligible world, have matter underlying their form.[91] In fact, matter itself is intelligible or spiritual, not corporeal.[92] Corporeality and materiality are two different things. There are various gradations of matter, to be sure; for the prime matter as it emerges from the essence of the Creator pervades all existence from highest to lowest, and the further it extends from its origin the less spiritual and the more corporeal it becomes until in the sublunar world we have in the matters of its particular objects, corporeal matter, *i. e.*, matter affected with quantity and magnitude and figure and color.[93] Like Plotinus, Gabirol conceives of the universe as a process of a gradually descending series of existences or worlds, as the Kabbalistic writers term them; these cosmic existences radiating or flowing out of the superabundant light and goodness of the Creator. The two extremes of this graded universe are God at the one end, and the corporeal world at the other. Intermediate between these are the spiritual substances, Intelligence, Soul and Nature.[94] Man as a microcosm, a universe in little, partakes of both the corporeal and intermediate worlds, and hence may serve as a model of the constitution of the macrocosm, or great universe. His body is typical of the corporeal world, which consists of the lowest matter, viz., that which has no other form except that of corporeality, or extension, and the forms of figure, color, and so on, borne on top of the extension.[95]

Body as such is at rest and is not capable of action. To act it needs an agent. Hence it needs an agency to compose its parts and hold them together. We call this agency Nature. Man's body also grows, is nourished and propagates its kind as do plants. This likewise must have its non-corporeal cause. This we call vegetative soul. Man has also sense perception and local motion like the animals. The principle or substance causing this is the animal soul. Man also thinks and reasons and reflects. This is brought about by the rational soul. Finally, man has a still higher function than discursive thought. The latter has to search and to pass from premise to conclusion, whereas the apprehension of the intelligence takes place "without seeking, without effort, and without any other cause except its own essence, because it is full of perfection." In other words, it is immediate intellectual intuition of which Gabirol speaks here. The Intelligence is capable of this because it has in itself, constituting its essence, all the forms of existence, and knowledge means possession of the forms of the things known.

As man is typical of the universe, it follows that there are cosmic existences corresponding to the principles or powers just enumerated in man, and the relation of the latter to the former is that of the particular to the general. Hence there is a cosmic Intelligence, a cosmic soul embracing the rational, the animal and the vegetative parts, and a cosmic nature. Of these the more perfect is the cause of the less perfect; hence the order in which we named them represents the order of causation or of emanation from the prime source.

The lowest of these emanations is the matter which sustains extension or magnitude, and with it the process ceases. This matter is no longer the source of an additional form of existence. The various qualities and attributes which inhere in this corporeal matter are caused by the spiritual substances above. For like the prototype of all generosity and goodness the First Essence or God, every one of the spiritual substances proceeding from him has the same tendency of imparting its form or forms to the substance next below it. But the forms thus bestowed are no longer the same as they are in the essence of the bestowing substance, as it depends upon the recipient what sort of form it will receive. An inferior receiving substance will receive a superior form in an inferior way. That is, the form which in the substance above the one in question is contained in a spiritual and unitary manner, will be transformed in the substance below it into something less spiritual, less unified, and more nearly corporeal, *i. e.*, visible and tangible. Hence the visible and tangible, and in general the sensible qualities of particular things in the sublunar world, are in reality descended from a line of spiritual ancestors in the forms of the simple substances, Intelligence, Soul and Nature. But it is their distance from the prime source, which increases with every transmission of influence, together with the cruder nature of the receiving substance, that makes the resulting forms corporeal and sensible. The matter may be made clear if we use the analogy of light, which is invisible as long as it is in air because it penetrates it, but becomes visible when it comes in contact with a gross body which it cannot penetrate. It then remains on the surface condensed, and becomes visible to the senses.

We thus see that the higher substance acts upon the lower and contains all that is found in the latter, though in a more perfect and simple manner. The lower substances flow from the higher and yet the latter are not diminished in their essence and power.[96]

That ordinary material objects are composed of matter and form is admitted and we need not now prove it, as we have already discussed the subject in the Introduction, where we gave an outline of the Aristotelian philosophy. The principle peculiar to Gabirol is that not merely the material objects of the sublunar world, but that the intelligible or spiritual substances also are composed of matter and form.[97] Whenever two things have something in common and something in which they differ, that which they have in common is the matter, that in which they differ is the form. Two things absolutely simple must be prime to each other, i. e., they must have nothing in common, for if they have anything in common they have everything in common, and they are no longer two things but one. Hence a spiritual substance must be composite, for it must have something by which it differs from a corporeal substance, and something, viz., substantiality, which it has in common with it. In the same way the intelligible substances, Intelligence and Soul, have their substantiality in common, and they differ in form. Hence they are composed of matter and form, and the matter must be the same in all the intelligible substances; for their differences are due to their forms, hence if their matters also differed, they would have to differ in form, but matter as such has no form. Hence matter in itself is everywhere the same.

As the Intelligence is the highest existence next to God, and is composed of matter and form, these are respectively the universal matter and universal form, embracing all subsequent matters and forms.[98] Hence the Intelligence in knowing itself knows everything, as everything is contained in it. And as it is prior to everything and the cause of everything it has an immediate knowledge of all things without effort or searching.

But what is the origin of universal matter and universal form which, in constituting Intelligence, are the fundamental principles of all

existence? [99]   The answer is they come from the First Essence, God.
Unity comes before duality or plurality, and there is no true unity
except in God.   Whatever issues from him is *ipso facto*, as a product
which is not God, affected with duality.   Matter and Form is this
duality.   Their union is necessary and real, and it is only in thought
that we can keep them apart.   In reality they form a unit, their union
varying in perfection according as they are nearer or further away
from their origin.   Hence the union is closest in Intelligence, the first
divine emanation, and least close in corporeal objects of the sublunar
world, where plurality is the order of the day.

This process by which universal matter and form issue from God
may be called creation. [100]   But we must conceive of it on the analogy
of water flowing from a fountain in continued and uninterrupted succession.   The only difference is that the emanation from God takes
place without motion and without time.

The union of universal form and universal matter must be thought
of as a stamping of the form upon the matter.   Matter has in itself
no actual or definable existence.   It serves merely as a *tabula rasa*,
as a potential background, as an empty receptacle, as a reflecting
mirror for form to be written, filled out, impressed or reflected therein
or upon.   Hence we may view God as the spectator, universal matter
as the mirror, and universal form as the reflection of the spectator in
the glass.   God himself does not enter the glass, only his reflection is
outlined therein.   And as matter and form are really the whole world,
it would follow that the universe is a reflection of God, though God
remains in himself and does not enter the world with his essence.

We may also picture to ourselves this impression of form upon matter
on the analogy of speech.   The speaker's words impress ideas upon
the soul of the listener.   So God speaks and his Word or Will impresses
form upon matter.   The world is created by the Word or the Will [101]
of God.

In all these similes matter appears as something external to God,
upon which he impresses form.   But this is not strictly true, since
matter has no real existence without form, and has never so existed.
The existence of matter and form is simultaneous, and both come from
God, matter from his essence, form from his attribute, or his Wisdom,
or his Word, or his Will.   And yet in God, who is a perfect unity, es-

sence and attribute are one. It is the Will of God, not God himself, that must be regarded as the spectator, whose outline is reflected in the mirror of matter in the above simile. It is the Will of God that writes form upon the chart of matter, and thereby produces a world. It is in virtue of the Will that God is said to be in everything.

But what is this will of God as distinguished from God himself, since in God there can be no duality of any kind? Gabirol's answer is not clear or satisfactory. The will, he says, is identical with God if we consider it apart from its activity; considered as active it is different from the divine essence. Exactly to describe it is impossible, but the following is an approximation. It is a divine power producing matter and form, binding them together, pervading them throughout their extent above and below, as the soul pervades the body, and moving and ordering everything.

God himself, or the First Essence, can be known only through the Will as pervading everything, *i. e.*, through his effects in the world. And in this way too only his existence can be known but not his essence as he is in himself, because God is above everything and infinite. The soul may know Intelligence because though the latter is above the soul there is some similarity between them. But the First Essence has no similarity to Intelligence, therefore no intelligence can know it.

There is a kind of mystic knowledge by which man may come in touch with the spiritual substances and rise even to universal matter, which is above Intelligence. "If you wish to form a picture of these substances," the master says to the disciple in the "Fons Vitæ," "you must raise your intellect to the last intelligible, you must purify it from all sordid sensibility, free it from the captivity of nature and approach with the force of your intelligence to the last limit of intelligible substance that it is possible for you to comprehend, until you are entirely divorced from sensible substance and lose all knowledge thereof. Then you will embrace, so to speak, the whole corporeal world in your being, and will place it in one corner of your soul. When you have done this you will understand the insignificance of the sensible in comparison with the greatness of the intelligible. Then the spiritual substances will be before your eyes, comprehending you and superior to you, and you will see your own being as though you were those substances. Sometimes it will seem to you that you

are a part of them by reason of your connection with corporeal substance; and sometimes you will think you are all of them, and that
there is no difference between you and them, on account of the union
of your being with their being, and the attachment of your form to
their forms." The pupil assures the teacher that he has followed this
advice and seen the whole corporeal world floating in the spiritual substances as a small boat in the sea, or a bird in the air. "When you
have raised yourself to the first universal matter," replies the
teacher, "and illumined its shadow, you will see there the wonder of
wonders. Pursue this therefore diligently and with love, because this
is the purpose of the existence of the human soul, and in this is great
delight and extreme happiness." [102]

But Gabirol does not promise a knowledge of the Most High even
through this royal road of ecstasy, unless we suppose that in the promise of seeing in universal matter the wonder of all wonders there may
be a covert allusion to a glimpse of the deepest secret of all, the essence
of God.

All knowledge is according to Gabirol embraced in the following
three topics, (1) Matter and Form, (2) the Active Word or Will, (3) the
First Essence or God. By far the larger part of the "Fons Vitæ" is
devoted to the first subject. Only brief hints are given of the second
and third, and Gabirol refers us to a special work of his on the Will,
which he says he wrote. There is no trace of any such treatise. At
any rate it is clear from the little that is contained on the Divine Will
in the "Fons Vitæ" that the Will forms an important element in
Gabirol's philosophy. This is the more remarkable because it is not
an essential element in Neo-Platonism, upon which Gabirol's system
is based. Nay, the doctrine of a divine will scarcely has any place
in the form of emanation taught by Plotinus. The cosmic process is
conceived there as necessary and impersonal. And but for the introduction of the Will in the "Fons Vitæ" we should be forced to
understand Gabirol in the same way. The difficulty in Neo-Platonism
is that God is at the same time transcendent and, through his powers
or emanations, immanent in the world. God is above all being and
at the same time is the cause of and pervades all existence. Gabirol
must have felt not merely this purely philosophical difficulty, but as
a Jew, Pantheism as well as impersonalism must have been objection-

able to him. Hence he mitigates both by introducing the divine will as mediating between God and the world. This brings God in closer and more personal touch with his creation. The cosmic process is not a necessary and impersonal flow or radiation but a voluntary activity having a purpose. The solution is unsatisfactory, as all such solutions are bound to be, because it introduces as many difficulties as it solves. The nature of this divine Will is ambiguous. If it is God's will, and God is the One in whom there can be no distinctions, we have only a new word, and nothing is solved. If on human analogy we are inclined to take the will seriously, we are endangering God's unity. This dilemma Gabirol does not succeed in removing. His system still has a strong flavor of Pantheism, and moreover his identification of the Will of God with the Wisdom and the Word of God, and his hypostatization of the latter as in a sense a being distinct from God, reminds us strongly of Philo's Logos, which became the Logos of Christianity, the second person in the Trinity. This is the reason why William of Auvergne, bishop of Paris in the thirteenth century, regarded Avicebron as a Christian. And these same reasons were no doubt adequate to estrange Jewish readers, as Abraham ibn Daud expressly tells us about himself, though his terms are general (see above, p. 62).

Gabirol is also the author of an ethical work which he composed in 1045. Though of little importance philosophically, or perhaps because of this, the "Tikkun Middot ha-Nefesh" (Improvement of the Qualities of the Soul) fared much better than its more important companion, the "Mekor Hayim." Not only did it have the privilege of a Hebrew translation at the hands of the father of translators, Judah ibn Tibbon, but the original Arabic itself is still extant and was recently published with an English translation by Stephen S. Wise (1901).[103] The Hebrew translation also had the good fortune of being reprinted several times. This is due to the fact that the "Tikkun Middot ha-Nefesh" is a popular work, dealing with morals, and does not go into metaphysical questions. It is full of Biblical citations, which stamps it as Jewish; and there are also in it quotations from Arabic writers serving to illustrate the argument and lending variety and interest to the style.

The larger question of the aim of human life is touched on in the

"Fons Vitæ." We are told there that the ultimate aim of man's existence is that the soul should unite with the upper world to which it belongs.[104] The particular human soul is according to Gabirol a part, though not in a physical sense, of the cosmic soul, which is one of the universal spiritual substances (see above, p. 66). Hence its own real existence is spiritual and eternal, and independent of the body. Its entrance into the body obscures its spiritual vision, though it does not lose all touch with the higher world from which it came. The senses and the data of sense perception are not an end in themselves; they are only a means for the soul through them to recall the higher knowledge which was its own in its spiritual existence, and thereby win its return to the intelligible world. Man's duty therefore in this world is to strive to attain this higher life for his soul. This is brought about by means of *knowledge* and *practice*. This knowledge has to do with knowing all things as they really are, and particularly the intelligible substances and the Prime Essence. Practice signifies to keep away as far as possible from things of sense, which are foreign to the soul and might injure it. What more particularly the things are which are beneficial to the soul, and what are injurious, we learn from Gabirol's ethical treatise. Man's soul has a higher and a lower nature. The higher power is the reason or rational soul, the lower is the animal or vegetative soul; and man's business is to see that the reason rules over the lower nature.

Gabirol does not give us any test by which we can tell whether a given act or feeling belongs to the lower or higher nature except to say that the appetites are diseases of the body which must be cured; that they do not belong to the rational soul, and to satisfy them is not the attainment of a good. Gabirol's method of treating virtue and vice, or rather the virtues and the vices, is to relate them to the five senses and the four humors in man, which in turn correspond to the four elements, fire, air, water, earth, and the four primitive qualities, hot, cold, moist, dry. This division of the elements, the humors, the qualities and the senses was a commonplace of the physiological and medical science of the time. We have met it in Isaac Israeli (see above, p. 3), and it goes back to Aristotle and Galen and Hippocrates. The originality, though a queer one to be sure, of Gabirol is to bring the ethical qualities of man into relation with all these. The approximations are forced in every instance and often ludicrous. Instead of attempting to give a psychological analysis of the qualities in question, he lays stress on their physical basis in one of the five senses, as we shall see presently.

The great world, we are told, was created out of the four elements, and similarly man, the microcosm, also consists of four natures corresponding to the elements. Thus the four humors, upon the harmonious combination of which the health of man's body depends, viz., blood, phelgm, black gall, and red gall, correspond respectively to air, water, earth, fire. Man is endowed besides with five senses. If he is wise he will use his senses properly and in the right measure, like a skilful physician who calculates carefully what proportion of each drug should be prescribed.

The sense of sight is the noblest of the senses, and is related to the body as the sun to the world. The philosophers have a wonderful saying concerning the eye that there are spiritual tints in the soul which are visible in the movements of the eyelids—pride and haughtiness, humility and meekness. Accordingly the ethical qualities due to the sense of sight are pride, meekness, modesty and impudence, besides the subordinate qualities derived from these.

Pride is common in a person of a warm disposition in whom the red gall predominates. Many wise men exhibit this quality out of place, fools adopt it until they are mastered by it, and it is prevalent in youth. It may be useful when it keeps a man away from vice and unworthy things, inspiring him to rise to nobility of character and the service of God. But generally it is useless and leads to many evils, especially if it causes one to be self-opinionated, refusing to seek the advice of anyone. When a man sees this quality gaining mastery over him, he should consider the origin and end of existing things. When he sees that all things are destined to pass away, and himself likewise, his pride will change to humility.

Meekness is closer to virtue than the quality mentioned before, because he who possesses it withholds his desire from seeking gratification. It is a quality manifested by the prophets and leads to honor. "The fruits of lowliness," a philosopher has said, "are love and tranquillity." Contentment is of a kind with meekness. The greatest riches are contentment and patience. He who esteems his rank but lightly enhances man's estimation of his dignity. A wise man has said, "Be humble without cringing, and manly without being arro-gant. Arrogance is a wilderness and haughtiness a taking refuge therein, and altogether a going astray."

Modesty is connected with humility but is superior to it, for it is a sister of reason, and reason, as everybody knows, is the most important quality, which separates man from beast and brings him near to the angels. You never see a modest person without sense, or a person of good sense who is not modest. A man must be modest not only before others but also to himself. Modesty and faithfulness, it is said, are closely related, and the one cannot be had truly without the other.

The impudent man is disliked by God and by man, even if he be wise and learned. If one has this quality it is the duty of his friend and associate to break him of it by reproving him. It is of value only when used in defence of the Torah and in behalf of God and the truth.

Space will not permit us to treat in detail of the other senses and the virtues and vices depending upon them, but we shall indicate briefly Gabirol's method of relating the ethical qualities to the physical senses.

Thus the sense of hearing, which is next in importance to sight has as its qualities hate, love, mercy and cruelty. It takes some fine insight, he says, to see the connection of these qualities with the sense of hearing, but the intelligent and discerning reader will find this hint sufficient. I hope he will not blame me, Gabirol continues, if I do not bring together all the reasons and the scriptural passages to prove this, for human flesh is weak, especially in my case on account of my vexatious experiences and disappointments. We find in the Bible love associated with hearing: "*Hear*, O Israel . . . and thou shalt *love* the Lord thy God" (Deut. 6, 4). Hate follows hearing in the phrase: "When Esau heard the words of his father . . . and Esau hated Jacob" (Gen. 27, 34–41). Mercy is related to hearing in Exod. (22, 26), "And I will hear for I am merciful." Finally cruelty is to refuse to listen, as we find in the case of Pharaoh (Ex. 9, 12), "And the Lord hardened the heart of Pharaoh, and he hearkened not unto them."

In a similar manner Gabirol proves that the sense of smell has four qualities, anger, favor, envy, wide-awakeness; the sense of taste, the four qualities, joy, sorrow, regret, calmness; while liberality, niggardliness, courage and cowardice are related to the sense of touch.

The relation of the ethical qualities to the senses, humors, elements and primitive physical qualities is exhibited in the following table, as it appears in the Arabic text of the "Aslah al-Ahlak," the original title of Gabirol's ethical work.

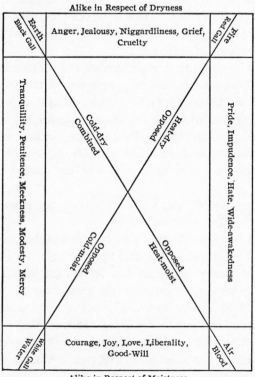

Alike in Respect of Dryness

Anger, Jealousy, Niggardliness, Grief, Cruelty

Earth / Black Gall

Fire / Red Gall

Tranquility, Penitence, Meekness, Modesty, Mercy

Cold-dry Combined

Heat-dry Opposed

Pride, Impudence, Hate, Wide-awakedness

Cold-moist Opposed

Heat-moist Opposed

Water / White Gall

Air / Blood

Courage, Joy, Love, Liberality, Good-Will

Alike in Respect of Moistness

Among Gabirol's religious poems there is one which interests us particularly because it bears traces of the philosophy of the " Fons Vitæ." It is the most important of his hymns and is found in the prayer-book of the Sephardic ritual for the Day of Atonement. "The Royal Crown," as the poem is entitled, is an appeal to God for mercy and forgiveness, and is based upon the contrast between the greatness of God and the insignificance of man. The first part is therefore devoted to a poetical description of God's attributes and the wonders of the cosmic system, as conceived in the astronomical science of the day. A few quotations will give us an idea of the style and character of the hymn and its relation to the "Fons Vitæ."

"Thine are the mysteries, which neither fancy nor imagination can comprehend; and the life, over which dissolution hath no power. Thine is the *Throne* exalted above all height; and the habitation concealed in the eminence of its recess. Thine is the existence, from the shadow of whose light sprung every existing thing; of which we said, under its protecting shadow shall we live. . . .

"Thou art One, the first of every number, and the foundation of all structure. Thou art One, and in the mystery of the Unity all the wise in heart are astonished; for they cannot define it. Thou art One, and thy Unity can neither be lessened nor augmented; for nothing is there wanting or superfluous. Thou art One, but not such a one as is estimated or numbered; for neither plurality, nor change, form, nor physical attribute, nor name expressive of thy quality, can reach thee. . . ."

In the same way he treats God's other attributes, existent, living, great, mighty. Then he continues:

"Thou art light, and the eyes of every pure soul shall see thee; for the clouds of iniquity alone hide thee from her sight. . . . Thou art most high, and the eye of the intellect desireth and longeth for thee; but it can only see a part, it cannot see the whole of thy greatness. . . .

"Thou art God, who by thy Divinity supportest all things formed; and upholdest all creatures by thy Unity. Thou art God, and there is no distinction between thy godhead, unity, eternity or existence; for all is one mystery; and although each of these attributes is variously named, yet the whole point to one end.

"Thou art wise, and wisdom, which is the *fountain of life*, floweth from thee; and compared with thy wisdom, the knowledge of all mankind is folly. Thou art wise; and didst exist prior to all the most ancient things; and wisdom was reared by thee. Thou art wise; and hast not learned aught from another, nor acquired thy wisdom from anyone else. Thou art wise; and from thy wisdom thou didst cause to emanate a ready *will*, an agent and artist as it were, to draw existence out of non-existence, as light proceeds from the eye. Thou drawest from the source of light without a vessel, and producest everything without a tool."

Then follows a description of the constitution of the sublunar world, the terrestrial sphere consisting of part earth, part water, and being surrounded by the successive spheres of air and fire. Then follow in order the spheres of the Moon, Mercury, Venus, Sun, Mars, Jupiter, Saturn, the spheres of the fixed stars, and the outermost sphere embracing all and giving to the entire heaven the diurnal motion from east to west. He then continues:

"Who can understand thy tremendous mysteries, when thou didst exalt above the ninth orb, the sphere of the *Intelligence;* that is the inner temple; for the tenth shall be holy to the Lord. This is the sphere which is exalted above all the highest, and which no imagination can reach; and there is the hiding-place, wherein is the canopy for thy glory. . . .

"O Lord! who can come near thy understanding, when thou didst place on high above the sphere of the Intelligence the *Throne of thy glory*, where is the glorious dwelling of the hiding-place; there also is the mystery and the *foundation* (matter); so far the intellect may reach and no further; for above this art thou greatly exalted upon thy mighty throne, where no man may come up to thee. . . .

"Who can comprehend thy power, when thou didst create from the splendor of thy glory a pure lustre? From the rock of rocks was it hewn, and dug from the hollow of the cave. Thou also didst bestow on it the spirit of wisdom, and didst call it soul. Thou didst form it hewn from the flames of intellectual fire, so that its spirit burneth as fire within it. Thou didst send it forth to the body to serve and guard it; it is as fire in the midst of it, and yet doth not consume it; for *from the fire of the soul the body was created*, and called into existence from nothing, because the Lord descended thereto in fire."

Here we see the Intelligence spoken of as standing above the heavenly spheres. This clearly represents the cosmic Intelligence as a creation of God, "which is exalted above all the highest," hence the first product of God's light. And yet the *Throne of Glory* is said to be placed even above the sphere of the Intelligence. He speaks of it as the mystery and the foundation (Yesod), beyond which the intellect cannot reach. This is apparently a contradiction, but becomes clear when we learn what is meant by the Throne of Glory, and by "founda-tion." In the "Fons Vitæ" Gabirol tells us that matter receives form from the First Essence through the medium of the Will, which latter therefore, as it bestows form upon matter, sits in it and rests upon it. And hence, he says, matter is as it were the stool (cathedra) of the One. The word "yesod" (foundation) which Gabirol applies in the "Keter Malkut" (Royal Crown) to the Throne of Glory is the same that Falaquera uses for matter throughout in his epitome of the "Mekor Hayim." Hence it is clear that the Throne of Glory which is above the Intelligence is nothing else than Gabirol's matter. And we know from the "Fons Vitæ" that matter is really prior to Intelli-gence as it exists in the knowledge of God, but that in reality it never was, as a creation, without form; and that with form it constitutes the Intelligence. Finally there is also a reference in the poem to the will as emanating from God's wisdom, and like an "agent and artist draw-ing existence out of non-existence as light proceeds from the eye." The process of creation is thus compared with the radiation of light in the sentence just quoted, and likewise in the following: "Thou drawest from the source of light without a vessel, and producest everything without a tool."

We do not know whether Gabirol wrote any commentaries on the Bible—none are extant, nor are there any references to such works—but from his exegetical attempts in his ethical work discussed above (p. 71 ff.) and from citations by Abraham ibn Ezra of Gabirol's ex-planations of certain passages in Scripture, we gather that like Philo of Alexandria before him and Maimonides and a host of philosophical commentators after him, he used the allegorical method to reconcile his philosophical views with the Bible, and read the former into the latter.[105]

Thus we are told that Eden represents the presence of God, the garden planted in Eden stands for the angelic beings or, according to another interpretation, for the world of sense. By the river which flows out of Eden is meant prime matter which issues from the essence of God according to the "Fons Vitæ." The four divisions of the river are the four elements; Adam is the rational soul, Eve, as the Hebrew name indicates, the animal soul, and the serpent is the vege-tative or appetitive soul. The serpent entices Adam to eat of the forbidden tree. This means that when the lower soul succeeds in controlling the reason, the result is evil and sin, and man is driven out of the Garden, *i. e.*, is excluded from his angelic purity and becomes a corporeal being.

It is clear from all this that Gabirol's omission of all reference to Jewish dogma in the " Fons Vitæ" was purely methodological. Philosophy, and religion or theology should be kept apart in a purely philosophical work. Apologetics or harmonization has its rights, but it is a different department of study, and should be treated by itself, or in connection with exegesis of the Bible.

While it is true that Gabirol's influence on subsequent Jewish philosophy is slight—at most we find it in Moses and Abraham ibn Ezra, Abraham ibn Daud and Joseph ibn Zaddik—traces of his ideas are met with in the mysticism of the Kabbala. Gabirol's " Fons Vitæ" is a peculiar combination of logical formalism with mystic obscurity, or profundity, according to one's point of view. The latter did not appeal to pure rationalists like Ibn Daud or Maimonides, and the former seemed unconvincing, as it was employed in a lost cause. For Neo-Platonism was giving way to Aristotelianism, which was adopted by Maimonides and made the authoritative and standard philosophy. It was different with the Kabbala. Those who were responsible for its spread in the thirteenth century must have been attracted by the seemingly esoteric character of a philosophy which sees the invisible in the visible, the spiritual in the corporeal, and the reflection of the unknowable God in everything. There are certain details also which are common to both, such as the analogies of irradiation of light or flowing of water used to represent the process of creation, the position of the Will, the existence of matter in spiritual beings, and so on, though some of these ideas are common to all Neo-Platonic systems, and the Kabbala may have had access to the same sources as Gabirol.

CHAPTER VI

BAHYA IBN PAKUDA

All that is known of the life of Bahya ben Joseph ibn Pakuda is that he lived in Spain and had the office of "Dayyan," or judge of the Jewish community. Not even the exact time in which he lived is yet determined, though the most reliable recent investigations make it probable that he lived after Gabirol and was indebted to the latter for some of his views in philosophy as well as in Ethics.[106] So far as traditional data are concerned we have equally reliable, or rather equally unreliable statements for regarding Bahya as an older contemporary of Gabirol (eleventh century), or of Abraham ibn Ezra (1088–1167). Neither of these two data being vouched for by any but their respective authors, who lived a long time after Bahya, we are left to such indirect evidence as may be gathered from the content of Bahya's ethical work, the "Duties of the Hearts." And here the recent investigations of Yahuda, the latest authority on this subject and the editor of the Arabic text of Bahya's masterpiece (1912), force upon us the conclusion that Bahya wrote after Gabirol. Yahuda has shown that many passages in the "Duties of the Hearts" are practically identical in content and expression with similar ideas found in a work of the Arab philosopher Gazali (1059–1111). This leaves very little doubt that Bahya borrowed from Gazali and hence could not have written before the twelfth century.

To be sure, there are arguments on the other side, which would give chronological priority to Bahya over Gabirol,[107] but without going into the details of this minute and difficult discussion, it may be said generally that many of the similarities in thought and expression between the two ethical works of Gabirol and Bahya rather point in favor of the view here adopted, namely, that Bahya borrowed from Gabirol, while the rest prove nothing for either side. In so far as a reader of the "Duties of the Hearts" recognizes here and there an idea met with in Gabirol's "Fons Vitæ," there can scarcely be any doubt that the latter is the more original of the two. Gabirol did not borrow his philosophy or any part thereof from Bahya. Despite its Neo-Platonic character the "Fons Vitæ" of Gabirol is the most independent and original of Jewish mediæval productions. The "Duties of the Hearts" owes what originality it has to its ethics, which is the chief aim of the work, and not at all to the introductory philosophical chapter. As we shall see later, the entire chapter on the existence and unity of God, which introduces the ethical teachings of Bahya, moves in the familiar lines of Saadia, Al Mukammas, Joseph al Basir and the other Jewish Mutakallimun. There is besides a touch of Neo-Platonism in Bahya, which may be due to Gabirol as well as to Arabic sources. That Bahya did not borrow more from the "Fons Vitæ" than he did is due no doubt to the difference in temperament between the two men. Bahya is not a mystic. Filled as he is with the spirit of piety and warmth of heart—an attitude reflected in his style, which helped to make his work the most popular moral-religious book in Jewish literature—there is no trace of pantheism or metaphysical mysticism in his nature. His ideas are sane and rational, and their expression clear and transparent. Gabirol's high flights in the "Fons Vitæ" have little in common with Bahya's modest and brief outline of the familiar doctrines of the existence, unity and attributes of God, for which he claims no originality, and which serve merely as the background for his contribution to religious ethics. That Bahya should have taken a few leading notions from the "Fons Vitæ," such as did not antagonize his temperament and mode of thinking, is quite possible, and we shall best explain such resemblances in this manner.

As Abraham ibn Ezra in 1156 makes mention of Bahya and his views,[108] we are safe in concluding that the "Duties of the Hearts" was written between 1100 and 1156.

As the title of the work indicates, Bahya saw the great significance of a distinction made by Mohammedan theologians and familiar in their ascetic literature, between outward ceremonial or observance, known as "visible wisdom" and "duties of the limbs," and inward intention, attitude and feeling, called "hidden wisdom" and "duties of the hearts." [109] The prophet Isaiah complains that the people are diligent in bringing sacrifices, celebrating the festivals and offering prayer while their hands are full of blood. He informs them that such conduct is an abomination to the Lord, and admonishes them to wash themselves, to make themselves clean, to put away the evil of their deeds from before God's eyes; to cease to do evil; to learn to do well, to seek for justice, to relieve the oppressed, to do justice to the fatherless, to plead for the widow (Isa. 1, 11–17). This is a distinction between duties to God and duties to one's fellow man, between religious ceremony and ethical practice. Saadia makes a further distinction—also found in Arabic theology before him—between those commandments and prohibitions in the Bible which the reason itself approves as right or condemns as wrong—the rational commandments—and those which to the reason seem indifferent, and which revelation alone characterizes as obligatory, permitted or forbidden—the so-called " traditional commandments."

Bahya's division is identical with neither the one nor the other. Ethical practice may be purely external and a matter of the limbs, quite as much as sacrifice and ceremonial ritual. On the other hand, one may feel profoundly moved with the spirit of true piety, love of God and loyalty to his commandments in the performance of a so-called "traditional commandment," like the fastening of a "mezuzah" to the door-post. Bahya finds room for Saadia's classification but it is with him of subordinate importance, and is applicable only to the "duties of the limbs." Among these alone are there some which the reason unaided by revelation would not have prescribed. The "duties of the heart" are all rational. Like all precepts they are both positive and negative. Examples of positive duties of the heart are, belief in a creator who made the world out of nothing; belief in his unity and incomparability; the duty to serve him with all our heart, to trust in him, to submit to him, to fear him, to feel that he is watching our open and secret actions, to long for his favor and direct our actions for his name's sake; to love those who love him so as to be near unto him, and to hate those who hate him. Negative precepts of this class are the opposites of those mentioned, and others besides, such as that we should not covet, or bear a grudge, or think of forbidden things, or desire them or consent to do them. The common characteristic of all duties of the heart is that they are not visible to others. God alone can judge whether a person's feeling and motives are pure or the reverse.

That these duties are incumbent upon us is clear from every point of view. Like Saadia Bahya finds the sources of knowledge, particularly of the knowledge of God's law and religion, in sense, reason, written law and tradition. Leaving out the senses which are not competent in this particular case, the obligatory character of the duties of the heart is vouched for by the other three, reason, law, tradition.

From reason we know that man is composed of soul and body, and that both are due to God's goodness. One is visible, the other is not. Hence we are obliged to worship God in a two-fold manner; with visible worship and invisible. Visible worship represents the duties of the limbs, such as prayer, fasting, charity, and so on, which are carried out by the visible organs. The hidden worship includes the duties of the heart, for example, to think of God's unity, to believe in him and his Law, to accept his worship, etc., all of which are accomplished by the thought of the mind, without the assistance of the visible limbs.

Besides, the duties of the limbs, the obligation of which no one doubts, are incomplete without the will of the heart to do them. Hence it follows that there is a duty upon our souls to worship God to the extent of our powers.

The Bible is just as emphatic in teaching these duties as the reason. The love of God and the fear of God are constantly inculcated; and in the sphere of negative precepts we have such prohibitions as, "Thou shalt not covet" (Exod. 20, 17); "Thou shalt not take vengeance, nor bear any grudge" (Lev. 19, 18); "Thou shalt not hate thy brother in thy heart" (ib. 17); "You shalt not go astray after your own heart" (Num. 15, 39); "Thou shalt not harden thy heart nor shut thy hand from thy needy brother" (Deut. 15, 7), and many others.

Rabbinical literature is just as full of such precepts as the Bible, and is if possible even more emphatic in their inculcation. Witness such sayings as the following: "Heaven regards the intention" (Sanh. 106b): "The heart and the eye are two procurers of sin" (Jer. Berak. 1), and many others, particularly in the treatise Abot.

The great importance of these duties is also made manifest by the fact that the punishment in the Bible for unintentional misdeeds is more lenient than for intentional, proving that for punishment the mind must share with the body in the performance of the deed. The same is true of reward, that none is received for performing a good deed if it is not done "in the name of heaven."

They are even more important than the duties of the limbs, for unlike the latter the obligation of the duties of the heart is always in force, and is independent of periods or circumstances. Their number, too, is infinite, and not limited, as are the duties of the limbs, to six hundred and thirteen.

And yet, Bahya complains, despite the great importance of these duties, very few are the men who observed them even in the generations preceding ours, not to speak of our own days when even the external ceremonies are neglected, much more so the class of precepts under discussion. The majority of students of the Torah are actuated by desire for fame and honor, and devote their time to the intricacies of legalistic discussion in Rabbinic literature, and matters unessential, which are of no account in the improvement of the soul; but they neglect such important subjects of study as the unity of God, which we ought to understand and distinguish from other unities, and not merely receive parrot fashion from tradition. We are expressly commanded (Deut. 4, 39), "Know therefore this day, and reflect in thy heart, that the Eternal is the God in the heavens above, and upon the earth beneath: there is none else." Only he is exempt from studying these matters whose powers are not adequate to grasp them, such as women, children and simpletons.

Moreover Bahya is the first, he tells us, among the post-Talmudical writers, to treat systematically and *ex professo* this branch of our religious duties. When I looked, he says, into the works composed by the early writers after the Talmud on the commandments, I found that their writings can be classified under three heads. First, exposition of the Torah and the Prophets, like the grammatical and lexicographical treatises of Ibn Janah, or the exegetical works of Saadia. Second, brief compilations of precepts, like the works of Hefez ben Yazliah and the responsa of some geonim. Third, works of a philosophico-apologetic character, like those of Saadia, Al Mukammas and others, whose purpose it was to present in an acceptable manner the doctrines of the Torah, to prove them by logical demonstration, and to refute the criticisms and erroneous views of unbelievers. But I have not seen any book dealing with the "hidden wisdom." [110]

Here we see clearly the purpose of Bahya. It is not the rationalization of Jewish dogma that he is interested in, nor the reconciliation of religion and philosophy. It is the purification of religion itself from within which he seeks to accomplish. Sincerity and consistency in our words and our thoughts, so far as the service of God is concerned, is the fundamental requirement and essential value of the duties of the heart. To be sure this cannot be attained without intelligence. The knowledge of God and of his unity is a prerequisite for a proper understanding and an adequate appreciation of our religious duties. Philosophy therefore becomes a necessity in the interest of a purer and truer religion, without reference to the dangers threatening it from without.

Having found, he continues in the introduction to the "Duties of the Hearts," that all the three sources, reason, Bible and tradition, command this branch of our religious duties, I tried to think about them and to learn them, being led from one topic to another until the subject became so large that I feared I could not contain it all in my memory. I then determined to write the subject down systematically in a book for my own benefit as well as for the benefit of others. But I hesitated about writing it on account of my limitations, the difficulty of the subject and my limited knowledge of Arabic, the language in which I intended writing it because the majority of our people are best familiar with it. But I thought better of it and realized that it was my duty to do what I could even if it was not perfect; that I must not yield to the argument springing from a love of ease and disinclination to effort; for if everyone were to abstain from doing a small good because he cannot do as much as he would like, nothing would ever be done at all.

Having decided to compose the work, he continues, I divided the subject into ten fundamental principles, and devoted a section of the book to each principle. I endeavored to write in a plain and easy style, omitting difficult expressions, technical terms and demonstrations in the manner of the dialecticians. I had to make an exception in the first section dealing with the existence and unity of God, where the subtlety of the subject required the employment of logical and mathematical proofs. For the rest I made use of comparisons or similes, adduced support from the Bible and tradition, and also quoted the sages of other nations.[111]

We have already seen in the introduction that Bahya was indebted for his ideas to the ascetic and Sufic literature of the Arabs, and Yahuda, who is the authority in this matter of Bahya's sources, has shown recently that among the quotations of the wise men of other nations in Bahya's work are such as are attributed by the Arabs to Jesus and the gospels, to Mohammed and his companions, to the early caliphs, in particular the caliph Ali, to Mohammedan ascetics and Sufis.[112]

In selecting the ten general and inclusive principles, Bahya lays down as the first and most fundamental the doctrine of the deity, or as it is called in the works of the Kalam, the Unity. As God is a true unity, being neither substance nor accident, and our thought cannot grasp anything except substance or accident, it follows that we cannot know God as he is in himself, and that we can get a conception of him and of his existence from his creatures only. The second section is therefore devoted to an examination of creation. Then follow in order sections treating of the service of God, trust in God, action for the sake of God alone, submission to God, repentance, self-examination, separation from the pleasures of the world, love of God.

In his discussion of the unity of God, Bahya follows the same method as Saadia, and the Kalam generally, *i. e.*, he first proves that the world must have been created; hence there must be a creator, and this is followed by a demonstration of God's unity. The particular arguments, too, are for the most part the same, as we shall see, though differently expressed and in a different order. The important addition in Bahya is his distinction between God's unity and other unities, which is not found so strictly formulated in any of his predecessors, and goes back to Pseudo-Pythagorean sources in Arabian literature of Neo-Platonic origin.

In order to prove that there is a creator who created the world out of nothing we assume three principles. First, nothing can make itself. Second, principles are finite in number, hence there must be a first before which there is no other. Third, every composite is "new," *i. e.*, came to be in time, and did not exist from eternity.

Making use of these principles, which will be proved later, we proceed as follows: The world is composite in all its parts. Sky, earth, stars and man form a sort of house which the latter manages. Plants and animals are composed of the four elements, fire, air, water, earth. The elements again are composed of matter and form, or substance and accident. Their matter is the primitive "hyle," and their form is the primitive form, which is the root of all forms, essential as well as accidental. It is clear therefore that the world is composite, and hence, according to the third principle, had its origin in time. As, according to the first principle, a thing cannot make itself, it must have been made by some one. But as, in accordance with the second principle, the number of causes cannot be infinite, we must finally reach a first cause of the world before which there is no other, and this first made the world out of nothing.

Before criticising this proof, from which Bahya infers more than is legitimate, we must prove the three original assumptions.

The proof of the first principle that a thing cannot make itself is identical in Bahya with the second of the three demonstrations employed by Saadia for the same purpose. It is that the thing must either have made itself before it existed or after it existed. But both are impossible. Before it existed it was not there to make itself; after it existed there was no longer anything to make. Hence the first proposition is proved that a thing cannot make itself.

The proof of the second proposition that the number of causes cannot be infinite is also based upon the same principle as the fourth proof in Saadia for the creation of the world. The principle is this. Whatever has no limit in the direction of the past, *i. e.*, had no beginning, but is eternal *a parte ante*, cannot have any stopping point anywhere else. In other words, we as the spectators could not point to any definite spot or link in this eternally infinite chain, because the chain must have traversed infinite time to reach us, but the infinite can never be traversed. Since, however, as a matter of fact we can and do direct our attention to parts of the changing world, this shows that the world must have had a beginning.

A second proof of the same principle is not found in Saadia. It is as follows: If we imagine an actual infinite and take away a part, the remainder is less than before. Now if this remainder is still infinite, we have one infinite larger than another, which is impossible. If we say the remainder is finite, then by adding to it the finite part which was taken away, the result must be finite; but this is contrary to hypothesis, for we assumed it infinite at the start. Hence it follows that the infinite cannot have a part. But we can separate in thought out of all the generations of men from the beginning those that lived between the time of Noah and that of Moses. This will be a finite number and a part of all the men in the world. Hence, as the infinite can have no part, this shows that the whole number of men is finite, and hence that the world had a beginning.

This proof is not in Saadia, but we learn from Maimonides ("Guide of the Perplexed," I, ch. 75) that it was one of the proofs used by the Mutakallimun to prove the absurdity of the belief in the eternity of the world.

The third principle is that the composite is "new." This is proved simply by pointing out that the elements forming the composite are prior to it by nature, and hence the latter cannot be eternal, for nothing is prior to the eternal. This principle also is found in Saadia as the second of the four proofs in favor of creation.[113]

We have now justified our assumptions and hence have proved— what? Clearly we have only proved that this *composite* world cannot have existed *as such* from eternity; but that it must have been composed of its elements at some point in time past, and that hence there must be a cause or agency which did the composing. But there is nothing in the principles or in the demonstration based upon them which gives us a right to go back of the composite world and say of the elements, the simple elements at the basis of all composition, viz., matter and form, that they too must have come to be in time, and hence were created out of nothing. It is only the composite that argues an act of composition and elements preceding in time and by nature the object composed of them. The simple needs not to be made, hence the question of its having made itself does not arise. It was not made at all, we may say, it just existed from eternity.

The only way to solve this difficulty from Bahya's premises is by saying that if we suppose matter (or matter and form as separate entities) to have existed from eternity, we are liable to the difficulty involved in the idea of anything having traversed infinite time and reached us; though it is doubtful whether unformed matter would lend itself to the experiment of abstracting a part as in generations of men.

Be this as it may, it is interesting to know that Saadia having arrived as far as Bahya in his argument was not yet satisfied that he proved creation *ex nihilo*, and added special arguments for this purpose.

Before proceeding to prove the unity of God, Bahya takes occasion to dismiss briefly a notion which scarcely deserves consideration in his eyes. That the world could have come by accident, he says, is too absurd to speak of, in view of the evidence of harmony and plan and wisdom which we see in nature. As well imagine ink spilled by accident forming itself into a written book.[114] Saadia also discusses this view as the ninth of the twelve theories of creation treated by him, and refutes it more elaborately than Bahya, whose one argument is the last of Saadia's eight.

In the treatment of creation Saadia is decidedly richer and more comprehensive in discussion, review and argumentation. This was to be expected since such problems are the prime purpose of the "Emunot ve-Deot," whereas they are only preparatory, though none the less fundamental, in the "Hobot ha-Lebabot," and Bahya must have felt that the subject had been adequately treated by his distinguished predecessor. It is the more surprising therefore to find that in the treatment of the unity of God Bahya is more elaborate, and offers a greater variety of arguments for unity as such. Moreover, as has already been said before, he takes greater care than anyone before him to guard against the identification of God's unity with any of the unities, theoretical or actual, in our experience. There is no doubt that this emphasis is due to Neo-Platonic influence, some of which may have come to Bahya from Gabirol, the rest probably from their common sources.

We see, Bahya begins his discussion of the unity of God, that the causes are fewer than their effects, the causes of the causes still fewer, and so on, until when we reach the top there is only one. Thus, the number of individuals is infinite, the number of species is finite; the number of genera is less than the number of species, until we get to the highest genera, which according to Aristotle are ten (the ten categories). Again, the causes of the individuals under the categories are five, motion and the four elements. The causes of the elements are two, matter and form. The cause of these must therefore be one, the will of God. (The will of God as immediately preceding universal matter and form sounds like a reminiscence of the "Fons Vitæ".)

God's unity is moreover seen in the unity of plan and wisdom that is evident in the world. Everything is related to, connected with and dependent upon everything else, showing that there is a unitary principle at the basis.

If anyone maintains that there is more than one God, the burden of proof lies upon him. Our observation of the world has shown us that there is a God who made it; hence one, since we cannot conceive of less than one; but why more than one, unless there are special reasons to prove it?

Euclid defines unity as that in virtue of which we call a thing one. This means to signify that unity precedes the unitary thing by nature, just as heat precedes the hot object. Plurality is the sum of ones, hence plurality cannot be prior to unity, from which it proceeds. Hence whatever plurality we find in our minds we know that unity precedes it; and even if it occurs to anyone that there is more than one creator, unity must after all precede them all. Hence God is one.

This argument is strictly Neo-Platonic and is based upon the idealism of Plato, the notion that whatever reality or attributes particular things in our world of sense possess they owe to the real and eternal types of these realities and attributes in a higher and intelligible (using the term in contradistinction to sensible) world in which they participate. In so far as this conception is applied to the essences of things, it leads to the hypostatization of the class concepts or universals. Not the particular individual whom we perceive is the real man, but the typical man, the ideal man as the mind conceives him. He is not a concept but a real existent in the intelligible world. If we apply it also to qualities of things, we hypostatize the abstract quality. Heat becomes really distinct from the hot object, existence from the existent thing, goodness from the good person, unity from the one object. And a thing is existent and one and good, because it participates in Existence, Unity and Goodness. These are real entities, intelligible and not sensible, and they give to our world what reality it possesses.

Plotinus improved upon Plato, and instead of leaving these Ideas as distinct and ultimate entities, he adopted the suggestion of Philo and gathered up all these intelligible existences in the lap of the universal Reason, as his ideas or thoughts. This universal Reason is in Philo the *Logos*, whose mode of existence is still ambiguous, and is rather to be understood as the divine mind. In Plotinus it is the first stage in the unfoldment of the Godhead, and is a distinct *hypostasis*, though not a person. In Christianity it is the second person in the Trinity, incarnated in Jesus. In Israeli, Gabirol and the other Jewish Neo-Platonists, it occupies the same place as the *Nous* in Plotinus. In Bahya, whose taint of Neo-Platonism is not even skin deep, there is no universal Reason spoken of. But we do not really know what his ideas may have been on the subject, as he does not develop them in this direction.

To return to Bahya's arguments in favor of the unity of God, we proceed to show that dualism would lead to absurd conclusions. Thus if there is more than one creator, they are either of the same substance or they are not. If they are, then the common substance is the real creator, and we have unity once more. If their substances are different, they are distinct, hence limited, finite, composite, and hence not eternal, which is absurd.

Besides, plurality is an attribute of substance, and belongs to the category of quantity. But the creator is neither substance nor accident (attribute), hence plurality cannot pertain to him. But if he cannot be described as multiple, he must be one.

If the creator is more than one, it follows that either each one of them could create the world alone, or he could not except with the help of the other. If we adopt the first alternative, there is no need of more than one creator. If we adopt the second, it follows that the creator is limited in his power, hence, as above, composite, and not eternal, which is impossible. Besides, if there were more than one creator, it is possible that a dispute might arise between them in reference to the creation. But all this time no such thing has happened, nature being always the same. Hence God is one. Aristotle also agrees with us, for he applies in this connection the Homeric expression, "It is not good to have many rulers, let the ruler be one" (Iliad, II, 204; Arist., Metaphysics, XII, ch. 10, p. 1076a 4).[115]

So far as Bahya proves the unity of God he does not go beyond Saadia, some of whose arguments are reproduced by him, and one or two of a Neo-Platonic character added besides. But there is a decided advance in the analysis which follows, in which Bahya shows that there are various kinds of unity in our experience, and that the unity of God is unique.

We apply the term one to a class, a genus, a species, or an individual. In all of these the multiplicity of parts is visible. The genus animal contains many animals; the species man embraces a great many individual men; and the individual man consists of many parts and organs and faculties. Things of this sort are one in a sense and many in a sense.

We also apply the term one to an object in which the multiplicity of parts is not as readily visible as in the previous case. Take for example a body of water which is homogeneous throughout and one part is like another. This too is in reality composed of parts, matter and form, substance and accident. It is in virtue of this composition that it is subject to genesis and decay, composition and division, union and separation, motion and change. But all this implies plurality. Hence in both the above cases the unity is not essential but accidental. It is because of a certain appearance or similarity that we call a thing or a class one, which is in reality many.

Another application of the term one is when we designate by it the basis of number, the numerical one. This is a true one, essential as distinguished from the accidental referred to above. But it is mental and not actual. It is a symbol of a beginning which has no other before it.

Finally there is the real and actual one. This is something that does not change or multiply; that cannot be described by any material attribute, that is not subject to generation and decay; that does not move and is not similar to anything. It is one in all respects and the cause of multiplicity. It has no beginning or end, for that which has is subject to change, and change is opposed to unity, the thing being different before and after the change. For the same reason the real one does not resemble anything, for resemblance is an accident in the resembling thing, and to be possessed of accidents is to be multiple. Hence the true one resembles nothing. Its oneness is no accident in it, for it is a purely negative term in this application. It means not multiple.[116]

We have now shown that there is a creator who is one, and on the other hand we have analyzed the various meanings of the term one, the last of which is the most real and the purest. It remains now to show that this pure one is identical with the one creator. This can be proved in the following way. The world being everywhere composite contains the one as well as the many—unity of composition, plurality of the parts composed. As unity is prior by nature to plurality, and causes do not run on to infinity (see above, p. 87), the causes of the world's unity and multiplicity cannot be again unity and multiplicity of the same kind forever. Hence as multiplicity cannot be the first, it must be unity—the absolute and true unity before which there is no other, and in which there is no manner of multiplicity. But God is the one cause of the universe, as we have shown, hence God and this true unity are the same.

We can show this also in another way. Whatever is an accidental attribute in one thing is an essential element in some other thing. Thus heat is an accidental attribute in hot water. For water may lose its heat and remain water as before. It is different with fire. Fire cannot lose its heat without ceasing to be fire. Hence heat in fire is an essential element; and it is from fire that hot water and all other hot things receive their heat. The same thing applies to the attribute of unity. It is accidental in all creatures. They are called one because they combine a number of elements in one group or concept. But they are really multiple since they are liable to change and division and motion, and so on. Hence there must be something in which unity is essential, and which is the cause of whatsoever unity all other things possess. But God is the cause of the universe, hence he is this true and absolute unity, and all change and accident and multiplicity are foreign to him.[117]

This unity of God is not in any way derogated from by the ascription to him of attributes. For the latter are of two kinds, "essential" and "active." We call the first essential because they are permanent attributes of God, which he had before creation and will continue to have when the world has ceased to be. These attributes are three in number, Existing, One, Eternal. We have already proved every one of them.

Now these attributes do not imply change in the essence of God. They are to be understood in the sense of denying their opposites, *i. e.*, that he is not multiple, non-existent or newly come into being. They also imply each other as can easily be shown, *i. e.*, every one of the three implies the other two. We must understand therefore that they are really *one* in idea, and if we could find one term to express the thought fully, we should not use three. But the three do not imply multiplicity in God.

The "active" are those attributes which are ascribed to God by reason of his actions or effects on us. We are permitted to apply them to him because of the necessity which compels us to get to know of his existence so that we may worship him. The Biblical writers use them very frequently. We may divide these into two kinds: First, those which ascribe to God a corporeal form, such as (Gen. 1, 27), "And God created man in his image," and others of the same character. Second, those attributes which refer to corporeal movements and actions. These have been so interpreted by our ancient sages as to remove the corporeality from God by substituting the "Glory of God" for God as the subject of the movement or act in question. Thus, (Gen. 28, 13) "And behold the Lord stood above it," is rendered by the Aramaic translator, "and behold the *glory of God was present* above it." Saadia deals with this matter at length in his " Emunot ve-Deot," in his commentary on Genesis, and on the book "Yezirah." So there is no need of going into detail here. We are all agreed that necessity compels us to speak of God in corporeal terms so that all may be made to know of God's existence. This they could not do if the prophets had spoken in metaphysical terms, for not everyone can follow such profound matters. But having come to the knowledge of God in this simpler though imperfect way, we can then advance to a more perfect knowledge of him. The intelligent and philosophical reader will lose nothing by the anthropomorphic form of the Bible, for he can remove the husk and penetrate to the kernel. But the simple reader would miss a very great deal indeed if the Bible were written in the language of philosophy, as he would not understand it and would remain without a knowledge of God.

Despite its predominant anthropomorphism, however, the Bible does give us hints of God's spirituality so that the thoughtful reader may also have food for *his* thought. For example, such expressions as (Deut. 4, 15), "Take ye therefore good heed unto yourselves; for ye saw no manner of form on the day that the Lord spake unto you in Horeb out of the midst of the fire," and many others are meant to spur on the discriminating reader to further thought. The same applies to all those passages in which the word "name" is inserted before the word God as the object of praise to indicate that we do not know God in his essence. An example of this is, "And they shall bless the name of thy glory" (Neh. 9, 5). For the same reason the name of God is joined in the Bible to heaven, earth, the Patriarchs, in such phrases as the God of the heavens, the God of Abraham, and so on, to show that we do not know God's essence but only his revelation in nature and in history. This is the reason why after saying to Moses, "I am sent me unto you" (Ex. 3, 14), he adds (ib. 15), tell them, "the God of your fathers, the God of Abraham, the God of Isaac and the God of Jacob sent me unto you." The meaning is, if they cannot understand God with their reason, let them know me from history and tradition.[118]

In Bahya's treatment of the divine attributes we already have in brief the main elements which Maimonides almost a century later made classic, namely, the distinction between essential and active attributes, and the idea that the former are to be understood as denying their opposites, *i. e.*, as being in their nature not positive but negative. The outcome therefore is that only two kinds of attributes are applicable to God, negative and those which are transferred or projected from the effects of God's activity as they are visible in nature. Saadia had already made the distinction between essential and active attributes, but it was quite incidental with him, and not laid down at the basis of his discussion, but casually referred to in a different connection. Al Mukammas speaks of negative attributes as being more applicable to God than positive, as Philo had already said long before. But the combination of these two, negative and active, as the only kinds of divine attributes is not found in Jewish literature before Bahya.

It is worth noting also that Bahya does not lay down the three attributes, Power, Wisdom and Life as fundamental or essential in the manner of the Christians, the Arab Mutakallimun, and the Jewish Saadia. Bahya, as we have seen, regards as God's essential attributes, existence, unity, eternity. Herein, too, he seems to anticipate Maimonides who insists against the believers in essential attributes that the attributes, living, omnipotent, omniscient, having a will, are no more essential than any other, but like the rest of the qualities ascribed to God have reference to his activity in nature.[119]

We have now gone through Bahya's philosophical chapter giving us the metaphysical basis of his ethico-religious views. That his purpose is practical and not theoretical is clear from his definition of what he calls the "acknowledgment of the unity of God with full heart," not to speak of the title of the book itself, the meaning of which we explained at the beginning of this section, and the nine chapters in Bahya's work following upon the first, which constitute its real essence and purpose. To acknowledge the unity of God with full heart means, he tells us, that one must first know how to prove the existence and unity of God, to distinguish God's unity from every other, and then to make his heart and his tongue unite in this conception.[120] It is not a matter of the intellect merely, but of the heart as affecting one's practical conduct. The adequacy of the conception is destroyed not merely by thinking of God as multiple, or by worshiping images, sun, moon and stars; it is made null and void likewise by hypocrisy and pretence, as when one affects piety before others to gain their favor or acquire a reputation. The same disastrous result is brought about by indulging the low physical appetites. Here the worship of the appetites is brought into competition and rivalry with devotion to the one God.[121]

Our object being to trace the philosophical conceptions in mediæval Jewish literature, we cannot linger long in the study of the rest of Bahya's masterpiece, which is homiletical and practical rather than theoretic, and must content ourselves with a very brief résumé of its principal contents.

In studying the nature and attributes of God we reached the conclusion that while a knowledge of him is absolutely necessary for a proper mode of life, we cannot form an idea of him as he is in himself, and are left to such evidence as we can gather from the world of which he is the author. It becomes our duty, therefore, to study nature, as a whole and in its parts, conscientiously and minutely, in order to realize clearly the goodness and wisdom of God as exhibited therein. For various reasons we are apt to neglect this study and miss the insight and benefits arising therefrom. Chief among these hindering circumstances are our excessive occupations with the pleasures of this world, and the accidents and misfortunes to which mortal is heir, which blind him to his real good, and prevent him from seeing the blessing in disguise lurking in these very misfortunes.

But it is clear that man has a duty to study the divine goodness and wisdom as exhibited in nature, else of what use is his faculty of reason and intelligence, which raises him above the beast. If he neglects it, he places himself below the latter, which realizes all the functions of which it is capable. Bible and Talmud are equally emphatic in urging us to study the wonders of nature.

The variety of natural phenomena and the laws they exhibit give evidence of the personality of God and the existence of his will. A being without will, acting by necessity of nature, acts with unswerving uniformity.

Heaven and earth, plant and animal, all creatures great and small, bear witness, in their structure and relations, in their functions and mutual service and helpfulness, to the wisdom and goodness of God. Above all is this visible in man, the highest of earthly beings, the microcosm, the rational creature, the discoverer and inventor of arts and sciences. In the laws and statutes which were given to him for the service of God, and in the customs of other nations which take the place of our divine law, we see God's kindness to man in securing his comfort in this world and reward in the next.

Pride is the great enemy of man, because it prevents him from appreciating what he owes to God's goodness. Pride makes him feel that he deserves more than he gets, and blinds him to the truth.[122]

We all recognize the duty of gratitude to a fellow man who has done us a favor, although all such cases of benefit and service between man and man, not excepting even the kindness of a father to his child, will be found on examination to be of a selfish nature. The benefit to self may not in all cases be conscious, but it is always there. It is a father's nature to love his child as part of himself. Moreover, these human favors are not constant, and the person benefited stands comparatively on the same level of existence and worth as his benefactor. How much greater then is the duty incumbent upon us to appreciate God's favors which are not selfish, which are constant, and which are bestowed by the greatest of all beings upon the smallest of all in respect of physical strength.

The only way in which man can repay God for his kindness, and show an appreciation thereof is by submitting to him and doing those things which will bring him nearer to God. In order to realize this it is necessary to abandon the bad qualities, which are in principle two, love of pleasure and love of power. The means enabling one to obtain this freedom are to abstain from too much eating, drinking, idling, and so on, for the first, and from too much gossip, social intercourse, and love of glory for the second. It may be difficult to do this, but one must make up one's mind to it, like the invalid who is ready to lose a limb in order to save his life.

The problem of free will is perplexing indeed and interferes with the proper attitude toward God and his worship. The best way out of the difficulty is to act as if we were free, and on the other hand to have confidence in God as the author of everything.

We have seen that the reason bids us recognize our duty to God in return for his goodness to us. At the same time we are not left to the suggestions and promptings of the reason alone. We have a positive law prescribing our conduct and the manner and measure of expressing our gratitude to God. This is made necessary by the constitution of man's nature. He is a composite of body and spirit. The former is at home in this lower world and is endowed with powers and qualities which tend to strengthen it at the expense of the spirit, a stranger in this world. Hence the necessity of a positive law to cure the spirit from the ills of the body by forbidding certain kinds of food, clothing, sexual indulgence, and so on, which strengthen the appetites, and commanding such actions as prayer, fasting, charity, benevolence, which have the opposite tendency of strengthening the reason.

The positive law is necessary and useful besides because it prescribes the middle way, discouraging equally the extremes of asceticism and of self-indulgence. It regulates and defines conduct, and makes it uniform for old and young, intelligent and unintelligent. It institutes new occasions of worship and thanksgiving as history reveals new benefactions of God to his people in various generations. The law also contains matters which the reason alone would not dictate, and of which it does not understand the meaning. Such are the "traditional commandments." The reason why the law prescribes also some of the principles of the "rational commandments" is because at that time the people were so sunk in their animal desires that their minds were weakened, and there was need of putting both classes of commandments on the same level of positive prescription. But now the intelligent person observes them in accordance with their distinct origin, whereas the masses simply follow the law in both.

The admonition of the positive law serves as an introduction to the suggestions of our own reason and prepares the way for the latter. The first is absolutely necessary for the young, the women and those of weak intellectual power. To worship God not merely because the law prescribes it, but because reason itself demands it denotes a spiritual advance, and puts one in the grade of prophets and pious men chosen of God. In this world their reward is the joy they feel in the sweetness of divine service; in the next world they attain to the spiritual light which we cannot declare or imagine.[123]

One of the duties of the heart is to trust in God. Apart from the Bible which commands us to have trust in God, we can come to the same conclusion as a result of our own reflection. For in God alone are combined all the conditions necessary to confidence. He has the power to protect and help us, and the knowledge of our needs. He is kind and generous and has a love for us and an interest in our welfare, as we have shown in a previous discussion. Trust in God is of advantage religiously in giving a person peace of mind, independence and freedom to devote himself to the service of God without being worried by the cares of the world. He is like the alchemist who changes lead into silver, and silver into gold. If he has money he can make good use of it in fulfilling his duties to God and man. If he has not, he is grateful for the freedom from care which this gives him. He is secure against material worries. He does not have to go to distant lands to look for support, or to engage in hard and fatiguing labor, or to exploit other people. He chooses the work that is in consonance with his mode of life, and gives him leisure and strength to do his duty to God and man.

The suffering of the good and the prosperity of the bad, which apparently contradicts our conclusion, is a problem as old as the world, and is discussed in the Bible. There is no one explanation to cover all cases, hence no solution is given in the Bible. But several reasons may be brought forward for this anomaly. The righteous man may suffer by way of punishment for a sin he has committed. He may suffer in this world in order that he may be rewarded in the next. His suffering may be an example of patience and goodness to other people; especially in a bad generation, to show off their wickedness by contrast with his goodness. Or finally the good man may be punished for not rebuking his generation of evil doers. In a similar way we may explain the prosperity of the wicked.

Trust in God does not signify that one should neglect one's work, be careless of one's life, health and well-being, or abandon one's effort to provide for one's family and dependents. No, one must do all these things conscientiously, at the same time feeling that if not for the help of God all effort would be in vain. In the matter of doing one's duty and observing the commandments, whether of the limbs or the heart, trust in God can apply only to the last step in the process, namely, the realization in practice. He must trust that God will put out of the way all obstacles and hindrances which may prevent him from carrying out his resolutions. The choice and consent must come from a man's own will, which is free. The most he may do is to trust that God may remove temptations.

While it is true that good deeds are rewarded in this world as well as in the next, a man must not trust in his deeds, but in God. It may seem strange that there is no reference in the Bible to reward in the hereafter. The reasons may be the following. Not knowing what the state of the soul is without the body, we could not understand the nature of future reward, and the statement of it in the Bible would not have been a sufficient inducement for the people of that time to follow the commandments. Or it is possible that the people knew by tradition of reward after death, hence it was not necessary to specify it.

As knowledge of nature and of God leads to trust in him, so ignorance leads away from it. It is as with a child, who develops in his manner of trusting in things; beginning with his mother's breast and rising gradually as he grows older and knows more, until he embraces other persons and attains to trust in God.[124]

We said before (p. 83) that the duties of the limbs are imperfect unless accompanied by the intention of the heart. A man's motive must be sincere. It must not be his aim to gain the favor of his fellow-men or to acquire honor and fame. The observance of the prescribed laws must be motived by the sole regard for God and his service. This we call the "unity of conduct." The meaning is that a man's act and intention must coincide in aiming at the fulfilment of God's will. In order to realize this properly one must have an adequate and sincere conception of God's unity as shown above; he must have an appreciation of God's goodness as exhibited in nature; he must submit to God's service; he must have trust in God alone as the sole author of good and evil; and correspondingly he must abstain from flattering mankind, and must be indifferent to their praise and blame; he must fear God, and have respect and awe for him. When he is in the act of fulfilling his spiritual obligations, he must not be preoccupied with the affairs of this world; and finally he must always consult his reason, and make it control his desires and inclinations.[125]

Humility and lowliness is an important element conducive to "unity of conduct." By this is not meant that general helplessness in the face of conditions, dangers and injuries because of ignorance of the methods of averting them. This is not humility but weakness. Nor do we mean that timidity and loss of countenance which one suffers before a superior in physical power or wealth. The true humility with which we are here concerned is that which one feels constantly before God, though it shows itself also in such a person's conduct in the presence of others, in soft speech, low voice, and modest behavior generally, in prosperity as well as adversity. The truly humble man practices patience and forgiveness; he does good to mankind and judges them favorably; he is contented with little in respect to food and drink and the needs of the body generally; he endures misfortune with resignation; is not spoiled by praise, nor irritated by blame, but realizes how far he is from perfection in the one case, and appreciates the truth of the criticism in the other. He is not spoiled by prosperity and success, and always holds himself under strict account. God knows it, even if his fellowmen do not.

Humility, as we have described it, is not, however, incompatible with a certain kind of pride; not that form of it which boasts of physical excellence, nor that arrogance which leads a man to look down upon others and belittle their achievements. These forms of pride are bad and diametrically opposed to true humility. Legitimate mental pride is that which leads a person blessed with intellectual gifts to feel grateful to God for his favor, and to strive to improve his talents and share their benefits with others.[126]

Humility is a necessary forerunner of repentance and we must treat of this duty of the heart next. It is clear from reason as well as from the Law that man does not do all that is incumbent upon him in the service of God. For man is composed of opposite principles warring with each other, and is subject to change on account of the change of his mental qualities. For this reason he needs a law and traditional custom to keep him from going astray. The Bible also tells us that "the imagination of the heart of man is evil from his youth" (Gen. 8, 21). Therefore God was gracious and gave man the ability and opportunity to correct his mistakes. This is repentance.

True repentance means return to God's service after having succeeded in making the reason the master of the desires. The elements in repentance are, (1) regret; (2) discontinuance of the wrong act; (3) confession and request for pardon; (4) promise not to repeat the offence.

In respect to gravity of offence, sins may be divided into three classes: (1) Violation of a positive commandment in the Bible which is not punished by "cutting off from the community." For example, dwelling in booths, wearing fringes, and shaking the palm branch. (2) Violation of a negative commandment not so punished. (3) Violation of a negative commandment the penalty for which is death at the hands of the court, and being "cut off" by divine agency; for example, profanation of the divine name or false oath. In cases of the first class a penitent is as good as one who never sinned. In the second class he is even superior, because the latter has not the same prophylactic against pride. In the third class the penitent is inferior to the one who never sinned.

Another classification of offences is in two divisions according to the subject against whom the offence is committed. This may be a human being, and the crime is social; or it may be God, and we have sin in the proper sense of the term. Penitence is sufficient for forgiveness in the latter class, but not in the former. When one robs another or insults him, he must make restoration or secure the pardon of the offended party before his repentance can be accepted. And if the person cannot be found, or if he died, or is alive but refuses to forgive his offender, or if the sinner lost the money which he took, or if he does not know whom he robbed, or how much, it may be impossible for him to atone for the evil he has done. Still if he is really sincere in his repentance, God will help him to make reparation to the person wronged.[127]

Self-examination is conducive to repentance. By this term is meant taking stock of one's spiritual condition so as to know the merits one has as well the duties one owes. In order to do this conscientiously a man must reflect on the unity of God, on his wisdom and goodness, on the obedience which all nature pays to the laws imposed upon it, disregard of which would result in the annihilation of all things, including himself. A man should review his past conduct, and provide for his future life, as one provides for a long journey, bearing in mind that life is short, and that he is a stranger in this world with no one to help him except the goodness and grace of his maker. He should cultivate the habit of being alone and not seek the society of idlers, for that leads to gossip and slander, to sin and wrong, to vanity and neglect of God. This does not apply to the company of the pious and the learned, which should be sought. He should be honest and helpful to his friends, and he will get along well in this world. All the evils and complaints of life are due to the fact that people are not considerate of one another, and everyone grabs for himself all that he can, more than he needs. One should examine anew the ideas one has from childhood to be sure that he understands them in the light of his riper intellect. He should also study again the books of the Bible and the prayers which he learned as a child, for he would see them now in a different light. He must try to make his soul control his body, strengthening it with intellectual and spiritual food for the world to come. These efforts and reflections and many others of a similar kind tend to perfect the soul and prepare it to attain to the highest degree of purity, where the evil desire can have no power over her.[128]

In self-examination temperance or abstemiousness plays an important rôle. Let us examine this concept more closely. By abstemiousness in the special sense in which we use it here we do not mean that general temperance or moderation which we practice to keep our body in good order, or such as physicians prescribe for the healthy and the sick, bidding them abstain from certain articles of food, drink, and so on. We mean rather a more stringent abstemiousness, which may be called separation from the world, or asceticism. We may define this to mean abstention from all corporeal satisfactions except such as are indispensable for the maintenance of life.

Not everyone is required to practice this special form of temperance, nor is it desirable that he should, for it would lead to extinction of the human race. At the same time it is proper that there shall be a few select individuals, ascetic in their habits of life, and completely separated from the world, to serve as an example for the generality of mankind, in order that temperance of the more general kind shall be the habit of the many.

The object of God in creating man was to try the soul in order to purify it and make it like the angels. It is tried by being put in an earthy body, which grows and becomes larger by means of food. Hence God put into the soul the desire for food, and the desire for sexual union to perpetuate the species; and he made the reward for the satisfaction of these desires the pleasure which they give. He also appointed the "evil inclination" to incite to all these bodily pleasures. Now if this "evil inclination" gets the upper hand of the reason, the result is excess and ruin. Hence the need of general abstemiousness. And the ascetic class serve the purpose of reinforcing general temperance by their example.

But in the asceticism of the few there is also a limit beyond which one should not go. Here too the middle way is the best. Those extremists who leave the world entirely and live the life of a recluse in the desert, subsisting on grass and herbs, are farthest from the middle way, and the Bible does not approve of their mode of life, as we read in Isaiah (45, 18) "The God that formed the earth and made it; he that hath established it,—not in vain did he create it, he formed it to be inhabited." Those are much better who without leaving for the desert pass solitary lives in their homes, not associating with other people, and abstaining from superfluities of all kinds. But the best of all are those who adopt the mildest form of asceticism, who separate from the world inwardly while taking part in it outwardly, and assisting in the ordinary occupations of mankind. These are commended in the Bible. Witness the prayer of Jacob (Gen. 28, 20), the fasting of Moses forty days and forty nights on the mount, the fasting of Elijah, the laws of the Nazirite, Jonadab ben Rechab, Elisha, prescriptions of fasting on various occasions, and so on.[129]

The highest stage a man can reach spiritually is the love of God, and all that preceded has this as its aim. True love of God is that felt toward him for his own sake because of his greatness and exaltation, and not for any ulterior purpose.

The soul is a simple spiritual substance which inclines to that which is like it, and departs from what is material and corporeal. But when God put the soul into the body, he implanted in it the desire to maintain it, and it was thus affected by the feelings and desires which concern the health and growth of the body, thus becoming estranged from the spiritual.

In order that the soul shall attain to the true love of God, the reason must get the upper hand of the desires, all the topics treated in the preceding sections must be taken to heart and sincerely and conscientiously acted upon. Then the eyes of the soul will be opened, and it will be filled with the fear and the love of God.[130]

CHAPTER VII

PSEUDO-BAHYA

It had been known for a number of years that there was a manuscript treatise in Arabic on the soul, which was attributed on the title
page to Bahya. In 1896 Isaac Broydé published a Hebrew translation
of this work under the title "Torot ha-Nefesh," ("Reflections on the
Soul").[131] The original Arabic was edited by Goldziher in 1907.[132]
The Arabic title is "Ma'ani al-Nafs," and should be translated "Concepts of the soul," or "Attributes of the soul."

There seems little doubt now that despite the ascription on the
title page of the manuscript, the treatise is not a work of Bahya.
It is very unlikely that anything written by so distinguished an author as Bahya, whose "Duties of the Hearts" was the most popular
book in the middle ages, should have been so thoroughly forgotten
as to have left no trace in Jewish literature. Bahya as well as the
anonymous author refer, in the introductions to their respective works,
to their sources or to their own previous writings. But there is no
reference either in the "Duties of the Hearts" to the "Attributes of
the Soul," or in the latter to the former. A still stronger argument
against Bahya as the author of our treatise is that derived from the
content of the work, which moves in a different circle of ideas from
the "Duties of the Hearts." Our anonymous author is an outspoken
Neo-Platonist. He believes in the doctrine of emanation, and arranges
the created universe, spiritual and material, in a descending series of
such emanations, ten in number. The Mutakallimun he opposes as
being followers of the "Naturalists," who disagree with the philosophers as well as the Bible. Bahya, on the other hand, is a strict follower of the Kalam in his chapter on the "Unity," as we have seen
(p. 86), and the Neo-Platonic influence is very slight. There is no
trace of a graded series of emanations in the "Duties of the
Hearts."[133]

The sources of the "Attributes of the Soul" are no doubt the various

Neo-Platonic writings current among the Arabs in the tenth and eleventh centuries, of which we spoke in the Introduction (p. xx) and in the chapter on Gabirol (p. 63 f.). Gabirol himself can scarcely have had much influence on our author, as the distinctive doctrine of the "Fons Vitæ" is absent in our treatise. The reader will remember that matter and form, according to Gabirol, are at the basis not merely of the corporeal world, but that they constitute the essence of the spiritual world as well, the very first emanation, the Universal Intelligence, being composed of universal matter and universal form. As we shall see this is not the view of the "Attributes of the Soul." Matter here occupies the position which it has in Plotinus and in the encyclopædia of the Brethren of Purity. It is the fourth in order of emanations, and the composition of matter and form begins with the celestial sphere, which is the fifth in order. Everything that precedes matter is absolutely simple. At the same time it seems clear that he was familiar with Gabirol's doctrine of the will. For in at least two passages in the "Attributes of the Soul" (chs. 11 and 13) [134] we have the series, vegetative soul, spheral impression, [psychic power—omitted in ch. 13], universal soul, intellect, will.

The "Categories" of Aristotle is also clearly evident in the "Attributes of the Soul." It is the ultimate source of the definition of accident as that which resides in substance without being a part of it, but yet in such a way that without substance it cannot exist.[135] The number of the species of motion as six [136] points in the same direction. This, however, does not prove that the author read the "Categories." He might have derived these notions, as well as the list of the ten categories, from the writings of the Brethren of Purity. The same thing applies to the statement that a spiritual substance is distinguished from a corporeal in its capacity of receiving its qualities or accidents without limits.[137] This probably goes back to the De Anima of Aristotle where a similar contrast between the senses and the reason is used as an argument for the "separate" character of the latter. The doctrine of the mean in conduct [138] comes from the ethics of Aristotle. The doctrine of the four virtues and the manner of their derivation is Platonic,[139] and so is the doctrine of reminiscence, viz., that the soul recalls the knowledge it had in its previous life.[140]

Ibn Sina is one of the latest authors mentioned in our work; hence

it could not have been written much before 1037, the date of Ibn
Sina's death. The *terminus ad quem* cannot be determined.

As the title indicates, the anonymous treatise is concerned primarily
with the nature of the soul. Whatever other topics are found therein
are introduced for the bearing they have on the central problem. A
study of the soul means psychology as well as ethics, for a complete
determination of the nature of the soul necessarily must throw light
not only upon the origin and activity of the soul, but also upon its
purpose and destiny.

The first error, we are told, that we must remove concerning the soul,
is the doctrine of the "naturalists," with whom the Mu'tazilites
among the Arabs and the Karaites among the Jews are in agreement,
that the soul is not an independent and self-subsistent entity, but only
an "accident" of the body. Their view is that as the soul is a corporeal quality it is dependent for its existence upon the body and disappears with the latter. Those of the Mu'tazilites who believe in
"Mahad" (return of the soul to its origin), hold that at the time of
the resurrection God will bring the parts of the body together with its
accident, the soul, and will reward and punish them. But the resurrection is a distinct problem, and has nothing to do with the nature
of the soul and its qualities.

The true opinion, which is that of the Bible and the true philosophers, is that the soul is a spiritual substance independent of the
body; that it existed before the body and will continue to exist after
the dissolution of the latter. The existence of a spiritual substance
is proved from the presence of such qualities as knowledge and ignorance. These are opposed to each other, and cannot be the qualities of body as such, for body cannot contain two opposite forms at
the same time. Moreover, the substance, whatever it be, which bears
the attributes of knowledge and ignorance, can receive them without
limit. The more knowledge a person has, the more capable he is of
acquiring more. No corporeal substance behaves in this way. There
is always a limit to a body's power of receiving a given accident. We
legitimately conclude, therefore, that the substance which bears the
attributes of knowledge and ignorance is not corporeal but spiritual.[141]

To understand the position of the soul and its relation to the body,
we must have an idea of the structure and origin of the universe.

The entire world, upper as well as lower, is divided into two parts, simple and composite. The simple essences, which are pure and bright, are nearer to their Creator than the less simple substances which come after. There are ten such creations with varying simplicity, following each other in order according to the arrangement dictated by God's wisdom. As numbers are simple up to ten, and then they begin to be compound, so in the universe the ten simple substances are followed by composite.

The first of these simple creations, which is nearest to God, is called in Hebrew "Shekinah." The Torah and the Prophets call it "Name" (Exod. 23, 21), also "Kabod," Glory (Is. 59, 19). God gave his name to the nearest and first of his creations, which is the first light, and interpreter and servant nearest to him. Solomon calls it "Wisdom" (Prov. 8, 22); the Greeks, Active Intellect. The second creation is called by the Prophets, "the Glory of the God of Israel" (Ezek. 8, 9); by the Greeks, Universal Soul, for it moves the spheres through a natural power as the individual soul moves the body. The soul partakes of the Intelligence or Intellect on the side which is near to it; it partakes of Nature on the side adjoining the latter. Nature is the third creation. It also is an angel, being the first of the powers of the universal soul, and constituting the life of this world and its motion.

These three are simple essences in the highest sense of the word. They are obedient to their Creator, and transmit in order his emanation and the will, and the laws of his wisdom to all the worlds. The fourth creation is an essence which has no activity or life or motion originally, but only a power of receiving whatever is formed and created out of it. This is the *Matter* of the world. From it come the bodies which possess accidents. In being formed some of its non-existence is diminished, and its matter moves. It is called "hyle," and is the same as the darkness of the first chapter in Genesis. For it is a mistake to suppose that by darkness in the second verse of the first chapter is meant the absence of the light of the sun. This is accidental darkness, whereas in the creation story the word darkness signifies something elemental at the basis of corporeal things. This is what is known as matter, which on account of its darkness, *i. e.*, its imperfection and motionlessness, is the cause of all the blemishes and evils in the world. In receiving forms, however, it acquires motion; its darkness is somewhat diminished, and it appears to the eye through the forms which it receives.

The fifth creation is the celestial Sphere, where for the first time we have motion in its revolutions. Here too we have the first composition of matter and form; and the beginning of time as the measure of the Sphere's motion; and place. The sixth creation is represented by the bodies of the *stars*, which are moved by the spheres in which they are set. They are bright and luminous because they are near the first simple bodies, which were produced before time and place. The last four of the ten creations are the four elements, fire, air, water, earth. The element earth is the end of " creation." What follows thereafter is "formation" and "composition." By creation is meant that which results through the will of God from his emanation alone, and not out of anything, or in time or place. It applies in the strictest sense to the first three only. The fifth, namely the Sphere, already comes from matter and form, and is in time and place. The fourth, too, enters into the fifth and all subsequent creations and formations. Still, the term creation is applicable to the first ten, though in varying degrees, until when we reach the element earth, creation proper is at an end. This is why in the first verse in Genesis, which speaks of heaven and earth, the term used is " bara" (created), and not any of the other terms, such as "yazar," "'asah," "kanah," "pa'al," and so on, which denote formation.

From earth and the other elements were formed all kinds of minerals, like rocks, mountains, stones, and so on. Then plants and animals, and finally man.

Man who was formed last bears traces of all that preceded him. He is formed of the four elements, of the motions of the spheres, of the mixtures of the stars and their rays, of Nature, of the Universal Soul, the mother of all, of the Intellect, the father of all, and finally of the will of God. But the order in man is reversed. The first two creations, Intellect and Soul, appear in man last.

The soul of man, embracing reason and intellect, is thus seen to be a divine emanation, being related to the universal soul and Intellect. On its way from God to man it passes through all spheres, and every one leaves an impression upon her, and covers her with a wrapper, so to speak. The brightness of the star determines the ornament or "wrapper" which the soul gets from it. This is known to the Creator, who determines the measure of influence and the accidents attaching to the soul until she reaches the body destined for her by his will. The longer the stay in a given sphere the stronger the influence of the sphere in question; and hence the various temperaments we observe in persons, which determine their character and conduct. For at bottom the soul is the same in essence and unchangeable in all men, because she is an emanation from the Unchangeable. All individual differences are due to the spheral impressions. These impressions, however, do not take away from the soul its freedom of will.[142]

In the rest of his psychology and ethics the anonymous author follows Platonic theories, modified now and then in the manner of Aristotle. Thus we are told that the soul consists of three powers, or three souls, the vegetative, the animal and the rational. We learn of the existence of the vegetative soul from the nourishment, growth and reproduction evidenced by the individual. The animal soul shows its presence in the motions of the body. The existence of the rational soul we have already shown from the attributes of knowledge and ignorance.

The vegetative soul comes from certain spheral influences, themselves due to the universal soul, and ultimately to the will of God. It is the first of the three to make its appearance in the body. It is already found in the embryo, to which it gives the power of motion in its own place like the motion of a plant or tree. Its seat is in the liver, where the growth of the embryo begins. Its function ceases about the twentieth year, when the growth of the body reaches its limit.

The animal soul springs from the heart. Its functioning appears after birth when the child begins to crawl, and continues until the person loses the power of locomotion in old age. The rational soul resides in the middle of the brain. She knows all things before joining the body, but her knowledge is obscured on account of the material coverings which she receives on her way down from her divine source.[143]

The virtue of the vegetative soul is temperance; of the animal soul, courage; of the rational soul, wisdom. When these are harmoniously combined in the individual, and the two lower souls are controlled by the higher, there results the fourth virtue, which is justice, and which gives its possessor the privilege of being a teacher and a leader of his people. In Moses all these qualities were exemplified, and Isaiah (11, 1–4) in describing the qualities of the Messianic King also enumerates these four cardinal virtues. "The spirit of wisdom and understanding" represents wisdom, "the spirit of counsel and strength" stands for courage; "the spirit of knowledge and fear of the Lord" denotes temperance; and justice is represented in the phrase, "and he will judge the poor with righteousness." [144]

Virtue is a mean between the two extremes of excess and defect, each of which is a vice. Thus an excess of wisdom becomes shrewdness and cunning and deceit; while a defect means ignorance. The true wisdom consists in the middle way between the two extremes. Similarly courage is a mean between foolhardiness and rashness on the side of excess, and cowardice on the side of defect. Temperance is a mean between excessive indulgence of the appetites on one side and utter insensibility on the other. The mean of justice is the result of the harmonious combination of the means of the last three. If the rational soul has wisdom and the two other souls are obedient to it through modesty and courage, their substance changes into the substance of the rational soul, *i. e.*, their bad qualities are transformed into the four virtues just mentioned. Then the two lower souls unite with the rational soul and enjoy eternal happiness with it. On the other hand, if the rational soul follows the senses, its wisdom changes into their folly, its virtues into their vices, and it perishes with them. [145]

The immortality of the soul is proved as follows. Things composed of elements return back to their elements, hence the soul also returns to its own origin. The soul is independent of the body, for its qualities, thought and knowledge, are not bodily qualities, hence they become clearer and more certain after the soul is separated from the body than before, when the body obscured its vision like a curtain. The fact that a person's mind is affected when his body is ill does not show that the soul is dependent in its nature upon the body; but that acting as it does in the body by means of corporeal organs, it cannot perform its functions properly when these organs are injured.

Since death is a decree of God, it is clear that he has a purpose in changing the relations of body and soul. But if the soul comes to an end, this change would be a vain piece of work of which he cannot be guilty. Hence it follows that the destruction of the body is in order that we may exist in another similar form, similar to the angels.[146]

The purpose of the soul's coming into this world is in order that she may purify the two lower souls; also that she may know the value of her own world in comparison with this one, and in grieving for having left it may observe God's commandments, and thus achieve her return to her own world.

In the matter of returning to their own world after separation from the body, souls are graded according to the measure of their knowledge and the value of their conduct. These two conditions, ethical and spiritual or intellectual, are requisite of fulfilment before the soul can regain its original home. The soul on leaving this world is like a clean, white garment soaked in water. If the water is clean, it is easy to dry the garment, and it becomes even cleaner than it was before. But if the water is dirty, no amount of drying will make the garment clean.

Those souls which instead of elevating the two lower souls, vegetative and animal, were misled by them, will perish with the latter. Between the two extremes of perfection and wickedness there are intermediate stages, and the souls are treated accordingly. Those of the proud will rise in the air and flying hither and thither will not find a resting place. Those which have knowledge, but no good deeds, will rise to the sphere of the ether, but will be prevented from rising higher by the weight of their evil deeds, and the pure angels will rain down upon them arrows of fire, thus causing them to return below in shame and disgrace. The souls of the dishonest will be driven from place to place without finding any rest. Other bad souls will be punished in various ways. Those souls which have good deeds but no knowledge will be placed in the terrestrial paradise until their souls recall the knowledge they had in their original state, and they will then return to the Garden of Eden among the angels.[147]

CHAPTER VIII

ABRAHAM BAR HIYYA

Abraham bar Hiyya, the Prince, as he is called, lived in Spain in the first half of the twelfth century. He also seems to have stayed some time in southern France, though we do not know when or how long. His greatest merit lies not in his philosophical achievement which, if we may judge from the only work of a philosophical character that has come down to us, is not very great. He is best known as a writer on mathematics, astronomy and the calendar; though there, too, his most important service lay not so much in the original ideas he propounded, as in the fact that he was among the first, if not the first, to introduce the scientific thought current in the Orient and in Moorish Spain into Christian Europe, and especially among the Jews of France and Germany, who devoted all their energies to the Rabbinical literature, and to whom the Arabic works of their Spanish brethren were a sealed book.

So we find Abraham bar Hiyya, or Abraham Savasorda (a corruption of the Arabic title Sahib al-Shorta), associated with Plato of Tivoli in the translation into Latin of Arabic scientific works. And he himself wrote a number of books on mathematics and astronomy in Hebrew at the request of his friends in France who could not read Arabic. Abraham bar Hiyya is the first of the writers we have treated so far who composed a scientific work in the Hebrew language. All the others, with the exception of Abraham ibn Ezra, wrote in Arabic, as they continued to do until and including Maimonides.

The only one of his extant works which is philosophical in content is the small treatise "Hegyon ha-Nefesh," Meditation of the Soul.[148] It is a popular work, written with a practical purpose, ethical and homiletic in tone and style. The idea of repentance plays an important rôle in the book, and what theoretical philosophy finds place therein is introduced merely as a background and basis for the ethical and religious considerations which follow. It may be called a miniature "Duties of the Hearts." As in all homiletical compositions in Jewish literature, exegesis of Biblical passages takes up a good deal of the discussions, and for the history of the philosophic movement in mediæval Judaism the methods of reading metaphysical and ethical ideas into the Bible are quite as important as these ideas themselves.

The general philosophical standpoint of Abraham bar Hiyya may be characterized as an uncertain Neo-Platonism, or a combination of fundamental Aristotelian ideas with a Neo-Platonic coloring. Thus matter and form are the fundamental principles of the world. They existed potentially apart in the wisdom of God before they were combined and thus realized in actuality.[149] Time being a measure of motion, came into being together with the motion which followed upon this combination. Hence neither the world nor time is eternal. This is Platonic, not Aristotelian, who believes in the eternity of motion as well as of time. Abraham bar Hiyya also speaks of the purest form as light and as looking at and illuminating the form inferior to it and thus giving rise to the heavens, minerals and plants.[150] This is all Neo-Platonic. And yet the most distinctive doctrine of Plotinus and the later Neo-Platonists among the Arabs, the series of emanating hypostases, Intellect, Universal Soul, Nature, Matter, and so on, is wanting in the "Hegyon ha-Nefesh."[151] Form is the highest thing he knows outside of God; and the purest form, which is too exalted to combine with matter, embraces angels, seraphim, souls, and all forms related to the upper world.[152] With the exception of the names angel, seraphim, souls, this is good Aristotelian doctrine, who also believes in the movers of the spheres and the active intellect in man as being pure forms.

To proceed now to give a brief account of Abraham bar Hiyya's teaching, he thinks it is the duty of rational man to know how it is that man who is so insignificant was given control of the other animals, and endowed with the power of wisdom and knowledge. In order to gain this knowledge we must investigate the origins and principles of existing things, so that we may arrive at an understanding of things as they are. This the wise men of other nations have realized, though they were not privileged to receive a divine Torah, and have busied themselves with philosophical investigations. Our Bible recommends to us the same method in the words of Deuteronomy (4, 39), "Know therefore this day, and reflect in thy heart, that the Lord is God in the heavens above, and upon the earth beneath: there is none else." This means that if you understand thoroughly the order of things in heaven above and the earth beneath, you will at once see that God made it in his wisdom, and that he is the only one and there is no one beside him. The book of Job teaches the same thing, when it says (19, 26) "And from my flesh I shall behold God." This signifies that from the structure of the body and the form of its members we can understand the wisdom of the Creator. We need not hesitate therefore to study the works of the ancients and the wise men of other nations in order to learn from them the nature of existence. We have the permission and recommendation of Scripture.[153]

Starting from a consideration of man we see that he is the last of created things because we find in him additional composition over and above that found in other creatures. Man is a *"rational animal."* "Animal" means a body that grows and moves and at last is dissolved. "Rational" refers to the power of knowledge, of inferring one thing from another, and discriminating between good and evil. In this man differs from other animals. Descending in the scale of existence we find that the plant also grows and dies like the animal, but it does not move. Stones, metals and other inanimate bodies on the earth, change their forms and shapes, but unlike plants they have no power of growing or increasing. They are the simplest of the things on the earth. They differ from the heavenly bodies in that the latter never change their forms. Proceeding further in our analysis, we find that body, the simplest thing so far, means length, breadth and depth attached to something capable of being measured. This definition shows that body is also composed of two elements, which are theoretically distinct until God's will joins them together. These are "hyle" (matter)— what has no likeness or form, but has the capacity of receiving form —and form, which is defined as that which has power to clothe the hyle with any form. Matter alone is too weak to sustain itself, unless form comes to its aid. Form, on the other hand, is not perceptible to sense unless it clothes matter, which bears it. One needs the other. Matter cannot *exist* without form; form cannot *be seen* without matter. Form is superior to matter, because it needs the latter only to be seen but can exist by itself though not seen; whereas matter cannot *exist* without form. These two, matter and form, were hidden in God, where they existed potentially until the time came to produce them and realize them *in actu*.

Matter is further divided into two kinds. There is pure matter, which enters into the composition of the heavens, and impure matter, forming the substance of terrestrial bodies. Similarly form may be divided at first into two kinds; closed and sealed form, too pure and holy to be combined with matter; and open and penetrable form, which is fit to unite with matter. The pure, self-subsistent form gazes at and illuminates the penetrable form, and helps it to clothe matter with all the forms of which the latter is capable.

Now when God determined to realize matter and form *in actu*, he caused the pure form to be clothed with its splendor, which no hyle can touch. This gave rise to angels, seraphim, souls, and all other forms of the upper world. Not all men can see these forms or conceive them in the mind, because they do not unite with anything which the eye can perceive, and the majority of people cannot understand what they cannot perceive with their corporeal senses. Only those who are given to profound scientific investigations can understand the essence of these forms.

The light of this pure form then emanated upon the second form, and by the word of God the latter united with the pure matter firmly and permanently, so that there is never a change as long as they are united. This union gave rise to the bodies of the heavens (spheres and fixed stars) which never change their forms. Then the form united with the impure matter, and this gave rise to all the bodies in the sublunar world, which change their forms. These are the four elements, and the products of their composition, including plants.[154]

So far we have bodies which do not change their places. Then a light emanated from the self-subsisting form by the order of God, the splendor of which spread upon the heaven, moving from point to point, and caused the material form (*i. e.*, the inferior, so-called penetrable form) to change its place. This produced the stars which change their position but not their forms (planets). From this light extending over the heaven emanated another splendor which reached the body with changing form, giving rise to the three species of living beings, aquatic, aerial and terrestial animals, corresponding to the three elements, water, air, earth; as there is no animal life in fire.

We have so far therefore three kinds of forms. (1) The pure self-subsistent form which never combines with matter. This embraces all the forms of the spiritual world. (2) Form which unites with body firmly and inseparably. These are the forms of the heavens and the stars. (3) Form which unites with body temporarily. Such are the forms of the bodies on the earth. The forms of the second and third classes cannot exist without bodies. The form of class number one cannot exist with body. To make the scheme complete, there ought to be a fourth kind of form which can exist with as well as without body. In other words, a form which unites with body for a time and then returns to its original state and continues to exist without body. Reason demands that the classification should be complete, hence there must be such a form, and the only one worthy of this condition is the soul of man. We thus have a proof of the immortality of the soul.[155]

These are the ideas of the ancient sages, and we shall find that they are drawn from the Torah. Thus matter and form are indicated in the second verse of Genesis, "And the earth was *without form* (Heb. Tohu) and *void* (Heb. Bohu)." "Tohu" is matter; "Bohu" (בו הוא = בהו) signifies that through which matter gains existence, hence form. "Water" (Heb. Mayim) is also a general word for any of the various forms, whereas "light" (Heb. Or) stands for the pure subsistent form. By "firmament" (Heb. Rakia‘) is meant the second kind of form which unites with the pure matter in a permanent and unchangeable manner. "Let there be a *firmament* in the midst of the *waters*" (Gen. 1, 6) indicates that the "firmament" is embraced by the bright light of the first day, that is the universal form, from which all the other forms come. "And let it divide between *water* and *water*" (*ib.*) signifies that the "firmament" stands between the self-subsistent form and the third kind of form above mentioned, namely, that which unites with body and gives rise to substances changing their forms, like minerals and plants. The "luminaries" (Heb. Meorot) correspond to the second light mentioned above. We shall find also that the order of creation as given in Genesis coincides with the account given above in the name of the ancient sages.[156]

It would seem as if the self-subsisting form and the two lights emanating from it are meant to represent the Intellect, Soul and Nature of the Neo-Platonic trinity respectively, and that Abraham bar Hiyya purposely changed the names and partly their functions in order to make the philosophical account agree with the story of creation in Genesis.

With regard to the intellectual and ethical condition of the soul and its destiny, the speculative thinkers of other nations, arguing from reason alone and having no divine revelation to guide or confirm their speculations, are agreed that the only way in which the soul, which belongs to a higher world, can be freed from this world of body and change is through *intellectual excellence* and *right conduct*. Accordingly they classify souls into four kinds. The soul, they say, may have health, sickness, life, death. Health signifies *wisdom* or *knowledge*; sickness denotes *ignorance*. Life means the *fear of God* and *right conduct;* death is *neglect of God* and *evil practice*. Every person combines in himself one of the two intellectual qualities with one of the two ethical qualities. Thus we have four classes of persons. A man may be wise and pious, wise and wicked, ignorant and pious, ignorant and wicked. And his destiny after death is determined by the class to which he belongs. Thus when a man who is wise and pious departs this world, his soul by reason of its wisdom separates from the body and exists in its own form as before. Owing to its piety it will rise to the upper world until it reaches the pure, eternal form, with which it will unite for ever. If the man is wise and wicked, the wisdom of the soul will enable it to exist without body; but on account of its wickedness and indulgence in the desires of this world, it cannot become completely free from the creatures of this world, and the best it can do is to rise above the sublunar world of change to the world of the planets where the forms do not change, and move about beneath the light of the sun, the heat of which will seem to it like a fire burning it continually, and preventing it from rising to the upper light.

If the man is ignorant and pious, his soul will be saved from body in order that it may exist by itself, but his ignorance will prevent his soul from leaving the atmosphere of the lower world. Hence the soul will have to be united with body a second, and a third time, if necessary, until it finally acquires knowledge and wisdom, which will enable it to rise above the lower world, its degree and station depend-ing upon the measure of intellect and virtue it possesses at the time of the last separation from the body. The soul of the man who is both ignorant and wicked cannot be saved from the body entirely, and dies like a beast.

These are the views of speculative thinkers which we may adopt, but they cannot tell us what is the content of the terms *wisdom* and *right conduct.* Not having been privileged to receive the sacred Law, which is the source of all wisdom and the origin of rectitude, they cannot tell us in concrete fashion just what a man must know and what he must do in order to raise his soul to the highest degree possible for it to attain. And if they were to tell us what they understand by wisdom and right conduct, we should not listen to them. Our author-ity is the Bible, and we must test the views of the philosophers by the teaching of the Bible.

If we do this we find authority in Scripture also for belief in the immortality of the soul. Thus if we study carefully the expressions used of the various creations in the first chapter of Genesis, we notice that in some cases the divine command is expressed by the phrase, "Let there be . . . ," followed by the name of the thing to be created; and the execution of the command is expressed by the words, "And there was . . . ," the name of the created object being repeated; or the phrase may be simply, "And it was so," without naming the object. In other cases the expression "Let there be" is not used, nor the corresponding "And there was."

This variation in expression is not accidental. It is deliberate and must be understood. Upon a careful examination we cannot fail to see that where the expression "Let there be" is used, the object so created exists in this world permanently and without change. Thus, "Let there be light" (Gen. i, 3). If in addition we have the corre-sponding expression, "And there was," in connection with the same object and followed by its name, it means that the object will continue its everlasting existence in the next world also. Hence, "And there was light" (*ib.*). In the creation of the firmament and the luminaries we have the expression, "Let there be"; the corresponding expression at the end is in each case not, "And there was . . . ," but, "And it was so." This signifies that in this world, as long as it lasts, the firmament and luminaries are permanent and without change; but they will have no continuance in the next world. In the creation of the sublunar world we do not find the phrase, "Let there be," at all, but such expressions as, "Let the waters be gathered together" (*ib.* 9), "Let the earth produce grass" (*ib.* 11), and so on. This means that these things change their forms and have no permanent existence in this world. The phrase, "And it was so," recording the realization of the divine command, signifies that they do not exist at all in the next world.

The case is different in man. We do not find the expression, "Let there be," in the command introducing his formation; hence he has no permanence in this world. But we do find the expression, "And the man became (lit. *was*) a living soul" (*ib.* 2, 7), which means that he will have permanent existence in the next world. The article before the word man in the verse just quoted indicates that not every man lives forever in the next world, but only the good. What manner of man he must be in order to have this privilege, *i. e.*, of what nation he must be a member, we shall see later. This phase of the question the speculative thinkers cannot understand, hence they did not investigate it. Reason alone cannot decide this question; it needs the guidance of the Torah, which is divine.

Consulting the Torah on this problem, we notice that man is distinguished above other animals in the manner of his creation in three respects. (1) All other living beings were created by means of something else. The water or the earth was ordered to produce them. Man alone was made directly by God. (2) There are three expressions used for the creation of living things, "create" (Heb. bara), "form" (Heb. yazar), and "make" (Heb. 'asah). The water animals have only the first (*ib.* 1, 21), as being the lowest in the scale of animal life. Land animals have the second and the third, "formed" and "made" (*ib.* 1, 25; 2, 19). Man, who is superior to all the others, has all the three expressions (*ib.* 26, 27; 2, 7). (3) Man was given dominion over the other animals (*ib.* 1, 28).

As man is distinguished above the other animals, so is one nation distinguished above other men. In Isaiah (43, 7) we read: "Every one that is called by my name, and whom I have *created* for my glory; I have *formed* him; yea, I have *made* him." The three terms, created, formed, made, signify that the reference is to man; and we learn from this verse that those men were created for his glory who are called by his name. But if we inquire in the Bible we find that the nation called by God's name is Israel, as we read (*ib.* 1), "Thus said the Lord that created thee, O Israel, Fear not; for I have redeemed thee, I have called thee by thy name; thou art mine," and in many other passages besides. The reason for this is their belief in the unity of God and their reception of the Law. At the same time others who are not Israelites are not excluded from reaching the same degree through repentance.[157]

There is no system of ethics in Abraham bar Hiyya, and we shall in the sequel select some of his remarks bearing on ethics and pick out the ethical kernel from its homiletical and exegetical husk.

Man alone, he tells us, of all animal creation receives reward and punishment. The other animals have neither merit nor guilt. To be sure, their fortune in life depends upon the manner in which they respond to their environment, but this is not in the way of reward and punishment, but a natural consequence of their natural constitution. With man it is different, and this is because of the responsible position man occupies, having been given the privilege and the ability to control all animal creation.[158]

The psychological basis of virtue in Abraham bar Hiyya is Platonic in origin, as it is in Pseudo-Bahya, though we do not find the four cardinal virtues and the derivation of justice from a harmonious combination of the other three as in the Republic of Plato, to which Pseudo-Bahya is ultimately indebted.

Man has three powers, we are told, which some call three souls. One is the power by which he grows and multiplies like the plants of the field. The second is that by which he moves from place to place. These two powers he has in common with the animal. The third is that by which he distinguishes between good and evil, between truth and falsehood, between a thing and its opposite, and by which he acquires wisdom and knowledge. This is the soul which distinguishes him from the other animals. If this soul prevails over the lower two powers, the man is called meritorious and perfect. If on the other hand the latter prevail over the soul, the man is accounted like a beast, and is called wicked and an evil doer. God gives merit to the animal soul for the sake of the rational soul if the former is obedient to the latter; and on the other hand imputes guilt to the rational soul and punishes her for the guilt of the animal soul because she did not succeed in overcoming the latter.[159]

The question of the relative superiority of the naturally good who feels no temptation to do wrong, and the temperamental person who has to sustain a constant struggle with his passions and desires in order to overcome them is decided by Abraham bar Hiyya in favor of the former on the ground that the latter is never free from evil thought, whereas the former is. And he quotes the Rabbis of the Talmud, according to whom the reward in the future world is not the same for the two types of men. He who must overcome temptation before he can subject his lower nature to his reason is rewarded in the next world in a manner bearing resemblance to the goods and pleasures of this world, and described as precious stones and tables of gold laden with good things to eat. On the other hand, the reward of the naturally perfect who is free from temptation is purely spiritual, and bears no earthly traces. These men are represented as "sitting under the Throne of Glory with their crowns on their heads and delighting in the splendor of the Shekinah." [160]

His theodicy offers nothing remarkable. He cites and opposes a solution frequently given in the middle ages of the problem of evil. This is based on the assumption that God cannot be the cause of evil. How then explain the presence of evil in the world? There is no analysis or classification or definition of what is meant by evil. Apparently it is physical evil which Abraham bar Hiyya has in mind. Why do some people suffer who do not seem to deserve it? is the aspect of the problem which interests him. One solution that is offered, he tells us, is that evil is not anything positive or substantial. It is something negative, absence of the good, as blindness is absence of vision; deafness, absence of hearing; nakedness, absence of clothing. Hence it has no cause. God produces the positive forms which are good, and determines them to stay a definite length of time. When this time comes to an end, the forms disappear and their negatives take their place automatically without the necessity of any cause.

Abraham bar Hiyya is opposed to this solution of the problem, though he gives us no philosophic reason for it. His arguments are

Biblical. God is the cause of evil as well as good, and this is the meaning of the word "judgment" (Heb. Mishpat) that occurs so often in the Bible in connection with God's attributes. The same idea is expressed in Jeremiah (9, 23) "I am the Lord which exercise loving kindness, judgment and righteousness in the earth." Loving kindness refers to the creation of the world, which was an act of pure grace on the part of God. It was not a necessity. His purpose was purely to do kindness to his creatures and to show them his wisdom and power. Righteousness refers to the kindness of God, his charity so to speak, which every one needs when he dies and wishes to be admitted to the next world. For the majority of men have more guilt than merit. Judgment denotes the good and evil distributed in the world according to the law of justice. Thus he rewards the righteous in the next world, and makes them suffer sometimes in this world in order to try them and to double their ultimate reward. He punishes the wicked in this world for their evil deeds, and sometimes he gives them wealth and prosperity that they may have no claim or defence in the next world. Thus evil in this world is not always the result of misconduct which it punishes; it may be inflicted as a trial, as in the case of Job. Abraham bar Hiyya's solution is therefore that there is no reason why God should not be the author of physical evil, since everything is done in accordance with the law of justice.[161]

CHAPTER IX

JOSEPH IBN ZADDIK

Little is known of the life of Joseph ben Jacob ibn Zaddik. He lived in Cordova; he was appointed *Dayyan*, or Judge of the Jewish community of that city in 1138; and he died in 1149. He is praised as a Talmudic scholar by his countryman Moses ibn Ezra, and as a poet by Abraham ibn Daud and Harizi, though we have no Talmudic composition from his pen, and but few poems, whether liturgical or otherwise.[162] His fame rests on his philosophical work, and it is this phase of his career in which we are interested here. "Olam Katon" or "Microcosm" is the Hebrew name of the philosophical treatise which he wrote in Arabic, but which we no longer possess in the original, being indebted for our knowledge of it to a Hebrew translation of unknown authorship.[163] Maimonides knew Joseph ibn Zaddik favorably, but he was not familiar with the "Microcosm." In a letter to Samuel Ibn Tibbon, the translator of his "Guide of the Perplexed," Maimonides tells us that though he has not seen the "Olam Katon" of Ibn Zaddik, he knows that its tendency is the same as that of the Brothers of Purity (*cf.* above, p. 60).[164] This signifies that its trend of thought is Neo-Platonic, which combines Aristotelian physics with Platonic and Plotinian metaphysics, ethics and psychology.

An examination of the book itself confirms Maimonides's judgment. In accordance with the trend of the times there is noticeable in Ibn Zaddik an increase of Aristotelian influence, though of a turbid kind; a decided decrease, if not a complete abandonment, of the ideas of the Kalam, and a strong saturation of Neo-Platonic doctrine and point of view. It was the fashion to set the Kalam over against the philosophers to the disadvantage of the former, as being deficient in logical knowledge and prejudiced by theological prepossessions. This is attested by the attitude towards the Mutakallimun of Judah Halevi, Maimonides, Averroes. And Ibn Zaddik forms no exception to the rule. The circumstance that it was most likely from Karaite writings, which found their way into Spain, that Ibn Zaddik gained his knowledge of Kalamistic ideas, was not exactly calculated to prepossess him, a Rabbanite, in their favor. And thus while we see him in the manner of Saadia and Bahya follow the good old method, credited by Maimonides to the Mutakallimun, of starting his metaphysics with proofs of the world's creation, and basing the existence of God, his unity, incorporeality and other attributes on the creation of the world as a foundation, he turns into an uncompromising opponent of these much despised apologetes when he comes to discuss the nature of God's attributes, of the divine will, and of the nature of evil. And in all these cases the target of his attack seems to be their Karaite representative Joseph al-Basir, whose acquaintance we made before (p. 48 ff.).

He laid under contribution his predecessors and contemporaries, Saadia, Bahya, Pseudo-Bahya, Gabirol; and his sympathies clearly lay with the general point of view represented by the last, and his Mohammedan sources; though he was enough of an eclectic to refuse to follow Gabirol, or the Brethren of Purity and the other Neo-Platonic writings, in all the details of their doctrine; and there is evidence of an attempt on his part to tone down the extremes of Neo-Platonic tendency and create a kind of level in which Aristotelianism and Platonism meet by compromising. Thus he believes with Gabirol that all things corporeal as well as spiritual are composed of matter and form; [165] but when it comes to defining what the matter of spiritual things may be, he tells us that we may speak of the genus as the matter of the species—a doctrine which is not so Neo-Platonic after all. For we do not have to go beyond Aristotle to hear that in the definition of an object, which represents its *intelligible* (opposed to sensible) essence, the genus is like the matter, the difference like the form. Of the universal and prime matter underlying all created things outside of God, of which Gabirol says that it is the immediate emanation of God's essence and constitutes with universal form the Universal Intelligence, Ibn Zaddik knows nothing. Nor do we find any outspoken scheme of emanation, such as we see in Plotinus or with a slight modification in the cyclopœdia of the Brethren of Purity, or as it is presupposed in the "Fons Vitæ" of Gabirol. Ibn Zaddik does refer to the doctrine of the divine Will, which plays such an important rôle in the philosophy of Gabirol and of the Pseudo-Empedoclean writings, which are supposed to have been Gabirol's source.[166] But here, too, the negative side of Ibn Zaddik's doctrine is developed at length, while the positive side is barely alluded to in a hint. He takes pains to show the absurdity of the view that the divine will is a momentary entity created from time to time to make possible the coming into being of the things and processes of our world—a view held by the Mutakallimun as represented by their spokesman al-Basir, but when it comes to explaining his own view of the nature of the divine will, and whether it is identical with God or not, he suddenly becomes reticent, refers us to the writings of Empedocles, and intimates that the matter is involved in mystery, and it is not safe to talk about it too plainly and openly. Evidently Ibn Zaddik was not ready to go all the length of Gabirol's emanationism and Neo-Platonic mysticism.

The Aristotelian ideas, of which there are many in the "Microcosm," are probably not derived from a study of Aristotle's works, but from secondary sources. This we may safely infer from the way in which he uses or interprets them. An Aristotelian definition is a highly technical proposition in which every word counts, and requires a definition in turn to be understood. In the Aristotelian context the reader sees the methodical derivation of the concept; and the several technical terms making up the definition are made clear by illustrative examples. Aside from the context the proposition is obscure even in the original Greek. Now conceive an Arabic translation of an Aristotelian definition taken out of its context, and you do not wonder that it is misunderstood; particularly when the interpreter's point of view is taken from a school of thought at variance with that of Aristotle. This is exactly what happens to Ibn Zaddik. He quotes approvingly Aristotle's definition of the soul, and proceeds to interpret it in a manner not intended by the author of the "De Anima."[167] If he had read the context he could not have misunderstood the definition as he did.

Unlike his predecessors, Ibn Zaddik did not confine himself to a special topic in philosophy or to the metaphysical aspects of Judaism. Isaac Israeli and Gabirol discuss special questions in Physics and Metaphysics without bringing them into relation with Judaism or the text of the Bible. Saadia takes cognizance of philosophical doctrine solely with a view to establishing and rationalizing Jewish dogma, and only in so far as it may thus be utilized. Bahya and Abraham bar Hiyya confine their philosophical outlook within still narrower limits, having Jewish ethics as their primary concern. All of the latter make a feature of Biblical interpretation, which lends to their work the Jewish stamp and to their style the element of homeliness and variety. To this they owe in a measure their popularity, which, however, cannot be said for Abraham bar Hiyya, whose "Hegyon ha-Nefesh" was not printed until the second half of last century. The "Microcosm" of Ibn Zaddik is the first compendium of science, philosophy and theology in Jewish literature. And yet it is a small book; for Ibn Zaddik does not enter into lengthy discussions, nor does he adorn his style with rhetorical flourishes or copious quotations from Bible and Talmud. The "Olam Katon" is clearly meant for beginners, who require a summary and compendious view of so much of physics, psychology, metaphysics and ethics as will give them an idea of the position of man in the world, and his duties, theoretical and practical, in this life, that he may fulfil his destiny for which he was created. It is very possible that Ibn Zaddik modelled his work on the Encyclopædia of the Brethren of Purity, leaving out all that he regarded as unessential or objectionable and abridging the rest.

Accordingly, the "Microcosm" is divided into four parts. The first part treats of what is called in the Aristotelian classification of the sciences Physics, *i. e.*, the principles and constitution of the corporeal world and its processes. The second treats of man, including anthropology and psychology. The third is devoted to a discussion of the existence, unity, incorporeality and other attributes of God, based upon the doctrine of the creation of the world. This bears the stamp of the Kalam, and is indebted to the writings of Saadia, Bahya and Joseph al-Basir. It covers the topics usually treated by the Mutakallimun in the division of their works, known by the name of "Bab al Tauhid," treatise on Unity. The fourth part corresponds to the "Bab al Adl" of the Kalam, *i. e.*, the second division of Kalamistic works devoted to theodicy, or vindication of God's justice in his dealings with mankind. Hence it includes theological questions of an ethical nature, like freedom of the will, reasons for divine worship, the nature of reward and punishment, and so on.

The book was written, Ibn Zaddik tells us, in answer to the question of a pupil concerning the meaning of such terms as "perfection" and "permanent good," used by philosophers. They are not of this world these men say, and yet every man of intelligence should seek them. This is a very difficult subject, made more so by the small number of persons engaged in its study. Particularly in our own generation is this true, that the value of knowledge and investigation is not recognized. People are Jews in name only, and men only in outward appearance. Former ages were much superior in this regard.

Two fundamental requisites are necessary for the knowledge of our subject. They are the knowledge of God, and performance of his will. For this purpose we must understand the works of the philosophers. But these in turn require a knowledge of the preliminary sciences of arithmetic, geometry, music, astronomy, and logic. This takes a long time and is likely to weary the student, especially the beginner. I have therefore made it my purpose to show how a man can know himself, for from a knowledge of self he will come to a knowledge of all. Man is called "Microcosm," a world in miniature, because he has in him represented all the elements of the universe. His body resembles the corporeal world; his rational soul the spiritual world. Hence the importance of knowing himself, and hence the definition of philosophy as *a man's knowledge of himself*. Philosophy is the science of sciences and the end thereof, because it is the path to a knowledge of the Creator.[168]

Here we see at the outset Ibn Zaddik's Neo-Platonic tendency to make a short cut to knowledge through the study of man instead of the painful and laborious mastery of the preliminary sciences. And so it was that the Neo-Platonists added little to Aristotle's study of nature, concentrating their attention upon the intelligible or spiritual world.

The first thing we must do then is to show that the human body is similar to the corporeal world. This will require an analysis of the structure of the latter. But before examining the *objects* of knowledge, we must say a word about the process of knowing. Man perceives things in two ways—through sense and through intellect. His senses give him the accidents of things, the shell or husk, so to speak. He perceives color through sight, sound through hearing, odor through smell, and so on. It takes reason to penetrate to the essence of an object. Take as an example a book. The sense of sight perceives its color, and through the color its form. This is then apprehended by the power of imagination or representation. The latter in turn hands it over to the cogitative power of the rational soul, from the reflection ot which results the spiritual reality of the object, which is its knowledge. So we see that the reason knows the essence and reality of a thing, whereas the senses know only its husk and its accidents. This same thing is stated by the philosopher in another form. The senses, he says, know only the particular, the universal can be known by the intellect only. This is because the soul is fine and penetrating, while the body is gross, and can reach the surface only.

We may also classify knowledge from another point of view as necessary (or immediate), and demonstrated (or mediate). Necessary knowledge is that which no sane man can deny. Such knowledge may be of the senses, as the sight of the sun or the sound of thunder; or it may be of the reason, such as that the whole is greater than its parts. We may then enumerate four kinds of things known directly without the help of other knowledge. (1) The percepts of the senses. (2) Truths generally admitted by reason of their self-evidence. (3) Traditional truths, *i. e.*, truths handed down by a reliable and wise man, or by a community worthy of credence. (4) First principles or axioms. These four can be easily reduced to two; for traditional truths ultimately go back to the testimony of the senses; while first principles or axioms are included in self-evident propositions. We thus have two kinds of necessary or immediate knowledge, the data of sense, and self-evident propositions. The latter kind is superior to the former, because man shares sense knowledge with the lower animals; whereas rational propositions are peculiar to him alone.

Demonstrated knowledge is built upon necessary knowledge, and is derived from it by means of logical inference.[169]

We may now proceed to discuss the principles of the corporeal world. Matter is the foundation and principle of a thing. All things. natural as well as artificial, are composed of matter and form. Wood is the common matter of chair and bed. Their forms are different. So the common matter of the four elements is the prime matter endowed with the form of corporeality, *i. e.*, with the capacity of filling place. This form of corporeality makes the prime matter corporeal substance. Matter is relative to form, form is relative to matter.

Spiritual things also have matter and form. In corporeal artificial things like ring or bracelet, the matter is gold, the form is the form of ring or bracelet, the efficient cause is the art of the goldsmith, the final cause or purpose is the adornment. In spiritual things we may compare genus to matter, species to form, specific difference to efficient cause, the individual to the final cause.

Everything exists either by itself (*per se*) or in something else. Matter exists by itself, form exists in something else, in matter. Matter is potentially substance; after it assumes a form it becomes actual substance. In reality there is no matter without form, but in thought we can remove the form and leave the matter.

Substance may be described as that which bears opposite and changing qualities. No substance can be the opposite of another substance through its substantiality, but through its accidents; for opposition resides in quality. Matter receiving form is substance. Absolute substance is simple and spiritual, for it cannot be perceived through the five senses. When the philosophers say that all body is substance, and that the individual is a substance, they use substance in contradistinction to accident, meaning that the individual exists by itself, and needs not another for its existence, unlike accidents, which must have something to exist in.

This absolute substance, which is simple and spiritual, seems to be identical with Gabirol's "substantia quæ sustinet decem prædicamenta," the substance which supports the ten categories. Gabirol means by it that which remains of a corporeal substance when we take away from it everything that qualifies it as being here or there, of a particular nature or size, in a given relation, and so on.

The expression corporeal world includes the celestial spheres and all which is under them. To be sure, the body of the sphere is different from the other bodies in matter and form and qualities. It consists of a fifth nature, different from the four elements. It is not cold, or it would move downward like earth and water. It is not warm, or it would move upward like air and fire. It is not wet, for it would then roll like the waves of the sea. Nor is it dry, for it would condense and not move at all. Not being any one of these qualities, which constitute our four elements, the sphere is not a composite of them either; for the simple is prior to the composite, and we cannot regard the elements of the sublunar world as prior and superior to the spheres.

The sphere is neither light nor heavy. For light and heavy are relative terms. An object is heavy when out of its natural place, light when in its natural place. Thus a stone is heavy when it is away from the earth, which is its natural place, but is light when it comes to rest where it belongs. The sphere is never out of its place or in its place, as it moves constantly in a circle. Hence it is neither light nor heavy.

Ibn Zaddik's definition of light and heavy as being relative, and dependent on the relation of the object to its natural place is peculiar, and would lead him to say that fire and air are also heavy when out of their natural place, which is outside of, and above earth and water. But this does not seem in consonance with the Aristotelian use of these terms. According to Aristotle an object is heavy if its tendency is to move to the centre of the world; it is light if it moves away from the centre to the circumference. Hence earth and water are heavy, fire and air are light. The natural place of a body or element is that to which it has a tendency to move, or in which it has a tendency to rest, when left to itself. Hence a body will always move to its natural place when away from it and under no restriction; and its heaviness or lightness does not change with its position.

To continue, the sphere moves in a circle, the most perfect of all motions, having neither beginning nor end. It is more perfect than all bodies, and the knowledge of God is not hidden from it as it is hidden from us. Whatever moves in a circle must move around a body at rest; for if it moves around another moving body, this second body must have another body around which it moves, and this third body another, and so on *ad infinitum*, which is impossible. Hence the sphere moves around a body at rest. This is the earth.

The four elements of the sublunar world are, fire, air, water, earth. In their purity these elements have neither color nor taste, nor odor nor any other sensible property. For the elements are simple bodies, whereas the sensible qualities are the result of the composition of the elements. If air had color, we should see it as we see all colored things; and all other things would appear to us in the color of air, as is the case when we look through a colored glass. The same argument applies to water.

The elements change into each other. We see water changing under the effect of heat into vapor, and the vapor condenses again under the influence of cold and changes back to water, namely, rain. Air changes into fire when flint strikes iron. Fire cannot exist here unless it has something to take hold of; otherwise it changes into air. Earth and water change into each other very slowly, because earth is hard to change.

The basis of the four elements is a substance filling place as a result of its assuming the form of corporeality, *i. e.*, extension in three directions. Filling place, it moves; moving, it becomes warm. When its motion is completed, it necessarily comes to rest and becomes cold. Heat and cold are the active powers, wet and dry are the passive qualities, wet being associated with heat, dry with cold. The mixture of these qualities with the corporeal basis results in the four elements.

The three natures, mineral, plant, animal are composed of the four elements. When a seed is put in the ground it cannot grow without water, and sunshine and air. These form its food, and food is assimilated to the thing fed. Our bodies are composed of the four elements, because they are nourished by plants. The general process of the sublunar world is that of genesis and dissolution. The genesis of one thing is the dissolution of another. The dissolution of the egg is the genesis of the chicken; the dissolution of the chicken is the genesis of the four elements; for in the living being the elements are potential, and they become actual when the animal dies. This continuous process of genesis and dissolution proves that this world is not permanent, for the basis of its processes is change.[170]

The human body corresponds to the corporeal world, and is similar to it in its nature and matter. Man's body is subject to genesis and decay like other objects. It is composed of the elements and returns to them. It has in it the nature of minerals, plants and animals. It has the power of growth, sustenance and reproduction like plants. Man is like animal in having motion and sensation. He has the spirited power and the appetitive like other animals. His body is perfect because it has resemblances to all kinds of plants and animals. His body as a whole resembles great trees, his hair is like grass and shrubs.

Animals have various qualities according to the relation of the animal soul to the body. Thus the lion has strength, the lamb meekness, the fox shrewdness, and so on. Mankind includes all of these qualities. In the same way various animals have various instincts resembling arts, such as the weaving of the spider, the building of the bird and the bee, and so on. They also subsist on various foods. Man alone combines all arts and all kinds of food.

The human body has three dimensions like inanimate bodies. It is also similar to the bodies of plants and animals, and at the same time is distinguished alone among animals by its erect position. This is due to the fact that man's nature is proportionate, and his body is purer and finer than other bodies. Thus we see when oil is pure, its flame rises in a straight line; when the oil is impure the flame is not straight. Another thing proving that man's nature is superior to that of other animals is that the latter live in that element which is akin to their constitution—fish in water, birds in air, quadrupeds on land. Man alone can inhabit all three. Another reason for man's erect position is that he is a plant originating in heaven. Hence his head, which is the root, faces heaven.[171]

Man has three souls, a plant soul, an animal soul and a rational soul. He must have a plant soul to account for the fact that man grows like other plants and dies like them. For if he can grow without a plant soul, plants can do the same. And if this too is granted, then there is no reason why mountains and stones should not grow also. Again, if man can grow without a plant soul, he can live without an animal soul, and know without a rational soul, which is absurd.

The faculty of the vegetative soul is the appetitive power, whose seat is in the liver. Its subordinate powers are those of nutrition and growth. Through it man feels the need of food and other natural desires. He has this in common with the lower animals. It is the first power that appears in man while he is still in his mother's womb. First comes the power which forms the combined seed of the male and the female into a human being in its proper form and nature. In doing this it requires the assistance of the "growing" power, which begins its activity as soon as the first member is formed, and continues until the period of youth is completed. This power in turn needs the assistance of the nourishing power, which accompanies the other two from the beginning of their activity to the end of the person's life. All this constitutes the plant soul, and it must not be supposed that these powers are separated from one another, and that one is in one place and another in another place. *They are all spiritual powers derived from the universal powers in the upper world.*

When the form of the being is complete, the animal soul makes its appearance. This soul is carried in the spirit of the animal or man, which is found in the pure blood of the arteries. There are two membranes in every artery, making two passages, one for blood and the other for the spirit or wind. The seat of the animal soul is in the heart, and it is borne in the pure red blood. This is why we see in the heart two receptacles; in one is spirit, in the other, blood. Hence after death we find congealed blood in the one, while the other is empty. Death happens on account of the defective "mixture" of the heart. This means that the four humors of which the body is composed, namely, blood, yellow and black gall and phlegm, lose the proper proportionality in their composition, and one or other of them predominates. An animal does not die unless the mixture of the heart is injured, or the heart is wounded seriously. Death is also caused by disease or injury of the brain. For the brain is the origin of the nerves which control the voluntary activities by means of contraction and expansion. If the chest does not contract, the warm air does not come out; if it does not expand, the cold air does not come in; and if the air does not come in or out, the heart loses its proportionality, and the animal dies. The functions of the animal soul are sensation and motion. This motion may be active as well as passive. The active motions are those of the arteries, and the expansion and contraction of the chest which results in respiration. The passive motions give rise to the emotions of anger, fear, shame, joy, sorrow.

Anger is the motion of the spirit within the body toward the outside, together with the blood and the humors. This is found in animals also. Fear is the entrance of the soul within, leaving the surface of the body, and causing the extremities to become cold. Shame is a motion inward, and forthwith again outward. Sorrow is caused in the same way as fear, except that fear is sudden, while sorrow is gradual. This is why fear sometimes kills when the body is weak. Joy is motion outward. Joy may kill too, when it is very great, and the person is weak and without control. Joy is of the nature of pleasure, except that pleasure is gradual, while joy is sudden.

Pain is that feeling we have when we are taken out of our natural state and put into an unnatural. Pleasure is felt when we are restored to the natural. Take, for example, the heat of the sun. When a person is exposed to it, the sun takes him out of his natural state. Heat is then painful, and pleasure is produced by the thing which restores him to his natural state; in this case a cold spring and a drink of cold water. Similarly a person walking in the snow and cold air feels pain by reason of the cold taking him out of his natural state. Heat then gives him pleasure by restoring him. The same thing applies to hunger and thirst, sleeping and waking, and other things which give us pleasure and pain. Without pain there is no pleasure, and the pleasure varies in accordance with the antecedent pain.

Life is the effect of the animal soul. The disappearance of the effect does not necessarily involve the disappearance of the cause, as the disappearance of the smoke does not require the cessation of the fire. Death means simply the separation of the soul, not the destruction thereof. It does not follow because the human soul remains after the death of the body, that the soul of the ox and the ass continues likewise, for the two souls are different. Animals were created for the sake of man, whereas man exists for his own sake. Moreover, man's life is ultimately derived from his rational soul. For if the animal soul of man were the ultimate source of life, the rational soul too would be dependent for its life upon the former, and hence would be inferior to it, which is absurd. It remains then that *the rational soul gives existence to the animal soul in man.*

Sleep is the rest of the senses, as death is their entire cessation. The purpose of sleep is to give the brain rest so that the "spirit" of the soul should not be dissolved and the "mixture" of the body injured suddenly and cause death. The heart rests continually between contraction and expansion, hence it needs no special rest at night. Waking is the activity of the senses and the exercise of their functions to satisfy the desires of the body. The motions of the soul in the waking state are in the interest of the needs of the body. During sleep the soul looks out for itself, for its better world, being then free from the business of the body. If it is pure and bright, and the body is free from the remnant of food, and the thought is not depressed by sorrow and grief—then the soul is aroused in its desire for the future, and beholds wonderful things.[172]

No one can deny that man has a rational soul because speech is an attribute which man has above all other animals. The soul is not a corporeal thing, for if it were it would have to occupy place like body, and would have color and form and other qualities like body. Moreover, it would require something else to give it life like body. In other words, the soul would require another soul, and that soul another soul, and so on *ad infinitum*, which is impossible. Hence the soul is not a corporeal thing.

Nor can we say that the soul is *in* the body. For if it were, it would itself be body; since only body can fill the empty place in another body, as water fills a jar.

The soul is a substance and not an accident. An accident is a quality which makes its appearance in something else, and has no permanence. If then the rational soul is an accident of the body, it has no permanence, and man is sometimes rational and sometimes not. This is absurd, for in that case there could be no purpose in giving him commandments and statutes.

There are inseparable accidents to be sure, like the color of the Ethiopian's skin. But in that case we know the color is an accident despite its inseparability, from the fact that in other things color is an accident and may be removed. This will not apply to the reason. For we do not find anything in which reason is a removable accident. The moment you remove reason, you remove man, for reason is essential to man. The fact that as a result of an injury a man may lose his reason is no argument against us, for this happens only when an injury is inflicted on the brain, which is the reason's instrument. This accounts for the fact, too, that men in good health if given henbane to drink lose their reason, because the drink affects the brain. On the other hand, we see that those afflicted with a certain disease of the intestines, which causes their death, are more rational and brighter at the time of death than ever before, showing that the soul cannot be an accident depending upon the "mixture" of the body.

To regard the soul as an accident, while the body is a substance, would make the soul inferior to the body. This is absurd. For we have the body in common with the beasts; whereas it is in virtue of the reason that we are given commandments, and reward and punishment in the world to come.

If the soul is neither a corporeal thing nor an accident of body, it must be a spiritual substance. And the best definition of the soul is that of Aristotle, who says it is *a substance giving perfection to a natural organic body, which has life potentially*. Every phrase in this definition tells. "Substance" excludes the view that the soul is an accident. "Giving perfection" signifies that the soul is that which makes man perfect, bringing him to the next world, and being the purpose not merely of his creation and the composition of his body, but of the creation of matter as well. "Natural organic body" indicates that the body is an organon, or instrument in the function of the soul, the latter using the body to carry out its own purposes. The rational soul is like a king; the animal soul is like an official before the king, rebuking the appetitive soul.

In the discussion of the last paragraph we have a good example of the uncritical attitude of Ibn Zaddik toward the various schools of philosophical thought, particularly those represented by Plato and Aristotle. This attitude is typical of the middle ages, which appealed to authority in philosophy as well as in theology, and hence developed a harmonistic attitude in the presence of conflicting authorities. Aided by their defective knowledge of the complete systems of the ancient Greek philosophers, by the difficulties and obscurities incident to translations from an alien tongue, and by the spurious writings circulating in the name of an ancient Greek philosopher, the precise demarcation of schools and tendencies became more and more confused, and it was possible to prove that Plato and Aristotle were in entire agreement. Thus Ibn Zaddik has no scruple in combining (unconsciously, to be sure) Platonic and Neo-Platonic psychology with the Aristotelian definition representing quite a different point of view. The one is anthropological dualism, regarding the soul as a distinct entity which comes to the body from without. The other is a biological monism, in which the soul is the reality of the body, the essence of its functioning, which makes the potentially living body an actually living body. We cannot enter here into a criticism of the elements of the Aristotelian definition of the soul as rendered and interpreted by Ibn Zaddik, but will merely say that it misses completely the meaning of Aristotle, and shows that Ibn Zaddik did not take it from the "De Anima" of Aristotle, but found it without its context in some Arabic work.

To return from our digression, the three souls, Ibn Zaddik tells us, are spiritual powers; every one of them is a substance by itself of benefit to the body. The rational soul gets the name soul primarily, and the others get it from the rational soul. The *Intellect* is called soul because the rational soul and the Intellect have a common matter. And hence when the soul is perfected it becomes intellect. This is why the rational soul is called potential intellect. The only difference between them is one of degree and excellence. The world of Intellect is superior, and its matter is the pure light, Intellect in which there is no ignorance, because it comes from God without any intermediate agency.

Here we see just a touch of the Neo-Platonic doctrine of emanation, of which the Universal Intellect is the first. But it is considerably toned down and not continued down the series as in Plotinus or the Brethren of Purity.

The accidents of the soul are spiritual like the soul itself. They are, knowledge, kindness, goodness, justice, and other similar qualities. Ignorance, wrong, evil, and so on, are not the opposites of those mentioned above, and were not created with the soul like the others. They are merely the absence of the positive qualities mentioned before, as darkness is the absence of light. God did not create any defect, nor did he desire it. Evil is simply the result of the incapacity of a given thing to receive a particular good. If all things were capable of receiving goods equally, all things would be one thing, and the Creator and his creatures would be likewise one. This was not God's purpose.

There is a tacit opposition to the Mutakallimun in Ibn Zaddik's arguments against the view that the soul is an accident, as well as in his statement in the preceding paragraph that the bad qualities and evil generally are not opposites of the good qualities and good respectively, but that they are merely privations, absences, and hence not created by God. This is a Neo-Platonic doctrine. Pseudo-Bahya, we have seen (p. 108 f.), and Abraham bar Hiyya (p. 123 f.) adopt the Kalamistic view in the latter point, and solve the problem of evil differently.

The function of the rational soul is knowledge. The rational soul investigates the unknown and comprehends it. It derives general rules, makes premises and infers one thing from another. Man alone has this privilege. It is in virtue of the rational soul that we have been given commandments and prohibitions, and become liable to reward and punishment. Brute animals have no commandments, because they have no reason. The soul has reason only potentially, and man makes it actual by study. If the reason were actual originally in the soul, there would be no difference between the soul's condition in its own world and in this one; and the purpose of man, which is that he may learn in order to choose the right way and win salvation, would have no meaning.

The existence of many individual souls, all of which have the soul character in common, shows that there is a universal soul by virtue of which all the particular souls exist. This division of the universal soul into many individual souls is not really a division of the former in its essence, which remains one and indivisible. It is the bodies which receive the influence of the universal soul, as vessels in the sun receive its light according to their purity. Hence the existence of justice and evil, righteousness and wrong. This does not, however, mean to say that the reception of these qualities is independent of a man's choice. Man is free to choose, and hence he deserves praise and blame, reward and punishment.

The rational soul is destined for the spiritual world, which is a pure and perfect world, made by God directly without an intermediate agency. It is not subject to change or defect or need. God alone created this spiritual world to show his goodness and power, and not because he needed it. The world is not like God, though God is its cause. It is not eternal *a parte ante*, having been made out of nothing by God; but it will continue to exist forever, for it cannot be more perfect than it is. It is simple and spiritual. This applies also to the heavenly spheres and their stars.

Man is obliged to reason and investigate, as all nations do according to the measure of their capacities. No animal reasons because it has not the requisite faculty. But if man should neglect to exercise the power given him, he would lose the benefit coming therefrom and the purpose of his existence. There would then be no difference between him and the beast.

The first requisite for study and investigation is to deaden the animal desires. Then with the reason as a guide and his body as a model, man acquires the knowledge of the corporeal world. From his rational soul he comes to the knowledge of the existence of a spiritual world. Finally he will learn to know the Creator, who is the only real existent, for nothing can be said truly to exist, which at one time did not exist, or which at some time will cease to exist. When a man neglects this privilege which is his of using his reason, he forfeits the name man, and descends below the station of the beast, for the latter never falls below its animal nature.

It is very important to study the knowledge of God, for it is the highest knowledge and the cause of human perfection. The prophets are full of recommendations in this regard. Jeremiah says (31, 33), "They shall all know me, from the least of them even unto their greatest." Amos (5, 6) bids us "Seek for the Lord and you shall live." Hosea likewise (6, 3) recommends that "We may feel it, and strive to know the Lord." [173]

The first loss a man suffers who does not study and investigate is that he does not understand the real existence of God, and imagines he is worshipping a body. Some think God is light. But this is as bad as to regard him body. For light is an accident in a shining body, as is proved by the fact that the air receives the light of the sun, and later it receives the shadow and becomes dark. And yet these people are not the worst by any means, for there are others who do not trouble to concentrate their minds on God, and occupy their thoughts solely with the business and the pleasures of this world. These people we do not discuss at all. We are arguing against those who imagine they are wise men and students of the Kalam. In fact they are ignorant persons, and do not know what logic is and how it is to be used.

Before giving our own views of the nature and existence of God, we must refute the objectionable doctrines of these people. Joseph al-Basir in a work of his called "Mansuri" casts it up to the Rabbanites that in believing that God descends and ascends they are not true worshippers of God. But he forgets that his own doctrines are no better. Anyone who believes that God created with a newly created will and rejects by means of a newly created rejection has never truly served God or known him. Just as objectionable is their view that God is living but not with life residing in a subject, powerful but not with power, and so on. We shall take up each of these in turn.

The Mutakallimun refuse to believe that God's will is eternal, for fear of having a second eternal beside God. And so they say that whenever God wills, he creates a will for the purpose, and whenever he rejects anything he creates a " rejection " with which the objectionable thing is rejected. But this leads them to a worse predicament than the one from which they wish to escape, as we shall see. If God cannot create anything without having a will as the instrument in creating, and for this reason must first create a will for the purpose —how did he create this will? He must have had another will to create this will, and a third will to create the second, and so on *ad infinitum*, which is absurd. If he created the first will without the help of another will, why not create the things he wanted outright without any will? Besides, in making God will at a given time after a state of not willing, they introduce change in God.

As for the other dictum, that God is "living but not with life," "powerful but not with power," "knowing but not with knowledge," and so on; what do they mean by this circumlocution? If they say "living" to indicate that he is not dead, and add "but not with life," so as to prevent a comparison of him with other living things, why not say also, "He is body, but not like other bodies"? If the objection to calling him body is that body is composite, and what is composite must have been composed by someone and is not eternal, the same objection applies to "living." For "living" implies "breathing" and "possessed of sensation," hence also composite and created. If they reply, we mean life peculiar to him, we say why not also body peculiar to him? You see these people entangle themselves in their own sophisms, because they do not know what demonstration means.[174]

Having disposed of the errors of the Mutakallimun, we must now present our own method of investigation into the nature of God. To know a thing, we investigate its four causes—material, formal, efficient and final. What has no cause but is the cause of all things, cannot be known in this way. Still it is not altogether unknowable for this reason. Its essence cannot be known, but it may be known through its activities, or rather effects, which suggest attributes. We cannot therefore know concerning God *what* he is, nor *how* he is, nor *on account of what*, nor *of what kind*, nor *where*, nor *when*. For these can apply only to a created thing having a cause. But we can ask concerning him, *whether* he is; and this can best be known from his deeds.

We observe the things of the world and find that they are all composed of substance and accident, as we saw before (p. 131). These are correlative, and one cannot exist without the other. Hence neither precedes the other. But accident is "new" (*i. e.*, not eternal), hence so is substance. That accident is new is proved from the fact that rest succeeds motion and motion succeeds rest, hence accidents constantly come and go and are newly created.

Now if substance and accident are both new there must be something that brought them into being unless they bring themselves into being. But the latter is impossible, for the agent must either exist when it brings itself into being, or not. If it exists it is already there; if it does not exist, it is nothing, and nothing cannot do anything. Hence there must be a being that brought the world into existence. This is God.

God is one, for the cause of the many must be the one. If the cause of the many is the many, then the cause of the second many is a third many, and so on *ad infinitum;* hence we must stop with the one. God is to the world as unity is to number. Unity is the basis of number without being included in number, and it embraces number on all sides. It is the foundation of number; for if you remove unity, you remove number; but the removal of number does not remove unity. The one surrounds number on all sides; for the beginning of number is the one, and it is also the middle of number and the end thereof. For number is nothing but an aggregate of ones. Besides, number is composed of odds and evens, and one is the cause of odd as well as even.

If there were two eternal beings, they would either coincide in all respects, and they would be one and not two. Or they would differ. In the latter case, the world is either the work of both or of one only.

If of both, they are not omnipotent, and hence not eternal. If of one only, then the other does not count, since he is not eternal, and there is only one.

By saying God is one we do not mean that he comes under the category of quantity, for quantity is an accident residing in a substance, and all substance is "new." What we mean is that the essence of God is true unity, not numerical unity. For numerical unity is also in a sense multiplicity, and is capable of multiplication and division. God's unity is alone separate and one in all respects.

God is not like any of his creatures. For if he were, he would be possessed of quality, since it is in virtue of quality that a thing is said to be like another, and quality is an accident contained in a substance.

God is self-sufficient and not in need of anything. For if he needed anything at all, it would be first of all the one who created him and made him an existent thing. But this is absurd, since God is eternal. We might suppose that he needs the world, which he created for some purpose, as we sometimes make things to assist us. But this, too, is impossible. For if he were dependent upon the world for anything, he could not create it. It is different with us. We do not create things; we only modify matter already existing.

Again, if God created the world for his own benefit, then either he was always in need of the world, or the need arose at the time of creating. If he was always in need of the world, it would have existed with him from eternity, but we have already proved that the world is not eternal. If the need arose in him at the time of creation, as heat arises in a body after cold, or motion after rest, then he is like created things, and is himself "new" and not eternal. To say the need was always there, and yet he did not create it until the time he did would be to ascribe inability to God of creating the world before he did, which is absurd. For one who is unable at any given time, cannot create at all. It remains then that he does not need anything, and that he created the world by reason of his goodness and generosity and nothing else.

The question of God's will is difficult. The problem is this. If God's will is eternal and unchanging, and he created the world with his will, the world is eternal. If we say, as we must, that he created the world after a condition of non-creation, we introduce a change in God, a something newly created in him, namely, the will to create, which did not exist before. This is a dilemma. My own view is that since God's creating activity is his essence, and his essence is infinite and eternal, we cannot say he created *after* a condition of non-creation, or that he willed *after* a condition of non-willing, or that he was formerly not able. And yet we do not mean that the world is eternal. It was created a definite length of time before our time. The solution of the problem is that time itself was created with the world; for time is the measure of motion of the celestial sphere, and if there are no spheres there is no time, and no before and after. Hence it does not follow because the world is not eternal that *before* its creation God did not create. There is no *before* when the world is not.

We objected to the view of the Mutakallimun (p. 142), who speak of God creating a will on the ground that if he can create a will directly he can create the world instead. Our opinion is therefore that God's will is eternal and not newly created, for the latter view introduces creation in God. There is still the difficulty of the precise relation of the will to God. If it is different from God we have two eternals, and if it is the same as God in all respects, he changes when he creates. My answer is, it is not different from God in any sense, and there is no changing attribute in God. But there is a subtle mystery in this matter, which it is not proper to reveal, and this is not the place to explain it. The interested reader is referred to the book of Empedocles and other works of the wise men treating of this subject (*cf.* above, p. 64).

God created the world out of nothing, and not out of a pre-existent matter. For if the matter of the world is eternal like God, there is no more reason for supposing that God formed a world out of it than that it formed a world out of God.

The world is perfect. For we have repeatedly shown that its creation is due entirely to God's goodness. If then it were not perfect, this would argue in God either ignorance or niggardliness or weakness.[175]

Most of the ancients avoided giving God attributes for fear of making him the bearer of qualities, which would introduce plurality and composition in his essence. The proper view, however, is this. As

God's essence is different from all other essences, so are his attributes
different from all other attributes. His attributes are not different
from him; his knowledge and his truth and his power are his essence.
The way man arrives at the divine attributes is this. Men have
examined his works and learned from them God's existence. They
then reflected on this existent and found that he was not weak; so
they called him strong. They found his works perfect, and they called
him wise. They perceived that he was self-sufficient, without need
of anything, and hence without any motives for doing wrong. Hence
they called him righteous. And so on with the other attributes. All
this they did in order that people may learn from him and imitate
his ways. But we must not forget that all these expressions of God's
attributes are figurative. No one must suppose that if we do not
say he has life, it means he is dead. What we mean is that we cannot
apply the term living to God literally, in the sense in which we apply
it to other living things. When the Bible does speak of God as alive
and living, the meaning is that he exists forever. The philosopher
is right when he says that it is more proper to apply negative attributes to God than positive.[176]

Taking a glance at Ibn Zaddik's theology just discussed in its essential outlines, we notice that while he opposes vigorously certain
aspects of Kalamistic thought, as he found them in al-Basir, the
Karaite, his own method and doctrine are not far removed from the
Kalam. His proof of the creation of the world from its composite
character (substance and accident) is the same as one of Saadia,
which Maimonides cites as a Kalamistic proof. We have already
spoken of the fact that the method of basing one's theology upon the
creation of the world is one that is distinctive of the Kalam, as Maimonides himself tells us. And this method is common to Saadia,
Bahya and Ibn Zaddik. In his discussion of the attributes Ibn Zaddik
offers little if anything that is new. His attitude is that in the literal and positive sense no attribute can be applied to God. We can
speak of God negatively without running the risk of misunderstanding.
But the moment we say anything positive we do become thus liable
to comparing God with other things; and such circumlocutions as
the Kalamistic "Living without life," and so on, do not help matters,
for they are contradictory, and take away with one hand what they

give with the other. The Biblical expressions must be taken figuratively; and the most important point to remember is that God's essence cannot be known at all. The manner in which we arrive at the divine attributes is by transferring them from God's effects in nature to his own essence. All this we have already found in Bahya much better expressed, and Bahya is also without doubt the source of Ibn Zaddik's discussion of God's unity.

We must now review briefly the practical part of Ibn Zaddik's philosophy as it is found in the fourth part of the "Microcosm." In the manner of Bahya he points out the importance of divine service and obedience to the commandments of God, viewing man's duties to his maker as an expression of gratitude, which everyone owes to his benefactor. Like Bahya he compares God's benefactions with those of one man to another to show the infinite superiority of the former, and the greater duty which follows therefrom.

The commandments which God gave us like the act of our creation are for our own good, that we may enjoy true happiness in the world to come. As it would not be proper to reward a person for what he has not done, God gave man commandments. The righteous as well as the wicked are free to determine their own conduct, hence reward and punishment are just.

Like Saadia and Bahya before him, Ibn Zaddik makes use of the distinction (or rather takes it for granted) between rational and traditional commandments; pointing out that the latter also have a cause and explanation in the mind of God even though we may not know it. In some cases we can see the explanation ourselves. Take for instance the observance of the Sabbath. Its rational signification is two-fold. It teaches us that the world was created, and hence has a Creator whom we worship. And in the second place the Sabbath symbolizes the future world. As one has nothing to eat on the Sabbath day unless he has prepared food the day before, so the enjoyment of the future world depends upon spiritual preparation in this world.

In his conduct a man must imitate God's actions by doing good and mercy and kindness. Without the knowledge of God a person's good deeds are of no account and no better than the work of idolaters. In fact it is not possible to do good deeds without a knowledge of God, for he is the source of all good, and there is no true good without him.

When a fool is seen with good qualities such as mercy and benevolence, they are due to the weakness of his animal soul, the spirited part of his nature.   Similarly if this fool abstains from pleasures, it is because of the weakness of his appetitive soul.

Thus we see that knowledge comes first in importance; for knowledge leads to practice, and practice brings reward in the world to come.   As the purpose of man's creation is that he may enjoy the future life, wisdom or knowledge is the first requisite to this great end.

The four principal qualities constituting goodness or virtue are (1) knowledge of God's attributes; (2) righteousness or justice; (3) hope; (4) humility. All other good qualities are derived from these. Jeremiah names some of them when he says (9, 23), "I am the Lord who exercise kindness, justice and righteousness on the earth; for in these things I delight, saith the Lord."   Similarly Zephaniah (2, 3) bids us, "Seek ye the Lord, all ye meek of the earth, who have fulfilled his ordinances; seek righteousness, seek meekness."

The four qualities of wisdom or knowledge, righteousness, hope and humility are without doubt modified descendants of the four Platonic virtues, wisdom, courage, temperance and justice, which we still find in their original form and in their Platonic derivation and psychological origin in Pseudo-Bahya (*cf.* above p. 111).

Reward and punishment of the real kind, Ibn Zaddik thinks, are not in this world but in the next. In this way he accounts for the fact of the prosperity of the wicked and the sufferings of the righteous. Another proof that this world cannot be the place of final reward and punishment is that pleasure in this world is not a real good, but only a temporary respite from disease. Pain and pleasure are correlative, as we saw before (p. 136). In fact pleasure is not a good at all; for if it were, then the greater the pleasure, the greater the good, which is not true. Reward in the next world is not a corporeal pleasure at all.

The evil which happens to the righteous in this world is often a natural occurrence without reference to reward and punishment, and may be compared to the natural pleasures which men derive from the sense of sight and the other senses, and which have nothing to do with reward and punishment. Sometimes, too, this evil is inflicted upon the good man to forgive his sins. Real reward and punishment are in the future life, and as that life is spiritual, the reward as well as the punishment is timeless.

The Mutakallimun think that animals and little children are also rewarded in the next world for ill treatment, suffering and death which are inflicted upon them in this world. So we find in Joseph al Basir's Mansuri. But this is absurd. If the killing of animals is a wrong, God would not have commanded us to do it, any more than he ordered us to kill human beings in order that he may reward them later. Moreover, we should then deserve punishment for killing animals if that is wrong, and there would follow the absurdity that God commanded us to do that for which we deserve punishment. Besides, if the animals deserve reward and punishment, they should have been given commandments and laws like ourselves. If this was not done because animals are not rational, reward and punishment are equally out of place for the same reason.

When the soul leaves the body in death, if she exercised her reason in the pursuit of knowledge, she will continue her existence forever in the upper world. This is her happiness, her reward and her paradise, namely, to cleave to her own world, and to shine with the true light emanating from God directly. This is the end of the human soul. But if she did not exercise her reason and did not pursue right conduct, she will not be able to return to the spiritual world, for she will have lost her own spirituality. She will be similar to the body, desiring this world and its pleasures. Her fate will be to revolve forever with the sphere in the world of fire, without being able to return to her world. Thus she will be forever in pain, and homeless.

When the Messiah comes, the pious men of our nation, the Prophets, the Patriarchs and those who died for the sanctification of the name, *i. e.*, the martyrs, will be brought back to life in the body, and will never die again. There will be no eating and drinking, but they will live like Moses on the mountain basking in the divine light. The wicked will also be joined to their bodies and burned with fire.[177]

CHAPTER X

JUDAH HALEVI

In Judah Halevi the poet got the better of the rationalist. Not that Judah Halevi was not familiar with philosophical thinking and did not absorb the current philosophical terminology as well as the ideas contained therein. Quite the contrary. He shows a better knowledge of Aristotelian ideas than his predecessors, and is well versed in Neo-Platonism. While he attacks all those views of philosophers which are inconsistent to his mind with the religion of Judaism, he speaks in other respects the philosophic language, and even makes concessions to the philosophers. If the reason should really demand it, he tells us, one might adopt the doctrine of the eternity of matter without doing any harm to the essence of Judaism.[178] As for the claims of reason to rule our beliefs, he similarly admits that that which is really proved in the same absolute manner as the propositions in mathematics and logic cannot be controverted. But this opinion need cause one no difficulty as there is nothing in the Bible which opposes the unequivocal demands of the reason.[179] He cannot consistently oppose all philosophy and science, for he maintains that the sciences were originally in the hands of the Jews, and that it was from them that the Chaldeans borrowed them and handed them over to the Persians, who in turn transferred them to Greece and Rome, their origin being forgotten.[180] At the same time he insists that philosophy and reason are not adequate means for the solution of all problems, and that the actual solutions as found in the writings of the Aristotelians of his day are in many cases devoid of all demonstrative value. Then there are certain matters in theory as well as in practice which do not at all come within the domain of reason, and the philosophers are bound to be wrong because they apply the wrong method. Revelation alone can make us wise as to certain aspects of God's nature and as to certain details in human conduct; and in these philosophy must fail because as philosophy it has no revelation. With all due respect therefore to the philosophers, who are the most reliable guides in matters not conflicting with revelation, we must leave them if we wish to learn the truth concerning those matters in which they are incompetent to judge.

This characterization of Judah Halevi's attitude is brief and inadequate. But before proceeding to elaborate it with more detail and greater concreteness, it will be well to sketch very briefly the little we know of his life.[181]

Judah Halevi was born in Toledo in the last quarter of the eleventh century. This is about the time when the city was taken from the Mohammedans by the emperor Alphonso VI, king of Leon, Castile, Galicia and Navarre. At the same time Toledo remained Arabic in culture and language for a long while after this, and even exerted a great influence upon the civilization of Christendom. The Jews were equally well treated in Toledo by Mohammedan emir and Christian king. The youth of Halevi was therefore not embittered or saddened by Jewish persecutions. It seems that he was sent to Lucena, a Jewish centre, where he studied the Talmud with the famous Alfasi, and made friends with Joseph ibn Migash, Alfasi's successor, and Baruh Albalia, the philosopher. A poet by nature, he began to write Hebrew verses early, and soon became famous as a poet of the first order in no manner inferior to Gabirol. His living he made not from his verses, but like many others of his day by practicing the art of medicine. Later in life he visited Cordova, already in its decline through the illiberal government of the Almoravid dynasty. The rulers were strict religionists, implicit followers of the "fukaha," the men devoted to the study of Mohammedan religion and law; and scientific learning and philosophy were proscribed in their domains. Men of another faith were not in favor, and the Jews who, unlike the Christians, had no powerful emperor anywhere to take their part, had to buy their lives and comparative freedom with their hard earned wealth. Here Halevi spent some time as a physician. He was admitted in court circles, but his personal good fortune could not reconcile him to the sufferings of his brethren, and his letters give expression to his dissatisfaction. He wrote a variety of poems on subjects secular and religious; but what made him famous above all else was his strong nationalism, and those of his poems will live longest which give expression to his intense love for his people and the land which was once their own. That it was not mere sentiment with Judah Halevi he proved late in life when he decided to leave his many friends and his birthplace and go to Palestine to end his life on the soil of his ancestors. It was after 1140 that he left Spain for the East. Unfavorable winds drove him out of course to Egypt, and he landed at Alexandria. From there he went to Cairo at the invitation of his admirers and friends. Everywhere he was received with great honor, his fame preceding him, and he was urged to remain in Egypt. But no dissuasion could keep him from his pious resolve. We find him later in Damietta; we follow him to Tyre and Damascus, but beyond the last city all trace of him is lost. We know not whether he reached Jerusalem or not. Legend picks up the thread where history drops it, and tells of Judah Halevi meeting his death at the gates of the holy city as with tears he was singing his famous ode to Zion. An Arab horseman, the story goes, pierced him through with his spear.

This sketch of Halevi's life and character, brief and inadequate as it is, will prepare us to understand better his attitude to philosophy and to Judaism. His was not a critical intellect whose curiosity is not satisfied until the matter in dispute is proved in logical form. Reason is good enough in mathematics and physics where the objects of our investigation are accessible to us and the knowledge of their nature exhausts their significance. It is not so with the truths of Judaism and the nature of God. These cannot be known adequately by the reason alone, and mere knowledge is not enough. God and the Jewish religion are not simply facts to be known and understood like the laws of science. They are living entities to be acquainted with, to be devoted to, to love. Hence quite a different way of approach is necessary. And not everyone has access to this way. The method of acquaintance is open only to those who by birth and tradition belong to the family of the prophets, who had a personal knowledge of God, and to the land of Palestine where God revealed himself.[182]

We see here the nationalist speaking, the lover of his people and of their land and language and institutions. David Kaufmann has shown that Judah Halevi's anti-philosophical attitude has much in common with that of the great Arab writer Al Gazali, from whom there is no doubt that he borrowed his inspiration.[183]   Gazali began as a philosopher, then lost confidence in the logical method of proof, pointed to the contradictions of the philosophers, to their disagreements among themselves, and went over to the Sufis, the pietists and mystics of the Mohammedan faith.   There are a number of resemblances between Gazali and Halevi as Kaufmann has shown, and there is no doubt that skepticism in respect of the powers of the human reason on the one hand, and a deep religious sense on the other are responsible for the point of view of Gazali as well as Halevi.   But there is this additional motive in Halevi that he was defending a persecuted race and a despised faith against not merely the philosophers but against the more powerful and more fortunate professors of other religions.   He is the loyal son of his race and his religion, and he will show that they are above all criticism, that they are the best and the truest there are.   Maimonides, too, found it necessary to defend Judaism against the attacks of philosophy.   But in his case it was the Jew in him who had to be defended against the philosopher in him.   It was no external enemy but an internal who must be made harmless, and the method was one of reconciliation and harmonization.   It is still truer to say that with Maimonides both Judaism and philosophy were his friends, neither was an enemy.   He was attached to one quite as much as to the other.   And it was his privilege to reconcile their differences, to the great gain, as he thought, of both.   Judah Halevi takes the stand of one who fights for his hearth and home against the attacks of foreign foes.   He will not yield an inch to the adversary.   He will maintain his own.   The enemy cannot approach.

Thus Halevi begins his famous work "Kusari": "I was asked what I have to say in answer to the arguments of philosophers, unbelievers and professors of other religions against our own."   Instead of working out his ideas systematically, he wanted to give his subject dramatic interest by clothing it in dialogue form.   And he was fortunate in finding a historical event which suited his purpose admirably.

Some three or four centuries before his time, the king of the Chazars, a people of Turkish origin living in the Caucasus, together with his courtiers and many of his subjects embraced Judaism.   Hasdai ibn Shaprut, the Jewish minister and patron of learning of Cordova, in the tenth century corresponded with the then king of the Chazars, and received an account of the circumstances of the conversion. In brief it was that the king wishing to know which was the true religion invited representatives of the three dominant creeds, Judaism, Christianity and Mohammedanism, and questioned them concerning the tenets of their respective faiths. Seeing that the Christian as well as the Mohammedan appealed in their arguments to the truth of the Hebrew Bible, the king concluded that Judaism must be the true religion, which he accordingly adopted. This story gave Halevi the background and framework for his composition. He works out his own ideas in the form of a dialogue between the Jewish Rabbi and the king of the Chazars, in which the former explains to the king the essentials of the Jewish religion, and answers the king's questions and criticisms, taking occasion to discuss a variety of topics, religious, philosophical and scientific, all tending to show the truth of Judaism and its superiority to other religions, to philosophy, Kalam, and also to Karaism.

The story is, Halevi tells us, in the introduction to his book, that the king of the Chazars had repeated dreams in which an angel said to him, "Your intentions are acceptable to God, but not your practice." His endeavors to be faithful to his religion, and to take part in the services and perform the sacrifices in the temple in person only led to the repetition of the dream. He therefore consulted a philosopher about his belief, and the latter said to him, "In God there is neither favor nor hatred, for he is above all desire and purpose. Purpose and intention argue defect and want, which the fulfilment of the intention satisfies. But God is free from want. Hence there is no purpose or intention in his nature.

"God does not know the particular or individual, for the individual constantly changes, whereas God's knowledge never changes. Hence God does not know the individual man and, needless to say, he does not hear his prayer. When the philosophers say God created man, they use the word created metaphorically, in the sense that God is the cause of all causes, but not that he made man with purpose and intention.

"The world is eternal, and so is the existence of man. The character and ability of a person depend upon the causes antecedent to him. If these are of the right sort, we have a person who has the potentialities of a philosopher. To realize them he must develop his intellect by study, and his character through moral discipline. Then he will receive the influence of the 'Active Intellect,' with which he becomes identified so that his limbs and faculties do only what is right, and are wholly in the service of the active Intellect.

"This union with the active Intellect is the highest goal of man; and he becomes like one of the angels, and joins the ranks of Hermes, Æsculapius, Socrates, Plato, Aristotle. This is the meaning of the expression 'favor of God.' The important thing is to study the sciences in order to know the truth, and to practice the ethical virtues. If one does this, it matters not what religion he professes, or whether he professes any religion at all. He can make his own religion in order to discipline himself in humility, and to govern his relations to society and country. Or he can choose one of the philosophical religions. Purity of heart is the important thing, and knowledge of the sciences. Then the desired result will come, namely, union with the active intellect, which may also result in the power of prophecy through true dreams and visions."

The king was not satisfied with the statement of the philosopher, which seemed to him inadequate because he felt that he himself had the necessary purity of heart, and yet he was told that his practice was not satisfactory, proving that there is something in practice as such apart from intention. Besides, the great conflict between Christianity and Islam, who kill one another, is due to the difference in religious practice, and not in purity of heart. Moreover, if the view of the philosophers were true, there should be prophecy among them, whereas in reality prophecy is found among those who did not study the sciences rather than among those who did.

The king then said, I will ask the Christians and the Mohammedans. I need not inquire of the Jews, for their low condition is sufficient proof that the truth cannot be with them. So he sent for a Christian sage, who explained to him the essentials of his belief, saying among other things, We believe in the creation of the world in six days, in the descent of all men from Adam, in revelation and Providence, in short, in all that is found in the law of Moses and in the other Israelitish Scriptures, which cannot be doubted because of the publicity which was given to the events recorded therein. He also quoted the words of the gospel, I did not come to destroy any of the commandments of Israel and of Moses their teacher; I came to confirm them.

The king was not convinced by the Christian belief, and called a Mohammedan doctor, who in describing the specific tenets of Mohammedanism also mentioned the fact that in the Koran are quoted the Pentateuch and Moses and the other leaders, and the wonderful things they did. These, he said, cannot be denied; for they are well known.

Seeing that both Christian and Mohammedan referred to the law of Moses as true, and as evidence that God spoke to man, the king determined to call a Jewish sage also, and hear what he had to say.

The Jewish "Haber," as Judah Halevi calls him, began his discourse by saying, We Jews believe in the God of Abraham, Isaac and Jacob, who took the children of Israel out of Egypt, supported them in the wilderness, gave them the land of Canaan, and so on.

The king was disappointed and said, I had determined not to consult the Jews in this matter at all, because their abject condition in the world did not leave them any good quality. You should have said, he told the Jew, that you believe in him who created the world and governs it; who made man and provides for him. Every religionist defends his belief in this way.

The Jew replied, The religion to which you refer is a rational religion, established by speculation and argument, which are full of doubt, and about which there is no agreement among philosophers, because not all the arguments are valid or even plausible. This pleased the king, and he expressed a wish to continue the discourse. The Rabbi then said, The proper way to define one's religion is by reference to that which is more certain, namely, actual experience. Jews have this actual experience. The God of Abraham, Isaac and Jacob spoke to Moses and delivered the Israelites out of Egypt. This is well known. God gave Israel the Torah. To be sure, all others not of Israel who accept the Law will be rewarded, but they cannot be equal to Israel. There is a peculiar relation between God and Israel in which the other peoples do not share. As the plant is distinguished from the mineral, the animal from the plant, and man from the irrational animal, so is the prophetic individual distinguished above other men. He constitutes a higher species. It is through him that the masses became aware of God's existence and care for them. It was he who told them things unknown to them; who gave them an account of the world's creation and its history. We count now forty-five hundred years from the creation. This was handed down from Adam through Seth and Enos to Noah, to Shem and Eber, to Abraham, Isaac and Jacob, to Moses, and finally to us. Moses came only four hundred years after Abraham in a world which was full of knowledge of heavenly and earthly things. It is impossible that he should have given them a false account of the division of languages and the relations of nations without being found out and exposed.

The philosophers, it is true, oppose us by maintaining that the world is eternal. But the philosophers are Greeks, descended from Japheth, who did not inherit either wisdom or Torah. Divine wisdom is found only in the family of Shem. The Greeks had philosophy among them only during the short time of their power. They borrowed it from the Persians, who had it in turn from the Chaldeans. But neither before nor after did they have any philosophers among them.

Aristotle, not having any inherited tradition concerning the origin of the world, endeavored to reason it all out of his own head. Eternity was just as hard to believe in as creation. But as he had no true and reliable tradition, his arguments in favor of eternity seemed to him to be the stronger. Had he lived among a people who had reliable traditions on the other side, he would have found arguments in favor of creation, which is more plausible than eternity. Real demonstration cannot be controverted; and there is nothing in the Bible which opposes what the reason unequivocally demands. But the matter of eternity or creation is very difficult. The arguments on one side are as good as those on the other. And tradition from Adam to Noah and Moses, which is better than argument, lends its additional weight to the doctrine of creation. If the believer in the Torah were obliged to hold that there is a primitive eternal matter from which the world was made, and that there were many worlds before this one, there would be no great harm, as long as he believes that this world is of recent origin and Adam was the first man.[184]

We see now the standpoint of Judah Halevi, for the "Haber" is of course his spokesman. Philosophy and independent reasoning on such difficult matters as God and creation are after all more or less guess work, and cannot be made the bases of religion except for those who have nothing better. The Jews fortunately have a surer foundation all their own. They have a genuine and indisputable tradition. History is the only true science and the source of truth; not speculation, which is subjective, and can be employed with equal plausibility in favor of opposite doctrines. True history and tradition in the case of the Jews goes back ultimately to first hand knowledge from the very source of all truth. The prophets of Israel constitute a higher species, as much superior to the ordinary man as the ordinary man is to the lower animal, and these prophets received their knowledge direct from God. In principle Judah Halevi agrees with the other Jewish philosophers that true reason cannot be controverted. He differs with them in the concrete application of this abstract principle. He has not the same respect as Maimonides for the actual achievements of the unaided human reason, and an infinitely greater respect for the traditional beliefs of Judaism and the Biblical expressions taken in their obvious meaning. Hence he does not feel the same neccessity as Maimonides to twist the meaning of Scriptural passages to make them agree with philosophical theories.

According to this view Judah Halevi does not find it necessary with the philosophers and the Mutakallimun painfully to prove the existence of God. The existence of the Jewish people and the facts of their wonderful history are more eloquent demonstrations than any that logic or metaphysics can muster. But more than this. The philosophical view of God is inadequate in more ways than one. It is inaccurate in content and incorrect in motive. In the first place, they lay a great deal of stress on nature as the principle by which objects move. If a stone naturally moves to the centre of the world, they say this is due to a cause called nature. And the tendency is to attribute intelligence and creative power to this new entity as an associate of God. This is misleading. The real Intelligence is God alone. It is true that the elements, and the sun and moon, and the stars exert certain influences, producing heat and cold, and various other effects in things material, by virtue of which these latter are prepared for the reception of higher forms. And there is no harm in calling these agencies Nature. But we must regard these as devoid of intelligence, and as mere effects of God's wisdom and purpose.[185]

The philosopher denies will in God on the ground that this would argue defect and want. This reduces God to an impersonal force. We Jews believe God has will. The word we use does not matter. I ask the philosopher what is it that makes the heavens revolve continually, and the outer sphere carry everything in uniform motion, the earth standing immovable in the centre? Call it what you please, will or command; it is the same thing that made the air shape itself to produce the sounds of the ten commandments which were heard, and that caused the characters to form on the Tables of Stone.[186]

The motive of the philosopher is also different from that of the believer. The philosopher seeks knowledge only. He desires to know God as he desires to know the exact position and form of the earth. Ignorance in respect to God is no more harmful in his mind than ignorance respecting a fact in nature. His main object is to have true knowledge in order to become like unto the Active Intellect and to be identified with it. As long as he is a philosopher it makes no difference to him what he believes in other respects and whether he observes the practices of religion or not.[187]

The true belief in God is different in scope and aim. What God is must be understood not by means of rational proofs, but by prophetic and spiritual insight. Rational proofs are misleading, and the heretics and unbelievers also use rational proofs—those for example who believe in two original causes, in the eternity of the world, or in the divinity of the sun and fire. The most subtle proofs are those used by the philosophers, and they maintain that God is not concerned about us, and pays no attention to our prayers and sacrifices; that the world is eternal. It is different with us, who heard his words, his commands and prohibitions, and felt his reward and his punishment. We have a proper name of God, Jhvh, representative of the communications he made to us, and we have a conviction that he created the world. The first was Adam, who knew God through actual communication and the creation of Eve from one of his ribs. Cain and Abel came next, then Noah and Abraham, Isaac and Jacob, and so on to Moses and the Prophets, who came after him. All these called him Jhvh by reason of their insight. The people who received the teaching of the Prophets, in whom they believed, also called him Jhvh, because he was in communication with men; and the select among them saw him through an intermediate agency, called variously, Form, Image, Cloud, Fire, Kingdom, Shekinah, Glory, Rainbow, and so on, proving that he spoke to them.[188]

As the sun's light penetrates different objects in varying degrees, for example, ruby and crystal receive the sun's light in the highest degree; clear air and water come next, then bright stones and polished surfaces, and last of all opaque substances like wood and earth, which the light does not penetrate at all; so we may conceive of different minds varying in the degree to which they attain a knowledge of God. Some arrive only as far as the knowledge of "Elohim," while others attain to a knowledge of Jhvh, which may be compared to the reception of the sun's light in ruby and crystal. These are the prophets in the land of Israel. The conception involved in the name "Elohim" no intelligent man denies; whereas many deny the conception of Jhvh, because prophecy is an unusual occurrence even among individuals, not to speak of a nation. That is why Pharaoh said (Exod. 5, 2), "I know not Jhvh." He knew "Elohim," but not Jhvh, that is a God who reveals himself to man. "Elohim" may be arrived at by reasoning; for the reason tells us that the world has a ruler; though the various classes of men differ as to details, the most plausible view being that of the philosophers. But the conception of Jhvh cannot be arrived at by reason. It requires that prophetic vision by which a person almost becomes a member of a new species, akin to angels. Then the doubts he formerly had about " Elohim " fall away, and he laughs at the arguments which led him to the conception of God and of unity. Now he becomes a devotee, who loves the object of his devotion, and is ready to give his life in his love for him, because of the great happiness he feels in being near to him, and the misery of being away from him. This is different from the philosopher, who sees in the worship of God only good ethics and truth, because he is greater than all other existing things; and in unbelief nothing more than the fault of choosing the untrue.[189]

Here there is clearly a touch of religious poetry and mysticism, which reveals to us Halevi's real attitude, and we have no difficulty in understanding his lack of sympathy with what seemed to him the shallow rationalism of the contemporaneous Aristotelian, who fancied in his conceit that with a few logical formulæ he could penetrate the mysteries of the divine, when in reality he was barely enabled to skim the surface; into the sanctuary he could never enter.

Though, as we have just seen, Halevi has a conception of God as a personal being, acting with purpose and will and, as we shall see more clearly later, standing in close personal relation to Israel and the land of Palestine, still he is very far from thinking of him anthropomorphically. In his discussion of the divine attributes he yields to none in removing from God any positive quality of those ascribed to him in the Bible. The various names or appellatives applied to God in Scripture, except the tetragrammaton, he divides, according to their signification, into three classes, *actional, relative, negative*. Such expressions as "making high," "making low," "making poor," almighty, strong, jealous, revengeful, gracious, merciful, and so on, do not denote, he says, feeling or emotion in God. They are ascribed to him because of his visible acts or effects in the world, which we judge on the analogy of our own acts. As a human being is prompted to remove the misery of a fellowman because he feels pity, we ascribe all instances of divine removal of misery from mankind to a similar feeling in God, and call him merciful. But this is only a figure of speech. God does remove misery, but the feeling of pity is foreign to him. We call therefore the attribute merciful and others like it actional, meaning that it is God's acts which suggest to us these appellations.

Another class of attributes found in the Bible embraces such expressions as blessed, exalted, holy, praised, and so on. These are called relative, because they are derived from the attitude of man to God. God is blessed because men bless him, and so with the rest. They do not denote any essential quality in God. And hence their number does not necessitate plurality in God. Finally we have such terms as living, one, first, last, and so on. These too do not denote God's positive essence, for in reality God cannot be said to be either living or dead. Life as we understand it denotes sensation and motion, which are not in God. If we do apply to God the term living, we do so in order to exclude its negative, dead. Living means not dead; one means not many; first means not having any cause antecedent to him; last means never ceasing to be. Hence we call these attributes negative.[190]

We see that Judah Halevi is at one with Bahya and Joseph ibn Zaddik in his understanding of the divine attributes. The slight difference in the mode of classification is not essential.

This God chose Israel and gave them the ten commandments in order to convince them that the Law originated from God and not from Moses. For they might have had a doubt in their minds, seeing that speech is a material thing, and believe that the origin of a law or religion is in the mind of a human being, which afterwards comes to be believed in as divine. For this reason God commanded the people to purify themselves and be ready for the third day, when they *all* heard the word of God, and were convinced that prophecy is not what the philosophers say it is—a natural result of man's reason identifying itself with the Active Intellect through the help of the imagination, which presents true visions in a dream—but a real communication from God. Not only did they hear the word of God, but they saw the writing of God on the Tables of Stone.

This does not mean that we believe in the corporeality of God; Heaven forbid, we do not even think of the soul of man as corporeal. But we cannot deny the things recorded, which are well known. Just as God created heaven and earth, not by means of material tools as a man does, but by his will, so he might have willed that the air should convey articulate sounds to the ear of Moses, and that letters should be formed on the Tables of Stone to convey to the people the ideas which he wanted them to know. They might have happened in a still more wonderful way than I have been able to conceive.

This may seem like an unwarranted magnifying of the virtues of our people. But in reality it is true that the chain of individuals from Adam to Moses and thereafter was a remarkable one of godly men. Adam was surely a godlike man since he was made by the hand of God and was not dependent on the inherited constitution of his parents, and on the food and climate he enjoyed in the years of his growth. He was made perfect as in the time of mature youth when a person is at his best, and was endowed with the best possible soul for man. Abel was his successor in excellence, also a godly man, and so down the line through Seth and Noah, and so on. There were many who were unworthy and they were excluded. But there was always one in every generation who inherited the distinguished qualities of the

Adam line. And even when, as in the case of Terah, the individual was unworthy in himself, he was important as being destined to give birth to a worthy son, who would carry on the tradition, like Abraham. Among Noah's sons, Shem was the select one, and he occupied the temperate regions of Palestine, whereas Japheth went north and Ham went south—regions not so favorable to the development of wisdom.[191]

The laws were all given directly to Moses with all their details so that there is no doubt about any of them. This was absolutely necessary, for had there been any detail left out, a doubt might arise respecting it which would destroy the whole spiritual structure of Judaism. This is not a matter which philosophical reasoning can think out for itself. As in the natural generation of plant and animal the complexity of elements and conditions is so great that a slight tilting of the balance in the wrong direction produces disease and death, so in the spiritual creation of Israel the ceremonies and the laws are all absolutely essential to the whole, whether we understand it or not, and none could be left to speculation. All were given to Moses.

Moses addressed himself to his own people only. You say it would have been better to call all mankind to the true religion. It would be better also perhaps that all animals should be rational. You have forgotten what I said about the select few that worthily succeeded Adam as the heart of the family to the exclusion of the other members, who are as the peel, until in the sons of Jacob all twelve were worthy, and from them Israel is descended. These remarkable men had divine qualities which made them a different species from ordinary men. They were aiming at the degree of the prophet, and many of them reached it by reason of their purity, holiness and proximity to the Prophets. For a prophet has a great influence on the one who associates with him. He converts the latter by awakening in him spirituality and a desire to attain that high degree which brings visible greatness and reward in the world to come, when the soul is separated from the senses and enjoys the heavenly light. We do not exclude anyone from the reward due him for his good works, but we give preference to those who are near to God, and we measure their reward in the next world by this standard. Our religion consists not merely in saying certain words, but in difficult practices and a line of conduct which bring us near to God. Outsiders too may attain to the grade of wise and pious men, but they cannot become equal to us and be prophets.[192]

Not only is Israel a select nation to whom alone prophecy is given as a gift, but Palestine is the most suitable place in the world for communion with God, as a certain spot may be best for planting certain things and for producing people of a particular character and temperament. All those who prophesied outside of Palestine did so with reference to Palestine. Abraham was not worthy of the divine covenant until he was in this land. Palestine was intended to be a guide for the whole world. The reason the second Temple did not last longer than it did is because the Babylonian exiles did not sufficiently love their fatherland and did not all return when the decree of Cyrus permitted them to do so.[193]

Israel is the heart among the nations. The heart is more sensitive than the rest of the body in disease as in health. It feels both more intensely. It is more liable to disease than the other organs, and on the other hand it becomes aware sooner of agencies dangerous to its health and endeavors to reject them or ward them off. So Israel is among the nations. Their responsibility is greater than that of other nations and they are sooner punished. "Only you have I loved out of all the families of the earth," says Amos (3, 2), "therefore will I visit upon you all your iniquities." On the other hand, God does not allow our sins to accumulate as he does with the other nations until they deserve destruction. "He pardons the iniquities of his people by causing them to pass away in due order." As the heart is affected by the other organs, so Israel suffers on account of their assimilation to the other nations. Israel suffers while the other nations are in peace. As the elements are for the sake of the minerals, the minerals for the sake of the plants, the plants for the sake of the animals, the animals for the sake of man, so is man for the sake of Israel, and Israel for the sake of the Prophets and the pious men. With the purification of Israel the world will be improved and brought nearer to God.[194]

Associated with Israel and Palestine as a third privilege and distinction is the Hebrew language. This is the original language which God spoke to Adam. The etymologies of Biblical names prove it. It was richer formerly, and has become impoverished in the course of time like the people using it. Nevertheless it still shows evidence of superiority to other languages in its system of accents which shows the proper expression in reading, and in its wonderful system of vowel changes producing euphony in expression and variation in meaning.[195]

The highest type of man, we have seen, is the Prophet, for whose sake Israel and the whole of humanity exists. He is the highest type because he alone has an immediate knowledge of Jhvh as distinguished from "Elohim," the concept of universal cause and power, which the philosopher also is able to attain. Jhvh signifies, as we have seen, the personal God who performs miracles and reveals himself to mankind through the prophet. We wish to know therefore how Judah Halevi conceives of the essence and process of prophetic inspiration. We are already aware that he is opposed to the philosophers who regard the power of prophecy as a natural gift possessed by the man of pure intellect and perfect power of imagination. To these Aristotelians, as we shall have occasion to see more clearly later, the human intellect is nothing more than an individualized reflection, if we may so term it, of the one universal intellect, which is—not God, but an intellectual substance wholly immaterial, some nine or ten degrees removed from the Godhead. It is called the Active Intellect, and its business is to govern the sublunar world of generation and decay. As pure thought the Active Intellect embraces as its content the entire sublunar world in essence. In fact it bestows the forms (in the Aristotelian sense) upon the things of this world, and hence has a timeless knowledge of all the world and its happenings. The individualized reflection of it in the human soul is held there so long as the person is alive, somewhat as a drop of water may hold the moon until it evaporates, and the reflection is reabsorbed in the one real moon. So it is the Active Intellect which is the cause of all conceptual knowledge in man through its individualizations, and into it every human intellect is reabsorbed when the individual dies. Some men share more, some less in the Active Intellect; and it is in everyone's power, within limits, to increase and purify his participation in the influence of the Active Intellect by study and rigorous ethical discipline. The prophet differs from the ordinary man and the philosopher in degree only, not in kind. His knowledge comes from the influence of the Active Intellect as does the knowledge of the philosopher. The difference is that in the prophet's case the imagination plays an important rôle and presents concrete visions instead of universal propositions, and the identification with the Active Intellect is much closer.

This conception of prophecy, which in its essentials, we shall see, was adopted by Abraham ibn Daud, Maimonides and Gersonides, naturally would not appeal to Judah Halevi. Prophecy is the prerogative of Israel and of Palestine. The philosophers have nothing to do with it. A mere philosopher has no more chance of entering the kingdom of prophecy than a camel of passing through the eye of a needle.* Have the philosophers ever produced prophets? And yet, if their explanation is correct, their ranks should abound in them. Prophecy is a supernatural power, and the influence comes from God. The prophet is a higher species of mortal. He is endowed with an internal eye, a hidden sense, which sees certain immaterial objects, as the external sense sees the physical objects. No one else sees those forms, but they are none the less real, for the whole species of prophetic persons testify to their existence. In ordinary perception we tell a real object from an illusion by appealing to the testimony of others. What appears to a single individual only may be an illusion. If all persons agree that the object is there, we conclude it is real. The same test holds of the prophetic visions. All prophets see them. Then the intellect of the prophet interprets the vision, as our intellect interprets the data of our senses. The latter give us not the essence of the sensible object, but the superficial accidents, such as color, shape, and so on. It is the work of the reason to refer these qualities to the essence of the object, as king, sun. The same holds true of the prophet. He sees a figure in the form of a king or a judge in the act of giving orders; and he knows that he has before him a being that is served and obeyed. Or he sees the form in the act of carrying baggage or girded for work; and he infers that he is dealing with a being that is meant for a servant. What these visions really were it is not in all cases possible to know with certainty. There is no doubt that the Prophets actually saw the hosts of heaven, the spirits of the spheres, in the form of man. The word angel in the Bible (Heb. Mal'ak) means messenger. What these messengers or angels were we cannot tell with certainty. They may have been specially created from the fine elementary bodies, or they belonged to the eternal angels, who may be

* This simile represents Halevi's thought. He does not use this expression.

the same as the spiritual beings of whom the philosophers speak. We can neither reject their view nor definitely accept it. Similarly the expression, "The Glory of Jhvh," may denote a fine body following the will of God and formed every time it has to appear to a prophet, or it may denote all the angels and spiritual beings, Throne and Chariot and Firmament, and Ofannim and Galgalim, and other eternal beings constituting, so to speak, the suite of God.

Even such phrases as, "They saw the God of Israel" (Exod. 24, 10), "He saw the form of Jhvh" (Num. 12, 8), the Rabbinic expression "Maase Merkaba" (work of the divine chariot, *cf*. above, p. xvi), and the later discussions concerning the "Measure of the divine stature" (Shi'ur Komah), must not be rejected. These visual images representative of God are calculated to inspire fear in the human soul, which the bare conception of the One, Omnipotent, and so on, cannot produce.[196]

As Judah Halevi is unwilling to yield to the philosophers and explain away the supernaturalism of prophecy, maintaining rather on the contrary that the supernatural character of the prophetic vision is an evidence of the superior nature of Israel as well as of their land and their language, so he insists on the inherent value of the ceremonial law, including sacrifices. To Saadia, and especially to Bahya and Maimonides, the test of value is rationality. The important laws of the Bible are those known as the rational commandments. The other class, the so-called traditional commandments, would also turn out to be rational if we knew the reason why they were commanded. And in default of exact knowledge it is the business of the philosopher to suggest reasons. Bahya lays the greatest stress upon the commandments of the heart, *i. e.*, upon the purity of motive and intention, upon those laws which concern feeling and belief rather than outward practice. Judah Halevi's attitude is different. If the only thing of importance in religion were intention and motive and moral sense, why should Christianity and Islam fight to the death, shedding untold human blood in defence of their religion. As far as ethical theory and practice are concerned there is no difference between them. Ceremonial practice is the only thing that separates them. And the king of the Chazars was told repeatedly in his dreams that his intentions were good but not his practice, his religious practice. To be sure the ethical law is important in any religion, but it is not peculiar to religion as such. It is a necessary condition of social life, without which no association is possible, not even that of a robber band. There is honesty even among thieves. Religion has its peculiar practices, and it is not sufficient for an Israelite to observe the rational commandments alone. When the Prophets inveigh against sacrifices; when Micah says (6, 8), "He hath shewed thee, O man, what is good; and what doth the Lord require of thee, but to do justly, and to love mercy, and to walk humbly with thy God," they mean that the ceremonies alone are not sufficient; but surely a man is not fully an Israelite if he neglects the ceremonial laws and observes only the rational commandments. We may not understand the value of the ceremonial laws, the meaning of the institution of sacrifices. But neither do we understand why the rational soul does not attach itself to a body except when the parts are arranged in a certain manner and the elements are mixed in a certain proportion, though the reason needs not food and drink for itself. God has arranged it so, that only under certain conditions shall a body receive the light of reason. So in the matter of sacrifices God has ordained that only when the details of the sacrificial and other ceremonies are minutely observed shall the nation enjoy his presence and care. In some cases the significance of certain observances is clearer than in others. Thus the various festivals are also symbolic of certain truths of history and the divine government of the world. The Sabbath leads to the belief in the exodus from Egypt and the creation of the world; and hence inculcates belief in God.[197]

In his views of ethics Judah Halevi is more human than Bahya, being opposed to all manner of asceticism. The law, he says, does not demand excess in any direction. Every power and faculty must be given its due. Our law commends fear, love and joy as means of worshipping God; so that fasting on a fast day does not bring a man nearer to God than eating and drinking and rejoicing on a feast day, provided all is done with a view to honoring God. A Jewish devotee is not one who separates himself from the world. On the contrary, he loves the world and a long life because thereby he wins a share in the world to come. Still his desire is to attain the degree of Enoch or Elijah, and to be fit for the association of angels. A man like this feels more at home when alone than in company of other people; for the higher beings are his company, and he misses them when people are around him. Philosophers also enjoy solitude in order to clarify their thoughts, and they are eager to meet disciples to discuss their problems with them. In our days it is difficult to reach the position of these rare men. In former times when the Shekinah rested in the Holy Land, and the nation was fit for prophecy, there were people who separated themselves from their neighbors and studied the law in purity and holiness in the company of men like them. These were the Sons of the Prophets. Nowadays when there is neither prophecy nor wisdom, a person who attempted to do this, though he be a pious man, would come to grief; for he would find neither prophets nor philosophers to keep him company; nor enough to keep his mind in that high state of exaltation needed for communion with God. Prayer alone is not sufficient, and soon becomes a habit without any influence on the soul. He would soon find that the natural powers and desires of the soul begin to assert themselves and he will regret his separation from mankind, thus getting farther away from God instead of coming nearer to him.

The right practice of the pious man at the present day is to give all the parts of the body their due and no more, without neglecting any of them; and to bring the lower powers and desires under the dominion of the higher; feeding the soul with things spiritual as the body with things material. He must keep himself constantly under guard and control, making special use of the times of prayer for self-examination, and striving to retain the influence of one prayer until the time comes for the next. He must also utilize the Sabbaths and the festivals and the Great Fast to keep himself in good spiritual trim. In addition he must observe all the commandments, traditional, rational, and those of the heart, and reflect on their meaning and on God's goodness and care.[198]

Judah Halevi has no doubt of the immortality of the soul and of reward and punishment after death, though the Bible does not dwell upon these matters with any degree of emphasis. Other religions, he admits, make greater promises of reward after death, whereas Judaism offers divine nearness through miracles and prophecy. Instead of saying, If you do thus and so, I will put you in gardens after death and give you pleasures, our Law says, I will be your God and you will be my people. Some of you will stand before me and will go up to heaven, walking among the angels; and my angels will walk among you, protecting you in your land, which is the holy land, not like the other nations, which are governed by nature. Surely, he exclaims, we who can boast of such things during life are more certain of the future world than those whose sole reliance is on promises of the hereafter. It would not be correct, the Rabbi says to the king of the Chazars, who was tempted to despise the Jews as well as their religion because of their material and political weakness, to judge of our destiny after death by our condition during life, in which we are inferior to all other people. For these very people, like the Christians and Mohammedans, glory in their founders, who were persecuted and despised, and not in the present power and luxury of the great kings. The Christians in particular worship the man who said, "Whosoever smiteth thee on thy right cheek, turn to him the other also. And if a man . . . take away thy coat, let him have thy cloak also" (Matth. 5, 39). Accordingly our worth is greater in the sight of God than if we were prosperous. It is true that not all of us accept our miserable condition with becoming humility. If we did, God would not keep us so long in misery. But after all there is reward awaiting our people for bearing the yoke of the exile voluntarily, when it would be an easy matter for any one of us to become a brother to our oppressors by the saying of one word.

Our wise men, too, have said a great deal about the pleasures and sufferings awaiting us in the next world, and in this also they surpass the wise men of other religions. The Bible, it is true, does not lay stress on this aspect of our belief; but so much is clear from the Bible also, that the spirit returns to God. There are also allusions to the immortality of the soul in the disappearance of Elijah, who did not die, and in the belief of his second coming. This appears also from the prayer of Balaam, "Let me die the death of the righteous, and may my last end be like his" (Num. 23, 10), and from the calling of Samuel from the dead. The idea of paradise (Gan Eden) is taken from the Torah, and Gehenna is a Hebrew word, the name of a valley near Jerusalem, where fire always burned, consuming unclean bones, carcases, and so on. There is nothing new in the later religions which is not already found in ours.[199]

An important ethical problem which Judah Halevi discusses more thoroughly than any of his predecessors is that of free will, which he defends against fatalistic determinism, and endeavors to reconcile with divine causality and foreknowledge. We have already seen (p. xxi) that this was one of the important theses of the Mu'tazilite Kalam. And there is no doubt that fatalism is opposed to Judaism. A fatalistic determinist denies the category of the contingent or possible. He says not merely that an event is determined by its proximate cause, he goes further and maintains that it is determined long in advance of any of its secondary causes by the will of God. It would follow then that there is no way of preventing an event thus predetermined. If we take pains to avoid a misfortune fated to come upon us, our very efforts may carry us toward it and land us in its clutches. Literature is full of stories illustrating this belief, as for example the story of Œdipus. Against this form of belief Judah Halevi vindicates the reality of the contingent or possible as opposed to the necessary. No one except the obstinate and perverse denies the possible or contingent. His preparations to meet and avoid that which he hopes and fears prove that he believes the thing amenable to pains and precautions. If he had not this belief, he would fold his hands in resignation, never taking the trouble to supply himself with arms to meet his enemy, or with water to quench his thirst. To be sure, we may argue that whether one prepare himself or omit to do so, the preparation or neglect is itself determined. But this is no longer the same position as that maintained at the outset. For we now admit that secondary causes do play a part in determining the result, whereas we denied it at first. The will is one of these secondary causes. Accordingly Judah Halevi divides all acts or events into four classes, divine, natural, accidental and voluntary. Strictly divine events are the direct results of the divine will without any intermediate cause. There is no way of preparing for or avoiding these; not, that is, physically; but it is possible to prepare oneself mentally and morally, namely, through the secrets of the Torah to him who knows them.

Natural events are produced by secondary causes, which bring the objects of nature to their perfection. These produce their effects regularly and uniformly, provided there is no hindrance on the part

of the other three causes. An example of natural events would be the
growth of a plant or animal under favorable conditions. Accidental
events are also produced by secondary causes, but they happen by
chance, not regularly and not as a result of purpose. Their causes
are not intended for the purpose of bringing perfection to their chance
effects. These too may be hindered by any one of the other three
causes. An example of a chance event might be death in war. The
secondary cause is the battle, but its purpose was not that this given
person might meet his death there, and not all men die in war.

Finally, voluntary acts are those caused by the will of man. It is
these that concern us most. We have already intimated that the human will is itself a secondary cause and has a rôle in determining its
effect. It is true that the will itself is caused by other higher causes
until we get to the first cause, but this does not form a *necessary* chain
of causation. Despite the continuous chain of causes antecedent to
a given volition the soul finding itself in front of a given plan is
free to choose either of the two alternatives. To say that a man's
speech is as necessary as the beating of his pulse contradicts experience.
We feel that we are masters of our speech and our silence. The fact
that we praise and blame and love and hate a person according to
his deliberate conduct is another proof of freedom. We do not blame
a natural or accidental cause. We do not blame a child or a person
asleep when they cause damage, because they did not do the damage
deliberately and with intention. If those who deny freedom are
consistent, they must either refrain from being angry with a person
who injures them deliberately, or they must say that anger and praise
and blame and love and hate are delusive powers put in our souls in
vain. Besides there would be no difference between the pious and the
disobedient, because both are doing that which they are by necessity
bound to do.

But there are certain strong objections to the doctrine of freedom.
If man is absolutely free to do or forbear, it follows that the effects
of his conduct are removed from God's control. The answer to this
is that they are not absolutely removed from his control. They are
still related to him by a chain of causes.

Another argument against free will is that it is irreconcilable with
God's knowledge. If man alone is the master of his choice, God cannot

know beforehand what he will choose. And if God does know, the man cannot but choose as God foreknew he would choose, and what becomes of his freedom? This may be answered by saying that the knowledge of a thing is not the cause of its being. We do not determine a past event by the fact that we know it. Knowledge is simply evidence that the thing is. So man chooses by his own determination, and yet God knows beforehand which way he is going to choose, simply because he sees into the future as we remember the past.[200]

Judah Halevi's discussion of the problem of freedom is fuller than any we have met so far in our investigation. But it is not satisfactory. Apart from his fourfold classification of events which is open to criticism, there is a weak spot in the very centre of his argument, which scarcely could have escaped him. He admits that the will is caused by higher causes ending ultimately in the will of God, and yet maintains in the same breath that the will is not determined. As free the will is removed from God's control, and yet it is not completely removed, being related to him by a chain of causes. This is a plain contradiction, unless we are told how far it is determined and how far it is not. Surely the aspect in which it is not determined is absolutely removed from God's control and altogether uncaused. But Judah Halevi is unwilling to grant this. He just leaves us with the juxtaposition of two incompatibles. We shall see that Hasdai Crescas was more consistent, and admitted determinism.

We have now considered Judah Halevi's teachings, and have seen that he has no sympathy with the point of view of those people who were called in his day philosophers, *i. e.*, those who adopted the teachings ascribed to Aristotle. At the same time he was interested in maintaining that all science really came originally from the Jews; and in order to prove this he undertakes a brief interpretation of the "Sefer Yezirah" (Book of Creation), an early mystic work of unknown authorship and date, which Judah Halevi in common with the uncritical opinion of his day attributed to Abraham.[201] Not to lay himself open to the charge of inconsistency, he throws out the suggestion that the Sefer Yezirah represented Abraham's own speculations before he had the privilege of a prophetic communication from God. When that came he was ready to abandon all his former rationalistic lucubrations and abide by the certainty of revealed truth.[202]

We may therefore legitimately infer that Judah Halevi's idea was that the Jews were the originators of philosophy, but that they had long discarded it in favor of something much more valid and certain; whereas the Greeks and their descendants, having nothing better, caught it up and are now parading it as their own discovery and even setting it up as superior to direct revelation.

Natural science in so far as it had to do with more or less verifiable data could not be considered harmful, and so we find Judah Halevi taking pains to show that the sages of Rabbinical literature cultivated the sciences, astronomy in connection with the Jewish calendar; anatomy, biology and physiology in relation to the laws of slaughter and the examination of animal meat (laws of "Terefa").[203]

But so great was the fascination philosophy exerted upon the men of his generation that even Judah Halevi, despite his efforts to shake its authority and point out its inadequacy and evident inferiority to revelation, was not able wholly to escape it. And we find accordingly that he deems it necessary to devote a large part of the fifth book of the Kusari to the presentation of a bird's eye view of the current philosophy of the day. To be sure, he does not give all of it the stamp of his approval; he repeatedly attacks its foundations and lays bare their weakness. At the same time he admits that not every man has faith by nature and is proof against the erroneous arguments of heretics, astrologers, philosophers and others. The ordinary mortal is affected by them, and may even be misled for a time until he comes to see the truth. It is therefore well to know the principles of religion according to those who defend it by reason, and this involves a knowledge of science and theology. But we must not, he says, in the manner of the Karaites, advance all at once to the higher study of theology. One must first understand the fundamental principles of physics, psychology, and so on, such as matter and form, the elements, nature, Soul, Intellect, Divine Wisdom. Then we can proceed to the more properly theological matters, like the future world, Providence, and so on.

Accordingly Judah Halevi gives us in the sequel a brief account such as he has just outlined. It will not be worth our while to reproduce it all here, as in the first place Judah Halevi does not give it as the result of his own investigation and conviction, and secondly a good deal of it is not new; and we have already met it in more or less similar form before in Joseph ibn Zaddik, Abraham bar Hiyyah, and others. We must point out, however, the new features which we did not meet before, explain their origin and in particular indicate Judah Halevi's criticisms.

In general we may say that Judah Halevi has a better knowledge of Aristotelian doctrines than any of his predecessors. Thus to take one example, which we used before (p. 138), Aristotle's famous definition of the soul is quoted by Isaac Israeli, Saadia, Joseph ibn Zaddik as well as by Judah Halevi. Israeli does not discuss the definition in detail.[204] Saadia and Ibn Zaddik show clearly that they did not understand the precise meaning of the definition. Judah Halevi is the first who understands correctly all the elements of the definition. And yet it would be decidedly mistaken to infer from this that Judah Halevi studied the Aristotelian works directly. By a fortunate discovery of S. Landauer [205] we are enabled to follow Judah Halevi's source with the certainty of eyewitnesses. The sketch which he gives of the Aristotelian psychology is taken bodily not from Aristotle's De Anima, but from a youthful work of Ibn Sina. Judah Halevi did not even take the trouble to present the subject in his own words. He simply took his model and abridged it, by throwing out all argumentative, illustrative and amplificatory material. Apart from this abridgment he follows his authority almost word for word, not to speak of reproducing the ideas in the original form and order. This is a typical and extremely instructive instance; and it shows how careful we must be before we decide that a mediæval writer read a certain author with whose ideas he is familiar and whom he quotes.

In the sketch of philosophical theory Judah Halevi first speaks of the hyle ($\H{v}\lambda\eta$) or formless matter, which according to the philosophers was in the beginning of things contained within the lunar sphere. The "water" in the second verse of Genesis ("and the spirit of God moved upon the face of the water") is supposed by them to denote this primitive matter, as the "darkness" in the same verse and the "chaos" ("Tohu") in the first verse signify the absence of form and composition in the matter (the Aristotelian $\sigma\tau\acute{\epsilon}\rho\eta\sigma\iota\varsigma$). God then willed the revolution of the outermost sphere, known as the diurnal sphere, which caused all the other spheres to revolve with it, thereby producing changes in the hyle in accordance with the motions of the sphere. The first change was the heating of that which was next to the lunar sphere and making it into pure fire, known among the philosophers as "natural fire," a pure, fine and light substance, without color or burning quality. This became the sphere of fire. The part that was further away changed as a result of the same revolution into the sphere of air, then came the sphere of water, and finally the terrestrial globe in the centre, heavy and thick by reason of its distance from the place of motion. From these four elements come the physical objects by composition. The forms (in the Aristotelian sense) of things are imposed upon their matters by a divine power, the "Intellect, and Giver of Forms"; whereas the matters come from the hyle, and the accidental proximity of different parts to the revolving lunar sphere explains why some parts became fire, some air, and so on.

To this mechanical explanation of the formation of the elements Judah Halevi objects. As long as the original motion of the diurnal sphere is admittedly due not to chance but to the will of God, what is gained by referring the formation of the elements to their accidental proximity to the moving sphere, and accounting for the production of mineral, plant and animal in the same mechanical way by the accidental composition of the four elements in proportions varying according to the different revolutions and positions of the heavenly bodies? Besides if the latter explanation were true, the number of species of plants and animals should be infinite like the various positions and formations of the heavenly bodies, whereas they are finite and constant. The argument from the design and purpose that is clearly visible in the majority of plants and animals further refutes such mechanical explanation as is attempted by the philosophers. Design is also visible in the violation of the natural law by which water should always be above and around earth; whereas in reality we see a great part of the earth's surface above water. This is clearly a beneficent provision in order that animal life may sustain itself, and this is the significance of the words of the Psalmist (136, 6), "To him that stretched out the earth above the waters."

The entire theory of the four elements and the alleged composition of all things out of them is a pure assumption. Take the idea of the world of fire, the upper fire as they call it, which is colorless, so as not to obstruct the color of the heavens and the stars. Whoever saw such a fire? The only fire we know is an extremely hot object in the shape of coal, or as a flame in the air, or as boiling water. And whoever saw a fiery or aëry body enter the matter of plant and animal so as to warrant us in saying that the latter are composed of the four elements? True, we know that water and earth do enter the matter of plants, and that they are assisted by the air and the heat of the sun in causing the plant to grow and develop, but we never see a fiery or aëry body. Or whoever saw plants resolved into the four elements? If a part changes into earth, it is not real earth, but ashes; and the part changed to water is not real water, but a kind of moisture, poisonous or nutritious, but not water fit for drinking. Similarly no part of the plant changes to real air fit for breathing, but to vapor or mist. Granted that we have to admit the warm and the cold, and the moist and the dry as the primary qualities without which no body can exist; and that the reason resolves the composite objects into these primary qualities, and posits substances as bearers of these qualities, which it calls fire, air, water and earth—this is true conceptually and theoretically only. It cannot be that the primary qualities really existed in the simple state *extra animam*, and then all existing things were made out of them. How can the philosophers maintain such a thing, since they believe in the eternity of the world, that it always existed as it does now?

These are the criticisms of their theory of the elements. According to the Torah God created the world just as it is, with its animals and plants already formed. There is no need of assuming intermediate powers or compositions. The moment we admit that the world was created out of nothing by the will of God in the manner in which he desired, all difficulties vanish about the origin of bodies and their association with souls. And there is no reason why we should not accept the firmament, and the waters above the heaven, and the demons mentioned by the Rabbis, and the account of the days of the Messiah and the resurrection and the world to come.[206]

Another theory he criticizes is that developed by Alfarabi and Avicenna, the chief Aristotelians of the Arabs before Averroes. It is a combination of Aristotelianism with the Neo-Platonic doctrine of emanation, though it was credited as a whole to Aristotle in the middle ages. We have already seen in the Introduction (p. xxxiv) that Aristotle conceived the world as a series of concentric spheres with the earth in the centre. The principal spheres are eight in number, and they carry in order, beginning with the external sphere, (1) the fixed stars, (2) Saturn, (3) Jupiter, (4) Mars, (5) Mercury, (6) Venus, (7) Sun, (8) Moon. To account for the various motions of the sun and the planets additional spheres had to be introduced amounting in all to fifty-six. But the principal spheres remained those mentioned. Each sphere or group of spheres with the star it carries is moved by an incorporeal mover, a spirit or Intelligence, and over them all is the first unmoved mover, God. He sets in motion the outer sphere of the fixed stars, and so the whole world moves. There is nothing said in this of the origin of these spheres and their intelligible movers. On the other hand, in the Neo-Platonic system of Plotinus all existence and particularly that of the intelligible or spiritual world issues or emanates from the One or the Good. Intellect is the first emanation, Soul the second, Nature the third and Matter the last.

On account of the confusion which arose in the middle ages, as a result of which Neo-Platonic writings and doctrines were attributed to Aristotle, Alfarabi and Avicenna worked out a scheme which combined the motion theory of Aristotle with the doctrine of emanation of Plotinus. The theory is based upon a principle alleged to be Aristotle's that from a unitary cause nothing but a unitary effect can follow. Hence, said Avicenna, God cannot have produced directly all the world we see in its complexity. He is the direct cause of the first Intelligence only, or first angel as Judah Halevi calls him. This Intelligence contemplates itself and it contemplates its cause. The effect of the latter act is the emanation of a second intelligence or angel; the effect of the former is a sphere—that of the fixed stars, of which the first Intelligence is the mover. The second Intelligence again produces a third Intelligence by its contemplation of the First Cause, and by its self-contemplation it creates the second sphere, the sphere of Saturn, which is moved by it. So the process continues until we reach the sphere of the moon, which is the last of the celestial spheres, and the Active Intellect, the last of the Intelligences, having in charge the sublunar world.

This fanciful and purely mythological scheme arouses the antagonism of Judah Halevi. It is all pure conjecture, he says, and there is not an iota of proof in it. People believe it and think it is convincing, simply because it bears the name of a Greek philosopher. As a matter of fact this theory is less plausible than those of the "Sefer Yezirah"; and there is no agreement even among the philosophers themselves except for those who are the followers of the same Greek authority, Empedocles, or Pythagoras, or Aristotle, or Plato. These agree not because the proofs are convincing, but simply because they are members of a given sect or school. The objections to the theory just outlined are manifold. In the first place why should the series of emanations stop with the moon? Is it because the power of the First Cause has given out? Besides why should self-contemplation result in a sphere and contemplation of the First Cause in an Intelligence or angel? It should follow that when Aristotle contemplates himself he produces a sphere, and when he contemplates the First Cause he gives rise to an angel. Granting the truth of the process, one does not see why the mover of Saturn should not produce two more emanations, one by contemplating the Intelligence immediately above it, and the other by contemplating the first Intelligence, thus making four emanations instead of two.[207]

In his outline of the philosophers' psychology, which as we have seen (p. 175) is borrowed verbally from Avicenna, what is new to us is the exposition of the inner senses and the account of the rational faculty. We must therefore repooduce it here in outline together with Judah Halevi's criticism.

The three kinds of soul, vegetative, animal and rational, we have already met before. We have also referred to the fact that Judah Halevi analyzes correctly the well-known Aristotelian definition of the soul. We must now give a brief account of the inner senses as Judah Halevi took it from Avicenna. The five external senses, seeing, hearing, touching, smelling and tasting, give us merely colors, sounds, touch sensations, odors and tastes. These are combined into an object by the *common sense*, known also as the *forming power*. Thus when we see honey we associate with its yellow color a sweet taste. This could not be done unless we had a power which combines in it all the five senses. For the sense of sight cannot perceive taste, nor can color be apprehended by the gustatory sense. There is need therefore of a common sense which comprehends all the five external senses. This is the first internal sense. This retains the forms of sensible objects just as the external senses present them. Then comes the *composing power* or power of imagination. This composes and divides the material of the common sense. It may be true or false, whereas the common sense is always true. Both of these give us merely forms; they do not exercise any judgment. The latter function belongs to the third internal sense, the *power of judgment*. Through this an animal is enabled to decide that a given object is to be sought or avoided. It also serves to rectify the errors of reproduction that may be found in the preceding faculty of imagination. Love, injury, belief, denial, belong likewise to the judging faculty together with such judgments as that the wolf is an enemy, the child a friend. The last of the internal senses is that of *factual memory*, the power which retains the judgments made by the faculty preceding.

In addition to these sensory powers the animal possesses motor faculties. These are two, the *power of desire*, which moves the animal to seek the agreeable; and the *power of anger*, which causes it to reject or avoid the disagreeable. All these powers are dependent upon the corporeal organs and disappear with the destruction of the latter.

The highest power of the soul and the exclusive possession of man (the faculties mentioned before are found also in animals) is the rational soul. This is at first simply a potentiality. Actually it is a *tabula rasa*, an empty slate, a blank paper. But it has the power (or is the power) of acquiring general ideas. Hence it is called hylic or material intellect, because it is like matter which in itself is nothing actual but is potentially everything, being capable of receiving any form and becoming any real object. As matter receives sensible forms, so the material intellect acquires intelligible forms, *i. e.*, thoughts, ideas, concepts. When it has these ideas it is an *actual intellect*. It is then identical with the ideas it has, *i. e.*, thinker and thought are the same, and hence the statement that the actual intellect is "intelligent" and "intelligible" at the same time. As matter is the principle of generation and destruction the rational soul, which is thus shown to be an immaterial substance, is indestructible, hence immortal. And it is the ideas it acquires which make it so. When the rational soul is concerned with pure knowledge it is called the *speculative* or *theoretical intellect.* When it is engaged in controlling the animal powers, its function is conduct, and is called the *practical intellect.* The rational soul, *i. e.*, the speculative intellect, is separable from the body and needs it not, though it uses it at first to acquire some of its knowledge. This is proved by the fact that whereas the corporeal powers, like the senses, are weakened by strong stimuli, the reason is strengthened by hard subjects of thought. Old age weakens the body, but strengthens the mind. The activities of the body are finite; of the mind, infinite.

We must also show that while the rational soul makes use of the data of sense perception, which are corporeal, as the occasions for the formation of its general ideas, it is not wholly dependent upon them, and the sense data alone are inadequate to give the soul its intellectual truths. Empirical knowledge is inductive, and no induction can be more general and more certain than the particular facts from which it is derived. As all experience, however rich, is necessarily finite, empirical knowledge is never universally certain. But the soul does possess universally certain knowledge, as for example the truths of mathematics and logic; hence the origin of these truths can not be empirical. How does the soul come to have such knowledge? We must assume that there is a divine emanation cleaving to the soul, which stands to it in the relation of light to the sense of sight. It is to the illumination of this intellectual substance and not to the data of sense perception that the soul owes the universal certainty of its knowledge. This divine substance is the *Active Intellect.* As long as the soul is united with the body, perfect union with the Active Intellect is impossible. But as the soul becomes more and more perfect through the acquisition of knowledge, it cleaves more and more to the Active Intellect, and this union becomes complete after death. Thus the immortality of the soul is proved by reason. It is based upon the conviction that the soul is an immaterial substance and that its perfection lies in its acquisition of intellectual ideas.[208]

Judah Halevi cannot help admitting the fascination such speculation exercises upon the mind of the student. But he must warn him against being misled by the fame of such names as Plato and Aristotle, and supposing that because in logic and mathematics the philosophers give us real proofs, they are equally trustworthy in metaphysical speculation. If the soul is, as they say, an intellectual substance not limited in place and for this reason not subject to genesis and decay, there is no way to distinguish one soul from another, since it is matter which constitutes individual existence. How then can my soul be distinguished from yours, or from the Active Intellect and the other Intelligences, or from the First Cause itself? The souls of Plato and Aristotle should become one so that the one should know the secret thoughts of the other. If the soul gets its ideas through divine illumination from the Active Intellect, how is it that philosophers do not intuit their ideas at once like God and the Active Intellect, and how is it they forget?

Then as to their ideas about immortality. If immortality is a necessary phenomenon due to the intellectual nature of the soul and dependent upon the degree of intellectual knowledge it possesses, how much knowledge must a man have to be immortal? If any amount is sufficient, then every rational soul is immortal, for everybody knows at least the axioms of logic and mathematics, such as that things equal to the same thing are equal to each other, that a thing cannot both be and not be, and so on. If a knowledge of the ten categories is necessary, and of the other universal principles which embrace existence conceptually, though not practically, this knowledge can be gotten in a day, and it is not likely that a man can become an angel in a day. If on the other hand one must know everything not merely conceptually but in detail, no one can ever acquire universal knowledge and no one is immortal The philosophers may be excused because this is the best they can do with the help of pure reason. We may commend them for their mode of life in accordance with the moral law and in freedom from the world, since they were not bound to accept our traditions. But it is different with us. Why should *we* seek peculiar proofs and explanations for the immortality of the soul, since we have promises to that effect whether the soul be corporeal or spiritual? If we depend upon logical proof, our life will pass away without our coming to any conclusion.[209]

Judah Halevi takes issue also with the Mutakallimun. These, as we know, were Mohammedan theologians who, unlike the philosophers, were not indifferent to religion. On the contrary their sole motive in philosophizing was to prove the dogmas of their faith.

They had no interest in pure speculation as such. Judah Halevi has no more sympathy with them than with the philosophers. Owing to the fact that the Karaites were implicit followers of the Kalam and for other reasons, no doubt, more objective, he thinks less of them than he does of the philosophers. The only possible use, he tells us, of their methods is to afford exercise in dialectics so as to be able to answer the arguments of unbelievers. To the superficial observer the Mutakallim may seem to be superior to the prophet, because he argues, whereas the latter affirms without proving. In reality, however, this is not so. The aim of the Mutakallim is to acquire the belief which the prophet has by nature. But his Kalam may injure his belief instead of confirming it, by reason of the many difficulties and doubts it introduces. The prophet, who has natural belief, teaches not by means of dialectic discussion. If one has a spark of the true belief in his nature, the prophet by his personality will benefit him by a slight hint. Only he who has nothing of true belief in his nature must have recourse to Kalam, which may benefit him or injure.

Judah Halevi follows up this general comment by a brief sketch of the system of the Kalam, but we need not enter into this matter as there is little there that we do not already know, and there is no detailed criticism on the part of Judah Halevi.[210]

The Rabbi concludes his discourse with the king of the Chazars by declaring his intention to leave the land in order to go to Jerusalem. Although the visible Shekinah is no longer in Palestine, the invisible and spiritual presence is with every born Israelite of pure heart and deed; and Palestine is the fittest land for this communion, being conducive to purity of heart and mind.[211]

CHAPTER XI

1. Moses ibn Ezra

Among the Jewish Neo-Platonists must be included the two Ibn Ezras, Moses and Abraham. They were contemporary and came from Spain. Moses, the older of the two, was born at Granada about 1070 and died after 1138. Abraham, who travelled all over the world, was born at Toledo in 1092 and died in 1167. Neither is particularly famous as a philosopher. Moses's celebrity rests on his poetic productions, secular as well as religious, which are highly praised by Harizi, above even those of Halevi. Abraham is best known as a grammarian and Biblical commentator, particularly the latter, though his versatility is remarkable. Besides grammar and exegesis he wrote on mathematics, astronomy and astrology, on religious philosophy, and was a poet of no mean order; though, as Zunz says,[212] "flashes of thought spring from his words, but not pictures of the imagination."

All that is accessible in print of Moses Ibn Ezra's philosophical treatise is a Hebrew translation of extracts under the title "Arugat ha-Bosem" (Bed of Spices).[213] If we may judge of the rest of the work by these Hebrew fragments, we should say that philosophy was not Ibn Ezra's forte. He dabbled in it as any poet of that age did, but what caught his fancy was more the mysteriously sounding phrases of celebrated authorities like Pythagoras, Empedocles, Socrates, Plato, Aristotle, Hermes (whom he identifies with Enoch), than a strictly reasoned out argument. Accordingly the Hebrew selections consist of little more than a string of quotations on the transcendence and unknowableness of God, on the meaning of philosophy, on the position of man in the universe, on motion, on nature and on intellect. It is of historical interest to us to know that Moses ibn Ezra, so famous as a poet, was interested in philosophy, and that the views which appealed to him were those of Ibn Gabirol, whose "Fountain of Life" he knew, and from which he quotes a celebrated mystical passage. A few details will suffice to make this clear.

Man is a microcosm, a world in miniature, and there is nothing above or below, the counterpart of which is not found in man. There is no sphere, or star, or animal, or plant, or mineral, or power, or nature, but something similar, *mutatis mutandis*, is found in man. The ten categories, which according to the philosophers embrace all existence, are also found, all of them, in man. The perfection of man's creation points to a wise Creator. Man comes after multiplicity, God is before multiplicity. Man is like the great universe, and in both the spiritual cannot come in direct contact with the corporeal, but needs intermediating powers to bring the extremes together. In man soul and spirit stand between intellect and body.

Hence a man must know himself before he can know the universe, else he is like a person who feeds other people while he is himself hungry. To know the Creator, the soul must first know herself, and this is one of the definitions of philosophy, to know one's own soul. He who can strip his soul of his corporeal senses and worldly desires, and rise to the sphere will find there his reward. Other similarly ascetic and mystical expressions are quoted from Aristotle (!), Pythagoras, and "one of the modern philosophers." The last is none other than Ibn Gabirol, and the passage quoted is the same as that cited above, p. 69.

Unity precedes the unitary object as heat comes before the hot object. Unity alone is self-subsistent. Numerical unity is prior to two, and is the very root and essence of number. God's unity is above all other unities, hence it cannot be described, because it has no cause, being the cause of everything else. As our eye cannot see the sun by reason of its very brilliance, so our intellect cannot comprehend God because of the extreme perfection of his existence. The finite and imperfect cannot know the infinite and perfect. Hence no names can apply to God except metaphorically. When we say that God knows, we mean that he is knowledge itself, not that knowledge is an attribute which he possesses. Socrates (!) said in his prayers, "Thou art not far from me so that I should raise my voice to thee, nor art Thou near unto me that I should content myself with a low whisper and the meditation of the heart; nor art Thou on any side of me so that I may turn toward Thee; for nearness and distance have measure, but there is no measure between me and Thee. Thou art united with me and embracest me more closely than my intellect and soul."

He who knows most of the secret of the Creator, knows least; and he who knows least, knows most. As the limbs of the body and the senses cannot know the intelligible ideas because the latter are superior to them, so the intellect cannot know the essence of the Creator because he is above the sphere of the intellect. Although the intellect is spiritual, it cannot comprehend the Creator because he is above all intellectual powers, and is infinite. What is infinite has no division or multiplication, or part or whole.

The Gentiles make use of the anthropomorphic expressions in the Bible to annoy us, charging us with believing in a corporeal God. Would that we had strength to silence their impudence by a crushing reply. But alas! their tyranny prevents us from raising our voice. But it is still more aggravating to hear men of our own people, heretics, repeating the same charge against the Bible and Talmud, when they ought to know better, since the expressions in question are metaphorical. Saadia has made this sufficiently clear.

The Active Intellect is the first of God's creations. It is a power emanating from the Will. It is a simple, pure and transparent substance, bearing in itself the forms of all existing things. The human intellect is known as the passive intellect. The rational soul is a pure substance giving perfection to a natural body, etc. It is inferior to the intellect, and the animal soul is inferior to the rational. The soul is the horseman, the body represents the soldiers and the arms. As the horseman must take care of his arms that he may not be put to death, so the soul must take care of the body that she may not perish. And the senses must be taken into account, for the powers of the soul are dependent upon the powers of the body. If the food of the body is in proper proportion, the activity of the soul is proper and right. Similarly if one neglects moderation in food, he is bound to suffer morally and spiritually.

The above selections, which are representative of the accessible portion of Moses ibn Ezra's philosophical treatise, except that such recurring phrases have been omitted as "And the philosopher said," "And they say," etc., show that the work is nothing but a compilation of sayings on various philosophical topics, without any attempt on the author's part to think out the subject or any part thereof, for himself.

2. Abraham ibn Ezra

Abraham Ibn Ezra did not write any special work on philosophy, and his importance lies chiefly in his Biblical commentary, which unlike that of Rashi, is based upon a scientific and philological foundation. Ibn Ezra was thoroughly familiar with Arabic and well versed in the philological, scientific and philosophical studies cultivated by Arabs and Jews in his native land. For reasons not known to us— poverty was very likely one of them—he left his native Spain and wandered as far as Rome in the east, Egypt and Morocco in the south, and London in the north. Everywhere he was busy with literary activity, and as he wrote in Hebrew his purpose must have been, as the result certainly proved to be, the enlightenment of the non-Arabic speaking Jews of England, France and Italy, by bringing before them in a language that they knew the grammar of Hayyuj, the mathematics and astronony of the Greeks and the Arabs, the philosophy of Neo-Platonism, and the scientific and rationalistic spirit generally, as enlightened Spain had developed it in Jew and Arab alike.

We are interested here more particularly in Ibn Ezra's philosophical views. These are scattered through his Biblical commentaries and in a few other small works devoted to an investigation of the laws of the Pentateuch and the meaning of the names of God.[214] For though Ibn Ezra favors the philological method as the best way to arrive at the true meaning of Scripture, and decries allegory as well as Midrash when pushed too far, and though his commentary is for the most part based upon the philological method of interpretation, he was too much a child of his age to be able to refrain from finding in the Bible views akin to those he learned from Gabirol, the Brethren of Purity and what other philosophical literature of the Arabs he read and was influenced by. And so he, too, the grammarian and philologist, succumbed to the allegorical and symbolical method he condemned. Without denying the historical reality of the Garden of Eden, the Tree of Knowledge and the Tree of Life, he also sees in these expressions symbols of cosmological, psychological and ethical ideas. In the fashion of Philo he sees in Eden a representation of the higher world of the divinity, in the Garden the intermediate world of the spheres and Intelligences, in the river issuing from the Garden the substance of the sublunar world, in the four heads into which the river divides the four elements, and so on. He speaks of these symbolic meanings as the "secrets," and so we have the secret of the Garden, of the rivers, of the coats. And in the same way he speaks of the secret of the Cherubim, of the ark and the Tabernacle. These objects also symbolize metaphysical and cosmological truths. He was a believer in astrology, and laid this pseudo-science also under contribution in the interpretation of Holy Writ. Here the various numbers found in the Bible in connection with ritual prescriptions, the construction of the Tabernacle, and so on, were of great service to Ibn Ezra in his symbolizations. Like Philo and the Neo-Pythagoreans he analyzes the virtues and significances of the different numbers, and thus finds a symbol in every number found in the Bible. Writing as he did for the Jews of central Europe, who were not trained in secular science and philosophy, Ibn Ezra was not prepared to shock the sensibilities of his readers by his novel and, to them, heretical views; and hence he expressed himself in cryptic phrases and allusions, which often make his meaning difficult if not impossible to decipher. This, taken together with the fact that his views are not laid down anywhere systematically and in connected fashion, but are thrown out briefly, often enigmatically, in connection with the explanation of Biblical verses and phrases, accounts for the difference among critics concerning the precise doctrines of Abraham Ibn Ezra.

Of his predecessors among the Jewish philosophers Ibn Ezra shows closest relation to Solomon ibn Gabirol. He does not quote the "Fountain of Life," but he names its author as a great thinker and writer of poems, and shows familiarity with Gabirol's doctrines. Like Gabirol he says that all except God consists of substance (matter) and form. Not only the sublunar things, subject to generation and decay, but the higher incorporeal things, also, are in essence two, *i. e.*, are composed of two elements, subject and predicate. God alone is One; he is subject only and not predicate. And Ibn Ezra also has some allusion to the divine Will as taught by Gabirol.

In giving a connected sketch of Ibn Ezra's philosophical ideas, the most one can do is to collect all the sayings bearing upon our subject which are found scattered through Ibn Ezra's writings, and classify them and combine them into a connected whole. This has been done before by Nahman Krochmal [215] and by David Rosin,[216] and we shall follow the latter in our exposition here.

God is the One. He gives forms to all things, and is himself all things. God alone is the real existent, all else is an existent by virtue of him. Unity is the symbol of God because in number also the unit is the foundation of all number, and yet is not itself number. It exists by virtue of itself and needs not the numbers that come after. At the same time the unit is also all number, because all number is made up of the unit. God alone is one, because he alone is not composed of matter and form, as everything else is. God has neither likeness nor form, for he is the creator of all things, *i. e.*, of all likeness and form. He is therefore incorporeal. In God the subject knowing and the object of his knowledge are one and the same thing. Else he would not be one. In knowing himself, therefore, he knows the universe. God as the cause and creator of all things must know all things, the universal as well as the particular, the world soul as well as the various species, and even every single creature, but he knows the particular in a general way. For God knows only what is permanent, whereas the particular is constantly changing, hence he does not know the particular as such, but only as involved in the general and permanent.

As God is incorporeal he is not subject to corporeal accidents or human feelings. Hence the many expressions in the Bible which ascribe such accidents and feelings to God must be understood as metaphors. It is a psychological necessity for man wishing to communicate his ideas to other men to speak in human terms, whether he speak of beings and things inferior or superior to him. The result is that the metaphor he finds it necessary to employ either raises or lowers the object to which it refers. It elevates the sub-human and lowers the superhuman to the human. This is the explanation of such phrases as "the mouth of the earth" the "hand of the Jordan," the "head of the dust of the world," and so on, in which the figure is that of personification. And the fundamental explanation is the same in such phrases as "The Lord repented," "The Lord rested," "The Lord remembered," "He that dwelleth in heaven laughs," and so on, where the process is the reverse of personification. The motive common to both is to convey some idea to the reader.

The Hebrew word "bara," ordinarily translated "created," which implies to most people the idea of *creatio ex nihilo*, Ibn Ezra renders, in accordance with its etymology, to limit, to define, by drawing or incising a line or boundary. Having said this, Ibn Ezra, in his wonted mysterious manner, stops short, refusing to say more and preferring to mystify the reader by adding the tantalizing phrase, "The intelligent will understand." He means apparently to indicate that an eternal matter was endowed with form. In fact he seems to favor the idea of eternal creation and maintenance of the universe, the relation of which to God is as the relation of speech to the speaker, which exists only so long as the speaker speaks. The moment he ceases speaking the sounds cease to exist.

The two ideas of eternal emanation of the world from God after the manner of the Neo-Platonists and of an eternal matter which God endows with forms, are not really quite consistent, for the latter implies that matter is independent of God, whereas according to the former everything owes its existence and continuance to God, from whom it emanates. But it is difficult from the fragmentary and laconic sayings of Ibn Ezra to extract a consistent and certain system.

The world consists of three parts, three worlds Ibn Ezra calls them. The highest world consists of the separate Intelligences or angels, including the world-soul of which the human soul is a part. The intermediate world consists of the spheres, planets and fixed stars. Finally the lower world contains the four elements and the product of their various mixtures, minerals, plants, animals, man. These three worlds, Ibn Ezra appears to intimate in his oracular manner, are symbolized by the three divisions of the Tabernacle, the holy of holies typifying the world of spirits, the holy pointing to the spheres, while the outer court represents the sublunar world.

The highest world, the world of Intelligences and angels, is eternal, though it too is dependent upon God for its existence. The angels, too, are composed of matter and form, and their function is to move the bodies of the intermediate world, the spheres and their stars

Through the instrumentality of the heavenly bodies, the angels form the lower world. This amounts to saying that the corporeal world is the last stage in the descending series of emanations from the One, and is preceded by the heavenly bodies and the Intelligences. The angels are also the immediate agents in prophetic inspiration.

Not all mention of angels in the Bible, however, must be identified with a separate Intelligence or a spheral soul (for the latter too is called angel by Ibn Ezra). There are instances of the expression angel which refer to a momentary, special creation of a light or air for the special benefit of the people. This explains a number of theophanies in the Bible, such as the burning bush, "the glory of the Lord," the cloud in the wilderness, and so on.

The intermediate world of spheres is also eternal and consists of nine spheres, that of the Intelligences making up the perfect number ten. The nine spheres are arranged as follows, the spheres of the seven planets, the sphere of the fixed stars, and the diurnal sphere without stars, which gives the motion from east to west to the whole heaven.

The lower world, the sublunar and corporeal world of generation and decay, was created in time. This, however, does not mean that there was time before this creation, for time exists only with motion and change. Creation here signifies the formation of the chaotic matter. As God cannot come in contact with the material and changeable (we have already seen that he cannot know it as such), it follows that this lower world was not made directly by him, but by the angels, hence the word "Elohim" is used in the first chapter of Genesis, which means primarily the angels, and secondarily God as acting through the angels.

In this lower world man is the noblest creature. By means of his soul he may attain eternal life as an individual like God and the angels (*i. e.*, the Intelligences), whereas all other creatures of the lower world are permanent in species only but not as individuals. This is the meaning of the expression in Genesis, "Let us make man in our image," in the image, that is, of God and the angels. Man is a microcosm, a universe in little, for like the great universe he consists of a body animated by a soul.

As the noblest part of man is his soul, it becomes his duty to know it. He must know whether it is substance or accident, whether it will die when it is separated from the body, and for what purpose it was brought into union with the body. In order to learn all this one must first study the preparatory branches, grammar, logic, mathematics and physics. In the study of psychology we learn that man has three souls, vegetative, animal and rational, and the latter alone is immortal. It is a part of the world soul, having existed before it came into the body, and under favorable conditions will return again to the world soul when separated from the body. The condition which must be fulfilled by the soul before it can return to the world soul is the acquisition of wisdom, for this is the purpose for which it was put into the body, namely, in order that it may learn the work of its master and observe his commandments. There are many sciences, but they are related to each other, all leading up to the one highest science, the knowledge of God and his goodness. A person must advance gradually in studying the work of God from the knowledge of minerals, plants, animals, the human body, to the knowledge of the spheres and heavenly bodies, the causes of eclipses, etc., and from this he will gradually come to know God. The commandments of the Bible are also of importance for this purpose. To understand the secret of the commandments is to gain eternal life. For wisdom is the form of the soul, and hence the soul does not die like a body.

The reward of the soul is re-absorption in the world soul of which it is a part, and the punishment of the unworthy soul that neglected to acquire knowledge is destruction. What Ibn Ezra means by the Hebrew word "abad" (ordinarily rendered to perish, to be destroyed) is not clear. It is hard to see how a pre-existing soul can perish utterly. Rosin suggests that Ibn Ezra is alluding to transmigration,[217] but it is not clear.

We have seen that Ibn Ezra holds that the events of the sublunar world and the destinies of men are governed by the positions and motions of the heavenly bodies, which in turn are determined by the Intelligences or angels. The heavenly bodies, he tells us, follow necessary laws imposed upon them, and are not responsible for any good or evil which results to mankind from them, since the effects are not of their intention, and they cannot change them if they would. Accordingly it is foolish to pray to the heavenly bodies in order to appease them and prevent evil, as some of the heathen are accustomed to do. The motions of the heavenly bodies are determined and invariable, and no prayer will change them. This, however, does not mean to say that no one can escape the evil which is destined for him in the stars. Ordinarily, it is true, God does not know the particular individual as such. He knows him only as implied in the whole, and his destiny is determined accordingly. But there are exceptions when a person by developing his soul and intellect, as we saw above, succeeds in his lifetime in separating his soul from the corporeal and particular, and brings it into contact with the spiritual and universal. In that case he attracts to himself the special providence of God, which enables him to evade the evil threatened by his star, without in any way changing the star's natural course or ordinary effects. How this is done, Ibn Ezra illustrates by an example.[218] Suppose, he says, that it is fated according to the stars that a given city shall be flooded by a river and its inhabitants drowned. A prophet comes and warns them, urging them to repent of their evil ways before their fate is sealed. They obey him, return to God with all their heart and leave the city to offer prayer to God. The river rises in their absence, as often happens, and floods the city. The wolf is satisfied and the lamb is whole. The decree of the stars is not interfered with, and the good man is delivered from evil. In this way Ibn Ezra endeavors to reconcile natural law (or astrological fatalism) with the ethical purpose of divine providence. And he also vindicates free will and responsibility. The rational soul of man has power, he says, to counteract in part the indications of the stars, though it cannot annul them entirely. The punishment of the wicked is that they are left entirely to the fates determined for them by their constellations.

The highest good of man, we have seen, is the knowledge of God and his work. There are two ways of knowing God. One is through a study of nature, the work of God. This is described in the first part of the nineteenth Psalm, "The Heavens declare the glory of God; and the firmament showeth his handiwork." But there is a second and, in a sense, a better way of knowing God. This is derived from his revelation in the Law. As we are told in the second part of the above Psalm (*v.* 7), "The law of the Lord is perfect, restoring the soul." The law of the Lord restores the soul, Ibn Ezra says, by removing doubt from it. For the first method of knowing God, with all its importance for the man of wisdom and reason, is not fit for all persons; and not everything can be proved by reason. Revelation in the Law is necessary for the simple minded. "I am the Lord thy God" (Exod. 20, 2) is a hint to the philosopher, who need not depend on hearsay, for real knowledge is proved knowledge. But as not everyone is in a position to have such knowledge, the Bible adds, "which brought thee out of the land of Egypt." This all can understand, the simple minded as well as the philosopher. The Law has also a practical purpose, to strengthen the rational soul so as to prevent the body from gaining the upper hand.

God's messenger, through whom his will is made known, is the prophet. He seeks retirement so as to get in communion with God, and receives such influence as he is capable of getting. Moses was the greatest of the prophets. He was able to communicate with God whenever he chose, whereas the others had to wait until the inspiration came. The revelation of God to Moses was without an intermediary, and without visions and likenesses. Moses saw the things presented to him in their true form.

The laws may be divided into 1. Innate or rational laws, *i. e.*, laws planted by God in the mind of every rational being. There are many such in the Torah. All the laws of the Ten Commandments belong to this class, with the exception of the Sabbath. Hence all mankind believe in them, and Abraham observed them all before ever the Law was given on Sinai. 2. Hidden laws, *i. e.*, laws, the reason of which is not given. We must not suppose for a moment that there is any law which is against reason, Heaven forbid! We must observe them all, whether we understand the reason or not. If we find a law that apparently is unreasonable, we must assume that it has some hidden meaning and is not to be taken in its literal sense. It is our duty, then, to look for this hidden meaning, and if we cannot find it, we must admit that we do not understand it.

The laws may also be classified as 1. Commandments of the heart, 2. Commandments of the tongue, and 3. Commandments of action. An example of commandments of the heart is, "Thou shalt love the Lord thy God," "Thou shalt not hate thy brother in thy heart," and so on. To the commandments of the tongue belong the reading of the *Shema*, grace after meals, the priestly benediction, and so on. The laws of the third class are so numerous that there is no need of mentioning them. The laws of the heart are the most important of all. The reader will recognize in this two-fold classification Saadia's division of the laws into rational and traditional, and Bahya's classification of duties of the heart and duties of the limbs. This second class includes Ibn Ezra's second and third classes, tongue and action.[219]

The problem of evil Ibn Ezra solves by saying that from God comes good only. The world as a whole is good; evil is due to the defect of the object receiving higher influence. To argue that because of the small part of evil the whole world, which is good, should not have been created, is foolish.

The highest good of man is to develop his reason. As the traveller and the captive long to return to the land of their birth and be with their family, so the rational soul is eager to rise to the upper world which is not made of clay. This it can do only if it purifies itself from the uncleanness of corporeal desire which drags it down, and takes pains to know its own nature and origin, with the help of Wisdom whose eyes are undimmed. Then she will know the truth, which will remain indelibly impressed upon her when she separates from the body, where she was put for her own good. The suffering she underwent here for a time will give place to everlasting rest and joy. All man's work is vain, for man can neither create nor annihilate a substance. All his corporeal activity consists in combination and separation of accidents. The only thing of value is the fear of God. But no man can rise to this stage until he has ascended the ladder of wisdom, and has acquired understanding.[220]

More concretely the way to purify the soul from the body is by uniting the rational and spirited soul, as Plato has it, against the appetitive, and giving the reason the mastery over the spirited soul as well. A moderate degree of asceticism is to be recommended as favoring the emancipation of the soul from the tyranny of the body. This is the meaning of the institution of the Nazirite; and the offering he must bring after the expiration of his period is to atone for the sin of returning to a life of indulgence. But one should not go to extremes. Too much praying and fasting results in stupefaction. It is a mistake to develop one side of one's nature at the expense of another. Every one of the three souls (the rational, the spirited and the appetitive) must be given its due.

But the most important activity of man, which leads to eternal life and happiness, is the knowledge of God. This knowledge cannot be attained at once. It must be preceded by a study of one's own soul and of the natural sciences. Through a knowledge of oneself and nature, one arrives finally at a knowledge of God. The soul, originally a *tabula rasa*, is gradually perfected by the ideas which theoretical speculation acquires. These ideas are identified with the rational soul, and there results the acquired Intellect, which, as absolutely immaterial, is immortal and becomes one with the world soul of which it is a part. During life complete union with the spiritual world is impossible. Even Moses could only see the "rear part" of God. But when one has during life kept as far as possible away from the sensuous and corporeal, then at the time of death, when the soul is separated from the body, he will be completely absorbed in the world soul and possess the knowledge of God.

CHAPTER XII

ABRAHAM IBN DAUD

What was poison to Judah Halevi is meat to Abraham Ibn Daud. We must, he says, investigate the principles of the Jewish religion and seek to harmonize them with true philosophy. And in order to do these things properly a preliminary study of science is necessary. Nowadays all this is neglected and the result is confusion in fundamental principles, for a superficial and literal reading of the Bible leads to contradictory views, not to speak of anthropomorphic conceptions of God which cannot be the truth. Many of our day think that the study of philosophy is injurious. This is because it frequently happens in our time that a person who takes up the study of philosophy neglects religion. In ancient times also this happened in the person of Elisha ben Abuya, known by the name of Aher. Nevertheless science was diligently studied in Rabbinic times. Witness what was said concerning Rabbi Yohanan ben Zakkai, Samuel and the Synhedrin.[221] It cannot be that God meant us to abstain from philosophical study, for many statements in the Bible, such as those relating to freedom of the will, to the nature of God and the divine attributes, to the creation of the world, and so on, are a direct stimulus to such investigation. Surely mental confusion cannot be the purpose God had in mind for us. If he preferred our ignorance he would not have called our attention to these matters at all.[222]

This, as we see, is decidedly a different point of view from that of Judah Halevi. The difference between them is not due to a difference in their age and environment, but solely to personal taste and temperament. Toledo was the birthplace of Ibn Daud as it was of Halevi. And the period in which they lived was practically the same. Judah Halevi's birth took place in the last quarter of the eleventh century, whereas Ibn Daud is supposed to have been born about 1110, a difference of some twenty-five or thirty years. The philosopher whom Judah Halevi presents to us as the typical representative of his time

is an Aristotelian of the type of Alfarabi and Avicenna. And it is
the same type of philosophy that we meet in the pages of the "Emunah
Ramah" (Exalted Faith), Ibn Daud's philosophical work.[223] Whereas,
however, Judah Halevi was a poet by the grace of God, glowing with
love for his people, their religion, their language and their historic
land, Ibn Daud leaves upon us the impression of a precise thinker,
cold and analytical. He exhibits no graces of style, eloquence of dic-
tion or depths of enthusiasm and emotion. He passes systematically
from one point to the next, uses few words and technical, and moves
wholly in the Peripatetic philosophy of the day. In 1161, the same
year in which the Emunah Ramah was composed, he also wrote a
historical work, "Sefer Hakabala" (Book of Tradition), which we
have; and in 1180, regarded by some as the year of his death, he
published an astronomical work, which is lost. This gives an index
of his interests which were scientific and philosophic. Mysticism,
whether of the poetic or the philosophic kind, was far from his nature;
and this too may account for the intense opposition he shows to
Solomon Ibn Gabirol. On more than one occasion he gives vent to
his impatience with that poetic philosopher, and he blames him principally for two faults. Choosing to devote a whole book to one purely
metaphysical topic, in itself not related to Judaism, Gabirol, we are
told by Ibn Daud, gave expression to doctrines extremely dangerous
to the Jewish religion. And apart from his heterodoxy, he is philosophically incompetent and his method is abominable. His style is
profuse to the point of weariness, and his logic carries no conviction.[224]

While Abraham Ibn Daud is thus expressly unsympathetic to Gabirol and tacitly in disagreement with Halevi (he does not mention
him), he shows the closest relation to Maimonides, whose forerunner he
is. We feel tempted to say that if not for Ibn Daud there would have
been no Maimonides. And yet the irony of history has willed that
the fame of being the greatest Jewish philosopher shall be Maimonides's own, while his nearest predecessor, to whose influence he owed
most, should be all but completely forgotten. The Arabic original
of Ibn Daud's treatise is lost, and the Hebrew translations (there are
two) lay buried in manuscript in the European libraries until one of
them was published by Simson Weil in 1852.[225]

Abraham Ibn Daud is the first Jewish philosopher who shows an intimate knowledge of the works of Aristotle and makes a deliberate effort to harmonize the Aristotelian system with Judaism. To be sure, he too owes his Aristotelian knowledge to the Arabian exponents of the Stagirite, Alfarabi and Avicenna, rather than to the works of Aristotle himself. But this peculiarity was rooted in the intellectual conditions of his time, and must not be charged to his personal neglect of the sources. And Maimonides does nothing more than repeat the effort of Ibn Daud in a more brilliant and masterly fashion.

The development of the three religious philosophies in the middle ages, Jewish, Christian and Mohammedan, followed a similar line of progression. In all of them it was not so much a development from within, the unfolding of what was implicit and potential in the original germ of the three respective religions, as a stimulus from without, which then combined, as an integral factor, with the original mass, and the final outcome was a resultant of the two originally disparate elements. We know by this time what these two elements were in each case, Hellenic speculation, and Semitic religion in the shape of sacred and revealed documents. The second factor was in every case complete when the process of fusion began. Not so the first. What I mean is that not all of the writings of Greek antiquity were known to Jew, Christian and Mohammedan at the beginning of their philosophizing career. And the progress in their philosophical development kept equal step with the successive accretion of Greek philosophical literature, in particular Aristotle's physical, psychological and metaphysical treatises, and their gradual purgation of Neo-Platonic adhesions.

The Syrian Christians, who were the first to adopt Greek teachings, seem never to have gone beyond the mathematical and medical works of the Greeks and the logic of Aristotle. The Arabs began where their Syrian teachers ended, and went beyond them. The Mutakallimun were indebted to the Stoics,[226] the Pure Brethren to the Neo-Platonists; and it was only gradually that Aristotle became the sole master not merely in logic, which he always had been, but also in physics, metaphysics and psychology. Alfarabi, Avicenna and Averroes represent so many steps in the Aristotelization of Arabic philosophy.

Christian mediæval thought, which was really a continuation of the Patristic period, likewise began with Eriugena in the ninth century under Platonic and Neo-Platonic influences. Of Aristotle the logic alone was known, and that too only in small part. Here also progress was due to the increase of Aristotelian knowledge; though in this case it was not gradual as with the Arabs before them, but sudden. In the latter part of the twelfth and the early part of the thirteenth century, through the Crusades, through the Moorish civilization in Spain, through the Saracens in Sicily, through the Jews as translators and mediators, Aristotle invaded Christian Europe and transformed Christian philosophy. Albertus Magnus, Thomas Aquinas, Duns Scotus, William of Occam are the results of this transformation.

The same thing holds true of the Jews. Their philosophizing career stands chronologically between that of their Arab teachers and their Christian disciples. And the line of their development was similar. It was parallel to that of the Arabs. First came Kalam in Saadia, Mukammas, the Karaites Al Basir and Jeshua ben Judah. Then Neo-Platonism and Kalam combined, or pure Neo-Platonism, in Bahya, Gabirol, Ibn Zaddik and the two Ibn Ezras, Abraham and Moses. In Judah Halevi, so far as philosophy is represented, we have Neo-Platonism and Aristotelianism. Finally in Ibn Daud and Maimonides, Neo-Platonism is reduced to the vanishing point, and Aristotelianism is in full view and in possession of the field. After Maimonides the only philosopher who deviates from the prescribed path and endeavors to uproot Aristotelian authority in Judaism is Crescas. All the rest stand by Aristotle and his major domo, Maimonides.

This may seem like a purely formal and external mode of characterizing the development of philosophical thought. But the character of mediæval philosophy is responsible for this. Their ideal of truth as well as goodness was in the past. Knowledge was thought to have been discovered or revealed in the past,[227] and the task of the philosopher was to acquire what was already there and to harmonize contradictory authorities. Thus the more of the past literature that came to them, the greater the transformation in their own philosophy.

The above digression will make clear to us the position of Ibn Daud and his relation to Maimonides. Ibn Daud began what Maimonides finished—the last stage in the Aristotelization of Jewish thought. Why is it then that so little was known about him, and that his important treatise was neglected and practically forgotten? The answer is to be found partly in the nature of the work itself and partly in historical circumstances.

The greatest and most abiding interest in intellectual Jewry was after all the Bible and the Talmud. This interest never flagged through adversity or through success. The devotion paid to these Jewish classics and sacred books may have been fruitful in original research and intelligent application at one time and place and relatively barren at another. Great men devoted to their study abounded in one country and were relatively few in another. The nature of the study applied to these books was affected variously by historical conditions, political and economic; and the cultivation or neglect of the sciences and philosophy was reflected in the style of Biblical and Talmudical interpretation. But at all times and in all countries, under conditions of comparative freedom as well as in the midst of persecution, the sacred heritage of Israel was studied and its precepts observed and practiced. In this field alone fame was sure and permanent. All other study was honored according to the greater or less proximity to this paramount interest. In times of freedom and of great philosophic and scientific interest like that of the golden era in Spain, philosophical studies almost acquired independent value. But this independence, never quite absolute, waned and waxed with external conditions, and at last disappeared entirely. If Ibn Daud had made himself famous by a Biblical commentary or a halakic work, or if his philosophic treatise had the distinction of being written in popular and attractive style, like Bahya's "Duties of the Hearts," or Halevi's "Cusari," it might have fared better. As it is, it suffers from its conciseness and technical terminology. Add to this that it was superseded by the "Guide of the Perplexed" of Maimonides, published not many years after the "Emunah Ramah," and the neglect of the latter is completely explained.

Abraham ibn Daud tells us in the introduction to his book that it was written in response to the question of a friend concerning the problem of free will. The dilemma is this. If human action is determined by God, why does he punish, why does he admonish, and why does he send prophets? If man is free, then there is something

in the world over which God has no control. The problem is made
more difficult by the fact that Biblical statements are inconsistent,
and passages may be cited in favor of either of the theories in question.
This inconsistency is to be explained, however, by the circumstance
that not all Biblical phrases are to be taken literally—their very
contradiction is a proof of this. Now the passages which require
exegetic manipulation are in general those which seem opposed to
reason. Many statements in the Bible are in fact intended for the
common people, and are expressed with a view to their comprehension,
and without reference to philosophic truth. In the present instance
the objections to determinism are much greater and more serious
than those to freedom. In order to realize this, however, it is necessary
to investigate the principles of the Jewish religion and seek to harmonize them with true philosophy. This in turn cannot be done
without a preliminary study of science. A question like that of determinism and freedom cannot be decided without a knowledge of
the divine attributes and the consequences flowing from them. But
to understand these we must have a knowledge of the principles of
physics and metaphysics.[228] Accordingly Abraham Ibn Daud devotes
the entire first part of the "Emunah Ramah" to general physics and
metaphysics in the Aristotelian conception of these terms.

Concerning the kind of persons for whom he wrote his book, he
says, I advise everyone who is perfectly innocent, who is not interested
in philosophical and ethical questions like that of determinism and
freedom on the ground that man cannot grasp them; and is entirely
unconcerned about his ignorance—I advise such a person to refrain
from opening this book or any other of a similar nature. His ignorance
is his bliss, for after all the purpose of philosophy is conduct. On
the other hand, those who are learned in the principles of religion and
are also familiar with philosophy need not my book, for they know
more than I can teach them here. It is the beginner in speculation
who can benefit from this work, the man who has not yet been able
to see the rational necessity of beliefs and practices which he knows
from tradition.

That the principles of the Jewish religion are based upon philosophic foundations is shown in Deuteronomy 4, 6: "Keep therefore and do them; for this is your wisdom and your understanding

in the sight of the peoples, which shall hear all these statutes, and say, surely this great nation is a wise and understanding people." This cannot refer to the ceremonial precepts, the so-called "traditional" commandments; for there is nothing in them to excite the admiration of a non-Jew. Nor can it refer to the political and moral regulations, for one need not profess the Jewish or any other religion in order to practice them; they are a matter of reason pure and simple. The verse quoted can only mean that the other nations will be seized with admiration and wonder when they find that the fundamental principles of the Jewish religion, which we received by tradition and without effort, are identical with those philosophical principles at which they arrived after a great deal of labor extending over thousands of years.[229]

Ibn Daud is not consistent in his idea of the highest aim of man. We have just heard him say that the purpose of philosophy is conduct. This is true to the spirit of Judaism which, despite all the efforts of the Jewish philosophers to the contrary, is not a speculative theology but a practical religion, in which works stand above faith. But as an Aristotelian, Ibn Daud could not consistently stand by the above standpoint as the last word in this question. Accordingly we find him elsewhere in true Aristotelian fashion give priority to theoretical knowledge.

Judging from the position of man among the other creatures of the sublunar world, we come to the conclusion, he tells us, that that which distinguishes him above his surroundings, namely, his rational soul, is the aim of all the rest; and they are means and preparations for it. The rational soul has two forms of activity. It may face upward and receive wisdom from the angels (theoretical knowledge). Or it may direct its attention downwards and judge the other corporeal powers (practical reason). But it must not devote itself unduly or without system to any one occupation. The aim of man is wisdom, science. Of the sciences the highest and the aim of all the rest is the knowledge of God. The body of man is his animal, which leads him to God. Some spend all their time in feeding the animal, some in clothing it, and some in curing it of its ills. The latter is not a bad occupation, as it saves the body from disease and death, and so helps it to attain the higher life. But to think of the study of medicine as the aim of life and devote all one's time to it is doing injury to one's soul. Some spend their time in matters even less significant than this, *viz*, in studying grammar and language; others again in mathematics and in solving curious problems which are never likely to happen. The only valuable part here is that which has relation to astronomy. Some are exclusively occupied in "twisting threads." This is an expression used by an Arabian philosopher,[230] who compares man's condition in the world to that of a slave who was promised freedom and royalty besides if he made the pilgrimage to Mecca and celebrated there. If he made the journey and was prevented from reaching the holy city, he would get freedom only; but if he did not undertake the trip he would get nothing. The three steps in the realization of the purpose are thus: making the preparations for the journey, getting on the road and passing from station to station, and finally wandering about in the place of destination. One small element in the preparation for the journey is twisting the threads for the water bottle. Medicine and law as means of gaining a livelihood and a reputation represent the stage of preparing for the journey. They are both intended to improve the ills of life, whether in the relations of man to man as in law; or in the treatment of the internal humors as in medicine. Medicine seems more important, for on the assumption of mankind being just, there would be no need of law, whereas the need for medicine would remain. To spend one's whole life in legal casuistry and the working out of hypothetical cases on the pretext of sharpening one's wits, is like being engaged in twisting threads continually—a little is necessary, but a great deal is a waste of time. It would be best if the religious man would first learn how to prove the existence of God, the meaning of prophecy, the nature of reward and punishment and the future world, and how to defend these matters before an unbeliever. Then if he has time left, he may devote it to legalistic discussions, and there would be no harm.

Self-examination, in order to purify oneself from vices great and small, represents the second stage of getting on the road and travelling from station to station. The final stage, arriving in the holy city and celebrating there, is to have a perfect knowledge of God. He who attains this is the best of wise men, having the best of knowledge, which deals with the noblest subject. The reader must not expect to find it all in this book. If he reads this and does not study the subject for himself, he is like a man who spent his time in reading about medicine and cannot cure the simplest ailment. The knowledge of God is a form that is bestowed from on high upon the rational soul when she is prepared by means of moral perfection and scientific study. The prophet puts all three functions of the soul on the same level, and gives preference to knowledge of God. "Thus saith the Lord," says Jeremiah (9, 22), "Let not the wise man glory in his wisdom [rational soul], neither let the mighty man glory in his might [spirited soul], let not the rich man glory in his riches [nutritive soul]: but let him that glorieth glory in this, that he understandeth, and knoweth me. . . ." Jeremiah also recommends (*ib.*) knowing God through his deeds—"That I am the Lord which exercise loving-kindness"—in order that man may imitate him.[231]

We have now a general idea of Ibn Daud's attitude and point of view; and in passing to the details of his system it will not be necessary to rehearse all the particulars of his thought, much of it being common to all mediæval writers on Jewish philosophy. We shall confine ourselves to those matters in which Ibn Daud contributed something new, not contained in the writings of his predecessors.

Following the Aristotelian system, he begins by describing substance and accident and gives a list and characterization of the ten categories. This he follows up by showing that the classification of the ten categories lies at the basis of the 139th Psalm. It needs not our saying that it must be an extraordinary mode of exegesis that can find such things in such unusual places. But the very strangeness of the phenomenon bears witness to the remarkable influence exerted by the Aristotelian philosophy upon the thinking of the Spanish Jews at that time.[232]

From the categories he passes to a discussion of the most fundamental concepts in the Aristotelian philosophy, matter and form. And here his method of proving the existence of matter is Aristotelian and new. It is based upon the discussion in Aristotle's Physics, though not necessarily derived from there directly. Primary matter, he says, is free from all form. There must be such, for in the change of one thing to another, of water to air for example, it cannot be the *form* of water that receives the form of air; for the form of water disappears, whereas that which receives the new form must be there. Reason therefore leads us to assume a common substrate of all things that are subject to change. This is primary matter, free from all form. This matter being at the basis of all change and becoming, could not itself have come to be through a similar process, or we should require another matter prior to it, and it would not be the prime matter we supposed it to be. This last argument led Aristotle to the concept of an eternal matter, the basis of becoming for all else besides, itself not subject to any such process. It is an ultimate, to ask for the origin of which would signify to misunderstand the meaning of origin. All things of the sublunar world originate in matter, hence matter itself is the unoriginated, the eternal.

Ibn Daud as a Jew could not accept this solution, and so he cut the knot by saying that while it is true that matter cannot originate in the way in which the composite objects of the sublunar world come to be, it does not yet follow that it is absolutely ultimate and eternal. God alone is the ultimate and eternal; nothing else is. Matter is a relative ultimate; relative, that is, to the composite and changeable objects of our world; but it is itself an effect of God as the universal cause. God created it outright.

Prime matter, therefore, represents the first stage in creation. The next stage is the endowment of this formless matter with corporeality in the abstract, *i. e.*, with extension. Then come the specific forms of the four elements, then their compounds through mineral, plant and animal to man. This is not new; we have already met with it in Gabirol and Ibn Zaddik. Nor is the following significant statement altogether new, though no one before Ibn Daud expressed it so clearly and so definitely. It is that the above analysis of natural objects into matter, universal body, the elements, and so on, is not a physical division but a logical. It does not mean that there was a time when prime matter actually existed as such before it received the form of corporeality, and then there existed actually an absolute body of pure extension until it received the four elements. No, nothing has existence *in actu* which has not individuality, including not only form, but also accidents. The above analysis is theoretical, and the order of priority is logical not real. In reality only the complete compound of matter and form (the individual) exists.

Allusion to matter and form is also found in the Bible in Jeremiah (18, 1ff.), "Arise and go down to the potter's house . . . Then I went down to the potter's house, and, behold, he wrought his work on the wheels . . . Behold as the clay in the potter's hand . . . " [233]

The next important topic analyzed by Ibn Daud is that of motion. This is of especial importance to Ibn Daud because upon it he bases a new proof of the existence of God, not heretofore found in the works of any of his predecessors. It is taken from Aristotle's Physics, probably from Avicenna's treatises on the subject, is then adopted by Maimonides, and through his example no doubt is made use of by Thomas Aquinas, the great Christian Scholastic of the thirteenth century, who gives it the most prominent place in his "Summa Contra Gentiles."

Ibn Daud does not give Aristotle's general definition of motion as the "actualization of the potential qua potential" (*cf.* above, p. xxxii), but his other remarks concerning it imply it. Motion, he says, is applied first to movement in place, and is then transferred to any change which is gradual, such as quantitative or qualitative change. Sudden change is not called motion. As the four elements have all the same matter and yet possess different motions—earth and water moving downward, fire and air upward—it cannot be the matter which is the cause of their motions. It must therefore be the forms, which are different in different things.

Nothing can move itself. While it is true that the form of a thing determines the kind of motion it shall have, it cannot in itself produce that motion, which can be caused only by an efficient cause from without. The case of animal motions may seem like a refutation of this view, but it is not really so. The soul and the body are two distinct principles in the animal; and it is the soul that moves the body. The reason why a thing cannot move itself is because the thing which is moved is potential with reference to that which the motion is intended to realize, whereas the thing causing the motion is actual with respect to the relation in question. If then a thing moved itself, it would be actual and potential at the same time and in the same relation, which is a contradiction. The Bible, too, hints at the idea that every motion must have a mover by the recurring questions concerning the origin of prophetic visions, of the existence of the earth, and so on. Such are the expressions in Job (38, 36, 37): "Who hath put wisdom in the inward parts?" "Who can number the clouds by wisdom?" In Proverbs (30, 4): "Who hath established all the ends of the earth?" and in many passages besides.[234]

The question of infinity is another topic of importance for proving the existence of God. We proceed as follows: An infinite line is an impossibility. For let the lines $c\overline{a|b}d$ be infinite in the directions b, d. Take away from cd a finite length $=ce$, and pull up the line ed so that e coincides with c. Now if ed is equal to ab, and cd was also equal to ab by hypothesis, it follows that $ed = cd$, which is impossible, for ed is a part of cd. If it is shorter than cd and yet is infinite, one infinite is shorter than another infinite, which is also impossible. The only alternative left is then that ed is finite. If then we add to it the finite part ce, the sum, $ce + ed = cd$, will be finite, and cd being equal to ab by hypothesis, ab is also finite. Hence there is no infinite line. If there is no infinite line, there is no infinite surface or infinite solid, for we could in that case draw in them infinite lines. Besides we can prove directly the impossibility of infinite surface and solid by the same methods we employed in line.

We can prove similarly that an infinite series of objects is also an impossibility. In other words, infinite number as an actuality is impossible because it is a contradiction in terms. A number of things means a known number; infinite means having no known number. A series is something that has beginning, middle and end. Infinite means being all middle. We have thus proved that an actual infinite is impossible, whether as extension or number. And the Bible also alludes to the finiteness of the universe in the words of Isaiah (40, 12): "Who hath measured the waters in the hollow of his hand . . . ," intimating that the universe is capable of being measured.

We must prove next that no finite body can have an infinite power. For let the line ae $\overline{abcde}$ be a finite line having an infinite power. Divide into the several parts ab, bc, cd, de, etc. If every one of the parts has an infinite power, ab has an infinite power, ac a greater infinite power, ad a still greater, ae a still greater, and so on. But this is absurd, for there cannot be anything greater than the infinite. It follows then that each of the parts has a finite power; and as the sum of finites is finite, the line ae also has a finite power. All these principles we must keep in mind, for we shall by means of them prove later the existence and incorporeality of God.[235]

As the concepts of physics are essential for proving the existence of God, so are the principles of psychology of importance in showing that there are intermediate beings between God and the corporeal substances of the world. These are called in the Bible angels. The philosophers call them secondary causes.

Accordingly Ibn Daud follows his physical doctrines with a discussion of the soul. There is nothing new in his proof that such a thing as soul exists. It is identical with the deduction of Joseph Ibn Zaddik (*supra*, p. 134). Stone and tree and horse and man are all bodies and yet the last three have powers and functions which the stone has not, *viz.*, nutrition, growth and reproduction. Horse and man have in addition to the three powers above mentioned, which they have in common with tree, the powers of sensation and motion and imagination, which plants have not. Finally man is distinguished above all the rest of animal creation in possessing the faculty of intelligence, and the knowledge of art and of ethical discrimination. All these functions cannot be body or the result of body, for in that case all corporeal objects should have all of them, as they are all bodies. We must therefore attribute them to an extra-corporeal principle; and this we call soul. As an incorporeal thing the soul cannot be strictly defined, not being composed of genus and species; but we can describe it in a roundabout way in its relation to the body. He then gives the Aristotelian definition of the soul as "the [first] entelechy of a natural body having life potentially" (*cf.* above, p. xxxv).

Like many of his predecessors who treated of the soul, Ibn Daud also finds it necessary to guard against the materialistic theory of the soul which would make it the product of the elemental mixture in the body, if not itself body. This would reduce the soul to a phenomenon of the body, or in Aristotelian terminology, an accident of the body, and would deprive it of all substantiality and independence, not to speak of immortality. How can that which is purely a resultant of a combination of elements remain when its basis is gone? Accordingly Ibn Daud takes pains to refute the most important of these phenomenalistic theories, that of Hippocrates and Galen. Their theory in brief is that the functions which we attribute to the soul are in reality the results of the various combinations of the four elementary qualities, hot, cold, moist, dry. The more harmonious and equable the proportion of their union, the higher is the function resulting therefrom. The difference between man and beast, and between animal and plant is then the difference in the proportionality of the elemental mixture. They prove this theory of theirs by the observation that as long as the mixture is perfect the activities above mentioned proceed properly; whereas as soon as there is a disturbance in the mixture, the animal becomes sick and cannot perform his activities, or dies altogether if the disturbance is very great. The idea is very plausible and a great many believe it, but it is mistaken as we shall prove.

His refutation of the "accident" or "mixture" theory of the soul, as well as the subsequent discussion of the various functions, sensuous and rational, of the tripartite soul, are based upon Ibn Sina's treatment of the same topic, and we have already reproduced some of it in our exposition of Judah Halevi. We shall therefore be brief here and refer only to such aspects as are new in Ibn Daud, or such as we found it advisable to omit in our previous expositions.

His main argument against the materialistic or mechanistic theory of the soul is that while a number of phenomena of the growing animal body can be explained by reference to the form of the mixture in the elementary qualities, not all aspects can be thus explained. Its growth and general formation may be the result of material and mechanical causes, but not so the design and purpose evident in the similarity, to the smallest detail, of the individuals of a species, even when the mixture is not identical. There is no doubt that there is wisdom here working with a purpose. This is soul. There is another argument based upon the visible results of other mixtures which exhibit properties that cannot be remotely compared with the functions we attribute to the soul. The animal and the plant exhibit activities far beyond anything present in the simple elements of the mixture. There must therefore be in animals and plants something additional to the elements of the mixture. This extra thing resides in the composite of which it forms a part, for without it the animal or plant is no longer what it is. Hence as the latter is substance, that which forms a part of it is also substance; for accident, as Aristotle says, is that which resides *in* a thing but not as forming a part of it.

We have now shown that the soul is substance and not accident. We must still make clear in which of the four senses of the Aristotelian substance the soul is to be regarded. By the theory of exclusion Ibn Daud decides that the soul is substance in the sense in which we apply that term to "form." The form appears upon the common matter and "specifies" it, and makes it what it is, bringing it from potentiality to actuality. It is also the efficient and final cause of the body. The body exists for the sake of the soul, in order that the soul may attain its perfection through the body. As the most perfect body in the lower world is the human body, and it is for the sake of the soul, it follows that the existence of the sublunar world is for the sake of the human soul, that it may be purified and made perfect by science and moral conduct.

While we have proved that soul is not mixture nor anything like it, it is nevertheless true that the kind of soul bestowed upon a given body depends upon the state of the mixture in the elementary qualities of that body. Thus we have the three kinds of soul, vegetative, animal and human or rational. We need not follow Ibn Daud in his detailed descriptions of the functions of the several kinds of soul, as there is little that is new and that we have not already met in Joseph Ibn Zaddik and Judah Halevi. Avicenna (Ibn Sina) is the common source for Halevi and Ibn Daud, and the description of the inner senses is practically identical in the two, with the slight difference that Halevi attributes to the "common sense" the two functions which are divided in Ibn Daud between the common sense and the power of representation.

The soul is not eternal. It was created and bestowed upon body. When a body comes into being, the character of its mixture determines that a soul of a certain kind shall be connected with it. The other alternatives are (1) that the soul existed independently before the body, is then connected with the body and dies with the death of the latter; or (2) it remains after the death of the body. The first alternative is impossible; because if the soul is connected with the body in order to die with it, its union is an injury to the soul, for in its separate existence it was free from the defects of matter. The second alternative is equally impossible; for if the soul was able to exist without the body before the appearance of the latter and after its extinction, of what use is its connection with the body? Far from being of any benefit, its union with the body is harmful to the soul, for it is obliged to share in the corporeal accidents. Divine wisdom never does anything without a purpose.

The truth is that the soul does not exist before the body. It arises at the same time as, and in connection with body, realizing and actualizing the latter. Seed and sperm have in them the possibility of becoming plant and animal respectively. But they need an agent to bring to actuality what is in them potentially. This agent—an angel or a sphere, or an angel using a sphere as its instrument—bestows forms upon bodies, which take the places of the previous forms the bodies had. The sphere or star produces these forms (or souls) by means of its motions, which motions ultimately go back to the first incorporeal mover, by whose wisdom forms are connected with bodies in order to perfect the former by means of the latter.

Now the human soul has the most important power of all other animals, that of grasping intelligibles or universals. It is also able to discriminate between good and evil in conduct, moral, political and economic. The human soul, therefore, has, it seems, two powers, *theoretical* and *practical*. With the former it understands the simple substances, known as angels in the Bible and as "secondary causes" and "separate intelligences" among the philosophers. By this means the soul rises gradually to its perfection. With the practical reason it attends to noble and worthy conduct. All the other powers of the soul must be obedient to the behests of the practical reason. This in turn is subservient to the theoretical, putting its good qualities at the disposition of the speculative reason, and thus helping it to come into closer communion with the simple substances, the angels and God. This is the highest power there is in the *world of nature*.

We must now show that the rational power in man is neither itself body nor is it a power residing in a corporeal subject. That it is not itself body is quite evident, for we have proved that the lower souls too, those of animals and plants, are not corporeal. But we must show concerning the rational power that it is independent of body in its activity. This we can prove in various ways. One is by considering the object and content of the reason. Man has general ideas or universal propositions. These are not divisible. An idea cannot be divided into two halves or into parts. Reason in action consists of ideas. Now if reason is a power residing in a corporeal subject, it would be divisible like the latter. Take heat as an example. Heat is a corporeal power, *i. e.*, a power residing in a body. It extends through the dimensions of the body, and as the latter is divided so is the former. But this is evidently not true of general ideas, such as that a thing cannot both be and not be, that the whole is greater than its part, and so on. Hence the rational power is independent of body.

Ibn Daud gives several other proofs, taken from Aristotle and Avicenna, to show that reason is independent, but we cannot reproduce them all here. We shall, however, name one more which is found in the "De Anima" of Aristotle and is based on experience. If the reason performed its thinking by means of a corporeal organ like the external senses, the power of knowing would be weakened when confronted with a difficult subject, and would thereby be incapacitated from exercising its powers as before. This is the case with the eye, which is dazzled by a bright light and cannot see at all, or the ear, which cannot hear at all when deafened by a loud noise. But the case of knowledge is clearly different. The more difficult the subject the more is the power of the reason developed in exercising itself therein. And in old age, when the corporeal organs are weakened, the power of reason is strongest.

Although it is thus true that the rational soul is independent of the body, nevertheless it did not exist before the body any more than the lower souls. For if it did, it was either one soul for all men, or there were as many souls as there are individual men. The first is impossible; for the same soul would then be wise and ignorant, good and bad, which is impossible. Nor could the separate souls be different, for being all human souls they cannot differ in essence, which is their common humanity. But neither can they differ in accidental qualities, for simple substances have no accidents. They cannot therefore be either one or many, *i. e.*, they cannot be at all before body.

Nor must we suppose because the reason exercises its thought functions without the use of a corporeal organ that it appears full fledged in actual perfection in the person of the infant. Experience teaches otherwise. The perfections of the human soul are in the child potential. Later on by divine assistance he acquires the first principles of knowledge about which there is no dispute, such as that two things equal to the same thing are equal to each other, that two contrary predicates cannot apply to the same subject at the same time in the same relation, and so on. Some of these are the fundamental principles of mathematics, others of other sciences. Then he progresses further and learns to make premises and construct syllogisms and argue from the known to the unknown. We have thus three stages in the development of the reason. The first potential stage is known as the *hylic* or *potential intellect*. The second is known as the *actual intellect*, and the third is the *acquired intellect*. If not for the body the person could not make this progress. For without body there are no senses, and without senses he would not see how the wine in the barrel ferments and increases in volume, which suggests that quantity is accident and body is substance. Nor would he learn the distinction between quality and substance if he did not observe a white garment turning black, or a hot body becoming cold. There is need therefore of the body with its senses to lead to a knowledge of the universals. But this knowledge once acquired, the soul needs not the body for its subsequent existence; and as the soul is not a corporeal power, the death of the body does not cause the extinction of the soul.

Some think that because the soul is the form of the body it is dependent upon it and cannot survive it, as no other form survives its substance. But this inference is not valid. For if the human soul is included in the statement that no form survives its matter, we assume what we want to prove, and there is no need of the argument. If it is not as a matter of fact included, because it is the question at issue, its comparison with the other observed cases is simply a matter of opinion and not decisive.

The reader will see that the problem of the rational soul gave Ibn Daud much concern and trouble. The pre-existence of the soul as Plato teaches it did not appeal to him for many reasons, not the least among them being the statement in Genesis (2, 7), "And God breathed into his nostrils the breath of life," which seems to favor the idea of the soul originating with the body; though, to be sure, a harmless verse of this kind would not have stood in his way, had he had reason to favor the doctrine of pre-existence. Immortality was also a dogma which he dared not deny. The arguments against it seemed rather strong.

From the doctrine of the soul's origin with the body and its being fitted to the material composition of the latter, would seem to follow the soul's extinction with the death of the body. The same result was apparently demanded by the observation that the intellect develops as the body matures, and that without the senses and their data there would be no intellect at all. The fluctuation of intellectual strength with the state of bodily health would seem to tend to the same end, against the doctrine of immortality. Moreover, the Aristotelian definition of the soul as the entelechy or form of the body, if it applies to the rational faculty as well as to the lower powers, implies necessarily that it is a form like other forms and disappears with the dissolution of its substance. To avoid all these pitfalls Ibn Daud insists upon the incorporeal character of the reason's activity, *i. e.*, its independence of any corporeal organ, and its increasing power in old age despite the gradual weakening of the body. He admits that its development is dependent on the data of sense perception, but insists that this is not incompatible with its freedom from the body when fully developed and perfected. As for its being a form of body, not all forms are alike; and it is not so certain that the rational power is a form of body. Neither the difficulties nor the solution are of Ibn Daud's making. They are as old as Aristotle, and his successors grappled with them as best they could.

There is still the question of the manner of the soul's survival. The same reasons which Ibn Daud brings forward against the possibility of the existence of many souls before the body, apply with equal cogency to their survival after death. If simple substances having a common essence cannot differ either in essence or in accident, the human souls after the death of the body must exist as one soul, and what becomes of *individual* immortality, which religion promises? Ibn Daud has not a word to say about this, and it is one of the weak points religiously in his system as well as in that of Maimonides, which the critics and opponents of the latter did not fail to observe.

Before leaving the problem of the soul Ibn Daud devotes a word to showing that metempsychosis is impossible. The soul of man is suited to the character of his elemental mixture, which constitutes the individuality of his body. Hence every individual's body has its own peculiar soul. A living person cannot therefore have in him a soul which formerly resided in a different body unless the two bodies are identical in all respects. But in that case it is not transmigration but the re-appearance of the same person after he has ceased to be. But this has never yet happened.

Finally Ibn Daud finds it necessary to defend the Bible against those who criticize the Jews on the ground that there is no mention of the future world and the existence of the soul after death in the Biblical writings. All the rewards and punishments spoken of in the Bible, they say, refer to this world. His answer offers nothing new. Judah Halevi had already tried to account for this phenomenon, besides insisting that altogether devoid of allusion to the future world the Bible is not. Ibn Daud follows in Halevi's footsteps (*cf.* above, p. 170).[236]

Abraham Ibn Daud closes the first, the purely scientific part of his treatise, by a discussion of the heavenly spheres and their motions. In accordance with the view of Aristotle, which was shared by the majority of writers throughout the middle ages, he regards the spheres with their stars as living beings, and their motions as voluntary, the result of will and purpose, and not simply " natural," *i. e.*, due to an unconscious force within them called nature. One of his arguments to prove this is derived from the superiority of the heavenly bodies to our own. Their size, their brightness and their continued duration are all evidence of corporeal superiority. And it stands to reason that as the human body, which is the highest in the sublunar world, has a soul that is nobler than that of plant or animal, so the heavenly bodies must be endowed with souls as much superior to the human intellect as their bodies are to the human body. The Bible alludes to this truth in the nineteenth Psalm, "The heavens declare the glory of God. . . . There is no speech nor language. . . ." The last expression signifies that they praise God with the intellect. There are other passages in the Bible besides, and particularly the first chapter of Ezekiel, which make it clear that the heavenly bodies are living and intelligent beings; not, to be sure, in the sense of taking nourishment and growing and reproducing their kind and making use of five senses, but in the sense of performing voluntary motions and being endowed with intellect.[237]

We have now concluded our preliminary discussion of the scientific principles lying at the basis of Judaism. And our next task is to study the fundamental doctrines of Jewish theology which form the highest object of knowledge, dealing as they do with God and his attributes and his revelation. The first thing to prove then is the existence of God, since we cannot define him. For definition means the designation of the genus or class to which the thing defined belongs, whereas God cannot be put in a class. As the essence of a thing is revealed by its definition, we cannot know God's essence and are limited to a knowledge of his existence.

The principles for this proof we have already given. They are that a thing cannot move itself, and that an actual infinite series is impossible. The argument then proceeds as follows: Nothing can move itself, hence everything that moves is moved by something other than itself. If this is also moving, it must be moved by a third, and so on *ad infinitum*. But an actual infinite series of things moving and being moved is impossible, and unless we ultimately arrive at a first link in this chain, all motion is impossible. Hence there must be a first to account for the motion we observe in the world. This first must not itself be subject to motion, for it would then have to have another before it to make it move, and it would not be the first we supposed it to be. We have thus proved, therefore, the existence of a *primum movens immobile*, a first unmoved mover.

We must now show that this unmoved mover is incorporeal. This we can prove by means of another principle of physics, made clear in the first part. We showed there that a finite body cannot have an infinite power. But God is infinite. For, being immovable, his power is not affected by time. Hence God cannot be body.

This proof, as we said before, is new in Jewish philosophy. In Bahya we found a proof which bears a close resemblance to this one (*cf.* above, p. 87); but the difference is that Bahya argues from being, Ibn Daud from motion. Bahya says if a thing is, some cause must have made it to be, for a thing cannot make itself. As we cannot proceed *ad infinitum*, there must be a first which is the cause of the existence of everything else. The objection here, of course, is that if a thing cannot make itself, how did the first come to be.

The Aristotelian proof of Ibn Daud knows nothing about the origin of being. As far as Aristotle's own view is concerned there is no *temporal* beginning either of being or of motion. Both are eternal, and so is matter, the basis of all genesis and change. God is the eternal cause of the eternal motion of the world, and hence of the eternal genesis and dissolution, which constitutes the life of the sublunar world. How to reconcile the idea of eternal time and eternal motion with the doctrine that an actual infinite is impossible we shall see when we treat Maimondes (p. 251). Ibn Daud does not adopt eternity of motion even hypothetically, as Maimonides does. But this merely removes the difficulty one step. For the infinity which is regarded impossible in phenomena is placed in God. But another more serious objection is the adoption of an Aristotelian argument where it does not suit. For the argument from motion does not give us a creator but a first mover. For Aristotle there is no creator, and his proof is adequate. But for Ibn Daud it is decidedly inadequate. We are so far minus a proof that God is a creator *ex nihilo*. Ibn Daud simply asserts that God created matter, but this argument does not prove it. As to the incorporeality of God Aristotle can prove it adequately from the eternity of motion. If a finite body (and there is no such thing as an infinite body) cannot have an infinite power, God, whose causing eternal motion argues infinite power, is not a body. Ibn Daud's attempt to prove God's infinity without the theory of infinite motion on the ground that time cannot affect what is immovable, is decidedly less satisfactory. On the whole then this adoption of Aristotle's argument from motion is not helpful, as it leads to eternity of matter, and God as the mover rather than the Creator. Gersonides was frank enough and bold enough to recognize this consequence and to adopt it. We shall see Maimonides's attitude when we come to treat of his philosophy.

Ibn Daud may have been aware of the inadequacy of his argument from motion, and therefore he adds another, based upon the distinction between the "possible existent" and the "necessary existent" —a distinction and an argument due to Alfarabi and Avicenna. A possible existent is a thing whose existence depends upon another, and was preceded by non-existence. It may exist or not, depending upon its cause; hence the name *possible* existent. A necessary existent is one whose existence is in itself and not derived from elsewhere. It is a necessary existent because its own essence cannot be thought without involving existence. Now the question is, Is there such a thing as a necessary existent, or are all existents merely possible? If all existents are possible, we have an infinite series, every link of which is dependent for its existence upon the link preceding it; and so long as there is no first there is nothing to explain the existence of any link in the chain. We must therefore assume a first, which is itself not again dependent upon a cause prior to it. This is by definition a necessary existent, which is the cause of the existence of everything else. This proof is compatible with God as a Creator.

Having shown the existence and incorporeality of God we must now prove his unity. We shall base this proof upon the idea of the necessary existent. Such an existent cannot have in it any multiplicity; for if it has, its own essence would not be able to keep the elements together, and there would be need of an external agent to do this. But in this case the object would be dependent upon something else, which is incompatible with the idea of a necessary existent.

Nor is it possible there should be two necessary existents; for the necessary existent, we have just shown, must be of the utmost simplicity, and hence cannot have any attribute added to its essence. Now if there is a second, there must be something by which the first differs from the second, or they are identical. Either the first or the second therefore would not be completely simple, and hence not a necessary existent.

We have thus shown that God is one both in the sense of simple and in the sense of unique. To have a clear insight into the nature of his unity, we must now show that nothing else outside of God is really one, though we apply the term one to many things. No one will claim that a collective is one; but neither is an individual really one, for an individual man, for example, consists of many organs. You might think that a homogeneous and continuous elementary mass like air or water is one. But this is not true either, for everything that is corporeal is composed of matter and form. If then we set aside corporeal objects and aim to find real unity in mathematical entities like line and surface, which are not corporeal, we are met with the difficulty that line and surface are divisible, and hence potentially multiple. But neither are the simple intellectual substances, like the angels, true ones; for they are composed of their own possible existence and the necessary existence they acquire from another. The only being therefore that may be a true one is that which is not corporeal and not dependent upon another for its existence.

Considering the question of unity from a different aspect, in its relation, namely, to the thing designated as one, we find that unity never forms the essence of anything called by that name; but is in every case an accident. Thus if it were the essence of man as man that he is one, there could not on the one hand be many men, and on the other there could not also at the same time be one horse, one tree, one stone. In God his unity cannot be an accident, since as simple he has no accidents. Hence his unity is his essence. And if we examine the matter carefully we find that it is a negative concept. It involves two things. First, that every other unity involves plurality in some form or another. And second that being unlike anything else, he cannot bear having other things associated with him to make the result many, as we can in the case of man. A, for example, is one; and with B, C, and D he becomes many. This is not applicable to God.[238]

The divine attributes form the next topic we must consider. Here Ibn Daud offers little or nothing that is essentially new. He admits neither essential nor accidental attributes, for either would bring plurality and composition in the nature of God. The only attributes he admits are negative and relative. When we speak of God as cause we do not place any special entity in his essence, but merely indicate the dependence of things upon him. The truest attributes are the negative, such as that he is not body, that his existence is not dependent upon another, and so on; the only difficulty being that negative attributes, though removing many doubts, do not give us any positive information. All the anthropomorphic attributes in the Bible endowing God with human functions like sleeping and waking, or ascribing to him human limbs, eyes, ears, hands, feet, etc., must be understood metaphorically. For the Bible itself warns us against corporealizing God, "Take ye therefore good heed unto yourselves; for ye saw no manner of form on the day that the Lord spake unto you in Horeb" (Deut. 4, 15). When the Bible speaks of God's anger and favor, the meaning is that good deeds bring man near to God and cause happiness which is known as paradise ("Gan Eden"), and bad deeds remove far away from God and lead to misfortune, called Gehenna. It is like the apparent motion of the trees and the mountains to the traveller, when in reality it is he that is moving. So here God is said to approach and depart, to be angry with and favor, when in reality it is man who by his deeds comes near to God or departs far from him. When we assign many attributes to God we do not mean that there is any multiplicity in his nature. This cannot be. It is like the case of a man whose eyes are not properly co-ordinated. He sees double when there is only one. So we too suffer from intellectual squinting, when we seem to see many attributes in the one God.

The most common and most important attributes are the following eight: One, existent, true, eternal, living, knowing, willing, able. It can be easily shown (and Ibn Daud does proceed to show, though we shall not follow him in his details) that all these are at bottom negative. Unity means that there is nothing like him and that he is indivisible. Eternal means he is not subject to change or motion. True means he will never cease existing and that his existence does not come from another, and so on with the rest.

He closes his discussion of the attributes by intimating that he has more to say on this topic, but had better be content with what has been said so far, for a more thorough discussion of these matters in a book might do harm to those who do not understand and interpret the author's words incorrectly. This reminds us of Maimonides's adjuration of the reader to keep what he finds in the "Guide of the Perplexed" to himself and not to spread it abroad. Philosophy clearly was a delicate subject and not meant for intellectual babes, whose intellectual digestion might be seriously disturbed.[239]

We have now concluded our theory of God and his attributes; and in doing so we made use of principles of physics, such as matter and form, potentiality and actuality, motion and infinity. The next step is to prove the existence and nature of intermediate spiritual beings between God and the corporeal objects of the superlunar and sublunar worlds, called angels in the Bible, and secondary causes by the philosophers. For this purpose we shall have to apply the principles we have proved concerning the soul and the motions of the heavenly bodies. We have proved above that the human soul is at first in the child intelligent potentially and then becomes intelligent actually.

This requires an agent, in whom the end to which the potential is proceeding is always actual. As the rational soul is neither body nor a corporeal power, this actual agent cannot be either of these, hence it is neither a sphere nor the soul of a sphere, but it must be a simple substance called *Active Intellect*. The prophets call it "Holy Spirit" ("Ruah Ha-Kodesh"). We thus have a proof of the existence of at least one such simple intellectual substance, or angel, the relation of which to the human soul is as that of light to vision. Without light vision is potential, light makes it actual. So the active intellect makes the potential soul actual and gives it first the axioms, which are universally certain, and hence could not have originated by induction from experience.

Similarly we can prove the existence of other simple substances from the motions of the heavenly spheres. We have already shown that the spheres are living beings and endowed with souls. But souls, while causing motion in their bodies are at the same time themselves in a sort of psychic motion. This must be caused by unmoved movers, or intellects, who are also the causes of the souls. To make this difficult matter somewhat clearer and more plausible, we may instance an analogy from familiar experience. A ship is made by the shipbuilder, who is its corporeal cause. But there is also an incorporeal cause, likewise a ship, *viz.*, the ship in the mind of the shipbuilder. The analogy is imperfect, because the incorporeal ship in the mind of the builder cannot produce an actual corporeal ship without the builder employing material, such as wood, iron, etc., and in addition to that expending time and physical exertion on the material. But if he had the power to give the form of a ship to the material as soon as the latter was prepared for it without time and physical manipulation, we should have an instance of what we want to prove, namely, the existence of simple immaterial substances causing forms to emanate upon corporeal existences. This is the nature of the active intellect in its relation to the soul of man, and it is in the same way that the philosophers conceive of the motions of the heavenly spheres. God is the first unmoved mover. The angels or simple substances stand next to him; and they, too, are always actual intelligences, and move the heavenly bodies as the object of love and desire moves the object loving it without itself being moved. The heavenly bodies move therefore because of a desire to perfect themselves, or to become like unto their movers.

So far Ibn Daud agrees with the philosophers, because the doctrines so far expounded are not incompatible with the Bible. But when the philosophers raise the question, How can the many originate from the One, the manifold universe from the one God, and attempt to answer it by their theory of successive emanations, Ibn Daud calls a halt. The human mind is not really so all-competent as to be able to answer all questions of the most difficult nature. The doctrine of successive emanations is that elaborated by Alfarabi and Avicenna, which we have already seen quoted and criticized by Judah Halevi (*cf.* above, p. 178 f.). It is slightly more complicated in Ibn Daud, who speaks of the treble nature of the emanations after the first Intelligence—an intelligence, a soul and a sphere—whereas in Halevi's account there were only two elements, the soul not being mentioned.[240]

We have so far dealt with the more theoretical part of theology and religion, so much of it as may be and is accepted by nations and religions other than Jews. It remains now to approach the more practical and the more specifically Jewish phases of religion; though in the purely ethical discussions and those relating to Providence we have once more a subject of general application, and not exclusively Jewish.

As the introduction to this second part of the subject, Abraham Ibn Daud devotes a few words to the theoretical defence of tradition, or rather of mediate knowledge. He does so by analyzing the various kinds of knowledge. Knowledge, he says, is either intelligible or sensible. Sensible knowledge is either directly perceived by the subject or received by him from another who perceived it directly, and whom he believes or not as the case may be. That is why some things believed by some people are not believed by others. The ignorant may think that this weakness is inherent in matters received from others. As a matter of fact such indirect knowledge is at the basis of civilization and makes it possible. If every man were to judge only by what he sees with his own eyes, society could never get along; there would be no way of obtaining justice in court, for the judge would not put credence in witnesses, and the parties would have to fight out their differences, which would lead to bloodshed and the disruption of social life. The different attitude of different persons to a given matter of belief is due not necessarily to the uncertainty of the thing itself, but to the manner in which the object of the belief came down to us. If a thing rests upon the testimony of one man, its warrant is not very strong. But if a whole nation witnessed an event, it is no longer doubtful, unless we suppose that the account itself is due to one writer, and the event never happened. We shall discuss these matters in the sequel.[241]

Having justified in a general way the knowledge derived from the testimony of others by showing that society could not exist without depending upon such knowledge; though admitting at the same time that caution should be exercised and criticism in determining what traditional testimony is valid or not, we now take up one of these traditional phenomena which plays perhaps the most important rôle in Jewish theology, namely, the phenomenon of prophecy. Before discussing the traditional aspect of this institution and its purpose in the history of religion we must consider it from its natural and psychological aspect.

The explanation of Ibn Daud—it was not original with him, as we have already seen the non-religious philosopher in Halevi's Cusari giving utterance to the same idea, and in Jewish philosophy Israeli touches on it—the explanation of Ibn Daud is grounded in his psychology, the Aristotelian psychology of Avicenna. The first degree of prophecy, he says, is found in true dreams, which happen to many people. Just as waking is a state of the body in which it uses the external as well as the internal senses, so sleeping is a state of the body in which the soul suppresses the external senses by putting them to sleep, and exercises its "natural" powers only, such as the beating of the heart pulse, respiration, and so on. The internal senses are also at work during sleep, or at least some of them. In particular the power of imagination is active when the external senses are at rest. It then makes various combinations and separations and brings them to the common sense. The result is a dream, true or false. When the senses are weak for one reason or another this power becomes active and, when not controlled by the reason, produces a great many erroneous visions and ideas, as in the delusions of the sick.

The Deity and the angels and the Active Intellect have a knowledge of the past, present and future, and we already know that the soul, *i. e.*, the rational soul, receives influence from the Active Intellect as a natural thing in every person. Now just as it gets from it science and general ideas, so it may receive a knowledge of hidden things if the soul is adequately prepared. The reason it cannot receive information of hidden things from the Active Intellect in its waking state, is because the soul is then busy in acquiring knowledge through the senses. In sleep, too, it may be prevented by the thick vapors rising from the food consumed during the day, or by anxiety due to want of food or drink. The imagination also sometimes hinders this process by the constant presentation of its foolish combinations to the common sense. But sometimes this power comes under the control of the reason, and then the rational soul is prepared to receive hidden things from the Active Intellect. In those cases the imagination transforms these facts into images, which are true dreams. If they concern an individual or a particular event, we do not call them prophecy, or at least the share of prophecy they may have is very small. We call them prophetic dreams when they concern important matters and have reference to a whole nation or nations, and come to pass in the distant future. An example of such a dream is that recorded in Laniel 7, 1.

Sometimes the information comes to the prophet without the aid of an image, when the reason prevails over the imagination, like the dream of Abraham at the "covenant of the pieces" (Gen. 15, 12ff.). Sometimes, also, the activity of the senses does not prevent the prophet from seeing the hidden things of the future, and he receives prophetic inspirations while awake. The prophet sometimes faints as he is overcome by the unusual phenomenon, at other times he succeeds in enduring it without swooning. All these cases can be illustrated from the Bible, and examples will readily occur to the reader who is familiar with the various instances and descriptions of prophetic visions and activities in Scripture.

The purpose of prophecy is to guide the people in the right way. With this end in view God inspires a proper man as a prophet and gives him superior powers to perform miracles. Not every man is capable of prophecy, only one who has a pure soul. For the most part the prophetic gift is innate, at the same time study and good associations help to develop this power in him who has it. Witness the "company of prophets," whose example inspired Saul (1 Sam. 19, 20), and Elisha as the disciple of Elijah.

While we thus see Ibn Daud, unlike Halevi, adopting the philosophical explanation of prophecy, which tries to bring it within the class of natural psychological phenomena and relates it to dreams, he could not help recognizing that one cannot ignore the supernatural character of Biblical prophecy without being untrue to the Bible. He accordingly adds to the above naturalistic explanation a number of conditions which practically have the effect of taking the bottom out of the psychological theory. If Judah Halevi insists that only Israelites in the land of Palestine and at the time of their political independence had the privilege of the prophetic gift, we realize that such a belief is of the warp and woof of Halevi's innermost sentiment and thinking, which is radically opposed to the shallow rationalism and superficial cosmopolitanism of the "philosophers" of his day. But when the champion of Peripateticism, Abraham Ibn Daud, after explaining that prophecy is of the nature of true dreams, and though in most cases innate, may be cultivated by a pure soul through study and proper associations—repeats with Judah Halevi that the time and the place are essential conditions and that Israelites alone are privileged in this respect, he is giving up, it seems to us, all that he previously attempted to explain. This is only one of the many indications which point to the essential artificiality of all the mediæval attempts to harmonize a given system of philosophy with a supernaturalistic standpoint, such as is that of the Bible. It is not in this way that the Bible is to be saved if it needs saving.[242]

The next practical question Ibn Daud felt called upon to discuss was that of the possibility of the Law being repealed, abrogated or altered. This he found it necessary to do in order to defend the Jewish standpoint against that of Christianity in particular. How he will answer this question is of course a foregone conclusion. We are only interested in his manner of argument. He adopts a classification of long standing of the Biblical laws into rational and traditional. The first, he says, are accepted by all nations and can never be changed. Even a band of thieves, who disregard all laws of right and wrong as they relate to outsiders, must observe them in their own midst or they cannot exist. These laws bring people of different nationalities and beliefs together, and hence there can be no change in these. Nor can there be any alteration in that part of the Law which is historical in content. An event of the past cannot be repealed.

It only remains therefore to see whether abrogation may possibly be compatible with the nature of the traditional or ceremonial laws. Without arguing like the philosophers that change of a divine law is incompatible with the nature of God, which is unchangeable, our sages nevertheless have a method of explaining such phrases as, "And it repented the Lord that he had made man" (Gen. 6, 6), so as to reconcile the demands of reason with those of tradition. Now if there were laws of the traditional kind stated in the Bible without any indication of time and without the statement that they are eternal, and afterwards other laws came to change them, we should say that the Lord has a certain purpose in his laws which we do not know, but which is revealed in the new law taking the place of the old. But as a matter of fact the Bible states explicitly in many cases that the laws are not to be changed, "A statute for ever throughout your genera-tions" (Num. 10, 8, and *passim*). Arguments from phrases like, "Your new moons and your appointed feasts my soul hateth, etc." (Is. 1, 14), have no validity, for there is no indication here that sacri-fices are abolished. The meaning of Isaiah is that sacrifices in con-junction with wrong living are undesirable.

Our opponents also argue that Biblical expressions to the effect that the laws are eternal prove nothing, for we know of similar in-stances in which promises have been withdrawn as in the priesthood of Eli's family and the royalty of the house of David, where likewise eternity is mentioned. We answer these by saying, first, that in David's case the promise was withdrawn only temporarily, and will return again, as the Prophets tell us. Besides the promise was made only conditionally, as was that made to Eli. But there is no state-ment anywhere that the Law is given to Israel conditionally and that it will ever be taken away from them.

The claim of those who say that the laws of the Old Testament were true, but that they were repealed and the New Testament took its place, we meet by pointing to a continuous tradition against their view. We have an uninterrupted tradition during two thousand four hundred and seventy-two years that there was a man Moses who gave a Law accepted by his people and held without any break for two thousand four hundred and seventy-two years. We do not have to prove he was a genuine prophet since they do not deny it.

Some of them say that in the captivity in Babylon the old Law was forgotten and Ezra made a new law, the one we have now. This is absurd. The law could not have been forgotten, for the people did not all go into captivity at one time. They were not all put to death; they were led into exile in a quiet fashion, and there were great men among them like Hananiah, Mishael, Azariah, Daniel and others who surely could not have forgotten the Law. Besides Ezra could never have had the consent of all the people scattered everywhere if he had made a law of his own. As a matter of fact the Law as we have it is the same in all details throughout the world.[243]

The next problem we must consider is the perennial one—the problem of evil and of freedom. It is the purpose of the entire book, as Ibn Daud tells us in his introduction.

The further a thing is removed from matter the more perfect is its knowledge. For, as we have already said, it is matter that hinders knowledge. All defect and evil is the result of the potential. Hence the farther a thing is removed from potentiality the more perfect it is and the freer it is from defect. God's essence is the most perfect thing there is; and as he knows his essence, his is the most perfect knowledge. God knows, too, that his perfection is not stationary in him, but that it extends and communicates itself to all other things in order. And the further a thing is from him the less is its perfection and the greater is its imperfection. We have thus a graduated series, at one end the most perfect being, at the other the least perfect, viz., matter.

Now it is impossible from any point of view, either according to reason or Bible or tradition, that evil or defect should come from God. Not by reason, for two contradictories in the same subject are impossible. Now if good and evil both came from God, he would have to be composite just like man, who can be the cause of good and evil, the one coming from his rational power, the other from the spirited or appetitive. But God is simple and if evil comes from him, good cannot do so, which is absurd. Besides, the majority of defects are privational in character and not positive, like for example darkness, poverty, ignorance, and so on, which are not things, but the negations of light, wealth, wisdom, respectively. Being negative, not positive, they are not *made* by any body.

One may argue that it is in the nature of man that he should have understanding and perfection; and if God deprives him of it, he does evil. The answer is that the evil in the world is very small in comparison with the good. For evil and defect are found only in things composed of the elements, which have a common matter, receiving forms in accordance with the mixture of the elementary qualities in the matter. Here an external cause sometimes prevents the form from coming to the matter in its perfection. The seed, for example, depends upon the character of the soil which it finds for its growth. Now it does not follow that God was bound to give things the highest perfection possible. For in that case all minerals would be plants, all plants animals, all animals men, all men angels; and there would be no world, but only God and a few of the highest angels. In order that there shall be a world, it was necessary to make a graduated series as we actually have it. And as a matter of fact the very defects in the material composites are a good when we have in view not the particular thing but the whole. Thus if all men were of a highly intellectual type, there would be no agriculture or manual labor.

Now there are men whose temperament is such that they cannot distinguish between right and wrong, and they follow their inclinations. To counteract these bad qualities God gave his commandments and warnings. This shows that it is not impossible to oppose these evil tendencies, for in that case the commandments would be useless. The acts of man come neither under the category of the *necessary*, nor under that of the *impossible*, but under the category of the *possible*.

There are two senses in which we may understand the term possible. A thing may be possible subjectively, *i. e.*, in relation to our ignorance, though objectively it may be necessary and determined. Thus we in Spain do not know whether the king of Babylon died to-day or not; and so far as we are concerned, it is possible that he is dead or that he is alive. In reality it is not a question of possibility but of necessity. God knows which is true. The same thing applies to the occurrence of an eclipse in the future for the man who is ignorant of astronomy. Such possibility due to ignorance does not exist in God.

But there is another sense of the word possible; the sense in which an event is objectively undetermined. An event is possible if there is nothing in the previous chain of causation to determine the thing's happening in one way rather than another. The result is then a matter of pure chance or of absolute free will. Now God may make a thing possible in this objective sense, and then it is possible for him also. If you ask, but is God then ignorant of the result? We say, this is not ignorance. For to assume that it is, and that everything should be determined like eclipses, and that God cannot create things *possible*, means to destroy the order of the world, of this world as well as the next. For why shall man engage in various occupations or pursue definite lines of conduct since his destiny is already fixed?

The truth of the matter is that there are several orders of causes. Some are directly determined by God, and there is no way of evading them; others are entrusted to nature, and man is able to enjoy its benefits and avoid its injuries by proper management. A third class contains the things of chance, and one may guard against these also. So we are bidden in the Bible to make a parapet on the roofs of our houses to guard against the possibility of falling down. Finally there is the fourth class, those things which depend upon the free choice of the individual. Right and wrong conduct are matters of choice, else there would be no use in prophets, and no reward and punishment. When a person makes an effort to be good, his desire increases, and he obtains assistance from the angels.

Since freedom is supported by reason, Scripture and tradition, the passages in the Bible which are in favor of it should be taken literally, and those against it should be interpreted figuratively. When the Bible says that God hardened Pharaoh's heart, it means simply that Pharaoh was allowed to proceed as he began. All the ancient sages of our nation were in favor of freedom.[244]

If we compare the above discussion of the problem of freedom with that of Judah Halevi (above, p. 171), we see that Ibn Daud is more consistent, whatever we may think of his success in solving the insoluble problem. He frankly insists on the absolute freedom of the will and on the reality of the objectively contingent, not shrinking before the unavoidable conclusion that the events which are the results of such freedom or chance are no more known beforehand to God than they are to man. And he tries to avoid the criticism of attributing imperfection to God by insisting that not to be able to foretell the contingent is not ignorance, and hence not an imperfection. The reader may think what he pleases of this defence, but there seems to be a more serious difficulty in what this idea implies than in what it explicitly says.

If the contingent exists for God also, it follows that he is not the complete master of nature and the world. To say as Ibn Daud does that God made the contingent, *i. e.*, made it to be contingent, sounds like a contradiction, and reminds one of the question whether God can make a stone so big that he cannot lift it himself.

His proofs in favor of freedom and the contingent are partially identical with those of Judah Halevi, but in so far as he does not explicitly admit that the will may itself be influenced by prior causes he evades, to be sure, the strongest argument against him, but he does so at the expense of completeness in his analysis. Halevi is less consistent and more thorough, Ibn Daud is more consistent, because he fails to take account of real difficulties.

In the final outcome of their respective analyses, Halevi maintains God's foreknowledge at the expense of absolute freedom, or rather he does not see that his admissions are fatal to the cause he endeavors to defend. Ibn Daud maintains absolute freedom and frankly sacrifices foreknowledge; though his defence of freedom is secured by blinding himself to the argument most dangerous to that doctrine.

Abraham Ibn Daud concludes his " Emunah Ramah " by a discussion of ethics and the application of the principles thus discovered to the laws of the Bible. He entitles this final division of his treatise, "Medicine of the Soul," on the ground that virtue is the health of the soul as vice is its disease. In his fundamental ethical distinctions, definitions and classifications he combines Plato's psychology and the virtues based thereon with the Aristotelian doctrine of the mean, which he also applies in detail. He omits wisdom as one of the Platonic virtues and, unlike Plato for whom justice consists in a harmony of the other three virtues and has no psychological seat peculiar to it, Ibn Daud makes justice the virtue of the rational soul.

The end of practical philosophy is, he says, happiness. This is attained, first, by good morals; second, by proper family life; and third, by means of correct social and political conduct.

The human soul consists of three principal faculties, vegetative, animal, rational. Corresponding to these the principal virtues and vices are also three. The vegetative power, whose functions are nourishment, growth and reproduction, is related to appetite, and is called the appetitive soul. The animal power as being the cause of sensation, voluntary motion, cruelty, revenge, mercy and kindness, is called the spirited soul, because these qualities are dependent upon the energy or weakness of the spirit. The rational power has two aspects. One is directed upwards and is the means of our learning the sciences and the arts. The other aspect is directed downwards, and endeavors to control (successfully or not as the case may be), the two lower powers of the soul, guarding them against excess and defect. This function we call conduct, and virtue is the mean between the two extremes of too much and too little. The mean of the appetitive power is temperance; of the spirited power, bravery and gentleness; of the rational soul, justice.[245]

Justice consists in giving everything its due without excess or defect. Justice is therefore the highest of all qualities, and is of value not merely in a person's relations to his family and country, but also in the relations of his powers one to another. The rational power must see to it that the two lower faculties of the soul get what is their due, no more and no less. This quality has an important application also in the relations of a man to his maker. It is just that a person should requite his benefactor as much as he received from him, if possible. If he cannot do this, he should at least thank him. Hence the reason for divine worship, the first of commandments. This quality, the greatest of men possessed in the highest degree. Moses "said to him that did the wrong, wherefore smitest thou thy fellow? " (Ex. 2, 13). And when the shepherds came and drove away the daughters of the priest of Midian, "Moses stood up and helped them, and watered their flock" (*ib.* 17). This is the reason why God sent him to deliver Israel.

God showed the care he had of his nation by revealing himself to them, and thus showing them the error of those who think that God

gave over the rule of this world to the stars, and that he and the angels
have no further interest in it. Hence the first commandment is "I
am the Lord thy God," which is followed by "You shall have no other
gods," "Thou shalt not take the name of the Lord thy God in vain"
(Ex. 20, 2ff.). "Remember the Sabbath day" is for the purpose of
condemning the belief in the eternity of the world, as is evident from
the conclusion, "For in six days the Lord made heaven and earth,
the sea, and all that in them is . . . " (*ib.* 11). "Honor thy father
and thy mother" (*ib.* 12) is intended to inculcate the duty of honoring
the cause of one's being, including God. Thus the first five commandments all aim to teach the revelation and Providence of God. The
rest deal with social and political conduct, especially the last one,
"Thou shalt not covet," which is important in the preservation of
society.

The commandment to love God involves the knowledge of God,
for one cannot love what one does not know. A man must know therefore God's attributes and actions. He must be convinced likewise
that no evil comes from God, or he cannot love him as he should.
He may fear him but not with the proper fear. For there are two kinds
of fear, and the one that is commanded is fear of majesty and awe,
not fear of punishment.

Divine service means not merely prayer three times a day, but
constant thought of God. To develop and train this thought of God
in us we are commanded to put on phylacteries and fringes, and to
fasten the "mezuzah" to our door posts. For the same reason we
celebrate the festivals of Passover, Tabernacles, Hanukkah and
Purim, as a remembrance of God's benefits to our people. All these
observances are ultimately based upon the duty of thanking our
benefactor, which is part of justice, the highest of the virtues.

Among moral virtues we are also commanded to practice suppres-
sion of anger, and its inculcation is emphasized by making it a divine
attribute, "The Lord, the Lord, a God full of compassion and gracious . . ." (Ex. 34, 6). Other virtues of the same kind are, not to
repay evil for evil, not to be jealous, to practice humility like Moses,
and so on. In fact all the virtues laid down by ethical philosophers are
found better expressed in the Bible.

In respect to family virtues, we are bidden to care for and protect the members of our family, wife, children and slaves. Of social virtues we have love of our neighbor, honesty in dealing, just weights and measures, prohibition of interest and of taking a pledge from the poor, returning a find to the loser, and a host of other teachings.

There are, however, some of the traditional laws, the purpose of which is not known, especially the details of sacrifices and the like. In explanation of these we must say that the law consists of a rule of life composed of several parts. First is belief; second, moral qualities; third, family life; fourth, social and political life; fifth, the commandments above referred to, which we shall characterize as dictated by divine wisdom, though we do not understand them. Not all the parts of the Law are of the same order of value. The fundamental portion and the most important is that dealing with belief. Next in importance are the laws governing social and moral conduct, without which society is impossible. That is why all nations agree about these; and there is honesty even among thieves. The last class of commandments, whose purpose is not known, are the least in importance, as is clear also from statements in the Bible, such as, "I spake not unto your fathers, nor commanded them in the day that I brought them out of the land of Egypt, concerning burnt offerings or sacrifices. . . ." (Jer. 7, 22). At the same time we cannot deny that there are some reasons for their observance. Thus sacrifice leads to repentance as a result of reflection, even if the person does not confess his sin, as he is bidden to do in certain cases.

In fact there is one aspect which gives this class of commandments even greater importance than the social duties. It is the principle of implicit obedience even when we do not see the value of the commandment. I do not mean that a man should not study science, particularly what concerns the knowledge of God. This is not to be recommended. But when a man is convinced that there is such a thing as genuine prophecy, showing God's providence, as we see in the case of Moses who delivered his nation, performed wonders for them and was always honored and believed—he should not balk at the acceptance of some laws given by such a divine man simply because he does not understand them. Abraham is a good example. For when God promised him that Isaac would become a great nation, and then commanded him to sacrifice his only child, he did not ask any questions and was ready to do God's behest. His example is meant to be followed by all. This is the purpose of these subtle command-ments, which are made with wisdom. Through them we may see the difference between belief and unbelief.[246]

The above discussion is extremely typical of the rationalistic atti-tude of Ibn Daud and his school, which includes such men as Mai-monides, Gersonides and others. Reason, theory, science, explana-tion—these are the important considerations in things philosophical, as well as things religious. Theory is more important than practice, and belief stands higher than mere conduct. No wonder that Maimon-ides was not satisfied until he elaborated a creed with a definite num-ber of dogmas. Dogmas and faith in reason go together. It is the mystic who is impatient of prescribed generalities, for he is constantly refreshed by the living and ever flowing stream of individual experi-ence. The rationalist has a fixed unchangeable Idea or reason or method, whose reality and value consists in its unity, permanence and immutability. In favor of this hypostatised reason, the ration-alist Ibn Daud is ready to sacrifice so fundamental an institution as sacrifice in the face of the entire book of Leviticus, pretending that a single verse of Jeremiah entitles him to do so. But the Jew Ibn Daud in the end asserted himself, and he finds it necessary to admit that in a sense these non-rational laws may be of even greater importance than the rational; not, however, as a simple believer might say, be-cause we must not search the wisdom of God, but for the reason that unreasoned obedience is itself a virtue.

In conclusion we remind the reader that Ibn Daud was the precursor of Maimonides, touching upon, and for the most part answering every question treated by his more famous successor. Ibn Daud was the first to adopt Aristotelianism for the purpose of welding it with Ju-daism. He showed the way to follow. Maimonides took his cue from Ibn Daud and succeeded in putting the latter in the shade. Historic justice demands that Ibn Daud be brought forward into the light and given the credit which is deservedly his due.

CHAPTER XIII

With Maimonides we reach the high water mark of mediæval Jewish philosophy. He was by far the most comprehensive mind of mediæval Jewry, and his philosophy was the coping stone of a complete system of Judaism. In his training and education he embraced all Jewish literature, Biblical and Rabbinic, as well as all the science and philosophy of his day. And his literary activity was fruitful in every important branch of study. He was well known as a practicing physician, having been in the employ of the Caliph's visier at Cairo (Fostat), and he wrote on medical theory and practice. He was versed in mathematics and astronomy, and his knowledge of these subjects served him in good stead not merely as an introduction to theology and metaphysics, but was of direct service in his studies and writings on the Jewish calendar. It goes without saying that he knew logic, for this was the basis of all learning in mediæval times; but in this branch, too, Maimonides has left us a youthful treatise,[247] which bears witness to his early interest in science and his efforts to recommend its study as helpful to a better understanding of Jewish literature.

But all these activities and productions were more or less side issues, or preparations for a *magnum opus*, or rather *magna opera*. From his youth we can trace the evident purpose, not finally completed until toward the end of his brilliant and useful career,—the purpose to harmonize Judaism with philosophy, to reconcile the Bible and Talmud with Aristotle. He was ambitious to do this for the good of Judaism, and in the interest of a rational and enlightened faith. Thus in his commentary on the Mishna,[248] the earliest of his larger works, he had already conceived the idea of writing a composition of a harmonizing nature, *viz.*, to gather all the homiletical disquisitions of the Talmud (the "derashot") and explain them in a rationalistic manner so as to remove what appears on the surface to be offensive to sound reason. But instead of proceeding at once to the performance of this cherished object of his philosophic ambition, he kept it in his bosom, brooding over it during a life of intense literary and practical activity, until it was in the end matured and brought to fruition in a manner quite different from that at first intended. The book explanatory of the Rabbinic legends was given up for reasons which will appear later. But the object that work was to realize was carried out in a much more effective manner because it was delayed, and was published toward the end of his life as the systematic and authoritative pronouncement of the greatest Jew of his time. The "Guide of the Perplexed" would not have attracted the attention it did, it would not have raised the storm which divided Jewry into two opposed camps, if it had not come as the mature work of the man whom all Jewry recognized as the greatest Rabbinic authority of his time. Others had written on philosophy before Maimonides. We have in these pages followed their ideas—Saadia, Gabirol, Ibn Zaddik, Abraham Ibn Daud. The latter in particular anticipated Maimonides in almost all his ideas. None had the effect of upsetting the theological equilibrium of Jewry. Everyone had his admirers, no doubt, as well as his opponents. Gabirol was forgotten, Ibn Zaddik and Ibn Daud were neglected, and Jewish learning continued the even tenor of its course. Maimonides was the first to make a profound impression, the first who succeeded in stirring to their depths the smooth, though here and there somewhat turbid, Rabbinic waters, as they flowed not merely in scientific Spain and Provence, or in the Orient, but also in the strictly Talmudic communities of northern France. It was the Commentary on the Mishna and the Talmudic code known as the "Yad ha-Hazaka" that was responsible for the tremendous effect of the "More Nebukim" ("Guide of the Perplexed").

In these two Rabbinical treatises, and particularly in the "Yad ha-Hazaka," the Rabbinic Code, Maimonides showed himself the master of Rabbinic literature. And all recognized in him the master mind. Having been written in Hebrew the Code soon penetrated all Jewish communities everywhere, and Maimonides's fame spread wherever there were Jews engaged in the study of the Talmud. His fame as a court physician in Egypt and as the official head of Oriental Jewry enhanced the influence of his name and his work. Jealousy

no doubt had its share in starting opposition to the Code itself even
before the publication of the "Guide," and during the lifetime of
its author. When the "More Nebukim" was translated from the
original Arabic into Hebrew, so that all could read it, and Maimonides
was no longer among the living, the zealots became emboldened and
the storm broke, the details of which, however, it is not our province
to relate.

For completeness' sake let us set down the facts of his life. Moses
ben Maimon was born in the city of Cordova on the fourteenth of
Nissan (30th of March) at one o'clock in the afternoon, on a Sabbath
which was the day before Passover, in the year 1135. It is not often
that the birth of a mediæval Jewish writer is handed down with such
minute detail. Usually we do not even know the year, to say nothing
of the day and the hour. Cordova had long fallen from its high estate.
It was no longer the glorious city of the days before the Almoravid
conquest. And it was destined to descend lower still when the fanati-
cal hordes of the Almohades renewed the ancient motto of the early
Mohammedan conquerors, "The Koran or the Sword."

Maimonides was barely thirteen when his native city fell into the
hands of the zealots from Morocco, and henceforth neither Jew nor
Christian dared avow his faith openly in Cordova. Adoption of
Islam, emigration or death were the choices held out to the infidel.
Many Jews adopted the dominant faith outwardly—that was all that
was demanded of them—while in the secret of their homes they observed Judaism. Some emigrated, and among them was the family
of Moses' father. For a time they wandered about from city to city
in Spain, and then crossed over to Fez in Morocco. This seems to us
like going from the frying pan into the fire, for Fez was the lion's den
itself. The conquerors of Cordova came from Morocco. And there
seems to be some evidence too that the Maimon family had to appear
outwardly as Mohammedans. Be that as it may, Maimonides did not
stay long in Fez. On the 18th of April, 1165, the family set sail for
Palestine, and after a month's stormy voyage they arrived in Acco.
He visited Jerusalem and Hebron, but did not find Palestine a promising place for permanent residence and decided to go to Egypt. He
settled in Old Cairo (Fostat), and with his brother David engaged in
the jewel trade. His father died soon after, and later his brother met

an untimely death when the ship on which he was a passenger on one of his business trips was wrecked in the Indian Ocean. Thereafter Maimonides gave up the jewel business and began to practice medicine, which at first did not offer him more than the barest necessities. But in the course of time his fame spread and he was appointed physician to Saladin's grand visier Alfadhil. He was also made spiritual head *
of the Jews of Egypt, and what with his official duties as court physician, leader of the Jewish community, practicing physician among the people, and his literary activities, Jewish and secular, Rabbinical and scientific, he was a busy man indeed; so much so that he dissuades Samuel Ibn Tibbon, the translator of the "Guide," from paying him a visit on the ground that he would scarcely have time to spare to see him, much less to enter into scientific discussions with him.[249] Maimonides died on Monday, December 13 (20 Tebeth), 1204.

The philosophy of Maimonides is contained in the "Guide of the Perplexed," his last great work, which was published in Arabic in 1190.[250] Some philosophic and ethical material is also found in the introductory chapters of his commentary on the Mishnaic treatise "Abot" (the so-called "Eight Chapters"—"Shemonah Perakim"),[251] in the introduction to the eleventh chapter (Helek) of the Talmudic treatise "Sanhedrin," and in the introductory sections of the Code ("Hilkot Yesode ha-Torah" and "Hilkot Deot"). Here, however, the treatment is popular and elementary, and is intended for popular consumption. He lays down results in their simplest form without discussing their origin or the arguments *pro* and *con*. The "Guide of the Perplexed," on the other hand, is intended for a special class of persons, for the sophisticated; for those who are well trained in science and philosophy, not to speak of Bible and Talmud, and are as a result made uneasy by the apparent disagreement of philosophical teaching with the ideas expressed in the Biblical and Rabbinic writings. His purpose is deliberately apologetic and concordistic. The work is not a treatise of science or philosophy. The latter are presupposed. He introduces philosophic principles, Aristotelian or Kalamistic, only with a view to their relation to Jewish theology. And he either accepts them, provisionally or absolutely, if he regards them as proven, as true and useful; or he refutes and rejects them if untenable. In the

* Not a paid post.

former case he shows by proper interpretation that similar principles are taught in Bible and Talmud; in the latter he contents himself by proving that Aristotle or the Mutakallimun, as the case may be, did not prove their point.

His method, in general, of quieting the doubts of the "perplexed" is the old one—as old as Philo and beyond—of regarding Biblical phrases as metaphors and allegories, containing an esoteric meaning beside or opposed to the literal. Accordingly he lays the greatest stress on the explanation of Scriptural "homonyms," as he calls them, borrowing an Aristotelian term. A homonym is a word which has more than one meaning; a word which denotes several things having nothing in common. Thus when I apply the word dog to the domestic animal we know by that name, as well as to Sirius, known as the dog-star, I use dog as a homonym. The star and the animal have nothing in common. So the word "merciful," one of the attributes of God in the Bible, is a homonym. That is, we denote by the same word also a quality in a human being; but this quality and that which is denoted by the same word when applied to God have nothing in common. They are not merely different in degree but in kind. In fact, as Maimonides insists, there is really nothing *in* God corresponding to the word merciful.

There are besides certain passages in the Bible which while having an acceptable meaning when taken literally, contain besides a deeper signification which the practiced eye can detect. Thus in the description of the harlot in the seventh chapter of Proverbs there is beside the plain meaning of the text, the doctrine of matter as the cause of corporeal desires. The harlot, never faithful to one man, leaving one and taking up with another, represents matter which, as Aristotle conceives it, never is without form and constantly changes one form for another.

There is really nothing new in this, and Philo apart, whom Maimonides did not know, Ibn Daud anticipated Maimonides here also in making use of the term "homonym" as the basis of this method of interpretation.[252] But whereas Ibn Daud relegates the chapter treating of this principle to a subordinate place, his interest being as he tells us primarily ethical—to solve the problem of free will; Maimonides places it in the very centre of his system. The doctrine of attributes as leading to a true conception of God,—of God as absolutely incorporeal

and without any resemblance or relation whatsoever to anything else—
is the very keystone of Maimonides's philosophical structure. His
purpose is to teach a spiritual conception of God. Anything short of
this is worse than idolatry. He cannot reconcile the Bible to such a
view without this "homonymic" tool. Hence the great importance of
this in his system; and he actually devotes the greater part of the first
book of the "Guide" to a systematic and exhaustive survey of all
terms in the Bible used as homonyms.[253] All this is preparatory to his
discussion of the divine attributes.

This consideration will account also for the fact that, systematic
and logical thinker as he was, he perpetrates what might appear at
first sight as a logical blunder. Instead of first proving the existence
of God and then discussing his nature and attributes, as Saadia,
Bahya, Ibn Daud and others did before him, he treats exhaustively
of the divine attributes in the first book, whereas the proof of the
existence of God does not appear until the second book. This inver-
sion of the logical order is deliberate. Maimonides's method is directed
ad hominem. The Jews for whom he wrote his "Guide" did not
doubt the existence of God. But a great many of them had an inadequate idea of his spiritual nature. And apparently the Bible counte-
nanced their anthropomorphism. Hence Maimonides cast logical
considerations to the wind, and dealt first with that which was nearest
to his heart. The rest could wait, this could not.

I promised in my commentary on the Mishna, he tells us in the
introduction to the "Guide," to explain the allegories and "Midrashim" in two works to be entitled "The Book of Reconciliation"
and "The Book of Prophecy." But after reflecting on the matter
a number of years I decided to desist from the attempt. The reasons
are these. If I expressed my explanations obscurely, I should have
accomplished nothing by substituting one unintelligible statement
for another. If, on the other hand, I were really to make clear the
matters that require explanation, the result would not be suitable
for the masses, for whom those treatises were intended. Besides,
those Midrashim when read by an ignorant man are harmless because
to such a person nothing is impossible. And if they are read by a
person who is learned and worthy, one of two things is likely to happen.
Either he will take them literally and suspect the author of ignorance,

which is not a serious offence; or he will regard the legendary statements as containing an esoteric meaning and think well of the author
—which is a good thing, whether he catch the meaning intended or
not. Accordingly I gave up the idea of writing the books mentioned.
In this work I am addressing myself to those who have been philosophizing; who are believers in the Bible and at the same time know
science; and are perplexed in their ideas on account of the homonymous terms.

Having made clear Maimonides's chief interest and purpose in his
masterpiece we need not follow his own method of treatment, which
often gives the impression of a studied attempt to conceal his innermost ideas from all but the initiated. At least he is not willing that
anyone who has not taken the trouble carefully to study and scruti-
nize every chapter and compare it with what precedes and follows,
should by a superficial browsing here and there arrive at an understanding of the profound problems treated in the work. He believes
that the mysterious doctrines passing by the name of "Maase Bereshit"
and "Maase Merkaba" in the Talmud (*cf.* Introduction, p. xvi)
denote respectively Physics and Metaphysics—the very sciences
of which he treats in the "Guide." Accordingly he tells us that following the instructions of the Rabbis he must not be expected to give
more than bare allusions. And even these are not arranged in order
in the book, but scattered and mixed up with other subjects which he
desires to explain. For, as he says, "I do not want to oppose the divine intention, which concealed the truths of his being from the
masses."

"You must not suppose," he continues, " that these mysteries are
known to anybody completely. By no means. But sometimes the
truth flashes upon us and it is day; and then again our natural constitution and habits shut them out, and we are again in darkness. The
relative proportion of light and darkness which a person enjoys in
these matters, makes the difference in the grade of perfection of great
men and prophets. The greatest of the prophets had comparatively
little if any darkness. With those who never see light at all, namely
the masses of the people, we have nothing to do in this book."

Finally he adjures the reader not to explain to anyone else the novel
ideas found in his work, which are not contained in the writings of

his predecessors. Heaven knows, he exclaims, I hesitated long before writing this book, because it contains unknown matters, never before treated by any Jewish writer in the "Galut." But I relied on two Rabbinic principles. One is that when it is a question of doing something for a great cause in a critical time, it is permitted to transgress a law. The other is the consciousness that my motives are pure and unselfish. In short, he concludes, I am the man who, when he finds himself in a critical position and cannot teach truth except by suiting one worthy person and scandalizing ten thousand fools, chooses to say the truth for the benefit of the one without regard for the abuse of the great majority.

As we are not bound by Maimonides's principle of esoterism and mystery, nor are we in fear of being an offence and a stumbling block to the fools, we shall proceed more directly in our exposition of his philosophy; and shall begin with Maimonides's general ideas on the need of science for intelligent faith and the relation thereto of Jewish history and literature.

The highest subject of study is metaphysics or theology, the knowledge of God (*cf.* below, p. 285). This is not merely not forbidden in the Bible, but it is directly commanded. When Moses says, "That I may know thee, to the end that I may find grace in thy sight" (Exod. 33, 13), he intimates that only he finds favor with God who knows him, and not merely who fasts and prays.[254] Besides, the commandment, "Thou shalt love the Lord thy God," cannot be fulfilled without a study and understanding of the whole of nature.[255] Thus, as we shall see, it is only by a study of physics that we come to understand that affection is a defect and must therefore be removed from the conception of God. The same thing applies to the ideas of potentiality and actuality. We should not know what they signify without a study of physics, nor should we understand that potentiality is a defect and hence not to be found in God. It is therefore a duty to study both physics and metaphysics for a true knowledge of God.[256] At the same time we must recognize that human reason has a limit and that there are matters which are beyond its ken. Not to realize this and to deny what has not been proved impossible is dangerous, and may lead a man astray after the imagination and the evil desires which quench the light of the intellect. And it is this the Bible and the Rabbis had in mind in such passages as, "Hast thou found honey? eat so much as is sufficient for thee; lest thou be filled therewith, and vomit it " (Prov. 25, 16); or in the following from the Mishna, "Whoever pries into four things, had better not come into the world, *viz.*, what is above and what is below, what was before and what will be after " (Hagigah, ch. 2). The meaning is not, as some fools think, that the Rabbis forbid the use of the reason entirely to reach what is in its power. It is *abuse* of the reason that they prohibit, and neglect of the truth that the human reason has a limit.[257]

Accordingly while the study of metaphysics and the explanation of the allegories of Scripture are thus shown to be a necessity of intelligent belief, it is not proper to begin with these difficult subjects. One must first be mature intellectually and possessed of the preliminary sciences. Otherwise the study of metaphysics is likely not merely to confuse the mind in its belief, but to destroy belief entirely. It is like feeding an infant on wheat bread and meat and wine. These are not bad in themselves, but the infant is not prepared to digest them. That is why these matters are given in the Bible in the form of allegories, because the Bible is intended for all—men, women and children —not because metaphysical ideas are injurious in themselves, as some fools imagine, who believe they are wise men. For beginners it is sufficient that they have the right view by tradition and know the existence of certain beings, without being able to prove the opinions they hold, or to understand the essence of the being in the existence of which they believe. This they will acquire gradually if they are capable.[258]

There are five causes preventing the study of metaphysics on the part of the general masses. First, the difficulty of the subject itself. Second, the limitations of all people's minds at the beginning. Third, the great amount of preparatory training that is necessary, and which everybody is not ready to undertake, however eager he may be to know the results. And to study metaphysics without preliminary training is worse than not to study it at all. For there is nothing in existence except God and his creation. To know God's existence and what is and is not proper to ascribe to him we must examine his creation; and thus arithmetic, the nature of number, and the properties of geometrical figures help us a great deal in determining what attributes are inapplicable to God. Even much more important for metaphysics is the study of spherical astronomy and physics, which throw light on the relation of God to the world. Then there are some theoretical topics which, while not directly of help in metaphysics, are useful in training the mind and enabling it to know what is true demonstration. One who wishes therefore to undertake the study of metaphysics, must first study logic, then the mathematical sciences in order, then physics, and not until he has mastered all these introductory branches should he take up metaphysics. This is too much for most people, who would die in the midst of their preparatory studies, and if not for tradition would never know whether there is a God or not, not to speak of knowing what attributes are applicable to him and what are not.

The fourth cause which keeps people away from the study of metaphysics is their natural disposition. For it has been shown that intellectual qualities are dependent upon moral; and the former cannot be perfect unless the latter are. Now some persons are temperamentally incapable of right thinking by reason of their passionate nature; and it is foolish to attempt to teach them, for it is not medicine or geometry, and not everybody is prepared for it. This is the reason, too, why young men cannot study it, because of the passions which are still strong in them. Finally as a fifth reason, the necessities of the body and its luxuries, too, stand in the way of a person's devoting enough time and attention to this subject.[259]

Like many others before him, Christians as well as Jews, Maimonides also believed that in ancient times the Jews diligently cultivated the sciences, which were gradually forgotten on account of foreign domination. Maimonides adds another reason for their disappearance, namely, that they were not disseminated abroad. They were confined to a select few and were not put down in writing but handed down by word of mouth. As a result only a few hints are found in the Talmud and Midrashim, where the kernel is small and the husk large, so that people mistake the husk for the kernel.[260]

He then traces the history of philosophical thinking in Jewish mediæval literature from the time of the Geonim, and tells us that the little that is found of the Kalam concerning the Unity of God and related topics in the works of some of the Geonim and the Karaites in the East is borrowed from the Mutakallimun of the Mohammedans and constitutes a small fraction of the writings of the latter on this subject. The first attempt in this direction among the Moslems was that of the party known as the Mu'tazila, whom our people followed. Later came the party of the Ashariya with different opinions which, however, were not adopted by any of our people. This was not due, he tells us, to a deliberate decision in favor of the Mu'tazila, but solely to the historical accident of their chronological priority. On the other hand, the Spanish Jews of Andalusia adopted the views of the philosophers, *i. e.*, the Aristotelians, so far as they are not in conflict with our religion. They do not follow the Mutakallimun, and hence what little of the subject is found in the works of the later writers of this class resembles our own method and views.[261]

There seems no doubt that whatever other Spanish writers Maimonides had in mind, whose works are not extant, his characterization fits admirably the "Emunah Ramah" of Abraham Ibn Daud (*cf.* above, p. 217), and in a less degree it is also true of Ibn Gabirol, Bahya, Judah Halevi, Moses and Abraham Ibn Ezra. Bahya as we saw above (p. 86) still retains a good deal of Kalamistic material and so does Ibn Zaddik (p. 126). As for Mukammas, Saadia and the two Karaites Al Basir and Jeshua ben Judah, we have seen (pp. 17, 24, 48, 56) that they move wholly in the ideas of the Mutakallimun. It becomes of great interest for us therefore to see what Maimonides thinks of these Islamic theologians, of their origins, of their methods and of their philosophical value. Maimonides's exposition and criticism of the principles of the Mutakallimun is of especial interest, too, because up to recent times his sketch of the tenets of this school was the only extensive account known; and it has not lost its value even yet. We shall, however, be obliged to abridge his detailed exposition in order not to enlarge our volume beyond due limits. Besides, there is no occasion for repeating what we have already said of the Kalam in our Introduction (p. xxi ff.); though the account there given was not taken from Maimonides and does not follow his order.

Maimonides is aware that the Arabs are indebted to the Christians, Greeks as well as Syrians. The Mu'tazila and Ashariya, he says, base their opinions upon premises and principles borrowed from Greek and Syrian Christians, who endeavored to refute the opinions of the philosophers as dangerous to the Christian religion. There was thus a Christian Kalam prior to the Mohammedan.[262] Their method was to lay down premises favorable to their religion, and by means of these to refute the opinions opposed to them. When the Mohammedans came upon the scene and translated the works of the philosophers, they included in their work of translation the refutations composed by the Christians. In this way they found the works of Philoponus, Yahya ben Adi and others; and adopted also the opinions of the pre-Socratic philosophers, which they thought would be of help to them, though these had already been refuted by Aristotle, who came after. Such are the atomic theory of matter and the belief in the existence of a vacuum. These opinions they carried to consequences not at all contemplated by their authorities, who were closer to the philosophers.

To characterize briefly the methods of the Mutakallimun, Maimonides continues, I would say that the first among them, the Greeks and the Mohammedans, did not follow reality, but adopted principles which were calculated to help them in defending their religious theses, and then interpreted reality to suit their preconceived notions. The later members of the school no longer saw through the motives of their predecessors and imagined their principles and arguments were *bona fide* refutations of philosophical opinions.

On examination of their works I found, he continues, that with slight differences they are all alike. They do not put any trust in reality and nature. For, they say, the so-called laws of nature are nothing more than the order of events to which we are accustomed. There is no kind of necessity in them, and it is conceivable they might be different. In many cases the Mutakallimun follow the imagination and call it reason. Their method of procedure is as follows. They first state their preliminary principles, then they prove that the world is "new," *i. e.*, created in time. Then they argue that the world must have had an originator, and that he is one and incorporeal. All the Mutakallimun follow this method, and they are imitated by those of our own people who follow in their footsteps.

To this method I have serious objections, continues Maimonides, for their arguments in favor of the creation of the world are not convincing unless one does not know a real demonstration from a dialectical or sophistic. The most one can do in this line is to invalidate the arguments for eternity. But the decision of the question is by no means easy, as is shown by the fact that the controversy is three thousand years old and not yet settled. Hence it is a risky policy to build the argument for the existence of God on so shaky a foundation as the "newness" of the world. The best way then, it seems to me, is to prove God's existence, unity and incorporeality by the methods of the philosophers, which are based upon the eternity of the world. Not that I believe in eternity or that I accept it, but because on this hypothesis the three fundamental doctrines are validly demonstrated. Having proved these doctrines we will then return to the problem of the origin of the world and say what can be said in favor of creation.[263]

This is a new contribution of Maimonides. All the Jewish writers before Halevi followed in their proofs of the existence of God the method designated by Maimonides as that of the Kalam. Judah Halevi criticised the Mutakallimun as well as the philosophers in the interest of a point of view all his own (p. 176 ff., 182). Ibn Daud tacitly ignored the Kalam and based his proof of the existence of God upon the principles of motion as exhibited in the Aristotelian Physics, without, however, finding it necessary to assume even provisionally the eternity of motion and the world (p. 217 ff.). His proof of the incorporeality of God is, as we have seen (*ibid.*), weak, just because he does not admit the eternity of motion, which alone implies infinity of power in God and hence incorporeality. Maimonides is the first who takes deliberate account of the Mutakallimun, gives an adequate outline of the essentials of their teaching and administers a crushing blow to their principles as well as their method. He then follows up his destructive criticism with a constructive method, in which he frankly admits that in order to establish the existence, unity and incorporeality of God—the three fundamental dogmas of Judaism—beyond the possibility of cavil, we must make common cause with the philosophers even though it be only for a moment, until they have done our work for us, and then we may fairly turn on our benefactors and taking advantage of their weakness, strike them down, and upon their lifeless arguments for the eternity of the world establish our own more plausible theory of creation. The attitude of Maimonides is in brief this. If we were certain of creation, we should not have to bother with the philosophers. Creation implies the existence of God. But the question cannot be strictly demonstrated either way. Hence let us prove the existence of God on the least promising hypothesis, namely, that of eternity, and we are quite secure against all possible criticism.

Of the twelve propositions of the Mutakallimun enumerated by Maimonides as the basis of their doctrine of God, we shall select a few of the most important.[264]

1. *The Theory of Atoms.* The entire universe is made up of indivisible bodies having no magnitude. Their combination produces magnitude and corporeality. They are all alike. Genesis and dissolution means simply the combination or rather aggregation of atoms and their separation. These atoms are not eternal, as Epicurus believed them to be, but created.

2. This atomic theory they extend from magnitude to time. Time also according to them is composed of moments or atomic units of time. Neither magnitude, nor matter, nor time is continuous or infinitely divisible.

3. Applying these ideas to motion they say that motion is the passage of an atom of matter from one atom of place to the next in an atom of time. It follows from this that one motion is as fast as another; and they explain the apparent variation in speed of different motions, as for example when two bodies cover unequal distances in the same time, by saying that the body covering the smaller distance had more rests in the intervals between the motions. The same thing is true in the flight of an arrow, that there are rests even though the senses do not reveal them. For the senses cannot be trusted. We must follow the reason.

Maimonides's criticism of the atomic theory of matter and motion just described is that it undermines the bases of geometry. The diagonal of a square would be the same length as its side. The properties of commensurability and incommensurability in lines and surfaces, of rational and irrational lines would cease to have any meaning. In fact all that is contained in the tenth book of Euclid would lose its foundation.

4. The atom is made complete by the accidents, without which it cannot be. Every atom created by God, they say, must have accidents, such as color, odor, motion, and so on, except quantity or magnitude, which according to them is not accident. If a substance

has an accident, the latter is not attributed to the body as a whole, but is ascribed to every atom of which the body is composed. Thus in a white body every atom is white, in a moving body every atom is in motion, in a living body every atom is alive, and every atom is possessed of sense perception; for life and sense and reason and wisdom are accidents in their opinion like whiteness and blackness.

6. Accident does not last more than one moment of time. When God creates an atom he creates at the same time an accident with it. Atom without accident is impossible. The accident disappears at the end of the moment unless God creates another of the same kind, and then another, and so on, as long as he wants the accident of that kind to continue. If he ceases to create another accident, the substance too disappears.

Their motive in laying down this theory of accidents is in order to destroy the conception that everything has a peculiar nature, of which its qualities and functions are the results. They attribute everything directly to God. God created a particular accident at this moment, and this is the explanation of its being. If God ceases to create it anew the next moment, it will cease to be.

7. All that is not atom is accident, and there is no difference between one kind of accident and another in reference to essentiality. All bodies are composed of similar atoms, which differ only in accidents; and animality and humanity and sensation and reason are all accidents. Hence the difference between the individuals of the same species is the same as that between individuals of different species. The philosophers distinguish between essential forms of things and accidental properties. In this way they would explain, for example, why iron is hard and black, while butter is soft and white. The Mutakallimun deny any such distinction. All forms are accidents. Hence it would follow that there is no intrinsic reason why man rather than the bat should be a rational creature. Everything that is conceivable is possible, except what involves a logical contradiction; and God alone determines at every instant what accident shall combine with a given atom or group of atoms.

8. It follows from the above also that man has no power of agency at all. When we think we are dyeing a garment red, it is not we who are doing it at all. God creates the red color in the garment at the

time when we apply the red dye to it. The red dye does not enter the garment, as we think, for an accident is only momentary, and cannot pass beyond the substance in which it is.

What appears to us as the constancy and regularity of nature is nothing more than the will of God. Nor is our knowledge of to-day the same as that of yesterday. Yesterday's is gone and to-day's is created anew. So when a man moves a pen, it is not he who moves it. God creates motion in the hand, and at the same time in the pen. The hand is not the cause of the motion of the pen. In short they deny causation. God is the sole cause.

In respect to human conduct they are divided. The majority, and the Ashariya among them, say that when a person moves a pen, God creates four accidents, no one of which is the cause of the other. They merely exist in succession, but no more. The first accident is the man's will to move the pen; the second, his ability to move it; the third, the motion of the hand; the fourth, the motion of the pen. It follows from this that when a person does anything, God creates in him a will, the ability and the act itself, but the act is not the effect of the ability. The Mu'tazila hold that the ability is the cause of the effect.

9. *Impossibility of the Infinite.* They hold that the infinite is impossible in any sense, whether actual or potential or accidental. That an actual infinite is impossible is a matter of proof. So it can be and has been proved that the potential infinite is possible. For example extension is infinitely divisible, *i. e.*, potentially. As to the accidental infinite, *i. e.*, an infinity of parts of which each ceases to be as soon as the next appears, this is doubtful. Those who boast of having proved the eternity of the world say that time is infinite, and defend their view against criticism by the claim that the successive parts of time disappear. In the same way these people regard it as possible that an infinite number of accidents have succeeded each other on the universal matter, because here too they are not all present now, the previous having disappeared before the succeeding ones came. The Mutakallimun do not admit of any kind of infinite. They prove it in this way. If past time and the world are infinite, then the number of men who died up to a given point in the past is infinite. The number of men who died up to a point one thousand years before the

former is also infinite. But this number is less than the other by the number of men who died during the thousand years between the two starting points. Hence the infinite is larger than the infinite, which is absurd. If the accidental infinite were really impossible the theory of the eternity of the world would be refuted at once. But Alfarabi has shown that the arguments against accidental infinity are invalid.

10. *Distrust of the Senses*. The senses, they say, cannot be regarded as criteria of truth and falsehood; for many things the senses cannot see at all, either because the objects are so fine, or because they are far away. In other cases the senses are deceptive, as when the large appears small at a distance, the small appears great in the water, and the straight appears broken when partly in water and partly without. So a man with the jaundice sees everything yellow, and one with red bile on his tongue tastes everything bitter. There is method in their madness. The motive for this sceptical principle is to evade criticism. If the senses testify in opposition to their theories, they reply that the senses cannot be trusted, as they did in their explanation of motion and in their theory of the succession of created accidents. These are all ancient theories of the Sophists, as is clear from Galen.[265]

Having given an outline of the fundamental principles of the Mutakallimun and criticised them, Maimonides next gives their arguments based upon these principles in favor of creation in time and against eternity. It will not be worth our while to reproduce them here as they are not adopted by Maimonides, and we have already met some of them though in a somewhat modified form before (*cf.* above, pp. 29 ff.).[266]

The Kalamistic proofs for the unity of God are similarly identical for the most part with those found in Saadia, Bahya and others, and we need only mention Maimonides's criticism that they are inadequate unless we assume with the Mutakallimun that all atoms in the universe are of the same kind. If, however, we adopt Aristotle's theory, which is more plausible, that the matter of the heavenly bodies is different from that of the sublunar world, we may defend dualism by supposing that one God controls the heavens and the other the earth. The inability of the one to govern the domain of the other would not necessarily argue imperfection, any more than we who believe in the unity of God regard it as a defect in God that he cannot make a thing both be and not be. This belongs to the category of the impossible; and we should likewise class in the same category the control of a sphere that is independent of one and belongs to another. This is purely an *argumentum ad hominem*, for Maimonides does not regard the sublunar and superlunar worlds as independent of each other. He recognizes the unity of the universe.[267]

Maimonides closes his discussion of the Kalamistic system by citing their arguments for incorporeality, which he likewise finds inadequate, both because they are based upon God's unity, which they did not succeed in proving (Saadia, in so far as he relates the two, bases unity upon incorporeality), and because of inherent weakness.[268]

Having disposed of the arguments of the Mutakallimun, Maimonides proceeds to prove the existence, unity and incorporeality of God by the methods of the philosophers, *i. e.*, those who, like Alfarabi and Avicenna, take their arguments from Aristotle. The chief proof [269] is based upon the Aristotelian principles of motion and is found in the eighth book of Aristotle's Physics. We have already met this proof in Ibn Daud (*cf.* above, p. 217), and the method in Maimonides differs only in form and completeness, but not in essence. There is, however, this very important difference that Ibn Daud fights shy of Aristotle's theory of the eternity of motion and time, thus losing his strongest argument for God's infinite power and incorporeality (*cf.* p. 218); whereas Maimonides frankly bases his entire argument from motion (provisionally to be sure) upon the Aristotelian theory, including eternity of motion. With this important deviation there is not much in this part of the Maimonidean discussion which is not already contained, though less completely, in the "Emunah Ramah" of Abraham Ibn Daud. We should be tempted to omit these technical arguments entirely if it were not for the fact that it is in the form which Maimonides gave them that they became classic in Jewish philosophy, and not in that of Ibn Daud.

The second proof of God's existence, unity and incorporeality, that based upon the distinction between "possible" and "necessary" existent,[270] which has its origin in Alfarabi and Avicenna, is also found in Ibn Daud.[271] The other two proofs[272] are Maimonides's own, *i. e.*, they are not found in the works of his Jewish predecessors.

As in the exposition of the theory of the Mutakallimun Maimonides began with their fundamental principles, so here he lays down twenty-six propositions culled from the Physics and Metaphysics of Aristotle and his Arabian commentators, and applies them later to prove his points. He does not attempt to demonstrate them, expecting the reader to take them for granted, or to be familiar with them from a study of the philosophical sources. Ibn Daud presupposed less from his readers, having written as he said, for beginners; hence he proves many of the propositions which Maimonides lays down dogmatically. Possibly Maimonides expected his readers to be familiar with the work of his immediate Jewish predecessor.

The twenty-six propositions of the philosophers are as follows:

1. There can be no infinite object possessing magnitude.

2. There cannot be an infinite number of bodies possessing magnitude, all at the same time.

3. There cannot be an infinite chain of cause and effect, even if these links are not possessed of magnitude, for example, intellects.

4. Change is found in four categories. In substance—genesis and decay. In quantity—growth and diminution. In quality—qualitative change. In place—motion of translation.

5. All motion is change, and is the realization of the potential.

6. Motion may be *per se, per accidens,* forcible, partial, the latter coming under *per accidens.* An example of motion *per se* is the motion of a body from one place to the next; of motion *per accidens,* when the blackness of an object is said to move from one place to another. Forcible motion is that of the stone when it is forced upward. Partial motion is that of a nail of a ship when the ship moves.

7. Every changeable thing is divisible; hence every movable thing is divisible, *i. e.,* every body is divisible. What is not divisible is not movable, and hence cannot be body.

8. That which is moved *per accidens* is necessarily at rest because its motion is not in itself. Hence it cannot have that accidental motion forever.

9. A body moving another must itself be in motion at the same time.

10. Being in a body means one of two things: being in it as an accident, or as constituting the essence of the body, like a natural form. Both are corporeal powers.

11. Some things which are in a body are divided with the division of the body. They are then divided *per accidens*, like colors and other powers extending throughout the body. Some of the things which constitute the body are not divisible at all, like soul and intellect.

12. Every power which extends throughout a body is finite, because all body is finite.

13. None of the kinds of change mentioned in 4 is continuous except motion of translation; and of this only circular motion.

14. Motion of translation is the first by nature of the motions. For genesis and decay presuppose qualitative change; and qualitative change presupposes the approach of the agent causing the change to the thing undergoing the change. And there is no growth or diminution without antecedent genesis and decay.

15. Time is an accident following motion and connected with it. The one cannot exist without the other. No motion except in time, and time cannot be conceived except with motion. Whatever has no motion does not come under time.

16. Whatever is incorporeal cannot be subject to number, unless it is a corporeal power; in which case the individual powers are numbered with their matters or bearers. Hence the separate forms or Intelligences, which are neither bodies nor corporeal powers, cannot have the conception of number connected with them, except when they are related to one another as cause and effect.

17. Everything that moves, necessarily has a mover, either outside, like the hand moving the stone, or inside like the animal body, which consists of a mover, the soul, and a moved, the body proper. Every *mobile* of the last kind is called a self-moving thing. This means that the motor element in the thing is part of the whole thing in motion.

18. If anything passes from potentiality to actuality, the agent that caused this must be outside the thing. For if it were inside and there was no obstruction, the thing would never be potential, but always actual; and if there was an obstruction, which was removed, the agency which removed the obstruction is the cause which caused the thing to pass from potentiality to actuality.

19. Whatever has a cause for its existence is a "possible" existent in so far as itself is concerned. If the cause is there, the thing exists; if not, it does not. Possible here means not necessary.

20. Whatever is a necessary existent in itself, has no cause for its existence.

21. Every composite has the cause of its existence in the composition. Hence it is not in itself a necessary existent; for its existence is dependent upon the existence of its constituent parts and upon their composition.

22. All body is composed necessarily of two things, matter and form; and it necessarily has accidents, *viz.*, quantity, figure, situation.

23. Whatever is potential and has in it a possibility may at some time not exist as an actuality.

24. Whatever is potential is necessarily possessed of matter, for possibility is always in matter.

25. The principles of an individual compound substance are matter and form; and there must be an agent, *i. e.*, a mover which moves the object or the underlying matter until it prepares it to receive the form. This need not be the ultimate mover, but a proximate one having a particular function. The idea of Aristotle is that matter cannot move itself. This is the great principle which leads us to investigate into the existence of the first mover.

Of these twenty-five propositions, Maimonides continues, some are clear after a little reflection, some again require many premises and proofs, but they are all proved in the Physics and Metaphysics of Aristotle and his commentators. My purpose here is, as I said, not to reproduce the writings of the philosophers. I will simply mention those principles which we must have for our purpose. I must add, however, one more proposition, which Aristotle thinks is true and more deserving of belief than anything else. We will grant him this by way of hypothesis until we explain what we intend to prove. The proposition is:

26. Time and motion are eternal and actual. Hence there must be a body moving eternally and existing actually. This is the matter constituting the substance of the heavenly bodies. Hence the heavens are not subject to genesis and decay, for their motion is eternal. This presupposes the possibility of accidental infinity (*cf.* above, p. 251). Aristotle regards this as true, though it does not seem to me that he claims he has proved it. His followers and commentators maintain that it is a necessary proposition and demonstrated. The Mutakalli-

mun, on the other hand, think it is impossible that there should be an infinite number of states in succession (*cf. ibid.*). It seems to me it is neither necessary nor impossible, but possible. This is, however, not the place to discuss it.[273]

Now follows the classical proof of the existence of God from motion. It is in essence the same as that given by Ibn Daud, but much more elaborate. We shall try to simplify it as much as possible. The numbers in parentheses in the sequel refer to the preliminary propositions above given.

We start with something that is known, namely, the motion we see in the sublunar world, the motion which is involved in all the processes of genesis and decay and change generally. This motion must have a mover (25). This mover must have another mover to move it, and this would lead us to infinity, which is impossible (3). We find, however, that all motion here below ends with the motion of the heaven. Let us take an example. The wind is blowing through an opening in the wall. I take a stone and stop up the hole. Here the stone is moved by the hand, the hand by the tendons, the tendons by the nerves, the nerves by the veins, the veins by the natural heat, the natural heat by the animal soul, the animal soul by a purpose, namely, to stop the hole from which the wind comes, the purpose by the wind, the wind by the motion of the heavenly sphere. But this is not the end. The sphere must also have a mover (17). This mover is either outside the sphere it moves or within it. If it is something outside, it is either again a body like the sphere, or an incorporeal thing, a "Separate Intelligence." If the mover of the sphere is something within the sphere, two alternatives are again possible. The internal moving power of the sphere may be a corporeal force extended throughout the body of the sphere and divisible with it like heat, or an indivisible power like soul or intellect (10, 11). We thus have four possibilities in all. The mover of the heavenly sphere may be (a) a body external to the sphere; (b) a separate incorporeal substance; (c) an internal corporeal power divisible with the division of the sphere; (d) an internal indivisible power. Of these four, (a) is impossible. For if the mover of the sphere is another body, it is likewise in motion (9) and must have another to move it, which, if a body, must have another, and so on *ad infinitum*, which is impossible (2). The third hypothesis, (c), is likewise impossible. For as the sphere is a body it is finite (1), and its power is also finite (12), since it is divisible with the body of the sphere (11). Hence it cannot move infinitely (26). Nor can we adopt the last alternative, (d). For a soul residing within the sphere could not alone be the cause of continuous motion. For a soul that moves its body is itself in motion *per accidens* (6); and whatever moves *per accidens* must necessarily sometime stop (8), and with it the thing set in motion by it will stop also. There is thus only one alternative left, (b), *viz.*, that the cause of the motion of the sphere is a "separate" (*i. e.*, incorporeal) power, which is itself not subject to motion either *per se* or *per accidens;* hence it is indivisible and unchangeable (7, 5). This is God. He cannot be two or more, for "separate" essences which are not body are not subject to number unless one is cause and the other effect (16). It follows, too, that he is not subject to time, for there is no time without motion (15).

We have thus proved with one stroke God's existence as well as his unity and incorporeality. But, it will be observed, if not for the twenty-sixth proposition concerning the eternity of motion, which implies an infinite power, we should not have been forced to the alternative (b), and could have adopted (c) as well as (d). That is, we might have concluded that God is the soul of the heavenly sphere resident within it, or even that he is a corporeal force pervading the extension of the sphere as heat pervades an ordinary body. But we must admit that in this way we prove only the existence of a God who is the cause of the heavenly motions, and through these of the processes of genesis and decay, hence of all the life of our sublunar world. This is not the God of Jewish tradition, who creates out of nothing, who is the cause of the being of the universe as well as of its life processes. Maimonides was aware of this defect in the Aristotelian view, and he later repudiates the Stagirite's theory of eternal motion on philosophical as well as religious grounds. Before, however, we speak of Maimonides's attitude in this matter, we must for completeness' sake briefly mention three other proofs for the existence of God as given by Maimonides. They are not strictly Aristotelian, though they are based upon Peripatetic principles cited above and due to the Arabian commentators of Aristotle.

The second proof is as follows. If we find a thing composed of two elements, and one of these elements is also found separately, it follows that the other element is found separately also. Now we frequently find the two elements of *causing motion* and *being moved* combined in the same object. And we also find things which are moved only, but do not cause motion, as for example matter, or the stone in the last proof. It stands to reason therefore that there is something that causes motion without being itself subject to motion. Not being subject to motion, it is indivisible, incorporeal and not subject to time, as above.

The third proof is based upon the idea of necessary existence. There is no doubt that there are existing things, for example the things we perceive with our senses. Now either all things are incapable of decay, or all are subject to genesis and decay, or some are and some are not. The first is evidently untrue for we see things coming into, and passing out, of being. The second hypothesis is likewise untrue. For if all things are subject to genesis and decay, there is a possibility that at some time all things might cease to be and nothing should exist at all. But as the coming and going of individuals in the various species in the world has been going on from eternity, the possibility just spoken of must have been realized—a possibility that is never realized is not a possibility—and nothing existed at all at that moment. But in that case how could they ever have come into being, since there was nothing to bring them into being? And yet they do exist, as ourselves for example and everything else. There is only one alternative left, therefore, and that is that beside the great majority of things subject to genesis and decay, there is a being not subject to change, a necessary existent, and ultimately one that exists by virtue of its own necessity (19).

Whatever is necessary *per se* can have no cause for its existence (20) and can have no multiplicity in itself (21); hence it is neither a body nor a corporeal power (12).

We can also prove easily that there cannot be two necessary existents *per se*. For in that case the element of necessary existence would be something added to the essence of each, and neither would then be necessary *per se*, but *per* that element of necessary existence which is common to both.

The last argument against dualism may also be formulated as follows. If there are two Gods, they must have something in common—that in virtue of which they are Gods—and something in which they differ, which makes them two and not one. If each of them has in addition to divinity a differential element, they are both composite, and neither is the first cause or the necessary existent (19). If one of them only has this differentia, then this one is composite and is not the first cause.

The fourth proof is very much like the first, but is based upon the ideas of potentiality and actuality instead of motion. But when we consider that Aristotle defines motion in terms of potentiality and actuality, the fourth proof is identical with the first. It reads in Maimonides as follows: We see constantly things existing potentially and coming into actuality. Every such thing must have an agent outside (18). It is clear, too, that this agent was first an agent potentially and then became one actually. This potentiality was due either to an obstacle in the agent himself or to the absence of a certain relation between the agent and its effect. In order that the potential agent may become an actual agent, there is need of another agent to remove the obstacle or to bring about the needed relation between the agent and the thing to be acted upon. This agent requires another agent, and so it goes *ad infinitum*. As this is impossible, we must stop somewhere with an agent that is always actual and in one condition. This agent cannot be material, but must be a "separate" (24). But the *separate* in which there is no kind of potentiality and which exists *per se*, is God. As we have already proved him incorporeal, he is one (16).[274]

We must now analyze the expressions *incorporeal* and *one*, and see what in strictness they imply, and how our logical deductions agree with Scripture. Many persons, misled by the metaphorical expressions in the Bible, think of God as having a body with organs and senses on the analogy of ours. Others are not so crude as to think of God in anthropomorphic terms, nor are they polytheists, and yet for the same reason, namely, misunderstanding of Scriptural expressions, ascribe a plurality of essential attributes to God. We must therefore insist on the absolute incorporeality of God and explain the purpose of Scripture in expressing itself in anthropomorphic terms, and on the other hand emphasize the absolute unity of God against the believers in essential attributes.

Belief in God as body or as liable to suffer affection is worse than idolatry. For the idolater does not deny the existence of God; he merely makes the mistake of supposing that the image of his own construction resembles a being which mediates between him and God. And yet because this leads to erroneous belief on the part of the people, who are inclined to worship the image itself instead of God (for the people cannot discriminate between the outward act and its idea), the Bible punishes idolatry with death, and calls the idolater a man who angers God. How much more serious is the error of him who thinks God is body! He entertains an error regarding the nature of God directly, and surely causes the anger of God to burn. Habit and custom and the evidence of the literal understanding of the Biblical text are no more an excuse for this erroneous belief than they are for idolatry; for the idolater, too, has been brought up in his wrong ideas and is confirmed in them by some false notions. If a man is not himself able to reason out the truth, there is no excuse for his refusing to listen to one who has reasoned it out. A person is not an unbeliever for not being able to *prove* the incorporeality of God. He *is* an unbeliever if he thinks God is corporeal.[275]

The expressions in the Bible which have led many to err so grievously in their conceptions of God are due to a desire on the part of their authors to show all people, the masses including women and children, that God exists and is possessed of all perfection, that he is existent, living, wise, powerful, and active. Hence it was necessary to speak of him as body, for this is the only thing that suggests real existence to the masses. It was necessary to endow him with motion, as this alone denotes life; to ascribe to him seeing, hearing, and so on, in order to indicate that he understands; to represent him as speaking, in order to show that he communicates with prophets, because to the minds of common people this is the only way in which ideas are communicated from one person to another. As we are active by our sense of touch, God, too, is described as doing. He is given a soul, to denote that he is alive. Then as all these activities are among us done by means of organs, these also are ascribed to God, as feet, hands, ear, eye, nose, mouth, tongue, voice, fingers, palm, arm. In other words, to show that God has all perfections, certain senses are ascribed to him; and to indicate these senses the respective organs are related to them, organs of motion to denote life, of sensation to denote under-standing, of touch to denote activity, of speech to denote revelation. As a matter of fact, however, since all these organs and perceptions and powers in man and animals are due to imperfection and are for the purpose of satisfying various wants for the preservation of the individual or the species, and God has no wants of any kind, he has no such powers or organs.[276]

Having disposed of crude anthropomorphism we must now take up the problem of attributes, which endangers the unity. It is a self-evident truth that an attribute is something different from the essence of a thing. It is an accident added to the essence. Otherwise it is the thing over again, or it is the definition of the thing and the explanation of the name, and signifies that the thing is composed of these elements. If we say God has many attributes, it will follow that there are many eternals. The only belief in true unity is to think that God is one simple substance without composition or multiplicity of elements, but one in all respects and aspects. Some go so far as to say that the divine attributes are neither God's essence nor anything outside of his essence. This is absurd. It is saying words which have nothing corresponding to them in fact. A thing is either the same as another, or it is not the same. There is no other alternative. The imagination is responsible for this error. Because bodies as we know them always have attributes, they thought that God, too, is made up of many essential elements or attributes.

Attributes may be of five kinds:

1. The attributes of a thing may be its definition, which denotes its essence as determined by its causes. This everyone will admit cannot be in God, for God has no cause, hence cannot be defined.

2. An attribute may consist of a part of a definition, as when we say, "man is rational," where the attribute rational is part of the definition of man, " rational animal " being the whole definition. This can apply to God no more than the first; for if there is a part in God's essence, he is composite.

3. An attribute may be an expression which characterizes not the essence of the thing but its quality. Quality is one of the nine cate-gories of accident, and God has no accidents.

4. An attribute may indicate relation, such as father, master, son,

slave. At first sight it might seem as if this kind of attribute may be applicable to God; but after reflection we find that it is not. There can be no relation of time between God and anything else; because time is the measure of motion, and motion is an accident of body. God is not corporeal. In the same way it is clear that there cannot be a relation of place between God and other things. But neither can there be any other kind of relation between God and his creation. For God is a necessary existent, while everything else is a possible existent. A relation exists only between things of the same proximate species, as between white and black. If the things have only a common genus, and still more so if they belong to two different genera, there is no relation between them. If there were a relation between God and other things, he would have the accident of relation, though relation is the least serious of attributes, since it does not necessitate a multiplicity of eternals, nor change in God's essence owing to change in the related things.

5. An attribute may characterize a thing by reference to its effects or works, not in the sense that the thing or author of the effect has acquired a character by reason of the product, like carpenter, painter, blacksmith, but merely in the sense that he is the one who made a particular thing. An attribute of this kind is far removed from the essence of the thing so characterized by it; and hence we may apply it to God, provided we remember that the varied effects need not be produced by different elements in the agent, but are all done by the one essence.

Those who believe in attributes divide them into two classes, and number the following four as *essential* attributes, not derived from God's effects like "creator," which denotes God's relation to his work, since God did not create himself. The four essential attributes about which all agree are, living, powerful, wise, possessed of will. Now if by wise is meant God's knowledge of himself, there might be some reason for calling it an essential attribute; though in that case it implies "living," and there is no need of two. But they refer the attribute wise to God's knowledge of the world, and then there is no reason for calling it an essential attribute any more than the word "creator," for example. In the same "powerful" and "having will" cannot refer to himself, but to his actions. We therefore hold that just as we do not say that there is something additional in his essence by which he created the heavens, something else with which he created the elements, and a third with which he created the Intelligences, so we do not say that he has one attribute with which he exercises power, another with which he wills, a third with which he knows, and so on, but his essence is simple and one.[277]

Four things must be removed from God: (1) corporeality, (2) affection, (3) potentiality, (4) resemblance to his creatures. The first we have already proved. The second implies change, and the author of the change cannot be the same as he who suffers the change and feels the affection. If then God were subject to affection, there would be another who would cause the change in him. So all want must be removed from him; for he who is in want of something is potential, and in order to pass into actuality requires an agent having that quality *in actu*. The fourth is also evident; for resemblance involves relation. As there is no relation between God and ourselves, there is no resemblance. Resemblance can exist only between things of the same species. All the expressions including "existent" are applied to God and to ourselves in a homonymous sense (*cf*. above, p. 240). The use is not even analogical; for in analogy there must be some resemblance between the things having the same name, but not so here. Existence in things which are determined by causes (and this includes all that is not God), is not identical with the essence of those things. The essence is that which is expressed in the definition, whereas the existence or non-existence of the thing so defined is not part of the definition. It is an accident added to the essence. In God the case is different. His existence has no cause, since he is a necessary existent; hence his existence is identical with his essence. So we say God exists, but not with existence, as we do. Similarly he is living, but not with life; knowing, but not with knowledge; powerful, but not with power; wise, but not with wisdom. Unity and plurality are also accidents of things which are one or many as the case may be. They are accidents of the category of quantity. God, who is a necessary existent and simple cannot be one any more than many. He is one, but not with unity. Language is inadequate to express our ideas of God. Wishing to say he is not many, we have to say he is one; though one as well as many pertains to the accidents of quantity. To correct the inexactness of the expression, we add, "but not with unity." So we say "eternal" to indicate that he is not "new," though in reality eternal is an accident of time, which in turn is an accident of motion, the latter being dependent upon body. In reality neither "eternal" nor "new" is applicable to God. When we say one, we mean merely that there is none other like him; and when Scripture speaks of him as the first and the last, the meaning is that he does not change.

The only true attributes of God are the negative ones. Negative attributes, too, by excluding the part of the field in which the thing to be designated is not contained, bring us nearer to the thing itself; though unlike positive attributes they do not designate any part of the thing itself. God cannot have positive attributes because he has no essence different from his existence for the attributes to designate, and surely no accidents. Negative attributes are of value in leading us to a knowledge of God, because in negation no plurality is involved. So when we have proved that there is a being beside these sensible and intelligible things, and we say he is existent, we mean that his non-existence is unthinkable. In the same way living means not dead; incorporeal is negative; eternal signifies not caused; powerful means not weak; wise—not ignorant; willing denotes that creation proceeds from him not by natural necessity like heat from fire or light from the sun, but with purpose and design and method. All attributes therefore are either derived from God's effects or, if they have reference to himself, are meant to exclude their opposites, *i. e.*, are really negatives. This does not mean, however, that God is devoid of a quality which he might have, but in the sense in which we say a stone does not see, meaning that it does not pertain to the nature of the stone to see.[278]

All the names of God except the tetragrammaton designate his activities in the world. Jhvh alone is the real name of God, which belongs to him alone and is not derived from anything else. Its meaning is unknown. It denotes perhaps the idea of necessary existence. All the other so-called divine names used by the writers of talismans and charms are quite meaningless and absurd. The wonderful claims these people bespeak for them are not to be believed by any intelligent man.[279]

The above account of Maimonides's doctrine of attributes shows us that he followed the same line of thought as his predecessors. His treatment is more thorough and elaborate, and his requirements of the religionist more stringent. He does not even allow attributes of relation, which were admitted by Ibn Daud. Negative attributes and those taken from God's effects are the only expressions that may be applied to God. This is decidedly not a Jewish mode of conceiving of God, but it is not even Aristotelian. Aristotle has very little to say about God's attributes, it is true, but there seems no warrant in the little he does say for such an absolutely transcendental and agnostic conception as we find in Maimonides. To Aristotle God is pure form, thought thinking itself. In so far as he is thought we may suppose him to be similar in kind, though not in degree, to human thought. The only source of Maimonides's ideas is to be sought in Neo-Platonism, in the so-called Theology of Aristotle which, however, Maimonides never quotes. He need not have used it himself. He was a descendant of a long line of thinkers, Christian, Mohammedan and Jewish, in which this problem was looked at from a Neo-Platonic point of view; and the Theology of Aristotle had its share in forming the views of his predecessors. The idea of making God transcendent appealed to Maimonides, and he carried it to the limit. How he could combine such transcendence with Jewish prayer and ceremony it is hard to tell; but it would be a mistake to suppose that his philosophical deductions represented his last word on the subject. As in Philo so in Maimonides, his negative theology was only a means to a positive. Its purpose was to emphasize God's perfection. And in the admission, nay maintenance, of man's inability to understand God lies the solution of the problem we raised above. Prayer *is* answered, man *is* protected by divine Providence; and if we cannot understand how, it is because the matter is beyond our limited intellect.

Having discussed the existence and nature of God, our next problem is the existence of angels and their relation to the "Separate Intelligences" of the philosophers. In this matter, too, Ibn Daud anticipated Maimonides, though the latter is more elaborate in his exposition as well as criticism of the extreme philosophic view. He adopts as much of Aristotelian (or what he thought was Aristotelian) doctrine as is compatible in his mind with the Bible and subject to rigorous demonstration, and rejects the rest on philosophic as well as religious grounds.

The existence of separate intelligences he proves in the same way as Ibn Daud from the motions of the celestial spheres. These motions cannot be purely "natural," *i. e.*, unconscious and involuntary like the rectilinear motions of the elements, fire, air, water and earth, because in that case they would stop as soon as they came to their natural place, as is true of the elements (*cf.* above, p. xxxiii); whereas the spheres actually move in a circle and never stop. We must therefore assume that they are endowed with a soul, and their motions are conscious and voluntary. But it is not sufficient to regard them as irrational creatures, for on this hypothesis also their motions would have to cease as soon as they attained the object of their desire, or escaped the thing they wish to avoid. Neither object can be accomplished by circular motion, for one approaches in this way the thing from which one flees, and flees the object which one approaches. The only way to account for continuous circular motion is by supposing that the sphere is endowed with reason or intellect, and that its motion is due to a desire on its part to attain a certain conception. God is the object of the conception of the sphere, and it is the love of God, to whom the sphere desires to become similar, that is the cause of the sphere's motion. So far as the sphere is a body, it can accomplish this only by circular motion; for this is the only continuous act possible for a body, and it is the simplest of bodily motions.

Seeing, however, that there are many spheres having different kinds of motions, varying in speed and direction, Aristotle thought that this difference must be due to the difference in the objects of their conceptions. Hence he posited as many separate Intelligences as there are spheres. That is, he thought that intermediate between God and the rational spheres there are pure incorporeal intelligences, each one moving its own sphere as a loved object moves the thing that loves it. As the number of spheres were in his day thought to be fifty, he assumed there were fifty separate Intelligences. The mathematical sciences in Aristotle's day were imperfect, and the astronomers thought that for every motion visible in the sky there must be a sphere, not knowing that the inclination of one sphere may be the cause of a number of apparent motions. Later writers making use of the more advanced state of astronomical science, reduced the number of Intelligences to ten, corresponding to the ten spheres as follows: the seven planetary spheres, the sphere of the fixed stars, the diurnal sphere embracing them all and giving all of them the motion from east to west, and the sphere of the elements surrounding the earth. Each one of these is in charge of an Intelligence. The last separate Intelligence is the Active Intellect, which is the cause of our mind's passing from potentiality to actuality, and of the various processes of sublunar life generally.

These are the views of Aristotle and his followers concerning the separate Intelligences. And in a general way his views, says Maimonides, are not incompatible with the Bible. What he calls Intelligences the Scriptures call angels. Both are pure forms and incorporeal. Their rationality is indicated in the nineteenth Psalm, "The heavens declare the glory of God." That God rules the world through them is evident from a number of passages in Bible and Talmud. The plural number in "Let *us* make man in our image" (Gen. 1, 26), "Come, let *us* go down and confuse their speech" (*ib.* 11, 7) is explained by the Rabbis in the statement that "God never does anything without first looking at the celestial 'familia.'" (Bab. Talm. Sanhedrin 38b.) The word "looking" ("Mistakkel") is striking; [280] for it is the very expression Plato uses when he says that God looks into the world of Ideas and produces the universe. [281]

For once Maimonides in the last Rabbinic quotation actually hit upon a passage which owes its content to Alexandrian and possibly Philonian influence. Having no idea of the Alexandrian School and of the works of Philo and his relation to some theosophic passages in the Haggadah, he made no distinction between Midrash and Bible, and read Plato and Aristotle in both alike, as we shall see more particularly later.

Maimonides's detailed criticism of Aristotle we shall see later. For the present he agrees that the philosophic conception of separate Intelligences is the same as the Biblical idea of angels with this exception that according to Aristotle these Intelligences and powers are all eternal and proceed from God by natural necessity, whereas the Jewish view is that they are created. God created the separate Intelligences; he likewise created the spheres as rational beings and implanted in them a desire for the Intelligences which accounts for their various motions.

Now Maimonides has prepared the ground and is ready to take up the question of the origin of the world, which was left open above. He enumerates three views concerning this important matter.

1. *The Biblical View.* God created everything out of nothing. Time itself is a creation, which did not exist when there was no world. For time is a measure of motion, and motion cannot be without a moving thing. Hence no motion and no time without a world.

2. *The Platonic View.* The world as we see it now is subject to genesis and decay; hence it originated in time. But God did not make it out of nothing. That a composite of matter and form should be made out of nothing or should be reduced to nothing is to the Platonists an impossibility like that of a thing being and not being at the same time, or the diagonal of a square being equal to its side. Therefore to say that God cannot do it argues no defect in him. They believe therefore that there is an eternal matter, the effect of God to be sure, but co-eternal with him, which he uses as the potter does the clay.

3. *The Aristotelian View.* Time and motion are eternal. The heavens and the spheres are not subject to genesis and decay, hence they were always as they are now. And the processes of change in the lower world existed from eternity as they exist now. Matter is not subject to genesis and decay; it simply takes on forms one after the other, and this has been going on from eternity. It results also from his statements, though he does not say it in so many words, that it is impossible there should be a change in God's will. He is the cause of the universe, which he brought into being by his will, and as his will does not change, the universe has existed this way from eternity.

The arguments of Aristotle and his followers by which they defend their view of the eternity of the world are based partly upon the nature of the world, and partly upon the nature of God. Some of these arguments are as follows:

Motion is not subject to beginning and end. For everything that comes into being after a state of non-existence requires motion to precede it, namely, the actualization from non-being. Hence if motion came into being, there was motion before motion, which is a contradiction. As motion and time go together, time also is eternal.

Again, the prime matter common to the four elements is not subject to genesis and decay. For all genesis is the combination of a pre-existing matter with a new form, namely, the form of the generated thing. If therefore the prime matter itself came into being, there must be a previous matter from which it came, and the thing that resulted must be endowed with form. But this is impossible, since the prime matter has no matter before it and is not endowed with form.

Among the proofs derived from the nature of God are the following: If God brought forth the world from non-existence, then before he created it he was a creator potentially and then became a creator actually. There is then potentiality in the creator, and there must be a cause which changed him from a potential to an actual creator.

Again, an agent acts at a particular time and not at another because of reasons and circumstances preventing or inducing action. In God there are no accidents or hindrances. Hence he acts always.

Again, how is it possible that God was idle an eternity and only yesterday made the world? For thousands of years and thousands of worlds before this one are after all as yesterday in comparison with God's eternity.

These arguments Maimonides answers first by maintaining that Aristotle himself, as can be inferred from his manner, does not regard his discussions favoring the eternity of the world as scientific demonstrations. Besides, there is a fundamental flaw in Aristotle's entire attitude to the question of the ultimate principles and beginnings of things. All his arguments in favor of eternity of motion and of the world are based upon the erroneous assumption that the world as a whole must have come into being in the same way as its parts appear now after the world is here. According to this supposition it is easy to prove that motion must be eternal, that matter is not subject to genesis, and so on. Our contention is that at the beginning, when God created the world, there were not these laws; that he created matter *out of nothing*, and then made it the basis of all generation and destruction.

We can also answer the arguments in favor of eternity taken from the nature of God. The first is that God would be passing from potentiality to actuality if he made the world at a particular time and not before, and there would be need of a cause producing this passage.

Our answer is that this applies only to material things but not to immaterial, which are always active whether they produce visible results or not. The term action is a homonym (*cf.* above, p. 240), and the conditions applying to it in the ordinary usage do not hold when we speak of God.

Nor is the second argument conclusive. An agent whose will is determined by a purpose external to himself is subject to influences positive and negative, which now induce, now hinder his activity. A person desires to have a house and does not build it by reason of obstacles of various sorts. When these are removed, he builds the house. In the case of an agent whose will has no object external to itself this does not hold. If he does not act always, it is because it is the nature of will sometimes to will and sometimes not. Hence this does not argue change.[282]

So far our results have been negative. We have not proved that God did create the world in time; we have only taken the edge off the Aristotelian arguments and thereby shown that the doctrine of creation is not impossible. We must now proceed to show that there are positive reasons which make creation a more plausible theory than eternity.

The gist of Maimonides's arguments here is that the difference between eternity and creation resolves itself into a more fundamental difference between an impersonal mechanical law as the explanation of the universe and an intelligent personality acting with will, purpose and design. Aristotle endeavors to explain all motions in the world above the moon as well as below in terms of mechanics. He succeeds pretty well as far as the sublunar world is concerned, and no one who is free from prejudice can fail to see the cogency of his reasoning. If he were just as convincing in his explanation of celestial phenomena on the mechanical principle as he is in his interpretation of sublunar events, eternity of the world would be a necessary consequence. Uniformity and absolute necessity of natural law are more compatible with an eternal world than with a created one. But Aristotle's method breaks down the moment he leaves the sublunar sphere. There are too many phenomena unaccounted for in his system.

Aristotle tries to find a reason why the heavens move from east to west and not in the opposite direction; and his explanation for the difference in speed of the motions of the various spheres is that it is due to their relative proximity to the outer sphere, which is the cause of this motion and which it communicates to all the other spheres under it. But his reasons are inadequate, for some of the swift moving spheres are below the slow moving and some are above. When he says that the reason the sphere of the fixed stars moves so slowly from west to east is because it is so near to the diurnal sphere (the outer sphere), which moves from east to west, his explanation is wonderfully clever.[283] But when he infers from this that the farther a sphere is from the fixed stars the more rapid is its motion from west to east, his conclusion is not true to fact. Or let us consider the existence of the stars in the spheres. The matter of the stars must be different from that of the spheres, for the latter move, whereas the stars are always stationary. Now what has put these two different matters together? Stranger still is the existence and distribution of the fixed stars in the eighth sphere. Some parts are thickly studded with stars, others are very thin. In the planentary spheres what is the reason (since the sphere is simple and uniform throughout) that the star occupies the particular place that it does? This can scarcely be a matter of necessity. It will not do to say that the differences in the motions of the spheres are due to the separate Intelligences for which the respective spheres have a desire. For the Intelligences are not bodies, and hence do not occupy any position relative to the spheres. There must therefore be a being who determines their various motions.

Further, it is argued on the philosophical side that from a simple cause only a simple effect can follow; and that if the cause is composite, as many effects will follow as there are simple elements in the cause. Hence from God directly can come only one simple Intelligence. This first Intelligence produces the second, the second produces the third, and so on (*cf.* above, p. 178). Now according to this idea, no matter how many Intelligences are produced in this successive manner, the last, even if he be the thousandth, would have to be simple. Where then does composition arise? Even if we grant that the farther the Intelligences are removed from the first cause the more composite they become by reason of the composite nature of their ideas or thoughts, how can we explain the emanation of a sphere from an Intelligence, seeing that the one is body, the other Intellect? Granting again this also on the ground that the Intelligence producing the sphere is composite (since it thinks itself and another), and hence one of its parts produces the next lower Intelligence and the other the sphere, there is still this difficulty that the part of the Intelligence producing the sphere is simple, whereas the sphere has four elements—the matter and the form of the sphere, and the matter and the form of the star fixed in the sphere.

All these are difficulties arising from the Aristotelian theory of mechanical causation, necessity of natural law and eternity of the world. And they are all removed at a stroke when we substitute intelligent cause working with purpose, will and design. To be sure, by finding difficulties attaching to a theory we do not disprove it, much less do we prove our own. But we should follow the view of Alexander, who says that where a theory is not proved one should adopt the view which has the least number of objections. This, we shall show, is the case in the doctrine of creation. We have already pointed out a number of difficulties attaching to the Aristotelian view, which are solved if we adopt creation. And there are others besides. It is impossible to explain the heavenly motions as a necessary mechanical system. The hypotheses made by Ptolemy to account for the apparent motions conflict with the principles of the Aristotelian Physics. According to these principles there is no motion of translation, *i. e.*, there is no change of place, in the heavenly spheres. Also there are three kinds of motion in the world, toward the centre (water, earth), away from the centre (air, fire) and around the centre (the celestial spheres). Also motion in a circle must be around a fixed centre. All these principles are violated in the theories of the epicycle and eccentric, especially the first. For the epicycle is a sphere which changes place in the circumference of the large sphere.

Finally, an important objection to the doctrine of eternity as taught by Aristotle, involving as it does necessity and absolute changelessness of natural phenomena, is that it subverts the foundations of religion, and does away with miracles and signs. The Platonic view (*cf.* above, p. 269) is not so bad and does not necessitate the denial of miracles; but there is no need of forcing the Biblical texts to that opinion so long as it has not been proved. As long as we believe in creation all possible

questions concerning the reasons for various phenomena such as prophecy, the various laws, the selection of Israel, and so on, can be answered by reference to the will of God, which we do not understand.
If, however, the world is a mechanical necessity, all these questions
arise and demand an answer.[284]

It will be seen that Maimonides's objections to eternity and mechanical necessity (for these two are necessarily connected in his mind), are
twofold, philosophic and religious. The latter objection we may conceive Maimonides to insist upon if he were living to-day. Mechanical
necessity as a universal explanation of phenomena would exclude free
will and the efficacy of prayer as ordinarily understood, though not
necessarily miracles, if we mean by miracle simply an extraordinary
phenomenon not explicable by the laws of nature as we know them,
and happening only on rare occasions. But in reality this is not what
we mean by miracle. A miracle is a discontinuity in the laws of nature
brought to pass on a special occasion by a personal being in response
to a prayer or in order to realize a given purpose. In this sense miracles are incompatible with the doctrine of necessity, and Maimonides's objections hold to-day, except for those to whom religion is independent of the Bible, tradition or any external authority.

As concerns the scientific objections, the case is different. We may
allow Maimonides's negative criticism of the Aristotelian arguments,
namely, that they are not convincing. His positive criticism that
Aristotle's interpretation of phenomena on the mechanical principle
does not explain all the facts is not valid. Aristotle may be wrong
in his actual explanations of particular phenomena and yet be correct
in his method. Modern science, in fact, has adopted the mechanical
method of interpreting phenomena, assuming that this is the only way
in which science can exist at all. And if there is any domain in which
mechanical causation is still denied, it is not the celestial regions about
which Maimonides was so much concerned—the motions of the heavenly bodies have been reduced to uniformity in accordance with natural law quite as definitely as, and in some cases more definitely than,
some terrestrial phenomena—but the regions of life, mind and will.
In these domains the discussion within the scientific and philosophic
folds is still going on. But in inanimate nature modern science
has succeeded in justifying its method by the ever increasing number

of phenomena that yield to its treatment. Maimonides fought an obsolete philosophy and obsolete scientific principles. It is possible that he might have found much to object to in modern science as well, on the ground that much is yet unexplained. But an objection of this sort is captious, particularly if we consider what Maimonides desires to place in science's stead. Science is doing its best to classify all natural phenomena and to discover the uniformities underlying their behavior. It has succeeded admirably and is continually widening its sphere of activity. It has been able to predict as a result of its method. The principle of uniformity and mechanical necessity is becoming more and more generally verified with every new scientific discovery and invention.

And what does Maimonides offer us in its stead? The principle of intelligent purpose and design. This, he says, is not open to the objections which apply to the Aristotelian principles and methods. It is as if one said the coward is a better man than the brave warrior, because the latter is open to the danger of being captured, wounded or killed, whereas the former is not so liable. The answer obviously would be that the only way the coward escapes the dangers mentioned is by running away, by refusing to fight. Maimonides's substitution is tantamount to a refusal to fight, it is equivalent to flight from the field of battle.

Aristotle tries to explain the variation in speed of the different celestial motions, and succeeds indifferently. Another man coming after Aristotle and following the same method may succeed better. This has actually been the case. Leverrier without ever looking into a telescope discovered Neptune, and told the observers in what part of the heavens they should look for the new planet. Substitute Maimonides's principle, and death to science! Why do the heavenly bodies move as they do? Maimonides replies in effect, because so God's wisdom has determined and his wisdom is transcendent. There is no further impulse to investigation in such an answer. It is the reply of the obscurantist, and it is very surprising that Maimonides the rationalist should so far have forgotten his own ideal of reason and enlightenment. He is here playing into the hands of those very Mutakallimun whom he so severely criticises. They were more consistent. Distrustful of the irreligious consequences of the philosophical theories of Aristotle and his Arabian followers, they deliberately denied causation and natural law, and substituted the will of God as interfering continuously in the phenomena of nature. A red object continues red because and as long as God creates the "accident" red and attaches it to the atoms of which the object is composed. Fire taking hold of wood burns it and reduces it to ashes because God wills at the particular moment that this shall be the result. The next moment God may will otherwise and the fire and the wood will lie down in peace together and no harm done. This makes miracles possible and easy. Maimonides would not think of going so far; he has no names harsh enough to describe this unscientific, unphilosophic, illogical, irrational, purely imaginary procedure. But we find that he is himself guilty of the same lack of scientific insight when he rejects a method because it is not completely successful, and substitutes something else which will always be successful because it will never tell us anything at all and will stifle all investigation. Were Maimonides living in our day, we may suppose he would be more favorably inclined to the mechanical principle as a scientific method.

Having laid the philosophical foundations of religion in proving the existence, unity and incorporeality of God, and purposeful creation in time, Maimonides proceeds to the more properly religious doctrines of Judaism, and begins with the phenomenon of prophecy. Here also he follows Aristotelian ideas as expressed in the writings of the Arabs Alfarabi and Avicenna, and was anticipated among the Jews by Ibn Daud. His distinction here as elsewhere is that he went further than his model in the manner of his elaboration of the doctrine.

He cites three opinions concerning prophecy:

1. *The Opinion of the Masses.* God chooses any person he desires, be he young or old, wise or ignorant, and inspires him with the prophetic spirit.

2. *The Opinion of the Philosophers.* Prophecy is a human gift and requires natural aptitude and hard preparation and study. But given these qualifications, and prophecy is sure to come.

3. *The Opinion of Judaism.* This is very much like that of the philosophers, the only difference being that a man may have all the qualifications and yet be prevented from prophesying if God, by way of punishment, does not desire that he should.

Prophecy is an inspiration from God, which passes through the mediation of the Active Intellect to the rational power first and then to the faculty of the imagination. It is the highest stage a man can attain and is not open to everyone. It requires perfection in theoretical wisdom and in morals, and perfect development of the imaginative power. This latter does its work when the senses are at rest, giving rise to true dreams, and producing also prophetic visions. Dream and prophecy differ in degree, not in kind. What a man thinks hard in his waking state, that the imagination works over in sleep. Now if a person has a perfect brain; develops his mind as far as a man can; is pure morally; is eager to know the mysteries of existence, its causes and the First Cause; is not susceptible to the purely animal desires, or to those of the spirited soul ambitious for dominion and honor—if a man has all these qualifications, he without doubt receives through his imagination from the Active Intellect divine ideas. The difference in the grade of prophets is due to the difference in these three requirements—perfection of the reason, perfection of the imagination and perfection of moral character.

According to the character and development of their reasons and imaginations men may be divided into three classes.

1. Those whose rational faculties are highly developed and receive influences from the Active Intellect, but whose imagination is defective constitutionally, or is not under the influence of the Active Intellect. These are wise men and philosophers.

2. When the imagination also is perfect in constitution and well developed under the influence of the Active Intellect, we have the class of prophets.

3. When the imagination alone is in good condition, but the intellect is defective, we have statesmen, lawgivers, magicians, dreamers of true dreams and occult artists. These men are so confused sometimes by visions and reveries that they think they have the gift of prophecy.

Each of the first two classes may be further divided into two according as the influence from above is just sufficient for the perfection of the individual himself, or is so abundant as to cause the recipient to seek to impart it to others. We have then authors and teachers in the first class, and preaching prophets in the second.

Among the powers we have in varying degrees are those of courage and divination. These are innate and can be perfected if one has them in any degree. By means of the power of divination we sometimes guess what a person said or did under certain conditions, and guess truly. The result really follows from a number of premises, but the mind passes over these so rapidly that it seems the guess was made instantaneously. The prophet must have these two faculties in a high degree. Witness Moses braving the wrath of a great king. Some prophets also have their rational powers more highly developed than those of an ordinary person who perfects his reason by theoretical study. The same inspiration which renders the activity of the imagination so vivid that it seems to it its perceptions are real and due to the external senses—this same inspiration acts also upon the rational power, and makes its ideas as certain as if they were derived by intellectual effort.

The prophetic vision (Heb. Mar'ah) is a state of agitation coming upon the prophet in his waking state, as is clear from the words of Daniel, "And I saw this great vision, and there remained no strength in me: for my comeliness was turned in me into corruption, and I retained no strength" (Dan. 10, 8). In vision also the senses cease their functions, and the process is the same as in sleep.

Whenever the Bible speaks of prophecy coming to anyone, it is always through an angel and in a dream or vision, whether this is specifically stated or not. The expression, "And God came to . . . in a dream of the night," does not denote prophecy at all. It is merely a dream that comes to a person warning him of danger. Laban and Abimelech had such dreams, but no one would credit these heathens with the prophetic power.

Whenever an angel is met in Scripture speaking or communicating with a person, it is always in a dream or vision. Examples are, Abraham and the three men, Jacob wrestling with the angel, Balaam and the ass, Joshua and the angel at Jericho;—all these were in a dream or vision. Sometimes there is no angel at all, but merely a voice that is heard by such as are not deserving of prophecy, for example Hagar, and Manoah and his wife.

The prophets see images in their visions. These images are sometimes interpreted in the vision itself; sometimes the interpretation does not appear until the prophet wakes up. Sometimes the prophet sees a likeness, sometimes he sees God speaking to him, or an angel; or he hears an angel speaking to him, or sees a man speaking to him, or sees nothing at all but only hears a voice.

In this way we distinguish eleven grades of prophecy. The first two are only preparatory, not yet constituting one who has them a prophet.

1. When one is endowed by God with a great desire to save a community or a famous individual, and he undertakes to bring it about, we have the first grade known as the "Spirit of God." This was the position of the Judges. Moses always had this desire from the moment he could be called a man, hence he killed the Egyptian and chided the two quarreling men, and delivered the daughters of Jethro from the shepherds, and so on. The same is true of David. Not everyone, however, who has this desire is a prophet until he succeeds in doing a very great thing.

2. When a person feels something come upon him and begins to speak—words of wisdom and praise or of warning, or relating to social or religious conduct—all this while in a waking state and with full consciousness, we have the second stage called the "Holy Spirit." This is the inspiration which dictated the Psalms, the Proverbs, Ecclesiastes, Song of Songs, Daniel, Job, Chronicles and the other sacred writings (Hagiographa). Balaam's discourses also belong to this class. David, Solomon and Daniel belong here, and are not in the same class with Isaiah, Jeremiah, Nathan, Ahiah, and so on. God spoke to Solomon through Ahiah the Shilonite; at other times he spoke to him in a dream, and when Solomon woke up, he knew it was a dream and not a prophecy. Daniel's visions were also in dreams. This is why his book is classed in the third division of the Biblical writings (Hagiographa), and not in the second (Prophets).

3. This is the first grade of real prophecy, *i. e.*, when a prophet sees a picture in a dream under the proper conditions, and the picture is explained to him in the dream itself. Most of the dreams of Zechariah are of this nature.

4. When he hears speech in a prophetic dream, but does not see the speaker, as happened to Samuel in the beginning of his career.

5. When a man speaks to him in a dream, as we find in some

of the prophecies of Ezekiel, "And the man said unto me, son of man. . . ."

6. When an angel speaks to him in a dream. This is the condition of most prophets, as is indicated in the expression, "And an angel of God said to me in a dream."

7. When it seems to him in a prophetic dream as if God is speaking to him; as we find in Isaiah, "I saw the Lord . . . and he said, whom shall I send and who will go for us" (Isa. 6, 1, 8).

8. When a *vision* appears to him and he sees pictures, like Abraham at the covenant of the pieces (Gen. 15).

9. When he hears words in a vision, as in the case of Abraham, "And, behold, the word of the Lord came unto him saying, This man shall not be thine heir" (Gen. 15, 4).

10. When he sees a man speaking to him in a prophetic vision. Examples, Abraham in the plain of Mamre, Joshua in Jericho.

11. When he sees an angel speaking to him in a vision, like Abraham in the sacrifice of Isaac. This is the highest degree of prophecy, excepting Moses. The next higher stage would be that a prophet should see God speaking to him in a vision. But this seems impossible, as it is too much for the imaginative faculty. In fact it is possible that in a vision speech is never heard at all, but only likenesses are seen. In that case the eleven grades are reduced to eight.

All the details of actions and travels that are described in prophetic visions must not be understood as having actually taken place, as for example Hosea's marrying a harlot. They appear only in the prophet's vision or dream. Many expressions in the prophets are hyperbolical or metaphorical, and must not be taken literally.

Moses was the greatest of the prophets. He alone received his communications direct from God. All the others got their divine messages through an angel. Moses performed his miracles before the whole people as no one else did. The standing still of the sun produced by Joshua was not in the presence of *all* the people. Besides it may be the meaning is that that day seemed to the people the longest of any they experienced in those regions. Moses alone, by reason of his superiority to all other prophets before or after, called the people to the Law. No one before him did this, though there were many prophets before Moses. Abraham taught a few people, and so did others. But no one like Moses said to the people, "The Lord sent me to you that you may do thus and so." After Moses all the prophets urge upon the people obedience to the law of Moses. This shows that the law of Moses will never change. For it is perfect, and any change in any direction would be for the worse.[285]

From the theoretical part of philosophy we pass to the practical. This includes ethics and other topics related thereto, theodicy, providence, free will and its compatibility with God's omniscience. To give his ethical doctrine a scientific character, Maimonides bases it upon a metaphysical and psychological foundation. The doctrine of matter and form gives him a convenient formula underlying his ethical discussion. Sin and vice are due to matter, virtue and goodness to form. For sensuous desires, which are due to matter, are at the basis of vice; whereas intellectual pursuits, which constitute the noblest activity of the soul, the form of the living body, lead to virtue. We may therefore state man's ethical duty in broad philosophical terms as follows: Despise matter, and have to do with it only so far as is absolutely necessary.[286] This is too general to be enlightening, and it is necessary to have recourse to psychology. Ethics has for its subject-matter the improvement and perfection of character. Making use of a medical analogy we may say that as it is the business of the physician to cure the body, so it is the aim of the moral teacher to cure the soul. We may carry this figure further and conclude that as the physician must know the anatomy and physiology of the body before he can undertake to cure it of its ills, so the moralist must know the nature of the soul and its powers or faculties.

In the details of his psychology Maimonides follows Alfarabi instead of Avicenna who was the model of Judah Halevi and Ibn Daud (pp. 175, 211).

The soul consists of five parts or faculties: the nutritive, the sensitive, the imaginative, the appetitive and the rational. The further description of the nutritive soul pertains to medicine and does not concern us here. The sensitive soul contains the well known five senses. The imaginative faculty is the power which retains the forms of sensible objects when they are no longer present to the external senses. It also has the function of original combination of sense elements into composite objects having no real existence in the outside world. This makes the imagination an unreliable guide in matters intellectual.

The appetitive faculty is the power of the soul by which a person desires a thing or rejects it. Acts resulting from it are the pursuit of an object and its avoidance; also the feelings of anger, favor, fear, courage, cruelty, pity, love, hate, and so on. The organs of these powers, feelings and activities are the members of the body, like the hand, which takes hold of an object; the foot, which goes toward a thing or away from it; the eye, which looks; the heart, which takes courage or is stricken with fear; and so with the rest.

The rational faculty is the power of the soul by which a person reflects, acquires knowledge, discriminates between a praiseworthy act and a blameworthy. The functions of the rational soul are practical and theoretical. The practical activity of the reason has to do with the arts directly, as in learning carpentry, agriculture, medicine, seamanship; or it is concerned with reflecting upon the methods and principles of a given art. The theoretical reason has for its subject-matter the permanent and unchangeable, what is known as science in the true sense of the term.[287]

Now as far as the commandments, mandatory and prohibitive, of the Bible are concerned, the only parts of the soul which are involved are the sensitive and the appetitive. For these are the only powers subject to control. The nutritive and the imaginative powers function in sleep as well in waking, hence a person cannot be held responsible for their activities, which are involuntary. There is some doubt about the rational faculty, but it seems that here too a person is responsible for the opinions he holds, though no practical acts are involved.

Virtues are divided into ethical and intellectual (dianoetic); and so are the contrary vices. The intellectual virtues are the excellencies of the reason. Such are *science*, which consists in the knowledge of proximate and remote causes of things; *pure reason*, having to do with such innate principles as the axioms; *the acquired reason*, which we cannot discuss here; *clearness of perception* and *quick insight*. The intellectual vices are the opposites or the contraries of these.

The ethical virtues are resident in the appetitive faculty. The sensitive soul is auxiliary to the appetitive. The number of these virtues is large. Examples are; temperance, generosity, justice, modesty, humility, contentment, courage, and so on. The vices of this class are the above qualities carried to excess, or not practiced to the required extent. The faculties of nutrition and imagination have neither virtues nor vices. We say a person's digestion is good or it is poor; his imagination is correct or it is defective, but we do not attach the idea of virtue or vice to these conditions.

Virtue is a permanent and enduring quality of the soul occupying an intermediate position between the two opposite extremes each of which is a vice, sinning by exceeding the proper measure of the golden mean or by falling short of it. A good act is that form of conduct which follows from a virtuous disposition as just defined. A bad act is the result of a tendency of the soul to either of the two extremes, of excess or defect. Thus temperance or moderation is a virtue. It is the mean between over-indulgence in the direction of excess, and insensibility or indifference in the direction of defect. The last two are vices. Similarly generosity is a mean between niggardliness and extravagance; courage is a mean between foolhardiness and cowardice; dignity is a mean between haughtiness and loutishness; humility is a mean between arrogance and self-abasement; contentment is a mean between avarice and slothful indifference; kindness is a mean between baseness and excessive self-denial; gentleness is a mean between irascibility and insensibility to insult; modesty is a mean between impudence and shamefacedness. People are often mistaken and regard one of the extremes as a virtue. Thus the reckless and the foolhardy is often praised as the brave; the man of no backbone is called gentle; the indolent is mistaken for the contented; the insensible for the temperate, the extravagant for the generous. This is an error. The mean alone is worthy of commendation.

The ethical virtues and vices are acquired as a result of repeated practice during a long time of the corresponding acts until they become a confirmed habit and a second nature. A person is not born virtuous or vicious. What he will turn out to be depends upon the way he is trained from childhood. If his training has been wrong and he has acquired a vicious disposition in a particular tendency, he may be cured. And here we may borrow a leaf from the book of medicine. As in bodily disease the physician's endeavor is to restore the disturbed equilibrium in the mixture of the humors by increasing the element that is deficient, so in diseases of the soul, if a person has a decided tendency to one of the vicious extremes, he must as a curative measure, for a certain length of time, be directed to practice the opposite extreme until he has been cured. Then he may go back to the virtuous mean. Thus if a person has the vice of niggardliness, the practice of liberality is not sufficient to cure him. As a heroic measure he must practice extravagance until the former tendency has left him. Then he may return to the liberal mean. The same thing applies to the other virtues, except that it is necessary to use proper judgment in the amount of practice of a vicious extreme necessary to bring about a satisfactory result. Too great deviation and too long continued from the mean would in some cases be dangerous, as likely to develop the opposite vice. Thus it is comparatively safe to indulge in extravagance as a cure for niggardliness; the reverse process must be used with caution. Care should likewise be taken in trying to wean a person away from a habit of insensibility to pleasure by means of a régime of indulgence. If it is not discontinued in time, he may become a pleasure seeker, which is even worse than total indifference.

It is in this way that we must explain the conduct of certain pious men and saints who were not content with following the middle way, and inclined to one extreme, the extreme of asceticism and self-abasement. They did this as a measure of cure, or because of the wickedness of their generation, whose example they feared would contaminate them by its contagion. Hence they lived a retired and solitary life, the life of a recluse. It was not meant as the normal mode of conduct, which would be as unwholesome to the soul as an invalid's drugs would be dangerous if taken regularly by a person of sound health.

The will of God is that we should follow the middle way and eat and drink and enjoy ourselves in moderation. To be sure, we must be always on our guard against slipping into the forbidden extreme, but it is not necessary for this purpose to inflict additional burdens upon ourselves or to practice mortification of the flesh and abstention from food and drink beyond what is prescribed in the Law. For many of the regulations in the Pentateuch have been laid down for this very purpose. The dietary laws, the laws of forbidden marriages, the laws of tithes, the laws prescribing that the corner of the field, the dropped and forgotten ears and the gleanings of the vintage should be left to the poor, the laws of the sabbatical year, the Jubilee, and the regulations governing charity—all these are intended to guard us against avarice and selfishness. Other laws and precepts are for the purpose of moderating our tendency to anger and rage, and so with all the other virtues and vices. Hence it is folly and overscrupulousness to add restrictions of one's own accord except in critical instances, as indicated above.

The purpose of all human life and activity is to know God as far as it is possible for man. Hence all his activities should be directed to that one end. His eating and drinking and sleeping and waking and motion and rest and pleasure should have for their object the maintenance of good health and cheerful spirits, not as an end in themselves, but as a means to intellectual peace and freedom from worry and care in order that he may have leisure and ability to study and reflect upon the highest truths of God. Good music, beautiful scenery, works of art, splendid architecture and fine clothing should not be pursued for their own sake, but only so far as they may be necessary to relieve the tedium and monotony of toil and labor, or as a curative measure to dispel gloom and low spirits or a tendency to melancholy. The same thing applies to the arts and sciences. Medicine is of assistance in maintaining bodily health and curing it of its ills. The logical, mathematical and physical sciences are either directly helpful to speculative theology, and their value is evident; or they serve to train the mind in deduction and analysis, and are thus indirectly of benefit for the knowledge of God.[288]

The ethical qualities similarly conduce to intellectual perfection, and the difference between one prophet and another is in large measure dependent upon relative ethical superiority. Thus when the Rabbis say that Moses saw God through a luminous mirror, and the other prophets through a non-luminous, the meaning is that Moses had intellectual and moral perfection, so far as a human being is capable of having them, and the only partition separating him from a complete vision of God was his humanity. The other prophets had other defects besides, constituting so many additional partitions obscuring the divine view.[289]

Some foolish astrologers are of the opinion that a man's character is determined in advance by the position of the stars at the time of his birth. This is a grave error, as can be shown from reason as well as tradition. The Bible as well as the Greek philosophers are agreed that a man's acts are under his own control, and that he himself and no one else is responsible for his virtues as well as his vices. It is true that a person's temperament, which is constitutional and over which he has no control, plays an important rôle in his conduct. There is no denying that men are born with certain tendencies. Some are born phlegmatic, some are passionate and hot-blooded. One man has a tendency to fearlessness and bravery, another is timid and backward. But while it is true that it is more difficult for the hot-blooded to develop the virtue of temperance and moderation than it is for the phlegmatic, that it is easier for the warm-tempered to learn courage than it is for the cold-tempered—these are not impossible. Virtue, we have seen before, is not a natural state, but an acquired possession due to long continued discipline and practice. One man may require longer and more assiduous practice than another to acquire a certain virtue, but no matter what his inherited temperament, he can acquire it if he undertakes to do so, or if properly trained. If man's character and conduct were determined, all the commandments and prohibitions in the Bible would be in vain, for without freedom command has no effect. Similarly there would be no use in a person's endeavoring to learn any trade or profession; for if it is determined beforehand that a given individual shall be a physician or a carpenter, he is bound to be one whether he studies or not. This would make all reward and punishment wrong and unjust whether administered by man or by God. For the person so rewarded or punished could not help doing what he did, and is therefore not responsible. All our plans and preparations would on this supposition be useless and without meaning, such as building houses, acquiring food, avoiding danger, and so on. All this is absurd and opposed to reason as well as to sense. It undermines the foundation of religion and imputes wrong to God. The Bible says distinctly, "See, I have set before thee this day life and the good, death and the evil . . . therefore choose thou life. . . ." (Deut. 30, 15, 19.)

There are some passages in the Bible which apparently lend color to the idea that a person's acts are determined from on high. Such are the expressions used in relation to Pharaoh's conduct toward the Israelites in refusing to let them go out of Egypt. We are told there that God hardened the heart of Pharaoh that he should not let the Israelites go. And he did this in order to punish the Egyptians. The criticism here is twofold. First, these expressions indicate that a person is not always free; and second, it seems scarcely just to force a man to act in a certain way and then to punish him for it.

The explanation Maimonides gives to this passage is as follows: He admits that in Pharaoh's case there was a restriction of Pharaoh's freedom. But this was a penal measure and exceptional. Normally a man is free, but he may forfeit this freedom if he abuses it. So Pharaoh's primary offence was not that he would not let the children of Israel go out of Egypt. His sin consisted in his tyrannical treatment of Israel in the past, which he did of his own accord and as a result of free choice. His loss of freedom in complying with Moses's request to let the Israelites go was already in the nature of a punishment, and its object was to let all the world know that a person may forfeit his freedom of action as a punishment for abusing his human privilege. To be sure God does not always punish sin so severely, but it is not for us to search his motives and ask why he punishes one man in one way and another in another. We must leave this to his wisdom.

Another argument against free will is that it is incompatible with the knowledge of God. If God is omniscient and knows the future as well as the past and the present, he knows how a given person will act at a given moment. But since God's knowledge is certain and not liable to error, the person in question cannot help acting as God long foreknew he would act, and hence his act is not the result of his free will. Maimonides's answer to this objection is virtually an admission of ignorance. He takes refuge in the transcendence of God's knowledge, upon which he dwelt so insistently in the earlier part of his work (p. 260 ff.). God is not qualified by attributes as we his creatures are. As he does not live by means of life, so he does not know by means of knowledge. He knows through his own essence. He and his existence and his knowledge are identical. Hence as we cannot know his essence, we cannot have any conception of his knowledge. It is mistaken therefore to argue that because we cannot know a future event unless it is already determined in the present, God cannot do so.

His knowledge is of a different kind from ours, and he can do what we cannot.[290]

The next problem Maimonides takes up is the doctrine of evil. The presence of evil in the world, physical as well as moral, was a stumbling block to all religious thinkers in the middle ages. The difficulty seems to find its origin in Neo-Platonism, or, farther back still, in Philo of Alexandria, who identified God with the Good. If he is the Good, evil cannot come from him. How then account for the evil in the world? The answer that was given was extremely unsatisfactory. It was founded on a metaphysical distinction which is as old as Plato, namely, of matter as the non-existent. Matter was considered a principle without any definite nature or actual being, and this was made the basis of all imperfection, death, sin. Evil partakes of the non-existence of matter, it is nothing positive, but only a negation or privation of good as darkness is the absence of light; hence it needs no creator, it has no efficient cause, but only a deficient cause. In this way physical evil was accounted for. Moral evil as the result of man's inhumanity to man could easily be explained by laying it to the charge of man's free will or even to the free will of the fallen angels as Origen conceives it. This removes from God all responsibility for evil. We shall find that Maimonides has nothing essentially new to contribute to the solution of the problem.

Strictly speaking, he says, only a positive thing can be made, negation or privation cannot. We may speak loosely of the negative being produced when one removes the positive. So if a man puts out a light, we say he made darkness, though darkness is a negation.

Evil is nothing but the negation of the positive, which is good. All positive things are good. Hence God cannot be said to produce evil. The positive thing which he produces is good; the evil is due to defect in the thing. Matter also is good so far as it is positive, *i. e.*, so far as it causes continued existence of one thing after another. The evil in matter is due to its negative or privative aspect as the formless, which makes it the cause of defect and evil. All evil that men do to each other is also due to negation, namely, absence of wisdom and knowledge.

Many people think there is more evil in the world than good. Their mistake is due to the fact that they make the experience of the individ·

ual man the arbiter in this question, thinking that the universe was made for his sake. They forget that man is only a small fraction of the world, which is made by the will of God. Even so man should be grateful for the great amount of good he receives from God, for many of the evils of man are self-inflicted. In fact the evils befalling man come under three categories.

1. The evil that is incident to man's nature as subject to genesis and decay, *i. e.*, as composed of matter. Hence arise the various accidents to which man is liable on account of bad air and other natural causes. These are inevitable, and inseparable from matter, and from the generation of individuals in a species. To demand that a person of flesh and blood shall not be subject to impressions is a contradiction in terms. And with all this the evils of this class are comparatively few.

2. They are the evils inflicted by one man upon the other. These are more frequent than the preceding. Their causes are various. And yet these too are not very frequent.

3. These are the most common. They are the evils man brings upon himself by self-indulgence and the formation of bad habits. He injures the body by excess, and he injures the mind through the body by perverting and weakening it, and by enslaving it to luxuries to which there is no end. If a person is satisfied with that which is necessary, he will easily have what he needs; for the necessaries are not hard to get. God's justice is evident in affording the necessaries to all his creatures and in making all the individuals of the same species similar in power and ability.[291]

The next problem Maimonides discusses is really theoretical and should have its place in the discussion of the divine attributes, for it deals with the character of God's knowledge. The reason for taking it up here is because, according to Maimonides, it was an ethical question that was the motive for the formulation of the view of the opponents. Accordingly the problem is semi-ethical, semi-metaphysical, and is closely related to the question of Providence.

Observing that the good are often wretched and the bad prosperous, the philosophers came to the conclusion that God does not know individual things. For if he knows and does not order them as is proper, this must be due either to inability or to jealousy, both of which are impossible in God. Having come to this conclusion in the way in-

dicated, they then bolstered it up with arguments to justify it pos-
itively. Such are that the individual is known through sense and God
has no sensation; that the number of individual things is infinite, and
the infinite cannot be comprehended, hence cannot be known; that
knowledge of the particular is subject to change as the object changes,
whereas God's knowledge is unchangeable. Against us Jews they argue
that to suppose God knows things before they are connects knowledge
with the non-existent; and besides there would be two kinds of knowledge in God, one knowledge of potential things, and another of actual
things. So they came to the conclusion that God knows only species
but not individuals. Others say that God knows nothing except his
own essence, else there would be multiplicity in his nature. As the
entire difficulty, according to Maimonides, arose from the supposed
impropriety in the government of individual destinies, he first discusses the question of Providence and comes back later to the problem
of God's knowledge.[292]

He enumerates five opinions concerning Providence.

1. *The Opinion of Epicurus.* There is no Providence at all; everything is the result of accident and concurrence of atoms. Aristotle has
refuted this idea.

2. *The Opinion of Aristotle.* Some things are subject to Providence,
others are governed by accident. God provides for the celestial
spheres, hence they are permanent individually; but, as Alexander
says in his name, Providence ceases with the sphere of the moon.
Aristotle's doctrine concerning Providence is related to his belief in
the eternity of the world. Providence corresponds to the nature of
the object in question. As the individual spheres are permanent,
it shows that there is special Providence which preserves the spheres
individually. As, again, there proceed from them other beings which
are not permanent individually but only as species, namely, the species
of our world, it is clear that with reference to the sublunar world
there is so much Providential influence as to bring about the permanence of the species, but not of the individual. To be sure, the
individuals too are not completely neglected. There are various powers
given to them in accordance with the quality of their matters; which
powers determine the length of their duration, their motion, perception, purposive existence. But the other incidents and motions in

individual human as well as animal life are pure accident. When a storm scatters the leaves of trees, casts down some trunks and drowns a ship with its passengers, the incident is as accidental with the men drowned as with the scattered leaves. That which follows invariable laws Aristotle regards as Providential, what happens rarely and without rule is accidental.

3. *The View of the Ashariya.* This is the very opposite of the preceding opinion. The Ashariya deny all accident. Everything is done by the will of God, whether it be the fall of a leaf or the death of a man. Everything is determined, and a person cannot of himself do or forbear. It follows from this view that the category of the possible is ruled out. Everything is either necessary or impossible. It follows also that all laws are useless, for man is helpless, and reward and punishment are determined solely by the will of God, to whom the concepts of right and wrong do not apply.

4. *The Opinion of the Mu'tazila.* They vindicate man's power to do and forbear, thus justifying the commands and prohibitions, and the rewards and punishments of the laws. God does not do wrong. They also believe that God knows of the fall of a leaf, and provides for all things. This opinion, too, is open to criticism. If a person is born with a defect, they say this is due to God's wisdom, and it is better for the man to be thus. If a pious man is put to death, it is to increase his reward in the next world. They extend this to lower animals also, and say that the mouse killed by the cat will be rewarded in the next world.

The last three opinions all have their motives. Aristotle followed the data of nature. The Ashariya refused to impute ignorance to God. The Mu'tazila object to imputing to him wrong, or to denying reason, which holds that to cause a person pain for no offence is wrong. Their opinion leads to a contradiction, for they say God knows everything and at the same time man is free.

5. *The Opinion of our Law.* A fundamental principle of the law of Moses is that man has absolute freedom in his conduct, and so has an irrational animal. No one of our religion disputes this. Another fundamental principle is that God does no wrong, and hence all reward and punishment is justly given. There is only one exception mentioned bv the Rabbis, what they call "suffering for love," *i. e.*, mis-

fortunes which are not in the nature of punishment for sins committed, but in order to increase reward. There is no support, however, for this view in the Bible. All this applies only to man. Nothing is said in the Bible or in the Talmud of reward and punishment of animals. It was adopted by some of the later Geonim from the Muʿ-tazila.

After citing these five opinions on the nature of Providence, Maimonides formulates his own to the following effect:

My own belief in the matter, not as a result of demonstration, but based upon what seems to me to be the meaning of Scripture is that in the sublunar world man alone enjoys individual Providence. All other individual things besides are ruled by chance, as Aristotle says. Divine Providence corresponds to divine influence or emanation. The more one has of divine influence, the more one has of Providence. Thus in plants and animals divine Providence extends only to the species. When the Rabbis tell us that cruelty to animals is forbidden in the Torah, the meaning is that we must not be cruel to animals for our own good, in order not to develop habits of cruelty. To ask why God does not provide for the lower animals in the same way as he does for man, is the same as to ask why he did not endow the animals with reason. The answer would be, so he willed, so his wisdom decreed. My opinion is not that God is ignorant of anything or is incapable of doing certain things, but that Providence is closely related to reason. One has as much of Providence as he has of the influence of the divine reason. It follows from this that Providence is not the same for all individuals of the human species, but varies with the person's character and achievements. The prophets enjoy a special Providence; the pious and wise men come next; whereas a person who is ignorant and disobedient is neglected and treated like a lower animal, being left to the government of chance.[293]

Having disposed of the question of Providence, we may now resume the discussion undertaken above (p. 289) of the nature of God's knowledge. The idea that God does not know the particular things in our world below is an old one and is referred to in the Bible often. Thus, to quote one instance from the Psalms, the idea is clearly enunciated in the following passage, "And they say [sc. the wicked], How doth God know? And is there knowledge in the most High? Behold, these are the wicked; and, being alway at ease, they increase in riches. Surely in vain have I cleansed my heart, and washed my hands in innocency . . ." (73, 11–13). The origin of this notion is in human experience, which sees the adversity of the good and the prosperity of the wicked, though many of the troubles are of a man's own doing, who is a free agent. But this view is wrong. For ignorance of any kind is a defect, and God is perfect. David pointed out this when he said, "He that planted the ear shall he not hear? He that formed the eye shall he not see?" (94, 9). This means that unless God knows what the senses are, he could not have made the sense organs to perceive.

We must now answer the other metaphysical arguments against God's knowledge of particulars. It is agreed that no new knowledge can come to God which he did not have before, nor can he have many knowledges. We say therefore (we who are believers in the Torah) that with one knowledge God knows many things, and his knowledge does not change as the objects change. We say also that he knows all things before they come into being, and knows them always; hence his knowledge never changes as the objects appear and disappear. It follows from this that his knowledge relates to the non-existent and embraces the infinite. We believe this and say that only the absolutely non-existent cannot be known; but the non-existent whose existence is in God's knowledge and which he can bring into reality can be known. As to comprehending the infinite, we say with some thinkers that knowledge relates primarily to the species and extends indirectly to the individuals included in the species. And the species are finite. The philosophers, however, decide that there cannot be knowledge of the non-existent, and the infinite cannot be comprehended. God, therefore, as he cannot have new and changing knowledge knows only the permanent things, the species, and not the changing and temporary individuals. Others go still further and maintain that God cannot even know the permanent things, because knowledge of many things involves many knowledges, hence multiplicity in God's essence. They insist therefore that God knows only himself. My view is, says Maimonides, that the error of all these people is that they assume there is a relation of resemblance between our knowledge and God's knowledge. And it is surprising that the philosophers should be guilty of such an error, the very men who proved that God's knowledge is identical with his essence, and that our reason cannot know God's essence.

The difference between our knowledge and God's knowledge is that we get our knowledge from the data of experience, upon which it depends. Each new datum adds to our knowledge, which cannot run ahead of that which produces it. It is different in the case of God. He is the cause of the data of experience. The latter follow his knowledge, and not *vice versa*. Hence by knowing himself he knows everything else before it comes into being. We cannot conceive of his knowledge, for to do this would be to have it ourselves.[294]

The last topic Maimonides considers in his philosophical work is the reason and purpose of the commandments of the Bible, particularly the ceremonial precepts which apparently have no rational meaning. In fact there are those who maintain that it is vain to search for reasons of the laws where none are given in the Bible itself; that the sole reason in those cases is the will of God. These people labor under the absurd impression that to discover a rational purpose in the ceremonial laws would diminish their value and reduce them to human institutions. Their divine character and origin is attested in the minds of these people by their irrationality, by the fact that they have no human meaning. This is clearly absurd, says Maimonides the rationalist. It is tantamount to saying that man is superior to God; and that whereas a man will command only that which is of benefit, God gives orders which have no earthly use. The truth is quite the reverse, and all the laws are for our benefit.[295]

Accordingly Maimonides undertakes to account for all the laws of the Bible. The Law, he says, has two purposes, the improvement of the body and the improvement of the soul or the mind. The improvement of the soul is brought about by study and reflection, and the result of this is theoretical knowledge. But in order to be able to realize this perfectly a necessary prerequisite is the improvement of the body. This is inferior in value to perfection of the soul, but comes naturally and chronologically first as a means to an end. For bodily perfection one must have health and strength as far as one's constitution permits, and for this purpose a person must have his needs at all times. Social life is necessary for the supply of the individuals' needs, and to make social life possible there must be rules of right and wrong to be observed.[296]

Applying what has just been said to the Law, we may divide its contents broadly into four classes. (1) Precepts inculcating true beliefs and ideas, such as the existence of God, his unity, knowledge, power, will, eternity. (2) Legal and moral precepts, such as the inculcation of justice and a benevolent disposition for the good of society. (3) The narratives and genealogies of the Law. (4) The ceremonial prescriptions.

Of these the purpose of the first two divisions is perfectly clear and admitted by all. True beliefs and ideas regarding God and his government of the world are directly conducive to the highest end of man, knowledge and perfection of the soul. Honorable and virtuous conduct is a preliminary requisite to intellectual perfection. The genealogies and narratives of the Bible are also not without a purpose. They are intended to inculcate a theoretical doctrine or a moral, and to emphasize the one or the other, which cannot be done so well by a bare statement or commandment. Thus, to take a few examples, the creation of the world is impressed upon the reader beyond the possibility of a doubt by a circumstantial narrative of the various steps in the process, the gradual peopling of the earth by the multiplication of the human race descended from the first pair, and so on. The story of the flood and of the destruction of Sodom and Gomorrah has for its purpose to emphasize the truth that God is a just judge, who rewards the pious and punishes the wicked. The genealogy of the kings of Edom in Genesis (36, 31) is intended as a warning to Israel in the appointment of kings. These kings of the Edomites were all of them foreigners not of Edom, and it is probable that the history of their tyrannical rule and oppression of their Edomite subjects was well known to the people in Moses's time. Hence the point of the enumeration of the list of kings and their origin is to serve as a deterring example to the Israelites never to appoint as king of Israel a man who came from another nation, in accordance with the precept in Deuteronomy (17, 15), "Thou mayest not put a foreigner over thee, which is not thy brother." [297]

There remains the division of the ceremonial laws, which are the subject of dispute. The purpose in these precepts is not evident, and

opinions are divided as to whether they have any purpose. I will endeavor to show, says Maimonides, that these also have one or more of
the following objects: to teach true beliefs and opinions, to remove
injustice and to inculcate good qualities.

Abraham grew up among the Sabeans, who were star worshippers
and believers in the eternity of the world. The object of the law is to
keep men away from the erroneous views of the Sabeans, which were
prevalent in those days. The Sabeans believed that the worship of
the stars helps in the cultivation of the ground to make it fruitful.
For this reason they think highly of the husbandmen and laborers on
the land. They also respect cattle and prohibit slaughtering them because they are of benefit in the cultivation of the land. In the interest
of agriculture they instituted the worship of the stars, which they believed would cause the rain to fall and the earth to yield its fertility.
On this account we find the reverse of this in the Bible, telling us that
worship of the stars will result in lack of rain and infertility.

In the life of nature we see how one thing serves another, and certain
objects are not brought about except through certain others, and development is gradual. So, for example, a young infant cannot be fed
on meat and solid food, and nature provides milk in the mother's
breast. Similarly in governing the people of Israel, who were living
in a certain environment, God could not at once tear them away from
the habits of thought to which they were accustomed, but he led them
gradually. Hence as they were accustomed to sacrificing to the stars,
God ordered them to sacrifice to him, the object being to wean them
away from the idols in the easiest way possible. This is why the
prophets do not lay stress on the sacrifices. To be sure, it was not
impossible for God to form their minds so that they would not require
this form of training, and would see at once that God does not need
sacrifices, but this would have been a miracle. And while God does
perform miracles sometimes for certain purposes, he does not change
the nature of man; not because he cannot, but because he desires man
to be free and responsible. Otherwise there would be no sense in laws
and prophets.

Among the purposes of the law are abstention from self-indulgence
in the physical appetites, like eating and drinking and sensuous pleasure, because these things prevent the ultimate perfection of man, and

are likewise injurious to civil and social life, multiplying as they do sorrow and trouble and strife and jealousy and hate and warfare.

Another purpose is to inculcate gentleness and politeness and docility. Another is purity and holiness. External cleanliness is also recommended, but not as a substitute for internal. The important thing is internal purity, external takes a secondary place.

Maimonides ends the discussion of the Pentateuchal laws by dividing them into fourteen classes (following in this the divisions in his great legal code, the "Yad Ha-Hazakah") and explaining the purposes of each class. It will be useful briefly to reproduce the division here.

1. Those laws that concern fundamental ideas of religion and theology, including the duty of learning and teaching, and the institutions of repentance and fasting. The purpose here is clear. Intellectual perfection is the greatest good of man, and this cannot be attained without learning and teaching; and without wisdom there is neither good practice nor true opinion. Similarly honoring the wise, swearing by God's name, and not to swear falsely—all these lead to a firm belief in God's greatness. Repentance is useful to guard against despair and continuance in evil doing on the part of the sinner.

2. The precepts and prohibitions relating to idolatry. Here are included also the prohibition to mix divers kinds of seeds in planting, the prohibition against eating the fruit of a tree during the first three years of its growth, and against wearing a garment made of a mixture of wool and flax. The prohibition of idolatry is evident in its purpose, which is to teach true ideas about God. The other matters above mentioned are connected with idolatry. Magic is a species of idolatry because it is based on a belief in the direct influence of the stars. All practices done to produce a certain effect, which are not justified by a reason or at least are not verified by experience, are forbidden as being superstitious and a species of magic. Cutting the beard and the earlocks is forbidden on a similar ground because it was a custom of the idolatrous priests. The same thing applies to mixing of cotton and flax, to men wearing women's garments and *vice versa*, though here there is the additional reason, to prevent, namely, laxness in sexual morality.

3. The precepts relating to ethical and moral conduct. Here the purpose is clear, namely, to improve social life.

4. The rules relating to charity, loans, gifts, and so on. The purpose is to teach kindness to the poor, and the benefit is mutual, for the rich man to-day may be poor to-morrow.

5. Laws relating to injury and damages. The purpose is to remove wrong and injustice.

6. Laws relating to theft, robbery, false witnesses. The purpose is to prevent injury by punishing the offender.

7. The regulation of business intercourse, like loan, hire, deposits, buying and selling, inheritance, and so on. The purpose here is social justice to make life in society possible.

8. Laws relating to special periods, such as the Sabbath and the festivals. The purpose is stated in each case in the Law itself, and it is either to inculcate a true idea like the creation in the case of the Sabbath, or to enable mankind to rest from their labors, or for both combined.

9. The other practical observances like prayer, the reading of "Shema," and so on. These are all modes of serving God, which lead to true opinions concerning him, and to fear and love.

10. The regulations bearing upon the temple and its service. The purpose of these was explained above in connection with the institution of sacrifice, namely that it was a concession to the primitive ideas and customs of the people of those times for the purpose of gradually weaning them away from idolatry.

11. Laws relating to sacrifices. The purpose was stated above and under 10.

12. Laws of cleanness and uncleanness. The purpose is to guard against too great familiarity with the Temple in order to maintain respect for it. Hence the regulations prescribing the times when one may, and the occasions when one may not, approach or enter the Temple.

13. The dietary laws. Unwholesome food is forbidden, also unclean animals. The purpose in some cases is to guard against excess and self-indulgence. Some regulations like the laws of slaughter and others are humanitarian in their nature.

14. Forbidden marriages, and circumcision. The purpose is to guard against excess in sexual indulgence, and against making it an end in itself.[298]

To sum up, there are four kinds of human accomplishments or excellencies. (1) Acquisition of wealth, (2) Physical perfection, strength, beauty, etc., (3) Moral perfection, (4) Intellectual and spiritual perfection. The last is the most important. The first is purely external; the second is common to the lower animals; the third is for the sake of one's fellowmen, in the interest of society, and would not exist for a solitary person. The last alone concerns the individual himself. Jeremiah expresses this truth in his statement, "Thus saith the Lord, Let not the wise man glory in his wisdom, neither let the mighty man glory in his might, let not the rich man glory in his riches: but let him that glorieth glory in this, that he understandeth, and knoweth me, that I am the Lord which exercise loving kindness, judgment and righteousness in the earth" (Jer. 9, 22). "Wise man" in the above quotation means the man of good morals. The important thing, Jeremiah says, is to know God through his actions and to imitate him.[299]

Maimonides's ethics as well as his interpretation of the Pentateuchal laws is intellectualistic, as the foregoing account shows. And it is natural that it should be. The prevailing trend of thought in the middle ages, alike among the Arabs, Jews and Christians, was of this character. Aristotle was the master of science, and to him intellectual contemplation is the highest good of man. The distinction of man is his rational faculty, hence the excellence and perfection of this faculty is the proper function of man and the realization of his being. This alone leads to that "eudaimonia" or happiness for which man strives. To be sure complete happiness is impossible without the complete development of all one's powers, but this is because the reason in man is not isolated from the rest of his individual and social life; and perfection of mind requires as its auxiliaries and preparation complete living in freedom and comfort. But the aim is after all the life of the intellect, and the "dianoetic" virtues are superior to the practical. Theoretic contemplation stands far higher than practical activity. Add to this that Aristotle's God is pure thought thinking eternally itself, the universal mover, himself eternally unmoved, and attracting the celestial spheres as the object of love attracts the lover, without itself necessarily being affected, and the intellectualism of Aristotle stands out clearly.

Maimonides is an Aristotelian, and he endeavors to harmonize the intellectualism and theorism of the Stagirite with the diametrically opposed ethics and religion of the Hebrew Bible. And he is apparently unaware of the yawning gulf extending between them. The ethics of the Bible is nothing if not practical. No stress is laid upon knowledge and theoretical speculation as such. The wisdom and the wise man of the book of Proverbs no more mean the theoretical philosopher than the fool and the scorner in the same book denote the one ignorant in theoretical speculation. "The beginning of wisdom is the fear of the Lord." This is the keynote of the book of Proverbs, and its precepts and exhortations are practical and nothing else. That the Pentateuchal law is solely concerned with practical conduct, religious, ceremonial and moral, needs not saying. It is so absolutely clear and evident that one wonders how so clear-sighted a thinker like Maimonides could have been misled by the authority of Aristotle and the intellectual atmosphere of the day to imagine otherwise. The very passage from Jeremiah which he quotes as summing up his idea of the *summum bonum*, speaks against him, and he only succeeds in manipulating it in his favor by misinterpreting the word "wise." Whatever the wise man may denote in the book of Proverbs, here in Jeremiah he is clearly contrasted with the person who in imitation of God practices kindness, judgment and righteousness. The word does not denote the theoretical philosopher, to be sure, but it approximates it more closely than the expression describing the ideal man of Jeremiah's commendation.

It is in line with Maimonides's general rationalistic and intellectualistic point of view when he undertakes to find a reason for every commandment, where no reason is given in the Law. He shows himself in this an opponent of all mysticism, sentimentality and arbitrariness. Reason is paramount. The intellect determines the will, and not even God's will may be arbitrary. His will is identical with his reason, hence there is a reason in everything that he wills. We may not in every case succeed in finding the reason where he himself did not choose to tell us, but a reason there always is, and the endeavor on our part to discover it should be commended rather than condemned.

The details of his motivation of the ceremonial laws are very interesting, and in many cases they anticipated, though in a cruder

form, the more scientific theories of modern critics. Take his interpretation of the institution of sacrifices. Take away the personal
manner of expression, which might seem to imply that God spoke to
Moses in some such fashion as this: You and I know that sacrifices
have no inherent meaning or value. They rather smack of superstition and idolatry. But what can we do? We cannot, *i. e.*, we must
not, change the nature of these people. We must train them gradually
to see the truth for themselves. They are now on the level of their
environment, and believe in the efficacy of killing sheep and oxen to
the stars and the gods. We will use a true pedagogical method if
we humor them in this their crudity for the purpose of transferring
their allegiance from the false gods to the one true God. Let us then
institute a system of sacrifices with all the details and minutiæ of
the sacrificial systems of the heathens and star worshippers. We
shall impose this system upon our people for the time being, and in
the end as they grow wiser they will outgrow it—take away this mode
of expression in Maimonides's interpretation, which is not essential,
and the essence may be rendered in more modern terms thus. Man's
religion is subject to change and development and progress like all
his other institutions. The forms they successively take in the course
of their development are determined by the state of general intelligence and positive knowledge that the given race or nation possesses.
The same thing holds of religious development. The institution of
sacrifices is prevalent in all religious communities at a certain stage
in their career. It starts with human sacrifice, which is later discarded
and replaced by sacrifices of animals. And this is again in the course
of time discontinued, leaving its traces only in the prayer book,
which in Judaism has officially taken the place of the Temple service.

While the merit of Maimonides in foreshadowing this modern
understanding of ancient religion cannot be overestimated, it is clear
that in some of his other interpretations of Jewish ceremonial, he is
wide of the mark. His rationalism could not take the place of a knowledge of history. His motivation of the dietary laws on the score of
hygiene or of moderation and self-restraint is probably not true. Nor
is the prohibition against mixing divers seeds, or wearing garments
of wool and flax mixed, or shaving the corner of the beard, and so on,
due to the fact that these were the customs of the idolaters and their

priests. If Maimonides was bold enough to pull the sacrificial system down from its glorious pedestal in Jewish tradition and admit that being inherently nothing but a superstition, it was nevertheless instituted with such great pomp and ceremony, with a priestly family, a levitical tribe and a host of prescriptions and regulations, merely as a concession to the habits and prejudices of the people, why could he not apply the same method of explanation to the few prohibitions mentioned above? Why not say the ancient Hebrews were forbidden to mix divers seeds because they had been from time immemorial taught to believe that there was something sinful in joining together what God has kept asunder; and in order not to shock their sensibilities too rudely the new religion let them have these harmless notions in order by means of these to inculcate real truths?

Before concluding our sketch of Maimonides we must say a word about his Bible exegesis. Though the tendency to read philosophy into the Bible is as old as Philo, from whom it was borrowed by Clement of Alexandria and Origen and by them handed down to the other Patristic writers, and though in the Jewish middle ages too, from Saadia down, the verses of the Bible were employed to confirm views adopted from other considerations; though finally Abraham Ibn Daud in the matter of exegesis, too, anticipated Maimonides in finding the Aristotelian metaphysic in the sacred scriptures, still Maimonides as in everything else pertaining to Jewish belief and practice, so in the interpretation of the Bible also obtained the position of a leader, of the founder of a school and the most brilliant and most authoritative exponent thereof, putting in the shade everyone who preceded him and every endeavor in the same direction to which Maimonides himself owed his inspiration. Maimonides's treatment of the Bible texts and their application to his philosophical disquisitions is so much more comprehensive and masterly than anything in the same line done before him, that it made everything else superfluous and set the pace for manifold imitation by the successors of Maimonides, small and great. Reading the Bible through Aristotelian spectacles became the fashion of the day after Maimonides. Joseph Ibn Aknin, Samuel Ibn Tibbon, Jacob Anatoli, Joseph Ibn Caspi, Levi Ben Gerson and a host of others tried their hand at Biblical exegesis, and the Maimonidean stamp is upon their work.

We have already spoken of Maimonides's general attitude toward the anthropomorphisms in the Bible and the manner in which he accounts for the style and mode of expression of the Biblical writers. He wrote no special exegetical work, he composed no commentaries on the Bible. But his "Guide of the Perplexed" is full of quotations from the Biblical books, and certain sections in it are devoted to a systematic interpretation of those Biblical chapters and books which lend themselves most easily and, as Maimonides thought, imperatively to metaphysical interpretation. It is impossible here to enter into details, but it is proper briefly to point out his general method of treating the Biblical passages in question, and to state what these passages are.

We have already referred more than once to the Talmudic expressions "Maase Bereshit" (Work of Creation) and "Maase Merkaba" (Work of the Chariot). Maimonides says definitely that the former denotes the science of physics, *i. e.*, the fundamental notions of nature as treated in Aristotle's Physics, and the latter signifies metaphysics or theology, as represented in Aristotle's Metaphysics. The creation chapters in Genesis contain beneath their simple exterior of a generally intelligible narrative, appealing to young and old alike, women as well as children, a treatment of philosophical physics. And similarly in the obscure phraseology of the vision of Ezekiel in the first and tenth chapters of that prophet's book, are contained allusions to the most profound ideas of metaphysics and theology, concerning God and the separate Intelligences and the celestial spheres. As the Rabbis forbid teaching these profound doctrines except to one or two worthy persons at a time, and as the authors of those chapters in the Bible clearly intended to conceal the esoteric contents from the gaze of the vulgar, Maimonides with all his eagerness to spread abroad the light of reason and knowledge hesitates to violate the spirit of Bible and Talmud. His interpretations of these mystic passages are therefore expressed in allusions and half-concealed revelations. The diligent student of the "Guide," who is familiar with the philosophy of Aristotle as taught by the Arabs Alfarabi and Avicenna will be able without much difficulty to solve Maimonides's allusions, the casual reader will not. Without going into details it will suffice for our purpose to say that in the creation story Maimonides finds the Aristotelian doctrines of matter and form, of the four elements, of potentiality and actuality, of the different powers of the soul, of logical and ethical distinctions (the true and the false on one hand, the good and the bad on the other), and so on.[300]   In the Vision of Ezekiel he sees the Peripatetic ideas of the celestial spheres, of their various motions, of their souls, their intellects and the separate Intelligences, of the Active Intellect, of the influence of the heavenly bodies on the changes in the sublunar world, of the fifth element (the ether) and so on.[301]   Don Isaac Abarbanel has already criticized this attempt of Maimonides by justly arguing that if the meaning of the mysterious vision of Ezekiel is what Maimonides thinks it is, there was no occasion to wrap it in such obscurity, since the matter is plainly taught in all schools of philosophy.[302]   We might, however, reply that no less a man than Plato expresses himself in the Timæus in similarly obscure terms concerning the origin and formation of the world.   Be this as it may, Munk is certainly right when he says that if, as is not improbable, Ezekiel's vision does contain cosmological speculations, they have nothing to do with the Aristotelian cosmology, but must be related to Babylonian theories.[303]

Another favorite book of the Bible for the exegesis of philosophers was the book of Job.   In this Maimonides sees reflected the several views concerning Providence, divine knowledge and human freedom, which he enumerates (p. 290 ff.).[304]

The influence of Maimonides upon his contemporaries and immediate successors was indeed very great, and it was not confined to Judaism.   Christian Scholastics and Mohammedan theologians studied and used the Guide of the Perplexed.   Maimonides himself, it seems, though he wrote his "Guide" in the Arabic language, did not desire to make it accessible to the Mohammedans, fearing possibly that some of his doctrines concerning prophecy might be offensive to them. Hence he is said to have instructed his friends and disciples not to transliterate the Hebrew characters, which he in accordance with general Jewish usage employed in writing Arabic, into Arabic characters.   But he was powerless to enforce his desire and there is no doubt that such transcriptions were in use.   Samuel Tibbon himself, the Hebrew translator of the "Guide," made use of manuscript copies written in Arabic letters.   We are told that in the Mohammedan schools in the city of Fez in Morocco, Jews were appointed to teach Maimonides's philosophy, and there is extant in Hebrew translation a commentary by a Mohammedan theologian on the twenty-five philosophical propositions laid down by Maimonides as the basis of his proof of the existence of God (p. 254).[305]

The influence of Maimonides on Christian scholasticism is still greater. We have already said (p. 199 f.) that the philosophical renaissance in Latin Europe during the thirteenth century was due to the introduction of the complete works of Aristotle in Latin translation. These translations were made partly from the Arabic versions of the Mohammedans, partly from the Greek originals, which became accessible after the capture of Constantinople by the Crusaders in 1207.[306] Before this time the scope of philosophical research and investigation in Christian Europe was limited, and its basis was the Platonism of St. Augustine and fragments of Aristotle's logic. In general Platonism was favorable to Christian dogma. Plato according to Augustine came nearest to Christianity of all the ancient Greek philosophers.[307] And the dangers to Church doctrine which lurked in philosophical discussion before the thirteenth century were a tendency to Pantheism on the part of thinkers imbued with the Neo-Platonic mode of thought, and an undue emphasis either on the unity of God as opposed to the Trinity (Abélard), or on the Trinity at the expense of the unity (Roscellinus of Compiègne)—conclusions resulting from the attitudes of the thinkers in question on the nature of universals.

In the early part of the thirteenth century for the first time, the horizon of the Latin schoolmen was suddenly enlarged and brilliantly illumined by the advent of the complete Aristotle in his severe, exacting and rigorous panoply. All science and philosophy opened before the impoverished schoolmen, famished for want of new ideas. And they threw themselves with zeal and enthusiasm into the study of the new philosophy. The Church took alarm because the new Aristotle constituted a danger to accepted dogma. He taught the eternity of the world, the uniformity of natural law, the unity of the human intellect, denying by implication Providence and freedom and individual immortality. Some of these doctrines were not precisely those of Aristotle but they could be derived from Aristotelian principles if inter-

preted in a certain way; and the Arab intermediators between Aristotle and his Christian students had so interpreted him. Averroes in
particular, who gained the distinction of being the commentator *par
excellence* of Aristotle, was responsible for this mode of interpretation;
and he had his followers among the Masters of Arts in the University
of Paris. These and similar tendencies the Church was striving to
prevent, and it attempted to do this at first crudely by prohibiting
the study and teaching of the Physical and Metaphysical works of
Aristotle. Failing in this the Papacy commissioned three representatives of the Dominican order to expurgate Aristotle in order to render
him harmless. You might as well think of expurgating a book on
geometry! The task was never carried out. But instead something
more valuable for the welfare of the Church was accomplished in a
different way. Albertus Magnus and Thomas Aquinas undertook the
study of Aristotle and the interpretation of his works with a view to
harmonizing his teachings with the dogmas of Christianity. Albertus
Magnus began the task, Thomas Aquinas, his greater disciple, the
Maimonides of Christian philosophy, completed it. And in this under-
taking Maimonides was Thomas Aquinas's model.[308]

The Guide of the Perplexed was translated into Latin not long after
its composition.[309] Before Albertus Magnus, Alexander of Hales, the
Franciscan leader, and William of Auvergne, the Bishop of Paris, had
read and made use of Maimonides's philosophical masterpiece. Albertus Magnus was still more diligent in his adoption of Maimonidean
views, or in taking account of them, where he is opposed to their
adoption. But it remained for Thomas Aquinas, who made the most
systematic attempt in the mediæval schools to harmonize the philosophy of Aristotle with the doctrine of the Church, to use Maimonides
as his guide and model. Like Maimonides he employs Aristotelian
proofs for the existence of God, proofs based on the eternity of motion;
and like him Aquinas argues that if motion is not eternal and the world
was made in time, the existence of God is still more readily evident.
In his discussion of the divine attributes, of angels, of Providence, of
Prophecy, of free will, of the ceremonial laws in the Pentateuch,
Thomas Aquinas constantly takes account of Maimonides's views.
whether he agrees with them or not. It is no doubt an exaggeration
to say that there would have been no Aquinas if Maimonides had not

preceded him. For Aquinas had access to the works of Aristotle and his Arabian commentators, the former of whom he studied more diligently than Maimonides himself. But there is no doubt that the method of harmonizing Aristotelian doctrine with traditional teaching so far as the common elements of Judaism and Christianity were concerned was suggested to Aquinas by his Jewish predecessor. It is not our province here to go into details of the system of Aquinas to show wherein he agrees or disagrees with Maimonides, nor is it possible to do more than mention the fact that after Aquinas also, Duns Scotus, the head of the Franciscan school, had the "Guide" before him, and in comparatively modern times, such celebrities as Scaliger and Leibnitz speak of the Jewish philosopher with admiration and respect.[310]

That Maimonides's influence upon Jewish theology and thought was deep and lasting is a truism. The attitude of the prominent theologians and philosophers who succeeded him will appear in the sequel in connection with our treatment of the post-Maimonidean writers. Here a word must be said of the general effect of Maimonides's teaching upon Jews and Judaism throughout the dispersion. His fame as the greatest Jew of his time—great as a Talmudical authority, which appealed to all classes of Jewish students, great as a physician with the added glory of being a favorite at court, great as the head of the Jewish community in the East, and finally great as a philosopher and scientist—all these qualifications, never before or after united in the same way in any other man, served to make him the cynosure of all eyes and to make his word an object of notice and attention throughout the Jewish diaspora. What he said or wrote could not be ignored whether people liked it or not. They could afford to ignore a Gabirol even, or an Ibn Daud. But Maimonides must be reckoned with. The greater the man, the greater the alertness of lesser, though not less independent, spirits, to guard against the enslavement of all Judaism to one authority, no matter how great. And in particular where this authority erred in boldly adopting views in disagreement with Jewish tradition, as it seemed to many, and in setting up a new source of truth alongside of, or even above, the revelation of the Torah and the authority of tradition, to which these latter must be bent whether they will or no—his errors must be strenuously opposed and condemned without fear or favor. This was the view of the traditionalists, whose sole authorities in all matters of theology and related topics were the words of Scripture and Rabbinic literature as tradition had interpreted them. On the other hand, the rationalistic development during the past three centuries, which we have traced thus far, and the climax of that progress as capped by Maimonides was not without its influence on another class of the Jewish community, particularly in Spain and southern France; and these regarded Maimonides as the greatest teacher that ever lived. Their admiration was unbounded for his personality as well as his method and his conclusions. His opponents were regarded as obscurantists, who, rather than the object of their attack, were endangering Judaism. All Jewry was divided into two camps, the Maimunists and the anti-Maimunists; and the polemic and the struggle between them was long and bitter. Anathema and counter anathema, excommunication and counter excommunication was the least of the matter. The arm of the Church Inquisition was invoked, and the altar of a Parisian Church furnished the torch which set on flame the pages of Maimonides's "Guide" in the French capital. More tragic even was the punishment meted out to the Jewish informers who betrayed their people to the enemy. The men responsible had their tongues cut out.

The details of the Maimunist controversy belong to the general historian.[311] Our purpose here is to indicate in brief outline the general effect which the teaching of Maimonides had upon his and subsequent ages. The thirteenth century produced no great men in philosophy at all comparable to Moses Ben Maimon or his famous predecessors. The persecutions of the Jews in Spain led many of them to emigrate to neighboring countries, which put an end to the glorious era inaugurated three centuries before by Hasdai Ibn Shaprut. The centre of Jewish liberal studies was transferred to south France, but the literary activities there were a pale shadow compared with those which made Jewish Spain famous. Philosophical thought had reached its apogee in Maimonides, and what followed after was an attempt on the part of his lesser disciples and successors to follow in the steps of their master, to extend his teachings, to make them more widespread and more popular. With the transference of the literary centre from Spain to Provence went the gradual disuse of Arabic as the medium of philosophic and scientific culture, and the age of translation made its appearance. Prior to, and including, Maimonides all the Jewish thinkers whom we have considered, with the exception of Abraham Bar Hiyya and Abraham Ibn Ezra, wrote their works in Arabic. After Maimonides Hebrew takes the place of Arabic, and in addition to the new works composed, the commentaries on the "Guide" which were now written in plenty and the philosophico-exegetical works on the Bible in the Maimonidean spirit, the ancient classics of Saadia, Bahya, Gabirol, Halevi, Ibn Zaddik, Ibn Daud and Maimonides himself had to be translated from Arabic into Hebrew. In addition to these religio-philosophical works, it was necessary to translate those writings which contained the purely scientific and philosophical branches that were preliminary to the study of religious philosophy. This included logic, the various branches of mathematics and astronomy, medical treatises and some of the books of the Aristotelian corpus with the Arabic compendia and commentaries thereon. The grammatical and lexical treatises of Hayyuj and Ibn Janah were also translated. The most famous of the host of translators, which the need of the times brought forth, were the three Tibbonides, Judah (1120–1190), Samuel (1150–1230) and Moses (fl. 1240–1283), Jacob Anatoli (fl. 1194–1256), Shemtob Falaquera (1225–1290), Jacob Ben Machir (1236–1304), Moses of Narbonne (d. after 1362), and others. Some of these wrote original works besides. Samuel Ibn Tibbon wrote a philosophical treatise, "Ma'amar Yikkawu ha-Mayim," [312] and commentaries in the Maimonidean vein on Ecclesiastes and the Song of Songs. His greater fame rests on his translation of the "Guide of the Perplexed." He translated besides Maimonides's "Letter on Resurrection," the "Eight Chapters," and other Arabic writings on science and philosophy. Moses Ibn Tibbon was prolific as an original writer as well as a translator. Joseph Ibn Aknin (1160–1226), the favorite pupil of Maimonides, for whom the latter wrote his "Guide," is the author of treatises on philosophical topics, and of exegetical works on certain books of the Bible and on the Mishnic treatise, the "Ethics of the Fathers."[312a] Jacob Anatoli, in addition to translating Ptolemy's Almagest and Averroes's commentaries on Aristotle's logic, wrote a work, "Malmad ha-Talmidim," on philosophical homiletics in the form of a commentary on the Pentateuch.[313] Shemtob Falaquera, the translator of portions of Gabirol's

"Fons Vitæ," [314] is the author of a commentary on the "Guide," entitled "Moreh ha-Moreh," [315] and of a number of ethical and psychological works.[316] Jacob Ben Machir translated a number of scientific
and philosophical works, particularly on astronomy, and is likewise
the author of two original works on astronomy. Joseph Ibn Caspi
(1297–1340) was a very prolific writer, having twenty-nine works
to his credit, most of them exegetical, and among them a commentary
on the "Guide." [317] Moses of Narbonne wrote an important commentary on the "Guide," [318] and is likewise the author of a number of
works on the philosophy of Averroes, of whom he was a great admirer.
The translations of Judah Ibn Tibbon, the father of translators as
he has been called, go back indeed to the latter half of the twelfth
century, and Abraham Ibn Ezra translated an astronomical work as
early as 1160. But the bulk of the work of translation is the product
of the thirteenth and fourteenth centuries. The result of these translations was that scientific and philosophical works became accessible
to all those who knew Hebrew instead of being confined to the lands
of Arabian culture. Another effect was the enlargement of the Hebrew language and the development of a new Hebrew dialect with a
philosophical and scientific terminology. These translations so far
as they relate to pure science and philosophy were neglected in the
closing centuries of the middle ages, when conditions among the Jews
were such as precluded them from taking an interest in any but purely
religious studies. Continuous persecutions, the establishment of
the Ghettoes, the rise of the Kabbala and the opposition of the pietists
and mystics to the rationalism of the philosophers all tended to the
neglect of scientific study and to the concentration of all attention
upon the Biblical, Rabbinic and mystical literature. The Jews at
the close of the middle ages and the beginning of modern times with-
drew into their shell, and the science and learning of the outside had
little effect on them. Hence, and also for the reason that with the
beginning of modern times all that was mediæval was, in the secular
world, relegated, figuratively speaking, to the ash-heap, or literally
speaking to the mouldering dust of the library shelves—for both of
these reasons the very large number of the translations above mentioned were never printed, and they are still buried on the shelves of the
great European libraries, notably of the British Museum, the national

library of Paris, the Bodleian of Oxford, the royal library of Munich, and others. The reader who wishes to have an idea of the translating and commenting activity of the Jews in the thirteenth and following centuries in the domains of logic, philosophy, mathematics, astronomy, medicine and folklore is referred to the monumental work of the late Moritz Steinschneider, the prince of Hebrew Bibliographers, "Die Hebräischen Uebersetzungen des Mittelalters und die Juden als Dolmetscher," (The Hebrew translations of the middle ages, and the Jews as dragomen) Berlin, 1893, containing 1077 pages of lexicon octavo size devoted to brief enumerations and descriptions of extant editions and manuscripts of the translations referred to.[319]

CHAPTER XIV

HILLEL BEN SAMUEL

In the post-Maimonidean age all philosophical thinking is in the nature of a commentary on Maimonides whether avowedly or not. The circle of speculation and reflection is complete. It is fixed by the "Guide of the Perplexed," and the efforts of those who followed Maimonides are to elaborate in his spirit certain special topics which are treated in his masterpiece in a summary way. In the case of the more independent thinkers like Levi ben Gerson we find the further attempt to carry out more boldly the implications of the philosophical point of view, which, as the latter thought, Maimonides left implicit by reason of his predisposition in favor of tradition. Hasdai Crescas went still farther and entirely repudiated the authority of Aristotle, substituting will and emotion for rationalism and logical inference. Not knowledge of God as logically demonstrated is the highest aim of man, but love of God. But even in his opposition Crescas leans on Maimonides's principles, which he takes up one by one and refutes. Maimonides was thus the point of departure for his more rigorous followers as well as for his opponents. In the matter of external sources philosophical reflection after Maimonides was enriched in respect to details by the works of Averroes on the Arabic side and those of the chief Christian scholastics among the Latin writers. Albertus Magnus and Thomas Aquinas furnished some material to men like Hillel of Verona in the thirteenth century and Don Isaac Abarbanel in the fifteenth. Maimonides was limited to the Aristotelian expositions of Alfarabi and Avicenna. The works of Averroes, his contemporary, he did not read until toward the end of his life. After his death Averroes gained in prestige and influence until he succeeded in putting into the shade his Arabian predecessors and was regarded by Jew and Christian alike as the Commentator of Aristotle *par excellence.* His works were rapidly translated into Hebrew and Latin, and the Jewish writers learned their Aristotle from Averroes. The knowledge of the Arabic language was gradually disappearing among the Jews of Europe, and they were indebted for their knowledge of science and philosophy to the works translated. Philosophy was declining among the Arabs themselves owing to the disfavor of the powers that be, and many of the scientific writings of the Arabs owe their survival to the Hebrew translations or transcriptions in Hebrew characters which escaped the proscription of the Mohammedan authorities.

The one problem that came to the front as a result of Averroes's teaching, and which by the solution he gave it formed an important subject of debate in the Parisian schools of the thirteenth century, was that of the intellect in man, whether every individual had his own immortal mind which would continue as an individual entity after the death of the body, or whether a person's individuality lasted only as long as he was alive, and with his death the one human intellect alone survived. This was discussed in connection with the general theory of the intellect and the three kinds of intellect that were distinguished by the Arabian Aristotelians, the material, the acquired and the active. The problem goes back to Aristotle's psychology, who distinguishes two intellects in man, passive and active (above, p. xxxvi). But the treatment there is so fragmentary and vague that it gave rise to widely varying interpretations by the Greek commentators of Aristotle, Alexander of Aphrodisias and Themistius, as well as among the Arabs, Alfarabi, Avicenna and Averroes. The latter insisted on the unity of the intellect for the human race, thereby destroying individual immortality, and this Averroistic doctrine, adopted by some Masters of Arts at the University of Paris, was condemned among other heresies, and refuted in the writings of Albertus Magnus and Thomas Aquinas. Maimonides does not discuss these problems in detail in his "Guide." He drops a remark incidentally here and there, and it would appear that for him too, as for Averroes, the intellect when in separation from the body is not subject to individual distinction, that there cannot be several human intellects, since matter is the principle of individuation and the immaterial cannot embrace a number of individuals of the same species.[320] The problem of immortality he does not treat *ex professo* in the "Guide." Hence this was a matter taken up by his successors. Hillel ben Samuel as well as Levi ben Gerson discuss this question in detail.

Hillel ben Samuel does not tower as a giant in mediæval Jewish literature. His importance is local, as being the first devotee of Jewish learning and philosophy in Italy in the middle of the thirteenth century, at the close of a period of comparative ignorance. The Italian Jews before his time contributed little to knowledge and learning despite their external circumstances, which were more favorable than in some other countries. Hillel ben Samuel (1220–1295) was a strong admirer of Maimonides and undertook to comment on the "Guide of the Perplexed." He defended Maimonides against the aspersions of his opponents, and was so confident in the truth of his master's teachings that he proposed a conference of the learned men of Jewry to judge the works and doctrines of Maimonides and to decide whether the "Guide" should be allowed to live or should be destroyed. Another interest attaching to Hillel ben Samuel is that he was among the first, if not the first Jew who by his knowledge of Latin had access to the writings of the scholastics, to whom he refers in his "Tagmule ha-Nefesh" (The Rewards of the Soul) as the "wise men of the nations." He was also active as a translator from the Latin.

His chief work, which entitles him to brief notice here, is the "Tagmule ha-Nefesh" just mentioned.[321] He does not offer us a system of philosophy, but only a treatment of certain questions relating to the nature of the soul, its immortality and the manner of its existence after the death of the body, questions which Maimonides passes over lightly. With the exception of the discussion relating to the three kinds of intellect and the question of the unity of the acquired intellect for all mankind, there is not much that is new or remarkable in the discussion, and we can afford to pass it by with a brief notice.

Men of science know, he tells us in the introduction, that the valuable possession of man is the soul, and the happiness thereof is the final purpose of man's existence. And yet the number of those who take pains to investigate the nature of the soul is very small, not even one in a hundred. And even the few who do undertake to examine this subject are hindered by various circumstances from arriving at the truth. The matter itself is difficult and requires long preparation and preliminary knowledge. Then the vicissitudes of life and the shortness of its duration, coupled with the natural indolence of man when it comes to study, completely account for the lack of true knowledge on this most important topic.

Induced by these considerations Hillel ben Samuel undertook to collect the scattered notices in the extensive works of the philosophers and arranged and expounded them briefly so as not to discourage those who are in search of wisdom. His purpose is the knowledge of truth, which is an end in itself. He desires to explain the existence of the soul, its nature and reward. The soul is that which makes man man, hence we should know the nature of that which makes us intelligent creatures, else we do not deserve the name.

Another reason for the importance of knowing the nature of the soul is that error in this matter may lead to more serious mistakes in other departments of knowledge and belief. Thus if a man who calls himself pious assumes that the soul after parting from the body is subject to corporeal reward and punishment, as appears from a literal rendering of passages in Bible and Talmud, he will be led to think that the soul itself is corporeal. And since the soul, it is believed, comes from on high, the upper world must have bodies and definite places, and hence the angels too are bodies. But since the angels are emanations from the divine splendor, God too is body! Thus you see how serious are the consequences of a belief, in itself perhaps not so dangerous, as that of the corporeality of the soul.[322]

We must first prove the existence of the soul. This can be shown in various ways. We see that of natural bodies some take food, grow, propagate their like, while others, like stones, do not do these things. This shows that the powers and functions mentioned cannot be due to the corporeal part of the objects performing them, else stones, too, would have those powers, as they are also corporeal like the rest. There must therefore be a different principle, not body, which is responsible for those activities. We call it soul.

As all existents are divided into substance and accident, the soul must be either the one or the other. Now an accident, according to Aristotle, is that which may be or not be without causing the being or destruction of the object in which it is. But the body cannot be a living body without the soul. Hence the soul is not an accident; it is therefore a substance. Substance may be corporeal or incorporeal. The soul cannot be a corporeal substance, for all body is divisible, and subject to motion and change, whereas the soul, as will be shown later, is not movable, not changeable and not divisible. It might seem that the soul is subject to motion, since it descends into the body and rises again when it leaves the body. But this is not so. Descent and ascent when thus applied to the soul are metaphorical. The union of soul and body is not a spatial relation. The upper world from which the soul comes is not corporeal, hence there is no such thing as place there, nor anything limited by space. Hence the coming of the soul from the spiritual world and its return thither are not motions at all. The relation of the soul to the body is as that of form to matter, as Aristotle says.

Granted that the soul's union with and separation from the body are not motions, is not the soul subject to motion while in the body? Hillel's answer is that it is not, and he proves his point in the prescribed fashion by making use of Aristotle's classification of motion into (1) genesis and (2) decay, (3) increase and (4) diminution, (5) qualitative change and (6) motion proper, or motion of translation. He then undertakes to show that the soul can have none of the kinds of motion here enumerated. The arguments offer nothing striking or interesting, and we can afford to omit them. It is worth while, however, to refer to his interpretation of emotion. The passage of the soul from joy to grief, from anger to favor, might seem to be a kind of motion. Hillel answers this objection by saying that these emotions do not pertain to the soul as such. Their primary cause is the state of mixture of the humors in the body, which affects certain corporeal powers in certain ways; and the soul shares in these affections only so far as it is united with the body. In its own nature the soul has no emotions.

We can also prove that the soul is not divisible. For a divisible thing must have parts. Now if the soul is divided or divisible, this means either that every part of the soul, no matter how small, has the same powers as the whole, or that the powers of the soul are the resultant of the union of the parts. The first alternative is impossible, for it leads us to the absurd conclusion that instead of one soul every person has an infinite number of souls, or at least a great number of souls. The second alternative implies that while the soul is not actually divided, since its powers are the summation of the parts, which form a unit, it is potentially divisible. But this signifies that at some time this potential divisibility will be realized (or potentiality would be vain and meaningless) and we are brought back to the absurdity of a multiplicity of souls in the human body.

Having shown that the soul is not movable, changeable or divisible, we are certain of its incorporeality, and we are ready to give a definition of the soul. Hillel accordingly defines the soul as "a stage of emanation, consisting of a formal substance, which subsists through its own perfection, and occupies the fourth place in the emanatory process, next to the Active Intellect. Its ultimate source is God himself, who is the ultimate perfection and the Good, and it emanates from him indirectly through the mediation of the separate Powers standing above it in the scale of emanation. The soul constitutes the first entelechy of a natural body." [323]

The above definition is interesting. It shows that Hillel did not clearly distinguish the Aristotelian standpoint from the Neo-Platonic, for in the definition just quoted, the two points of view are combined. That all mediæval Aristotelianism was tinged with Neo-Platonism especially in the doctrine of the Active Intellect, is well known. But in Hillel's definition of the soul we have an extreme form of this peculiar combination, and it represents a step backward to the standpoint of Pseudo-Bahya and Ibn Zaddik. The work of Ibn Daud and Maimonides in the interest of a purer Aristotelianism seems not to have enlightened Hillel. The Neo-Platonic emanation theory is clearly enunciated in Hillel's definition. The soul stands fourth in the series. The order he has in mind is probably (1) God, (2) Separate Intelligences, (3) Active Intellect, (4) Soul. We know that Hillel was a student of the Neo-Platonic "Liber de Causis" (*cf.* above, p. xx), having translated some of it into Hebrew, and he might have imbibed his Neo-Platonism from that Proclean book.

Continuing the description of the soul in man, he says that the noblest part of matter, *viz.*, the human body, is endowed with the rational soul, and becomes the subject of the powers of the latter. Thereby it becomes a man, *i. e.*, a rational animal, distinguished from all other animals, and similar to the nature of the angels.

The Active Intellect causes its light to emanate upon the rational soul, thus bringing its powers out into actuality. The Active Intellect, which is one of the ten degrees of angels, is related to the rational power in man as the sun to the power of sight. The sun gives light, which changes the *potentially* seeing power into *actually* seeing, and the potentially visible object into the actually visible. Moreover, this same light enables the sight to see the sun itself, which is the cause of the actualization in the sight. So the Active Intellect gives something to the rational power which is related to it as light to the sight; and by means of this something the rational soul can see or understand the Active Intellect itself. Also the potentially intelligible objects become through this influence actually intelligible, and the man who was potentially intelligent becomes thereby actually intelligent.

Intellect ("sekel") in man is distinguished from *wisdom* ("hokmah"). By the former power is meant an immediate understanding of abstract principles. The latter is *mediate* understanding. Wisdom denotes speculation about universals through inference from particulars. Intellect applies directly to the universals and to their influence upon the particulars.[324]

Hillel next discusses the live topic of the day, made popular by Averroes, namely, whether there are in essence as many individual souls as there are human bodies, or, as Averroes thought, there is only one universal soul, and that its individualizations in different men are only passing incidents, due to the association of the universal soul with the human body, and disappear when the body dies. The "sages of the Gentiles," Hillel tells us, regard Averroes's notion as heretical, and leading besides to the absurd conclusion that the same soul is both rewarded and punished; a view which upsets all religion. Averroes employs a number of arguments to prove his point, among them being the following. If there are many souls, they are either all existing from eternity or they are created with the body. The first is impossible, for since the soul is a form of the body, we should have actually an infinite number of forms, and this would necessitate the actual existence of an infinite number of bodies also; else the existence of these souls for the purpose of joining the bodies would be in vain. But it is absurd to suppose that there has been from eternity an infinite number of bodies created like the number of souls, and yet they have not become real bodies with souls until now.

The second alternative is also impossible. For if there are many souls which came into being with the bodies, they either came from nothing or from something. From nothing is impossible, for nothing comes from nothing except by way of creation, which is a miracle; and we do not believe in miracles unless we have to. That they came from something is also impossible; for this something can be neither matter nor form. It cannot be matter, for form, the actual and superior, cannot come from the potential and inferior. It cannot be form, for then form would proceed from form by way of genesis and dissolution, which is not true. Matter is the cause of generation and dissolution, not form. We are thus forced to the conclusion that the soul is one and eternal, one in substance and number; and that it becomes many only *per accidens*, by virtue of the multiplicity of its receiving subjects, comparable to the light of the one sun, which divides into many rays.

The Bible cannot help us to decide this question, for its expressions can be interpreted either way. Hillel then undertakes to adjudicate between the contending views by striking a compromise. He feels that he is contributing to the solution of an important problem by an original suggestion, which he says is to be found nowhere else expressed with such clearness and brevity.

Here again Hillel's Neo-Platonic tendencies are in evidence. For he assumes both a universal soul and a great number of individual souls emanating from it in a descending series. The objection that forms cannot come from other forms by way of generation and dissolution, Hillel says, is not valid, for no such process is here involved. Generation and dissolution is peculiar to the action of body upon body, which is by contact. A *spiritual* form acts upon other forms not through contact, because it is not limited by time or place. We know concerning the Intelligences that each comes from the one previous to it by way of emanation, and the same thing applies to the issue of many human souls from the one universal soul. After death the rational part of every soul remains; that part which every soul receives from the Active Intellect through the help of the *possible* or *material intellect*, and which becomes identified with the Active and separate Intellect. This is the part which receives reward and punishment, whereas the one universal soul from which they all emanate is a divine emanation, and is not rewarded or punished.[325]

We must now discuss further the nature of the three grades of intellect. For this it will be necessary to lay down three preliminary propositions.

1. There must be an intellect whose relation to the material intellect is the same as that of the object of sense perception is to the sense. This means that just as there must be a real and actual object to arouse the sense faculty to perceive, so there must be an actual intelligible object to stir the rational power to comprehend.

2. It follows from 1 that as the material sense has the power of perceiving the sensible object, so the material intellect has the power of perceiving this other intellect.

3. If it has this power, this must at some time be realized *in actu.* Therefore at some time the material intellect is identified with the other intellect, which is the Active Intellect.

We must now prove 1. This is done as follows: We all know that we are potentially intelligent, and it takes effort and pains and study to become actually intelligent. In fact the process of intellection has to pass several stages from sense perception through imagination. Now our intellect cannot make itself pass from potentiality to actuality. Hence there must be something else as agent producing this change; and this agent must be actually what it induces in us. Hence it is an active intellect.

The material intellect has certain aspects in common with the sense faculty, and in certain aspects it differs. It is similar to it in being receptive and not active. But the mode of receptivity is different in the two. As the intellect understands all forms, it cannot be a power residing in a body in the sense of extending through it and being divided with the division of the body, as we see in some of the powers of sense. This we can prove as follows:

1. If the intellect were receptive in the same manner as the senses, it would receive only a definite kind of form, as for example the sense of sight does not receive taste.

2. If the intellect were a power in body and had a special form, it could not receive that form, just as for example if the eye were colored, it could not perceive colors.

3. If the intellect were a corporeal power, it would be affected by its object and injured by a powerful stimulus, as is the case in the

senses of sight and hearing. A dazzling light injures the eye, a deafening noise injures the ear, so that thereafter neither sense can perform its normal function properly. This is not true with the intellect. An unusually difficult subject of thought does not injure the intellect.

4. If the intellect were similar in its activity to sense perception, it would not be self-conscious, as the sense faculties cannot perceive themselves.

5. The intellect, if it were like sense, would not be able to comprehend a thing and its opposite at the same time, or it would do so in a confused manner, as is the case in the powers of sense.

6. The intellect perceives universals; the sense, particulars.

This being the case, there is a difference of opinion as to the nature of the material intellect. Some say that it has no definite nature in itself except that of possibility and capacity, though it is different from other possibilities in this respect that it is not resident in, and dependent upon a material subject like the others. That is why Aristotle says that the material intellect is not anything before it intellects; that it is in its essence potential with reference to the *intelligibilia*, and becomes actual when it understands them actually.

Themistius says it is not any of the existents actually, but a potential essence receiving material forms. Its nature is analogous to that of prime matter; hence it is called *material* intellect. It is best to call it possible intellect. Being a potential existent it is not subject to generation and dissolution any more than prime matter.

Alexander of Aphrodisias thinks the material intellect is only a capacity, *i. e.*, a power in the soul, and appears when the soul enters the body, hence is not eternal *a parte ante*.

Averroes holds that the possible intellect is a separate substance, and that the capacity is something it has by virtue of its being connected with the body as its subject. Hence this capacity is neither entirely distinct from it nor is it identical with it. According to him the possible intellect is not a part of the soul.

Which of these views is correct, says Hillel, requires discussion, but it is clear that whichever of these we adopt there is no reason opposing the conjunction of the possible intellect with the Active. For if it is an eternal substance, potential in its nature, like primary matter, then it becomes actual when it understands the intelligible objects. The same is true if it is a capacity residing in the soul.

Hillel is thus of the opinion in this other question debated in those days, whether the intellect of man is capable of conjunction during life with the angelic Active Intellect, that it is. The Active Intellect, he says, in actualizing the material intellect influences it not in the manner of one body acting upon another, *i. e.*, in the manner of an efficient or material cause, but rather as its formal or final cause, leading it to perfection. It is like the influence which the separate Intelligences receive from one another, the influence of emanation, and not a material influence comparable to generation. This reception of influence from the Active Intellect on the part of the potential is itself conjunction. It means that the agent and the thing acted upon become one, and the same substance and species. The material intellect becomes a separate substance when it can understand itself.[326]

Before taking up the more theological problem of reward and punishment, he devotes the last section of the theoretical part of his book to a discussion of the relation of the possible or material intellect to the rest of the human soul. This problem also arose from Averroes's interpretation of the Aristotelian psychology, and is closely related to the other one of the unity of the human intellect. It is needless for us to enter into the technical details which are a weariness to the flesh of the modern student, but it is worth while to state briefly the motives underlying the opposing views. Averroes, who had no theological scruples, interpreted Aristotle to mean that the part of the soul which was intimately associated with the body as its form, constituting an indissoluble organism in conjunction with it, embraced its lower faculties of sense, imagination and the more concrete types of judgment. These are so intimately bound up with the life of the body that they die with its death. The reason on the other hand, which has to do with immaterial ideas, or intelligibles as they called them, is eternal and is not the form of the body. It is a unitary immaterial substance and is not affected by the life or death of the body. To be sure it comes in contact with the human soul during the life of the body, thus bringing into existence an individualized human reason as a passing episode. But this individualized phase of the intellect's life is dependent upon the body and ceases when the body dies, or is reabsorbed in the universal intellect.

The theological implications of this view were that if there is any reward and punishment after death, it would either have to be administered to the lower faculties of the soul, which would have to be made immortal for the purpose, or if the rational soul is the subject of retribution, this cannot affect the individual, as there is no individual rational soul. Hence the Christian opponents of Averroes, like Albertus Magnus and Thomas Aquinas (Hillel speaks of them here as the "Religionists," or the "Sages who believe in religion"), endeavored to vindicate for the Aristotelian definition of the soul as the form of the body, also the rational part, thus maintaining the view that the reason too has an individual existence both during life and after death. Thomas Aquinas, as a truer interpreter of Aristotle, goes so far as to maintain that the Active Intellect itself is also a part of the human soul, and not one of the angelic separate Intelligences. Neither Maimonides nor Hillel ben Samuel, nor any other Jewish philosopher was able to depart so widely from their Arabian masters or to undertake an independent study of Aristotle's text, as to come to a similar conclusion. Hence the Active Intellect in Jewish Philosophy is unanimously held to be the last of the Angelic substances, and the proximate inspirer of the prophet. The discussion therefore in Hillel's work concerns the possible intellect, and here he ventures to disagree with Averroes and decides in favor of the possible intellect as a part of the soul and the subject of reward and punishment.[327]

Concerning the nature of reward and punishment after death opinions are divided. Some think that both reward and punishment are corporeal. Some say reward is spiritual, punishment is corporeal; while a small number are of the opinion that both are spiritual. Hillel naturally agrees with the latter and gives reasons for his opinion. If the soul, as was shown before, is incorporeal, immaterial and a *formal* substance, it cannot be influenced by corporeal treatment. For corporeal influence implies motion on the part of agent and patient, and the pervasion of the influence of the former through the parts of the latter; whereas a spiritual substance has no parts. Besides, if reward and punishment are corporeal, and Paradise is to be taken literally, then why separate the soul from the body, why not reward the living

person with eternal life and give him the enjoyment of paradise while
on earth? The effect would be much greater upon the rest of mankind,
who would see how the righteous fare and the wicked. The objection
that this would make people mercenary does not hold, for they are
mercenary in any case, since they expect reward; whether in this life
or in the next makes no difference. Reward must therefore be spiritual, and so must punishment, since the two go together.[328]

When God in his kindness favored the human race by giving them
a soul, which he united with the body, he also gave them the possibility
of attaining eternal happiness. For this purpose he arranged three
grades of ascent, *viz.*, the three intellects spoken of above, the material
or possible intellect, the acquired intellect (this is the actual functioning of the possible intellect and the result thereof) and the active intellect. The second intellect is partly speculative or theoretical and
partly practical. The theoretical intellect studies and contemplates
all intelligible existents which are separate from matter. There is
nothing practical in this contemplation, it is just the knowledge of
existents and their causes. This is called the science of truth, and is
the most important part of philosophy.

The practical intellect is again divided into the *cogitative* and the
technological. The former decides whether a thing should be done or
not, and discriminates between the proper and the improper in human
actions and qualities. It is important as a guide to the happiness of
the soul because it instructs the appetitive power in reference to those
things which are subject to the will, and directs it to aim at the good
and to reject the evil.

The technological intellect is that by which man learns arts and
trades. The practical intellect is also theoretical in the sense that it
has to think in order to discriminate between the proper and the improper, and between the beneficial and injurious in all things pertaining
to practice. The difference between the speculative and practical
intellects is in the respective objects of their comprehension, and
hence is accidental and not essential. The objects of the theoretical
intellect are the true and the false; of the practical, the good and the
bad. The acquired intellect gives these intelligibles to the soul through
the possible intellect, and is intermediate between the latter and the
Active Intellect. which is one of the separate Intelligences above soul.

The Active Intellect watches over the rational animal that he may attain to the happiness which his nature permits.

Men differ according to their temperamental composition and their human conduct. This leads to differences in the power of understanding and in the amount of influence received from the Active Intellect. Hillel quotes Maimonides in support of his view that the prophetic stage is an emanation of glory from God through the medium of the Active Intellect, which exerts its influence upon the rational power and upon the imagination, so that the prophet sees his vision objectified *extra animam*. The three conditions requisite for prophecy are perfection in theory, perfection in imagination and perfection in morals. The first without the second and third produces a philosopher; the second without the first and third gives rise to a statesman or magician.

It is important to know, he tells us, that the cultivation of the reason and imagination alone is not sufficient. Practice of the commandments is very important. Hence a man must guide properly the two powers of sense perception and desire, which are instruments of the rational power. For, as Maimonides says in his commentary on Aboth (*cf.* p. 282), all observance and violation of the commandments, good and bad qualities depend upon those two powers. Without a proper training of these the influence of the active intellect upon the reason and imagination may lead to evil.

Beginning with sense perception a man must train all his five senses to attend only to what is good and to turn away from evil. When he satisfies his sensuous desires, he must do this in order to preserve his body that he may be enabled to serve God in the best possible way.

The same applies to the power of desire. This is the power which directs one to pursue the agreeable and shun the disagreeable. From it proceed also courage, confidence, anger, good will, joy, sorrow, humility, pride. All these qualities must be used in the service of God. If a man do this, he will attain the grade of an angelic being even during life, and will be able to perform miracles like the prophets and the sages of the Talmud.

After death the souls of such men reach even a higher degree than they had before entering the body, as a reward for not allowing themselves to be degraded by their corporeal desires, but on the contrary directing these to higher aims.[329]

As for the nature of reward and punishment more particularly, we may say that the soul of the wicked loses all the glory promised to her and descends to a position lower than was hers originally. She is expelled from the land of life and remains in darkness forever, without returning to her original station. Knowing what she has lost, she will feel continuous distress, sorrow and fear, for the power of imagination remains with the soul after death. But there is no physical burning with fire. On the other hand, the soul of the righteous will return to God.

The doctrine of the resurrection and the explanation for it are a further proof that the soul after death is not punished corporeally. The motive of the resurrection is that the soul and body may receive their compensation together as in life. If then the retribution of the soul is corporeal, there is no need of resurrection.[330]

Hillel then proceeds to show that the words of the Rabbis which seem to speak for corporeal retribution are not to be taken literally. In this connection it is worth while to reproduce his classification of the contents of the Talmud and his attitude toward them. He enumerates six classes.

1. Passages in the Talmudic and Midrashic literature which must be taken literally. These are the discussions of the *Halaka* (the legal and ceremonial portions). To pervert these from their literal meaning, or to maintain that the *intention* of the law is the important thing and not the practice of the ceremony, is heresy and infidelity; though it is meritorious to seek for an explanation of every law, as the Rabbis themselves do in many instances.

2. Passages which should be understood as parables and allegories with a deeper meaning. These are the peculiar *Haggadahs*, or the strange interpretations of Biblical verses where no ceremonial precept is involved.

3. Statements similar to those of the Prophetical books of the Bible, which were the result of the influence of the Active Intellect and came to the sages in a dream or in the waking state, speaking of the future in an allegorical manner. These are the extraordinary tales found in the Talmud, which cannot be understood literally, as

they involve a violation of the order of nature; and no miracle must be believed unless for a very important reason.

4. The homilies addressed to the people on the occasion of holidays for the purpose of exhorting them to divine worship and observance of the Law. Many of these are hyperbolical in their expression, especially in the promises concerning the future blessings in store for the people. These were in the nature of encouragement to the people to make their burdens easier to bear. Here belong also unusual interpretations of Biblical verses, explanations which do not give the original meaning of the verse in question, but are suggested in order to interest the people. We must add, too, stories of the good things that came to pious people in return for their piety. These must be taken for the most part literally, unless they are clearly improbable.

5. Jokes and jests by way of relief from the strain of study. Hyperboles belong here.

6. Narratives of miracles done for pious people, such as reviving the dead, punishing with death by means of a word, bringing down rain, and so on. All these must be taken literally. To disbelieve is heresy. This is true only where the alleged miracles were done for a high purpose, otherwise we need not believe them.

The reason the Bible and the Talmud express themselves in corporeal terms concerning reward and punishment is in order to frighten the people and to impress them with the terrible punishment consequent upon wrongdoing. The people do not understand any reward and punishment unless it is physical and corporeal. In reality spiritual existence is more real than physical.[331]

CHAPTER XV

Among the men who devoted themselves to philosophical investigation in the century and a half after Maimonides's death, the greatest and most independent was without doubt Levi ben Gerson or Gersonides, as he is also called. There were others who were active as commentators, translators and original writers, and who achieved a certain fame, but their work was too little original to merit more than very brief notice in these pages. Isaac Albalag[331a] (second half of thirteenth century) owes what reputation he enjoys to the boldness with which he enunciated certain doctrines, such as the eternity of the world and particularly the notion, well enough known among the Averroists of the University of Paris at that time and condemned by the Church, but never before announced or defended in Jewish philosophy—the so-called doctrine of the twofold truth. This was an attitude assumed in self-defence, sincerely or not as the case may be, by a number of scholastic writers, who advanced philosophic views at variance with the dogma of the Church. They maintained that a given thesis might be true and false at the same time, true for philosophy and false for theology, or vice versa.[332] Shem Tob Falaquera (1225–1290) is a more important man than Albalag. He was a thorough student of the Aristotelian and other philosophy that was accessible to him through his knowledge of Arabic. Munk's success in identifying Avicebron with Gabirol (p. 63) was made possible by Falaquera's translation into Hebrew of extracts from the "Fons Vitæ." Of great importance also is Falaquera's commentary of Maimonides's "Guide," which, with that of Moses of Narbonne (d. after 1362), is based upon a knowledge of Arabic and a thorough familiarity with the Aristotelian philosophy of the Arabs, and is superior to the better known commentaries of Shemtob, Ephodi, and Abarbanel. Falaquera also wrote original works of an ethical and philosophical character.

Joseph Ibn Caspi (1297–1340) is likewise a meritorious figure as a commentator of Maimonides and as a philosophical exegete of Scripture. But none of these men stands out as an independent thinker with a strong individuality, carrying forward in any important and authoritative degree the work of the great Maimonides. Great Talmudic knowledge, which was a necessary qualification for national recognition, these men seem not to have had; and on the other hand none of them felt called upon or able to make a systematic synthesis of philosophy and Judaism in a large way.

Levi ben Gerson (1288–1344) was the first after Maimonides who can at all be compared with the great sage of Fostat. He was a great mathematician and astronomer; he wrote supercommentaries on the Aristotelian commentaries of Averroes, who in his day had become the source of philosophical knowledge for the Hebrew student; he was thoroughly versed in the Talmud as his commentary on the Pentateuch shows; and he is one of the recognized Biblical exegetes of the middle ages. Finally in his philosophical masterpiece "Milhamot Adonai" (The Wars of the Lord),[333] he undertakes to solve in a thoroughly scholastic manner those problems in philosophy and theology which Maimonides had either not treated adequately or had not solved to Gersonides's satisfaction. That despite the technical character and style of the "Milhamot," Gersonides achieved such great reputation shows in what esteem his learning and critical power were held by his contemporaries. His works were all written in Hebrew, and if he had any knowledge of Arabic and Latin it was very limited, too limited to enable him to make use of the important works written in those languages.[334] His fame extended beyond the limits of Jewish thought, as is shown by the fact that his scientific treatise dealing with the astronomical instrument he had discovered was translated into Latin in 1377 by order of Pope Clement VI, and his supercommentaries on the early books of the Aristotelian logic were incorporated, in Latin translation, in the Latin editions of Aristotle and Averroes of the 16th century.[335]

Levi ben Gerson's general attitude to philosophical study and its relation to the content of Scripture is the same as had become common property through Maimonides and his predecessors. The happiness and perfection of man are the purpose of religion and knowledge.

This perfection of man, or which is the same thing, the perfection of the human soul, is brought about through perfection in morals and in theoretical speculation, as will appear more clearly when we discuss the nature of the human intellect and its immortality. Hence the purpose of the Bible is to lead man to perfect himself in these two elements—morals and science. For this reason the Law consists of three parts. The first is the legal portion of the Law containing the 613 commandments, mandatory and prohibitive, concerning belief and practice. This is preparatory to the second and third divisions of the Pentateuch, which deal respectively with social and ethical conduct, and the science of existence. As far as ethics is concerned it was not practicable to lay down definite commandments and prohibitions because it is so extremely difficult to reach perfection in this aspect of life. Thus if the Torah gave definite prescriptions for exercising and controlling our anger, our joy, our courage, and so on, the results would be very discouraging, for the majority of men would be constantly disobeying them. And this would lead to the neglect of the other commandments likewise. Hence the principles of social and ethical conduct are inculcated indirectly by means of narratives exemplifying certain types of character in action and the consequences flowing from their conduct. The third division, as was said before, contains certain teachings of a metaphysical character respecting the nature of existence. This is the most important of all, and hence forms the beginning of the Pentateuch. The account of creation is a study in the principles of philosophical physics.[336]

As to the relations of reason and belief or authority, Levi ben Gerson shares in the optimism of the Maimonidean school and the philosophic middle age generally, that there is no opposition between them. The priority should be given to reason where its demands are unequivocal, for the meaning of the Scriptures is not always clear and is subject to interpretation.[337] On the other hand, after having devoted an entire book of his "Milhamot" to a minute investigation of the nature of the human intellect and the conditions of its immortality, he disarms in advance all possible criticism of his position from the religious point of view by saying that he is ready to abandon his doctrine if it is shown that it is in disagreement with religious dogma. He developed his views, he tells us, because he believes that they are in agreement with the words of the Torah.[338] This apparent contradiction is to be explained by making a distinction between the abstract statement of the principle and the concrete application thereof. In general Levi ben Gerson is so convinced of man's prerogative as a rational being that he cannot believe the Bible meant to force upon him the belief in things which are opposed to reason. Hence, since the Bible is subject to interpretation, the demands of the reason are paramount where they do not admit of doubt. On the other hand, where the traditional dogma of Judaism is clear and outspoken, it is incumbent upon man to be modest and not to claim the infallibility of direct revelation for the limited powers of logical inference and deduction.

We must now give a brief account of the questions discussed in the "Milhamot Adonai." And first a word about Gersonides's style and method. One is reminded, in reading the Milhamot, of Aristotle as well as Thomas Aquinas. There is no rhetoric and there are no superfluous words. All is precise and technical, and the vocabulary is small. One is surprised to see how in a brief century or so the Hebrew language has become so flexible an instrument in the expression of Aristotelian ideas. Levi ben Gerson does not labor in the expression of his thought. His linguistic instrument is quite adequate and yields naturally to the manipulation of the author. Gersonides, the minute logician and analyst, has no use for rhetorical flourishes and figures of speech. The subject, he says, is difficult enough as it is, without being made more so by rhetorical obscuration, unless one intends to hide the confusion of one's thought under the mask of fine writing.[339] Like Aristotle and Thomas Aquinas, he gives a history of the opinions of others in the topic under discussion, and enumerates long lists of arguments *pro* and *con* with rigorous logical precision. The effect upon the reader is monotonous and wearisome. Aristotle escapes this by the fact that he is groping his way before us. He has not all his ideas formulated in proper order and form ready to deliver. He is primarily the investigator, not the pedagogue, and the brevity and obscurity of his style pique the ambitious reader and spur him on to puzzle out the meaning. Not so Thomas Aquinas and the scholastics generally. As the term scholastic indicates, they developed their method in the schools. They were expositors of what was ready made, rather than searchers for the new. Hence the question of form was an important one and was determined by the purpose of presenting one's ideas as clearly as may be to the student. Add to this that the logic of Aristotle and the syllogism was the universal method of presentation and the monotony and wearisomeness becomes evident. Levi ben Gerson is in this respect like Aquinas rather than like Aristotle. And he is the first of his kind in Jewish literature. Since the larger views and problems were already common property, the efforts of Gersonides were directed to a more minute discussion of the more technical details of such problems as the human intellect, prophecy, Providence, creation, and so on. For this reason, too, it will not be necessary for us to do more than give a brief résumé of the results of Gersonides's lucubrations without entering into the really bewildering and hairsplitting arguments and distinctions which make the book so hard on the reader.

We have already had occasion in the Introduction (p. xxxvi) to refer briefly to Aristotle's theory of the intellect and the distinction between the passive and the active intellects in man. The ideas of the Arabs were also referred to in our treatment of Judah Halevi, Ibn Daud and Maimonides (pp. 180 f., 213 f., 282). Hillel ben Samuel, as we saw (p. 317 ff.), was the first among the Jews who undertook to discuss in greater detail the essence of the three kinds of intellect, material, acquired and active, as taught by the Mohammedan and Christian Scholastics, and devoted some space to the question of the unity of the material intellect. Levi ben Gerson takes up the same question of the nature of the material intellect and discusses the various views with more rigor and minuteness than any of his Jewish predecessors. His chief source was Averroes. The principal views concerning the nature of the possible or material intellect in man were those attributed to Alexander of Aphrodisias, the most important Greek commentator of Aristotle (lived about 200 of the Christian Era), Themistius, another Aristotelian Greek commentator who lived in the time of Emperor Julian, and Averroes, the famous Arabian philosopher and contemporary of Maimonides. All these three writers pretended to expound Aristotle's views of the passive intellect rather than propound their own. And Levi ben Gerson discusses their ideas before giving his own.

Alexander's idea of the passive intellect in man is that it is simply a capacity residing in the soul for receiving the universal forms of material things. It has no substantiality of its own, and hence does not survive the lower functions of the soul, namely, sensation and imagination, which die with the body. This passive intellect is actualized through the Active Intellect, which is not a part of man at all, but is identified by Alexander with God. The Active Intellect is thus pure form and actuality, and enables the material or possible intellect in man, originally a mere potentiality, to acquire general ideas, and thus to become an intellect with a content. This is called the actual or acquired intellect, which though at first dependent on the data of sense, may succeed later in continuing its activity unaided by sense perception. And in so far as the acquired intellect thinks of the purely immaterial ideas and things which make up the content of the divine intellect (the Active Intellect), it becomes identified with the latter and is immortal. The reason for supposing that the material intellect in man is a mere capacity residing in the soul and not an independent substance is because as having the capacity to receive all kinds of forms it must itself not be of any form. Thus in order that the sense of sight may receive all colors as they are, it must itself be free from color. If the sight had a color of its own, this would prevent it from receiving other colors. Applying this principle to the intellect we make the same inference that it must in itself be neutral, not identified with any one idea or form, else this would color all else knocking for admission, and the mind would not know things as they are. Now a faculty which has no form of its own, but is a mere mirror so to speak of all that may be reflected in it, cannot be a substance, and must be simply a power inherent in a substance and subject to the same fate as that in which it inheres. This explains the motive of Alexander's view and is at the same time a criticism of the doctrine of Themistius.

This commentator is of the opinion that the passive intellect of which Aristotle speaks is not a mere capacity inherent in something else, but a real spiritual entity or substance independent of the lower parts of the soul, though associated with them during the life of the body, and hence is not subject to generation and destruction, but is eternal. In support of this view may be urged that if the passive intellect were merely a capacity of the lower parts of the soul, we should expect it to grow weaker as the person grows older and his sensitive and imaginative powers are beginning to decline; whereas the contrary is the case. The older the person the keener is his intellect. The difficulty, however, remains that if the human intellect is a real substance independent of the rest of the soul, why is it that at its first appearance in the human being it is extremely poor in content, being all but empty, and grows as the rest of the body and the soul is developed?

To obviate these difficulties, Averroes in his commentary on the *De Anima* of Aristotle practically identifies (according to Levi ben Gerson's view of Averroes) the material intellect with the Active Intellect. The Active Intellect according to him is neither identical with the divine, as Alexander maintains, nor is it a part of man, as Themistius and others think, but is the last of the separate Intelligences, next to the spiritual mover of the lunar sphere. It is a pure actuality, absolutely free from matter, and hence eternal. This Active Intellect in some mysterious manner becomes associated with man, and this association results in a temporary phase represented by the material intellect. As a result of the sense perceptions, images of the external objects remain in the imagination, and the Active Intellect takes hold of these images, which are potentially universal ideas, and by its illumination produces out of them actual ideas and an intellect in which they reside, the material intellect. The material intellect is therefore the result of the combination of the Active Intellect with the memory images, known as *phantasmata* (φαντάσματα), in the human faculty of imagination. So long as this association exists, the material intellect receives the intelligible forms as derived from the *phantasmata*, and these forms are represented by such ideas as "all animal is sensitive," "all man is rational," *i. e.*, ideas concerning the objects of this world. This phase of man's mind ceases when the body dies, and the Active Intellect alone remains, whose content is free from material forms. The Active Intellect contemplates itself, a pure intelligence. At the same time it is possible for man to identify himself with the Active Intellect as he acquires knowledge in the material intellect, for the Active Intellect is like light which makes the eye see. In seeing, the eye not merely perceives the form of the external object, but indirectly also receives the light which made the object visible. In the same way the human soul in acquiring knowledge as implicit in its *phantasmata*, at the same time gets a glimpse of the spiritual light which converted the *phantasma* into an explicit idea (*cf.* above, p. 320). When the soul in man perfects itself with all the knowledge of this world it becomes identified with the Active Intellect, which may be likened to the intellect or soul of the corporeal world.

In this combination of the views of Alexander and Themistius Averroes succeeds in obviating the criticisms levelled at the two former. That the power of the material intellect grows keener with age though the corporeal organs are weaker, supports Averroes's doctrine as against Alexander, to whom it is a mere capacity dependent upon the mixture of the elements in the human body. But neither is he subject to the objection applying to Themistius's view, that a real independent entity could scarcely be void of all forms and a mere receptacle. For the material intellect as it really is in itself when not in combination with the human body is not a mere receptacle or empty potentiality. It is the Active Intellect, which combines in itself all immaterial forms and thinks them as it thinks itself. It is only in its individualized aspect that it becomes a potential intellect ready to receive all material forms.

But what Averroes gains here he loses elsewhere. There are certain considerations which are fatal to his doctrine. Thus it would follow that theoretical studies which have no practical aim are useless. But this is impossible. Nature has put in us the ability as well as the desire to speculate without reference to practical results. The pleasure we derive from theoretical studies is much greater than that afforded by the practical arts and trades. And nature does nothing in vain. Theoretical studies must therefore have some value. But in Averroes's theory of the material intellect they have none. For all values may be divided into those which promote the life of the body and those which lead to the final happiness of man. The former is clearly not served by those theoretical speculations which have no practical aim. On the contrary, they hinder it. Deep students of the theoretical sciences forego all bodily pleasures, and often do without necessities. But neither can there be any advantage in theoretical speculation for ultimate human happiness. For human happiness according to Averroes (and he is in a sense right, as we shall see later) consists in union with the Active Intellect. But this union takes place as a matter of course according to his theory at the time of death, whether a man be wise or a fool. For the Active Intellect then absorbs the material.

Another objection to Averroes's theory is the following. If the material intellect is in essence the same as the Active Intellect, it is a separate, immaterial substance, and hence is, like the Active Intellect, one. For only that which has matter as its substratum can be _quantitatively_ differentiated. Thus A is numerically different from B, though A and B are both men (_i. e._, _qualitatively_ the same), because they are corporeal beings. Forms as such can be differentiated qualitatively only. Horse is different from ass in quality. Horse as such and horse as such are the same. It follows from this that the material intellect, being like the Active Intellect an immaterial form, cannot be numerically multiplied, and therefore is one only. But if so, no end of absurdities follows. For it means that all men have the same intellect, hence the latter is wise and ignorant at the same time in reference to the same thing, in so far as A knows a given thing and B does not know it. It would also follow that A can make use of B's sense experience and build his knowledge upon it. All these inferences are absurd, and they all follow from the assumption that the material intellect is in essence the same as the Active Intellect. Hence Averroes's position is untenable.[340]

Gersonides then gives his own view of the material intellect, which is similar to that of Alexander. The material intellect is a capacity, and the prime matter is the ultimate subject in which it inheres. But there are other powers or forms inhering in matter prior to the material intellect. Prime matter as such is not endowed with intellect, or all things would have human reason. Prime matter when it reaches the stage of development of the imaginative faculty is then ready to receive the material intellect. We may say then that the sensitive soul, of which the imaginative faculty is a part, is the subject in which the material intellect inheres. The criticism directed against Alexander, which applies here also, may be answered as follows. The material intellect is dependent upon its subject, the sensitive soul, for its existence only, not for the manner of receiving its knowledge. Hence the weakening or strengthening of its subject cannot affect it directly at all. Indirectly there is a relation between the two, and it works in the reverse direction. When the sensitive powers are weakened and their activities diminish, there is more opportunity for the intellect to monopolize the one soul for itself and increase its own activity, which the other powers have a tendency to hinder, since the soul is one for all these contending powers. It follows of course that the material intellect in man is not immortal. As a capacity of the sensitive soul, it dies with the latter. What part of the human soul it is that enjoys immortality and on what conditions we shall see later. But before we do this, we must try to understand the nature of the Active Intellect.[341]

We know now that the function of the Active Intellect is to actualize the material intellect, *i. e.*, to develop the capacity which the latter has of extracting general ideas from the particular memory images (phantasmata) in the faculty of imagination, so that this capacity, originally empty of any content, receives the ideas thus produced, and is thus constituted into an *actual* intellect. From this it follows that the Active Intellect, which enables the material intellect to form ideas, must itself have the ideas it induces in the latter, though not necessarily in the same form. Thus an artisan, who imposes the form of chair upon a piece of wood, must have the form of chair in his mind, though not the same sort as he realizes in the wood. Now as all the ideas acquired by the material intellect constitute one single activity so far as the end and purpose is concerned (for it all leads to the perfection of the person), the agent which is the cause of it all must also be one. Hence there are not many Active Intellects, each responsible for certain ideas, but one Intellect is the cause of all the ideas realized in the material intellect. Moreover, as this Active Intellect gives the material intellect not merely a knowledge of separate ideas, but also an understanding of their relations to each other, in other words of the systematic unity connecting all ideas into one whole, it follows that the Active Intellect has a knowledge of the ideas from their unitary aspect. In other words, the unity of purpose and aim which is evident in the development of nature from the prime matter through the forms of the elements, the plant soul, the animal soul and up to the human reason, where the lower is for the sake of the higher, must reside as a unitary conception in the Active Intellect.

For the Active Intellect has another function besides developing the rational capacity in man. We can arrive at this insight by a consideration undertaken from a different point of view. If we consider the wonderful and mysterious development of a seed, which is only a piece of matter, in a purposive manner, passing through various stages and producing a highly complicated organism with psychic powers, we must come to the conclusion, as Aristotle does, that there is an intellect operating in this development. As all sublunar nature shows a unity of purpose, this intellect must be one. And as it cannot be like one of its products, it must be eternal and not subject to generation and decay. But these are the attributes which, on grounds taken from the consideration of the intellectual activity in man, we ascribed to the Active Intellect. Hence it *is* the Active Intellect. And we have thus shown that it has two functions. One is to endow sublunar nature with the intelligence and purpose visible in its processes and evolutions; the other is to enable the rational power in man to rise from a *tabula rasa* to an actual intellect with a content. From both these activities it is evident that the Active Intellect has a knowledge of sublunar creation as a systematic unity.

This conception of the Active Intellect, Levi ben Gerson says, will also answer all the difficulties by which other philosophers are troubled concerning the possibility of knowledge and the nature of definition. The problems are briefly these. Knowledge concerns itself with the permanent and universal. There can be no real knowledge of the particular, for the particular is never the same, it is constantly changing and in the end disappears altogether. On the other hand, the universal has no real existence outside of the mind, for the objectively real is the particular thing. The only really existing man is A or B or C; man in general, man that is not a particular individual man, has no objective extra-mental existence. Here is a dilemma. The only thing we can really know is the thing that is not real, and the only real thing is that which we cannot know. The Platonists solve this difficulty by boldly declaring that the universal ideas or forms are the real existents and the models of the things of sense. This is absurd. Aristotle's solution in the Metaphysics is likewise unsatisfactory. Our conception, however, of the Active Intellect enables us to solve this problem satisfactorily. The object of knowledge is not the particular thing which is constantly changing; nor yet the logical abstraction which is only in the mind. It is the real unity of sublunar nature as it exists in the Active Intellect.

The problem of the definition is closely related to that of knowledge. The definition denotes the essence of every individual of a given species. As the individuals of a given species have all the same definition, and hence the same essence, they are all one. For what is not in the definition is not real. Our answer is that the definition represents that unitary aspect of the sublunar individuals which is in the Active Intellect. This aspect is also in a certain sense present in every one of the individual objects of nature, but not in the same manner as in the Active Intellect.[342]

We are now ready to take up the question of human immortality. The material intellect as a capacity for acquiring knowledge is not immortal. Being inherent in the sensitive soul and dependent for its acquisition of knowledge upon the memory images (phantasmata) which appear in the imagination, the power to acquire knowledge ceases with the cessation of sense and imagination. But the knowledge already acquired, which, we have shown above, is identical with the conceptions of sublunar nature in the Active Intellect, is indestructible. For these conceptions are absolutely immaterial; they are really the Active Intellect in a sense, and only the material is subject to destruction. The sum of acquisition of immaterial ideas constitutes the *acquired* or *actual intellect*, and this is the immortal part of man.

Further than this man cannot go. The idea adopted by some that the human intellect may become identified completely with the Active Intellect, Levi ben Gerson rejects. In order to accomplish this, he says, it would be necessary to have a complete and perfect knowledge of all nature, and that too a completely unified and wholly immaterial knowledge just as it is in the Active Intellect. This is clearly impossible. But it is true that a man's happiness after death is dependent upon the amount and perfection of his knowledge. For even in this life the pleasure we derive from intellectual contemplation is greater the more nearly we succeed in completely concentrating our mind on the subject of study. Now after death there will be no disturbing factors such as are supplied in this world by the sensitive and emotional powers. To be sure this lack will also prevent the acquisition of new knowledge, as was said before, but the amount acquired will be there in the soul's power all at once and all the time. The more knowledge one has succeeded in obtaining during life, the more nearly he will resemble the Active Intellect and the greater will be his happiness.[343]

The next topic Levi ben Gerson takes up is that of prognostication. There are three ways in which certain persons come to know the future, *dreams, divination* and *prophecy*. What we wish to do is to determine the kind of future events that may be thus known beforehand, the agency which produces in us this power, and the bearing this phenomenon has on the nature of events generally, and particularly as concerns the question of chance and free will.

That there is such knowledge of future events is a fact and not a theory. Experience testifies to the fact that there are certain people who are able to foretell the future, not as a matter of accident or through a chance coincidence, but as a regular thing. Diviners these are called, or fortune tellers. This power is even better authenticated in prophecy, which no one denies. We can also cite many instances of dreams, in which a person sees a future event with all its particulars, and the dream comes true. All these cases are too common to be credited to chance. Now what does this show as to the nature of the events thus foreseen? Clearly it indicates that they cannot be chance happenings, for what is by chance cannot be foreseen. The only conclusion then to be drawn is that these events are determined by the order of nature. But there is another implication in man's ability to foretell the future, namely, that what is thus known to man is first known to a higher intellect which communicates it to us.

The first of these two consequences leads us into difficulties. For if we examine the data of prognostication, whether it be of dream, divination or prophecy, we find that they concern almost exclusively such particular human events as would be classed in the category of the contingent rather than in that of the necessary. Fortune tellers regularly tell people about the kind of children they will have, the sort of things they will do, and so on. In prophecy similarly Sarah was told she would have a son (Gen. 18, 10). We also have examples of prognostication respecting the outcome of a battle, announcement of coming rain,—events due to definite causes—as well as the prediction of events which are the result of free choice or pure accident, as when

Samuel tells Saul that he will meet three men on tne way, who will give him two loaves of bread, which he will accept; or when the prophet in Samariah tells the prophet in Bethel that he will be killed by a lion. The question now is, if these contingent things can be known in advance, they are not contingent; and if these are not, none are. For the uniform events in nature are surely not contingent. If then those events usually classed as contingent and voluntary are not such, there is no such thing as chance and free will at all, which is impossible.

Our answer is that as a matter of fact those contingent happenings we call luck and ill luck do often come frequently to certain persons, whom we call lucky or unlucky, which shows that they are not the result of pure chance, and that there is some sort of order determining them. Moreover, we know that the higher in the scale of being a thing is, the more nature takes care to guard it. Hence as man is the highest being here below, it stands to reason that the heavenly bodies order his existence and his fortune. And so the science of astrology, with all its mistakes on account of the imperfect state of our knowledge, does say a great many things which are true. This, however, does not destroy freedom and chance. For the horoscope represents only one side of the question. Man was also endowed with reason and purpose, which enable him whenever he chooses to counteract the order of the heavenly bodies. In the main the heavenly bodies by their positions and motions and the consequent predominance of certain elemental qualities in the sublunar world over others affect the temperaments of man in a manner tending to his welfare. The social order with its differentiation of labor and occupation is worked out wonderfully well—better than the system of Plato's Republic—by the positions and motions of the heavenly bodies. If not for this, all men would choose the more honorable trades and professions, there would be no one to do the menial work, and society would be impossible. At the same time there are certain incidental evils inherent in the rigid system which would tend to destroy certain individuals. To counteract these unintended defects, God endowed man with reason and choice enabling him to avoid the dangers threatening him in the world of nature.

The solution of our problem then is this. These human events have a twofold aspect. They are determined so far as they follow from the order of the heavenly bodies; and in so far they can be foretold. They are undetermined so far as they are the result of individual choice, and in so far they cannot be known beforehand. There are also pure chance events in inanimate nature, bearing no relation to human fortune. These cannot be foretold.[344]

We said above that there must be an intellect which knows these contingent events predicted in dreams, divination and prophecy and imparts a knowledge of them to these men. This can be no other than the Active Intellect, whose nature we discussed above. For the Active Intellect knows the order of sublunar things, and gives us a knowledge of them in the ideas of the material intellect. Moreover, he is the agent producing them through the instrumentality of the heavenly bodies. Hence the heavenly bodies are also his instrument in ordering those contingent events which are predicted in dreams and prophetic visions.

The purpose of this information is to protect man against the evil destined for him in the order of the heavenly bodies, or in order that he may avail himself of the good in store for him if he knows of it.

There is a difference in kind between prophecy on the one hand and divination and dream on the other. Prophecy comes from the Active Intellect directly acting on the material intellect. Hence only intelligent men can be prophets. Divination and dream come from the Active Intellect indirectly. They are caused by the heavenly bodies, and the action is on the imagination. The imagination is more easily isolated from the other parts of the soul in young people and simpletons. Hence we find examples of dreams and divination among them.[345]

In discussing the problem of God's knowledge, Gersonides takes direct issue with Maimonides. The reader will recall that the question turns upon the knowledge of particulars. Some philosophers go so far as to deny to God any knowledge of things other than his own essence; for the known is in a sense identified with the knower, and to bring in a multiplicity of ideas in God's knowledge would endanger his unity. Others, however, fell short of this extreme opinion and admitted God's knowledge of things other than himself, but maintained that God cannot know particulars for various reasons. The particular is perceived by sense, a material faculty, whereas God is immaterial.

Particulars are infinite and cannot be measured or embraced, whereas knowledge is a kind of measuring or embracing. The particulars are not always existing, and are subject to change. Hence God's knowledge would be subject to change and disappearance, which is impossible. If God knows particulars how is it that there is often a violation of right and justice in the destinies of individual men? This would argue in God either inability or indifference, both of which are impossible.

Maimonides insists on God's knowledge of all things of which he is the creator, including particulars. And he answers the arguments of the philosophers by saying that their objections are valid only if we assume that God's knowledge is similar to ours, and since with us it is impossible to know the material except through a material organ, it is not possible in God. As we cannot comprehend the infinite; as we cannot know the non-existent, nor the changing without a change in our knowledge, God cannot do so. But it is wrong to assume this. God's knowledge is identical with his essence, which these same philosophers insist is unlike anything else, and unknowable. Surely it follows that his knowledge is also without the least resemblance to our knowledge and the name alone is what they have in common. Hence all the objections of the philosophers fall away at one stroke. *We* cannot in one act of knowing embrace a number of things differing in species; God can, because his knowledge is one. *We* cannot know the non-existent, for our knowledge depends upon the thing known. God can. *We* cannot know the infinite, for the infinite cannot be embraced; God can. *We* cannot know the outcome of a future event unless the event is necessary and determined. If the event is contingent and undetermined we can only have opinion concerning it, which may or may not be true; we are uncertain and may be mistaken. God can know the outcome of a contingent event, and yet the event is not determined, and may happen one way or the other. Our knowledge of a given thing changes as the thing itself undergoes a change, for if our knowledge should remain the same while the object changes, it would not be knowledge but error. In God the two are compatible. He knows in advance how a given thing will change, and his knowledge never changes, even though that which was at one moment potential and implicit becomes later actual and explicit.

At this point Gersonides steps in in defence of human logic and sanity. He accuses Maimonides of not being quite honest with himself. Maimonides, he intimates, did not choose this position of his own free will—a position scientifically quite untenable—he was forced to it by theological exigencies.[346] He felt that he must vindicate, by fair means or foul, God's knowledge of particulars. And so Gersonides proceeds to demolish Maimonides's position by reducing it *ad absurdum*.

What does Maimonides mean by saying that God knows the contingent? If he means that God knows that the contingent may as contingent happen otherwise than as he knows it will happen, we do not call this in us knowledge, but opinion. If he means that God knows it will happen in a certain way, and yet it may turn out that the reverse will actually take place, then we call this in our case error, not knowledge. And if he means that God merely knows that it may happen one way or the other without knowing definitely which will happen, then we call this in our experience uncertainty and perplexity, not knowledge. By insisting that all this is in God knowledge because, forsooth, God's knowledge is not like our knowledge, is tantamount to saying that what is in us opinion, uncertainty, error, is in God knowledge—a solution far from complimentary to God's knowledge.

Besides, the entire principle of Maimonides that there is no relation of resemblance between God's attributes and ours, that the terms wise, just, and so on, are pure homonyms, is fundamentally wrong. We attribute knowledge to God because we know in our own case that an intellect is perfected by knowledge. And since we have come to the conclusion on other grounds that God is a perfect intellect, we say he must have knowledge. Now if this knowledge that we ascribe to God has no resemblance whatsoever to what we understand by knowledge in our own case, the ground is removed from our feet. We might as well argue that man is rational because solid is continuous. If the word knowledge means a totally different thing in God from what it means in us, how do we know that it is to be found in God? If we have absolutely no idea what the term means when applied to God, what reason have we for preferring knowledge as a divine attribute to its opposite or negative? If knowledge does not mean knowledge, ignorance does not mean ignorance, and it is just the same whether we ascribe to God the one or the other.

The truth is that the attributes we ascribe to God do have a resemblance to the same attributes in ourselves; only they are primary in God, secondary in ourselves, *i. e.*, they exist in God in a more perfect manner than in us. Hence it is absurd to say that what would be in us error or uncertainty is in God knowledge. Our problem must be solved more candidly and differently. There are arguments in favor of God's knowing particulars (Maimonides gives some), and there are the arguments of the philosophers against the thesis. The truth must be between the two, that God knows them from one aspect and does not know them from another. Having shown above that human events are in part ordered and determined by the heavenly bodies, and in part undetermined and dependent upon the individual's choice, we can now make use of this distinction for the solution of our problem. God knows particulars in so far as they are ordered, he does not know them in so far as they are contingent. He knows that they are contingent, and hence it follows that he does not know which of the two possibilities will happen, else they would not be contingent. This is no defect in God's nature, for to know a thing as it is is no imperfection. In general God does not know particulars as particulars but as ordered by the universal laws of nature. He knows the universal order, and he knows the particulars in so far as they are united in the universal order.

This theory meets all objections, and moreover it is in agreement with the views of the Bible. It is the only one by which we can harmonize the apparent contradictions in the Scriptures. Thus on the one hand we are told that God sends Prophets and commands people to do and forbear. This implies that a person has freedom to choose, and that the contingent is a real category. On the other hand, we find that God foretells the coming of future events respecting human destiny, which signifies determination. And yet again we find that God repents, and that he does not repent. All these apparent contradictions can be harmonized on our theory. God foretells the coming of events in so far as they are determined in the universal order of nature. But man's freedom may succeed in counteracting this order, and the events predicted may not come. This is signified by the expression that God repents.[347]

Levi ben Gerson's solution, whatever we may think of its scientific or philosophic value, is surely very bold as theology, we might almost say it is a theological monstrosity. It practically removes from God the definite knowledge of the outcome of a given event so far as that outcome is contingent. Gersonides will not give up the contingent, for that would destroy freedom. He therefore accepts free will with its consequences, at the risk of limiting God's knowledge to events which are determined by the laws of nature. Maimonides was less consistent, but had the truer theological sense, namely, he kept to both horns of the dilemma. God is omniscient and man is free. He gave up the solution by seeking refuge in the mysteriousness of God's knowledge. This is the true religious attitude.

The question of Providence is closely related to that of God's knowledge. For it is clear that one cannot provide for those things of which he does not know. Gersonides's view in this problem is very similar to that of Maimonides, and like him he sees in the discussions between Job and his friends the representative opinions held by philosophers in this important problem.

There are three views, he says, concerning the nature of Providence. One is that God's providence extends only to species and not to individuals. The second opinion is that God provides for every individual of the human race. The third view is that some individuals are specially provided for, but not all. Job held the first view, which is that of Aristotle. The arguments in favor of this opinion are that God does not know particulars, hence cannot provide for them. Besides, there would be more justice in the distribution of goods and evils in the world if God concerned himself about every individual. Then again man is too insignificant for God's special care.

The second view is that of the majority of our people. They argue that as God is the author of all, he surely provides for them. And as a matter of fact experience shows it; else there would be much more violence and bloodshed than there is. The wicked are actually punished and the good rewarded. This class is divided into two parts. Some think that while God provides for all men, not all that happens to a man is due to God; there are also other causes. The others think that every happening is due to God. This second class may again be divided according to the manner in which they account for those facts in experience which seem to militate against their view. Maintaining that every incident is due to God, they have to explain the apparent deviation from justice in the prosperity of the wicked and the adversity of the righteous. One party explains the phenomenon by saying that the prosperity and the adversity in these cases are only seeming and not real; that they in fact are the opposite of what they seem, or at least lead to the opposite. The second party answers the objection on the ground that those we think good may not really be such, and similarly those we think bad may not really be bad. For the way to judge a person's character is not merely by his deeds alone, but by his deeds as related to his temperament and disposition, which God alone knows. Eliphaz the Temanite belonged to those who think that not all which happens is due to God; that folly is responsible for a man's misfortune. Bildad the Shuchite believed that all things are from God, but not all that seems good and evil is really so. Zophar the Naamathite thought we do not always judge character correctly; that temperament and disposition must be taken into account.

Of these various opinions the first one, that of Aristotle, cannot be true. Dreams, divination, and especially prophecy contradict it flatly. All these are given to the individual for his protection (*cf.* above, p. 342). The second opinion, namely, that God's providence extends to every individual, is likewise disproved by reason, by experience and by the Bible. We have already proved (p. 345) that God's knowledge does not extend to particulars as such. He only knows things as ordered by the heavenly bodies; and knows at the same time that they may fail to happen because of man's free will. Now if God punishes and rewards every man according to his deeds, one of two things necessarily follows. Either he rewards and punishes according to those deeds which the individual is determined to do by the order of the heavenly bodies, or according to the deeds the individual actually does. In the first case there would be often injustice, for the person might not have acted as the order of the heavenly bodies indicated he would act, for he is free to act as he will. The second case is impossible, for it would mean that God knows particulars as particulars—a thesis we have already disproved. Besides, evil does not come from God directly, since he is pure form and evil comes only from matter. Hence it cannot be said that he punishes the evil doer for his sin.

Experience also testifies against this view, for we see the just suffer and the wicked prosper. The manner in which Eliphaz, Bildad and Zophar wish to defend God's justice will not hold water. Man's own folly will account perhaps for some evils befalling the righteous and some good coming to the wicked. But it will not account for the failure of the good man to get the reward he deserves, and of the wicked to receive the punishment which is his due. The righteous man often has troubles all his life no matter how careful he is to avoid them, and correspondingly the same is true of the wicked, that he is prosperous, despite his lack of caution and good sense. To avoid these objections as Eliphaz does by saying that if the wicked man himself is not punished, his children will be, is to go from the frying pan into the fire. For it is not just either to omit to punish the one deserving it, or to punish another innocent man for him. Nor is Zophar's defence any better. For the same man, with the same temperament and disposition, often suffers more when he is inclined to do good, and is prosperous when he is not so scrupulous. Bildad is no more successful than the other two. The evils coming to the righteous are often real and permanent. But neither does the Bible compel us to believe that God looks out for all individuals. This is especially true in reference to punishment, as can be gathered from such expressions as "I will hide my face from them, and they shall be given to be devoured" (Deut. 31, 17), or "As thou hast forgotten the law of thy God, so will I myself also forget thy children" (Hosea 4, 6). These expressions indicate that God does not punish the individuals directly, but that he leaves them to the fate that is destined for them by the order of the heavenly bodies. True there are other passages in Scripture speaking of direct punishment, but they may be interpreted so as not to conflict with our conclusions.

Having seen that neither of the two extreme views is correct, it remains to adopt the middle course, namely, that some individuals are provided for specially, and others not. The nearer a person is to the Active Intellect, the more he receives divine providence and care. Those people who do not improve their capabilities, which they possess as members of the species, are provided for only as members of the species. The matter may be put in another way also. God knows all ideas. Man is potentially capable of receiving them in a certain manner. God, who is actual, leads man from his potentiality to actuality. When a man's potentialities are thus realized, he becomes similar to God, because when ideas are actualized the agent and the thing acted upon are one. Hence the person enjoys divine providence at that time. The way in which God provides for such men is by giving them knowledge through dream, divination or prophecy or intuition or in some other unconscious manner on the individual's part, which knowledge protects him from harm. This view is not in conflict with the truth that God does not know particulars as such. For it is not to the individual person as such that providence extends as a conscious act of God. The individualization is due to the recipient and not to the dispenser. One may object that after all since it is possible that bad men may have goods as ordered by the heavenly bodies, and good men may have misfortune as thus ordered, when their attachment to God is loosened somewhat, there is *injustice* in God if he could have arranged the heavenly spheres differently and did not, or *incapacity* if he could not. The answer is briefly that the order of the spheres does a great deal of good in maintaining the existence of things. And if some little evil comes also incidentally, this does not condemn the whole arrangement. In fact the evils come from the very agencies which are the authors of good. The view of providence here adopted is that of Elihu the son of Barachel the Buzite in the book of Job (ch. 32), and it agrees also with the opinion of Maimonides in the "Guide of the Perplexed" (*cf.* above, p. 292).[348]

Instead of placing his cosmology at the beginning of his system and proceeding from that as a basis to the other parts of his work, the psychology and the ethics, Levi ben Gerson, whose "Milhamot Hashem" is not so much a systematic work as an aggregation of discussions, reversed the process. He begins as we have seen with a purely psychological analysis concerning the nature of the human reason and its relation to the Active Intellect. He follows up this discussion with a treatment of prognostication as exhibiting some of the effects of the Active Intellect upon the reason and imagination of man. This is again followed by a discussion of God's knowledge and providence. And not until all these psychological (and in part ethical) questions have been decided, does Levi ben Gerson undertake to give us his views of the constitution of the universe and the nature and attributes of God. In this discussion he takes occasion to express his dissatisfaction with Aristotle's proofs of the existence of the spheral movers and of the unmoved mover or God, as inadequate to bear the structure which it is intended to erect upon them. It will be remembered that the innovation of Abraham Ibn Daud and Maimonides in making Jewish philosophy more strictly Aristotelian than it had been consisted in a great measure in just this introduction of the Aristotelian proof of the existence of God as derived from the motions of the heavenly bodies. Levi ben Gerson's proofs are teleological rather than mechanical. Aristotle said a moving body must have a mover outside of it, which if it is again a body is itself in motion and must have a mover in turn. And as this process cannot go on *ad infinitum*, there must be at the end of the series an unmoved mover. As unmoved this mover cannot be body; and as producing motion eternally, it cannot be a power residing in a body, a physical or material power, for no such power can be infinite. Gersonides is not satisfied with this proof. He argues that so far as the motions of the heavenly bodies are concerned there is no reason why a physical power cannot keep on moving them eternally. The reason that motions caused by finite forces in our world come to a stop is because the thing moved is subject to change, which alters its relation to its mover; and secondly because the force endeavors to move the object in opposition to its own tendency, in opposition to gravity. In the case of the heavenly bodies neither of these conditions is present. The relation of the mover to the moved is always the same, since the heavenly bodies are not subject to change; and as they are not made of the four terrestrial elements they have no inherent tendency to move in any direction, hence they offer no opposition to the force exerted upon them by the mover. A finite power might therefore quite conceivably cause eternal motion. Similarly an unmoved mover cannot be body, to be sure, but it may be a physical power like a soul, which in moving the body is not itself moved by that motion. Aristotle's proofs therefore are not sufficient to produce the conviction that the movers of the spheres and God himself are separate Intelligences.[349]

Gersonides accordingly follows a different method. He argues that if a system of things and events exhibits perfection not here and there and at rare intervals but regularly, the inference is justified that there is an intelligent agent who had a definite purpose and design in establishing the system. The world below is such a system. Hence it has an intelligent agent as its author. This agent may be a separate and immaterial intelligence, or a corporeal power like a soul. He then shows that it cannot be a corporeal power, for it would have to reside in the animal sperm which exhibits such wonderful and purposive development, or in the parent animal from which the sperm came, both of which, he argues, are impossible. It remains then that the cause of the teleological life of the sublunar world is an immaterial power, a separate intellect. This intellect, he argues further, acts upon matter and endows it with forms, the only mediating power being the natural heat which is found in the seed and sperm of plants and animals. Moreover, it is aware of the order of what it produces. It is the Active Intellect of which we spoke above (p. 337). The forms of terrestrial things come from it directly, the heat residing in the seed comes from the motions of the spheres. This shows that the permanent motions of the heavenly bodies are also intelligent motions, for they tend to produce perfection in the terrestrial world and never come to a standstill, which would be the case if the motions were "natural" like those of the elements, or induced against their nature like that of a stone moving upward. We are justified in saying then that the heavenly bodies are endowed with intellects and have no material soul. Hence their movers are pure Intelligences, and there are as many of them as there are spheres, *i. e.*, forty-eight, or fifty-eight or sixty-four according to one's opinion on the astronomical question of the number of spheres.

Now as the Active Intellect knows the order of sublunar existence in its unity, and the movers of the respective spheres know the order of their effects through the motions of the heavenly bodies, it follows that as all things in heaven above and on the earth beneath are related in a unitary system, there is a highest agent who is the cause of all existence absolutely and has a knowledge of all existence as a unitary system.[350]

The divine attributes are derived by us from his actions, and hence they are not pure homonyms (*cf.* p. 240). God has a knowledge of

the complete order of sublunar things, of which the several movers
have only a part. He *knows* it as *one*, and knows it eternally without
change. His *joy* and *gladness* are beyond conception, for our joy also
is very great in understanding. His is also the perfect *Life*, for understanding is life. He is the most real *Substance* and *Existent*, and he
is *One*. God is also the most real *Agent*, as making the other movers
do their work, and producing a complete and perfect whole out of
their parts. He is also properly called *Bestower*, *Beneficent*, *Gracious*,
Strong, *Mighty*, *Upright*, *Just*, *Eternal*, *Permanent*. All these attributes, however, do not denote multiplicity.[351]

From God we now pass again to his creation, and take up the problem which caused Maimonides so much trouble, namely, the question
of the origin of the world. It will be remembered that dissatisfied
with the proofs for the existence of God advanced by the Mutakallimun, Maimonides, in order to have a firm foundation for the central
idea of religion, tentatively adopted the Aristotelian notion of the
eternity of motion and the world. But no sooner does Maimonides
establish his proof of the existence, unity and incorporeality of God
than he returns to the attack of the Aristotelian view and points out
that the problem is insoluble in a strictly scientific manner; that
Aristotle himself never intended his arguments in favor of eternity
to be regarded as philosophically demonstrated, and that they all
labor under the fatal fallacy that because certain laws hold of the
world's phenomena once it is in existence, these same laws must have
governed the establishment of the world itself in its origin. Besides,
the assumption of the world's eternity with its corollary of the necessity and immutability of its phenomena saps the foundation of all
religion, makes miracles impossible, and reduces the world to a ma-
chine. Gersonides is on the whole agreed with Maimonides. He
admits that Aristotle's arguments are the best yet advanced in the
problem, but that they are not convincing. He also agrees with Maimonides in his general stricture on Aristotle's method, only modifying
and restricting its generality and sweeping nature. With all this,
however, he finds it necessary to take up the entire question anew
and treats it in his characteristic manner, with detail and rigor, and
finally comes to a conclusion different from that of Maimonides,
namely, that the world had an origin in time, to be sure, but that it

came not *ex nihilo* in the absolute sense of the word *nihil*, but developed from an eternal formless matter, which God endowed with form. This is the so-called Platonic view.

We cannot enter into all his details which are technical and fatiguing in the extreme, but we must give a general idea of his procedure in the investigation of this important topic.

The problem of the origin of the world, he says, is very difficult. First, because in order to learn from the nature of existing things whether they were created out of a state of non-existence or not, we must know the essence of existing things, which is not easy. Secondly, we must know the nature of God in order to determine whether he could have existed first without the world and then have created it, or whether he had to have the world with him from eternity. The fact of the great difference of opinion on this question among thinkers, and the testimony of Maimonides that Aristotle himself had no valid proof in this matter are additional indications of the great difficulty of the subject.

Some think the world was made and destroyed an infinite number of times. Others say it was made once. Of these some maintain it was made out of something (Plato); others, that it was made out of absolute nothing (Philoponus, the Mutakallimun, Maimonides and many of our Jewish writers). Some on the other hand, namely, Aristotle and his followers, hold the world to be eternal. They all have their defenders, and there is no need to refute the others since Aristotle has already done this. His arguments are the best so far, and deserve investigation. The fundamental fallacy in all his proofs is that he argues from the laws of genesis and decay in the parts of the world to the laws of these processes in the world as a whole. This might seem to be the same criticism which Maimonides advances, but it is not really quite the same, Maimonides's assertion being more general and sweeping. Maimonides says that the origin of the world as a whole need not be in any respect like the processes going on within its parts; whereas Gersonides bases his argument on the observed difference in the world between wholes and parts, admitting that the two may be alike in many respects.

In order to determine whether the world is created or not, it is best to investigate first those things in the world which have the appearance of being eternal, such as the heavenly bodies, time, motion, the form of the earth, and so on. If these are proven to be eternal, the world is eternal; if not, it is not. A general principle to help us distinguish a thing having an origin from one that has not is the following: A thing which came into being in time has a purpose. An eternal thing has no purpose. Applying this principle to the heavens we find that all about them is with a purpose to ordering the sublunar world in the best way possible. Their motions, their distances, their positions, their numbers, and so on are all for this purpose. Hence they had a beginning. Aristotle's attempts to explain these conditions from the nature of the heavens themselves are not successful, and he knew it. Again, as the heavenly bodies are all made of the same fifth element (the Aristotelian ether), the many varieties in their forms and motions require special explanation. The only satisfactory explanation is that the origin of the heavenly bodies is not due to nature and necessity, which would favor eternity, but to will and freedom, and the many varieties are for a definite purpose. Hence they are not eternal.[352]

Gersonides then analyzes time and motion and proves that Aristotle to the contrary notwithstanding, they are both finite and not infinite. Time belongs to the category of quantity, and there is no infinite quantity. As time is dependent on motion, motion too is finite, hence neither is eternal. Another argument for creation in time is that if the world is eternal and governed altogether by necessity, the earth should be surrounded on all sides by water according to the nature of the lighter element to be above the heavier. Hence the appearance of parts of the earth's surface above the water is an indication of a break of natural law for a special purpose, namely, in order to produce the various mineral, plant and animal species. Hence once more purpose argues design and origin in time.

Finally if the world were eternal, the state of the sciences would be more advanced than it is. A similar argument may be drawn from language. Language is conventional; which means that the people existed before the language they agreed to speak. But man being a social animal they could not have existed an infinite time without language. Hence mankind is not eternal.[353]

We have just proved that the world came into being, but it does not necessarily follow that it will be destroyed. Nay, there are reasons to show that it will not be destroyed. For there is no destruction except through matter and the predominance of the passive powers over the active. Hence the being that is subject to destruction must consist of opposites. But the heavenly bodies have no opposites, not being composite; hence they cannot be destroyed. And if so, neither can the sublunar order be destroyed, which is the work of the heavenly bodies. There is of course the abstract possibility of their being destroyed by their maker, not naturally, but by his will, as they were made; but we can find no reason in God for wishing to destroy them, all reasons existing in man for destroying things being inapplicable to God.[354]

That the world began in time is now established. The question still remains, was the world made out of something or out of nothing? Both are impossible. The first is impossible, for that something out of which the world was made must have had some form, for matter never is without form, and if so, it must have had some motion, and we have a kind of world already, albeit an imperfect one. The second supposition is also impossible; for while form may come out of nothing, body cannot come from not-body. We never see the matter of any object arise out of nothing, though the form may. Nature as well as art produces one corporeal thing out of another. Hence the generally accepted principle, "*ex nihilo nihil fit.*" Besides it would follow on this supposition that before the world came into existence there was a vacuum in its place, whereas it is proved in the Physics that a vacuum is impossible. The only thing remaining therefore is to say that the world was made partly out of something, partly out of nothing, *i. e.*, out of an absolutely formless matter.

It may be objected that to assume the existence of a second eternal thing beside God is equivalent to a belief in dualism, in two gods. But this objection may be easily answered. Eternity as such does not constitute divinity. If all the world were eternal, God would still be God because he controls everything and is the author of the order obtaining in the world. In general it is the qualitative essence that makes the divine character of God, his wisdom and power as the source of goodness and right order in nature. The eternal matter of which we are speaking is the opposite of all this. As God is the extreme of perfection so is matter the extreme of imperfection and defect. As God is the source of good, so is matter the source of evil. How then can anyone suppose for a moment that an eternal formless matter can in any way be identified with a divine being?

Another objection that may be offered to our theory is that it is an established fact that matter cannot exist at all without any form, whereas our view assumes that an absolutely formless matter existed an infinite length of time before the world was made from it. This may be answered by saying that the impossibility of matter existing without form applies only to the actual objects of nature. God put in sublunar matter the nature and capacity of receiving all forms in a certain order. The primary qualities, the hot and the cold and the wet and the dry, as the forms of the elements, enable this matter to receive other higher forms. The very capacity of receiving a given form argues a certain form on the part of the matter having this capacity; for if it had no form there would be no reason why it should receive one form rather than another; whereas we find that the reception of forms is not at random, but that a given form comes from a definite other form. Man comes only from man. But this does not apply to the prime matter of which we are speaking. It may have been without form. Nay, it is reasonable to suppose that as we find matter and form combined, and we also find pure forms without matter, *viz.*, in the separate Intelligences,—it is reasonable to suppose that there is also matter without form.

Finally one may ask if the world has not existed from eternity, what determined the author to will its existence at the time he did and not at another? We cannot say that he acquired new knowledge which he had not before, or that he needed the world then and not before, or that there was some obstacle which was removed. The answer to this would be that the sole cause of the creation was the will of God to benefit his creatures. Their existence is therefore due to the divine causality, which never changes. Their origin in time is due to the nature of a material object as such. A material object as being caused by an external agent is incompatible with eternity. It must have a beginning, and there is no sense in asking why at this time and not before or after, for the same question would apply to any other time. Gersonides cites other objections which he answers, and then he takes up one by one the Aristotelian arguments in favor of eternity and refutes them in detail. We cannot afford to reproduce them here as the discussions are technical, lengthy and intricate.[355]

Having given his philosophical cosmology, Gersonides then undertakes to show in detail that the Biblical story of creation teaches the same doctrine. Nay, he goes so far as to say that it was the Biblical account that suggested to him his philosophical theory. It would be truer to say that having approached the Bible with Aristotelian spectacles, and having no suspicion that the two attitudes are as far apart as the poles, he did not scruple to twist the expressions in Genesis out of all semblance to their natural meaning. The Biblical text had been twisted and turned ever since the days of Philo, and of the Mishna and Talmud and Midrash, in the interest of various schools and sects. Motives speculative, religious, theological, legal and ethical were at the basis of Biblical interpretation throughout its long history of two millennia and more—the end is not yet—and Gersonides was swimming with the current. The Bible is not a law, he says, which forces us to believe absurdities and to practice useless things, as some people think. On the contrary it is a law which leads us to our perfection. Hence what is proved by reason must be found in the Law, by interpretation if necessary. This is why Maimonides took pains to interpret all Biblical passages in which God is spoken of as if he were corporeal. Hence also his statement that if the eternity of the world were strictly demonstrated, it would not be difficult to interpret the Bible so as to agree. But in the matter of the origin of the world, Gersonides continues, it was not necessary for me to force the Biblical account. Quite the contrary, the expressions in the Bible guided me to my view.[356]

Accordingly he finds support for his doctrine that the world was not created *ex nihilo*, in the fact that there is not one miracle in the Bible in which anything comes out of nothing. They are all instances of something out of a pre-existent something. The miracle of the oil in the case of Elisha is no exception. The air changed into oil as it entered the partly depleted vessel. The six days of creation must not be taken literally. God's creation is timeless, and the six days indicate the natural order and rank in existing things proceeding from the cause to the effect and from the lower to the higher. Thus the movers of the heavenly bodies come before the spheres which they move as their causes. The spheres come before the terrestrial elements for the same reason. The elements are followed by the things composed of them. And among these too there is a certain order. Plants come before animals, aquatic animals before aerial, aerial before terrestrial, and the last of all is man, as the most perfect of sublunar creatures. All this he reads into the account of creation in Genesis. Thus the *light* spoken of in the first day represents the angels or separate Intelligences or movers of the spheres, and they are distinguished from the *darkness* there, which stands for the heavenly bodies as the matters of their movers, though at the same time they are grouped together as one day, because the form and its matter constitute a unit. The *water*, which was divided by the firmament, denotes the prime formless matter, part of which was changed into the matter of the heavenly bodies, and part into the four terrestrial elements. Form and matter are also designated by the terms "Tohu" and "Bohu" in the second verse in Genesis, rendered in the Revised Version by "without form" and "void." And so Gersonides continues throughout the story of creation, into the details of which we need not follow him.[357]

The concluding discussion in the Milhamot is devoted to the problem of miracles and its relation to prophecy. Maimonides had said that one reason for opposing the Aristotelian theory of the eternity of the world is that miracles would be an impossibility on that assumption. Hence Maimonides insists on creation *ex nihilo*, though he admits that the Platonic view of a pre-existent matter may be reconciled with the Torah. Gersonides, who adopted the doctrine of an eternal matter, finds it necessary to say by way of introduction to his treatment of miracles that they do not prove creation *ex nihilo*. For as was said before all miracles exhibit a production of something out of something and not out of nothing.

To explain the nature of miracles, he says, and their authors, it is necessary to know what miracles are. For this we must take the Biblical records as our data, just as we take the data of our senses in determining other matters. On examining the miracles of the Bible we find that they may be classified into those which involve a change of substance and those in which the substance remains the same and the change is one of quality or quantity. An example of the former is the change of Moses's rod into a serpent and of the water of Egypt into blood; of the latter, Moses's hand becoming leprous, and the withering of the hand of Jeroboam. We may further divide the miracles into those in which the prophet was told in advance, as Moses was of the ten plagues, and those in which he was not, as for example the reviving of the dead by Elijah and many other cases. Our examination also shows us that all miracles are performed by prophets or in relation to them. Also that they are done with some good and useful purpose, namely, to inculcate belief or to save from evil.

These data will help us to decide who is the author of miracles. Miracles cannot be accidental, as they are performed with a purpose; and as they involve a knowledge of the sublunar order, they must have as their author one who has this knowledge, hence either God or the Active Intellect or man, *i. e.*, the prophet himself. Now it is not reasonable to suppose that God is the author of miracles, for miracles come only rarely and are of no value in themselves but only as a means to a special end, as we said before. The laws of nature, however, which control all regular events all the time, are essentially good and permanent. Hence it is not reasonable to suppose that the Active Intellect who, as we know, orders the sublunar world, has more important work to do than God. Besides if God were the author of miracles, the prophet would not know about them, for prophetic inspiration, as we know (p. 342), is due to the Active Intellect and not directly to God.

Nor do we need waste words in proving that man cannot be the author of miracles, for in that case the knowledge of them would not come to him through prophetic inspiration, since they are due to his own will. Besides man, as we have seen, cannot have a complete knowledge of the sublunar order, and hence it is not likely that he can control its laws to the extent of changing them.

There is therefore only one alternative left, namely, that the author of miracles is the same as the inspirer of the prophets, the controlling spirit of the sublunar world, whose intellect has as its content the unified system of sublunar creation as an immaterial idea, namely, the Active Intellect, of whom we have spoken so often. The prophet knows of the miracles because the Active Intellect, who is the author of them, is also the cause of the prophetic inspiration. This will account too for the fact that all miracles have to do with events in the sublunar world and are not found in the relations and motions of the heavenly bodies. The case of Joshua causing the sun and moon to stand still is no exception. There was no standing still of the sun and moon in that case. What is meant by the expressions in Joshua 10 is that the Israelites conquered the enemy in the short time that the sun occupied the zenith, while its motion was not noticeable for about an hour, as is usually the case about noon. In the case of Isaiah moving the sun ten degrees back for Hezekiah (Isai. 38, 8), there was likewise no change in the motion of the sun, but only in that of the cloud causing the shadow.

Miracles cannot be of regular occurrence, for if natural phenomena and laws were changed by miracle as a regular thing, it would signify a defect in the original order. Miracles cannot take place to violate the principle of contradiction, hence there can be no miracles in reference to mathematical truths, nor in matters relating to the past. Thus a miracle cannot make a thing black and white at the same time; nor a plane triangle whose angles are less than two right angles; nor is it possible by miracle now to make it not to have rained in Jerusalem yesterday, when as a matter of fact it did rain. For all these involve a denial of the logical law of contradiction that a thing cannot be and not be at the same time.[358]

A prophet is tested (1) by being able to foretell miracles before they come, and (2) by the realization of his prophetic messages. The question is raised concerning the statement of Jeremiah that one may be a true prophet and yet an evil prophecy may remain unfulfilled if the people repent. Does this mean that a good prophecy must always come true? In that case a good deal of what comes within the category of the possible and contingent becomes determined and necessary! The answer is that a good prophecy too sometimes fails of realization, as is illustrated in Jacob's fear of Esau after he was promised protection by God. But this happens more rarely on account of the fact that a man endeavors naturally to see a good prophecy realized, whereas he does his best to counteract an evil prophecy.[359]

Gersonides's entire discussion of miracles shows a deep seated motive to minimize their extent and influence. The study of science and philosophy had the effect of planting in the minds of the mediæval philosophers a great respect for reason on the one hand and natural law on the other. A study of history, archæology and literary criticism has developed in modern times a spirit of scepticism regarding written records of antiquity. This was foreign to mediæval theologians generally. No one doubted for a moment the accuracy of the Biblical records as well as their inspiration in every detail. Hence prophecy and miracles had to be explained or explained away. Interpretation held the place of criticism.

CHAPTER XVI

The chronological treatment of Jewish philosophy which we have followed makes it necessary at this point to take up a Karaite work of the fourteenth century that is closely modelled upon the "Guide of the Perplexed." In doing this we necessarily take a step backward as far as the philosophical development is concerned. For while it is true that the early Rabbanite thinkers like Saadia, Bahya, Ibn Zaddik and others moved in the circle of ideas of the Mohammedan Mutakallimun, that period had long since been passed. Judah Halevi criticized the Kalam, Ibn Daud is a thorough Aristotelian, and Maimonides gave the Kalam in Jewish literature its deathblow. No Rabbanite after Maimonides would think of going back to the old arguments made popular by the Mutakallimun—the theory of atoms, of substance and accident in the Kalamistic sense of accident as a quality which needs continuous creation to exist any length of time, the denial of law and natural causation, the arguments in favor of creation and the existence of God based upon creation, the doctrine of the divine will as eternal or created, residing in a subject or existing without a subject, the world as due to God's will or to his wisdom, the nature of right and wrong as determined by the character and purpose of the act or solely by the arbitrary will of God—these and other topics, which formed the main ground of discussion between the Mu'tazilites and the Ashariya, and were taken over by the Karaites and to a less extent by the early Rabbanites in the tenth and eleventh centuries, had long lost their significance and their interest among the Rabbanite followers of Maimonides. Aristotelianism, introduced by Alfarabi, Avicenna and Averroes among the Arabs, and Ibn Daud and Maimonides among the Jews, dominated all speculative thought, and the old Kalam was obsolete and forgotten. Gersonides no longer regards the Kalamistic point of view as a living issue. He ignores it entirely. His problems as we have seen are those raised by the Averroistic system. In this respect then a reading of Aaron ben Elijah's "Ez Hayim" (Tree of Life) [360] affects us like a breath from a foreign clime, like the odor of a thing long buried. And yet Aaron ben Elijah was a contemporary of Levi ben Gerson. He was born about 1300, and died in 1369. He lived in Nicomedia, Cairo, Constantinople. The reason for the antiquated appearance of his work lies in the fact that he was a Karaite, and the Karaites never got beyond the Mu'tazilite point of view. Karaism was only a sect and never showed after the days of Saadia anything like the life and enthusiastic activity of the great body of Rabbanite Judaism, which formed the great majority of the Jewish people. The Karaites had their important men in Halaka as well as in religious philosophy and Biblical exegesis. Solomon ben Yeroham, Joseph Ha-Maor (Al-Kirkisani), Joseph Al Basir (p. 48 ff.), Jeshua ben Judah (p. 55 ff.), Yefet Ha-Levi, Judah Hadassi, Aaron ben Joseph—all these were prominent in Karaitic literature. But they cannot be compared to the great men among the Rabbanites. There was no Maimonides among them. And Aaron ben Elijah cherished the ambition of being to the Karaites what Maimonides was to the Rabbanites. Accordingly he undertook to compose three works representing the three great divisions of Karaitic Judaism—a book of Laws, a work on Biblical exegesis and a treatise on religious philosophy. The last was written first, having been composed in 1346. The "Sefer Ha-Mizvot," on the religious commandments, was written in 1354, and his exegetical work, known as "Keter Torah" (The Crown of the Law) was published in 1362. It is the first that interests us, the "Ez Hayyim." As was said before, this book is closely modelled upon the "More Nebukim," though the arrangement is different, being more logical than that of the "Guide." Instead of beginning, as Maimonides does, with interpreting the anthropomorphic expressions in the Bible, which is followed by a treatment of the divine attributes, long before the existence of God has been proved or even the fundamental principles laid down upon which are based the proofs of the existence of God, Aaron ben Elijah more naturally begins with the basal doctrines of physics and metaphysics, which he then utilizes in discussing the existence of God. As Maimonides brought to a focus all the speculation on philosophy and religion as it was handed down to him by Arab and Jew, and gave it a harmonious and systematic form in his masterpiece; so did Aaron ben Elijah endeavor to sum up all Karaitic discussion in his work, and in addition declare his attitude to Maimonides. The success with which he carried out this plan is not equal. As a source of information on schools and opinions of Arabs and Karaites, the "Ez Hayyim" is of great importance and interest. But it cannot in the least compare with the "Guide" as a constructive work of religious philosophy. It has not the same originality or any degree remotely approaching it. The greater part of the Aristotelian material seems bodily taken from Maimonides, and so is the part dealing with the anthropomorphic expressions in the Bible. There is a different point of view in his exposition of the Mu'tazilite physics, which he presents in a more systematic and favorable light than Maimonides, defending it against the strictures of the latter. But everywhere Aaron ben Elijah lacks the positiveness and commanding mastery of Maimonides. He is not clear what side of a question to espouse. For the most part he places side by side the opposed points of view and only barely intimates his own attitude or preference. Under these circumstances it will not be necessary for us to reproduce his ideas *in extenso*. It will be sufficient if we indicate his relation to Maimonides in the problems common to both, adding a brief statement of those topics which Aaron ben Elijah owes to his Karaite predecessors, and which Maimonides omits.

His general attitude on the relation of religion or revelation to reason and philosophy is somewhat inconsistent. For while he endeavors to rationalize Jewish dogma and Scriptural teaching like Maimonides, and in doing so utilizes Aristotelian terminology in matters physical, metaphysical, psychological, ethical and logical, he nevertheless in the beginning of his work condemns philosophy as well as philosophers, meaning of course the Aristotelians.[361] He nowhere expressly indicates the manner of reconciling this apparent contradiction. But it would seem as if he intended to distinguish between the philosophical method and the actual teachings of the Aristotelians. Their method he approves, their results he condemns. The Aristotelians taught the eternity of the world, the immutability of natural law, God's ignorance of particulars and the absence of special Providence. These doctrines must be condemned. Maimonides too rejects these extreme teachings while praising Aristotle and maintaining that philosophy was originally a possession of the Israelitish people, which they lost in the exile. Aaron ben Elijah is not willing to follow the philosophers as far as Maimonides. He admits positive attributes in God, which Maimonides rejects; he admits an absolute will in God and not merely a relative like Maimonides; he extends God's providence to all individuals including irrational creatures, whereas Maimonides limits special providence to the individuals of the human species, and so on. And so he condemns the philosophers, though he cannot help using their method and even their fundamental doctrines, so far as they are purely theoretical and scientific. He is willing to go the full length of the Aristotelians only in the unity and incorporeality of God, though here too he vindicates sense perception to God, *i. e.*, the knowledge of that which we get through our sense organs. He too like the philosophers insists on the importance of the reason as the instrument of truth and knowledge. Abraham was the first, he tells us, who proved the existence of God with his intellect. Then came the law of Moses, which strengthened the same idea. The Gentiles hated and envied Israel for their superiority and their true opinions; hence they endeavored to refute their ideas and establish others in their stead. This was the work of the ancient Greek philosophers, who are called enemies in the Bible (Psalms 139, 21). At the time of the second Temple, seeing that the Jewish religion and its teachings were true, they took advantage of the advent of Jesus to adopt his false teachings, thus showing their hatred and envy of Israel. At the same time, however, they were obliged to borrow some views and methods of proof from Israel, for religion as such is opposed to philosophy. Still the true nature of God was unknown to them. Then came the Arabs, who imitated the Christians in adopting a belief different from Judaism, at the same time borrowing views from the Bible. These are the *Mu'tazila* and the *Ashariya*. Later when on account of the exile differences arose among the Jews, there were formed the two parties of the Karaites and the Rabbanites. The Karaites followed the Mu'tazila, and so did some of the Rabbanites, because their views coincided with those of the Bible, from which they were borrowed. The views of the philosophers as being opposed to the Bible they naturally rejected. Nevertheless some Rabbanites adopted the views of the philosophers, though believing in the Bible. This is a mistake, for even the Christians rejected the views of the philosophers.[362]

Here we see clearly the difference in general attitude between Aaron ben Elijah and Maimonides. The latter has no use whatsoever for the Mu'tazila. He realizes the immeasurable superiority of the Aristotelians (this is the meaning of the word philosophers in mediæval Jewish and Arabic literature). His task is therefore to harmonize the Bible with Aristotelian doctrine wherever possible. Aaron ben Elijah is still, in the fourteenth century, a follower of the Kalam, and believes the Mu'tazila are closer to Scripture than Aristotle. He is two centuries behind Maimonides philosophically, and yet he has the truer insight because less debauched by Aristotelian learning.

As was said before, Aaron ben Elijah follows a more logical arrangement in the disposition of his work than Maimonides. In reality it is the old arrangement of the Kalamistic works (cf. p. 24). The purpose of all Jewish investigators, he says, is the same, namely, to prove the existence and nature of God, but there is a difference among them in the method of proving God's existence. Some base their proofs on the assumption of the creation of the world, others on that of the world's eternity. The Mutakallimun follow the former method, the philosophers, the latter. Their respective views of the origin of the world are determined by their opinions concerning the principles of existence and the existent, that is, the fundamental principles of physics and metaphysics. Accordingly Aaron ben Elijah finds it necessary to give a preliminary account of the Kalamistic as well as the philosophic theories, as Maimonides did before him (p. 249 ff.). It is not necessary for us to reproduce here his sketch of the philosophical views, as we know them sufficiently from our studies of Ibn Daud and Maimonides. But it will be of value to refer to his account of the Kalamistic principles, though we have already discussed them in the introduction (p. xxi) and in our study of Maimonides (p. 249 ff.). This is due principally to the fact that Aaron ben Elijah endeavors to defend the Mutakallimun against Maimonides's charge that they were influenced by preconceived notions and allowed their religious views to dictate to them their interpretation of nature, instead of letting the latter speak for itself. Thus Maimonides specifically accuses them of having adopted the atomic theory of the pre-Aristotelian philosophers not because they were really and independently convinced of its scientific truth—how could that be since Aristotle proved it impossible?—but because on this theory they could prove the creation of the world, which they must at all hazards maintain as a religious dogma fundamental in its nature, since upon it is based the proof of the existence of God.

Aaron ben Elijah denies this charge, maintaining the philosophical honesty of the Mutakallimun. Epicurus too, he says, believed in the atomic theory, though he regarded the world as eternal. Hence there is no necessary connection between atoms and creation.[363] The atomic theory is defensible on its own merits, and the motives of the Mutakallimun in adopting it are purely scientific, as follows: According to the Mutakallimun there are only body or substance and its accidents or qualities. This is the constitution of material objects. There are, however, two kinds of qualities or attributes, *viz.*, "characters," and accidents. Characters are such attributes as are essential to body and without which it cannot exist. Accidents may disappear, while body continues. Since, then, body may exist with or without accidents, there must be a cause which is responsible for the attachment of accidents to body when they are so attached. This cause we call "union." When a body is "united" with accidents it owes this to the existence of a certain something, a certain property, let us say, in it which we have called "union." Hence when the body is "separated" from accidents, when it is without accidents, it is because there is no "union." Further, every body possessed of magnitude or extension is divisible, hence it must have "union" to hold its parts together. But this "union" is not essential to all existents; for we have seen that its function is to unite accidents with body. And as accidents are separable while body may continue to exist without them, "union" disappears together with the accidents. Bodies without "union" are therefore possible and real. But we have just seen that all bodies possessing magnitude have "union." It follows therefore that if there are "union"-less bodies, they are without magnitude, and hence atoms. This is the proof of the atomic theory and it has nothing to do with the matter of the origin of the world.[364] As a matter of fact the Mutakallimun believe that the atoms were created *ex nihilo.* But the creation of the world can be proved whichever view we adopt concerning the nature of the existent, whether it be the atomic theory of the Mutakallimun or the principles of matter and form of the Aristotelians. The important principle at the basis of this proof is the well-known Kalamistic one that if an object cannot do without an attribute originating in time, the object itself has its origin in time. Now on either view of the constitution of the existent, body must have form or accidents respectively, and as the latter are constantly changing, body or matter has its origin in time, hence the world is not eternal.

Besides, not to speak of the inconclusive character of the philosophical arguments in favor of eternity and the positive arguments for creation (all or most of which we have already met in our previous studies, and need not therefore reproduce Aaron ben Elijah's version of them), the philosophers themselves without knowing it are led to contradict themselves in their very arguments from the assumption of eternity. The doctrine of creation follows as a consequence from their own presuppositions. Thus on the basis of eternity of motion they prove that the heavenly spheres are endowed with soul and intellect, and their motions are voluntary and due to conceptions which they endeavor to realize (*cf.* p. 267). This makes the sphere a composite object, containing the elements, *sphericity, soul, intellect.* Everything composite is a *possible* existent, because its existence depends upon the existence of its parts. What is a possible existent may also not exist. Moreover, that which is possible must at some time become actual. Hence the sphere must at some time have been non-existent, and it required an agent to bring it into being. We are thus led to contradict our hypothesis of eternity from which we started.[365]

Creation is thus established, and this is the best way to prove the existence, unity and incorporeality of God. Maimonides attempts to prove creation from the peculiarities of the heavenly motions, which cannot be well accounted for on the theory of natural causes. Adopting the latter in the main, he makes an exception in the case of the spherical motions because the philosophers cannot adequately explain them, and jumps to the conclusion that here the philosophical appeal to mechanical causation breaks down and we are dealing with teleology, with intelligent design and purpose on the part of an intelligent agent. This leads to belief in creation. But this argument of Maimonides is very weak and inconclusive. Ignorance of causes in a special case, due to the limitations of our reason, proves nothing. Mechanical causes may be the sole determinants of the heavenly motions even though the philosophers have not yet discovered what they are (*cf.* above, p. 270 ff.).[366]

Nor is Maimonides to be imitated, who bases his proof of the existence of God on the theory of eternity. The Bible is opposed to it. The Bible begins with creation as an indication that this is the basis of our knowledge of God's existence, revelation and providence. This is the method Abraham followed and this is what he meant when he swore by the "most high God, the creator of heaven and earth " (Gen. 14, 22). Abraham arrived at this belief through ratiocination and endeavored to convince others. The same thing is evident in the words of Isaiah (40, 26), "Lift up your eyes on high and see who created these." He was arguing with the people who believed in eternity, and proved to them the existence of God by showing that the world is created. All these indications in the Bible show that the doctrine of creation is capable of apodeictic proof.[367]

The reader will see that all this is directed against Maimonides, though he is not mentioned by name. Maimonides claimed against the Mutakallimun that it is not safe to base the existence of God upon the theory of creation, because the latter cannot be strictly demonstrated. And while he believed in it himself and gave reasons to show why it is more plausible than eternity, he admitted that others might think differently; and hence based his proofs of God's existence on the Aristotelian theory of eternity in order to be on the safe side. It is never too late to prove God's existence if the world is created. We must be sure of his existence, no matter what the fate of our cosmological theories might be. This did not appeal to the Karaite and Mutakallim, Aaron ben Elijah. His idea is that we must never for a moment doubt the creation of the world. To follow the procedure of Maimonides would have the tendency of making people believe that the world may be eternal after all, as happened in fact in the case of Gersonides. Aaron ben Elijah will not leave a way open to such a heresy.

In the doctrine of attributes Aaron ben Elijah likewise maintains

the views of the Mu'tazilite Karaites against the philosophers, and
especially against Maimonides.   The general problem is sufficiently
familiar to us by this time, and we need only present the salient points
in the controversy.   The question is whether there are any positive
attributes which may be applied to God as actually denoting his
essence—hence *positive essential* attributes.   Maimonides denied it,
the Karaites affirmed it.   The arguments for Maimonides's denial we
saw before (p. 262 f.).   And his conclusion is that the only attributes
that may be applied to God are the negative, and those positive ones
which do not denote any definite thing corresponding to them in God's
essence, but are derived from the effects of God's unitary and simple
being on the life of man and nature.   He is the author of these effects,
and we characterize him in the way in which we would characterize
a human being who would do similar things; but this must not be
done.

Aaron ben Elijah insists that there are positive essential attributes,
which are the following five: Omnipotent, Omniscient, Acting with
Will, Living, Existent.   He agrees with Maimonides that these essential attributes must be understood in a manner not to interfere with
God's simplicity and unity, but is satisfied that this can be done.   For
we must not conceive of them as additions to God's essence, nor as so
many distinct elements composing God's essence, but as representing
the multiplicity of powers issuing from him without detriment to his
unity.   We call them essential attributes, meaning that they are the
essence of God, but not that they are different from each other and
each makes up part of God's essence.   We do not know God's essence,
and these terms are simply transferred from our human experience,
and do not indicate that God's activity can be compared to ours in
any sense.

The five attributes above named are all identical with God's simple
essence.   "Living" denotes ability to perceive, hence is identical with
"Omniscient."   "Acting with will" likewise denotes just and proper
action, which in turn involves true insight.   Hence identity of will and
knowledge.   "Omnipotent" also in the case of an intellectual being
denotes the act of the intellect *par excellence*, which is knowledge.
And surely God's existence is not distinct from his essence, else his
existence would be caused, and he would not be the necessary existent

all agree him to be. It follows then that God is one, and his essence is nevertheless all these five attributes.

There are all the reasons in the world why we should apply attributes to God. The same reason as we have for applying names to anything else exists for giving names to God. In fact it would be correct to say that we should have more names for God than for anything else, since in other things we can avoid naming them by pointing to them, as they can be perceived by the senses. Not so God. We are forced to use words in talking about him. God has given himself names in the Bible, hence we may do the same.

Maimonides and his school endeavor to obviate the criticisms of the philosophers, who are opposed to all attributes, by excluding all but negative terms. But this does not help the matter in the least. A negative attribute is in reality no different from a positive, and in the end leads to a positive. Thus if we say "not mineral," "not plant," we clearly say "animal." The advocates of negative attributes answer this criticism by saying that they understand pure negation without any positive implications, just as when we say a stone is "not seeing," we do not imply that it is blind. But this cannot be, for when they say God is "not ignorant," they do not mean that he is not "knowing" either, for they insist that he is power and knowledge and life, and so on. This being the case, it is much more proper to use positive attributes, seeing that the Prophets do so. When they say that the Prophets meant only to exclude the negative; that by saying, "Able," "Knowing," they meant to exclude "weak" "ignorant," they *ipso facto* admit that by excluding the latter we posit the former.

The arguments against positive essential attributes we can easily answer. By saying that certain attributes are essential we do not claim to know God's essence. All we know is God's existence, which we learn from his effects, and according to these same effects we characterize God's existence by means of attributes of which also we know only the existence, not the essence. For we do not mean to indicate that these terms denote the same thing in God as they denote in us. They are homonyms, since in God they denote essence, whereas in us they are accidents. The plurality of attributes does not argue plurality in God, for one essence may perform a great many acts, and hence we may characterize the essence in accordance with those acts.

The error of composition arises only if we suppose that the various acts point to various elements in their author. Of the various kinds of terms those only are applicable to God which denote pure essence or substance like knowledge, power; and those denoting activity like creating, doing, and so on.[368]

In reference to the will of God Aaron ben Elijah refuses to agree with the peculiar view of the Mutakallimun; but unlike Maimonides, who can afford to ignore their discussions entirely and dismiss their fanciful notion with a word ("Guide," I. 75, proof 3), Aaron ben Elijah takes up the discussion seriously. The Mutakallimun (or the Asbariya, according to Aaron ben Elijah) were in dread of anything that might lend some semblance to eternity of the world. Hence they argued, If the will of God is identical with his essence like the other essential attributes, it follows that as his essence is eternal and unchangeable so is his will. And if we grant this, then the objects of his will too must be eternal and unchangeable, and we have the much abhorred doctrine of the eternity of the world. To avoid this objectionable conclusion they conceived of God's voluntary acts as due to an external will. But this external will also offered diffi- ficulties. It cannot be a power or quality residing in God as its sub- ject, for God is not a material substance bearing accidents. It can- not be a quality inherent in another subject, for then it would not be God's will at all; it would be the will of this other being, and God's acts would be determined by someone else. They were thus forced to assume a subject-less will newly created with every act of God. This notion Aaron ben Elijah rejects on the ground that a subject-less will is an impossibility. An accident must have a subject, and will im- plies life as its subject. Besides, the relation between God and this subject-less accident, will, would be the cause of much logical difficulty. Aaron ben Elijah therefore accepts the ordinary sane view that the will of God is identical with his essence; that God wills through his own essence. And he does not fear that this will lead to eternity of the world. He identifies God's will with his wisdom, and God's wisdom with right action. As we do not know the essence of God's wisdom, so we do not know how it is that it prompts him to realize his will at one time and not at another, though his will is always the same.[369]

Aaron ben Elijah also follows his party in attributing to God sense perception, not, to be sure, the same kind of perception as we have, acquired by means of corporeal organs; for this is impossible in God for many reasons. God is not corporeal, and he cannot be affected or changed by a corporeal stimulus. But it is clear beyond a doubt that nothing can be more absurd than to suppose that the creator of the sense organs does not understand the purpose which they serve and the objects which they perceive. What we mean then is that the objects which we perceive with our senses God also perceives, though in an incorporeal manner. Hence it does not follow that there is any change in God due to the external object he perceives, nor that the multiplicity of objects involves plurality in God; for even our power of perception is one, though it perceives many things and opposite. We conclude then that God has perception as well as intelligence, but they are not two distinct powers in him. It is the object perceived that determines the power percipient. Hence one and the same power may be called perception when we are dealing with a sensible object, and intelligence when it has an intelligible as its object.[370]

In his discussion of the nature of evil we once more are brought in contact with Kalamistic views recalling the old Karaite works of the eleventh century (*cf.* pp. 52, 57). Thus the notion that good and bad are adjectives applied to acts not in view of their inherent character, which is *per se* neither good nor bad, but solely to indicate that they have been commanded or forbidden; the idea that only the dependent subject can do wrong, but not the master, since his will is the source of all right and wrong—these views are frequently discussed in the Mu'tazilite works of Arabs and Karaites. The Rabbanites scarcely ever mention them. Aaron ben Elijah enumerates six views on the nature of evil, with all of which except the last he disagrees. The opinion named above that an act is made good or bad by being commanded or prohibited, he refutes as follows: Such a view removes the very foundation of good and bad. For if the person in authority chooses to reverse his order, the good becomes bad, and the bad good, and the same thing is then good and bad, which is absurd. Besides, if there are two authorities giving opposite orders, the same act is good and bad at the same time. To say that God's command alone determines the character of an act is incorrect, because as long as commanding and prohibiting as such determine the goodness or badness of an act, the person issuing the command is immaterial. We do say quite generally that an act which God commands is good, and one which he prohibits is bad; but we mean by this merely that the command or prohibition is an indication to us, who are ignorant of the true nature of acts.

Again, on this theory of the value of acts, what will you do with such an act as the investigation of the existence and nature of God? Surely such an important matter cannot be indifferent. It must be good or bad. And yet we cannot apply to it the above test of command and prohibition, for this test implies the existence of God, which the act endeavors to prove. It follows therefore that the value of an act is inherent in it and not determined and created by command and prohibition.

Aaron ben Elijah is similarly dissatisfied with another view, which regards evil as a negation. We have heard this opinion before and we know that Maimonides adopted it (p. 288). Its motive as we know is to remove from God the responsibility for evil. If evil is nothing positive it is not caused by the activity of an agent. All essential activity is good, and all the acts of God are good. Evil consists in the absence of good; it is due to matter, and does not come from God. Aaron ben Elijah objects properly that as good is a positive act, a doing of something positive, so is evil, even on the theory of its negative character, a removal of something positive, hence a positive act. Besides, granting all that the opponent claims, the argument should work both ways, and if God is not held responsible for the evil in the world because it is mere privation, why should man be held responsible for doing evil, *i. e.*, for removing the positive? He clinches his argument by quoting Isaiah (5, 20), "Woe unto those who say of evil it is good, and of good it is evil . . . that put bitter for sweet, and sweet for bitter." Good and evil are placed parallel with sweet and bitter, which are both positive. Hence the Bible is opposed to the negative conception of evil.

His own view is that good and evil are qualities pertaining to an act by reason of its own nature, but these are not absolute conceptions like true and false. The good and the bad are conventional constructs, and the value of an act is relative to the end or purpose it serves. The purpose of human convention in regarding certain acts as good and others as bad is the protection of the human race. An act which conduces to human welfare is good, one that militates against it is bad. Still there are instances in which an act generally regarded as bad may assume a different character when in the given instance it serves a good purpose, as for example when pain is inflicted to obviate more serious danger. The surgeon, who amputates a leg to save the patient's life, does good, not evil. The judge, who punishes the criminal with imprisonment or death for the protection of society and to realize justice, does good, not evil. In this way we must explain the evil which God brings upon man. God cannot be the cause of evil. For evil in man is due to want or ignorance. Neither is found in God, hence he has no motive to do wrong. All the evil of which we complain is only apparent. In reality it is good, because it is either brought upon us to prevent still greater evils, or it is in the nature of just punishment for wrongdoing. In either case it is a good.[371]

Aaron ben Elijah's discussion of Providence follows closely the plan of the corresponding arguments in Maimonides. The problem is treated by both in connection with God's knowledge, and both maintain that the real motive of those who denied God's knowledge of particulars is their observation of apparent injustice in the happenings of this world (*cf.* above, p. 289). Both again preface their own views of the question of Providence by a preliminary statement of the various opinions held by other sects. Here too the two accounts are in the main similar, except that Aaron ben Elijah is somewhat more detailed and names a few sects not mentioned by Maimonides, among them being the Manicheans and the followers of the Syrian Gnostic Bardesanes. In their own views, however, Aaron ben Elijah and Maimonides differ; the latter approaching the view of Aristotle, the former that of the Mu'tazila.

Maimonides as we know (p. 292) denies special providence for the individuals of the sublunar world with the exception of man. In the case of the lower animals, the species alone are protected by divine providence, hence they will continue forever, whereas the individual animals are subject to chance. Man, as a rational animal, is an exception. He is a free and responsible agent, hence he is under divine guidance and is rewarded and punished for his conduct. The extent of the divine care depends upon the degree to which the individual develops his reason, actualizing his potential intellect.

Aaron ben Elijah argues that this view is erroneous, for it is not proper to make a distinction between God's knowledge and his providence. If it would argue imperfection in God not to *know* certain things, the same objection applies to limiting his providence, and the two should be coextensive. To say that God's providence extends to superior and important things and ignores the inferior is to make God guilty of injustice. Aaron ben Elijah believes therefore that Providence extends to all individuals, including animals. And he quotes the Bible in his support, "The Lord is good to all, and his mercies are over all his works," (Ps. 145, 9), and, "Thou shalt not plough with an ox and an ass together " (Deut. 22, 10). Maimonides, he says, was led to his opinion by his idea that death and suffering always involve sin; and not being able to apply this dictum to the suffering of animals that are slaughtered, he removed Providence from their individuals entirely. When the Bible orders us to consider the feelings of the animal, he says the object is to train our own faculties in mercy, and prevent the formation of habits of cruelty, not for the sake of the animal. But he cannot remove all difficulties in this way. What will he do with the case of a person born crippled, and the sufferings of little children? The idea that death and suffering in all cases involve sin must be given up. Maimonides is also wrong when he says that reward is purely intellectual and is dependent upon the development of the "acquired intellect." It would follow from this that right conduct as such is not rewarded; that it serves merely as a help to realizing the acquired intellect. All this is opposed to Biblical teaching.[372]

The prosperity of the wicked and the adversity of the righteous Aaron ben Elijah endeavors to explain as follows. The prosperity of the wicked may be due to former good deeds; or by way of punishment, that he may continue in his evil deeds and be punished more severely. It may be in order that he may use the good fortune he has in whatever way he pleases, for good or ill. Finally his good fortune may be given him as a matter of grace, like his creation. Correspondingly we may explain the adversity of the righteous in a similar manner. It may be due to former sins. If he has no sins, his sufferings may be intended to test him in order to add to his reward.

If he dies without having enjoyed life, he will be rewarded in the next world. The pleasures of this world must not be considered. For since they are given as a matter of grace, they may come or not without involving any injustice. When a man has both good deeds and sins, he may be rewarded for his good deeds and punished for his bad, or he may be paid according to the element which predominates. Those who are born crippled and the sufferings of children will be rewarded later. In reference to the slaughter of animals, Aaron ben Elijah does not agree with the Mu'tazila that the animals will be recompensed for their undeserved sufferings. There is no immortal part in animals, hence no reward after death. He can assign no reason for their sufferings except that men need them for food, but he sees nothing wrong in taking an animal's life for food, for as the life of animals was given to them as a matter of grace, there is no wrong in taking it away. However, to inflict pain in a way different from the manner permitted by God is wrong.[373]

Aaron ben Elijah lays great stress upon what he considers an important difference of opinion between the Rabbanites and the Karaites concerning the nature and purpose of divine punishment. The Rabbanites according to him insist that "there is no death without sin, nor suffering without guilt," whereas the Karaites admit that some of the sufferings of the righteous are not in the nature of punishment at all, but are what are known as "chastisements of love." Their purpose is to increase the man's reward later in the future world, and at the same time they have a pedagogical value in themselves in strengthening the person spiritually. Accordingly Aaron ben Elijah, who in the main follows the opinions of the Karaites, differs with the Rabbanites and particularly Maimonides in the interpretation of the "trials" of Adam, Abraham, Job.

So far as Job is concerned, we know the opinions of Maimonides on the subject. In his "Guide of the Perplexed" he interprets the book of Job in connection with his discussion of Providence (cf. above, p. 304). In the general nature of suffering the idea of "chastisement of love" is quite familiar to the Rabbis, though Maimonides does not care to insist on it, claiming that there is no support for it in the Bible. The idea of "trial" according to him is neither that God may know what he did not know before; nor is it to make a man suffer

that he may be rewarded later. The purpose of trial is that mankind
may know whatever it is desired to teach them in a given case. In
the trial of Abraham when he was told to sacrifice Isaac, there was a
two-fold reason; first, that all may know to what extent the love of
God may go in a pious man; and second to show that a prophet is
convinced of the reality of his visions as an ordinary person is of the
data of his senses.[374]

The book of Job is to Maimonides a treatise on Providence, and
the five characters in the drama represent the various opinions on
the nature of Providence as they were held by different schools of
philosophy and theology in Maimonides's day. Job has the Aristotelian view that God cares nothing for man. Eliphaz represents the
correct Jewish view that everything is reward or punishment for
merit and demerit. Bildad maintains the Mu'tazilite opinion that
many misfortunes are for the purpose of increasing reward in the
world to come. Zophar stands for the view of the Ashariya that
all is to be explained by reference to the will of God, and no questions
should be asked. Elihu finally insists that the individual man is the
object of the divine care, but that we must not compare God's providence with our own interest in, and care for things; that there is no
relation at all between them except in name (cf. above, p. 304). The
Rabbis, who do not make of Job a philosopher, naturally do not understand the matter as Maimonides does, but they nevertheless agree
with him that Job deserved the punishment he received. The Karaites
on the other hand classed Job's sufferings with "chastisements of love,"
which would mean that Job was a perfect man and did not deserve
any punishment. The sole motive for inflicting pain and tribulation
upon him was to reward him the more later.

Aaron ben Elijah agrees in the main with his Karaite predecessors
that Job was not punished for any fault he had committed. He does
not see in the arguments of Job's friends any difference of opinion
on the general question of Providence, and Job was not an Aristotelian.
Unlike Aristotle, he did believe in God's care for man, as is evident
from such statements as (Job 10, 10), "Behold like milk didst thou
pour me out, and like cheese didst thou curdle me." The Karaites, he
holds, are correct in their main contention that Job's sufferings were
not in the nature of punishment for previous guilt and wrongdoing,

but they are mistaken in supposing that Job was altogether right in his conception of the meaning and reason of his sufferings; that they had no other purpose except to increase his reward in the future. Aaron ben Elijah then explains his own view of "trial."

Man, he says, is composed of body and soul, and must therefore endeavor to gain this world and the next. If he is punished for guilt or offence, the punishment corresponds to the offence. Corporeal guilt is followed by corporeal punishment, spiritual guilt by spiritual punishment. Adam offended spiritually and was punished spiritually by being driven from the Garden of Eden as will be explained later. Abraham endeavored to do justice to both the constituent parts of his being; and hence God in his kindness, wishing to strengthen Abraham spiritually, gave him the opportunity in the trial of Isaac. At the same time the physical suffering was compensated by the promise to Abraham of the continuity of Isaac's descendants. Job's sufferings were of the same kind, except that they came to him without his knowledge and without his being told their purpose. And at first he thought they were in order to give him future reward, but without any use in themselves. Later he discovered that they benefited him directly by increasing his spiritual strength.[375]

Aaron ben Elijah differs also from Maimonides in reference to the purpose of the world. Maimonides maintains that while there is sense in inquiring for the purpose of the parts of the world, the question of the ultimate purpose of the world as a whole is meaningless. The purpose of a given event or law of nature lies in its relation to the other events and laws, hence there is a relative purpose in particular things; thus, given the existence of animals they must have food, sense perception, and so on. But if we ask why the universe as a whole, the only answer that can be given is God's wisdom, which we do not understand. In particular Maimonides will not admit that the world is for the sake of man, as this view clashes with experience and makes it impossible to explain a great many phenomena in nature, which are distinctly of no benefit to man and take no cognizance of his interests.[376] Aaron ben Elijah agrees with Maimonides that God's wisdom rather than his arbitrary will, as the Ashariya maintain, must be appealed to in answering the question of the purpose of the world. But he is inclined to regard man as the purpose of the lower world, admitting that we cannot know the purpose of the higher worlds of the spheres and Intelligences, as they transcend the powers of our comprehension.[377]

We can pass over Aaron ben Elijah's discussion of prophecy very briefly because there is no new attitude or contribution in his views. Without saying it, he reluctantly perhaps, leans upon Maimonides, and with apparent variations in form really adopts the classification of the "Guide" (p. 277). He gives no psychological explanation of prophecy because he disagrees with the philosophers, to whom prophecy is a purely natural gift which cannot fail to manifest itself when the requisite conditions are there, namely, perfection in intellect and imagination. In fact when he gives the different views on the nature of prophecy, he refuses to identify what seems to stand in his book for the view of Maimonides (the fourth view) with that of the followers of the Mosaic law. Whereas Maimonides following the philosophers insists on the two important elements in prophecy, namely, intellect and imagination, adding thereto also moral perfection, Aaron ben Elijah in giving the opinion of those who follow the law of Moses, says nothing of the imagination. He insists only on perfection in intellect and in ethical character. This difference is, however, only apparent; and further on he refers to the imagination as an important element, which determines, in its relation to the reason, the character of a man as a prophet or a mere statesman or philosopher —all in the manner of Maimonides.

His idea of the purpose of prophecy he develops, as it seems, with an eye to the criticism of the Brahmins of India, whom he quotes as denying prophecy, though admitting Providence, on the ground that it can serve no purpose. The reason alone, they say, is sufficient to decide what is right and what is wrong. Accordingly Aaron ben Elijah meets their objection as follows: It is true that man might have gotten along without prophecy through the laws which his own reason established for right and wrong, good and evil. Those who followed these rational laws would have attained long life, and the others would have perished. But a good man living in a bad environment would have been involved in the downfall of the majority, which would not be just. Hence it was necessary that God should warn the man, that he might save himself. This is the first beginning of prophecy. Witness Noah and Lot. Abraham was a great advance on his predecessors. He endeavored to follow God's will in respect to both body and soul. Hence God saved him from the danger to which he was exposed in Ur of the Chaldees, and wanted to benefit his descendants also that they should perfect their bodies and their souls. This is impossible for a whole nation without special laws to guide them. This is particularly true of the "traditional" laws (ceremonial), which are not in themselves good or bad, but are disciplinary in their nature.

A prophet must have both intellectual and ethical perfection. For he must understand the nature of God in order to communicate his will; and this cannot be had without previous ethical perfection. Hence the twofold requirement. This is the reason, he says, why we do not believe in the religions of Jesus and Mohammed, because they were not possessed of intellectual perfection. And besides they tend to the extinction of the human species by reason of their monastic and celibate ideal. They were misled by the asceticism of the prophets, who meant it merely as a protest against the material self-indulgence of the time, and called attention to the higher life. But those people in their endeavor to imitate the prophets mistook the means for the end, with the result that they missed both, perfection of soul as well as of body, and merely mortified the flesh, thinking it the will of God. Hence, Aaron ben Elijah continues, we shall never accept a religion which does not preach the maintenance of this world as well as of the next. Not even miracles can authenticate a religion which preaches monasticism and celibacy.

Moses was superior to the other prophets. All the others received their messages in a vision or a dream, Moses had his inspiration while awake. The others were inspired through the medium of an angel, *i. e.*, through the imagination, hence their language abounds in allegories and parables. Moses did not use the imagination, hence the plain character of his speech. The others were overcome by the vision and physically exhausted, as we read in Daniel (10, 17), "There remained no strength in me, and no breath was left in me." Moses was free from this weakness—"And the Lord spoke unto Moses face to face, as a man speaketh unto his neighbor" (Exod. 33, 11). The others required preparation, Moses did not. Moses's testimony, too, was stronger than that of all the rest. His authority in the end was made

plain to all the people directly and openly, so that there remained not
a shred of a doubt. This is why we accept his law and no other, because none is so well authenticated. The Law cannot change without
implying that the standard of perfection has changed, or the world has
changed, or God's knowledge has changed. All this is impossible.
The Law says besides, "Thou shalt not add thereto, and thou shalt
not diminish therefrom" (Deut. 13, 1). Therefore, concludes Aaron
ben Elijah the Karaite, we do not believe in the oral or traditional law
because of the additions to, and subtractions from, the written law
which it contains.[378]

Aaron ben Elijah agrees with Maimonides that all the commandments of the Bible, including the ceremonial laws, have a purpose and
are not due to the arbitrary will of God. The ceremonial laws are
for the sake of the rational, serving a pedagogical and disciplinary
purpose, and the Law as a whole is for the purpose of teaching the
truth and inculcating the good. He goes further than Maimonides
in vindicating the rational and ethical purpose of all the details of the
various laws, and not merely of the several commandments as a whole
(cf. above, p. 294).[379]

A problem that occupied the minds of the Mutakallimun, Arabs
as well as Karaites, but which Maimonides does not discuss, is the
purpose of God's giving commandments to those who he knew would
remain unbelievers, and refuse to obey. That God's knowledge and
man's freedom co-exist and neither destroys the other, has already
been shown.[380] If then God knows, as we must assume, that a given
person will refuse to obey the commandments, what is the use of
giving them to him? And granting that for some reason unknown to
us they have been given, is it just to punish him for disobedience when
the latter might have been spared by not giving the man in question
any commandments?

Aaron ben Elijah answers these questions by citing the following
parallel. A man prepares a meal for two guests and one does not come.
The absence of the guest does not make the preparation improper, for
the character of the act does not depend upon the choice of the guest
to do or not to do the desire of the host. The invitation was proper
because the host meant the guest's benefit. To be sure, the case is not
quite parallel, and to make it so we must assume that the host expects

that the guest will not come. His intention being good, the invitation is proper. In our problem knowledge takes the place of expectation. God does not merely expect, he knows that the man will not obey. But as God's desire is to benefit mankind and arouse them to higher things, the command is proper, no matter what the person chooses to do.

To punish the man for disobedience is not unjust because God intended to benefit him by the command. If he disobeyed, that is his lookout. If the benefit could have been had without the command, then the punishment would be unjust, but not otherwise.

If only good men were commanded and the rest ignored, the danger would be that the former being thereby assured of reward, might be tempted to do wrong; and the others in despair might be worse than they would be under ordinary circumstances. God saw that man has evil tendencies, and needs warning and guidance from without. And just as he gave men understanding and ability to believe though he knew that a given person would not avail himself thereof, so he gave all men commandments, though he knew that some would not obey.[381]

The rest of the book is devoted to such questions as reward and punishment after death, immortality of the soul, the problem of the soul's pre-existence, the nature of the future life, repentance—questions which Maimonides left untouched in the " Guide " on the ground that whatever religion and tradition may say about them, they are not strictly speaking scientific questions, and are not susceptible to philosophical demonstration.

Aaron ben Elijah proves that there must be reward and punishment after death. For as man is composed of body and soul, there must be reward for each according as man endeavors to maintain and perfect them. Thus if a man cares for his body alone, he will be rewarded in his body, *i. e.*, in this world. The other man who looks out for both body and soul must have the same reward in this world as the other, since their physical efforts were similar. At the same time he must have something over and above the other in the nature of compensation for his soul, and this must be in the next world.

The prosperity of the wicked and the misery of the righteous are also to be explained in part, as we have seen (p. 376), by reference to their respective destinies in the next world, where the inequalities of this world will be adjusted.

Finally, material reward cannot be the consequence of intellectual and spiritual merit; it would mean doing the greater for the sake of the smaller. And besides the soul is not benefited by physical goods and pleasures, and would remain without reward. Hence there must be another kind of reward after death. In order to deserve such reward the soul must become wise. At the same time the common people, who observe the ceremonial commandments, are not excluded from a share in the world to come, because the purpose of these laws is also intellectual and spiritual, as we said before (p. 382), and hence their observance makes the soul wise, and gives it immortality. This last comment is clearly directed against the extreme intellectualism of Maimonides and Gersonides, according to whom rational activity alone confers immortality (p. 339).[382]

The considerations just adduced imply the immortality of the soul, to which they lend indirect proof. But Aaron ben Elijah endeavors besides to furnish direct proof of the soul's continuance after the death of the body. And the first thing he does is to disarm the criticism of the philosophers, who deny immortality on the ground that the soul being the form of the body, it must like other material forms cease with the dissolution of the things of which they are the forms. He answers this by showing that the soul as the cause of knowledge and wisdom—immaterial faculties—is itself immaterial. Being also the cause of the body's motion, it is not itself subject to motion, hence not to time, and therefore not destructible like a natural form. Besides the composition of body and soul is different from that of matter and form in the ordinary sense. For in the former case each of the constituent parts is already a composite of matter and form. The body has both matter and form, and the soul has likewise. For the acquired intellect is the form of the soul, which is the matter. Other proofs are as follows: The rational soul performs its functions without help from the body, hence it is independent in its existence. The proof of the last statement is that the power of the rational soul is not limited, and does not become weary, as a corporeal power does. Hence it can exist without the body. Again, as the corporeal powers grow stronger, the intellectual powers grow weaker, and *vice versa* as the corporeal powers grow weaker in old age, the intellect grows stronger. Hence the soul is independent of the body, and when the physical powers cease entirely in death, the intellect is at its height.[383]

The question of the soul's pre-existence before coming in contact with the body, Aaron ben Elijah answers in the affirmative, though his arguments in favor of the opposite view are stronger. His sole argument in favor of its pre-existence is that the soul, being a self-subsisting substance and not an accident, is not dependent upon the body, and must have existed before the body. The consequence which some have drawn from this supposition combined with the soul's immortality, namely, that the soul is eternal, he refuses to adopt. The soul existed before the body, but like all things which are not God it was created in time.

Though we have thus seen that the soul existed before the body, it is mistaken to suppose that it was completely developed. For though the gradual progress in knowledge and understanding as the individual matures proves nothing for the soul's original imperfection, as we may account for this progress by the gradual adaptation of the physical elements to the functions of the soul, there is a more valid objection. If the soul was perfectly developed before entering the body, all souls should be alike when they leave it, which is not the case. We come to the conclusion therefore that the soul does acquire knowledge while in contact with the body. The human soul is a unit, and from its connection with the body arise the various powers, such as growth, life, reason. When the soul is separated from the body, those powers which functioned with the aid of the body perish; the others remain.[384]

In the matter of eschatology Aaron ben Elijah gives a number of views without declaring himself definitely for any of them. The main difference among the three points of view quoted concerns the possibility of the resurrection of the body, and the meaning of the terms "revival of the dead" ("Tehiyat ha-metim") and "the world to come" ("Olam ha-ba"). Aaron ben Elijah seems to incline to the first, in favor of resurrection.

We must endeavor, he says, to get some notion of final reward and punishment. For without any idea of its nature a man's hope or fear is taken away from him, and he has no motive for right conduct. To be sure it is not possible to get a clear understanding of the matter, but some idea we must have. The first view which he seems to favor is that *revival of the dead* and *world to come* are the same thing; that the end of man is the resurrection of the body and its reunion with the soul. This is the future life, and this is meant by reward and punishment. There is Biblical support for this view in such expressions as, "Thy dead shall live, thy dead bodies shall arise" (Isa. 26, 19). "The Lord killeth, and maketh alive; he bringeth down to the grave and bringeth up" (1 Sam. 2, 6). There is nothing to object in this, he says, for the same God who made man of the dust can revive him after death. Besides, there seems to be a logical propriety in bringing soul and body together for reward and punishment just as they were during conduct in life. When the soul is once reunited with the body in the resurrection, it is never separated again. The expression "*garden* of Eden" for paradise is a figure of speech for eternal life free from pain.

The second opinion is expressed by those who do not believe in bodily resurrection. The end of man according to these is the return of the soul to the world of souls. This is the meaning of "world to come"; and "revival of the dead" means the same thing. For it is not possible that the soul should be reunited with the body, which is temporary in its nature and subject to dissolution. Besides, the body has organs, such as those of food and reproduction, which would be useless in the future life. The advocates of this theory also believe in transmigration of souls as a punishment. Aaron ben Elijah rejects metempsychosis on the ground that there is some relation between a soul and its body, and not every body can receive every soul.

Aaron ben Elijah also quotes without comment the classification, already familiar to us (p. 119), of human souls into (1) dead, (2) alive, (3) healthy, and (4) sick. Death denotes evil deeds; life, good deeds; health, intellectual knowledge; disease, ignorance. This classification is applied in determining the destiny of the soul after death. If one is alive and healthy, *i. e.*, has knowledge and good deeds, he has a share in the world to come. If he is healthy and dead (knowledge + evil deeds), the soul is kept in an intermediate world forever. If he is alive and sick (good deeds + ignorance), the soul rises to the upper air, whence it returns again and again to the body until it acquires wisdom to be able to rise to the world of angels. If he is dead and sick (evil deeds + ignorance), the soul dies like an animal.

Finally, the third opinion is a combination of resurrection and "future world." Seeing that some of the functions of the soul are performed with the help of the body, while others are not, the advocates of this view maintain that the soul will be rewarded in both conditions—with the body, in resurrection, without the body, in the world to come.

If a man has merits and demerits, his good and evil deeds are balanced against each other, and the surplus determines his reward on punishment according to its nature.[385]

CHAPTER XVII

The influence of Aristotle on Jewish thought, which began as early as Saadia and grew in intensity as the Aristotelian writings became better known, reached its high water mark in Ibn Daud, Maimonides and Gersonides. To Maimonides Aristotle was the indisputable authority for all matters pertaining to sublunar existence, but he reserved the right to differ with the Stagirite when the question concerned the heavenly spheres and the influences derived from them. Hence he denied the eternity of motion and the fundamental principle at the basis of this Aristotelian idea, that necessity rules all natural phenomena. In his doctrine of creation in time, Maimonides endeavored to defend God's personality and voluntary and purposeful activity. For the same reason he defended the institution of miracles. Gersonides went further in his rationalistic attitude, carried the Aristotelian principles to their inevitable conclusions, and did not shrink from adopting to all intents and purposes the eternity of the world (strictly speaking the eternity of matter), and the limitation of God's knowledge to universals. Aristotle's authority was now supreme, and the Bible had to yield to Aristotelian interpretations, as we have seen abundantly. Maimonides and Gersonides were the great peaks that stood out above the rest; but there was any number of lesser lights, some who wrote books and still more who did not write, taking the great men as their models and looking at Jewish literature and belief through Aristotelian spectacles. Intellectualism is the term that best describes this attitude. It had its basis in psychology, and from there succeeded in establishing itself as the ruling principle in ethics and metaphysics. As reason and intellect is the distinguishing trait of man—the part of man which raises him above the beast—and as the soul is the form of the living body, its essence and actuating principle, it was argued that the most important part of man is his rational soul or intellect, and immortality was made dependent upon theoretical ideas. Speculative study made the soul; and an intellect thus constituted was immortal, for it was immaterial. The heavenly world, consisting of the separate Intelligences and culminating in God, was also in its essence reason and intellect. Hence thought and knowledge formed the essence of the universe. By thought is man saved, and through thought is he united with the Most High. All else that is not pure thought acquires what value it has from the relation it bears to thought. In this way were judged those divisions of Judaism that concerned ceremony and ethical practice. Their value consisted in their function of promoting the ends of the reason.

Judah Halevi, influenced by Al Gazali, had already before Maimonides protested against this intellectualistic attitude in the name of a truer though more naïve understanding of the Bible and Jewish history. But Judah Halevi's nationalism and the expression of his poetical and religious feelings and ideas could not vie with the dominating personality of Maimonides, whose rationalistic and intellectualistic attitude swept everything before it and became the dominant mode of thinking for his own and succeeding ages. It remained for Hasdai Crescas (born in Barcelona, in 1340), who flourished in Christian Spain two centuries after Maimonides and over a half century after Gersonides, to take up the cudgels again in behalf of a truer Judaism, a Judaism independent of Aristotle, and one that is based more upon the spiritual and emotional sides of man and less upon the purely intellectual, theoretical and speculative. Himself devoid of the literary power and poetic feeling of Judah Halevi, Crescas had this in common with the mediæval national poet that he resented the domination of Jewish belief and thought by the alien Greek speculation. In a style free from rhetoric, and characterized rather by a severe brevity and precision, he undertakes to undermine the Aristotelian position by using the Stagirite's own weapons, logical analysis and proof. His chief work is the "Or Adonai," Light of the Lord.[386]

Agreeing with all other Jewish writers that the existence of God is the basis of Judaism, he sees in this very fact a reason why this principle cannot be regarded as one of the six hundred and thirteen commandments. For a commandment implies the existence of one who commands. Hence to regard the belief in the existence of God as a commandment implies the very thing which the commandment expresses. The existence of God therefore as the basis of all commandments cannot itself be a commandment. Besides only those things can form the objects of a command which can be controlled by the will. But a matter of belief like the existence of God is not subject to will, it is a matter of fact and of proof.[387]

Maimonides, as we know, based his proofs of the existence, unity and incorporeality of God upon twenty-six philosophical propositions taken from the works of Aristotle and his Arabian interpreters. As he was not writing a book on general philosophy, Maimonides simply enumerates twenty-five propositions, which he accepts as proved by Aristotle and his followers. To these he adds provisionally another proposition, number twenty-six, concerning the eternity of motion, upon which he bases his proof of the existence of God in order to be safe from all criticism. In the sequel he discusses this last proposition and shows that unlike the other twenty-five, it is not susceptible of rigid demonstration, and the arguments in favor of the origin of motion and the world in time are more plausible.

Crescas goes further than Maimonides, and controverts most of the other propositions as well, maintaining in particular against Aristotle and Maimonides that an infinite magnitude *is* possible and exists actually; that there *is* an infinite fullness or void outside of this world, and hence there *may* be many worlds, and it need not follow that the elements would pour in from one world into the next, so that all earth should be together in the centre, all fire together in the outer circumference, and the intermediate elements, air and water, between these two. The elements may stay in their respective worlds in the places assigned to them. It will not be worth our while to wade through all the technical and hair-splitting discussions of these points. The results will be sufficient for our purpose.

The proof of the existence of an unmoved mover in Aristotle and Maimonides is based upon the impossibility of a regress to infinity. If Hasdai Crescas admits the infinite, the Aristotelian proof fails. Similarly God's unity in Maimonides is among other things based upon the finiteness of the world and its unity. If infinite space is possible outside of this world, and there may be many worlds, this proof fails for God's unity. So Crescas takes up in detail all the Maimonidean proofs of the existence, unity and incorporeality of God and points out that they are not valid because in the first place they are based upon premises which Crescas has refuted, and secondly were the premises granted Maimonides's results do not follow from them.[388] It remains then for Crescas to give his own views on this problem which, he says, the philosophers are unable to solve satisfactorily, and the Bible alone is to be relied upon. At the same time he does give a logical proof which in reality is not different from one of the proofs given by Maimonides himself. It is based upon the distinction insisted upon by Alfarabi and Avicenna between the "possible existent" and the "necessary existent." Whatever is an effect of a cause is in itself merely possible, and owes the necessity of its existence to its cause. Now, argues Crescas, whether the number of causes and effects is finite or infinite, there must be one cause of all of them which is not itself an effect. For if all things are effects they are "possible existents" as regards their own nature, and require a cause which will make them exist rather than not. This self-subsisting cause is God.[389]

He then endeavors to prove the unity of God in the two senses of the term; unity in the sense of simplicity, and unity in the sense of uniqueness. Unity as opposed to composition—the former sense of the term—is neither the same as the essence of a thing, nor is it an accident added to the essence. It cannot be essence, for in that case all things called one would have the same essence. Nor is it accident, for that which defines and separates the existing thing is truly called substance rather than accident; and this is what unity does. Accordingly Crescas defines unity as something essential to everything actually existing, denoting the absence of plurality. This being true, that existent which is before all others is most truly called one. Also that being which is most separated from other things is best called one.[390]

Crescas disagrees with Maimonides's opinion that no positive attributes can be applied to God, such as indicate relation to his creatures, and so on. His arguments are that we cannot avoid relation to creatures even in the term "cause," which Maimonides admits; and in the attributes of action—the only kind of positive attributes allowed by Maimonides—it is implied that before a given time God did not do a particular thing, which he did later, a condition in God which Maimonides will not admit. Besides, if there are no positive attributes, what could be the meaning of the tetragrammaton, about which Maimonides has so much to say? If it expressed a negative attribute, why was its meaning kept so secret? Crescas's own view is that there are positive attributes, and that there is a relation between God and his creatures, though not a similarity, as they are far apart, the one being a necessary existent, the other a possible existent; one being infinite, the other finite.[391]

We must now try to show that God is one in the sense that there are no other Gods besides. We may proceed as follows: If there are two Gods, one of them controls only part of the world or he does not control it at all. The first is impossible because the unitary world must be due to one agent. But there may be more than one world and hence more than one agent. This is, however, answered by the thought that being infinite in power one could control them all. There is still another alternative, *viz.*, that one agent controls the whole world and the other does nothing. Here speculation can go no further, and we must have recourse to Scripture, which says, "Hear, O Israel, the Lord our God, the Lord is One." [392] We see here that Crescas is interested in discrediting the logic chopping of the philosophers. No merely logical argument, is his idea, can give us absolute certainty even in so fundamental a doctrine as the unity of God. Like Judah Halevi, Crescas took his inspiration from Algazali, whose point of view appealed to him more than that of Maimonides and Gersonides, who may be classed with Alfarabi, Avicenna and Averroes.

Having discussed the fundamental principles of all religion and philosophy, namely, the existence and nature of God, Crescas next takes up the following six fundamental dogmas of Judaism, God's knowledge of existing things, Providence, Power, Prophecy, Freedom, Purpose.

There are three things to be remembered in the matter of God's knowledge. He knows the infinite, for he knows particulars. He knows the non-existent, as he knows the future; and his knowledge of the contingent does not remove its contingent character. Maimonides and Gersonides had difficulty with this problem and we know their respective solutions. Gersonides, for reasons metaphysical as well as ethical, does not scruple to limit God's knowledge to universals. Maimonides endeavors to reconcile the dilemma by throwing the blame upon our limited understanding. In God's knowledge which is *toto cœlo* different from ours, and of which we have no conception, all oppositions and contradictions find their ultimate harmony. Crescas, as we might naturally expect, agrees with Maimonides in this matter rather than with Gersonides. To limit God's knowledge is opposed to the Bible, and would involve us in greater difficulties than those we endeavor to escape.[393]

Related to the question of God's knowledge is the problem of Providence. For God must know the individual or thing for which he provides, and if God has no knowledge of particulars, there can be no such thing as special providence. This latter as we know is virtually the opinion of Gersonides (*cf.* p. 345). Crescas, we have seen, defends God's knowledge of particulars, hence he sees no difficulty in special providence on this score. He takes, however, the term in a broad sense. All evidence of design in nature, all powers in plant and animal which guide their growth, reproduction and conservation are due to God's providence. Providence, he says, is sometimes exercised by God directly, without an intermediate voluntary agent, sometimes with such mediation. God's relations to Moses and to the Israelites in Egypt at the time of the tenth plague were without intermediate agency. In all other cases there is mediation of angels, or prophets, or wise men, or, according to some, the heavenly bodies, which are living and intelligent beings.

Providence itself is of different kinds. There is the most general and natural exhibited in the equipment of the various species of plant and animal life for their protection and growth and conservation. There are the more special powers found in the human race. These forms of providence have little to do with the person's deserts. They are purely dependent upon the constitution and influence of the stars. Then there is the more special providence of the Jewish nation, then of the male members of this nation, and of the priests and the levites. Finally comes the special providence of the individual, who is rewarded and punished according to his conduct. The reward and punishment of this world are not strictly controlled by conduct, the reward and punishment of the next world are. In this last remark Crescas cuts the knot which has been the cause of so much discussion in religious philosophy. If the real reward and punishment are in the next world,

the prosperity of the wicked and the adversity of the righteous in
this world do not form so great a problem. At the same time an
explanation of this peculiar phenomenon is still wanting. For surely
the righteous man does not deserve to *suffer* for his righteousness,
even though his good deeds will not go unrewarded in the next world.
In this discussion also Crescas takes issue with the intellectualistic
point of view of Maimonides and particularly Gersonides. The
solution of these men that evil does not come from God directly
but by accident and by reason of matter, and the corollary drawn
therefrom that God does not punish the wicked directly, that he merely
neglects them, leaving them to the accidents of nature and chance,
Crescas does not approve. Nor is he more favorably inclined to the
theory that the good man is provided for because the more he culti-
vates his mind, the more closely he comes in contact with God, in
whom are contained actually all the ideas of which man has some
potentially. His main criticism is that the theory is opposed to clear
statements in the Bible, which imply special and individual reward
and punishment in a miraculous and supernatural manner, which
cannot be due to intellectual perfection, nor to the order of the heavenly bodies. Besides, if a man who is highly intellectual did much
wrong, he should be punished in his soul, but on the intellectualist
theory such a soul is immortal and cannot be destroyed.

Accordingly Crescas goes back to the religious doctrine of reward
and punishment as ordinarily understood. God rewards and punishes
because man obeys or disobeys his will and command. The com-
plaint raised on account of the misery of the good and the prosperity
of the wicked he answers by saying that real reward and punishment
are in the next world. The goods and evils of this world are also to be
considered, and he gives the ordinary excuses for the apparent deviation from what ought to be, such as that evil is sometimes a good in
disguise and *vice versa;* that one sometimes inherits evil and good from
one's parents; that the individual is sometimes involved in the destinies of the majority, and so on, and so on. Evil in the sense of moral
evil, *i. e.,* wrong, does not come from God, it is true, but punishment
does come from God, and as its aim is justice, it is a good, not an
evil. The providence extended to Israel is greatest. There is more
Providence in Palestine than elsewhere, not because there is any

difference in the relation on God's side, but there is on the side of the man enjoying this providence. His character and disposition change with the place, and similarly with the time and the season. Hence certain seasons of the year, like that about the time of the Day of Atonement, are more propitious for receiving God's providence.[394]

Another fundamental doctrine of Judaism is God's omnipotence. Weakness would be a defect. Hence God can do everything except the contradictory. His power is infinite not merely in duration, but also in intensity. From Aristotle's proof of the necessity of an immovable mover as based upon the eternity of motion (p. 256 f.), we gather only that God's power is infinite in duration; whereas our doctrine of creation *ex nihilo* shows that there is no relation at all between God's power and the work he does; hence his power is infinite. This is shown also in the miracles, some of which took place instantaneously, as the destruction of the first born in Egypt at midnight precisely. Crescas insists that the ass of Balaam did speak, and refers with disapproval to those who doubt it and say it was in a vision (Gersonides).[395]

In his discussion of Prophecy the interest lies once more in his anti-intellectualistic attitude. Maimonides agrees with the philosophers that the prophetic power is a psychological process attainable by the man who in addition to moral perfection possesses a highly developed intellect and power of imagination. To anticipate the objection that if this be so, why are there no prophets among the philosophers, Maimonides adds that divine grace is necessary besides, and that if this is lacking, one may have all the qualifications and yet not be a prophet. Crescas sees the forced nature of this explanation, and once more frankly returns to the plain intent of Scripture and Jewish tradition that the prophet is the man chosen by God because he is a student of the Torah and follows its commandments, and because he cleaves to God and loves him. The prophet receives his inspiration from God directly or through an intermediate agent, and the information received may concern any topic whatsoever. It is not to be limited to certain topics to the exclusion of others, as Gersonides tries to make out; and its purpose is to give guidance to the prophet himself or to others through him.[396]

The most original contribution of Crescas to philosophical theory is his treatment of the ever living problem of freedom. So fundamental has it seemed for Judaism to maintain the freedom of the will that no one hitherto had ventured to doubt it. Maimonides no less than Judah Halevi, and with equal emphasis Gersonides, insist that the individual is not determined in his conduct. This seemed to be the only way to vindicate God's justice in reward and punishment. But the idea of man's freedom clashed with the doctrine of God's omniscience. If nothing in the past determines a man's will in a given case, then up to the moment of the act it is undetermined, and no one can know whether a given act will take place or its opposite. On the other hand, if God does know everything in the future as well as in the past, man is no longer free to act in a manner contrary to God's foreknowledge. This difficulty was recognized by Maimonides as well as by Gersonides, and they solved it in different ways. Maimonides gives up neither God's omniscience nor man's absolute freedom, and escapes the dilemma by taking refuge in his idea of God's transcendence. Human knowledge is incompatible with human freedom; God's knowledge is not like human knowledge, and we have no conception what it is. But it is consistent with human freedom. Gersonides, who objects to Maimonides's treatment of the divine attributes, and insists that they must resemble in kind though not in degree the corresponding human attributes, can avoid the difficulty only by a partial blunting of the sharp points of either horn of the dilemma. Accordingly he maintains freedom in all its rigor, and mitigates the conception of omniscience. God's omniscience extends only to the universal and its consequences; the contingent particular is by definition not subject to foreknowledge, and hence it argues no defect in God's knowledge if it does not extend to the undetermined decisions of the will.

Crescas embraces the other horn of the dilemma. God's omniscience must be maintained in all its rigor. It is absurd to suppose that the first universal and absolute cause should be ignorant of anything pertaining to its effects. Is man then not free? Has he no choice at all, no freedom in the determination of his conduct? If so how justify God's reward and punishment, if reward and punishment are relative to conduct and imply responsibility? Crescas's answer is a compromise. Determinism is not fatalism. It does not mean that a given person is preordained from eternity to act in a given way, no matter what the circumstances are. It does not mean that command and advice and warning and education and effort and endeavor are useless and without effect. This is contradicted by experience as well as by the testimony of Scripture. But neither is it true on the other hand that a person's will and its conduct are causeless and undetermined until the moment of action. This idea is equally untrue to reason and experience. We know that every effect has a cause and the cause has a cause, and this second cause has again a cause, until we reach the first necessary cause. Two individuals similar in every respect would have the same will unless there is a cause which makes them different. We have already intimated that God's foreknowledge, which we cannot deny, is incompatible with absolute freedom, and in the Bible we have instances of God's knowing future events which are the results of individual choice, as in the case of Pharaoh. The only solution then is that the act of will is in a sense contingent, in a sense determined. It is contingent in respect to itself, it is determined by its cause, *i. e.*, the act is not fated to take place, cause or no cause. If it were possible to remove the cause, the act would not be; but given the cause, the effect is necessary. Effort is not in vain, for effort is itself a cause and determines an effect. Commandments and prohibitions are not useless, for the same reason. Reward and punishment are not unjust, even though antecedent causes over which man has no control determine his acts, any more than it is unjust that fire burns the one who comes near it, though he did so without intention. Reward and punishment are a necessary consequence of obedience and disobedience.

This is a bold statement on the part of Crescas, and the analogy between a man's voluntary act in ethical and religious conduct and the tendency of fire to burn irrespective of the person's responsibility in the matter can be valid only if we reduce the ethical and religious world to an impersonal force on a plane with the mechanism of the physical world order. This seems a risky thing to do for a religionist. And Crescas feels it, saying that to make this view public would be dangerous, as the people would find in it an apology for evil doers, not understanding that punishment is a natural consequence of evil. This latter statement Crescas does not wish to be taken in its literal strictness, nor should the analogy with the burning fire be pressed too far. For it would then follow even if a person is physically compelled to do evil that he would be punished, just as the fire would not refrain from burning a person who was thrown into it by force. The determination of the will, he says, must not be felt by the agent as a constraint and compulsion, else the act is not free and no punishment should follow; for command and prohibition can have no effect on a will constrained. Reward and punishment have a pedagogical value generally, even if in a given case they are not deserved. Even though in reality every act is determined, still where there is no external compulsion the person is so identified with the deed that it is in a real sense the product of his own soul, bringing about a union with, or separation from God; and hence reward and punishment are necessarily connected with it. Where there is external compulsion, on the other hand, the act is not in reality his own and hence no reward or punishment.

The question arises, however, why should there be punishment for erroneous belief and opinion? These have nothing to do with the will, and are determined if anything is, *i. e.*, the person having them is constrained to believe as he does by the arguments, over which he has no control. This matter offers no difficulty to those who, like Maimonides and Gersonides, regard intelligence as the essence of the soul, and make immortality dependent upon intellectual ideas. A soul acquiring true ideas, they say, becomes *ipso facto* immortal. It is not a question of right and wrong or of reward and punishment. But this is not the Biblical view, and if it were true, there would be no need of the many ceremonial regulations. Geometry would play a greater rôle in immortality than the Torah. Crescas's answer is that reward and punishment in this case are not for the belief itself, but rather for the pleasure one finds in it and the pains one takes to examine it carefully. Even in conduct one is not rewarded or punished for deeds directly, but for the intention and desire. Deed without intention is not punished. Intention without deed is; though the two together call for the greatest punishment or reward. "A burnt offering," say the Rabbis, "atones for sinful thoughts; sin committed through compulsion is not punished." [397]

It is of interest here to know that Spinoza, as has been shown by Joel,[398] owed his idea of man's freedom to Crescas. He also like Crescas denies the absolute indeterminism of a person's conduct that is insisted upon by the majority of the mediæval Jewish philosophers. And Joel shows moreover that Spinoza's final attitude to this question as found in his Ethics was the outcome of a gradual development, and the result of reading Crescas. In some of his earlier writings he insists that anything short of absolute omniscience in God is unthinkable. He sees the difficulty of reconciling this with man's freedom, but is not ready to sacrifice either, and like Maimonides decides that we must not deny it simply because we cannot understand it. Later, however, he maintains that God's omniscience and man's freedom are absolutely incompatible, and solves the difficulty in a manner similar to that of Crescas by curtailing freedom as formerly understood.

The next topic of which it is necessary to have a clear idea for a complete understanding of Judaism, is the purpose of the Law, and in general the purpose of man. Here also appears clearly the anti-intellectualism of Crescas and his disagreement with Maimonides and Gersonides. The final purpose of the Law is of course, he says, a good. The Bible teaches us to perfect our morals; it inculcates true beliefs and opinions; and it promises by means of these happiness of body and happiness of soul. Which of these four is the ultimate end? Clearly it must be the best and most worthy. And it seems as if this quality pertains to the eternal happiness of the soul, to which as an end the other three tend. Corporeal happiness is a means to the perfection of the soul since the latter acts through the means of bodily organs. Similarly moral perfection assists in purifying the soul. As for perfection in ideas, some think that it alone makes the soul immortal by creating the acquired intellect, which is immaterial and separate, and enjoys happiness in the next world incomparably greater than the joy we feel here below in the acquisition of knowledge. There is a difference of opinion as to the subject-matter which bestows immortality. According to some it is all knowledge, whether of sublunar things or of the separate substances. According to others it is only the knowledge of God and the angels that confers immortality. All these views are wrong from the Scriptural as well as the philosophical point of view.

The Bible makes it clear repeatedly that eternal life is obtained by performance of the commandments; whereas according to the others practical observance is only a means and a preparation to theory, without which practice alone is inadequate. According to Scripture and tradition certain offences are punished with exclusion from eternal life, and certain observances confer immortality, which have nothing to do with theoretical truths.

But philosophically too their views are untenable. For it would follow from their opinions that the purpose of the Law is for something other than man, for the acquired intellect is "separate," and hence cannot be the form of man. It is different in kind from man, for unlike him it is eternal as an individual. Besides it is not true that the acquired intellect is made as a substance by its ideas, while being separate from the material intellect; for as immaterial it has no matter as its subject from which it could come into being. It must therefore come into being *ex nihilo*, which is absurd.

And there are other reasons against their view. For if all knowledge confers immortality, one may acquire it by studying geometry, which is absurd. And if this privilege can be gained only by a knowledge of God and the separate substances, the objection is still greater; for, as Maimonides has shown, the only knowledge that may be had of these is negative; and it is not likely that such imperfect knowledge should make an eternal intellect.

If then theoretical knowledge does not lead to immortality as they thought, and the other perfections are preparatory to theoretical, it follows that the ultimate purpose of the Law and of man is attained primarily neither by theory alone nor by practice alone, but by something else, which is neither quite the one nor the other. It is the love and fear of God. This is demanded alike by Scripture, tradition and philosophy. That it is the view of religion is clear enough from the many passages in the Bible urging love of God. But it is also demanded by philosophy. For the soul is a spiritual substance, hence it is capable of separation from the body and of existing by itself forever, whether it has theoretical knowledge or not; since it is not subject to decay, not being material. Further, the perfect loves the good and the perfect; and the greater the good and the perfection the greater the love and the desire in the perfect being. Hence the perfect soul loves God with the greatest love of which it is capable. Similarly God's love for the perfect soul, though the object as compared with him is low indeed, is great, because his essence and perfection are great. Now as love is the cause of unity even in natural things, the love of God in the soul brings about a unity between them; and unity with God surely leads to happiness and immortality. As love is different from intellectual apprehension, the essence of the soul is love rather than intelligence.

There are many Talmudical passages confirming this view logically derived. We are told that the souls of the righteous enjoy the splendor of the Shekinah, and the wicked suffer correspondingly. This agrees with our conception of immortality and not with theirs. For enjoyment is impossible on their showing, though they try to make it plausible. Pleasure is different from apprehension; and as the essence of the acquired intellect is apprehension, there is no room for the pleasure, the intellect being simple. According to our view love is rewarded with pleasure. The pleasure we feel here below in intellectual work (Gersonides, p. 339) proves nothing, for it is due to the effort and the passing from potential knowledge to actual knowledge, *i. e.*, to the process of learning. Proof of this is that we find no pleasure in axioms and first principles, which we know without effort. But the acquired intellect after the death of the body does not learn any new truths, hence can have no pleasure.

The Rabbis also speak of definite places of reward and punishment, which cannot apply to the acquired intellect, since it is a "separate" substance and can have no place. The soul as we understand it can have a place, just as it is connected with the body during life.

The Rabbis often speak of the great reward destined for school children. But surely the acquired intellect cannot amount to much in children. The truth is that the soul becomes mature and complete as soon as it acquires the rational faculty in the shape of the first principles or axioms. Then it is prepared for immortality as a natural thing without regard to reward.

The purpose of the soul as we showed is to love God. This object the Bible attains by the commandments, which may be classified with reference to their significance in seven groups. They exalt God; they show his great kindness to us; they give us true ideas concerning the nature of God; they call our attention to his providence; they give us promises of corporeal and spiritual reward; they call our attention to God's miracles in order to keep our attention from flagging; and finally they command love of God and union with him as the final aim of man.[399]

In addition to the six fundamental doctrines of Judaism mentioned above (p. 392), there are true beliefs which are essential to Judaism, and the denial of which constitutes heresy; though they are not as fundamental as the other six, in the sense that the Law would continue to exist without them. They are (1) Creation, (2) Immortality, (3) Reward and Punishment, (4) Resurrection, (5) Eternity of the Law, (6) The superiority of Moses to the other prophets, (7) The priest's learning the future through the Urim and Tumim, (8) Belief in the Messiah. The list of thirteen articles of the creed given by Maimonides (cf. below, p. 409) is open to criticism. If he meant fundamental dogmas, there are not as many as thirteen; there are no more than seven or eight—the six mentioned before (p. 392), and, if one chooses, the existence of God, making seven, and revelation as the eighth. On the other hand, if Maimonides meant to include "true beliefs," there are more than fifteen, the six enumerated above (p. 392), existence of God and revelation, and the eight "true beliefs" named at the head of this section, not counting a great many specific commandments.[400]

Having made this criticism of Maimonides's thirteen articles, Crescas proceeds to discuss every one of the eight true beliefs named at the beginning of the last paragraph. For our purpose it will not be necessary to reproduce the minute arguments here. We will select a few of the more important topics and state briefly Crescas's attitude.

The doctrine of creation formed the central theme in Maimonides and Gersonides. It was here, as we have seen, that Maimonides stopped short in his devotion to Aristotle and took pains to show that the arguments of the latter in favor of eternity are not valid, and that Aristotle knew it. He endeavored to show, moreover, that the doctrine of creation can be made more plausible than its opposite, and hence since creation is essential to Judaism, it must be regarded as a fundamental dogma. Gersonides could not see his way clear to accepting creation *ex nihilo*, among other things because as matter cannot come from form, the material world cannot come from God. Accordingly he compromised by saying that while the present world as it is is not eternal, it came from a primitive "hyle" or matter, which was eternal. Thus our world is dependent for its forms upon God, for its matter upon the prime and eternal "hyle."

Here Crescas takes up the problem and points out that whether we accept or not an eternal "hyle," everything that exists must be dependent upon God as the only necessary existent. Everything outside of him, be it eternal matter or not, is only a possible existent and owes its existence to God. Creation *ex nihilo* means no more. To be sure, if we assume that the existence of the world and its emanation from God is eternal, because his relation to his product is the same at all times, it will follow that the emanation of the world from God is a necessary process. But necessity in this case does not exclude will, nay it implies it. For the only way in which anything can come from a rational cause is by way of conception. The rational cause forms a conception of the world order and of himself as giving existence to this world order as a whole and in its parts. Will means no more than this. This will also solve the old philosophic difficulty, how can the many come from the One. Our answer is that the good God created a good world. The goodness of the world is its unity, *i. e.*, the parts contribute to making a whole which is good. On the other hand, an agent is perfectly good when he acts with will. God's will also makes miracles possible. Moreover, eternal creation is not inconsistent with continued creation, and we have creation *ex nihilo* every moment. Maimonides is wrong therefore when he thinks that eternity would upset Judaism and make miracles impossible. Creation in time is therefore not a fundamental dogma with which Judaism stands and falls. At the same time it is a true belief as taught in the first verse of Genesis.[401]

Another of the true beliefs is reward and punishment. This consists of two kinds, corporeal and spiritual. Corporeal is spoken of in the Bible and is not opposed to reason. For as the purpose of creation is to do man good and enable him to achieve perfection, it stands to reason that God would remove any obstacles in the way of man's perfecting himself, and this is the kind of reward mentioned first, "All the diseases which I put upon the Egyptians I shall not put upon thee, for I the Lord am thy healer" (Exod. 15, 26). Punishment is primarily for the same purpose.

As for spiritual reward and punishment, they are not mentioned specifically in the Bible, but the Talmud is full of it. Rationally they can be explained as follows. As the soul is spiritual and intellectual, it enjoys great pleasure from being in contact with the world of spirit and apprehending of the nature of God what it could not apprehend while in the body. On the other hand, being restrained from the world of spirit and kept in darkness gives it pain; and this may lead to its ultimate destruction. The essence of the soul, as was said above, is not intellectuality, but love and desire; hence pain may destroy it.

The reason spiritual reward and punishment, which is the more important of the two, is not mentioned in the Bible, is because it was taken as a matter of fact. Corporeal reward and punishment was not so regarded, hence the need of specifying it.

A difficulty that presents itself is, How is it consistent with justice to punish the soul by itself, when it was the composite of body and soul that sinned? This may be answered by saying that the soul is the form of the body and does not change when separated. Hence, being the more important of the two elements composing man, it receives the more important punishment, namely, spiritual.

Besides, it is true that the composite also receives compensation. And this is the purpose of resurrection.[402]

Resurrection of the body is not universal, but is reserved only for some, as is clear from the passage in Daniel (12, 2), "And many of those that sleep in the dust of the earth shall awake, some to ever-lasting life, and some to disgrace and everlasting abhorrence." At the same time it is difficult to know who these some are. It cannot be the perfect and the good only, since some of those rising will go "to disgrace and everlasting abhorrence." We can decide this better later, when we have learned more of resurrection.

The variety of opinions concerning the time of the resurrection Crescas endeavors to reconcile by supposing that all agreed it would take place as soon as the Temple was built, but that the Messiah would precede the building of the Temple by some length of time.

The purpose of the resurrection is to strengthen belief in those who have it and to impress it upon those who have it not. At the time of the resurrection those who come back to life will tell the living how they fared when their souls left their bodies. Another purpose of resurrection is, as mentioned above, in order to reward and punish the composite of body and soul which acted during life.

The dogma of resurrection is regarded so seriously by the Rabbis, who exclude the unbeliever in it from a portion in the world to come, because in this act is completed the form of man; and because thereby is realized the justice of God, and the faith is strengthened in the minds of the believers.

It seems at first sight impossible that the elements of the body, which were dispersed at the time of the body's death and formed part of other substances, can be gathered together again. But it is not really so strange, for in the first place God may so arrange matters that these elements may be in a position to return. Besides, this is not really necessary. It is quite sufficient that God create a body exactly like the first in temperament and form, and endow it with the old soul, which will then behave like the old person; and being endowed with memory besides, the identity of personality will be complete.

For the purpose of showing God's justice and strengthening man's faith it is sufficient to resurrect the perfectly good and the completely bad. The intermediate classes do not deserve this extraordinary miracle, and their spiritual reward will be sufficient.[403]

CHAPTER XVIII

JOSEPH ALBO (1380–1444)

Of the post-Maimonidean philosophers Crescas is the last who contributes original views of philosophical value. Joseph Albo, of Monreal in Aragon, is of little importance as a philosopher. He rehashes the problems which occupied a Maimonides, a Gersonides and a Crescas, and sides now with one, now with the other. He benefited by the writings of his predecessors, particularly Maimonides, Crescas, and Simon Duran; [403a] and the philosophical discussions in the last three sections of his "Book of Roots" ("Sefer Ikkarim") give the impression of an eclectic compilation in the interest of a moderate conservatism. The style is that of the popularizer and the homilist; and to this he owes his popularity, which was denied his more original teacher, Crescas.

But philosophy as such was not Albo's forte, nor was it his chief interest. While it is true that all the Jewish thinkers of the middle ages were for a great part apologetes, this did not prevent a Maimonides or a Gersonides from making a really thorough and disinterested study of science and philosophy; and often their scientific and philosophic conviction was so strong that the *apologia* was *pro philosophia sua* rather than *pro Judaismo*. The central theme therefore in the majority of Albo's philosophical predecessors was the equally metaphysical and theological, of God and his attributes. These were proved by reason and confirmed by Scripture and tradition. Judaism had to be formulated and defended with a view not so much to the dangers threatening from Christianity and Mohammedanism as to those endangering all religions alike, namely, the opinions of science and philosophy as taught especially by the Aristotelians. Hence Maimonides treated for the most part of the same problems as the Mohammedan Mutakallimun before him, and Thomas Aquinas the Christian had no scruple in making the Jewish philosopher's method his own when he undertook to defend the Catholic faith "contra Gentiles."

Different were the circumstances as well as the attitude of Joseph Albo. The purely philosophic interest was not strong in his day. He was not confronted by the necessity of proving the existence and incorporeality of God by reason. No one doubted these things and they had been abundantly written about in times gone by. In the interest of completeness and for the benefit of those who were not trained in technical philosophy, Albo found it desirable to restate the results of previous discussions of these topics in a style more accessible to the readers of his day. But the central interest in his age was shifted. It was a time of religious disputations and forced conversions. Albo himself had taken part in such a disputation held at Tortosa in 1413–14, and he had to defend Judaism against Christianity. He had to show his own people that Judaism was the true religion and Christianity spurious. Hence it was religion as such he had to investigate, in order to find what marks distinguished a divine law from a human, and a genuine divine law from one that pretended to be such. To make this investigation logically complete he had to show that there must be such a thing as a divine law, and that no such law can be conceived without assuming certain basal beliefs or dogmas. A discussion of religious dogma was essential, for upon the nature of these fundamental beliefs depended one's judgment of a given law and its character as divine or human, genuine or spurious. Hence the title of Albo's treatise, "Book of [religious] Roots [dogmas]." And while it is true that Maimonides, the systematizer and codifier, could not fail to put down in his commentary on the Mishna a list of articles of the Jewish creed, nothing is said of this in his philosophical work, the "Guide of the Perplexed." With Albo the establishment of the fundamental dogmas is the central theme.

At the same time Albo was anticipated even in this, his more original contribution. Crescas, his teacher, had written, beside the "Or Adonai," a work against Christianity.[404] And in the "Or Adonai" itself he devotes considerable space to the question of the fundamental dogmas of Judaism, and takes occasion to criticize Maimonides for his faulty method in the selection of the thirteen articles, on the ground that he did not distinguish between what was fundamental and what was derivative. This suggestion gave Albo his cue, which he developed in his own way.[404a]

Human happiness, Albo tells us, depends upon theory and practice, as Aristotle says. But the human mind is inadequate to know by itself the truth touching these two. Hence there is need of something superior to the human mind which will define right practice and the true ideas. This can be only by divine guidance. Hence everyone must be able to tell the divine legislation from those which are not divine. For this it is necessary to know what are the principles without which a divine law cannot exist. This is the purpose of the book, to explain the essential principles of a divine law.[405]

A knowledge of the principles of religion would seem easy, for all people profess some religion or other, and hence are presumed to know upon what their religions are based. But this question has not been treated adequately before, and there is no agreement among previous writers about the number of the principles or their identity. Some say there are thirteen (Maimonides), some say twenty-six, some six (Crescas), without investigating what are the principles of divine religion generally. For we must distinguish between the general principles which pertain to divine legislation as such and hence are common to all religions, and special principles which are peculiar to a particular religion.

Seeing the importance of this subject, Albo continues, I undertook this investigation. I came to the conclusion that there are three general principles of divine religion, existence of God, Revelation, and Reward and Punishment after death. Then there are special principles peculiar to a particular religion. From the general principles ("Ikkarim") follow particular or derivative principles ("Shorashim.") [406]

The investigation of the principles of religion is a delicate matter because one is in danger of being reckoned an infidel if he denies what is considered by others a fundamental dogma. Thus according to Maimonides the belief in the Messiah is fundamental, and he who denies it is a heretic and has no share in the world to come. And yet Rabbi Hillel in the Talmud (Sanhedrin, 99a) said, "Israel need expect no Messiah, for they had the benefit of one in the days of Hezekiah, King of Judah." On the other hand, Maimonides does not regard creation *ex nihilo* as fundamental, whereas others do; and to their mind Maimonides is open to the charge of unbelief.

The truth is that only he is an unbeliever who deliberately and knowingly contradicts the Bible. A person who believes in the Bible but is led mistakenly to misinterpret it, and denies real principles because he thinks the Bible does not require us to believe them as principles, or does not require us to believe them at all, is guilty of error and in need of forgiveness, but is not a heretic.[407]

Having thus defined his attitude and purpose, Albo proceeds to criticize the list of dogmas laid down by Maimonides and modified by Crescas, and then defends his own view. A fundamental principle ("Ikkar," lit. root) is one upon which something else depends and without which this latter cannot exist. Maimonides counts thirteen principles of Judaism as follows: (1) Existence of God, (2) Unity, (3) Incorporeality, (4) Eternity, (5) He alone must be worshipped, (6) Prophecy, (7) Superiority of the prophecy of Moses, (8) Revelation, (9) Immutability of the Law, (10) God's Omniscience, (11) Reward and Punishment, (12) Messiah, (13) Resurrection.[408] This list is open to criticism. If Maimonides intended to admit strict principles only without which Judaism cannot exist, we understand why he named (1), (6), (8), (10), (11), which are general principles of any divine religion, and (7) and (9) as special principles of Judaism. But we cannot see why he included (2) and (3). For while they are true, and every Jew should believe them, Judaism can be conceived as existing without them. It is still more strange that (5) should be counted as a principle. To be sure, it is one of the ten commandments, "Thou shalt have no other Gods before me. . . . Thou shalt not bow thyself down to them, nor serve them" . . . (Exod. 20, 35), but Judaism can be conceived to exist even with the belief in a mediator. Similarly it is not clear why (13) should be considered as a fundamental dogma. On the other hand, he omitted Tradition and Free Will as beliefs essential to any divine religion.

If, in defence of Maimonides, we say that he intended to name not only fundamental principles, but also true beliefs, whether fundamental or derivative, then there are many others he might have mentioned, such as creation *ex nihilo*, belief in miracles, that God rests in Israel through the Torah, and so on.

Another writer counts twenty-six principles, including everything that occurred to his mind, such as the attributes of eternity, wisdom, life, power, will and others, counting paradise and hell as two, and other

absurd ideas.   Others again,[409] criticizing Maimonides's principles,
reduce them to six, *viz.* (1) God's knowledge, (2) Providence, (3)
Power, (4) Prophecy, (5) Free Will, (6) Purpose, adding thereto the
three proved by Maimonides, God's existence, unity and incorporeality.
The objection to this list is that it does not contain the special dogmas
of Judaism, and does not give us a principle by which we can distinguish between the genuine and spurious divine religion.   For the dogmas named in the above list give us the *necessary* requirements for a
divine law, but not the *sufficient*.   We may have all these principles and
yet not have a divine religion.   As to Free Will and Purpose, they are
essential to divine legislation to be sure, but not *qua* divine; they are
also essential to a conventional human law.   Divine religion has a
special purpose peculiar to it.[410]

Having laid bare the defects in the attempts at a list of fundamental
dogmas of Judaism made by his predecessors, Albo categorically lays
down the following three principles as fundamental to divine religion:
(1) Existence of God, (2) Providence, and reward and punishment,
(3) Revelation.

To justify this statement Albo finds it necessary to make clear
what is meant by divine law or religion, and what relation it bears
to other laws, not divine.   This necessitates an explanation of existing laws and their motives and causes.

Animal life, we are told, may be divided into three classes according
to the mode of living adopted by each.   Beasts of prey live separately
and not in groups.   Mankind must live in communities, as one individual is dependent upon the work of another, and social life is essential
to their existence.   Intermediate between beast of prey and man are
the gregarious animals, which keep together not as a matter of necessity, as is the case in man, but for convenience, for the sake of being
together.   Man is social by nature; and in order to make communal
life possible, there must be some order in the community which prohibits violence, robbery, and so on.   This is known as "natural law."
In addition to this there are in many places "conventional laws,"
made by kings and emperors, regulating more carefully and with
greater detail than the natural law the affairs of the members of the
community.

But this is not all.   There is still another kind of law due directly to God's providence. The providence of God is seen even in the lower animals, in the constitution of their bodies, not merely in matters essential to the preservation of the animal, but also in the interest of comfort and convenience, as for example the duplication of the sense organs. It stands to reason therefore that there is a divine influence which provides for man even to a greater degree. This providence may extend only to one individual, but this person brings about the perfection of the race; just as in the individual man the heart is instrumental in giving life to all the other limbs. The law which is promulgated through this person is a "divine law."

The term "law" ("Dat") applies to any system of directions embracing a large aggregate of men, whether it contains many commands or one. There are thus three kinds of law, natural, conventional and divine. Natural law is the same for all persons, times and places. Conventional law is ordered by a wise man or men in conformity with the necessity of the persons, times and places, as the reason dictates, without special divine suggestion. Divine law is ordered by God through a prophet. The purpose of natural law is to remove wrong and promote right, keeping men from robbery and theft so that society may be able to exist. Conventional law goes further and tends to remove the unseemly and to promote the becoming. Divine law has for its purpose to guide men to true happiness, which is the happiness of the soul and its eternal life. It points out the way to follow to reach this end, showing what is the true good for man to pursue, and what is the real evil which one must shun; though it also lays down the law of right and wrong like the other two.[411]

The conventional law is inferior to the divine in a number of ways.

The conventional law only orders human conduct for the purpose of improving social life, but does not concern itself with perfection in theoretical speculation and knowledge, which leads the soul to eternal life. The divine law embraces both the parts upon which human perfection depends, conduct and theory. It embraces the becoming and unbecoming (practice), and the true and untrue (theory). As the Psalmist has it, "The Law of the Lord is perfect, restoring the soul" (Psal. 19, 8).

The conventional law, being human, cannot always decide with certainty what is becoming and what unbecoming. It is liable to error. This is particularly the case in matters of theory, such as the creation or eternity of the world. The divine law gives us certainty in all things, "The testimony of the Lord is sure, making wise the simple" (*ib.*).

The person guided by the conventional law is not sure that he is always guided aright; hence he cannot feel the satisfaction and the joy of the man whose guide is the divine law, making him certain of being right—"The precepts of the Lord are upright, rejoicing the heart" (*ib.* 9).

The conventional law can give general rules only, but is unable to advise in a particular case. So Aristotle in the Ethics points out that virtue is a mean, but he cannot determine exactly the proper measure at a given time. This is the function of the divine law—"The commandment of the Lord is clear, enlightening the eyes" (*ib.*).

The conventional law is subject to change in the course of time. Witness the marriage of sisters in the early period of Adam and Abel. The divine law alone does not change—"The fear of the Lord is pure, enduring for ever" (*ib.* 10).

The conventional law cannot estimate exactly the merited amount and kind of reward and punishment; whereas, "The ordinances of the Lord are the truth; they are just altogether" (*ib.*).[412]

Freedom and Purpose are principles of conventional law. Without freedom there is no sense in giving orders. For this reason Freedom and Purpose are not correctly given as fundamental dogmas of divine law, for while the latter cannot get along without them, they are not peculiar to divine law as such, but are common also to conventional law. This is why Maimonides omitted Freedom in his creed. The same is true of Purpose in general. The divine law, however, has a special purpose, perfection and eternal life, hence Maimonides did include it in his list.[413]

The fundamental dogmas of divine law are, as we said before, Existence of God, Revelation, Reward and Punishment. It is evident that there cannot be a divine law without the first two. The third is also necessary; for the purpose of divine law must be a perfection greater than the conventional law can accomplish. This is eternal life, and is signified by Reward and Punishment.

As all agree that the Law of Moses is divine, it is proper to use it as a standard in order to discover what a divine law must have. Accordingly if we examine the first four chapters of Genesis, we find the principle of the existence of God in chapter one, describing creation. The second and third chapters give evidence of revelation, or communication of God with man for the purpose of directing his conduct. Finally in the Cain incident in chapter four is illustrated the third dogma of Reward and Punishment.[414]

Creation *ex nihilo* is a true belief but not a fundamental principle. For though the Aristotelian view of eternity is heretical, as it takes away the possibility of miracles, nay even the possibility of Moses and the Messiah (for these could exist only after the lapse of an infinite number of individuals), one who believes like Plato in a primitive matter is not necessarily in contradiction with the Biblical miracles, for they were not *ex nihilo* [415] (*cf.* above, p. 358).

It is not sufficient to believe in the three principles mentioned to be considered a believer and to be entitled to a share in the world to come. One must believe also in the derivative principles following from them. Thus from the existence of God follow his unity and incorporeality. And if a man does not believe in incorporeality, he disbelieves in the real nature of God, and it is as if he denied the original principle.

The derivative principles ("Shorashim" = roots) are as follows. From existence of God are derived four: (1) Unity, (2) Incorporeality, (3) Independence of time, (4) Freedom from defects. From Revelation are derived three: (1) God's knowledge, (2) Prophecy, (3) Authenticity of God's messenger. From Reward and Punishment is derived one— Providence in the sense of special Providence. In all there are eleven dogmas.[416]

A particular commandment of the Law is not reckoned either as a fundamental principle or as a derivative. He who trangresses it is a sinner and is punished for his misdeed, but is not a heretic who loses his share in the world to come, unless he denies that the commandment in question is from God. In that case he comes in the category of those who deny revelation. Similarly the belief in tradition is not a principle because it is a particular commandment. Unity of God is a principle though it is apparently a special commandment, because the term unity contains two concepts; first, that God is one and there is not another like him; second, that being one and free from any multiplicity or composition, he is the cause of all the multiplicity in the world. The latter is not a particular commandment, but a principle derived from the existence of God. The former is a particular commandment. If particular commandments were regarded as principles, we should have as many principles as there are commandments in the Bible.[417]

The above distinction between the two senses of the term unity, one of which is rationally derived from the existence of God, whereas the other not being so derivable is not a principle, and is given in the Bible as a special commandment, is clearly due to Crescas, who after a few attempts at proving the unity of God in the sense of excluding dualism, gives it up as incapable of proof logically, and falls back upon the testimony of Scripture, "Hear, O Israel, the Lord our God, the Lord is One." The other sense of the word unity Crescas proves by reason. Hence Albo counts it among the derivative principles (*cf.* above, p. 392).

If a particular commandment is not a principle, which means that a fundamental or derivative dogma cannot itself be a commandment, but must lie at the basis of all commandments, the question arises whence come these principles, and who is to warrant their truth. In the sciences we know that the basal principles of a given science are not proved in that science itself, but are borrowed from another science in which they are proved. Thus physics takes the concepts of substance and accident from metaphysics. In turn the latter takes the idea of a first mover from physics. Among the laws, too, the conventional law takes its principles, freedom and purpose, from political philosophy. Whence does divine law take its principles? The existence of God can be demonstrated philosophically from premises going back to axioms and first principles. But this is not true of Prophecy and Providence.

The answer Albo gives to this question is that of Judah Halevi and Crescas. The principles of the divine law are known empirically, *i. e.*, by experience. Adam knew of the existence of God, of prophecy and reward and punishment from personal experience. Similarly Noah and Abraham. Nowadays we know the law by tradition, but the majority of the principles thus known are so certain that there is neither difference of opinion nor doubt entertained by anyone concerning them. Such is the status for example of the principle of

Revelation. Other principles again, like the existence of God, are, as was said before, known by theoretical speculation.[418]

To find out whether a religion professing to be of divine origin is really so or not, it must be examined first with reference to the three fundamental, and the other derivative principles. If it opposes them, it is spurious and not genuine. If it is not opposed to the principles in question, it must be further examined with a view to determining whether the promulgator is a genuine messenger of God or not. And the test here must be a direct one. Miracles and signs are no conclusive proof of prophecy, and still less do they prove that the person performing them is a messenger sent by God to announce a law. They merely show that the person is considered worthy of having miracles performed through him, provided the miracles are genuine and not performed through magic. The test of the prophet and the messenger of God must be as direct as it was in the case of Moses, where the people actually saw that he was addressed by God and commissioned with a message for them.[419]

This opinion of Albo is clearly intended as a defence of Judaism against Christianity's claim that Jesus performed miracles, a claim which the Rabbis of the middle ages were inclined to recognize.

In addition to the three fundamental and eight derivative principles of divine legislation, there are six dogmas, which every follower of the Mosaic law must believe. They are (1) Creation *ex nihilo*, (2) Superiority of Moses to other prophets, (3) Immutability of the Law, (4) That human perfection can be attained by any one of the commandments of the Law, (5) Resurrection, (6) Messiah.

Creation *ex nihilo* is neither a fundamental nor a derivative principle of religion generally or of Judaism specially because, as we saw before (p. 413), they can exist without this dogma. At the same time it is a truth which it behooves every religionist and particularly every Jew to believe. It follows from the principle of the existence of God. If God cannot create *ex nihilo*, there is a defect in him. For creation *ex nihilo* is admitted in a certain sense even by those who hold that the world is eternal. They admit that God is the cause of everything else; hence matter is his effect through the mediation of the separate Intellect. But how can a separate Intellect be the cause of matter if there is no creation *ex nihilo*. This *is ex nihilo* as much as anything can be. To say that we can find no reason why he should create at a particular time rather than at another, and hence the world must be eternal, is no argument; for this reasoning can apply only to action from necessity. Voluntary action is just of this kind, that it takes place at a particular time.

In the above argument for creation the reader will not fail to see reminiscences of Maimonides as well as Crescas (*cf.* pp. 271 and 403).

The superiority of Moses to other prophets is not essential to Judaism, nevertheless it behooves every Jew to believe it, as it is included in the principle of Revelation, and the Bible tells us, "And there arose not a prophet since then in Israel like unto Moses" (Deut. 34, 10).

The Immutability of the Law will be treated in detail later. Here it will suffice to say that while it is not a *sine qua non* of Judaism, every Jew should believe it, as it is included in the derivative principle of the Authenticity of God's messenger.

It stands to reason that human perfection can be attained by the performance of any one of the commandments of the Law. For if it requires the performance of all the commandments for this purpose, then the Law of Moses makes it more difficult to reach perfection than the previous laws, which is not in consonance with the statement of the Rabbis that "God gave Israel so many laws and commandments because he wished to make them meritorious" (Tal. Bab. Makkot, 23 b).

Resurrection will be treated more at length later. It must be believed because it has been accepted by Israel and has come down to us by tradition. The same thing applies to the belief in the Messiah. This is also a traditional belief and is related to the principle of Reward and Punishment, though it is not like the latter indispensable either to religion in general or to Judaism in particular.[420]

The difference, it will be seen, between Albo and Maimonides in the question of Jewish dogmas is simply one of classification and grading. Albo includes in his enumeration all the thirteen dogmas of Maimonides with the exception of the fifth, namely, that God alone be worshipped, but instead of placing them all on the same level of importance as equally essential to the structure of Judaism, as Maimonides apparently intended, Albo divides them into three categories of descending rank as follows: fundamental principles, derived principles, true beliefs. Of Maimonides's list the last two, Messiah and Resurrection, belong to the last category. None the less Albo believed strictly in both and held it incumbent upon every Jew to believe in them. It was only a question of the status of a person who mistakenly denies these true beliefs. According to Maimonides, it would seem, he would be called a heretic and be excluded from a share in the world to come equally with one who denied the existence of God; whereas according to Albo a person so guilty is a sinner and needs forgiveness, but is not a heretic. Of the other eleven dogmas of Maimonides, (1), (8) and (11) are placed by Albo in his first class, (2), (3), (4), (6) and (10) belong to the second class, while (7) and (9) come under true beliefs along with Messiah and Resurrection. The difference between the first and the second class is purely logical and not practical. As we saw before (p. 413), one who denies incorporeality (a principle of the second class) disbelieves in the true nature of God, which is tantamount to denying the principle of the existence of God.

Before concluding this general discussion of the fundamental dogmas of religion and Judaism, Albo undertakes to answer two questions which must have been near his heart, and which were on the tongues no doubt of a great many honest people in those days of religious challenge and debate. The first question is, Is it proper, or perhaps obligatory, to analyze the fundamental principles of one's religion, to see if they are true; and if one finds another religion which seems to him better, is one permitted to adopt it in place of his own? Albo sees arguments against both sides of the dilemma. If a man is allowed to analyze his religion and to choose the one that seems best to him, it will follow that a person is never stable in his belief, since he is doubting it, as is shown by his examination. And if so, he does not deserve reward for belief, since belief, as Albo defines it elsewhere (Pt. I, ch. 19), means that one cannot conceive of the opposite being true. Again, if he finds another religion which he thinks better and is allowed to exchange his own religion for the new one, he will never be sure of any religion; for he may find a third still better, and a fourth, and so on, and as he cannot examine all the possible religions, he will remain without any religious convictions.

On the other hand, if he is not allowed to investigate the foundations of his belief, it follows either that all religions alike bring their believer happiness, no matter how contradictory they are, which is absurd; or God would seem unfair if only one religion leads its devotees to happiness and no one is allowed to change his religion for one that seems to him the true one.

The answer of Albo to this interesting question is characteristic. It shows that he armored himself in advance, before he risked such a delicate question. He makes it clear that it really does not expose to any danger the religion of Judaism, the mother of the other two, which they came to supersede. If all religions in the world, Albo tells us, were opposed to one another, and regarded each other as untrue, the above difficulty would be real. But it is not so. All religions agree in respect to one of them that it is divine; but they say that it is superseded. Hence every religionist who is not a Jew must investigate his religion to see if it is justified in opposing the religion which is acknowledged to be divine. Similarly the professor of the admittedly divine religion should investigate to see if his religion is temporary or eternal. In this investigation he must first see if the religion conforms to the principles of divine religion above mentioned. If it does this and in addition endeavors to order human affairs in accordance with justice, and leads its devotees to human perfection, it is divine. It is still, however, possible that it is the work of a wise man of good character. It is therefore necessary to investigate the character of the promulgator, to find out whether he is a genuine divine messenger or not. This test, as was said above (p. 415), must be a direct test and not an indirect.[421]

The other question is whether there can be more than one divine religion. Apparently there can be only one, since the giver is one, and the recipients are of one species. But in reality the receivers vary in temperament according to difference in inheritance and environment. Hence there may be a difference in the law according to the character of the people for whom it is intended. Since, however, the difference is due to the receiver and not to the giver, it must reside in those elements which are dependent upon the receiver, *i. e.*, in particulars and details, not in the principles, fundamental or derived. So the Noachite and the Mosaic laws differ only in details, not in fundamental principles.[422]

We have now completed the exposition of the part of Albo's teaching that may be called distinctly his own. And it seems he was aware that he had nothing further to teach that was new, and would have been content to end his book with the first part, of which we have just given an account. But his friends, he tells us in the concluding remarks to the first part of the "Ikkarim,"[423] urged him to proceed further and discuss in detail the principles, fundamental and derived, the true beliefs and the so-called "branches," which he barely enumerated in the first part. He was persuaded by their advice and added the other three sections, each devoted to one of the three fundamental dogmas and the corollaries following from it. Here Albo has nothing new to teach. He follows the beaten track, reviews the classic views of Maimonides, takes advantage of the criticisms of Gersonides and Crescas, and settles the problems sometimes one way sometimes another, without ever suggesting anything new. Accordingly it will not be worth our while to reproduce his discussions here. It will suffice briefly to indicate his position on the more important problems.

The second section deals with the existence of God and the derived principles and branches growing out from this root. In proving the existence of God he refers to Maimonides's four proofs (*cf.* p. 257 ff.), and selects the third and fourth as really valid and beyond dispute. The first and second are not conclusive; the one because it is based upon the eternity of motion, which no Jew accepts; the other because the major premise is not true. It does not follow if one of the two elements a, b, of a composite $a+b$ is found separately, that the other must be found existing separately likewise.[424]

We have seen that from the principle of the existence of God follow four derivative dogmas, unity, incorporeality, independence of time, freedom from defects. We are now told that from these secondary roots issue a number of branches. From Unity it follows that no attributes either essential or accidental can be applied to God, such as wisdom, strength, generosity, and so on, for they would cause multiplicity. From incorporeality we infer that God is not subject to corporeal affections like fear, sorrow, joy, grudge, and so on. Independence of time implies infinite power and want of resemblance to other things. Freedom from defect implies absence of such qualities as ignorance, weakness, and so on.[425]

In the discussion of the divine attributes Albo has nothing new to offer, but instead he argues forward and backward, now with Maimonides, now against him, reproducing a good deal of Maimonides's classification, embodying some material of Bahya on unity, and after this rambling and not very consistent discussion, he comes to the conclusion that none but active and negative attributes are applicable to God; and yet some essential attributes too must be his, but these must be understood as implying only the aspect of perfection, and not that other aspect of attribute which is responsible for multiplicity.[426]

He asks the question so often asked before, How can multiplicity come from unity? And after giving Ibn Sina's scheme of the emanation of the Intelligences one after the other, and criticizing it in the manner of Gazali and Maimonides, he gives his own solution that the variety and multiplicity of the world tends to one end, which is the order of the world. And thus are reconciled plurality and unity. (*cf.* Gersonides above, p. 351).[427]

He discusses the question of angels or Intellects, gives the views of the philosophers concerning their nature and number, each being the effect of the superior and the cause of the inferior, and objects to their idea on the ground that these cannot be the same as the Biblical angels, who are messengers of God to mankind. He then gives his own view that the number of angels is infinite, not as the philosophers say ten or fifty, and that they are not related to each other as cause and effect, but that though they are immaterial Intellects they are individuated and differentiated according to the degree of understanding they have of God.[428]

In discussing the second fundamental principle, Revelation, Albo argues in the good old fashion that man is the noblest creature of the sublunar world, and the most distinctive and noblest part of man— his form and essence—is the theoretical reason. Hence the purpose of man must be the realization of the theoretical intellect. At the same time, and with little consistency, Albo takes the part of Judah Halevi and Crescas, employing their arguments, without naming them, that the philosophers and the philosophizing theologians are wrong who make human immortality, perfection and happiness depend solely upon intellectual activity. He comes to the conclusion, therefore, that spiritual understanding, which gives perfection of soul when in combination with practice, is not acquisition of ideas but the intention of doing the will of God in the performance of good deeds, and not that of pleasure or reward.[429]

This being so, it becomes an important question what are the practices which tend to human perfection, and what are those which tend the other way. In general we may conclude, as like desires and rejoices in like, that those deeds which give the soul pleasure before and after performance are good and helpful, while those which cause subsequent pain, regret and sorrow are bad, and tend away from the soul's perfection.

But the criterion of pleasure and pain just suggested is not sufficient as a guide in conduct, for a great deal depends upon a man's temperament. What a hot-blooded man may commend and find pleasure in, the phlegmatic temperament will object to, and will feel discomfort in doing. Besides, as the good deed is always a mean between two extremes, which it is hard to measure precisely; and as the good deed is that which pleases God, and beyond generalities we cannot tell what does, and what does not please God, since we do not know his essence, it was necessary for man's sake that God should reveal his will to mankind through a prophet. Thus Revelation is proved by reason.[430]

This leads to the problem of prophecy, one of the derivative principles of Revelation. The divine influence from which man gets a knowledge of the things pleasing and displeasing to God, he cannot obtain without the divine will. Instead of magic, divination, and communication with evil spirits and the dead, which the ancient heathen employed in order to learn the future, God sent prophets to Israel, to tell the people of the will of God. Foretelling the future was only secondary with them. Prophecy is a supernatural gift, whether it takes place with the help of the imagination or not. If it were a natural phenomenon dependent upon the intellectual power of the individual and his faculty of imagination, as the philosophers and some Jewish theologians think, there should have been prophets among the philosophers.

Here again we see Albo adopt the view of Halevi and Crescas against the intellectualism of Maimonides and Gersonides. His further classification of the grades of prophecy is based upon Maimonides, though Albo simplifies it. Instead of eleven Albo recognizes four grades in all, including that of Moses. The great majority of mankind, he says, stop with the ability to analyze, such as is exhibited in the analysis of things into matter and form, and so on, though not all of them go so far. But there are some few who go farther and are enabled to speak words of wisdom and to sing praises to God without being able to account for the power. This is the holy spirit ("Ruah ha-Kodesh"). Some go still farther, and through the strength of their reason and imagination they dream true dreams and receive prophecies; though, the imagination having the upper hand, they struggle very hard and tremble and faint, almost losing their soul. This is the first stage of prophecy. The second stage is when the imagination and reason are equal. In that case there is no struggle or fainting. Visions come to the prophet at night in dreams, or in a revery at daytime. The forms that appear are not real, but the meanings they convey are. Such are the figures of women, horses, basket of summer fruit, and so on, in the visions of Zechariah and Amos. The third stage is when the reason gets the better of the imagination and there are no forms or images, but real essences and ideas, like the visions of Ezekiel, which represent real things in the secrets of nature and divinity. The prophet in this stage also hears an angel speaking to him and giving him information of importance to himself or others. In all these cases the will of God is essential. No preparation can replace it. Finally the fourth stage is reached when the imagination does not come into play at all. In this stage there is no angel or form, and the message comes to the prophet at daytime while he is awake. He hears a voice telling him what he desires to know; and whenever he chooses he can summon this power. Moses alone attained to this final stage. Outside of the prophets, the righteous and the pious have various degrees of power according to the degree of their union with God. Some can in this way influence the powers of nature to obey them, as a person can, by thinking of food, make his mouth water. So they can by taking thought cause rain and storm. Others can bring down fire from above and revive the dead.

Through the influence of a prophet the gift of prophecy may sometimes rest upon individuals who are themselves unprepared and unworthy. Witness the revelation on Sinai where the entire people, six hundred thousand in number, were endowed with the spirit of prophecy, and that too of the highest degree, like Moses himself. The prophetic medium reflects the spirit of prophecy on others as a smooth surface reflects the light of the sun upon dark bodies. This is why prophecy is found only in Israel and in Palestine, because the ark and the Tables of Stone, upon which the Shekinah rests, reflect the divine spirit upon those who are worthy and have in them something resembling the contents of the ark, namely, the Torah and the commandments.[431]

Among the true beliefs we have seen (p. 416) that Immutability of the Law is related to the principle of Revelation. Hence this is the place to discuss this question. Can a divine religion change with time or not? It would seem at first sight that it cannot. For the giver expresses his will in the Law, and his will never changes. The receivers are the same, *i. e.*, the same nation, and a nation does not change. Finally the purpose of the Law or religion is to give people true opinions, and these never change.

And yet on further reflection there seems no reason why religion should not change with the change of the recipient, as the physician changes his prescription with the progress of the patient, and as a matter of fact we find that the commandments given to Adam were different from those given to Noah and to Abraham and to Moses. Adam was not allowed to eat meat, Noah was. Abraham was commanded circumcision. High places were at first permitted and later forbidden. Maimonides makes the immutability of the Law a fundamental dogma, relying upon the commandment, "Thou shalt not add thereto, and thou shalt not diminish therefrom" (Deut. 13, 1). But in the first place the verse refers to changes in the mode of observing the laws; and besides, it says nothing about God himself changing the Law.

The phrases "an eternal statute," "throughout your generations," "it is a sign for ever," are no proof of the eternity of the Law; for not all commandments have these expressions attached, and this shows rather that the others are subject to change. Besides, the expressions, " for eternity," and so on, are not to be taken absolutely. They are often used to express finite periods of time.

After the Babylonian Exile two changes were made. They changed the characters in which the Bible was written, and the order and names of the months, beginning with Tishri instead of Nisan. There is no reason, therefore, why other laws might not change, too. We need not, then, regard Immutability of the Law as a fundamental dogma with Maimonides. Hasdai Crescas also classes it with true beliefs and not with fundamental principles.

Albo resolves the problem as follows: A matter that is revealed by God himself cannot be changed by a prophet unless it is changed by God himself. The first two commandments, "I am the Lord thy God, &c.," and "Thou shalt not have other gods, &c.," were heard by the people directly from God without the intervention of Moses, hence they cannot be changed by any prophet. It follows therefore that the three fundamental dogmas, existence of God, Revelation and Reward and Punishment can never be changed by a prophet, for they are implied in the first two commandments, which were heard from God himself. The rest of the commandments, as they were heard from God through the interpretation of Moses, can be changed by a prophet as a temporary measure. The other laws which were given by Moses may be changed by a later prophet even permanently. But the prophet must be greater than Moses, and he must show this by the greatness, number, publicity and permanence of his miracles, which must excel those of Moses. He must likewise show that he was sent by God to change the Law, as clearly as Moses proved that he was sent to give it. But it is unlikely that any such prophet will come, for the Torah says that there never was or will be any prophet like Moses.[432]

Before discussing the third fundamental dogma, Albo finds it desirable to dispose first of a few other problems implied by this dogma, one of which, God's knowledge, was postponed to this place, though it is connected with Revelation, because it cannot well be separated in discussion from the problem of Freedom. Providence is the other related problem, which is derived from the dogma of Reward and Punishment.

There is nothing that is new in Albo's treatment of knowledge and Freedom. He insists like Maimonides that God must be omniscient, and on the other hand the contingent cannot be denied, and neither can freedom. He gives the stock arguments, which it is not necessary to reproduce at this late hour. And his solution is that of Maimonides that in God human freedom and divine Omniscience are reconcilable because God's knowledge is not our knowledge.[433]

Nor is there anything original in Albo's discussion of the problem of Providence. He recognizes with Maimonides and others that a strong argument against special Providence is the observed inequality between the destinies of men and their apparent merits. And he endeavors in the well worn method to give reasons and explanations for this inequality which will not touch unfavorably God's justice or his special Providence. The reasons are such as we met before and we shall not repeat them. Albo also gives a few positive arguments to prove the reality of special Providence for man. He sees in various natural and human phenomena evidence of deviation from the merely "natural" as demanded by the principles of Aristotle's Physics or the laws of uniformity. This shows special Providence. Thus the existence of dry earth, the heaviest element, above water, cannot be accounted for by the laws of Physics. The phenomenon of rain cannot be reduced to law, hence it argues will and purpose and Providence. Admonition in dreams is direct evidence of special Providence, and it is scarcely likely that man, who has special equipment above the other animals in his reason, should not also receive special care above that which the lower animals have. Now they are protected in the species, hence man is provided for as an individual.[434]

Having disposed of the auxiliary dogmas, Albo takes up the fundamental principle of Reward and Punishment. He cites various opinions on the subject, which are dependent upon the idea one entertains concerning the nature of the soul. Thus if one holds that the human soul is not different in kind from the animal soul, it follows that as there is no reward and punishment for the animal, there is none for man. And if one regards the human soul as merely a capacity or possibility of intelligence he must necessarily conclude that the soul perishes with the body and there is no spiritual reward and punishment after death. The only reward there is must therefore be corporeal, during life. On the other hand, our general experience, which brings before us many cases of good men suffering and bad men enjoying prosperity, would seem to argue against corporeal reward and punishment in this world. This taken together with the philosophical opinion that the soul is an immaterial and indestructible substance gives rise to the third view that the only recompense is spiritual after death. None of these views is satisfactory to Albo. The first two because they are based upon an erroneous notion of the soul. All agree, philosophers as well as theologians, that the human soul is different in kind from the soul of the animal; and it is likewise admitted that the human soul is immortal. His criticism of the third view so far as it is based upon the intellectualist idea that the thing of highest value is intellectual effort, and the only reward is immortality which intellectual activity engenders, is similar to that of Halevi and Crescas in its endeavor to refute this notion and to substitute for it the religious view that the soul is an independent substance having a capacity for intelligence *in God's service*. The degree in which a person realizes this service determines his reward and punishment. The argument from experience Albo does not answer here, but we may suppose he regards it as answered by what he said in his discussion of Providence, where he tries to account for the prosperity of the wicked and the adversity of the righteous.

Albo's own view accordingly is that which he also attributes to the Bible that there is a twofold reward, in this world and in the next. There is still a difference of opinion concerning the nature of the true and ultimate reward, whether it is given to the soul alone, or to body and soul combined in resurrection. He quotes Maimonides's opinion, with whom he agrees, that the real reward is purely spiritual enjoyed by the soul alone. To be sure, after the coming of the Messiah the bodies of the righteous will be resurrected to make known abroad God's wonders, or to give these people bodily pleasure for the pain they suffered during life, or to give them additional opportunity to acquire perfection so that they may have a greater reward later. But this state of resurrected life will last only for a time, and then all will die again, and the souls will enjoy spiritual life forever.

The other opinion, held by Nachmanides, is that the real and ultimate reward is that of body and soul united to everlasting life. Albo is not satisfied with this view, his objections being among others that if only the perfect are resurrected, the rest will remain without any reward at all, not to mention the difficulty that it is not likely that the human body—a perishable thing—will change into a matter that will last forever.

As to the nature of reward and punishment after death, Albo tells us that reward will consist in the soul's realization that its endeavors in this world were correct, and in the next world it will be prepared to join the spiritual beings, which will give it great joy. The erring soul will find itself in a position where it will still desire the corporeal pleasures of this world, but will not be able to have them for want of corporeal organs. At the same time it will also entertain the other more natural desire of a spiritual substance to join the other spiritual beings in the other world. This feeling too it will not be able to satisfy because of its want of perfection. This division of desires unsatisfied will cause the soul excruciating torture, and this is its punishment.[435]

CONCLUSION

Our task is done. We have now reached the limit we have assigned ourselves. We have traced objectively and with greater or less detail the rationalistic movement in mediæval Jewry from its beginnings in the ninth and tenth centuries in Babylon among the Karaites and Rabbanites to its decline in Spain and south France in the fifteenth century. We have followed its ascending curve from Saadia through Gabirol, Bahya and Ibn Daud to its highest point in Maimonides, and we likewise traced its descent through Gersonides, Crescas and Albo. We took account of its essential nature as being a serious and conscientious attempt to define a Jewish *Weltanschauung* in the midst of conflicting claims of religions and philosophies. The Jewish sacred writings had to be studied and made consistent with themselves in regard to certain ethical and metaphysical questions which forced themselves upon the minds of thinking men. In this endeavor it was necessary to have regard to the system of doctrine that was growing up among their Mohammedan neighbors and masters—itself inherited from Greece—and adjust its teachings to those of Judaism. The adjustment took various forms according to the temperament of the adjuster. It embraced the extremes of all but sacrificing one of the two systems of doctrine to the other, and it counted among its votaries those who honestly endeavored to give each claim its due. The system of Judaism was the same for all throughout the period of our investigation, excepting only the difference between Karaites and Rabbanites. This was not the case with the system of philosophic doctrine. There we can see a development from Kalam through Neo-Platonism to Aristotelianism, and we accordingly classified the Jewish thinkers as Mutakallimun, Neo-Platonists or Aristotelians, or combinations in varying proportions of any two of the three systems mentioned.

It was not our province to treat of the mystic movement in mediæval Jewry as it developed in the Kabbalistic works and gained the ground yielded in the course of time by the healthier rationalism. To complete the picture it will suffice to say that as the political and economic conditions of the Jews in the fourteenth and fifteenth centuries deteriorated, and freedom and toleration were succeeded by persecution and expulsion, the Jews became more zealous for their own spiritual heritage as distinguished from foreign importations; philosophy and rationalism began to be regarded askance, particularly as experience showed that scientific training was not favorable to Jewish steadfastness and loyalty. In suffering and persecution those who stuck to their posts were as a rule not the so-called enlightened who played with foreign learning, but the simple folk who believed in Torah and tradition in the good old style. The philosophical and the scientific devotees were the first to yield, and many of them abandoned Judaism.[436] Thus it was that mysticism and obscurantism took the place of enlightenment as a measure of self-defence. The material walls of the Ghetto and the spiritual walls of the Talmud and the Kabbala kept the remnant from being overwhelmed and absorbed by the hostile environment of Christian and Mohammedan. The second half of the fourteenth, and the fifteenth century were not favorable to philosophical studies among the Jews, and the few here and there who still show an interest in science and philosophy combine with it a belief in Kabbala and are not of any great influence on the development of Judaism.

Shemtob ben Joseph ibn Shemtob (ab. 1440) author of a work entitled "Emunot," [437] is a strong opponent of Greek science and philosophy. He is not content with attacking the lesser lights and extremists like Albalag or Gersonides or Abraham ibn Ezra. He goes to the very fountain-head of Jewish Aristotelianism and holds Maimonides responsible for the heresies which invaded the Jewish camp. He takes up one doctrine after another of the great Jewish philosopher and points out how dangerous it is to the true Jewish faith. Judah Halevi and Nachmanides represent to him the true Jewish attitude. The mysteries of the Jewish faith are revealed not in philosophy but in the Kabbala, which Maimonides did not study, and which he would not have understood if he had studied it, for he had no Kabbalistic tradition.

Unlike Shemtob, his son Joseph ben Shemtob (d. 1480) [438] shows great admiration for Aristotle and Maimonides. But he is enabled to

do so by lending credence to a legend that Aristotle in his old age re-
canted his heretical doctrines, in particular that of the eternity of the
world. Joseph ben Shemtob made a special study of Aristotle's Ethics,
to which he wrote a commentary, and endeavored to show that the
Stagirite's ethical doctrines had been misunderstood; that the highest
good of man and his ultimate happiness are to be sought according
to Aristotle not in this world but in the next. It was likewise a misunderstanding, he thinks, when Maimonides and others make Aristotle deny special Providence. True science is not really opposed to
Judaism. At the same time he too like his father realizes the danger
of too much scientific study, and hence agrees with Solomon ben Adret
that the study of philosophy should be postponed to the age of matu-
rity when the student is already imbued with Jewish learning and
religious faith.

The son of Joseph, bearing the name of his grandfather, Shemtob ben Joseph (fl. ab. 1461–89), followed in his father's
footsteps,[439] and wrote a commentary on the "Guide of the
Perplexed" of Maimonides, whom he defends against the attacks of
Crescas.

Isaac ben Moses Arama (1420–1494)[440] is the author of a
philosophico-homiletical commentary on the Pentateuch entitled,
"Akedat Yizhak," and a small treatise on the relations of philosophy
and theology. He was also interested in Kabbala and placed Jewish
revelation above philosophy.

Don Isaac Abarbanel (1437–1508),[441] the distinguished Jewish statesman who went with his brethren into exile at the time of the expulsion
of the Jews from Spain in 1492, was a prolific writer on Biblical exegesis and religious philosophy. Though a great admirer of Maimonides, on whose "Guide" he wrote a commentary, and whose thirteen
articles of the creed he defended against the strictures of Crescas and
Albo, he was nevertheless an outspoken opponent of the rationalistic
attitude and has no phrases strong enough for such men as Albalag,
Gersonides, Moses of Narbonne and others, whom he denounces as
heretics and teachers of dangerous doctrines. He does not even spare
Maimonides himself when the latter attempts to identify the traditional "Maase Bereshit" and "Maase Merkaba" with the Aristotelian Physics and Metaphysics (cf. above, p. 303 f.), and adopts Kab-

balistic views along with philosophic doctrines. He is neither original nor thoroughly consistent.

His son Judah Leo Abarbanel (1470–1530) [442] is the author of a philosophical work in Italian, "Dialoghi di Amore," (Dialogues of Love), which breathes the spirit of the Renaissance of the fifteenth and sixteenth centuries in Italy. It is under the influence of Plato and Plotinus and identifies God with love, which is regarded as the essential principle of all life and activity in the world, including even the inorganic natural processes. There is no attempt made to construct a Jewish philosophy, and though all evidence is against it, some have made it out that Judah Abarbanel was a convert to Christianity.

In the same country, in Italy, Judah ben Yechiel Messer Leon of Mantua [443] (1450–1490) made a name for himself as a student of Cicero and of mediæval Latin scholasticism. He wrote a rhetoric in Hebrew based upon Cicero and Lactantius, and composed logical works based upon Aristotle's Latin text and Averroes. As an original student of philosophy he is of no importance.

Two members of the Delmedigo family of Crete, Elijah (1460–1498) and Joseph Solomon,[444] are well known as students of philosophy and writers on philosophical and scientific subjects.

Thus the stream of philosophical thought which rose among the Jews in Babylonia and flowed on through the ages, ever widening and deepening its channel, passing into Spain and reaching its high water mark in the latter half of the twelfth century in Maimonides, began to narrow and thin out while spreading into France and Italy, until at last it dried up entirely in that very land which opened up a new world of thought, beauty and feeling in the fifteenth century, the land of the Renaissance. Jewish philosophy never passed beyond the scholastic stage, and the freedom and light which came to the rest of the world in the revival of ancient learning and the inventions and discoveries of the modern era found the Jews incapable of benefiting by the blessings they afforded. Oppression and gloom caused the Jews to retire within their shell and they sought consolation for the freedom denied them without in concentrating their interests, ideals and hopes upon the Rabbinic writings, legal as well as mystical. There have appeared philosophers among the Jews in succeeding centuries, but they either philosophized without regard to Judaism and in opposition to its fundamental dogmas, thus incurring the wrath and exclusion of the synagogue, or they sought to dissociate Judaism from theoretical speculation on the ground that the Jewish religion is not a philosophy but a rule of conduct. In more recent times Jewry has divided itself into sects and under the influence of modern individualism has lost its central authority making every group the arbiter of its own belief and practice and narrowing the religious influence to matters of ceremony and communal activity of a practical character. There are Jews now and there are philosophers, but there are no Jewish philosophers and there is no Jewish philosophy.

BIBLIOGRAPHY[1]

GENERAL WORKS

SOLOMON MUNK, Mélanges de Philosophie Juive et Arabe, Paris, 1859, pp. 461–511. A brief historical résumé of philosophical authors and books. German translation by Beer, Philosophie und philosophische Schriftsteller der Juden, Leipzig, 1852. English translation by Isidor Kalisch, Philosophy and Philosophical Authors of the Jews, Cincinnati, 1881.

A. SCHMIEDL, Studien über jüdische, insonders jüdisch-arabische Religions-philosophie, Wien, 1869.

MORITZ EISLER, Vorlesungen über die jüdischen Philosophen des Mittelalters (3 parts), Wien, 1870–84.

DAVID KAUFMANN, Geschichte der Attributenlehre in der jüdischen Religionsphilosophie des Mittelalters von Saadia bis Maimuni, Gotha, 1877.

SIMEON BERNFELD, דעת אלהים, תולדות הפלוסופיא הדתית בישראל, Warsaw, 1897.

S. HOROVITZ, Die Psychologie bei den jüdischen Religions-Philosophen des Mittelalters, von Saadia bis Maimuni, Breslau, 1898–1912 (includes so far Saadia, Gabirol, Ibn Zaddik, Abraham ibn Daud).

J. POLLAK, "Entwicklung der arabischen und jüdischen Philosophie im Mittelalter" in Archiv für Geschichte der Philosophie, vol. xvii (1904), pp. 196–236, 433–459.

UEBERWEG-BAUMGARTNER, Grundriss der Geschichte der Philosophie, vol. II, 10th ed., Berlin, 1915, pp. 385–403.

DAVID NEUMARK, Geschichte der jüdischen Philosophie des Mittelalters, nach Problemen dargestellt, vol. I, Berlin, 1907, vol. II, part I, Berlin, 1910.

IGNAZ GOLDZIHER, Die jüdische Philosophie in Allgemeine Geschichte der Philosophie, von W. Wundt, etc. (Die Kultur der Gegenwart I, 5), pp. 70–77 (2nd ed., pp. 301–337).

KALAM IN JEWISH PHILOSOPHY

MARTIN SCHREINER, Der Kalam in der jüdischen Literatur, Berlin, 1895.

ISAAC ISRAELI

JACOB GUTTMANN, Die philosophischen Lehren des Isaak ben Salomon Israeli, Münster i. W. 1911.

[1] This bibliography contains a selection of the more important works of exposition. For original sources see the notes.

Al Mukammas

Abraham Harkavy, in Russian periodical *Woskhod*, Sept. 1898.

Saadia

Jacob Guttmann, Die Religionsphilosophie des Saadia, Göttingen, 1882.
D. J. Engelkemper, Saadja Gaon's religionsphilosophische Lehre über die heilige Schrift, übersetzt und erklärt, Münster, 1903.

Joseph Al Basir

P. F. Frankl, Ein Mu'tazilitischer Kalam aus dem 10, Jahrhundert, Wien, 1872.
Miksa Klein, Júszuf Al-Baszîr, Al-Kitâb Al-Muhtavî, Budapest, 1913.
Ernö Morgenstern, Júszuf Al-Baszîr, Al Kitâb Al Muhtavî, Budapest, 1913.

Jeshua ben Judah

Martin Schreiner, Studien über Jeschu'a ben Jehuda, Berlin, 1900.

Solomon ibn Gabirol

S. Munk, Mélanges, etc., Paris, 1859, pp. 151–306.
Seyerlen, in Zeller's Theologische Jahrbücher, vols. XV and XVI.
Jacob Guttmann, Die Philosophie des Salomon ibn Gabirol, Göttingen, 1889.
David Kaufmann, Studien über Salomon ibn Gabirol, Budapest, 1899.

Bahya ibn Pakuda

David Kaufmann, "Die Theologie des Bachja ibn Pakuda," in "Gesammelte Schriften von David Kaufmann" (ed. Brann), vol. II, Frankfurt a. M., 1910, pp. 1–98.
J. H. Hertz, Bachya, The Jewish Thomas à Kempis, New York, 1898 (in Sixth Biennial Report of the Jewish Theological Seminary Association).

Psuedo-Bahya

Jacob Guttmann, "Eine bisher unbekannte, dem Bachja ibn Pakuda zugeignete Schrift," *Monatschrift f. G. u. W. d. J.*, vol. XLI (1897), p. 241 ff.

Abraham bar Hiyya

Jacob Guttmann, in *Monatschrift f. G. u. W. d. J.*, 1900.

Joseph ibn Zaddik

Max Doctor, Die Philosophie des Joseph ibn Zaddik, nach ihren Quellen, insbesondere nach ihren Beziehungen zu den Lauteren Brüdern und zu Gabirol untersucht, Münster, 1895.

Leopold Weinsberg, Der Mikrokosmos, ein angeblich im 12. Jahrhundert von dem Cordubenser Joseph ibn Zaddik verfasstes philosophisches System, nach seiner Echtheit untersucht, Breslau, 1888.

Judah Halevi

Ad. Frankl-Grün, Sie Ethik des Juda Halevi, Bilin, s. a.

David Kaufmann, Jehuda Halewi, Versuch einer Charakteristik, Breslau, 1877; reprinted in *Gesammelte Schriften* (ed. Brann), Frankfurt a. M., 1910, vol. II, pp. 99–151.

David Neumark, Jehuda Hallevi's Philosophy in its Principles, Cincinnati, 1908.

Julius Guttmann, "Das Verhältniss von Religion und Philosophie bei Jehuda Halewi," in Israel Lewy's *Festschrift* (ed. Brann and Elbogen), Breslau, 1911, pp. 327–358.

Abraham ibn Ezra

Nachman Krochmal, מורה נבוכי הזמן, Warsaw, 1894, p. 266 ff.

David Rosin, "Die Religionsphilosophie Abraham ibn Esras," in *Monatschrift f. G. u. W. d. J.*, vols. XLII (1898) and XLIII (1899).

G. Orschansky, Abraham ibn Esra als Philosoph, Breslau, 1900.

Abraham ibn Daud

Gugenheimer, Die Religionsphilosophie des R. Abraham ben David ha-Levi nach dessen noch ungedruckter Schrift *Emuna Rama* in ihrem inneren und historischen Zusammenhange entwickelt, Augsburg, 1850.

Jacob Guttmann, Die Religionsphilosophie des Abraham ibn Daud aus Toledo, Göttingen, 1897.

Maimonides

M. Joel, Die Religionsphilosophie des Mose ben Maimon, Breslau, 1876.

Simon B. Scheyer, Das Psychologische System des Maimonides, Frankfurt a. M., 1845.

David Rosin, Die Ethik des Maimonides, Breslau, 1876.

Moses ben Maimon, sein Leben, seine Werke und sein Einfluss, herausgegeben von der Gesellschaft zur Förderung der Wissenschaft des Judenthums, Band I, Leipzig, 1908.

Louis-Germain Lévy, Maimonide, Paris, 1911 (Les Grands Philosophes).

J. Münz, Moses ben Maimon, sein Leben und seine Werke, Frankfurt a. M., 1912.

M. JOEL, Verhältniss Albert des Grossen zu Moses Maimonides, Breslau, 1876.

JACOB GUTTMANN, "Der Einfluss der Maimonidischen Philosophie auf das christliche Abendland," in *Moses ben Maimon* (see above), pp. 135–230.

DAVID KAUFMANN, "Der "Führer" Maimûni's in der Weltliteratur," *Archiv für Geschichte der Philosophie*, vol. XI (1898), pp. 335–376; reprinted in *Gesammelte Schriften* (ed. Brann), Frankfurt a. M., 1910, vol. II, pp. 152–189.

J. P. WICKERSHAM CRAWFORD, "The *Vision Delectable* of Alfonso de la Torre and Maimonides' *Guide of the Perplexed*," *Publications of the Modern Language Association of America*, XXVIII, 2 (1913), pp. 188–212.

ISAAC HUSIK, "An Anonymous Medieval Christian Critic of Maimonides," *Jewish Quarterly Review*, New Series, vol. II, 1911, pp. 159–190.

GERSONIDES

M. JOEL, Lewi ben Gerson als Religionsphilosoph, Breslau, 1862.

ISIDORE WEIL, Philosophie Religieuse de Levi ben Gerson, Paris, 1868.

BENZION KELLERMANN, Die Kämpfe Gottes von Lewi ben Gerson, Uebersetzung und Erklärung des handschriftlich revidierten Textes, Erster Teil, Berlin, 1914. Contains the German translation of the first book of the *Milhamot Adonai*. The translation is faulty in many places, as the present writer has shown in an article entitled, "Studies in Gersonides," which appeared in the *Jewish Quarterly Review*, New Series, VIII (1917–18), 113 f., 231 f.

HASDAI CRESCAS

M. JOEL, Don Chasdai Creskas' religionsphilosophische Lehren in ihrem geschichtlichen Einflusse dargestellt, Breslau, 1866.

PHILIPP BLOCH, Die Willensfreiheit von Chasdai Kreskas, München, 1879.

JULIUS WOLFSOHN, Der Einfluss Gazâlî's auf Chisdai Crescas, Frankfurt a. M., 1905.

DAVID NEUMARK, "Crescas and Spinoza," in Commemoration of the Fifth Centenary of the Publication of the *Or Adonai;* in *Year Book of the Central Conference of American Rabbis*, XVIII, 1908, pp. 277–318.

JOSEPH ALBO

SAMUEL BACK, Joseph Albo's Bedeutung in der Geschichte der jüdischen Religionsphilosophie, Breslau, 1869.

JAULUS, in *Monatschrift f. G. u. W. d. J.*, 1874, p. 462 ff.

A. TÄNZER, Die Religionsphilosophie Joseph Albo's nach seinem Werke *Ikkarim* systematisch dargestellt und erläutert, Frankfurt a. M., 1896.

Biblical Exegesis

W. Bacher, Die Bibelexegese der jüdischen Religionsphilosophen des Mittelalters vor Maimûni, Budapest, 1892.

Idem., "Die Jüdische Bibelexegese vom Anfange des zehnten bis zum Ende des fünfzehnten Jahrhunderts," Treves, 1892, reprinted from Winter und Wünsche, *Die jüdische Literatur seit Abschluss des Kanons*, II, 239–339, where a full bibliography is given.

Idem., *Jewish Encyclopedia*, s. v. Bible Exegesis, §14–16.

Influence of Jewish Philosophy on Scholasticism

The works of Joel, Guttmann, Kaufmann, Crawford and Husik mentioned above under Maimonides; and besides

Jacob Guttmann, Das Verhältniss des Thomas von Aquino zum Judenthum und zur jüdischen Litteratur, Göttingen, 1891.

Idem., Die Scholastik des dreizehnten Jahrhunderts in ihren Beziehungen zum Judenthum und zur jüdischen Literatur, Breslau, 1902.

Additions

Atlas, Samuel, „לתורת ההכרה של הרמב"ם", בספר היובל לכבוד ד"ר מרדכי ברודא, כרך נ'ד', מכתבי המכון לחכמת ישראל בוורשה, Warsaw, 5691–1931.

Bamberger, Fritz, Die System des Maimonides, Berlin, 1935.

Baneth, D. H., "The Common Theological Source of Bahye ibn Pakuda and Ghazzali," in *Magnes Anniversary Volume*, pp. 23–30. Jerusalem, 1938.

Baneth, D. Z., לטרמינילוניה הפילוסופית של הרמב"ם in *Tarbiz*, VI (1935), 10–40.

Berger, Emil, Das Probelm der Erkenntnis in der Religionsphilosophie Jehuda Hallewis, Berlin, 1916.

Bieler, Majer, Der göttliche Wille (Logosbegriff) bei Gabirol, Würzburg, 1933.

Bluvstein, Jacob, Hebrew translation of Gabirol's *Fons Vitae*, Jerusalem, 1926.

Brunner, Peter, Probleme der Teleologie bei Maimonides, Thomas von Aquin und Spinoza, Heidelberg, 1928.

Cassuto, Umberto, "L'Origine della Filosofia ebraica medioevale," in *Dibattiti Filosofici, Atti del V. Congresso Italiano di Filosofia: Il Solco*. Città di Castello, 1925, pp. 228–234.

Diesendruck, Z., "Maimonides' Lehre der Prophetie," in *Israel Abrahams Memorial Volume*, pp. 74–134, Vienna, 1927.

Diesendruck, Z., "Die Teleologie bei Maimonides," *Hebrew Union College Annual*, V (1928), 415–534, Cincinnati.

Diesendruck, Z., "On the date of the Composition of the Moreh Nebukim," in *Hebrew Union College Annual*, XII-XIII (1937–38), 461–497.

Diesendruck, Z., "Maimonides' Theory of the Negation of Privation," in *Proceedings of the Am. Ac. for Jewish Research*, VI (1934–35), 139–151.

Diesendruck, Z., מורה לדורות, in *Moznaim*, III (1935), 347–369.

Diesendruck, Z., התכלית והתארים בתורת הרמב״ם, in *Tarbiz*, I, 106–125.

Diesendruck, Z., "Saadya's Formulation of the Time-Argument for Creation," in *Jewish Studies in Memory of George Alexander Kohut*, New York, 1935, pp. 145–158.

Dreyer, Karl, Die religiöse Gedankenwelt des Salomo ibn Gabirol. Leipzig, 1930.

Efros, Israel I., "Palquera's Reshit Hakmah and Alfarabi's Iḥṣa al 'Ulum," in *JQR*, N. S., 25 (1935), 227–235.

Efros, Israel I., מלות ההגיון, Maimonides' Treatise on Logic, New York, 1938.

Efros, Israel I., The Problem of Space in Jewish Mediaeval Philosophy, New York, 1917.

Efros, Israel I., Philosophical Terms in the Moreh Nebukim, New York, 1924.

Epstein, Isidore, "Judah Halevi as Philosopher," *JQR*, N. S. 25 (1935), 201–225.

Finkel, Joshua, Maimonides' Treatise on Resurrection (Text), New York, 1939.

Finkel, Joshua, Maimonides' Treatise on Resurrection, edited by S. W. Baron, 1941, 93–121.

Gebhardt, Carl, Leone Ebreo, Dialoghi di Amore, Heidelberg, 1929.

Golinski, Georg, Das Wesen des Religionsgesetzes in der Philosophie des Bachja ibn Pakuda, Berlin, n. d.

Gulkowitsch, Lazar, Das Wesen der Maimonidischen Lehre. Tartu, 1935.

Guttmann, Julius, "Chasdai Creskas als Kritiker der aristotelischen Physik," in *Festschrift zum siebzigsten Geburtstage Jacob Guttmanns*, pp. 28–54, Leipzig, 1915.

Guttmann, Julius, "Zur Gabirols allegorischer Deutung der Erzählung vom Paradies," in *MGWJ*, 80 (1936), 180–184.

Guttmann, Julius, "Zur Kritik der Offenbarungsreligion in der islamischen und jüdischen Philosophie," in *MGWJ*, 78 (1934), 456–464.

Guttmann, Julius, Die Philosophie des Judentums, Munich, 1933.

Guttmann, Julius, "Das Problem der Willensfreiheit by Hasdai Crescas und dem islamischen Aristotelikern," *Jewish Studies in Memory of George A. Kohut*, 1935, 325–349.

Heinemann, Isaac, "Abravanels Lehre vom Niedergang der Menschheit," in *MGWJ*, 82 (1938), 381–400.

Heinemann, Isaak, "Maimuni und die Arabischen Einheitslehrer," in *MGWJ*, 79 (1935), 102–148.

Heschel, Abraham, "Der Begriff der Einheit in der Philosophie Gabirols," in *MGWJ*, 82 (1938), 89–111.

HESCHEL, ABRAHAM, Maimonides, Eine Biographie, Berlin, 1935.

HESCHEL, ABRAHAM, "Das Wesen der Dinge nach der Lehre Gabirols," in *Hebrew Union College Annual*, 14 (1939), 359–385.

HUSIK, ISAAC, "Jewish Philosophy," in *Ency. Brit.*, 14th ed., 1929.

HUSIK, ISAAC, Sefer ha-'Ikkarim, critical Hebrew text, English translation and notes, 5 vols., Philadelphia, 1929–30.

HUSIK, ISAAC, "Joseph Albo, the last of the Jewish Mediaeval Philosophers," in *Proc. of the Am. Acad. for Jewish Research*, Phila., 1930.

HUSIK, ISAAC, "Maimonides and Spinoza on the Interpretation of the Bible," in *Supplement to the Journal Am. Orient. Soc.*, 55 (1935), 22-40.

KARO, JAKOB, Kritische Untersuchungen zu Levi ben Gersons (Ralbag) Widerlegung des Aristotelischen Zeitbegriffes, Leipzig, 1935.

KAUFMAN, JUDAH IBN SHMUEL, מורה נבוכים ... עם פירוש ... יהודה אבן שמואל, Tel-Aviv, pt. I, 1935, pt. II, 1938.

KLATZKIN, JACOB, Anthology of Jewish Philosophy (in Hebrew), Vol. I, Berlin, Eschkol, 1926.

KLATZKIN, JACOB, Thesaurus Philosophicus Linguae Hebraicae et Veteris et Recentioris (in Hebrew), Vols. I and II, Berlin, Eschkol, 1928.

KLAUSNER, "Solomon ibn Gabirol, Poet and Philosopher," Introduction (in Hebrew) to Bluvstein's Hebrew translation of the *Fons Vitae*, Jerusalem, 1926.

KOKOWZOFF, P., "The Date of Life of Bahya ibn Paqoda," in *Livre d'Hommage à la Memoire du Dr. Samuel Poznański*, pp. 13–21, Warsaw, 1927.

KÖNIG, MOSES, Die Philosophie des Jehuda Halevi und des Abraham ibn Daud, Berlin, 1929.

KOPLOWITZ, ERNST S., Die Abhängigkeit Thomas von Aquin von R. Moses ben Maimon, Würzburg, 1935.

MALTER, HENRY, Saadia Gaon, Life and Works, Philadelphia, 1921.

MALTER, HENRY, "Jewish Philosophy," in Hastings, *Encyclopedia of Religion and Ethics*, Vol. 9, pp. 873–877.

MARX, ALEXANDER, "Texts about Maimonides," in *JQR*, N. S. 25 (1935), 371–428.

NEUMARK, DAVID, Essays in Jewish Philosophy, Vienna, 1929.

NEUMARK, DAVID, "Saadya's Philosophy," in *Hebrew Union College Annual*, Vol. I, pp. 503–573, Cincinnati, 1924.

NEUMARK, DAVID, History of Mediaeval Jewish Philosophy (in Hebrew), Vol. I, Stiebel, N. Y., Warsaw, Moscow, 1921; Vol. II, Cin., 1929.

PFLAUM, HEINZ, "Die Idee der Liebe, Leone Ebreo," Tübingen, 1926.
Roth, Leon, *Spinoza, Descartes and Maimonides*, Oxford, 1924.
Uberweg-Geyer, Grundriss der Geschichte der Philosophie. Zweiter Teil, Berlin, 1928.

RAWIDOWICZ, SIMON, "Philosophy as a Duty," in *Moses Maimonides* (VIII Centenary Volume), ed. I. Epstein, London, 1935, pp. 179–188.

RAWIDOWITZ, SIMON, בעית ההגשמה לרס"נ ולרמב"ם in *Kenesset*, 1938, pp. 222–377.

RAWIDOWITZ, SIMON, שאלת מבנהו של "מורה נבוכים" in *Tarbiz*, VI (1935), 41–89.

RAWIDOWITZ, SIMON, אדם ואלוה (פרק בתורת האלהות של הרמב"ם), in *Moznaim*, III (1935), pp. 493–526.

RIEDL, JOHN O., "Maimonides and Scholasticism;" in *New Scholasticism* 10 (1936), 18–29.

ROSENTHAL, E., "Maimonides' conception of State and Society," in *Moses Maimonides* (VIII Centenary Volume), ed. I. Epstein, London, 1936, pp. 191–206.

ROTH, LEON, מלות ההגיון, Jerusalem, 1935.

SAMUELI, EPHRAIM, דון יצחק אברבנאל in *Kenesset*, 1938, pp. 295–321.

STRAUSS, LEO, "Eine Vermisste Schrift Parabes," in *MGWJ*, 80 (1936), 96–106.

STRAUSS, LEO, "On Abravanel's philosophical tendency and political teaching," in *Isaac Abravanel, Six Lectures*, Cambridge, University Press, 1837, pp. 93–129.

STRAUSS, LEO, Philosophie und Gesetz: Beiträge zum verständnis Maimunis und seiner Vorläufer. Berlin, 1935.

STRAUSS, LEO, "Quelques remarques sur la science politique de Maimuni et de Fârâbi," in *REJ*, 100 (1936), 1–37.

STRAUSS, LEO, "The Literary character of the Guide of the Perplexed," 1941, 37–91, in *Essays on Maimonides*, ed. S. W. Baron, New York, 1941, pp. 37–91.

STRAUSS, LEO, "Maimonides Lehre von der Prophetie und ihren quellen," in *Le Monde Oriental*, 28 (1934), 99–139.

TEICHER, JACOB, "Observations critiques sur l'interpretation traditionelle de la doctrine des attributs négatifs chez Maimonide," in *REJ*, 99 (1935), 56–67.

TEICHER, JACOB, "Studi preliminari sulla dottrina della conoscenza di Gersonide," in *Reale Accademia Nazionale dei Lincei*, Ser. VI, vol. VIII (1932), 500–510.

VENTURA, M., Le Kalâm et la Peripatétisme d'après le Kuzari. Paris. 1934.

VENTURA, M., La Philosophie de Saadia Gaon, Paris, 1934.

VENTURA, M., Maimonide: Terminologie logique, Paris, 1935.

WAXMAN, MEYER, דון יצחק אברבנאל in *Sefer ha-Shanah li-Yehudei Amerika*, New York, 1938.

WAXMAN, MEYER, "Maimonides as Dogmatist," in *Year Book of the Central Conference of Am. Rabbis*, 45 (1935), pp. 397–418.

WAXMAN, MEYER, The Philosophy of Don Hasdai Crescas, New York, 1920.

WEISS, ADOLF, Mose ben Maimon, Führer der Unschlüssigen, ins Deutsch übertragen und mit erklärenden Anmerkungen versehen (contains also a long introduction, pp. xix-cccxx), 3 vols., Leipzig, 1923.

WOLFSON, HARRY A., "Crescas on the Problem of Divine Attributes," in *JQR*, N. S., VII (1916), pp. 1–44, 175–221.

WOLFSON, HARRY A., "Note on Crescas' Definition of Time," in *JQR*, N. S., (1919), pp. 1–17.

WOLFSON, HARRY A., "Notes of Proofs of the Existence of God in Jewish Philosophy," in *Hebrew Union College Annual*, I, pp. 575–596, Cincinnati, 1924.

WOLFSON, HARRY A., "The Classification of Science in Mediaeval Jewish Philosophy," in *Hebrew Union College Jubilee Volume*, pp. 263–315. Cincinnati, 1925.

WOLFSON, HARRY A., "Additional Notes to Hebrew Union College Jubilee Volume," in *Hebrew Union College Annual*, III, pp. 371–375, Cincinnati, 1926.

WOLFSON, HARRY A., "The Problem of the Origin of Matter in Mediaeval Jewish Philosophy," in *Proceedings of the Sixth International Congress of Philosophy* (1926), pp. 602–608.

WOLFSON, HARRY A., Crescas' Critique of Maimonides, Cambridge, 1929.

WOLFSON, HARRY A., "The Internal Senses in Latin, Arabic and Hebrew Philosophic Texts," in *Harvard Theological Review*, 28 (1935), 69–133.

WOLFSON, HARRY A., "Isaac Israeli on the Internal Senses," in *Jewish Studies in Memory of George A. Kohut*, 1935, 583–598.

WOLFSON, HARRY A., "Maimonides on the Internal Senses," in *JQR*, N. S., 25 (1935), 441–467.

WOLFSON, HARRY A., Note on Maimonides' Classification of the Sciences, *JQR*, N. S., 26 (1936), 369–377.

WOLFSON, HARRY A., "The Aristotelian Predicables and Maimonides' Division of Attributes," *Essays and Studies in Memory of Linda R. Miller*, 1938, 201–234.

WOLFSON, HARRY A., "The Amphibolous Terms in Aristotle, Arabic Philosophy and Maimonides," in *Harvard Theological Review*, 31 (1938), 151–173.

ZEITLIN, S., Maimonides, New York, 1935.

For further references see the notes.

NOTES

[Black figures denote the page, the light figures the notes]

xv, 1. See below, p. 395 ff.

xvi, 2. Talm. Bab. Hagiga 11b.

3. Ibid.

4. See Zeller, Die Philosophie der Griechen, III, 2, 3d ed. p. 347; Maimonides, Guide of the Perplexed, I, ch. 71, beginning.

xvii, 5. See Wenrich, De Auctorum Graecorum Versionibus et Commentariis Syriacis, Arabicis, Armeniacis Persicisque, Leipzig, 1842, p. 4 ff; De Boer, Geschichte der Philosophie im Islam, Stuttgart, 1901, p. 17 ff (English translation by Jones, London, 1903, pp. 11–30). Duval, La Littérature Syriaque 2nd ed., Paris, 1900, ch. XIV, § 2, p. 253 ff.

xx, 6. See Dieterici, Die Theologie des Aristotles (Arabic text), Leipzig, 1882; German translation by the same, Leipzig, 1883.

7. See Bardenhewer, Die Pseudoaristotelische Schrift über das reine Gute, bekannt unter dem Namen Liber de causis, Freiburg i. Br., 1882.

8. See Valentinus Rose, Deutsche Literaturzeitung, 1883, p. 843.

9. See Husik, Judah Messer Leon's Commentary upon the "Vetus Logica," Leyden, 1906, p. 11, 97 note.

xxi, 10. For the following sketch of the Kalam see Goldziher, Vorlesungen über den Islam, Heidelberg, 1910, 100 ff, 127 f.

xxiv, 11. See below, p. 247.

xxv, 12. See Schreiner, Der Kalam in der jüdischen Literatur, Berlin, 1895, p. 3; ibid., Studien über Jeschu'a ben Jehuda, Berlin, 1900, p. 12 ff.

xxvi, 13. See L. Ginzberg, in Jewish Encyclopedia, s. v. "Anthropomorphism."

14. See Talm. Bab. Berakot, 33b.
‫מודים מודים משתקין אותו‬.

15. See Talm. Bab. Megillah, 25b.
‫הכל בידי שמים חוץ מיראת שמים‬.

16. Schreiner, Studien über Jeschu'a ben Jehudah, p. 15 note 2.

17. See Bab. Talm. Pesakim, 54a,
‫שבעה דברים נבראו קודם שנברא העולם‬
(‫ואלו הן תורה.... תורה דכתיב (משלי ח׳‬
‫ה׳ קנני ראשית דרכו.‬

18. Schreiner l. c. p. 12.

19. Ibid.

20. Schreiner, Der Kalam in der jüdischen Literatur, p. 3, 4.

xxvii, 21. Guide of the Perplexed, I, ch. 71.

22. See below, p. 246 ff.

23. See Goldziher, Vorlesungen über den Islam, p. 155 ff.

xxviii, 24. See Yahuda, Al-Hidāja 'Ilā Farā'id Al-Qulūb des Bachja ibn Joseph Ibn Paquda, Leyden, 1912, p. 53 ff.

xxxvii, 25. Cf. above, note 6.

1, 26. See Steinschneider, Die Hebräischen Uebersetzungen des Mittelalters und die Juden als Dolmetscher, Berlin, 1893, § 479 and notes.

1, 27. See Guttmann, Die Scholastik des dreizehnten Jahrhunderts in ihren Beziehungen zum Judenthum und zur jüdischen Literatur, Breslau, 1902, p. 55 ff.

28. Omnia Opera Ysaac, Lugduni, (Lyons), 1515.

2, 29. See ‫אגרות הרמב״ם‬, ed. Amsterdam, p. 14b.

30. S. Fried, Das Buch über die Elemente (‫ספר היסודות‬), Drohobycz, 1900.

31. Published by Hirschfeld in "Fest-schrift zum achtzigsten Geburtstag Moritz Steinschneiders," Leipzig, 1896, pp. 131–141; cf. also pp. 233–4.

32. See note 28 and the two preced-ing notes.

5, 33. ספר הרוח והנפש published by Steinschneider in the Hebrew periodi-cal הכרמל I, pp. 401–405. Cf. Gutt-mann, Die philosophischen Lehren des Isaak ben Salomon Israeli, Münster i. W., 1911, p. 31, note 1.

10, 34. Fried, ספר היסודות, p. 12f.

17, 35. Berlin, 1885, pp. 65, 77–83, 151–154.

36. See the Russian paper Woskhod, September, 1898.

24, 37. Arabic text edited by S. Landauer, Kitāb al-Amānāt wa'l-I'tiqādāt, Leyden 1880. The Hebrew translation of Judah ibn Tibbon has been published in many editions. The references in the following notes are to the Yozefov edition.

25, 38. Cf. below, p. 249 ff.

39. Pt. I, ch. 1, third argument, p. 58 of Yozefov edition.

40. Ibid., fourth argument, p. 59.

26, 41. Ibid., ch. 3, p. 63 ff.; cf. Gutt-mann, Die Religionsphilosophie des Saadia, Göttingen, 1882, p. 45 f.

42. Pt. II, chs. 9–12, pp. 95–101.

43. Pt. VI, ch. 1, p. 149.

44. Pt. II, ch. 2, pp. 88–9.

27, 45. Introduction, pp. 38–39.

46. Ibid., p. 40.

28, 47. Ibid., pp. 43–48.

48. Ibid., p. 48.

49. p. 49.

50. p. 51.

29, 51. Pt. I. Introduction, p. 54 f.

52. Ibid., ch. 1, p. 56.

30, 53. Ibid., p. 57.

54. Ibid., p. 58.

55. Ibid., p. 59.

31, 56. Ch. 2, p. 60 ff.

57. Ch. 3, third opinion, p. 66 ff.

32, 58. Ch. 4, pp. 80–82.

59. Pt. II, Introduction, p. 86.

60. Ibid., ch. 1, p. 88.

33, 61. Pt. I, ch. 3, fifth opinion, p. 68.

62. Pt. II, ch. 2, p. 89.

34, 63. Ibid., chs. 4–5, pp. 91–93.

64. See Graf, Die Philosophie und Gotteslehre des Jahjā ibn 'Adī und späteren Autoren, Münster, 1910, p. 32, note, p. 52.

35, 65. III, ch. 10, p. 122; V, ch. 8, p. 147; VII, ch. 2, p. 165.

66. II, chs. 9–12, pp. 95–102.

37, 67. VI, chs. 1–4, pp. 148–156.

38, 68. III, chs. 1–3, pp. 104–110.

40, 69. Ibid., chs. 4–5, pp. 110–113.

70. Ch. 6, pp. 113–114.

71. Chs. 7–9, pp. 114–121.

41, 72. IV, pp. 124–136.

42, 73. V, chs. 1–3, pp. 136–140.

43, 74. IX, chs. 1–4, pp. 185–190.

44, 75. VI, ch. 8, pp. 160–162.

45, 76. VII, chs. 1–9, pp. 162–174.

77. VIII, pp. 175–185.

78. IX, chs. 5–11, pp. 190–197.

46, 79. X, pp. 197–215.

48, 80. The following sketch is based upon Frankl, Ein Mu'tazilitischer Kalam aus dem 10ten Jahrhundert, Wien, 1872.

55, 81. The following sketch is based upon Schreiner, Studien über Jeschu'a ben Jehuda, Berlin, 1900.

60, 82. אגרות הרמב"ם (Letters of Maimonides), ed. Amsterdam, p. 14b.

61, 83. See Munk, Mélanges de Philosophie Juive et Arabe, Paris, 1859, p. 291 ff; Guttmann, Die Scholastik des Dreizehnten Jahrhunderts, Breslau, 1902, pp. 60–85. Id., Die Philosophie des Salomon ibn Gabirol, Göttingen, 1889, p. 54 ff. This last work and that of Munk represent the best ex-position and criticism of Gabirol's philosophy and of his sources and in-fluences.

62, 84. Cf. Baeumker, Avencebrolis Fons Vitae, Münster, 1892-95, Prolegomena.

63, 85. Jourdain, A., Recherches Critiques sur l'âge et l'origine des traductions Latines d' Aristote, 2 ed. Paris, 1843, p. 197 note.

86. Munk, Mélanges, etc. (see note 83), contains the Hebrew extracts of Falaquera. The Latin translation was published by Clemens Baeumker in the Beiträge zur Geschichte der Philosophie des Mittelalters, vol. I, pts. 2-4 (cf. above note 84). See also Seyerlen in Theologische Jahrbücher, edited by Zeller, XV and XVI.

64, 87. Cf. Munk, Le Guide des Égarés, II, p. 25, note 1, end.

88. See Kaufmann, Studien über Salomon ibn Gabirol, Budapest, 1899.

89. Baeumker, Fons Vitae, V, p. 313, 6.

65, 90. F. V. V, 333-335, Falaquera in Munk's Mélanges, V, §§ 67-69.

91. F. V. IV, 8 ff., Falaquera IV, § 1.

92. F. V. V, 296, 10.

93. F. V. IV, 243, 10.

94. F. V. III, p. 196, 5 ff., Falaq. III, § 10.

95. F. V. III, 208, 15; Falaq. III, § 44.

67, 96. F. V. III, 175, 10 ff.; Falaq. III, § 27 ff.

97. F. V. IV, 211, 9 ff., 213, 17 ff., 217, 11 ff., 218, 18; Falaq. IV, §§ 1-4 and ff.

98. F. V. V, 258, 19; 259, 1; 268, 8, 14, 15; 322, 12; Falaq. V, § 55.

68, 99. F. V. V, 306, 7 ff.; Falaq. V, § 34 ff.

100. F. V. V, 330, 15 ff.; Falaq. V, § 64 ff.

101. F. V. V, 326, 3 ff.; Falaq. V, § 60 ff.

70, 102. F. V. III, 204, 13 ff.; Falaq. III, § 37.

71, 103. S. Wise, "Improvement of the Moral Qualities," New York, 1901. (Columbia University Oriental Studies, vol. 1.)

72, 104. F. V. I, 4, 24 ff.; Falaq. I, § 2.

78, 105. See Munk, Mélanges, 166 ff.

80, 106. Yahuda, Prolegomena zu einer erstmaligen Herausgabe des Kitāb Al-Hidāja 'Ilā Farā'id Al-Qulūb, Frankfurt a. M., 1904, 12 ff.; *id.*, Al-Hidaja 'Ilā Faraid Al-Qulūb des Bachja ibn Joseph ibn Paqūda, Leyden, 1912, 63 f.

107. Neumark, Geschichte der jüdischen Philosophie des Mittelalters, I, Berlin, 1907, 485-493.

81, 108. In his commentary on Deut. 32, 39. Cf. Yahuda, Prolegomena, p. 12, note 2, where 35 should be corrected to 39.

109. Yahuda, Al-Hidaja, etc., p. 97.

85, 110. חובת הלבבות (Duties of the Hearts) ed. Warsaw, 1875, Introduction, pp. 9-28.

86, 111. Ibid., Introduction, 28-37.

112. Yahuda, Al-Hidāja, pp. 53-112.

88, 113. Duties of the Hearts, I, chs. 1-6, pp. 41-58.

89, 114. Duties, I, ch. 6, pp. 57-8.

92, 115. Ibid., ch. 7, pp. 58-69.

93, 116. Ch. 8, pp. 69-72.

117. Ch. 9, pp. 72-76.

95, 118. Ch. 10, pp. 76-84.

96, 119. Guide of the Perplexed I, ch. 53.

120. Duties, ch. 1, p. 44.

121. Ibid., ch. 10, end, p. 92 f.

97, 122. Duties, II, pp. 95-137.

99, 123. III, pp. 138-197.

101, 124. IV, pp. 198-256.

125. Duties, 2nd volume, part V, pp. 3-35.

102, 126. VI, pp. 36-58.

103, 127. VII, pp. 58-82.

104, 128. VIII, pp. 82-126.

105, 129. IX, pp. 126-150.

130. X, pp. 151-168.

106, 131. Broydé, Les Reflexions sur l'âme par Bahya ben Joseph ibn Pa-

kouda, Paris, 1896; Hebrew title, ספר
תורות הנפש.

132. Goldziher, Kitāb Ma'ānī al-
nafs, Berlin, 1907.

133. See Guttmann in " Monatschrift
für Geschichte und Wissenschaft des
Judenthums," XLI (1897), 241 ff.

107, 134. Arabic text, p. 41, 12 and
46, 2; Hebrew, p. 55, 1 and 61, 5.

135. Ch. 2, p. 4, 29 (Heb. p. 5, last
line).

136. Ibid., p. 6, 1 (Heb. p. 7, 3).

137. Ibid., p. 5, 16 f. (Heb. 6, 16 f.).

138. Ibid., ch. 9, p. 34, 13 ff. (Heb.
p. 44, 10).

139. Ch. 2, p. 6, 6 ff. (Heb. p. 7,
8 f.).

140. Ch. 12, p. 42, 23 (Heb. p. 56, 23).

108, 141. Chs. 1–2.

111, 142. Chs. 16–17.

143. Chs. 6 and 11–12.

112, 144. Ch. 2.

145. Ch. 9.

113, 146. Ch. 7.

147. Chs. 19 and 21.

114, 148. ספר הגיון הנפש, edited by
Freimann, Leipzig, 1860. German
title, Sefer Hegjon ha-Nefesch.

115, 149. p. 2a.

150. Ibid., also 4b.

151. See, however, below, p. **119**.

152. p. 2b.

116, 153. p. 1.

117, 154. pp. 1–2.

118, 155. pp. 4b–5a.

156. pp. 2b–4a.

122, 157. pp. 5b–8a.

158. p. 8b ff.

123, 159. p. 11a.

160. pp. 10–12.

124, 161. p. 30b ff.

125, 162. See Doctor, Die Philosophie
des Joseph ibn Zaddik, Münster, 1895,
pp. 1–3; Horovitz, Der Mikrokosmos
des Joseph Ibn Saddik, Breslau, 1903,
I–II.

163. Horovitz, Mikrokosmos, XIII,
ff.

164. Letters of Maimonides, **ed.**
Amsterdam, 14b.

126, 165. Horovitz, Mikrokosmos, 7,
24–8, 2.

127, 166. Ibid., 44–46; 53–54; cf. below, p. 145.

167. Ibid., p. 37, 2 ff.; cf. below,
p. 138.

129, 168. pp. 1–2.

130, 169. pp. 3–6.

133, 170. pp. 7–19.

134, 171. pp. 19–25.

137, 172. pp. 25–33.

141, 173. pp. 33–43.

142, 174. pp. 43–47.

145, 175. pp. 47–57.

146, 176. pp. 57–58.

149, 177. pp. 59–79.

150, 178. Al-Chazari, I, 67, **ed.**
Hirschfeld, Leipzig, 1887, p. 29,
24.

179. Ibid., p. 29, 19–20.

180. I, 63; II, 66; pp. 29 and 125.

151, 181. See Kaufmann, Jehuda
Halewi in " Gesammelte Schriften,"
Frankfurt a. M., 1910, vol. 2, pp. 99–
151.

152, 182. Al-Chazari IV, 13, 15; p.
253, 18 ff., 257, 6 ff.

153, 183. Kaufmann, Geschichte
der Attributenlehre in der jüdischen
Religionsphilosophie des Mittelalters,
Gotha, 1877, pp. 119–140.

157, 184. Al-Chazari I, 1–67, pp. 1–
29.

158, 185. Ibid., 70 ff., p. 31 ff.

159, 186. II, 6; p. 75, 22 ff.

187. IX, 13; p. 253, 18 ff.

160, 188. IV, 3; p. 229, 10 ff.

189. Ibid., 15 ff.; p. 257, 6 ff.

161, 190. II, 2–4; pp. 71–75.

163, 191. I, 87 ff.; p. 39 ff.

164, 192. I, 99 ff.; p. 53 ff.

193. II, 10 ff.; p. 77 ff.

194. Ibid., 36 ff.; p. 103 ff.

165, 195. Ibid., 68 f.; p. 125 f.

167, 196. IV, 3 ff.; p. 237, 9 ff.

168, 197. II, 26, p. 95; 48, p. **107 f.**

169, 198. Ibid., 50, p. 109, 24 f.; III, 1 ff., p. 141 ff.

170, 199. I, 109 ff.; p. 59 ff.

173, 200. V, 20 ff., p. 337 ff.

201. IV, 25, p. 267 ff.

202. Ibid., 27, p. 283 f.

174, 203. Ibid., 29 ff., p. 285 ff.

175, 204. See above, p. 8.

205. Zeitschrift der deutschen morgenländischen Gesellschaft, XXIX (1875), pp. 335–418.

177, 206. V, 1 ff., p. 295 ff.

179, 207. IV, 25, p. 281, 24 ff.

181, 208. V, 12, p. 311 ff.

182, 209. Ibid., 14, p. 323 ff.

183, 210. Ibid., 16 ff., p. 331 ff.

211. Ibid., 22 ff., p. 357 ff.

184, 212. Quoted by Bacher in Jewish Encyclopedia, s. v. Ibn Ezra, Abraham.

213. Published by Dukes in "Zion," II, Frankfurt a. M., 1842, pp. 117–123, 134–137, 157–159, 175. Cf. also Literaturblatt des Orients, X, 748, where Dukes publishes a brief passage from the "Arugat Habosem," not found in "Zion." He derived it from a different manuscript.

187, 214. Jesod Mora, published with German translation by M. Creizenach, Frankfurt a. M., and Leipzig, 1840. Hebrew title יסוד מורא. Sefer Ha-Schem, ed. Lippmann, 1834. Cf., Bacher, Jewish Encyclopedia, s. v.

189, 215. מורה נבוכי הזמן, Warsaw, 1894, ch. 17 (חכמת המסכן), pp. 266 ff.

216. Die Religionsphilosophie Abraham Ibn Esra's, in "Monatschrift für Geschichte und Wissenschaft des Judenthums," 42 and 43 (1898 and 1899).

192, 217. Ibid., 42 (1898), pp. 454–455.

193, 218. Commentary on Exod. 33, 21, towards the end of the long excursus.

195, 219. Commentary on Exod. 20, 2.

220. Introduction to his commentary on Ecclesiastes.

197, 221. Emunah Ramah (Heb. title אמונה רמה), published with German translation by Simson Weil, Frankfurt a. M., 1852, p. 2 (Heb.).

222. Em. Ram., p. 83.

198, 223. See note 221.

224. Em. Ram., 2–3.

225. See note 221.

199, 226. See Horovitz, Ueber den Einfluss der griechischen Philosophie auf die Entwicklung des Kalam, Breslau, 1909.

200, 227. But see below, p. 354, l. 31.

202, 228. Em. Ram., p. 1 ff.

203, 229. Ibid., 4.

204, 230. Al Gazali. Cf. Guttmann, Die Religionsphilosophie des Abraham ibn Daud aus Toledo, Göttingen, 1879, p. 117, note.

205, 231. Em. Ram., 44–46.

232. Ibid., 4–8.

207, 233. Ibid., 9–13.

208, 234. Ibid., 13–15.

209, 235. Ibid., 15–20.

216, 236. Em. Ram., 20–41.

237. Ibid., 41–43.

220, 238. Em. Ram., 44–51.

221, 239. Ibid., 51–57.

223, 240. Ibid., 57–69.

224, 241. Ibid., 69–70.

226, 242. Ibid., 70–75.

228, 243. Ibid., 75–81.

230, 244. Ibid., 93–98.

232, 245. See Guttmann, Die Religionsphilosophie des Abraham Ibn Daud, p. 220, note 2.

235, 246. Ibid., 98–104.

236, 247. באור מלות ההגיון, Breslau, 1828. For other editions and interesting information concerning this treatise see Steinschneider, Die Hebräischen Uebersetzungen des Mittelalters, Berlin, 1893, § 251, and Die Arabische Literatur der Juden, Frankfurt a. M., 1902, p. 208, 5.

248. Introduction to the eleventh chapter (ch. Helek) of the treatise Sanhedrin.

239, 249. Letters of Maimonides, ed. Amsterdam, pp. 13b–14.

250. The Arabic text was published with a French translation and extremely valuable notes by Solomon Munk, under the title, Le Guide des Égarés, 3 volumes, Paris, 1856–66. English translation by M. Friedländer in 3 vols., London, 1881–1885, re-issued in one volume, with omission of notes, London, 1910. For other translations, editions and commentaries see Kaufmann, "Der 'Führer' Maimûnis in der Weltliteratur," Archiv für Geschichte der Philosophie, XI (1898), pp. 335–376, republished in Kaufmann's Gesammelte Schriften ed. Brann, vol. 2, Frankfurt a. M., 1910, pp. 152–189. See also Friedländer's translation, London, 1910, p. XXVII ff.

251. The Arabic text was published with a German translation by M. Wolff under the title, Mûsâ Maimûni's Acht Kapitel, 2nd edition, Leyden, 1903. Hebrew text with English translation by Joseph I. Gorfinkle, The Eight Chapters of Maimonides on Ethics, New York, 1912 (Columbia University Oriental Studies, vol. VII).

240, 252. Emunah Ramah, p. 81 ff.

241, 253. Guide, I, chs. 1, 3-16, 18–30, 37–45, 64–67, 70.

243, 254. Ibid., ch. 54.

255. III, 28.

256. I, 55.

244, 257. I, 32.

258. Ibid., ch. 33.

245, 259. Ch. 34.

260. Ch. 71.

246, 261. Ibid.

247, 262. Cf., however, above, p. xxv f. (the view that Kalam originated in Judaism).

248, 263. Ch. 71.

249, 264. The following numbers do not correspond to those of Maimonides.

252, 265. Guide, I, 73.

266. Ibid., 74.

253, 267. Ibid., 75.

268. Ibid., 76.

269. See below, p. 257.

270. Below, p. 259.

271. Above, p. 218.

272. Below, p. 258, last line, and 260.

257, 273. Guide II, Introduction.

260, 274. Ibid., ch. 1.

261, 275. Ch. 36.

262, 276. Ch. 46.

264, 277. Ibid., chs. 51–53.

265, 278. Chs. 55–58.

279. Ch. 61.

268, 280. See Munk, Guide des Égarés II, p. 69, note 1.

281. Guide II, chs. 3–6.

271, 282. Chs. 13–18.

272, 283. Munk understands the preceding sentence differently. See his edition, vol. II, p. 157, note 2.

274, 284. Guide II, chs. 19–25.

281, 285. Ibid., chs. 32–48.

286. III, ch. 8.

282, 287. " Eight Chapters," ch. 1.

285, 288. Ibid., chs. 2–5.

289. Ch. 7.

288, 290. Ch. 8.

289, 291. Guide III, chs. 10–12.

290, 292. Ibid., ch. 16.

292, 293. Ibid., chs. 17–18.

294, 294. Ibid., chs. 19–21.

295. Ibid., chs. 26 and 31.

295, 296. Ibid., ch. 27.

297. Ibid., ch. 50.

298, 298. Ibid., chs. 29–50.

299, 299. Ibid., ch. 54.

304, 300. Ibid., II, ch. 30.

301. Ibid., III, chs. 1–7.

302. See Munk, Le Guide des Égarés, III, p. 8, note.

303. Ibid.

304. Guide III, chs. 22–23.

305, 305. See Kaufmann, Der Führer Maimûnis in der Weltliteratur in Archiv für Geschichte der Philosophie XI (1898) p. 314 f.; reprinted in Kaufmann's Gesammelte Schriften, ed. Brann, Frankfurt a. M., 1910, p. 158 f.

306. See Jourdain, Recherches critiques sur l'âge et l'origine des traductions Latines d'Aristote, 2nd ed., Paris, 1843. German transl. by Stahr, Halle, 1831.

305, 307. Augustine, De Civitate Dei, Book VIII, ch. 5, "Nulli nobis quam isti [sc., Platonici] propius accesserunt"; ch. 9, "Platonem de Deo ista sensisse, quae multum congruere veritati nostrae religionis agnoscunt."

306, 308. See Mandonnet, Siger de Brabant et l'Averroïsme Latin au XIIIᵐᵉ Siècle, Louvain, 1911, chs. 1–2; Isaac Husik, An Anonymous Medieval Christian Critic of Maimonides, Jewish Quarterly Review, New Series, vol. II, Phila. 1911, p. 159 ff.

309. See J. Perles, "Die in einer Münchener Handschrift aufgefundene erste lateinische Uebersetzung des Maimonidischen Führers", in Monatschrift für Geschichte und Wissenschaft des Judenthums, XXIV (1875), p. 9 ff.

307, 310. See M. Joel, Verhältniss Albert des Grossen zu Moses Maimonides, Breslau, 1876, in M. Joel, Beiträge zur Geschichte der Philosophie, Breslau, 1876. J. Guttmann, Das Verhältniss des Thomas von Aquino zum Judenthum und zur jüdischen Literatur, Göttingen, 1891; id., Die Scholastik des dreizehnten Jahrhunderts in ihren Beziehungen zum Judenthum und zur jüdischen Literatur, Breslau, 1902; id., Der Einfluss der Maimonidischen Philosophie auf das christliche Abendland, in "Moses ben Maimon," vol. I, Leipzig, 1908.

308, 311. See Graetz, History of the Jews, index volume, s. v., " Maimunist Controversy."

309, 312. Published by M. L. Bisliches, Pressburg, 1837.

312a. Edited by W. Bacher under the title "Sefer Musar," Berlin, 1910.

313. Published by the "Mekize Nirdamim" Society, Lyck, 1866.

310, 314. Published by Munk in Mélanges de Philosophie Juive et Arabe, Paris, 1859.

315. Published by Bisliches, Pressburg, 1837.

316. See Munk, Mélanges, p. 494, note 1; H. Malter, Shem Tob Palquera, in Jewish Quarterly Review, new series, vol. 1, pp. 151–181, 451–501.

317. Published by Werbluner, Josephi Kaspi . . . Commentaria hebraica in R. Mosis Maimonides Tractatum Dalalat al Haiirin, Frankfurt a. M., 1848.

318, Edited by Goldenthal, Wien, 1852.

311, 319. The English reader will also find a good deal of material in the pages of the Jewish Encyclopedia under the names of the translators and writers above mentioned.

313, 320. Guide I, ch. 74, 7th proof, end.

314, 321. Published by the "Mekize Nirdamim," Lyck, 1874.

315, 322. Tagm. Hanef. 1.

317, 323. Ibid., 1b–7b. The definition occurs, p. 7b, ll. 28 ff.

318, 324. Ibid., 8a.

319, 325. Ibid., 8a–10a.

322, 326. Ibid., 10a–13b.

323, 327. Ibid., 13b–19b.

324, 328. Ibid., 20a–21b.

326, 329. Ibid., 21b–24b.

330. Ibid., 24.

327, 331. Ibid., 25a–32.

328, 331a. See Heimann Auerbach, Albalag und seine Uebersetzung des Makâsid al-Gazzalis, Breslau, 1906, p. vii f.; Guttmann, Die Stellung des Simon ben Zemach Duran in der Geschichte der jüdischen Religionsphilosophie in Monatschrift für Geschichte und Wissenschaft des Judenthums, vol. LVII (1913), p. 184 f.

328, 332. See Maywald, Die Lehre von der zweifachen Wahrheit, Berlin, 1871; Mandonnet, Siger de Brabant et l'Averroïsme Latin au XIIIme Siècle, Louvain, 1911, vol. 1, p. 148 ff.

329, 333. First edition, Riva di Trento, 1560; modern edition, Leipzig, 1866. The references in the sequel are to the Leipzig edition.

334. See Husik, Judah Messer Leon's Commentary on the "Vetus Logica," Leyden, 1906, p. 11.

335. See Joel, Lewi ben Gerson als Religionsphilosoph, Breslau, 1862, p. 9 f. (in M. Joel, Beiträge zur Geschichte der Philosophie, Breslau, 1876).

330, 336. Introduction to Gersonides' commentary on the Pentateuch.

337. Introduction to "Milhamot Adonai," pp. 6–7.

331, 338. Milhamot I, ch. 14, p. 91.

339. Ibid., Introduction, p. 8.

336, 340. I, chs. 1–4, pp. 12–35.

337, 341. Ibid., ch. 5, pp. 35–36.

339, 342. Ch. 6, pp. 36–48.

340, 343. Ibid., chs. 10–12, pp. 61–88.

342, 344. Milhamot II, chs. 1–2, pp. 92–98.

345. Ibid., chs. 3, 5 and 6, pp. 98 f., 104, 111 f.

344, 346. Milhamot III, ch. 3, p. 132.

345, 347. III, chs. 1–6, pp. 120–150.

349, 348. IV, chs. 1–7, pp. 151–187.

350, 349. V, 3, ch. 6, p. 264 f.

351, 350. Ibid., chs. 4–6, pp. 247–264.

352, 351. Ch. 12, pp. 278–285.

354, 352. VI, 1, chs. 1–9, pp. 293–328.

353. Ibid., chs. 10–13, pp. 328–353; ch. 15, p. 356 f.

355, 354. Ch. 16, pp. 359–361.

357, 355. Chs. 17–28, pp. 362–416.

356. VI, 2, ch. 1, p. 419.

358, 357. VI, 2, chs. 1–8, pp. 418–441.

360, 358. Ibid., chs. 9–12, pp. 441–460.

359. Chs. 13–14, pp. 460–463.

363, 360. Published by Delitzsch **and** Steinschneider, Leipzig, 1841.

364, 361. Ez Hayim, p. 4.

366, 362. E. H., pp. 3–5.

367, 363. p. 15, l. 6 f., also p. 18, l. 10 f.

364. Ch. 4, pp. 12–13, l. 24.

368, 365. Ch. 9, pp. 26–27.

369, 366. p. 17, l. 16.

367. p. 33.

372, 368. Chs. 66–72, pp. 80–89.

369. Ch. 75, pp. 93–96.

373, 370. Chs. 76–78, pp. 96–99.

375, 371. Chs. 79–81, pp. 100–107.

376, 372. Chs. 82–89, pp. 107–133.

377, 373. Ch. 89, pp. 133–136.

378, 374. "Guide" III, 24.

379, 375. Ez Hayim, ch. 90, pp. 136–144.

376. "Guide" III, chs. 12, 13, 25 end.

380, 377. Ez Hayim, ch. 94, pp. 149–154.

382, 378. Chs. 96–100, pp. 160–176.

379. Chs. 101–102, pp. 177–181.

380. Ez Hayim, pp. 116–117.

383, 381. Ch. 103, pp. 181–185.

384, 382. Chs. 104–105, pp. 185–187.

385, 383. Ch. 106, p. 187 ff.; ch. 109, p. 194 ff.

384. Chs. 107–108.

387, 385. Chs. 110–112.

389, 386. Ed. Ferara, 1556 (no pagination).

390, 387. "Or Adonai," Introduction, pp. 6–7 (not numbered).

391, 388. Book I, sections 1–2.

389. Ibid., section 3, ch. 2.

390. Ibid., ch. 3.

392, 391. Ibid.

392. Ibid., ch. 4.

393, 393. Book II, section I.

395, 394. Ibid., section 2.

395. Section 3.

396. Section 4.

398, 397. Section 5.

398. See M. Joel, "Don Chasdai Creskas' religionsphilosophische Lehren,"

Breslau, 1866 (in M. Joel, Beiträge zur Geschichte der Philosophie, Breslau, 1876), p. 54 f.

402, 399. Or Adonai, II, section 6.

400. Ibid., III, introduction.

403, 401. Ibid., section 1.

404, 402. Section 3.

405, 403. Section 4.

406, 403a. Simon ben Zemach Duran (1361-1444). He was a relative of Gersonides, a Rabbinical authority, and the author of a scientific and philosophical work, entitled "Magen Abot." Unlike his more distinguished relative, Simon Duran was opposed to the extreme views adopted by such men as Albalag, Moses of Narbonne or Gersonides himself, and favored a return to the more moderate standpoint of Maimonides. Without laying any claim to originality his work shows wide reading and familiarity with the scientific and philosophic literature of the time. See Guttmann, " Die Stellung des Simon ben Zemach Duran in der Geschichte der jüdischen Religionsphilosophie," in Monatschrift für Geschichte und Wissenschaft des Judenthums, vol. 52 (1908), pp. 641-672, vol. 53 (1909), pp. 46-97, 199-228. From Guttmann's investigations it appears that Albo cannot claim any originality even for the reduction of the fundamental dogmas of Judaism to three. The first part of the "Ikkarim" turns out to be a compilation from Crescas and Duran, and is no more original than the rest of the book. When we consider that though he owes the central point of his contribution to Duran, Albo never mentions him, the charge of plagiarism brought against him is not far from justified. See below, p. 407.

407, 404. ביטול עקרי הנוצרים, published by Ephraim Deinard, Carney, N. J., 1904. The work was originally composed in Spanish, and was translated into Hebrew by Joseph Ibn Shemtob.

404a. See also note 403a.

408, 405. ספר העקרים, ed. Warsaw, 1877, pp. 13-14.

406. Ibid., pp. 14-17.

409, 407. pp. 21-25.

408. In the introduction to his commentary on the eleventh chapter of the Mishnic treatise Sanhedrin (chapter Helek).

410, 409. Crescas; cf. above, p. 392.

410. Ikkarim, I, ch. 3, pp. 25-31.

411, 411. Chs. 4-7, pp. 31-39.

412, 412. Ch. 8, pp. 39-46.

413. Ch. 9, pp. 46-48.

413, 414. Chs. 10-11, pp. 48-58.

415. Ch. 12, pp. 58-60.

416. Chs. 13 and 15, pp. 60-61 and 64-68.

414, 417. Ch. 14, pp. 61-64.

415, 418. Ch. 17, pp. 71-76.

419. Ch. 18, pp. 76-78.

416, 420. Ch. 23, pp. 84-86.

418, 421. Ch. 24, pp. 87-90.

422. Ch. 25, pp. 90-92.

419, 423. Ch. 26, p. 93.

424. Book II, chs. 4-5, pp. 107-114.

425. Ibid., ch. 7, pp. 117-118.

420, 426. Chs. 8-10, pp. 118-125.

427. Chs. 11-13, pp. 125-140.

428. Ch. 12, pp. 129-133.

421, 429. Book III, chs. 1-5, pp. 197-214.

430. Chs. 6-7, pp. 214-218.

423, 431. Chs. 8-11, pp. 218-228.

424, 432. Chs. 13-20, pp. 229-246.

433. Book IV, chs. 1-6, pp. 279-294.

425, 434. Chs. 7-15, pp. 294-313.

427, 435. Chs. 29-35, pp. 338-356.

429, 436. See Guttmann "Die Familie Schemtob in ihren Beziehungen zur Philosophie," Monatschrift für Geschichte und Wissenschaft des Judenthums, vol. 57 (1913), p. 177 ff.

437. See Guttmann as in preceding note.

438. See preceding note.

430, 439. See note 436.

440. See Jewish Encyclopedia s. v.

441. J. E. s. v.

431, 442. See Zimmels, "Leo Hebraeus, ein jüdischer Philosoph der Renaissance," Leipzig, 1886; Appel, "Leone Medigos Lehre vom Weltall und ihr Verhältniss zu griechischen und zeitgenössischen Anschauungen," in Archiv für Geschichte der Philosophie, vol. XX, pp. 387–400, 496–520; Munk, Mélanges, pp. 522–528.

443. Husik, "Judah Messer Leon's Commentary on the Vetus Logica," Leyden, 1906.

444. Jewish Encyclopedia, s. v.

LIST OF BIBLICAL AND RABBINIC QUOTATIONS

INDEX

Atheneum Paperbacks

TEMPLE BOOKS—*The Jewish Publication Society*

PHILOSOPHY AND RELIGION

Atheneum Paperbacks

STUDIES IN AMERICAN NEGRO LIFE